McGRAW-HILL SERIES IN

Sociology and Anthropology

RICHARD T. LaPIERE

Consulting Editor

POPULATION PROBLEMS

McGRAW-HILL SERIES IN

Sociology and Anthropology

RICHARD T. LaPIERE

Consulting Editor

Population Problems

WARREN S. THOMPSON

*Formerly, Director of Scripps Foundation for Research
in Population Problems, Miami University*

With the assistance of

EVANGELYN D. MINNIS

FOURTH EDITION

McGRAW-HILL BOOK COMPANY, INC.

NEW YORK   TORONTO   LONDON

1953

POPULATION PROBLEMS

46,983
May, 1964

PREFACE

The preceding edition of this book was issued during World War II (1942). At that time it was impossible to secure as much up-to-date material on population as was needed to keep current with population changes. In particular, the censuses of many countries were not taken, and the results for others were not published in the customary detail. Since 1940 much water has gone over the dam. A truly surprising amount of study of population questions has taken place during the past dozen years. As a consequence this revision does more than add new data. It is in many respects a new book. Almost all of it has been rewritten, and the author has tried to embody in his rewriting the more significant additions which have been made to our knowledge of population growth and changes in recent years.

Unfortunately, in the field of population study as in so many other fields of social science we do not yet possess enough information to make possible wholly objective interpretations and analyses when treating of many aspects of population growth and change. This means that we must often resort to opinions and to general observations when trying to assess the probable consequences of trends and changes in the population.

The author, as in the past, will do his best to be objective, but will frequently inject interpretations based on insufficient data and will even express value judgments where they seem to be called for. However, he will try to let the student know when he departs from rigid objective description and from the analysis of well-authenticated facts.

As in the preceding edition, no general bibliography will be included, but a few suggested readings will be appended to each chapter in addition to the specific references in the footnotes. Fortunately the increased interest in population matters has led to the accumulation of many general works on population in most college and public libraries where they are readily accessible under this heading. Another bibliographic change in this edition is the placing of all specific references in footnotes. But in order not to burden the reader with an undue number of notes and because of the increasing availability of good current bibliographies, yearbooks, and abstracts carrying current population materials, no effort has been made to document facts which the reader could easily find in these publications from other references in the text.

The decline in the need for documentation in a book of this character arising from the increased availability of references and actual data deserves more definite specification. *Population Index* (quarterly) first appeared under the title *Population Literature* in 1935. It has been expanded and improved over the years. It now provides a certain amount of current demographic data and at least one article of interest in addition to its excellent bibliography. Since it is available in most libraries, the author believes that it provides a better guide to current population materials than any book can do.

Since the war two other excellent periodicals have appeared, devoted chiefly to the discussion of population matters but also presenting some current population data and noting the publication of most of the more important books and articles on population: (1) *Population: Quarterly Review of the National Institute of Demographic Studies*, Paris, which began publication in January–March, 1946, and (2) *Population Studies*, published (quarterly) on behalf of the Population Investigating Committee by the Cambridge University Press (England), the first number being dated June, 1947. Both of these contain excellent articles dealing with many aspects of population study.

There is still no American journal devoted primarily to the publication of research and discussion in the field of population, although the journals devoted to sociology accept a considerable number of articles dealing with different aspects of population and other social-science journals occasionally accept articles on population which are believed to be of interest to their readers. *The Annals of the American Academy of Political and Social Science*, a bimonthly publication of the Academy, has from time to time devoted considerable space to different aspects of population growth and change.

As far as possible the data used here are taken from original sources, but considerable use has been made of the *Demographic Yearbook* and other statistical publications of the United Nations both because these publications make certain data available which would otherwise be difficult to obtain and also because the experts preparing these data for publication by the United Nations have been at great pains to render the data for different countries comparable to a high degree. As a rule in each volume of the *Demographic Yearbook* some particular subject is given detailed consideration, in addition to the annual data whose presentation constitutes the reason for the name.

Finally, the author wishes to call attention to a contemplated publication of the United Nations which should appear in the near future, probably to be entitled *Findings of Studies on the Relationships between Population Trends and Economic and Social Factors*. This should provide a résumé of great value to teachers and students interested in some particular aspect of these relationships.

It would also be desirable to have available for class use not only the publications already mentioned but several yearbooks for different countries and the current United States census volumes. Most of these national yearbooks contain a considerable amount of demographic material.

The author finds it impossible to make any adequate acknowledgment of his indebtedness to the members of the staff of the Scripps Foundation and to many other people for the direct help as well as for the suggestions and criticisms which have been of use to him in the rewriting of this book. His debt to one person is so great, however, that he has placed her name on the title page as a partial acknowledgment of her able and conscientious assistance at all stages of the work.

WARREN S. THOMPSON

CONTENTS

Part II: Consideration of the Population

x   CONTENTS

Part III. Natural Increase Fertility and Mortality

INTRODUCTION

Many factors have contributed to a growing interest in the growth and changes in population during the past three or four decades. It will not be possible here to do more than enumerate the chief of these factors in very general terms and to state briefly a few of the more important reasons why it is necessary to know something about population and its changes, not only from the standpoint of the student of social conditions but also from that of the average citizen who is being called upon more and more to participate in decisions in the making of which knowledge of population changes is essential to intelligent action. The aspects of population growth and change to which the discussion in this book will be devoted may be indicated by three questions. When thus summarized these questions must necessarily be very comprehensive and of such a broad character that they may at first seem rather meaningless. The body of the book will, therefore, be devoted to making different aspects of these questions more intelligible, *i.e.,* to the effort to present facts and observations, where necessary, relating to these three aspects of population growth and change and to interpret their significance. These questions are:

1. What changes are taking place in the size of populations, and how are changes in size effected? What is the significance of these changes from the standpoint of human welfare?

2. Where are people found, and what changes in their distribution in communities and areas are taking place? While the distribution of people in space over a given area cannot be treated apart from changes in the size of the total population of the area, it serves many practical purposes to think of the *distribution of population* in space as a somewhat separate aspect of population change. The distribution of population may also have a significant relation to human welfare.

3. What kind of people are found in any given population group, and how do those in one group differ from those in another? This is the study of the characteristics of population in different groups, and these characteristics often differ so much that if we do not know them we cannot understand the varying social conditions in these groups. Here again the characteristics of any given population are closely associated with its welfare and need careful analysis from this standpoint.

The remainder of this introductory chapter will be devoted to a brief statement of some of the reasons which have led to increased interest in these aspects of population change.

1

In the first place, the mere change in numbers in a community, in a nation, and even in the world as a whole creates new and different social situations which demand attention and hence increases interest in this aspect of population change. There is hardly a person of middle age, or above, in the United States who has not had his attention called directly to the fact that the size of his community has changed within his lifetime. As a consequence he, as a citizen, has been called upon to join with his fellows in making certain practical adjustments to these changes in the size of his community, of his state, and quite possibly of the region of which his state is a part.

It should be mentioned at this point that not all these changes in size have been increases. For the most part the urban communities have had to provide for large increases in population. This is especially true of the larger urban communities which we are coming to think of as metropolitan areas. On the other hand, in many rural communities, including a great many villages, the residents have had to adjust themselves and their institutions to a declining population. These changes in size of community have created new and often very perplexing problems as regards providing the public utilities needed for health and comfort, the schools considered essential to the training of the youth, the safety measures ensuring protection against fire and crime, and many other services now considered essential to good living.

Thus the rapid growth of a large urban community creates an increased need for schools, for playgrounds for children, for recreation areas for everybody, for an improved highway system, and so forth. The growth of suburban areas in turn creates a need for the integration of the governmental activities of the city with those of the suburbs by which it is surrounded and for finding some means by which the tax burdens of the different governmental units can be adjusted fairly. In rural communities where population has been declining the problems of providing better schools and roads and fire and police protection are made more difficult by this very fact, and if satisfactory services are to be provided a new type of organization must be developed. Thus almost every citizen is today made aware that changes in the size of the population in his community, his state, and so forth, do affect him and his family directly and that as a consequence he must take an interest in these size changes.

Many of the situations which arise because of changes in the size of population in local communities have their analogues in larger populations such as those of states, provinces, or nations. But there are also distinctive problems which arise from the changes in population in these larger areas, and while they do not come to the attention of the average citizen as directly as do local changes, they are no less important to his welfare.

In the United States the decision to take a decennial census arose out of the prevision of the need for an adjustment of legislative representation as population grew but grew at unequal rates in the several states. This problem of fair legislative representation arising from changes in the size of local populations is not confined to the United States. It exists in all countries having representative government where there have been significant differentials in rates of growth in different areas and regions. At this point a change in the size of the population within a given area becomes also a problem of the distribution of population within this area and will be discussed more fully below.

Many problems are also created by the fact that different nations and peoples have grown at different rates, so that, in so far as political power is dependent upon the size of the population, great changes have taken place during the last century and a half and are still taking place. At the time of the first census in the United States (1790) our population probably amounted to about one-forty-fifth of the population of Europe. At the present time it amounts to about one-fourth of that of Europe. In the early nineteenth century France's population was about the same size as that of the territory which later became the German Empire. At the outbreak of World War I (1914) the population of France was about 39.8 million and that of the German Empire was 67.8 million.[1] There is no need to continue these comparisons here. The point I am trying to make is that there have been large differentials in the growth of population in different political units and that these differentials have been important in bringing about changes in the political status of different nations and peoples and will continue to be important for some time in the future. I should like to make it clear, however, that I do not mean to imply that mere change in numbers is the only factor which affects the political status of nations and peoples— only that population changes are almost certain to be an important element in the situation.

Finally, as regards changes in the size of populations, it seems to me that the increasing scope and accuracy of information relating to the numbers of people in different areas has had an important effect in arousing wider interest in population matters. The very fact that the growth of population in France and Germany was known precisely contributed materially to the interest of the French and German people in population growth both at home and abroad. The same is true as regards interest in the growth of numbers within a country. In the United States, when people could compare the growth of New York City and New York State with that of Philadelphia and Pennsylvania, and so forth, knowledge of the size of the population took on added interest. Likewise as the practice of census taking spread, more and more people became interested in comparing the popula-

[1] Frank W. Notestein *et al., The Future Population of Europe and the Soviet Union,* p. 75, League of Nations, Geneva, 1944.

tion changes in their own country or community with those in other countries and communities. Thus changes in the size of populations both in absolute numbers and in relation to numbers in other communities and countries attracted increasing attention, and the significance of these changes is gradually coming to be considered worthy of study. The description of these changes in size, of the dynamics lying behind them, and the exploration of their significance constitute a main task in this book.

A second aspect of population change which has attracted more and more attention in recent years is that of the distribution of population. The changes in distribution of population in space arise chiefly as a consequence of the changes in the relative importance of the economic activities of different areas. Thus when the area now constituting Greater New York was primarily agricultural and when our foreign trade was small and there was no need for a national financial center, this area could support only a small population—smaller than could be supported in many other areas of like size having better soil and of easier access to nearby areas of greater natural resources. However, as the economy of the nation (and the world) became more complex and as the need arose for a large variety of economic activities serving the nation as a whole, New York was able to supply more and more of these needs, and it has continued to grow to its present vastness.

As our economy was transformed from one which depended almost completely upon agriculture to one in which manufacturing, commerce, and services claimed a larger and larger proportion of our efforts, the distribution of population changed apace, and the description and analysis of these changes constitutes another important part of our study of population. Changes in distribution, *i.e.*, in the relative size of communities and regions, take place, from the standpoint of demography, in two ways: (1) the population of one area may have a larger excess of births over deaths than that of another area and as a consequence may grow faster, and (2) people may move from one area to another (migrate), thus reducing the rate of growth in the area of emigration and raising it in the area of immigration. This statement of the effects of migration on the population growth of different areas is too simple, since there are conditions under which migration may have little effect on population growth either in the area of emigration or in that of immigration, particularly in the former area, but it will be allowed to stand for the present.

Another aspect of the distribution of population which is of increasing interest is that of the distribution of man over the earth to secure a more satisfactory relation between numbers and the natural resources on which man's economic welfare depends (Chap. XVII). This matter has received but little attention up to the present. It is becoming increasingly certain, however, that the vastly varying densities of population in different lands, coupled with the enormous variations in per capita resources, are raising many questions regarding the effect of the present distribution of population upon human welfare, particularly as regards its effects upon the peace of the world, as expanding peoples come to demand access to larger resources. The distribution of population in both its national and international aspects will be discussed in the proper connection. But it seems clear now that whether or not we desire it we must give careful consideration to the regional distribution of population in the world as a whole.

The distribution of population—where people live—may also have an effect on natality (births). This results from the fact that today in industrialized lands the distribution of population is closely associated with its willingness to rear enough children to keep numbers from declining. In large cities there are frequently too few children to keep population from declining, while in small communities, and especially in the open country, there are generally enough to keep population growing fairly rapidly. Whether this deficiency of births in cities is merely a passing phase of urbanization or is inherent in urban life in the modern world cannot yet be told. Certainly if it is the latter the distribution of population in different types of communities becomes of prime importance, since it will determine whether a people will survive, for with a declining proportion of the population living in small communities (including open country) it becomes increasingly difficult for this group to make up any deficiency of births which may arise among the people living in the larger urban communities.

Even before the voluntary control of conception was widespread in the cities, a number of people had come to realize that cities had to depend largely on migration for the maintenance of their numbers. In the period before about 1700 this was due not to the low birth rate but to the fact that the death rate was so high that it exceeded the birth rate. It seems unlikely that cities have ever produced enough children to maintain their own numbers or to add to them, except for a short period in modern times when the death rate had come under control to a considerable extent while the birth rate had been but little changed from earlier times and remained relatively high. This period lasted only a few decades.

It was noted in the preceding section that the more rapid growth of population in one area than in another created problems of maintaining the representative character of our legislative bodies. This problem is becoming increasingly acute in many different political units because of changes in the distribution of people within the different political units. In our states this problem often takes the form of rural areas being over-represented in the legislative bodies because of the relative decline, sometimes the absolute decline, of population in rural counties while the more urban counties have grown at a rapid pace and the area basis of representation remains almost unchanged. In cities where representation is by wards or other specific areas a similar difficulty frequently arises. Thus an allocation of legislative representation to a given area which was quite satisfactory at one time, because of the relative uniform density of population, becomes highly unsatisfactory as the distribution of population within the area concerned becomes less uniform and sometimes highly concentrated in small portions of it.

One should not close even a brief enumeration of the factors making it important for us to study the changes in the distribution of population and thus arousing our growing interest in them without mentioning the changes in the methods of warfare since about 1935. The development of the airplane as a bomb carrier and the discovery of the atom bomb have probably made it desirable to disperse more widely both the people and the vital industries of a nation. This is a new consideration with regard to the distribution of population, and although as yet it has received little attention it requires no prophet to foresee that if we do not work out some plan for preventing war we shall be forced to give these strategic considerations first place in planning the future distribution of people in our industrial and commercial centers. We dare not ignore the possibility that as long as war remains a threat to the freedom of any people the present concentration of people, of industry, and of the vital directive control of our economy in a few very large urban centers is extremely hazardous. The "man in the street" is gradually coming to recognize this situation and hence has an increasing interest in the distribution of the people over the land.

Finally, a word should be said about the increasing interest of business enterprises of all kinds in the distribution of population. It is obvious that where people are, there are workers and markets, and hence business cannot afford to remain indifferent to the changes in the distribution of population when new plants are being located, when sales plans are being developed, and when the central control organization of a business is being built up. The distribution of population and the changes taking place in it are of very vital concern to all of us, and there can be no doubt that we will devote more and more attention to this aspect of population change as time passes.

The third aspect of population study which accounts for much of the increased interest in this subject is our desire to know more about what kind of people we are, whether and in what way our characteristics are changing, and how these changes affect our social conditions. It was inevitable that as we found out that changes in what we call the *composition* of the population affected our lives in many ways we would be increasingly interested in them. The chief demographic characteristics of interest to us are age and sex, but race is also of importance in some populations, particularly so in the United States. However, there are many social and economic characteristics which are just as important to study carefully if we would understand the differences between communities and peoples. In many populations differences in social characteristics are of more significance than differences in purely demographic characteristics (age, sex, race), but differences between populations in the proportions of males and females, in the proportions of persons of different ages, and in the proportions belonging to the different racial groups often create considerable differences in the social conditions prevailing in different communities. These purely demographic traits are so important that a substantial portion of our study of population is concerned with describing and analyzing the effects of sex and age differences on various aspects of community life. However, the social and economic characteristics in respect of which there are often large differences between communities probably are more significant from the standpoint of their effects on the welfare of the people. The more important social and economic characteristics to be treated are marital status, educational status, occupational status, economic status, religious affiliation, rural and urban residence, nationality, language or mother tongue, and the quality of people—commonly thought of as eugenic quality. These characteristics are not irrevocably determined for every person by heredity as are the purely demographic characteristics noted above, although in individual cases they are sometimes so determined. Thus an hereditary *idiot* always has an educational status of *no grades of school completed*. For the most part, however, the social and economic characteristics of people are determined by the conditions under which they live. For many people, however, social status changes once or more during their lifetime, even when account is taken of the changes in status which usually accompany age changes. The most common types of change in the social characteristics or status of individuals in the United States are probably those connected with changes in occupational, economic, and educational status. When there are rather large differences between communities in the proportions of their populations having a given social and economic status, the social conditions in these communities are also likely to differ widely. It will be sufficient here to mention that a community in which few people are well educated will be quite different in many respects from one which contains a larger proportion of educated persons. Differences in income are also accompanied by differences in social conditions, as will be noted in due course. More and more we are coming to realize that differences between the composition of groups must be known if we are to understand the differences which are found in their social conditions. This study of the composition of the population is the third of the major aspects of population growth and change to be treated here.

Finally, I would insert a word of caution. Although I have spoken of three aspects of population study as though they were rather distinct, it is not possible to treat them separately, and if it were it would not be desirable to do so. I have already indicated that the growth of population in any given area cannot be understood without giving consideration to the changes in the distribution of population and vice versa, and also that this holds when considering the characteristics of the people in a given area. The manner of its growth—natural increase or migration—will determine to a large extent many of the characteristics of a population at different stages of development, and in turn its composition will have a marked effect on the growth and distribution of population.

In treating any aspect of population growth and change, or even in getting a cross section of status at a given moment, we should not forget that we are always dealing with a living, changing entity—an organic body, in which any change in any part has more or less effect on all other parts. It is therefore highly artificial to separate the study of the distribution of population from the study of its growth or its composition. But it is necessary as a practical matter to emphasize particular aspects of growth and change at certain points and times if we are to make progress in our study; hence this attempt to describe briefly what the author regards as the chief constituent elements to be kept in mind in the study of population questions and as the aspects of population change which account for the growing interest in this field of study.

CHAPTER I

POPULATION CONTROL IN PAST TIMES

To effect a satisfactory adjustment to environment has always required the major portion of man's efforts. Quite naturally the adjustment of his numbers to the resources he could use with the techniques available to him has constituted an extremely important part of his broader adjustment to all aspects of his environment. It is not in the least surprising, therefore, that many peoples have developed population practices which aimed at controlling their growth in numbers, at effecting a better distribution, and at securing a more desirable composition of the group. Indeed, when one studies the numerous practices affecting the growth of population among different peoples, one is impressed with the fact that the uncontrolled growth of population—that is, uncontrolled by man's mores, or by his deliberate acts, chiefly by the former—has been the unusual condition, while controlled growth has been quite general, although it has by no means always been successful in effecting a nice adjustment between numbers and the means of subsistence. However, this control has generally been unconscious and customary (group) rather than the result of deliberate individual choice.[1] On the other hand, *laissez faire* as a population policy, that is, the relative lack of customary group controls affecting the size of the group, seems to be of quite recent origin and no doubt can be explained like all other patterns of human reproduction as an attempted adjustment of particular groups to their own environments.

Patterns of reproduction in times past have generally been established, whether consciously or by the slow accretion of tradition, to serve one of four ends: (1) to slow up or prevent an increase in numbers; (2) to encourage an increase, or at least to ensure the continuation of the group at about the same size; (3) to improve the quality of the population; or (4) to secure a better distribution of people in relation to the resources available for their support. Most of the well-established patterns of reproduction have involved a combination of these practices, and the entire pattern may very well be called a *population policy* although not, as a rule, deliberately planned and adopted as such.

There is little doubt that throughout the greater part of human history

[1] Alexander Morris Carr-Saunders, *The Population Problem: A Study in Human Evolution,* pp. 476–477, Clarendon Press, Oxford, 1922.

restrictive practices have been more common than the others. This is probably due to the fact that whenever such practices were not in effect the group soon found itself in a position where it had difficulty in securing the necessities of life. Expansive practices have been less common than restrictive practices, probably because there was less need of them, there generally being a relatively rapid natural increase when economic conditions were fairly favorable and when restrictive practices were not resorted to. In other words, man has less often felt that an increase in his welfare was dependent upon his rapid growth in numbers than that his welfare was endangered by too rapid a growth.

One need make only a very simple arithmetical calculation to convince himself that an unrestricted increase of mankind, or even of any considerable part of it, has been a rare occurrence in human history and that such an increase could not continue for any great length of time even with a very small initial population. Supposing that man arose from a single pair and that his numbers doubled every 25 years, a rate of 2.81 per cent a year, it would require but a little over seven and one-half centuries for his numbers to approximate those now on the earth—about 2.4 billion. Clearly, an expansive population policy, if effective in producing unrestricted increase, could not have endured for more than a comparatively short time. It would have resulted in overcrowding not only in local groups having an unrestricted increase but in the world at large in the course of only a few centuries (Chap. XII). At any time within the past 4,000 years an unrestricted world-wide increase at this rate would have led to a far larger population in the course of three or four centuries than we now have.

1. RESTRICTIVE PRACTICES

As was said above, restrictive practices have constituted by far the most important element in population control in the history of the race. The means used to restrict population growth have been, and still are, extremely numerous. Only a few of the more important—those more widely practiced —can be discussed here.

Infanticide. Infanticide was an almost universal custom from very early times and is still quite common in many parts of the world.[2] Almost all the

[2] Herbert Aptekar, *Anjea: Infanticide, Abortion, and Contraception in Savage Society,* Chap. 7, W. Godwin, Inc., New York, 1931; *Encyclopaedia of Religion and Ethics,* 12 vols., ed. by James Hastings, with the assistance of John A. Selbie, Edin, Clark, and other scholars, Charles Scribner's Sons, New York, 1911–1921 (Index, 1927, separate); *Encyclopaedia of the Social Sciences,* ed. by Edwin R. A. Seligman, (Alvin Johnson, assoc. ed.), The Macmillan Company, New York, 1935; William Graham Sumner, *Folkways: A Study of the Sociological Importance of Usages, Manners, Customs, Mores, and Morals,* pp. 316–318, Ginn & Company, Boston, 1907.

so-called primitive peoples regularly practice infanticide and have done so for ages. Many Australian tribes, many tribes of American Indians, and some of the African peoples belong to this group. Indeed, it is such a common practice that one notices its absence rather than its presence when reading the accounts of explorers and anthropologists. It appears that not infrequently the proportion of infants thus made away with reaches one-half or even more. Among peoples having a more complex social organization infanticide has not been so common, but it was an approved practice among the ancient Greeks of certain communities and certainly was not rare among other Mediterranean peoples in those days. In Europe it was not until well into the Middle Ages that infanticide came to be looked upon as a crime, and there is much evidence that it is by no means absent from the modern world. The census of India, 1921,[3] shows that among certain groups where there is a tradition of female infanticide, the proportion of females is much smaller than in groups where there is no such tradition. These differences at times amount to as much as 15 per cent. It would appear probable that as late as 1921 there were some groups in India among whom infanticide was still practiced to some extent although there is no evidence that it was widespread or that the amount was large. There is also reason to believe that some infanticide exists in parts of China, since the sex ratios of children, i.e., the number of boys per 100 girls, are frequently so high that only a considerable amount of infanticide among girl babies or their deliberate neglect with intent of inducing early death would account for the large excess of boys, since it cannot be assumed that the ratio of male to female births is significantly higher in China than in Western countries, namely, 105 to 106 boy babies born to each 100 girl babies. In the past it is highly probable that infanticide has been one of the most effective of the practices designed to limit the growth of population.

Abortion. Abortion, like infanticide, has been practiced by many peoples for ages past.[4] Even today it remains a very important factor in reducing the birth rate in almost all parts of the world and is one of the most important checks that man has ever exercised on his growth in numbers. It is not at all improbable that the rather small number of children born to individual women among many primitive peoples and even in highly civilized countries [5] is due in a considerable measure to abortion.

There are, of course, no reliable statistics on induced abortions among those peoples having good demographic data, since induced abortion, except

[3] India, Census Commissioner, *India* (Census of India, 1921), Vol. 1, Pt. 1, Appendix 6, Superintendent of Government Printing, Calcutta, 1924.

[4] Aptekar, *op. cit.,* Chap. VI; Norman Edwin Himes, "Medical History of Contraception," *New England J. Medicine,* Vol. 210, No. 11, pp. 576–581, 1934.

[5] India, Census Commissioner, *op. cit.,* Appendix 7.

for urgent health reasons, is now a criminal offense in such countries (Chap. X). However, in spite of this fact the number of such abortions is very large. The author has been told on what he regards as good authority that in pre-Nazi days the number of induced abortions in Berlin each year considerably exceeded the number of births. A recent study in a maternity clinic in Hamburg showed that in 1947 and 1948 there were only 1.2 births per abortion and that in one medium-sized town in the British Zone (1947) the number of abortions exceeded the number of births.[6] Inghe[7] gives the number of illegal abortions in Sweden as 10,000. This may be compared with 130,000 live births. Legal abortions rose from 500 in 1939, when the new more liberal law was passed, to 1,600 in 1945. In the Soviet Union there was a very large increase in abortions in the larger cities when it was publicly sanctioned and a large increase in births after it was banned again in 1935.[8] In Japan, under the new eugenics law, the number of abortions is increasing rapidly.[9] There is little doubt, therefore, that abortion is still one of the leading methods of keeping down man's numbers.

Sexual Taboos. Until the last few centuries, sexual taboos of various kinds have also been quite effective in reducing the number of births among many peoples. These taboos have been particularly effective among peoples where the segregation of women, for frequent and often for prolonged periods, was quite common and where elaborate marriage and sexual codes led to prolonged periods of sexual continence on their part. Where remarriage of widows was discountenanced, that restriction also contributed materially to a reduction of the birth rate.[10] Since such sexual taboos scarcely exist in Europe and its settlements, we are apt to underestimate their importance in restricting births. There can be little doubt, however, that throughout most of human history they should be classed with infanticide and abortion in importance as restrictive practices.[11]

Treatment of the Aged and Ill. The killing of the aged and the killing or abandoning of the sick have likewise played a part in restricting population growth in times past, and the abandonment of the sick and helpless even now is by no means uncommon among tribal peoples at times of great hardship and catastrophe.

[6] Hans Harmsen, "Notes on Abortion and Birth Control in Germany," *Population Studies,* Vol. 3, No. 4, p. 404, 1950.

[7] Gunnar Inghe, "The Abortion Problem in Sweden," *Human Fertility,* Vol. 12, No. 2, pp. 40–43, 1947.

[8] Lewis A. Coser, "Some Aspects of Soviet Family Policy," *Am. J. Soc.,* Vol. 56, No. 5, p. 428, 1951.

[9] Population Problems Research Council, *The Population of Japan,* p. 14, The Mainichi Shimbun, Tokyo, 1950.

[10] Sumner, *op. cit.,* Chap. 9.

[11] Carr-Saunders, *op. cit.,* Chaps. 7 and 8.

Acceptance of Disaster. The passive acceptance of recurring catastrophes may also be regarded as a practice designed to prevent the too rapid growth of population. Professor Ross [12] cites the case of a Chinese official who did not want measures taken to avoid the almost yearly recurrence of the plague in his city because he regarded it as the best friend of those surviving its visitations. Molony quotes a South Indian farmer as saying, "In old days wars, pestilence, famine kept the population within manageable limits. You have stopped the working of Nature's laws, and saved alive myriads of people. What are you going to do with them?" [13]

War. Modern war cannot be regarded as a definite restrictive practice, as will be seen later (Chap. IV), but among tribal peoples war is often so large a part of the life of the tribe, or horde, that it can very legitimately be regarded as an important restrictive factor. Head-hunters, who must possess a given number of enemy heads before they marry; nomads, among whom the men must show their ability to steal cattle, in spite of the fact that their lives are endangered in every foray, before the women will take notice of them—these and many other peoples have warlike practices which certainly count as factors which restrict population growth.

Marriage Restrictions. Legal restrictions upon marriage, such as property and age qualifications and the consent of the lord of the manor, were in certain respects analogous to sexual taboos. They were probably not as effective as sexual taboos in reducing the birth rate, but they have been of sufficient importance as restrictive measures to deserve notice. They impeded easy marriage and led to high rates of infant mortality among children born to unmarried mothers, thus helping to keep down numbers.

Migration. The migration of a part of a group to new lands has frequently been resorted to in past times when the standards of the group could no longer be maintained on the resources of a given area. This sending out of colonists or of raiding armies which settled the lands that they conquered has certainly been one of the important elements of population policy among many peoples in times past, and migration is still regarded as an important outlet for surplus population if one may judge from the resentment expressed by peoples desiring to emigrate toward those peoples and countries that refuse to admit them. There has long been much difference of opinion as to whether emigration really relieves population pressure (Chaps. XIII and XIV), but whether it does or not, there is not the least doubt that many peoples have believed that it did and have encouraged it for this reason.

[12] Edward Alsworth Ross, *The Changing Chinese: The Conflict of the Oriental and Western Cultures in China,* p. 90, Century Company, New York, 1911.

[13] J. Chartres Molony, "Population Problems," *Contemporary Rev.,* Vol. 173, No. 5, 287, 1948.

Contraception. Methods of preventing conception have been known for ages (Genesis 38:8–9) [14] but as an important factor in determining the rate of population growth the practice of contraception appears to be fairly recent. Even now its effects are largely confined to Europe or the countries settled by Europeans. But it seems quite likely that this will not long be the case. Evidence is beginning to accumulate that the upper economic classes in the cities of many of the less industrialized countries are already practicing a small measure of contraception, and there is good reason to expect that such a movement will follow much the same course in these under-developed areas as in the West. In view of its very manifest advantages, as compared with most of the restrictive practices noted above, it seems highly probable that contraception and the "safe-period" method are destined to become the foundation stone of the modern restrictive practices needed to bring about a rational adjustment of numbers to resources and to maintain the quality of the population.

The point in enumerating the practices which have been and are being used to limit the growth of population is to call attention to the fact that practices for the control of population, for the better adjustment of numbers to the means available for their support, are almost as old as the race. Man has seldom, if ever, refrained from interfering with his power to reproduce if he has felt that he could thereby reduce the hardship and suffering which the pressure of numbers on subsistence inflicted upon him. But at any given time the restrictive practices he followed were more likely to be the result of tribal or community experience developed over a long period of time than of a deliberate policy adopted consciously with restriction of numbers as its avowed purpose. Today in the Western world actual restrictive practices are largely the consequence of the deliberate intent of married couples to keep their families to the size they feel they can support at the level of living they consider desirable. Such restriction is not based on the community concept of the "general welfare" which underlay most of the traditional restrictive practices in the past.

2. EXPANSIVE PRACTICES

Practices calculated to increase the population more rapidly have been far less common in human history than those intended to prevent its too rapid increase. In general it would appear that they have been rather closely associated with some important cultural change in the life of the group which, temporarily at least, seemed to make it desirable that the group should expand more rapidly than it had been expanding in the recent past. The encouragements to more rapid increase as a rule consisted largely in

[14] Norman Edwin Himes, *Medical History of Contraception,* Chaps. 2–4, The Williams & Wilkins Company, Baltimore, 1936.

removing the restraints on population increase which have been discussed above. This, of course, constitutes a tacit and often unconscious recognition of man's tendency to reproduce at a rapid rate if this tendency is not controlled by restrictive practices sanctioned by the group.

Larger Resources. From early historical times and no doubt long before, the access to new economic resources seems to have had a strongly stimulating effect on population growth. This seems to have been true for peoples in all stages of cultural development—hunters, shepherds, agriculturists, and industrial peoples. When larger resources became available, it is more than likely that restrictive practices which may have been in use at the time these lands were acquired would tend to be sloughed off and the policy of the group would tend to change into "be fruitful and multiply and replenish the earth" (Genesis 9:1). But it should be noted that the improved economic conditions resulting from a larger and more certain supply of the necessities of life would of itself almost always reduce the death rate and thus increase the rate of growth, since it usually had little or no effect on the birth rate. If it had any effect on the birth rate, it was probably to increase the birth rate to some extent by encouraging earlier marriage. Consequently, all policies, public or private, which resulted in making larger economic opportunities available to the masses have been very potent factors in encouraging population growth. There is little doubt, for example, that the land policy of this country which was consciously pursued from about 1790 to 1890, namely, making family-sized farms readily available, was a very potent factor in determining the growth of our population. The expansion of job opportunities in industry, commerce, and the services during the past three-quarters of a century also acted in much the same way after land settlement was practically completed. With the spread of contraceptive information, however, there is some reason to believe that large families, except in rare cases, are a thing of the past and that improved economic opportunity will do little to encourage the raising of families of more than three or four children. But as long as the growth of population was determined chiefly by the height of the death rate, because the birth rate was almost universally high and fluctuated less than the death rate, the improvement of economic conditions was a powerful stimulant of population growth.

Need for Defense. Another situation which would encourage practices intended to increase the population would be one where the defense of their homeland seemed to demand a larger population to beat off invaders.

Dynastic and National Interests. At times rulers and dynasties have desired large numbers of subjects in order to render themselves formidable to their foes, to enable them to seize adjacent lands which were desired, or to enhance the prestige of their families and their countries or empires. It is well known that Augustus tried to reform the manner of life of the Roman people, particularly those of the upper classes that were being imitated by the lower classes, so that restrictive practices would be abandoned. Other rulers have also occasionally encouraged their people to raise large families. But by and large such direct efforts seem to have been singularly devoid of results, because the rulers failed to recognize the fact that the high death rate was the chief reason for the slow growth of population and that as long as nothing was done to reduce it there was little chance of more rapid population growth.

In the last two or three centuries the rise and spread of nationalism and the expansion of empires have also had an important effect on the attitudes of people toward population growth and have, in some cases, tended to encourage population increase. Clearly, soldiers and workers are needed for nationalistic or imperialistic expansion, and consequently, because the expansion of the power of the nation depended in part upon increasing numbers, a whole complex of social attitudes was developed which was favorable to the growth of population.

Religion. Another cultural factor which has at times encouraged population growth is religion. (No effort will be made to define this term.) When a tribal people adopted an expansive policy, as did the Jews, there is little doubt that it was rather closely associated with their religious beliefs. This was also the case in China and India, where reproductive practices were developed which served religious purposes or beliefs as well as what was conceived of as the general welfare. The duty taught by some religions to spread their beliefs has not infrequently led them into militant activities in which the success of the propaganda depended largely on the size of their armies.

The actual growth of population in religious groups probably came about chiefly as a consequence of gaining control of larger resources, although the suppression or reduction of restrictive practices such as infanticide, abortion, sexual taboos, and so forth, no doubt also had some influence. Thus Christianity gradually reduced the effectiveness of these restrictive practices in the Western world, but this action seems to have had comparatively little effect on the increase of population until the economic conditions became favorable to the reduction of the death rate as will be shown in Chaps. IV and V.

3. EUGENIC PRACTICES

Little can be said on this subject, as eugenic considerations have not generally been of much moment in the determination of population practices in the past. There are, of course, some well-known examples of eugenic selection in the population practices of different peoples. In Sparta the children selected for exposure were "weaklings"—those who did not seem likely to contribute to the military strength of the state. Infanticide has probably always tended to do away with the weaker and the deformed babies. However, when infanticide was a conscious policy for keeping down numbers it must always have borne more heavily upon the children born later in the family than on those born earlier and thus have reduced somewhat its eugenic effects. There is no evidence showing that later-born children are less fit physically or mentally than those born earlier. As a eugenic policy there can be little question that natural infant mortality has done far more than infanticide to eliminate weaklings. But here, too, later-born children have, as a rule, suffered higher mortality than earlier-born children, and infant mortality has probably had less eugenic significance than is commonly assumed. There has, of course, always been more or less prejudice against the crippled or malformed child. It is probable, therefore, that in addition to the hazard of their natural handicap such children have been neglected as compared with normal children and that their death rate has always been relatively high. The same "selective" death rate also probably operated against those who were "queer" mentally, although at times the "queer" were regarded as favored by the supernatural powers. Recently, however, the direct elimination of those who were visibly weak at birth has not been as rigorous as formerly, although it is doubtful whether this has increased their rate of reproduction to any great extent. There is much popular misconception of the rate at which the mentally handicapped reproduce [15] (Chap. XXI).

The eugenic selection to which man has hitherto been subject has been exercised by the natural rigors of his life far more than by his following any practices consciously adopted. The visions of a superrace arising from the breeding of selected stocks which have often intrigued the utopians have never gained any support from the masses, nor do they seem likely to gain it in the near future, for the right to mate and rear children as seems best to them is a highly cherished personal prerogative not to be relinquished lightly.

4. PRACTICES AFFECTING THE DISTRIBUTION OF POPULATION

As far as the author can ascertain, no people has ever developed a clearcut policy regarding its distribution, but there have been numerous occasions on which the better distribution of population was a factor in determining the decisions of groups regarding migration and probably regarding war with neighboring groups. Abraham and Lot decided to part company (Genesis 13:9) so that both groups would have better pastures. Similar decisions must have been taken on thousands of occasions of which there is no record. When land for hunting, pasture, or agriculture is almost the sole

[15] Paul Popenoe, "Eugenic Sterilization in California. Fecundity of the Insane," *J. Heredity,* Vol. 19, No. 2, p. 77, 1928.

basis of man's livelihood, it is obvious that the distribution of population over the land is of such great importance that it must always have been of much concern to all peoples even in the days when population was very sparse according to our ideas. Much of the warfare mankind has engaged in over the ages must also have arisen out of different ideas as to how the land should be divided between different peoples, *i.e.*, out of efforts to change the distribution of particular groups in a given area. Such struggles are still going on.

There have also been times when statesmen and philosophers were concerned over the distribution of population between city and country; between trade, manufacturing, and agricultural production; and between different parts of the nation or empire. However, it can scarcely be said that any policy has anywhere been consciously adopted which was calculated to bring about a changed distribution. It has, of course, been said that Rome's downfall was caused by the latifundia—great estates, all the produce of which, beyond subsistence for the slaves, went to the absentee owners living in the city—and by the excessive urbanization of population in many of the provinces of the empire, but so far as is known no policy likely to result in the redistribution of the population was ever seriously undertaken.

It is also true that every social system leads to its own peculiar distribution of population; for example, population is quite differently distributed both spatially and industrially in England and in France. But it can scarcely be said that the distribution actually achieved in either is the result of any definite policy; it is rather an accidental by-product of the striving for other aims with the techniques available at a given time and to a particular people. It is, therefore, not misstating the situation to say that only now are we becoming conscious of the need for policies regarding the distribution of population if we are to achieve the largest measure of welfare for the mass of the people in any land. We are only beginning to ask whether or not it is socially desirable to have most of the people live in more or less crowded cities; whether or not our highly centralized cities are the most efficient form of economic association for the prosecution of industry and trade that can be devised in the modern world; whether or not it is good to have millions and millions of people living in crowded slums when it is possible to scatter them over areas where they can have some contact with nature. In a word, it is becoming more and more clear that the distribution of population does affect its welfare in many ways, and hence that any population policy developed today must give careful attention to the grouping of the people within the nation.

While there is no doubt that from time immemorial man has had much interest in almost all aspects of population growth and change which affected his welfare and at times his very existence, and while he has made many adjustments in his mores and institutions affecting population growth with a view to furthering his welfare, it is nevertheless essentially true to say that only quite recently in his history has he begun to study population growth with a view to conscious and deliberate control over the processes of growth and change.

As has been already noted, there has also been a considerable speculation over a long period of time by statesmen and philosophers about many aspects of population growth, but there has only recently, as history goes, been much serious study of population growth and changes in relation to human welfare. Since, in the author's opinion, this modern era in the investigation of population in its relation to human welfare was greatly stimulated by the work of Malthus, the speculations of his precursors will be passed over with only occasional mention, although they were of great value to Malthus himself. Moreover, Malthus' own work must be treated very briefly and inadequately, but enough will be said to indicate why he came to be regarded as the "father" of modern population study.

Suggestions for Supplementary Reading

CARR-SAUNDERS, ALEXANDER MORRIS: *The Population Problem: A Study in Human Evolution,* 516 pp., Clarendon Press, Oxford, 1922.

Encyclopaedia of the Social Sciences, ed. by Edwin R. A. Seligman (Alvin Johnson, assoc. ed.), The Macmillan Company, New York, 1935.

HIMES, NORMAN EDWIN: *Medical History of Contraception,* 521 pp., The Williams and Wilkins Company, Baltimore, 1936.

LANDIS, PAUL H.: *Population Problems,* 500 pp., American Book Company, New York, 1943. Treats on most of the matters discussed in this book and is useful at many points.

SUMNER, WILLIAM GRAHAM: *Folkways: A Study of the Sociological Importance of Usages, Manners, Customs, Mores, and Morals,* Chaps. 7 and 9, Ginn & Company, Boston, 1907.

WESTERMARCK, EDWARD: *The History of Human Marriage,* 5th ed., 3 vols., Allerton Book Company, New York, 1922.

Some of the references in footnotes are repeated at the end of a chapter as suggestions for supplementary reading because they contain matter bearing upon the general theme of the chapter as well as information on the specific point for which they are cited. The others are additional suggestions of a more general character. These supplementary references are seldom repeated, even though a number of them discuss matters treated in several chapters.

Chapter II

THE POPULATION DOCTRINES OF MALTHUS

Malthus published the 1st edition of his essay on population in 1798.[1] It was a short treatise and owed

its origin to a conversation with a friend [probably his father], on the subject of Mr. Godwin's Essay, on avarice and profusion, in his Enquirer. . . .[2] The only authors from whose writings I had deduced the principle, which formed the main argument of the essay, were Hume, Wallace, Dr. Adam Smith, and Dr. Price; and my object was to apply it to try the truth of those speculations on the perfectibility of man and society, which at that time excited a considerable portion of the publick attention.[3]

1. MALTHUS' THESIS

The argument of Malthus in the 1st edition referred to in the preceding quotation is developed as follows:

I think I may fairly make two postulata.
First, That food is necessary to the existence of man.
Secondly, That the passion between the sexes is necessary, and will remain nearly in its present state.[4]

Assuming then, my postulata as granted, I say, that the power of population is indefinitely greater than the power in the earth to produce subsistence for man.
Population, when unchecked, increases in a geometrical ratio. Subsistence increases only in an arithmetical ratio. A slight acquaintance with numbers will shew the immensity of the first power in comparison of the second.[5]

[1] Thomas Robert Malthus, *An Essay on the Principle of Population as It Affects the Future Improvement of Society, with Remarks on the Speculations of Mr. Godwin, M. Condorcet, and Other Writers,* 396 pp., a facsimile reprint in *First Essay on Population, 1798,* with notes by James Bonar, Printed for the Royal Economic Society, Macmillan & Company, Ltd., London, 1926.
[2] *Ibid.,* p. i.
[3] Quoted by Bonar, in his notes to the facsimile edition, from the preface to the 2d edition of the Essay issued in 1803. *Ibid.,* p. xiv.
[4] *Ibid.,* p. 11.   [5] *Ibid.,* pp. 13–14.

The ratios Malthus had in mind were:

        Geometrical: 1, 2, 4, 8, 16, 32, etc.

        Arithmetical: 1, 2, 3, 4, 5, 6, etc.

The 2d edition of the Essay was several times as long as the 1st, and Malthus has this to say about it as compared with the 1st:

> In the course of this inquiry [*i.e.*, in preparing the second edition], I found that much more had been done, than I had been aware of, when I first published the essay. The poverty and misery arising from a too rapid increase of population, had been distinctly seen, and the most violent remedies proposed, so long ago as the times of Plato and Aristotle. And of late years, the subject had been treated in such a manner by some of the French Economists, occasionally by Montesquieu, and, among our own writers, by Dr. Franklin, Sir James Steuart, Mr. Arthur Young, and Mr. Townsend, as to create a natural surprise, that it had not excited more of the publick attention.[6]

It was the 2d edition of the Essay, and those which followed it, which made it proper to call Malthus the father of modern population study. In these he brought together a really large amount of data, considering what was available in his day, supporting his argument that the reason population did not grow much faster than it actually did was the hardship ("vice and misery") man suffered because of his tendency to outgrow his means of subsistence. Hunger and disease were the chief *positive* checks which kept down man's numbers, *i.e.*, the chief factors in keeping the death rate high. But in the 2d edition he recognized "another check to population [as] possible, which does not strictly come under the head either of vice or misery." This is the *preventive* check through which the birth rate might be reduced. Malthus thought of the preventive check as operating chiefly, perhaps wholly, through late marriage and abstinence within marriage, as the following quotation shows:

> With regard to the preventive check to population, though it must be acknowledged that that branch of it which comes under the head of moral restraint, does not at present prevail much among the male part of society, yet I am strongly disposed to believe that it prevails more than in those states which were first considered; and it can scarcely be doubted that in modern Europe a much larger proportion of women pass a considerable part of their lives in the exercise of this virtue than in past times and among uncivilised nations. But however this may be, if we consider only the general term which implies principally a delay of the marriage union from prudential considerations, without reference to consequences, it may be considered in this light as the most powerful of the checks which in

[6] *Ibid.,* Bonar's notes, pp. xiv–xv.

modern Europe keep down the population to the level of the means of subsistence.[7]

It does not appear from this that Malthus thought of contraception as a possible preventive check, although he must have known of the propaganda for it being carried on by Francis Place, Richard Carlile, and others. Place had begun active propaganda by 1823, and the preceding year he had published a defense of Malthus' views refuting Godwin's "perfectionism." It seems highly unlikely, therefore, that Malthus did not know that contraception was being put forward as a preventive check to population growth which if effectively practiced would substantially reduce the birth rate. We can only conclude (1) that Malthus did not believe contraception would become an effective preventive check within marriage and therefore did not believe that it merited serious discussion; or (2) that he regarded it as merely a means of avoiding the consequences of extramarital relations and as such disapproved of it so strongly that he did not wish to give it the publicity of being noticed; or (3) that he regarded any deliberate attempt to reduce the birth rate except through postponed marriage as vice and therefore classed it as a positive check. In any event, it appears that he did not believe there was any serious likelihood that the preventive check would effectively reduce the birth rate.

2. SOCIAL AND ECONOMIC CONDITIONS IN MALTHUS' TIME

In order to understand Malthus' work better, it will be well to call attention very briefly to some of the social conditions influencing his thought. The most common means used to check population growth in earlier times had, long before Malthus' time, come to be regarded in Western Europe as morally reprehensible (infanticide and abortion) or as foolish (sexual taboos). Over the centuries these changes had probably tended to raise the birth rate in this part of the world. There were also certain contemporary changes taking place in the social organization of Western Europe (for example, some small improvement of the living conditions of the lower classes in the population following the breakdown of feudalism and the beginning of modern industrial development) that were favorable to a higher rate of population increase because they reduced the death rate. Malthus was fully convinced that under the conditions existing in his day it was more than doubtful whether food and the other necessities of life

[7] Thomas Robert Malthus, *An Essay on Population,* Vol. 1, p. 315, J. M. Dent & Sons, Ltd., London; E. P. Dutton & Co., Inc., New York, n.d. (Everyman's Library, No. 692, reprinted from the 7th ed.). The 6th ed. of the Essay (1826) was the last to appear during Malthus' lifetime. But the 7th, which appeared after his death (1834), is commonly accepted as Malthus' work, and the above statements apply to this last edition.

(subsistence) could be increased fast enough to meet the needs of the off-spring that man not only was capable of producing but was quite likely to produce. Hence, he felt it incumbent upon him to expound his views regarding the way in which the human propensity to reproduce would inter-fere with the improvements in the living conditions of the mass of mankind which were coming to be expected by the "utopians" or "perfectionists." These people were, in Malthus' view, greatly exaggerating the possibilities of the increase in welfare that might arise from the application of scientific knowledge to agriculture and manufacturing because they were under-estimating the potentiality of human increase. Hence, they believed that a rate of improvement in the level of living was possible which Malthus thought was wholly unrealistic. This belief of Malthus at first rested chiefly on general considerations of the possible rate of increase of population on the one hand and of subsistence on the other.

In the 2d and later editions of the Essay he adduced a great body of facts to prove that when man had a relative abundance of subsistence his death rate fell and his rate of increase rose. He believed that with the birth rate prevailing in his day and with a reasonable abundance of subsistence, population could and would double each 25 years. As he showed in later editions of the Essay, it had probably been growing at about this rate in the United States for some decades. A natural increase of approximately 28 per 1,000 per year will double population in 25 years, and such a rate of increase could, in the absence of strong positive checks, take place with a birth rate of 43 and a death rate of 15. Today we have far more evidence than Malthus that such an increase not only is possible but has actually been attained occasionally for rather short periods under favorable living conditions. It was because Malthus was convinced that the alleviation of the positive checks to population growth would immediately be accompanied by a greater rate of population growth that he held any permanent improve-ment in the lot of mankind would be extremely difficult (at first, he thought impossible) to attain and even if attained would not continue for long.[8]

This very brief and inadequate statement of the differences between the 1st and 2d editions cannot be pursued further. It might be said, however, that to judge from the way in which he treated the 1st edition in his later writings he himself regarded it merely as a statement of the general prin-ciple of population growth and that he regarded the later editions as express-ing this principle more accurately and as providing the data needed to get a true view of the dynamics of population growth. In view of Malthus' own attitude toward the 1st edition, it seems odd that many of his critics have written as though they were unaware that this edition had ever been revised —or, one should say, rewritten.

[8] G. Talbot Griffith, *Population Problems of the Age of Malthus*, Chap. 4, Cam-bridge University Press, London, 1926.

It was noted in the first quotation from Malthus given above that the Essay was originally written to refute ideas regarding the probable rapidity and extent of the improvement of man's lot which the utopians and perfectionists were spreading abroad. Malthus was as interested in increasing human welfare as were the utopians, but he thought their enthusiasm should be tempered with reason based on fact—that it served no good purpose to encourage visions of improvement in manner of living which were utterly unattainable. Thus, while he was strongly humanitarian in his sympathies, he tried to be scientific in his evaluation of the probabilities of attaining the ease of living pictured by the utopians. He wanted the facts to speak for themselves, and in the author's opinion Malthus made good use of the facts which were available to him. Although many people lay the blame on Malthus for the doctrine of many of the classical economists that man's hardship and suffering are solely the result of his tendency to produce too many children, he certainly did not accept this view without qualifications. Moreover, he did not absolve from blame those employers who did all they could to enforce "the iron law of wages" because they regarded labor simply as a commodity to be bought in the market just like any other commodity.

Malthus recognized that the greed and the meanness of some employers increased the misery of the workers, and he most certainly did not regard the tendency of population to increase too rapidly for its own good as absolving the employer from the moral obligation to treat his employees as human beings rather than as chattels to be used for his own enrichment. But he did not think that man would attain freedom from hardship (the positive check) as long as he did not adopt the preventive check, i.e., did not reduce his birth rate, although he had no practical suggestion as to how this latter was to be accomplished.

As illustrating the way in which Malthus modified his theory to accord with facts, attention may be called to his recognition that under special conditions man could, for a time, increase subsistence as fast as, or even faster than, population could grow. The United States was his favorite example of a population growing very rapidly because it had access to large areas of new and fertile land and in consequence suffered much less than most countries from the operation of the positive checks. Malthus recognized that, for the duration of the expansion into new lands such as those of the United States, subsistence could increase at a very rapid rate and, like population, could double in about 25 years. The fact that man's numbers did not generally show such a rapid increase as in the United States merely proved that vice and misery, the positive checks, were responsible for man's relatively slow growth over long periods of time.

As already noted Malthus did recognize a second type of check to population growth—the preventive—but he did not believe that this would so reduce the birth rate of any people that the positive checks of vice and hardship could be rendered inoperative. In the author's opinion this was Malthus' first and most serious error, for although he lived until 1834 and although there was considerable discussion of contraception before that time, he never gave any evidence of recognizing that by its use a substantial reduction of the birth rate was a practical possibility. Some reasons for this failure have been suggested above. But whatever the reason, the fact is that Malthus did not see any considerable hope that the positive checks to population growth might be replaced by the preventive check and that man might adjust his growth to his ability to produce subsistence.

Malthus' second great error, in the author's opinion, was in failing to recognize more clearly the possibilities of increase in production growing out of the application of science to agriculture, manufacturing, and transportation. It is probable that the exaggerations of the perfectionists with regard to what could be accomplished in these respects helped to blind him to some extent to the probabilities of improvement. But Malthus was not an unthinking pessimist. He did believe that man could and would improve his living conditions. But he also believed that man's tendency to reproduce at a fairly rapid rate would increase the difficulty of improvement and would delay its realization.

In the opinion of the author, Malthus was essentially correct in his view that in the absence of effective preventive checks man, with only occasional and short-lived exceptions, would continue to suffer from the positive checks leading to a high death rate, that more children would be born than could be reared, and that the balance between numbers and subsistence would be maintained only by the excessive deaths arising from hardships.

Malthus' primary contribution to the study of population, and the one which in my opinion makes him the real father of modern population study, was his use of facts for the support of his general doctrine regarding the dynamics of population growth and change. He is more responsible than anyone else for bringing population study within the field of social science. Whereas it had been largely philosophical and speculative before his time, thenceforward, with only a few exceptions, men were to discuss the growth of population chiefly as a question of direct public concern about which action might be taken with a view to affecting human welfare. No longer could man's growth in numbers be looked upon as something which did not concern him because he could do nothing about it. The study of population was to become a proper field of investigation for man, with a view to greater control leading to greater welfare. Malthus' Essay could not have had this effect, of course, if the time had not been ripe for social science to begin to supersede social speculation and for man to undertake more actively the guidance of his own destiny. Malthus was a social scientist rather than a social philosopher. This is the reason we still find much of value in his work, although he made rather serious errors in evaluating the importance of contraception as a preventive check and also in evaluating the effect of science in increasing production.

Malthus had a sound factual foundation for maintaining that, under the conditions he knew, man suffered from the positive checks and that this condition would continue if he did not use effective preventive checks. We have much less reason to repeat Malthus' errors today, although, as a matter of fact, much the larger part of mankind still lives under the conditions described by Malthus in which only the severity of the positive checks prevents a far more rapid increase in numbers. Among these peoples the increase in numbers still proceeds at about the same pace as the increase in production, and there is consequently little or no improvement in level of living. Malthus deserves great credit for bringing this problem to the attention of people as well as for the calm and objective manner in which he analyzed the facts available to him and thus increased our understanding of one important element affecting human welfare. To dwell on Malthus' mistakes and to overlook his contribution to our understanding of social conditions in our day is altogether too common. It is to be hoped that as our work proceeds Malthus' place as an earnest and enlightened student of this particular social question will emerge more clearly and that we shall be able to appreciate him and his work more adequately.

3. MALTHUS ON OTHER ASPECTS OF POPULATION PROBLEMS

We find that, in addition to the ideas discussed above, Malthus expressed himself quite fully on numerous other aspects of population growth which are of considerable interest to us today. It would be doing him an injustice not to state his position on some of these more important problems, because it would give the impression that his thinking was less complete and his Essay less thorough, in the later editions, than was actually the case.

Malthus saw clearly that emigration was an important factor in population growth, and he discussed the effects both upon the mother country and upon the country of destination. From the standpoint of the country sending out emigrants he believed that such a policy, as a permanent means of relieving pressure, was useless since it would result almost immediately in somewhat earlier marriages and a greater number of births per marriage. In addition, if it did reduce pressure it would also reduce the death rate; hence, the pressure would soon be as great as or even greater than it ever had been. The following passages state his position plainly:

> The population of the United States of America, according to the fourth census, in 1820, was 7,861,710. We have no reason to believe that Great Britain is less populous at present for the migration of the small parent stock which produced these numbers. On the contrary, a certain degree of emigration is known to be favourable to the population of the mother

country. It has been particularly remarked that the two Spanish provinces from which the greatest number of people emigrated to America became in consequence more populous.[9]

Another passage will also throw light on Malthus' attitude toward emigration:

It is clear, therefore, that with any view of making room for an unrestricted increase of population, emigration is perfectly inadequate; but as a partial and temporary expedient, and with a view to the more general cultivation of the earth, and the wider extension of civilisation, it seems to be both useful and proper; and if it cannot be proved that governments are bound actively to encourage it, it is not only strikingly unjust, but in the highest degree impolitic in them to prevent it. There are no fears so totally ill-grounded as the fears of depopulation from emigration. The *vis inertiae* of the great body of the people, and their attachment to their homes, are qualities so strong and general that we may rest assured they will not emigrate unless, from political discontents or extreme poverty, they are in such a state as will make it as much for the advantage of their country as of themselves that they should go out of it. The complaints of high wages in consequence of emigrations are of all others the most unreasonable, and ought the least to be attended to. If the wages of labour in any country be such as to enable the lower classes of people to live with tolerable comfort, we may be quite certain that they will not emigrate; and if they be not such, it is cruelty and injustice to detain them.[10]

As regards the effect of immigration on the growth of a country, Malthus believed that whether or not it was of importance depended upon the circumstances of the particular case. The United States of America is his favorite example of a country increasing very rapidly in population from a relatively small immigration, owing to the ease of making a living. His "principle of population," however, would lead him to hold, logically, that if the demand for labor in any country were to any considerable extent supplied from without, the growth within the country by natural increase would be retarded, in the long run, because of the earlier time at which the pressure of numbers on subsistence would come into play and a higher death rate would ensue.

Malthus also foresaw that it was possible for a high degree of specialization in agriculture and other industries to develop in any country, provided that it could trade its products for those of other countries specializing along different lines, and hence that there was no inherent virtue in the

---

[9] Malthus, *An Essay on Population*, Vol. 1, p. 306. This same statement, using 1800 census figures instead of those for 1820, occurs on p. 56 in the 1st American edition of the Essay, printed from the 3d London edition in 1809.

[10] *Ibid.*, Vol. 2, p. 36.

mercantile system. The following quotations will give his ideas on this matter:

> It must ever be true that the surplus produce of the cultivators, taken in its most enlarged sense, measures and limits the growth of that part of the society which is not employed upon the land. Throughout the whole world the number of manufacturers, of merchants, of proprietors, and of persons engaged in the various civil and military professions, must be exactly proportioned to this surplus produce and cannot in the nature of things increase beyond it.[11]

> A country which excels in commerce and manufactures may purchase corn from a great variety of others; and it may be supposed, perhaps, that, proceeding upon this system, it may continue to purchase an increasing quantity, and to maintain a rapidly increasing population, till the lands of all the nations with which it trades are fully cultivated. As this is an event necessarily at a great distance, it may appear that the population of such a country will not be checked from the difficulty of procuring subsistence till after the lapse of a great number of ages.
> There are, however, causes constantly in operation which will occasion the pressure of this difficulty long before the event here contemplated has taken place, and while the means of raising food in the surrounding countries may still be comparatively abundant.[12]

Malthus believed, in consequence, that the country which depended on adventitious factors, such as skill and capital, could not long hope to maintain its place secure, as there were many forces at work to undermine its power. All countries accumulate capital as time goes on, and skill in work is easily acquired if there is any demand for it. Consequently, commercial and manufacturing countries were always in a more or less precarious position because of the potential rise of competition in other countries having abundance of land as well as other natural resources.

In reading his discussion of the relative advantages and disadvantages of countries largely given over to industry and commerce and of those having large reserves of land, one could almost imagine that he was reading a description of the present-day conditions confronting Great Britain, on the one hand, and Australia or Argentina, on the other. So clearly does Malthus depict the limitations of a nation which acts as manufacturer, middleman, and carrier and has small agricultural resources and the advantages of a nation which has a combined agricultural and commercial system, that one cannot but feel that he was very clear-sighted when he looked ahead and attempted to set forth the effects of commercial and agricultural systems, simple and combined, upon population growth.

[11] *Ibid.,* p. 76.   [12] *Ibid.,* p. 79.

From Malthus' view on the advantages and disadvantages of the industrial specialization of nations one may deduce his attitude toward the distribution of population, as between agriculture and other industries. It would be that a nation should be largely self-supporting if it wished to be reasonably independent of the vicissitudes of the fortunes of other nations. According to his view, any country which supported any considerable part of its population by imported food was doomed to suffer therefor sooner or later. He was also opposed to the growth of great towns as detrimental to both the health and the morals of the people and to the enduring strength of the nation.

Of the problem of eugenics, as it is studied today, Malthus knew nothing. The differential birth rate, or perhaps one had better say the differential *survival* rate, had not yet made the problem of quality stand out clearly. Malthus frequently mentions the fact that paupers and the improvident nearly always marry early and bring into the world an abundant progeny, while the prudent are cautious, marry late, and consequently have fewer children. It was probably even more true in his day than now that the death rate of the improvident was greatly in excess of that of the prudent, so that the number of the children of the improvident reaching maturity was not so much greater as the differences in birth rates might have led Malthus to suppose. So far was Malthus from feeling that there was any problem of quality involved in the difference of birth rates among the improvident and the prudent that he always urged celibacy and late marriages upon the prudent as the chief means of lessening the pressure of population. He was opposed to poor-law charity not because it allowed an inferior class to increase at the expense of a superior class (as is so often urged today) but because it increased the improvidence of the paupers and defeated its own ends by increasing the numbers dependent upon charity for support. The relief of poverty was like the labor of Sisyphus—it was unending—and, one may add, the better it succeeded at one time the greater was the disaster later on.

According to Malthus' view, there was but one sensible method of improving the conditions of the mass of the population, and that was to control the growth of population so that it would not increase as rapidly as the means of subsistence; the outlook for the future depended upon how effective the preventive check could be made, particularly that form of the preventive check which Malthus called "moral restraint."

4. PESSIMISTIC OUTLOOK

In the 1st edition of the Essay one may say that Malthus' pessimism was unmitigated and profound, because he did not believe that the preventive check could be made effective. But as time went on, he observed many circumstances which led him to believe that man could more or less control his growth in numbers if he would and that he was actually doing so to some extent. If he could do this, then there was no reason why his condition should not be steadily improved, even though there would always remain a certain amount of pressure on the means of subsistence. The following quotation from the close of the 7th edition of the Essay will give Malthus' final judgment regarding the "future improvement of society":

From a review of the state of society in former periods compared with the present, I should certainly say that the evils resulting from the principle of population have rather diminished than increased, even under the disadvantage of an almost total ignorance of the real cause. And if we can indulge the hope that this ignorance will be gradually dissipated, it does not seem unreasonable to expect that they will be still further diminished. The increase of absolute population, which will of course take place, will evidently tend but little to weaken this expectation, as everything depends upon the relative proportion between population and food, and not on the absolute number of people. In the former part of this work it appeared that the countries which possessed the fewest people often suffered the most from the effects of the principle of population; and it can scarcely be doubted that, taking Europe throughout, fewer famines and fewer diseases arising from want have prevailed in the last century than in those which preceded it.

On the whole, therefore, though our future prospects respecting the mitigation of the evils arising from the principle of population may not be so bright as we could wish, yet they are far from being entirely disheartening, and by no means preclude that gradual and progressive improvement in human society which, before the late wild speculations on this subject, was the object of rational expectation. . . .

It would indeed be a melancholy reflection that, while the views of physical science are daily enlarging, so as scarcely to be bounded by the most distant horizon, the science of moral and political philosophy should be confined within such narrow limits, or at best be so feeble in its influence, as to be unable to counteract the obstacles to human happiness arising from a single cause. But however formidable these obstacles may have appeared in some parts of this work, it is hoped that the general result of the inquiry is such as not to make us give up the improvement of human society in despair. The partial good which seems to be attainable is worthy of all our exertions; is sufficient to direct our efforts and animate our prospects. And although we cannot expect that the virtue and happiness of mankind will keep pace with the brilliant career of physical discovery; yet, if we are not wanting to ourselves, we may confidently indulge the hope that, to no unimportant extent, they will be influenced by its progress and will partake in its success.[13]

[13] *Ibid.*, pp. 261–262

If the preceding quotations and comments have succeeded even moderately well in presenting the more salient features in Malthus' thinking, it is clear that he has been greatly misrepresented by many people. Probably the chief sinners in this respect have been those who never read him carefully. There have been others, however, who have been unable to see any truth whatever in his position because they believed that the ratios would not hold. Furthermore, there are those today who seem to think that Malthus is responsible for all the practices now frequently called "neo-Malthusian," which they believe are harmful to the race, both physically and morally. Therefore, they hold that there is something inherently reprehensible in his doctrines. They fail to appreciate the fact that it is only because there is a large measure of truth in Malthus' doctrines that men feel the need of resorting to contraception to keep their families within reasonable limits. Those who do not believe in contraception should not cavil at Malthus, since he was only the expositor of what he believed to be facts; they should rather condemn nature, which has made man more fertile than he should be if he is to reproduce without hindrance and yet live in decency and comfort.

5. CONCLUSION

To the author it seems eminently just that all modern study of population problems should start from Malthus, even though the ideas that he set forth were not altogether original and were destined to be greatly modified and amended in the course of time. Malthus presented so clearly a useful point of view for the study of population that his work well deserves to be considered the point of departure for our study of population. He never thought for a moment that he had said the last word on any aspect of population questions, though he did believe in the fundamental antagonism of man's sex passion and his ability to produce the means of subsistence. It should also be borne in mind that in some parts of the Essay Malthus touched on most of the present-day problems of population and that in nearly every case this treatment is enlightening, if not final. Altogether, Malthus richly deserves the place of honor generally accorded him by those who are familiar with his work.

Suggestions for Supplementary Reading

BONAR, JAMES: *Malthus and His Work,* 438 pp., The Macmillan Company, New York, 1924.

FIELD, JAMES A.: *Essays on Population and Other Papers,* 440 pp., University of Chicago Press, Chicago, 1931.

GODWIN, WILLIAM: *Of Population: An Enquiry Concerning the Power of Increase in the Numbers of Mankind. Being an Answer to Mr. Malthus's Essay on That Subject,* 626 pp., Longman, Hurst, Rees, Orme, and Brown, London, 1820.

GRIFFITH, GROSVENOR TALBOT: *Population Problems of the Age of Malthus*, 276 pp., Cambridge University Press, London, 1926.

KEYNES, JOHN MAYNARD: *Essays in Biography*, 318 pp., Harcourt, Brace and Company, Inc., New York, 1933.

LEVIN, S. M.: "Malthus' Conception of the Checks to Population," *Human Biology*, May, 1938.

MALTHUS, THOMAS ROBERT: *An Essay on Population*, 2 vols., J. M. Dent & Sons, Ltd., London; E. P. Dutton & Co., Inc., New York, n.d. (Everyman's Library, Nos. 692–693).

————: *First Essay on Population, 1798*, 396 pp., with notes by James Bonar. Printed for the Royal Economic Society, Macmillan & Co., Ltd., London, 1926. A facsimile reprint.

PLACE, FRANCIS: *Illustrations and Proofs of the Principle of Population, Including an Examination of the Proposed Remedies of Mr. Malthus, and a Reply to the Objections of Mr. Godwin and Others*, ed. by Norman E. Himes, 354 pp., Houghton Mifflin Company, Boston, 1930.

STANGELAND, CHARLES EMIL: *Pre-Malthusian Doctrines of Population: A Study in the History of Economic Theory*, 356 pp., Columbia University Press, The Macmillan Company (agents), New York, 1904.

CHAPTER III

SOME POST-MALTHUSIAN THEORIES OF POPULATION

It was to be expected that, as shortcomings in Malthus' theory of population became apparent, as interest in social science increased, and as important changes took place in the structure of society (the development of an industrial society), there would be many attempts to develop a theory of population growth which would provide a more adequate explanation of the population changes which were taking place. In this chapter a few of these theories are summarized briefly in order to show the chief directions in which men have been reaching out for an explanation of the facts of population growth since Malthus' day.

Malthus had set a style in population theory, however, and the most important theories arising in England for some time followed his lead in searching for a "natural" tendency which would explain the actual growth of population and at the same time would not close the door to more optimistic conclusions regarding the influence of population growth on welfare than he had arrived at. No doubt the conditions arising out of the industrial revolution made many people feel that Malthus' pessimism, even the modified pessimism of his later years, was not justified and consequently that his theory must be discarded. This led to the propounding of several theories which were just as "natural" as his but which would not to the same degree preclude faith in human "progress" as an inevitable accompaniment of social development.

1. NATURAL THEORIES OF POPULATION GROWTH

Sadler. Sadler's theory was published during Malthus' lifetime. The following quotations outline his general position:

> The principle of human increase thus obtained may be very briefly enunciated and is simply this: The fecundity of human beings is, *caeteris paribus*, in the inverse ratio of the condensation of their numbers; and, still in direct contradiction to the theory now maintained [Malthus'], the variation in that fecundity is effectuated not by the wretchedness and misery but by the happiness and prosperity of the species. . . .

33

Excluding, of course, cases of extreme distress, a state of labour and privation is that most favourable to human fecundity. A dispersed and scanty population invariably implies that state; but as mankind advance from the hunting to the pastoral, and from thence to the agricultural stages of existence, and ultimately rise to the highest condition of civilization, labour becomes divided and consequently diminished in its duration and intensity, and many are liberated from its drudgeries, so as to devote themselves to other and more intellectual pursuits, or are rendered independent of it altogether; while the means of subsistence become progressively augmented, and ease and luxury more generally diffused. At every step the principle of increase contracts, and, as I contend, would pause at that precise point where it had secured the utmost possible degree of happiness to the greatest possible number of human beings.[1]

Just as Malthus believed that he had stated a natural principle or law of population growth which of necessity precluded faith in the rapid improvement of man's lot in this world, so Sadler believed that he had discovered a natural principle that furnished a rational basis for faith in the rapid perfectibility of man's lot. Again he says: "The law of population, by which the increase of mankind has been and still is, in all cases, regulated, is simply this: *The fecundity of human beings under similar circumstances, varies inversely as their numbers on a given space.*"[2]

The reader will no doubt have been somewhat confused by the use of the terms *fecundity* and *principle of increase* in the above quotations. In the last paragraph quoted, Sadler seems to have used fecundity in the sense in which it is generally used today, namely, as connoting the physiological capacity to conceive. However, when he used fecundity in the statement of Malthus' views (in the first paragraph quoted), to the effect that the variation in fecundity is "effectuated" not by wretchedness and misery but by happiness and prosperity, he was either using fecundity to mean actual reproduction, *i.e.*, fertility (Chap. VIII), or he failed to see any difference between the ability to conceive and the actual increase of population and hence misunderstood Malthus' views.

Malthus believed that the fecundity (ability to conceive) of the human race was high and that fertility (actual reproduction) was also high and would remain high unless a much more effective preventive check was developed than he was able to foresee. Hence, population growth was generally slow at most times only because of the operation of the social and economic conditions which he described as positive checks, *i.e.*, because of

[1] Michael Thomas Sadler, *Ireland: Its Evils and Their Remedies. Being a Refutation of the Errors of the Emigration Committee, and Others, Touching That Country. To Which Is Prefixed a Synopsis of the Original Treatise About to Be Published on the Law of Population; Developing the Real Principle on Which It Is Universally Regulated,* 2d ed., pp. xviii–xix, John Murray, London, 1829.

[2] *Ibid.,* p. xxviii.

a high death rate. Sadler apparently failed to grasp these points in Malthus' argument but thought he had found a different principle at work, namely, that fecundity—and here the author believes he really meant the ability to conceive—diminished as the density of population increased. Hence, he held that man's happiness, as far as it depended upon the ratio between the increase in production and the increase in population, was ensured by the very law of his growth. Such a theory furnished the basis of an easy optimism as regards man's economic future, for as soon as his numbers began to get dense, man would necessarily cease to reproduce as rapidly as he had been because he would lose the power to do so. Thus all would be well without any particular effort on man's part to control his growth.

Obviously, there are certain grave defects in this theory. So far as we can judge from facts which are available today, the Javanese, the Chinese, and the Hindus are among the most fecund as well as the most fertile of peoples, and at the same time they are among the most densely crowded of peoples. It is possible, of course, that Sadler is using "dense" in a different sense. There can be no reasonable doubt, however, of Sadler's failure to realize that Malthus had definitely shown that a population may be very fertile, i.e., that it can have a high birth rate and yet have little or no growth because of the high death rate. (A population cannot have high fertility without also being highly fecund, but it can be highly fecund without having high fertility.) Sadler must have known this, but since he was interested in proving that there was no antagonism between man's "natural" capacity to reproduce and his capacity to produce subsistence, he was led to hold that man's fecundity diminished as his capacity to produce increased.

Doubleday. Doubleday's theory is somewhat similar to that of Sadler but is expressed in terms of food rather than in terms of density. He stated it as follows:

> The *great general law* then, which, as it seems, really regulates the increase or decrease both of vegetable and of animal life, is this, that whenever a *species* or *genus* is *endangered*, a corresponding effort is invariably made by nature for its preservation and continuance, by an increase of fecundity or fertility; and that this especially takes place whenever such danger arises from a diminution of proper nourishment or food, so that consequently the state of depletion, or the deplethoric state, is favourable to fertility, and that on the other hand, the plethoric state, or state of repletion, is unfavourable to fertility, in the ratio of the intensity of each state, and this probably throughout nature universally, in the vegetable as well as the animal world; further, that as applied to mankind this law produces the following consequences, and acts thus:
>
> There is in all societies a constant increase going on amongst that portion of it which is the worst supplied with food; in short, amongst the poorest.
>
> Amongst those in the state of affluence, and well supplied with food and luxuries, a constant decrease goes on. Amongst those who form the mean

or medium between these two opposite states; that is to say, amongst those who are tolerably well supplied with good food, and not overworked, nor yet idle, population is stationary. Hence it follows that it is upon the *numerical proportion* which these three states bear to each other in any society that increase or decrease upon the whole depends.

In a nation where the affluence is sufficient to balance, by the decrease which it causes amongst the rich, the increase arising from the poor, population will be stationary. In a nation highly and generally affluent and luxurious, population will decrease and decay. In poor and ill-fed communities population will increase in the ratio of the poverty, and the consequent deterioration and diminution of the food of a large portion of the members of such communities. This is the real and great law of human population, and to show that it unquestionably is so, must be the aim of the following pages.[3]

Doubleday explicitly uses fecundity and fertility as interchangeable terms, but his principle of population makes no sense unless he really means that the capacity to reproduce, rather than actual reproduction, decreases as the food supply becomes abundant and varied and increases as it becomes scanty and monotonous. He argues that peoples who are heavy meat eaters are less fecund than those who subsist largely on grain and vegetables. Thus Doubleday finds a general law of population growth in the inverse relation between the abundance and variety of food and the ability to reproduce—the better the food, the lower the fecundity.

It requires but little acquaintance with the facts available regarding differences in fecundity to make it appear highly doubtful that such differences are group differences. They appear rather to be individual differences. There is no clear proof that differences in diet have any significant effect on the ability of people to reproduce, de Castro [4] to the contrary notwithstanding. There are, however, a good many physicians who believe that the overeating of rich foods does have a depressing effect upon the reproductive capacity of the individual, but inasmuch as this overeating is generally accompanied by many other conditions which might also reduce reproductive capacity, it cannot be said with certainty just what is the effective cause of lack of reproductive capacity in the overfed classes, if it is a fact. What is actually observed is a small number of births rather than a low capacity to conceive, and this low fertility is more likely to be voluntary than due to the inability to conceive. Doubleday like Sadler seems to have missed the main point of Malthus. It was the antagonism between actual fertility and the ability to rear the children born that led Malthus to his belief in the

[3] Thomas Doubleday, *The True Law of Population Shewn to Be Connected with the Food of the People*, 2d ed., pp. 5–7, George Pierce, London, 1847.

[4] Josué de Castro, *The Geography of Hunger*, pp. 71–72, Little, Brown & Company, Boston, 1952, revives Doubleday's theory and makes the appearance of giving it a scientific foundation.

general and continued operation of the positive checks. Neither Sadler nor Doubleday seems to have realized that a law of population growth must do more than account for changes in the reproductive capacity of a population unless it can be proved that such changes are large and take place so rapidly as to effect continual changes in the actual rate of growth. Malthus was trying to explain changes in growth which were actually observed, and he assumed an almost, if not entirely constant, level of fecundity. He also believed that the social conditions which prevailed in his day led to the realization of such a large part of the fecundity of the race that the level of fertility would remain high until these social conditions changed. Malthus realized clearly, as apparently neither Sadler nor Doubleday did, that the growth of population results from the difference between the birth rate and the death rate, and both of these are variables. He also assumed—and very properly, it seems to me—that human experience in the past had proved that the birth rate was less variable than the death rate, and hence that the actual rate of growth had generally depended on the level of the death rate. Both Sadler and Doubleday failed to recognize the fact that it was the actual growth of population that must be explained in any satisfactory "law" or "principle" of population such as they were searching for.

Spencer. Spencer's theory—that, as complexity of life increased, a reduction in fecundity takes place—belongs in the same group of theories as those of Sadler and Doubleday, because though it is directly at variance with them on certain points, it invokes a natural change in capacity to reproduce to explain changes in the growth of population. But Spencer finds the cause of this change in fecundity not in such simple factors as density of population and abundance of food but in the increase in the complexity of the social organization leading to an increased expenditure of energy in non-reproductive activities. To use his own terms there is in nature an antagonism between *individuation* and *genesis*. As the output of the individual's energy used in personal development increases, the amount of energy available for reproduction decreases. Hence, the more strenuous the adjustments the individual must make to ensure his own existence and success, the weaker are his efforts toward reproduction. The following quotation will help to make Spencer's position clear:

> That absolute or relative infertility is generally produced in women by mental labour carried to excess, is more clearly shown. Though the regimen of upper-class girls is not what it should be, yet, considering that their feeding is better than that of girls belonging to the poorer classes, while, in most other respects, their physical treatment is not worse, the deficiency of reproductive power among them may be reasonably attributed to the overtaxing of their brains—an overtaxing which produces a serious reaction on the physique. This diminution of reproductive power is not shown only by the greater frequency of absolute sterility; nor is it shown only in the

earlier cessation of child bearing; but it is also shown in the very frequent inability of such women to suckle their infants. In its full sense, the reproductive power means the power to bear a well-developed infant, and to supply that infant with the natural food for the natural period. Most of the flat-chested girls who survive their high-pressure education are incompetent to do this. Were their fertility measured by the number of children they could rear without artificial aid, they would prove relatively very infertile.[5]

As a consequence of the operation of a natural law, Spencer, like Sadler and Doubleday, foresees the disappearance of population pressure and its accompanying evils. When this time comes we shall have "a state of things requiring from each individual no more than a normal and pleasurable activity." [6] Spencer felt that he had found a law of population growth which would explain the facts of human growth and would fit into his general theory of the nature of evolution. Indeed, he says: "In the end, therefore, the obtainment of subsistence and discharge of all the parental and social duties will require just that kind and that amount of action needful to health and happiness." [7] One is inclined to believe that Spencer was probably more interested in developing a population theory consistent with his general biological views than in searching for the truth. Life does not appear to have the beautiful consistency of Spencer's theory. The easy optimism that it encourages scarcely seems justified in the light of our greater knowledge.

Gini. Gini's theory is more than a theory of population growth, for it is also a theory of social evolution in which the evolution of nations is closely linked to the changes in their rate of population growth. Gini believes that the different rates of increase in different classes or sections of the population may very rapidly change the biological traits of a population. He bases this belief on the well-established fact that a rather small proportion of one generation generally produces the majority of the succeeding generation.[8] The process of the growth of nations he describes as "the cyclical rise and fall of population." [9] This cycle of growth in a population is likened to the life cycle of the individual. There is first a period of extremely rapid growth, followed by a period of slower growth and mature achievement, which, in turn, passes into a period of senescence, during which numbers decline and the quality of a civilization deteriorates. Every nation in its youth is simple

[5] Herbert Spencer, *The Principles of Biology,* Vol. 2, pp. 485–486, D. Appleton & Company, Inc., New York, 1867–1868.

[6] *Ibid.,* p. 506.

[7] *Ibid.*

[8] Harris Foundation, *Population. Lectures on the Harris Foundation, 1929, by Corrado Gini . . . Shiroshi Nasu . . . Robert R. Kuczynski . . . Oliver Edwin Baker . . . ,* pp. 17–18, University of Chicago Press, Chicago, 1930.

[9] *Ibid.,* p. 4.

and undifferentiated in structure and has a high rate of fertility, because each generation springs from the people who are hereditarily most prolific. As a consequence, such a nation grows rapidly in numbers; and with this growth in numbers goes growth in complexity of organization, as manifested by the development of social classes and the growth of industrial and commercial activities. With increasing numbers, pressure of population begins to be felt, and expansion takes place through war or colonization or both.

In the next stage there is increasing complexity of social and economic organization, accompanied by a decrease in rate of growth which is due in part to the loss of the most energetic through war and colonization and in part to the increase in the proportion of the population in the upper classes, which are always less prolific than are the lower classes. The chief cause of slackening of population growth, however, is biological.[10] Gini believes that the biological factor in declining fertility is the fundamental factor and that it really underlies the influence of economic and social factors, which only *apparently* determine the decline in fertility. In other words, the decline in fertility (the actual number of children born) is due to a decline in fecundity (the ability to bear children). This decline in fertility is first manifested in the upper classes, but once it sets in there, it is only a comparatively short time before it becomes apparent in all classes. Indeed, with the absorption of the more energetic and prolific members of the lower classes into the upper classes, they, too, become relatively sterile, like the older portion of these classes, and do not revive the fertility of the class as a whole. Even the sterility of these climbers is not a consequence of the social conditions surrounding their climbing, according to Professor Gini; it is rather the outgrowth of the weakening of the reproductive instinct and is an inevitable phase of the cycle of population growth.

Professor Gini also holds that when the decline in reproduction sets in, there is a similar decline in the qualities of the individual, and that so far as one may judge, both of these follow upon some biological change in the hereditary qualities of the individual. To quote:

> The ideas set forth above throw new light on the phenomenon of the different rate of growth of the social classes, which has led many students in the past to fear progressive decline in the quality of the nations. On the contrary, we now see it is a providential mechanism for the elimination of those family stocks which have fulfilled the cycle of their evolution. . . .[11]

Even allowing that the word "providential" is not happily chosen, it yet appears that Gini believes in some inevitable and natural force which determines the rise and fall of populations. This he finds in the mixture of races and in the selection of new types arising from this mixture, thus looking to

---

[10] *Ibid.*, p. 23.   [11] *Ibid.*, pp. 24–25.

biological more than to social factors in human life for the explanation of man's growth in numbers and also of the distinctive characteristics of his civilizations.

No attempt will be made here to criticize Gini's general theory of population growth and of social evolution. It is, however, a matter of doubt whether or not one may accept as valid any theory of population growth which, for the explanation of human conduct, falls back upon those unknown and inscrutable natural forces over which we have little or no control. To do this savors somewhat of that mysticism of which there is always too much in the study of social science. The author's views on the forces determining population growth will be found in numerous places in what follows.

2. SOME SOCIAL THEORIES OF POPULATION GROWTH

Marx. Karl Marx took a view of the causes of poverty that he believed to be completely contrary to that of Malthus. I say "believed to be" because a careful perusal of Marx's views on population leads me to conclude that he never took the trouble to examine Malthus' doctrines carefully. He attributed to Malthus the view that all poverty and hardship were due to man's inherent tendency to grow in numbers faster than his production of subsistence would permit. As I have indicated above, I believe that Malthus considerably modified his views in the later editions of his Essay and recognized that man's growth in numbers to the limit of his subsistence was not an inevitable consequence of his nature, but that under the conditions of life that had generally prevailed in the past such growth did as a rule actually take place. Marx, on the other hand, claimed that man's tendency to press on the means of subsistence was due solely to the evils of the social systems which had prevailed up to his day. In his own words:

> It is the working population which, while effecting the accumulation of capital, also produces the means whereby it is itself rendered relatively superfluous, is turned into a relative surplus population; and it does so to an ever increasing extent. This is a law of population peculiar to the capitalist method of production; and, in fact, every method of production that arises in the course of history has its own peculiar, historically valid, law of population. It is only for plants and animals that there is a law of population in the abstract; and that only in so far as man does not interfere with them.[12]

As this statement indicates, Marx held that the poverty which so much concerned Malthus was entirely a consequence of unemployment, which

[12] Karl Marx, *Capital. A Critique of Political Economy. The Process of Capitalist Production,* translated from the 4th German ed. by Eden and Cedar Paul, pp. 697–698, International Publishers Co., New York, 1929.

was an inevitable accompaniment of the development of modern capitalism. It would also appear that poverty in past times would be explained by Marx entirely in terms of social conditions imposed by the capitalists of those times on the masses of the people. It seems to the author, however, that Marx would not have manifested such extreme bitterness toward Malthus and his doctrines [13] if he had felt as certain of his own position as he wished to appear. He must have had deep-seated doubts that Malthus' views could be refuted or he would not have gone to the trouble of trying to discredit them by ridicule and invective rather than by appealing to facts. Clearly Marx felt that much of the strength of his own argument against capitalism depended on denying any truth whatever to the position of Malthus that man's tendency to grow in numbers more rapidly than he could increase subsistence had a harmful effect upon the improvement of his manner of living. But all Marx really proved as regards population and its relation to poverty was that an amelioration of the lot of the British workingman of his day, the third quarter of the nineteenth century, was possible if the abuses of the system (capitalism) were lessened or abolished.

It has probably always been true that some improvement in the living conditions of the masses could be effected, at least temporarily, by the abolition of the abuses which accompany the development of every social system. Marx certainly did not prove that the uncontrolled growth of population was not an important factor in making possible many of the abuses of the capitalism of his day, or that these abuses were the inevitable consequence of capitalism alone and therefore could not be lessened or abolished unless the system itself were abolished.

In general character Marx's population doctrines resembled those of Godwin which originally provided the occasion for Malthus' Essay. Marx can find no natural law of population growth which inevitably operates in such a way as to prevent any lasting improvement in man's living conditions. In the opinion of the author, Malthus had also moved a considerable distance in this direction in the later editions of his Essay, although he always maintained that man's tendency to multiply was so strong that it would long continue to remain an obstacle to the rapid improvement of his welfare.

The author's own view is that Marx's statement, "In fact, every method of production that arises in the course of history has its own peculiar, historically valid, law of population," is essentially correct. But this is saying no more than that the social practices which determine population growth vary from time to time and place to place as the habits, the mores, and the economic conditions of peoples change. In his anxiety to prove the inherent viciousness of capitalism Marx seems to have ignored completely the possibility that the pressure of population on subsistence might arise even

[13] *Ibid.*, p. 679*n*.

under the system—socialism—he proposed to substitute for capitalism. He never examined with any care the factors affecting the actual growth of population, because the logic of his position, namely, that all the social evils of his day flowed from the capitalistic system, made it impossible for him to admit that there could be any pressure of population on the necessities of life which did not arise from the evil machinations of capitalists.

George. Henry George, like Marx, was interested in population theory only because he had a particular theory of social reform to set forth and felt that he needed to refute Malthus' theory of population growth to make his single-tax theory appear more plausible. George believed that, if the system of utilization of property in land were made over by the adoption of the single tax, there would be no danger of overpopulation and poverty for an indefinite period. He held that it was only because men did not have easy access to land that they could not find work which would enable them to support themselves and their families, however large, in decency and comfort. The application of the single tax to land, taking all its rental value for the government, would give access to the land to those who could use it best, and as a consequence, a very great increase in man's productive power would ensue. This would, of course, make it possible to support a vastly increased population and would postpone indefinitely, perhaps forever, the day when overpopulation and poverty would be man's lot. Indeed, George goes so far as to say that "unlike that of any other living thing, the increase of man involves the increase of his food," [14] and he implies that this will always be so if only man has easy access to the resources of the earth and is not prevented by customs and laws from exploiting them for his welfare. George's own statement of the law of population is as follows:

> If the real law of population is thus indicated, as I think it must be, then the tendency to increase, instead of being always uniform, is strong where a great population would give increased comfort, and where the perpetuity of the race is threatened by the mortality induced by adverse conditions; but weakens just as the higher development of the individual becomes possible and the perpetuity of the race is assured. In other words, the law of population accords with and is subordinate to the law of intellectual developments, and any danger that human beings may be brought into a world where they cannot be provided for arises not from the ordinances of nature, but from social maladjustments that in the midst of wealth condemn men to want. . . .[15]

I have placed George's theory with the social theories although he seems to assume like Spencer that fecundity and/or fertility will decrease as the

[14] Henry George, *Progress and Poverty: An Inquiry into the Cause of Industrial Depressions and of Increase of Want with Increase of Wealth. The Remedy*, p. 131, Doubleday, Doran & Company, Inc., New York, 1905.

[15] *Ibid.*, pp. 138–139.

intellectual development of the individual becomes possible. Like Marx he could not logically admit that the fertility of man might interfere with his welfare under the particular reform in social institutions he proposed, but unlike Marx he counted on the weakening of fecundity to be a help in the long run.

Dumont. Dumont's theory has been called the "theory of social capillarity." Briefly stated, it is that the individual, like oil in the wick of a lamp, tends to mount to higher levels in his social environment and that in this process of climbing he becomes less and less likely to reproduce himself; he is drawn out of his natural milieu and away from the family. As a consequence he loses interest in the family and in the welfare of the race. He becomes interested chiefly in climbing or moving in such a way as will benefit him personally, regardless of whether such movement will be of benefit to the community or the race. Dumont believes that in a society where movement from class to class is easily accomplished, social capillarity is as inevitable as gravity, for he says: "What gravity is to the physical world, capillarity is to the social order." He also regards this movement from class to class as directly related to the decline in birth rate, for he says: "The development of numbers in a nation is in inverse ratio to the development of the individual." [16]

Naturally, social capillarity is greater in a country where obstacles to movement from class to class are few; hence, in France, where democracy is well established, the movement is rapid, and the birth rate suffers greatly in consequence. Furthermore, in a democratic society, large cities exert a powerful attraction upon those living near them and thus increase the capillary movement of people; and since cities sterilize the people thus drawn in, they increase the speed of decline in the birth rate. People at a distance from centers of attraction and in occupations where individual ambition has little opportunity to develop are not drawn into this capillary movement so rapidly and hence are not likely to reduce their birth rate to the same degree. They will continue to increase while the ambitious climbers will die out.

In countries like India, where capillarity is small because of a rigid caste system, there is no tendency for the birth rate to decline and for population to die out. Just as a very solid substance (copper or iron) will prevent any considerable capillary movement in fluids, so a rigid social structure will prevent upward movement in society and will thus obviate the danger of individual development becoming so engrossing that the person has not time for the rearing of a family.

One is reminded of Spencer's theory of the antagonism between individuation and genesis. These two theories certainly have many points in com-

[16] Arsène Dumont, *La Morale basée sur la démographie,* p. 33, Schleicher Frères, Paris, 1901.

mon, although Dumont's theory allows for a much larger psychological element in determining the birth rate than does Spencer's. On this subject Dumont says: "From the moment when the imagination and the attraction of the ideal enter the scene, we find ourselves in the presence of a new principle of population." [17]

On the whole, this statement of the relation between individuation and genesis seems a decided improvement over Spencer's, but it still leaves much to be desired as a complete explanation of the decline of the birth rate even in France, and it is still more inadequate as applied to other countries. It does, however, have the merit of directing attention more closely to the actual social conditions of a people in the effort to find out the reasons for changes in their rates of growth.

Carr-Saunders. In his theory of population growth Carr-Saunders holds that man has always striven to attain the optimum number. "This is the number which—taking into consideration the nature of the environment, the degree of skill employed, the habits and customs of the people concerned, and all other relevant facts—gives the highest average return per head." Man's growth in numbers has, then, always been more or less controlled by him with a view to attaining this optimum which, of course, varies from time to time. The optimum "is not fixed once and for all. On the contrary, it is constantly varying as the conditions referred to vary and, as skill has tended to increase throughout history, so has the number economically desirable tended to increase." [18]

In brief, then, Carr-Saunders may be said to sponsor the theory that man's growth in numbers has been determined by his notions of the economically desirable numbers under his conditions of life. He so far accepts Malthus' view, that man has a tendency to increase faster than his means of subsistence, as to hold that without the use of definite means for slowing up his increase (abortion, infanticide, and so forth) he would never have approached the optimum number; but he believes that Malthus was wrong in supposing that man, having developed practices which gave him the optimum, was constantly pressing against his means of subsistence and that only vice and misery kept him from increasing more rapidly than he actually did.

Carr-Saunders' theory is especially interesting because it seems to have started a considerable discussion of the optimum population which has followed his lead—namely, discussion of the optimum population in purely economic terms. Carr-Saunders regards man's growth as quite within his control and as conditioned by the attitudes of mind that he has developed

[17] *Ibid.,* p. 35.
[18] Alexander Morris Carr-Saunders, *The Population Problem: A Study in Human Evolution,* p. 476, Clarendon Press, Oxford, 1922.

under the particular conditions of his life. On the whole, it would seem that this is, in the present state of our knowledge, a more scientific approach than the "natural" theories mentioned above.

3. IS THERE A LAW OF POPULATION GROWTH?

The foregoing statement of theories is, of course, incomplete, but selection has been made with a definite purpose in mind; namely, to show the two general types of theories that have predominated in the discussion of population growth since Malthus' day—*natural* theories and *social* theories. The former are based on the belief that there is something inherent in the nature of man, or of the world in which he lives, that determines his growth at a rate and in a direction largely or wholly beyond his control. This is apparently a seductive type of quest; biologists, in particular, appear eager to find the "law" of population growth. Once this is discovered and is given definite expression mathematically, the search for causes may be abandoned because nothing can be done about it. From such a law both what has happened in the past and what will happen in the future may be known, and we need not concern ourselves about the variations in tendencies shown because they are natural and therefore inevitable. It is not surprising that wherever and whenever men have thought about population, many have been eager to find the natural law of its growth; for this would give them a sure basis for reasoning on many related social problems.

In the social theories of population growth, on the other hand, the underlying assumption is that population growth is not subject to any immutable natural law but is rather the resultant of the social conditions (social here is used to include economic) in which a people finds itself. To one who accepts this view it would appear to be folly to search for a simple natural law of population growth; what should receive attention is rather the factors which determine its growth in a particular community at a particular time. The author believes that the social theorists are working in the right direction. This does not mean that Marx and George are any nearer right, except in their approach to the problem, than are Spencer and Doubleday. The man who has a particular reform to preach is as likely to twist facts so that they fit into his scheme of redemption as is the man who believes that he has discovered a law of nature and then seeks to verify it by observation. But it does seem eminently reasonable to hold that the way to discover the dynamics of population growth at any given time and place and in any given group is to study the environment of this group for elements which affect its birth rate and death rate as well as the fecundity of the people. When these are found, then we can tell with considerable accuracy whether or not man can exercise any effective control over his fertility and we shall also probably gain light on the methods by which control can be exercised. After all, social science can find its *raison d'être* only in the practical application of its findings to the welfare of man.

No attempt will be made in this book to develop a complete theory of population. The chief factors in population growth in the modern world will be studied in some detail on the assumption that there is no *natural* law of population growth but rather that the conditions of life, both physical and social, determine this growth and that it varies from group to group as these conditions vary. We shall expect, therefore, to find some valuable suggestions in practically every theory, but we shall not try to combine them into any consistent and comprehensive theory that will explain population growth at all times, in all places, and among all peoples.

Suggestions for Supplementary Reading

DOUBLEDAY, THOMAS: *The True Law of Population Shewn to Be Connected with the Food of the People,* 2d ed., 278 pp., George Pierce, London, 1847.

DUMONT, ARSÈNE: *La Morale basée sur la démographie,* 181 pp., Schleicher Frères, Paris, 1901.

GEORGE, HENRY: *Progress and Poverty: An Inquiry into the Cause of Industrial Depressions and of Increase of Want with Increase of Wealth. The Remedy,* 568 pp., Doubleday, Doran & Company, Inc., New York, 1905.

Harris Foundation: *Population. Lectures on the Harris Foundation, 1929, by Corrado Gini . . . Shiroshi Nasu . . . Robert R. Kuczynski . . . Oliver Edwin Baker . . .,* 312 pp., University of Chicago Press, Chicago, 1930.

LEVIN, S. M.: "Marx vs. Malthus," *Papers of the Michigan Academy of Science, Arts, and Letters,* Vol. 22, pp. 243–258, 1936 (published 1937).

MARX, KARL: *Capital. A Critique of Political Economy. The Process of Capitalist Production,* 927 pp., translated from the 4th German ed. by Eden and Cedar Paul, International Publishers Co., New York, 1929.

SADLER, MICHAEL THOMAS: *Ireland: Its Evils and Their Remedies. Being a Refutation of the Errors of the Emigration Committee, and Others, Touching That Country. To Which Is Prefixed a Synopsis of an Original Treatise About to be Published on the Law of Population: Developing the Real Principle on Which It Is Universally Regulated,* 2d ed., 464 pp., John Murray, London, 1829.

SPENCER, HERBERT: *The Principles of Biology,* 2 vols., D. Appleton & Company, Inc., New York, 1867–1868.

CHAPTER IV

FAMINE, DISEASE, AND WAR AS FACTORS
IN POPULATION GROWTH

These three factors comprise what Malthus regarded as the positive checks to population growth. He looked upon them as the chief causes of the high death rate which prevented population from growing rapidly at all times. It will be well, therefore, to examine their role in population growth in more detail both historically and currently.

1. FAMINE AND HUNGER

In spite of the restrictions on births embodied in the customs and traditions of peoples (Chap. I), there can be no doubt that among much the greater part of mankind the birth rate has always been high. Even today the birth rate remains high, perhaps at 35 to 40 or above, in the larger part of mankind. It follows, therefore, that from time immemorial the number of people living in any given area has been determined not so much by the level of the birth rate as by the level of the death rate (Chap. XI). The birth rate for any given group at any particular time was relatively stable when compared with the death rate, which depended very largely upon the plentifulness of game and/or the adequacy of agricultural production. For the past, and for much of the world even now, the author believes that Malthus was essentially right when he said that it was the positive checks —hardship—that kept population from growing faster than it actually did. In this section attention will be focused on famine and hunger as factors in keeping the death rate high, and hence in reducing the rate of population growth below what it would have been if there had been an abundance of food.

The author believes with Malthus that the lack of food has always been one of the most important causes of a high death rate among men. The folklore of almost all peoples is full of tales of dry seasons resulting in short crops; of late frosts in the spring interfering with planting or with normal growth; of early frosts in the fall damaging the harvest; of the failure of the salmon run; of the spoiling of crops in storage because they had not properly matured; of rainy cold seasons when crops could not be harvested; of the failure of certain tree crops as a result of uncontrollable blight; of the ravaging of the fields by locusts, grasshoppers, or other pests; or of the failure of the customary supply of food from any one of a dozen other natural causes. Food shortage has been one of the most constant worries of mankind in all past ages and is still imminent in a large part of the world.

The shortage of food takes two forms: (1) chronic and (2) acute. Of these, the former probably has been and still is the most deadly to man, although the latter is far more spectacular and has therefore received more than its due meed of attention from the public.

Chronic Lack of Food. In consequence of the constant pressure on the food supply in many parts of the world it is often said that half of the people in the world go to bed hungry every night. A recent survey by the Food and Agriculture Organization (FAO) of the United Nations shows that a large part of the people of the world do not have sufficient food to maintain health, while the data on food, income, and mortality show beyond doubt that the countries having small amounts of food available have much higher death rates than those having relatively large amounts.[1] Thus over one-half of the people in the world had a daily per capita calorie supply of food of less than 2,250, and most of these peoples had crude death rates (as estimated for about 1931) of 30 and over. The relatively small proportion of this group which had death rates of 25 or less was to be found in well-managed colonial areas, or in Central and South America.

At the other extreme those peoples having over 3,000 calories available daily had death rates of 14 or under, except France which, largely because of its high proportion of older people, had a death rate of 16. The average would be in the neighborhood of 12 to 14. Most of the countries with 2,250 to 2,499 calories available also had high death rates, although only about 35 per cent of these peoples had rates above 30. In general, the death rate declined as the number of calories available increased. A very rough estimate of the annual excess of deaths in the countries having less than 2,250 calories available as compared with those which would have occurred if they had had 3,000 or more calories available is 18 million, or over twice as many as would have occurred if they had been well fed. The author does not mean to say that the very low calorie intake in these countries is the sole cause of their excess mortality, but the evidence warrants the statement that a considerable proportion of this excess of deaths is due to inadequate diet. It is generally recognized today that underfeeding weakens the individual and renders him less resistant to disease, whether it be degenerative or acute. Hence, although it is impossible to draw a fine distinction between deaths which should be attributed to disease as a cause and those which should be attributed to chronic hunger, it must be recognized that a

[1] "Food, Income, and Mortality," *Population Index,* Vol. 13, No. 2, pp. 96–103, 1947; Food and Agriculture Organization of the United Nations, *World Food Survey,* Washington, D.C., 1946.

great many people who die of a specific disease would not have died at that time if they had not been suffering from chronic undernourishment. When death rates regularly exceed 25 per 1,000, we may be reasonably certain that undernourishment is one of the important factors at work. This is the reason for the statement made above that the chronic lack of food has probably been much more deadly to man than the acute lack, or famine. Hunger is probably the basic cause of millions of deaths annually each of which, from the medical standpoint, would be assigned to a particular disease.

malnutrition

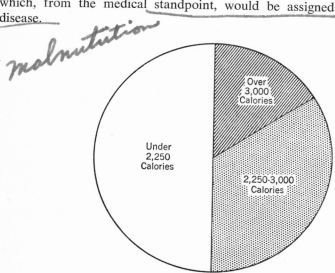

Fig. 4-1. Proportion of world's population with different food levels.

Acute Lack of Food. It would be both tedious and unprofitable to list all the famines that have occurred in any one country during historical times, but it may be of some interest merely to mention the numbers that have occurred within given periods in certain countries where the records have been searched rather carefully.

Walford lists 350 famines, 201 of which occurred in the British Isles between A.D. 10 and 1846. No doubt Walford's list is fairly complete for the British Isles, but it is only a beginning for most other lands.[2] In China "a study recently completed by the Student Agricultural Society of the University of Nanking brought to light the surprising and significant fact that between the years 108 B.C. and A.D. 1911 there were 1,828 famines, or one nearly every year in some one of the provinces." [3]

[2] Cornelius Walford, "The Famines of the World: Past and Present," *Royal Statis. Soc. J.,* Vol. 41, pp. 433–526, 1878.

[3] Walter H. Mallory, *China: Land of Famine,* p. 1, American Geographical Society, New York, 1926.

Walford is also authority for the statement that 31 famines occurred in India between 1769 and 1878, and it is by no means certain that he has listed all of them. Although no historical study of famines in India comparable to that just mentioned for China has been found, it seems only reasonable to assume that India, because its climate is of much the same general character as that of China, has had many hundreds of famines during the last 2,000 years and that untold millions of people have died as the consequence, both direct and indirect, of these famines. Moreover, it is highly probable that direct famine losses have always been highest in those areas where the chronic lack of food was greatest. Such areas almost never have any food reserves available for times of unusual shortage.

Since famine has been such an important factor in determining the growth of population in the world in the past and still is important for a large part of mankind, it may not be out of place to give some estimates of deaths in a few great famines to help us realize what a terrible calamity it is to peoples who depend almost solely upon local agriculture for their livelihood.

Effects of Particular Famines. China has had several famines about which a considerable amount is known. The worst in recent years appears to have been that which occurred as the result of a great drought in the years 1876 to 1879. The area affected was 300,000 square miles (about the area of New England, the Middle Atlantic states, Ohio, Indiana, and Illinois), and somewhere between 9 and 13 million people are supposed to have perished from hunger and the disease and violence accompanying prolonged want. In 1920 and 1921 not less than 20 million people were made destitute by crop failures, and in spite of the most efficient famine relief ever known in China, by which more than 7 million people were fed, at least 500,000 died of want. During 1929 and 1930 the newspapers reported that millions died of starvation and disease in northwestern China. Some reports placed the number of deaths as high as 4 million.

Scarcely had a fair crop in northwestern China eased matters there, when the most disastrous flood ever known covered many thousands of square miles along the Yangtze River and its tributaries. Crops were totally destroyed, and the number of deaths was very large, although the fact that relief could be brought by water to much of this area kept the toll far below what is usual under similar circumstances in China.

A little further back in Chinese history occurred disasters even worse than those just mentioned. Various authorities estimate that the Taiping Rebellion (1848 to 1864) resulted in the loss of 25 to 50 million lives, only a part of which, of course, was caused directly by famine. The Mohammedan Rebellion in western China (1861 to 1862) is also supposed to have so disrupted the normal course of life that widespread famine ensued and caused the deaths of several millions of people.

The history of China is replete with the stories of such disasters. Mallory is fully justified when he says: "In fact, the normal death rate [in China] may be said to contain a constant famine factor. Depleted vitality following years of want also tends to increase the death rate." [4]

The story is much the same for India as for China. Droughts are common, and almost every year some region suffers more or less from the shortage of food. In 1769 to 1770 there was a great famine in Bengal which is said to have carried off one-third of the total population, or about 10 million people. There is no way of checking such an estimate, but certainly several millions of people died at this time.[5] Other great famines occurred in 1803 to 1804 and in 1837 to 1838. The mortality resulting from them can only be guessed at, but the victims must certainly be counted by millions, if we take into account the aftereffects of these periods of want.

It may not be out of place to quote from a description of the great Indian famine of 1837 to 1838, as it will help us to understand the profound effects of such a calamity upon the growth of population. This description was written by a man who had access to the full official reports.

The famine of 1837 to 1838 was the last of the great desolating famines which characterized this epoch; like the Doji Bara in the Deccan, and the Chalisa in Upper India, it loosened the bonds of society, laid waste large tracts of country, and permanently modified the development of industry. It is the one famine of the old type of which we possess adequate detailed record; the reports of the local officers at various stages of the famine are, in many cases, still extant, and Mr. Girdlestone, in his "Past Famines in the Northwest Provinces," has given a history of it which covers 28 pages. The main features of the famine may be clearly traced, and they are unmistakably characteristic of the worst famines of this epoch. There had been a succession of bad harvests since 1832 which had caused considerable distress in various localities. The summer of 1837 brought a terrible drought. . . . July and August are described as having been absolutely rainless, and such were the anticipations of dearth that "in Aligarh the *baniyas* would not produce grain even when payment was offered at their own exorbitant prices." With the prospect of inevitable starvation at their homes, the people naturally began to wander; in August Bulandshahr was already being overwhelmed with emigrants from Marwar and Hariana. In September there were a few partial showers towards the south, but in the upper Doab this month was practically rainless. "The utter hopelessness of their case was enough in the minds of the lower classes to justify recourse to violence, and soon . . . neither grainboats nor storehouses were safe from attack, whilst the public roads were dangerous to travellers, owing to the number of armed men who were roaming about in quest of plunder."

[4] *Ibid.*

[5] Theodore Morison, *The Industrial Organization of an Indian Province,* p. 253, John Murray, London, 1918.

On October 20, John Lawrence wrote from Gurgaon: "I have never in my life seen such utter desolation as that which is now spread over the pergunnahs of Horul and Pulwul. The people have been feeding their cattle for the last two months on the leaves of trees, and, since this resource has failed, are driving them off." The difficulty of feeding the cattle is often mentioned. From Cawnpore in the beginning of 1838, Mr. Rose wrote: "There was not, I am told, in 1783 that total absence of vegetation which has caused the present dearth of cattle, and in milk the people then possessed a valuable article of food which is now wanting. . . . To those who have not witnessed the melancholy change it will scarcely be credible that an extensively-cultivated and thickly-populated country like the Doab could, by one year's drought, be reduced to its present state of waste and desolation. Flourishing villages, which last year contained from 300 to 400 cultivators, are now occupied by half a dozen starving beggars, and I have travelled for 20 miles in the pergunnahs adjoining the Jumnal, where there are no wells, without seeing a vestige of cultivation." . . . So long as the rich zemindars had the means, they fed their poor neighbours, and even went to the length of selling jewels and ornaments in order to raise money for the purchase of food. When their resources were exhausted and the *baniyas* proved inexorable, the poorer classes resorted to the jungle, in the hope of securing a meal from some of the wild trees. . . . Women were ready to sell their children for 2 or 3 seers of wheat, whilst their husbands and brothers waylaid and plundered travellers. Gold and silver were parted with at half their ordinary value, and brass and copper were esteemed worth their weight in grain. Artisans disposed of their tools at a quarter their cost price.[6]

But we need not go so far afield as China and India to find fairly recent examples of the way in which famine checks population growth or even reduces the numbers of a people. During the nineteenth century Ireland suffered from famine on several occasions. In the last great famine, 1846 to 1847, not less than 275,000 persons are supposed to have perished, while some place the number who died from starvation and the pestilence consequent upon it at over 1 million. Besides, nearly 1.2 million are supposed to have emigrated. The scarcity lasted for about six years, and the total population was reduced by about 2.5 million. Ireland also had other famines during the nineteenth century, and it is probably not far wrong to attribute a large part of the reduction in total population from 8,196,597 in 1841 to 4,390,219 in 1911 to these famines.

A recent famine, about which we have considerable information, occurred in Russia in 1918 to 1922. The American Relief Administration took the most active part in supplying outside help to the stricken areas. At the time of its greatest activity in August, 1922, the A.R.A. was feeding 10,491,297

[6] *Ibid.,* pp. 262–264.

people, and famine deaths had fallen to comparatively small figures. It has been estimated that, out of 30 to 40 million people who were affected by this famine, from 2 to 5 million perished from hunger. In some communities mortality was unbelievably high, running from 4 to 6 per cent a month when conditions were at their worst.[7] In other communities 25 to 50 per cent of the total population is supposed to have perished. Lorimer [8] is inclined to believe that possibly two-thirds, or 17 to 18 million, of the deficit in population growth in the Soviet Union between 1914 and 1926, which he estimates at 26 million, was due to disease, famine, and civil war. The larger part of this was probably due either directly or indirectly to famine, although there is no way of estimating this proportion with any precision.

In 1934 to 1935 there was another famine in Russia which seems to have killed millions but about which comparatively little is known because of the stringent censorship maintained. The census of Jan. 17, 1939, counted about 5.5 million fewer persons than would have been "expected" carrying forward the population from 1926 by the addition of births and the subtraction of deaths at "normal" rates.[9] By no means all of these died of famine, but there is no doubt that famine contributed significantly to this deficit of population between 1926 and 1939. In addition to these quite recent famines Russia also had severe famines in 1891, 1906, and 1911. In the past 60 years she has lost many millions of people from this cause.

Causes. This is not the place to go into a detailed discussion of the causes of famine. Quite obviously there is one general cause, namely, crop failure; but we must know more than this to understand the role that famine has played in the past and is likely to play in the future. Crop failure is usually more or less local in character. Even the great Russian, Indian, and Chinese famines of recent years have affected comparatively small areas in those countries, perhaps never more than 200,000 to 300,000 square miles at any given time. However, while people were dying by millions in Russia in 1921 and 1922 there were great surpluses of food in this country, in Australia, in Argentina, and indeed even in other parts of Russia. In 1930, with millions dying in northwestern China, rice was abundant and cheap in the lower Yangtze valley and wheat was a drug on the market in the United States and in all other large wheat-exporting areas. Local crop failure, therefore, need no longer mean starvation if a better distribution of food can be secured. Perhaps the chief obstacles to adequate famine relief at the present

[7] *Epidemiological Intelligence*, Pt. II, No. 5, pp. 54–55, League of Nations, Geneva, 1922.

[8] Frank Lorimer, *The Population of the Soviet Union: History and Prospects,* p. 40, League of Nations, Geneva, 1946.

[9] *Ibid.,* pp. 133–137.

time in the less industrialized lands are the lack of organization capable of bringing outside relief and the absence of adequate transportation facilities. There has been no considerable famine in any Western land since it has become possible to transport food quickly and cheaply from one locality to another and since governments have become strong enough to organize relief effectively.

In the 1920 and 1921 famine in China only about one-fourth to one-fifth as many people died as would have died a few years earlier, largely because some outside food could be taken to the sufferers in spite of the poor communication and transportation and the difficulties of organizing a supply service. Owing in part, but only in part, to internal political troubles, this service did not work as well in the 1929 to 1930 famine, and the number of deaths was far greater. The greater difficulty in reaching the most badly stricken area with outside supplies was an important factor in the relatively high death rate in the 1930 famine.

Today, as in the past, the lack of transport and of relief organization may be as important a cause of famine as is the actual failure of crops. This does not mean that all would be well with the world's food supply if we had better transportation facilities in all lands. Obviously the methods of agriculture, the kinds of soil, the climate, the economic organization of a people, the density of population, the social attitudes affecting diet, its religion, and many other factors have a definite relation to the available food supply. But one may say that today famine is extremely unlikely to occur in those countries which have good systems of transportation and where the economic system is capable of mobilizing outside resources for the assistance of the endangered areas, provided some additional catastrophe like war does not intervene.

Today there is little need to insist that war may result in famine or, more likely, in semistarvation and disease because of the disorganization of the facilities of production and distribution which accompany it and because of the disruption of the usual medical and sanitary services. Undoubtedly the Russian famine of 1918 to 1922 was greatly aggravated by Russian participation in World War I and by the civil war which followed. The 1929 to 1930 famine in China also claimed many tens of thousands of lives because of the internal strife which made relief impossible in certain areas.

It can be said with reasonable certainty that hunger and famine as a check on population growth can never be entirely eliminated until man does away with these basic causes—until he creates stores against crop shortages, stops wars, develops the means and the organization to supply famine sufferers, and last but not least learns to keep his numbers within the "means of subsistence" and thus eliminates malnutrition as a predisposing cause of disease.

2. DISEASE AND EPIDEMICS

From what has been said about hunger and famine it will be clear that until very recently they were always accompanied by a great deal of disease and sometimes by devastating epidemics. It is easy to understand how this came about, for famine of itself meant the disruption of most of the normal routine of life and led naturally to the breakdown of the customary safeguards of the community against disease. When people tear down their houses to sell the stones and timbers in order to get food, when they wander away from their usual abodes in hope of finding food elsewhere, when they gather in great crowds along the main highways and then scatter to the four winds, when they come together again in hastily organized camps to receive famine relief or are concentrated in camps to carry on public works instituted as relief measures, it can certainly occasion no surprise if disease breaks out and epidemics sweep over the land with deadly effect.

This close relation between famine and disease is well illustrated by the Soviet troubles of 1918 to 1922.[10] Certain diseases, particularly typhus, had broken out in epidemic form before the famine became severe. Demobilization of the army and the general disorganization of Russia incident to World War I and the Revolution helped to spread the disease still more rapidly because of the lack of any adequate control over the movements of the people. Scarcely had the epidemic situation begun to show signs of improvement in the winter of 1920 to 1921 when the country was stricken again by famine in the summer of 1921, and the mortality in the following winter rose to former levels.

It is, of course, utterly impossible to say whether famine or disease is the more deadly in such a situation. Is the death of a starving wretch who contracts cholera due to hunger or to cholera? No one can decide whether famine or disease is the cause of the deaths in a district where such great disorganization of economic and social life results from the presence of either that the other is certain to follow. All one can say is that practically every famine is accompanied or followed by disease and that the deaths caused directly by starvation are often fewer than those attributable, medically, to disease which is especially deadly to those who are undernourished.

The Black Death. But while disease is generally present at times of famine, it is not equally true that famine follows upon disease. This sometimes happens because of the great disturbance to social and economic life caused by disease, but quite frequently the effect is just the opposite. There are numerous instances in history when a great plague which has wiped out a considerable part of the population has made life much easier for the sur-

---

[10] Frank Alfred Golder and Lincoln Hutchinson, *On the Trail of the Russian Famine,* pp. 18–19, Stanford University Press, Stanford, Calif., 1927.

vivors for some years or even for some decades because more land was available per capita than before and because real wages rose as a consequence of the scarcity of labor. This was very clearly the case in England after the great plague of 1348. Cheyney describes the economic effects of this epidemic as follows:

The lords of manors might seem at first thought to have reaped advantage from the unusually high death rate. The heriots collected on the death of tenants were more numerous; reliefs paid by their successors on obtaining the land were repeated far more frequently than usual; much land escheated to the lord on the extinction of the families of free tenants, or fell into his hands for redisposal on the failure of descendants of villains or cotters. But these were only temporary and casual results. In other ways the diminution of population was distinctly disadvantageous to the lords of manors. They obtained much lower rents for mills and other such monopolies, because there were fewer people to have their grain ground and the tenants of the mills could therefore not make as much profit. The rents of assize or regular periodical payments in money and in kind made by free villain tenants were less in amount, since the tenants were fewer and much land was unoccupied. The profits of the manor courts were less, for there were not so many suitors to attend, to pay fees, and to be fined. The manor court rolls for these years give long lists of vacancies of holdings, often naming the days of the deaths of the tenants. Their successors are often children, and in many cases whole families were swept away and the land taken into the hands of the lord of the manor. Juries appointed at one meeting of the manor court are sometimes all dead by the time of the next meeting. There are constant complaints by the stewards that certain land "is of no value because the tenants are all dead"; in one place that a water-mill is worthless because "all the tenants who used it are dead"; in another that the rents are £7 14s. less than in the previous year because fourteen holdings, consisting of 102 acres of land are in the hands of the lord; in still another the rents of assize which used to be £20 are now only £2 and the court fees have fallen from 40 to 5 shillings "because the tenants there are dead." . . .

The demand for laborers remained approximately as great as it had been before. The number of laborers, on the other hand, was vastly diminished. They were therefore eagerly sought for by employers. Naturally they took advantage of their position to demand higher wages, and in many cases combined to refuse to work at the old accustomed rates. A royal ordinance of 1349 states that "because a great part of the people, especially of workmen and servants, have lately died in the pestilence, many, seeing the necessity of masters and great scarcity of servants, will not serve unless they may receive excessive wages." A contemporary chronicler says that "laborers were so elated and contentious that they did not pay any attention to the command of the king, and if anybody wanted to hire them he was bound to pay them what they asked, and so he had his choice either to lose his harvest and crops or give in to the proud and covetous desires of the workmen." [11]

Such a pestilence, without doubt, left the survivors, particularly in the laboring classes, in a far better economic position than they had been. The fact that a statute of laborers designed to prevent workmen from demanding higher wages because of the scarcity of laborers was enacted and reenacted no less than 14 times in the century following the Black Death shows pretty conclusively that this plague had greatly thinned England's population.

Hecker in his account of the Black Death (1348) gives figures which seem incredible, but they are so generally accepted that we may repeat a few of them here.[12] All Europe was devastated. London is supposed to have lost 100,000; Venice, 100,000; Florence, 60,000; and Paris, 50,000. The populations of these cities at that time are not known, but it is not unlikely that nearly one-half of their people perished within the space of a few months. The island of Cyprus is said to have been practically depopulated; Italy is thought to have lost at least half of its people, England about one-third, France about one-third. Eastern Europe did not suffer so severely as western and southern Europe. For the entire continent it is quite generally agreed that not less than one-fourth of the people perished in a few months. The loss amounted to no less than 25 million, and it appears to have been close on to three and a half centuries before Europe's population again attained the numbers that it had possessed in the middle of the fourteenth century. Of course during this period parts of the Continent suffered more or less frequently from epidemics of one kind or another, but nothing approaching the Black Death again devastated the whole continent.

Influenza in India. It is extremely difficult for us today to realize how a great epidemic may thin out a population and for how long a time its effects may be felt. Those of us who went through the influenza epidemic of 1918 and 1919 can recall how people died in our own neighborhoods without being able to secure the services of a physician, how whole families were occasionally stricken and were unable to call aid of any kind, and how helpless the physicians were in dealing with a disease that was relatively unknown to them. But in spite of what seem to us the terrible ravages of influenza, it raised the death rate in the registration area of the United States only 5 or 6 per 1,000 above normal and caused only about 500,000 excess deaths. This was about one-half of 1 per cent of our population at that time. The ravages of this disease in the United States should not be minimized, but when we compare our experience with India's at the same time

[11] Edward P. Cheyney, *An Introduction to the Industrial and Social History of England,* rev. ed., pp. 88–90, The Macmillan Company, New York, 1925.

[12] J. F. K. Hecker, *The Epidemics of the Middle Ages,* translated by B. G. Babington, pp. 22–24, George Woodfall (The Sydenham Society), London, 1844.

and with the experiences of other countries in the past, we find that we suffered hardly at all. In India the number of influenza deaths will never be known, but the lowest estimate seems to be 8 million and the highest about 15 million. Since the increase of population in the decade 1911 to 1921 was only about 3.8 million, while it amounted to almost 21 million in the decade 1901 to 1911 and to almost 34 million from 1921 to 1931, and since the influenza epidemic was the greatest although not the only catastrophe in the decade 1911 to 1921, it seems likely that it may have killed or prevented the birth of 15 to 20 million during this decade. Even such an estimate allows for famine deaths or deaths from other epidemics of 10 million or more if it is assumed that the increase between 1921 and 1931 is fairly normal.

But great as has been the devastation wrought by recent epidemics, their effects appear almost negligible, even in India, when compared with those of earlier times. In past ages people had little or no knowledge of the nature of disease or of the sanitary precautions necessary to prevent its spread; nor had they the economic means to devote to improving sanitary arrangements even if they had had the knowledge.

Plague in London. It may be interesting in this connection to quote from the description of the London plague of 1665 by Defoe, who was four years old at the time and who must have listened to the firsthand accounts of some of the survivors and read descriptions written by eyewitnesses. Like the quotation from Cheyney, it will help us visualize the disruption of life consequent upon a great epidemic.

> At the beginning of the plague, when there was now no more hope but that the whole city would be visited; when, as I have said, all that had friends or estates in the country retired with their families, and when, indeed, one would have thought the very city itself was running out of the gates, and that there would be nobody left behind, you may be sure, from that hour, all trade except such as related to immediate subsistence, was, as it were, at a full stop.
>
> I might be more particular as to this part, but it may suffice to mention, in general, all trades being stopt, employment ceased, the labour, and, by that, the bread of the poor, were cut off; and at first, indeed, the cries of the poor were most lamentable to hear; though, by the distribution of charity, their misery that way was gently abated. Many, indeed, fled into the country; but thousands of them having stayed in London, till nothing but desperation sent them away, death overtook them on the road, and they served for no better than the messengers of death; indeed, others carrying the infection along with them, spread it very unhappily into the remotest parts of the kingdom.
>
> The women and servants that were turned off from their places were employed as nurses to tend the sick in all places; and this took off a very great number of them.

And which, though a melancholy article in itself, yet was a deliverance in its kind, namely, the plague, which raged in a dreadful manner from the middle of August to the middle of October, carried off in that time thirty or forty thousand of these very people, which had they been left, would certainly have been an insufferable burden, by their poverty; that is to say, the whole city could not have supported the expense of them, or have provided food for them; and they would, in time, have been even driven to the necessity of plundering either the city itself, or the country adjacent, to have subsisted themselves, which would first or last, have put the whole nation, as well as the city, into the utmost terror and confusion.[13]

This plague is supposed to have killed not less than 100,000 in the city of London out of a probable population of 400,000. But because of the great exodus from the city in the early weeks of the epidemic it amounted perhaps to one-third or one-half of the actual residents of the city during its visitation.

Diseases Not of Plague Proportions. It would be very easy to give examples of epidemics from all parts of the world not commonly regarded as plagues in which millions upon millions of people have met an untimely end. Measles has killed many thousands of American Indians, tuberculosis has practically depopulated some of the South Sea Islands, while syphilis has wrought havoc in many quarters. India and China are never wholly free from the most deadly diseases in some part of their vast territories, and from Africa come reports of frequent epidemics among the Negro tribes which lay waste areas greater than many European states. Man always has been at the mercy of many kinds of disease about whose control he has known nothing.

It would be a great mistake, however, to think of the great epidemics which attract wide attention as the only diseases exacting their toll from man. In the aggregate there is no doubt that lesser epidemic or even endemic diseases have been far more important in keeping down population growth than the catastrophic epidemics. Thus it is supposed that there were probably not less than 150,000 cases of typhus each year in Russia prior to World War I and that deaths amounted to from 15,000 to 20,000 annually. This is certainly a considerable drain and, entirely aside from the great epidemics such as that of 1918 to 1922, when 2 to 3 million died from this disease, accounts for a considerable slowing up in the rate of Russia's population growth. Cholera is also endemic in Russia and during the last century has probably caused about 2,250,000 deaths. Of course some of these occurred at times of great epidemics. But if we think of the ravages of smallpox, malaria, scarlet fever, typhoid fever, yellow fever, and many other diseases which have but recently come under control, even in the most highly industrialized countries, we can readily appreciate the fact that the unspectacular

[13] Daniel Defoe, *History of the Plague in London, 1665* . . . , pp. 69–71, George Bell & Sons, Ltd., London, 1905.

epidemic has been so common in man's life that it has long since ceased to attract his attention. As long as typhus took a regular yearly toll little attention was paid to it, and as long as smallpox caused a regular death rate of 3 to 6 in 1,000 no particular concern was felt over its ever-present depredations.

In a Chinese community where an experiment in the registration of births and deaths was carried out under the author's direction, the death rate for the year Sept. 1, 1933, to Aug. 31, 1934, was 52.0 per 1,000.[14] The field worker actually on the ground assured the author that though this was considered a bad year it was not regarded as *especially* bad. The year in which there was not an epidemic of typhoid, or cholera, or dysentery, or smallpox, or of several of these was the unusual year. Epidemics of bubonic plague, or pneumonic plague, or influenza, or typhus would be worthy of remembrance but not those of the diseases which were always with them and which only resulted in a 50 to 60 per cent increase in the "normal" death rate.

3. WAR

There are two views regarding the effects of war on population growth which are quite common and which are diametrically opposed: one is to the effect that war has little influence on the growth of population, and the other is to the effect that war has done much to keep down man's numbers throughout his entire history and that our recent experiences prove that it can and does cause tremendous losses in population.

Nature of War Losses. It seems probable that the first view mentioned arises largely from the observations of the recent world wars, in which the losses of life have unquestionably been huge but in which there seems to have been only a momentary pause in population growth. This view has been in part supported by a rather widespread belief that "nature" saw to it that war losses were quickly made up by (1) causing an increase in the proportion of boy babies born (the normal sex ratio at birth is 105 to 106 boys to 100 girls), buttressed by (2) inducing a rise in the birth rate following a war. There is no clear evidence that sex ratios at birth are significantly affected by war, but there is abundant evidence that crude birth rates are quite likely to rise following a war, at least in modern times. The reasons for the rise in the birth rate are to be found largely in the disruption of the normal processes of population growth during the war and the effort to revert to "normal" conditions following it.

The decline in the birth rate during a war arises chiefly from the fact that relatively large numbers of men are mobilized for long periods, thus separat-

[14] Warren S. Thompson and C. M. Chiao, *An Experiment in the Registration of Vital Statistics in China*, p. 49, Scripps Foundation for Research in Population Problems, Oxford, Ohio, 1938.

ing many husbands and wives and also preventing many of the marriages which would normally occur during this period. As a consequence the normal processes of reproduction are disrupted to a greater or lesser extent for large numbers of couples during their most fertile years. Naturally this disruption of family life is reflected to a greater or lesser extent in the birth rate during the war, the extent depending on the degree and the length of the disruption of the normal life in the given community.

Table 4-1. Ratio of Male to Female Births in Selected Countries before and after World Wars I and II [1]

Country	1947–1949	1936–1940	1920–1922	1911–1913
Japan	105.8	105.1	104.3	104.2
New Zealand	105.4	104.2	105.4	105.3
England and Wales	106.1	105.4	105.1	103.9
France	106.6	104.8	105.3	104.3
Italy	106.0	105.5	105.6	105.3
Finland	106.1	105.7	106.0	106.8
United States	105.4	105.3	105.7	
Sweden	106.0	105.6	105.5	105.9
Netherlands	106.4	105.8	105.9	105.0

[1] Japan, 1947, 1936 to 1938; England and Wales, 1948 to 1949; France, 1943 to 1945, 1938 to 1940; Italy, 1946 to 1948; Finland, 1945 to 1946; Sweden, 1945 to 1948; Netherlands, 1936 to 1939.

Following the war and the demobilization of the military forces, married couples come together again and the soldiers not married hasten to establish families to compensate for the postponement caused by the war. Hence, there is almost certain to be a considerable rise in the marriage rate immediately following the war and in due course in the birth rate. It is by no means inevitable, however, that the increase in births following a war will make up for the decrease in them during the war, to say nothing of filling the gaps in population left by direct war losses (men killed in action, those dying as a result of wounds and brutal treatment in prison camps, and so forth) and by the excess of civilian deaths due to the hardships arising out of war.

The truth of these two views of the effect of war can best be brought out by examining more closely some of the facts which seem to be well established regarding modern wars as well as some of the rather common beliefs regarding the effects of warfare in earlier times.

In the past much of the warfare of mankind took place between relatively small groups and often assumed the form of almost continual forays into the hunting areas of surrounding clans and tribes, or of small expeditions to steal cattle or grain, or of somewhat larger and better organized efforts to drive one's neighbors out of lands which appeared desirable either as pasture or for agriculture. As civil organization replaced tribal organization and the areas inhabited by civil groups became more definitely fixed, the number of persons involved in any given war tended to increase, but it is by no means certain that the effects of war on the growth of population became proportionally greater. There is little doubt, however, that throughout human history war has had a depressing effect on population growth for the time being, although it is certainly arguable that, in the long run, the deaths caused by war directly merely equal those which would have occurred from hunger and disease a little later if there had been no war. Deaths directly due to war would be less noticeable where there was continual intertribal warfare than where organized armies entered the field because the attrition due to the former would not be concentrated within a short period of time (months or a few years).

Losses Due to Different Types of War. The extent to which war has even temporarily depressed population growth has usually depended upon the degree to which it actually disrupted the normal processes of living. The greater the degree of disruption, through invasion and the forced migration of masses of people, the more likely were hunger and disease to take heavy toll in addition to the actual killing of soldiers and civilians by the invading forces. There can be little doubt that in such a war as that of the United Nations in Korea the deaths of civilians would greatly outnumber military losses, even though much food and medical service were supplied to the Koreans. In addition, it is not improbable that crop yields throughout the country would be so reduced by the disruption of war that famine or semi-famine would continue to stalk the land in deadly fashion for some time to come unless much more aid were supplied from without.

There can be no reasonable doubt that in times past many tribes, as well as many small groups of peoples organized on a civil basis, have been wiped out entirely by war and its aftermath, but even such catastrophes may have had comparatively little effect upon the total number of the persons in the affected areas a few decades later, since the conquerors may have multiplied at a rate which soon filled the gap left by the destroyed peoples. But there have been other instances in which the population destroyed by war was many decades in recovering its former numbers. The Thirty Years' War (1618 to 1648) is supposed to have left much of Germany almost depopulated and so weakened that it did not recover its former numbers for at least a century and probably longer. The author has been told that many communities in South and Central China which were wiped out at the time of the Taiping Rebellion (1848 to 1864) had not recovered their numbers six to eight decades later.

It should be noted that, although the wars just cited are said to have caused great losses, only a small fraction of the total losses can properly be called military losses. In the past as well as at present, famine and disease have been the constant accompaniments of organized warfare on any but the smallest scale, and there is little doubt that they have, as a rule, claimed far more lives than were lost in battle. Thus war has probably been far more deadly than the direct military losses indicate and has had the over-all effect of temporarily reducing the size of many populations. It would be impossible, however, to prove that the population of Germany, or of Europe as a whole, was smaller in A.D. 1800 because of the Thirty Years' War, or even because of the Black Death, than it would have been if there had been no such catastrophes. In A.D. 1700, however, few people acquainted with the devastation caused by the Thirty Years' War would have been disposed to deny that it had reduced the size of the population in southern Germany. The same general position must be taken as regards the effects of particular famines and epidemics in the past even when they were not directly connected with wars.

Losses in World War I. An examination of what happened to population growth as a consequence of World Wars I and II will aid in understanding the effects of wars in the modern world. Many people have looked at the population figures for European countries collectively and severally for 1910 to 1911 and 1920 to 1921 and have noted that collectively the population increased somewhat during this interval. They have also noted that in only a few countries did population fail to grow during this decade, and that even in France there was only a small decrease. This has led some of them to believe that even World War I, great as was its devastation, had little or no effect on Europe's population growth. Several comments need to be made on these figures.

In the first place, one needs to be careful as regards particular countries to see that the same area is included at both times. For example, France had a population of 39,600,000 in 1911 and of 39,210,000 in 1921. But in 1921 Alsace and Lorraine were a part of France and contained 1,710,000 people, whereas in 1911 they were a part of Germany.[15] Thus France actually lost over 2 million during the decade, although a casual glance at the census figures might easily lead the layman to conclude that she lost only about 400,000. The student of population would not make such a mistake, and official publications call attention to the changes in the areas enumerated at different censuses, but it is easy for the general reader to make such a mistake and quite erroneous impressions may thus become current. The effects of World War I on population growth must be examined more closely if we would get a true picture of its influence in this respect.[16]

[15] Statistique Générale de la France. *Résultats statistiques du recensement général de la population, 1921,* Vol. 1, Pt. 1, p. 75, Imprimerie Nationale, Paris, 1923.

[16] The brief discussion here will follow that in Frank W. Notestein *et al., The Future Population of Europe and the Soviet Union,* Chap. 3, League of Nations, Geneva, 1944. The data are assembled there in more detail than can be given here.

On the eve of World War I, Europe west of Russia had a population of approximately 319 million. Military losses are estimated at about 6.6 million. Excess civilian deaths during the war years are reckoned at about 5.0 million, and the deficit of births after allowing for the smaller number of infant deaths amounted to about 10.8 million. Thus the total war losses amounted to about 22.4 million. Since it seems reasonable to estimate that this part of Europe would have had a natural increase (excess of births over deaths) of 33 to 35 million if there had been no war, the war losses as calculated were about two-thirds as large as this natural increase.

Table 4-2. Birth Rates as Affected by War

Country	World War II[1]			World War I[2]		
	Postwar, 1947– 1949	War, 1940– 1944	Prewar, 1937– 1939	Postwar, 1920– 1924	War, 1915– 1919	Prewar, 1910– 1914
England and Wales.........	18.3	15.5	14.9	21.4	19.4	24.2
France...................	21.1	14.9	14.9	19.8	11.3	18.8
Belgium.................	17.5	13.9	15.6	20.9	13.6	22.2
Germany................	16.9[3]	17.3[3]	19.6	23.1	16.8	28.2
Austria.................	17.4	19.1	15.8	22.6	15.8	29.6
Hungary................	19.8[3]	19.3[3]	19.8	30.0	20.2	35.0
Italy....................	21.2	20.8	23.4	30.0	22.7	32.0
Bulgaria................	24.0[3]	22.1	22.8	39.6	26.6	39.2
Romania................	....	23.2	29.6	36.8	31.9[3]	41.8
Japan...................	33.6	30.1	28.2	34.8	32.4	33.6
United States[4]............	25.8	23.1	18.9	26.8	28.4	29.8
Netherlands.............	25.6	21.8	20.3	26.5	25.5	28.2
Sweden.................	18.2	17.7	14.9	20.3	20.7	23.7
Norway.................	20.5	17.7	15.4	23.4	24.2	25.6
Denmark................	20.4	20.3	18.0	23.1	23.8	26.4
Spain...................	21.9	22.0	19.8	30.3	29.0	31.3
Australia................	23.3	19.4	17.5	24.4	25.7	27.7
New Zealand............	25.6	21.4	18.0	23.0	24.4	26.2
Switzerland.............	19.0	17.9	15.1	19.9	18.6	23.8

[1] *Demographic Yearbook, 1951,* Table 7, United Nations, New York, 1952.
[2] France, Bureau de la Statistique Générale, *Annuaire statistique de la France, 1913,* p. 168*, *1929,* p. 214*, Imprimerie Nationale, Paris; Institut International de Statistique, *Annuaire international de statistique,* Vol. 5, pp. 47, 119, W. P. Van Stockum & Fils, The Hague, 1921; and New Zealand, Census and Statistics Office, *New Zealand Official Yearbook, 1926,* p. 109, Government Printer, Wellington, 1926.
[3] Federal Republic, 1947–1949, Germany, 1940–1943; Hungary, 1947–1948, 1940–1943; Bulgaria; 1947; Romania, 1915, 1918, and 1919.
[4] U.S. Federal Security Agency, National Office of Vital Statistics, "Births and Birth Rates in the Entire United States, 1909–1948," *Vital Statistics—Special Reports, Selected Studies,* Vol. 33, No. 8, p. 141, 1948.

The actual increase of population in this part of Europe had for some decades been reduced by a rather large net emigration; hence, the actual increase of population from 1910 to 1920 would probably have been several million less than the natural increase—perhaps 6 to 8 million less, as was the case in the preceding decade (1900 to 1910). The actual increase in population of this part of Europe during the war decade was only about 8.0 million, or 2.6 per cent. In addition to war losses there was still a net emigration of about 4.6 million. This was probably 2 to 3 million under what it would have been if there had been no war. Therefore, it can be said that in round numbers the population of Europe west of Russia was about 20 million less in 1920 than it would have been but for the war. Moreover, Notestein calculates that even the neutral countries in this area had war losses, as that term is used here, approximating 0.73 million.

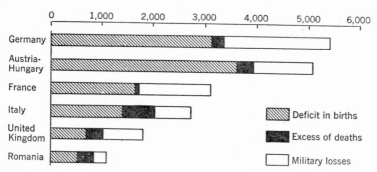

Fig. 4-2. Population deficits as a result of World War I (shown in thousands). (From Frank W. Notestein *et al., The Future Population of Europe and the Soviet Union,* p. 75, League of Nations, Geneva, 1944.)

It should be emphasized that the excess of civilian deaths and the deficit of births charged to war must necessarily be estimates based on assumptions regarding how many deaths and births would have occurred if there had been no war and that such estimates, particularly those for births, may very well be in error by a considerable amount. But the important fact in this estimate of war losses to Central and Western Europe is not that the figure used may be in error by 1 million or even somewhat more in either direction but that about 70 per cent of the normal natural increase for the decade 1910 to 1920 was lost on account of the war. Perhaps this is not a large proportional loss compared with that due to many other catastrophes suffered by man, but it affected a huge population of over 300 million in which hunger and disease had already pretty well come under public control.

Outside of Europe, some war losses were also suffered by Japan, the United States, Canada, Australia, New Zealand, and South Africa, but they were small as compared with those of Europe. In these countries the excess of deaths must be attributed in major part—in the United States, almost entirely—to the great influenza epidemic of 1918, which may or may not have been related to the war. There is certainly no clear evidence that it was so related. Moreover, in these countries the number of births was also affected to some extent by the war. War losses in these non-European countries may have amounted to 1 million or more.

The largest war losses suffered by any belligerent in World War I were probably those of Russia. Lorimer [17] accepts 2.0 million as a reasonable figure for Russia's military losses 1914 to 1917 but makes no estimates for the excess of civilian deaths and the deficit in births during this period. He does, however, calculate that in addition to the military deaths just noted there was a deficit of about 10.0 million births between 1914 and 1926 (date of first Soviet Union census) and an excess of about 16 million deaths. Since he is disposed to think that only about one-third of this total (about 9.5 million) occurred during the war (1914 to 1917), the deficit of births and excess of deaths for this period would amount to about 7.5 million. (In his estimates of Russia's war losses in the preceding edition of this book, the author included the losses of 1918 and 1919 as war losses.) The remaining losses between 1914 and 1926 (18 to 19 million) are discussed in preceding sections under the heading of Famine and Hunger and under that of Disease and Epidemics.

If Russia's population was about 140.4 million in 1914 [18] and if she suffered losses of 9 to 10 million (1914 to 1917), then Russia like Europe to the west lost about 7 per cent of her 1914 population, which under normal conditions she would have replaced in about three and a half years.

Losses in World War II. Up to the present the author has been unable to find any comprehensive discussion of war losses in World War II. There is no doubt, however, that in Western Europe such losses were small as compared with those in World War I. In France strictly military losses (about 200,000) were perhaps little more than one-seventh as large as in World War I, but to these must be added deaths of war prisoners and labor deportees and civil victims of war in France. Even so, these direct victims of the war (about 600,000) were less than one-half as numerous as military losses in World War I. Excess mortality not included in the categories given above was somewhat greater in World War II than in World War I, but the deficit of births, which was about one-fourth greater than military losses in World War I, turned into an excess of 36,000 annually over the number to be expected from a constant production of children per family averaging the same as for the years 1932 to 1939.[19]

[17] Lorimer, *loc. cit.*

[18] *Ibid.*, p. 37.

[19] Paul Vincent, "Conséquences de six années de guerre sur la population française," *Population*, Vol. 1, No. 3, pp. 429–440, 1946.

German military losses (territory of 1937) probably amounted to somewhat more than 3 million, one-half greater than such losses in World War I (territory of 1914). Sauvy and Lederman have estimated that in the neighborhood of 400,000 persons may have been killed in the aerial bombing of Germany and that the excess of deaths in the civilian population was of about the same magnitude, while the deficit of births amounted to about 1 million.[20] Thus the total war losses of Germany (area of 1937) may have been about 4.8 million. Admittedly these figures involve considerable estimating and make use of assumptions as to what normal vital rates would have been, but the author thinks they are reasonable. Thus even for Germany, because of the higher birth rate, the losses attributable to World War II up to the end of the war were probably somewhat smaller (perhaps 600,000) than in World War I.

The effects of World War II on the population growth of the United Kingdom were similar to its effects on France; military losses were considerably smaller than in World War I, the excess of civilian deaths was smaller, and the deficit of births was less. The Netherlands, Norway, and Denmark, which were neutral in World War I but were occupied by Germany in World War II, had substantial war losses; but in spite of these differences the war losses of the Western European countries were considerably less in World War II than in World War I, and the outstanding difference is found in the relatively normal birth rates maintained in most of these countries during the war, although the fact that military losses of the United Kingdom and France were relatively light in World War II should not be overlooked.

But if the Western countries of Europe escaped with lighter losses in World War II than in World War I, this was not the case for most of the countries in Central and Eastern Europe. Poland is supposed to have lost 5 to 6 million through civilian and military losses, perhaps one-fifth to one-sixth of her prewar population.[21] The deficit of births is not included. Yugoslavia probably lost over 10 per cent of her prewar population (about 1.6 million) and Greece almost one-half million, or about 7 per cent of her population, without taking account of the deficit of births in either case. But it should be noted that in contrast to World War I the birth rate remained closer to its normal level in all countries among both belligerent and neutral peoples during World War II. In a number of countries it was higher during the war than during most of the preceding decade.

Thus far nothing has been said about the war losses of the Soviet Union during World War II. There are no even reasonably satisfactory data regarding these. Estimates vary greatly and necessarily reflect the views of the

[20] Alfred Sauvy and Sully Lederman, "La Guerre biologique (1933–1945): population de l'Allemagne et des pays voisins," *Population*, Vol. 1, No. 3, pp. 471–488, 1946.

[21] Grzegorz Frumkin, "Pologne: dix années d'histoire démographique," *Population*, Vol. 4, No. 4, p. 706, 1949.

estimators regarding the effects of the different factors operating to raise deaths and reduce births. In the absence of facts these judgments must be regarded as guesses. Quite reasonable arguments can be advanced in favor of widely different results. Because of the light the discussion of the probable war losses of the Soviet Union will throw on the way war may affect population growth, they will be treated in greater detail than those of other belligerents.

The Soviet census of Jan. 17, 1939, gave the population as 170,467,000. In the interval between this census and the German attack on the Soviet Union (almost two and one-half years), the population would normally have increased by about 7.5 million. Thus at the time of this attack it seems reasonable to assume a population of about 178 million. In 1939 and 1940 large annexations were made to the Soviet Union. It is probable that they contained between 21 and 22 million persons.[22] Thus the Soviet Union as of the time of the German attack probably contained in the neighborhood of 200 million people and was growing at the rate of between 3 and 4 million per year. Had there been no war it is reasonable to suppose that this enlarged Soviet Union would have grown by at least 13.5 million and probably by somewhat more between the German attack in June, 1941, and January, 1946 (four and one-half years). Annexations during and after the war would have added another 1.5 to 2.0 million; hence, Timasheff's estimate of 218.4 million on Jan. 1, 1946,[23] for the territory of the Soviet Union at that time, if unaffected by war, is certainly not unreasonable, although possibly a little high.

The real question, then, is, what was the actual population on Jan. 1, 1946? Timasheff comes to the conclusion that the actual population was only 181 million. He arrives at this figure by an analysis of electoral data and data relating to children of school age, using these to aid in making estimates of civilian deaths in excess of normal and the deficit of births below that to be expected in the absence of war. His division of total losses amounting to 37.5 million is (1) military losses, 7.0 million; (2) emigration, 1.3 million; (3) birth deficit, 10.9 million; and (4) civilian deaths, 18.3 million.[24] The figures in (1) and (2) will probably not be much disputed, since they seem well within reason, considering the conditions that prevailed. The birth deficit (3) is a different matter. This would amount to from one-fourth to one-third of all the births to be expected under normal conditions and is considerably larger (perhaps 1 to 2 million) than the deficit in births as calculated by Lorimer for World War I and its aftermath of revolution and famine. This of course proves nothing. As favoring a high estimate of deficit in births during the war years, the very complete mobilization of Soviet

[22] N. S. Timasheff, "The Postwar Population of the Soviet Union," *Am. J. Soc.*, Vol. 54, No. 2, p. 149, 1948.

[23] *Ibid.*, p. 153.   [24] *Ibid.*, p. 155.

military strength during much of this period may be cited and also the fact that, because of the vast territory overrun by the Germans and the evacuation of tremendous numbers of civilians whose whereabouts were unknown to the members of their families in the military forces, furloughs, even if given, would have had little influence in maintaining the birth rate. It can very plausibly be argued, therefore, that a decline of one-fourth to one-third in the number of births from the beginning of 1942 to the beginning of 1946 is well within the limits of reasonable expectation and that the relatively small decline in births in Western Europe during the war arose from conditions quite different from those prevailing in the Soviet Union. But it should be clearly understood that in the absence of facts we can only express personal judgments. The author can only say that, taking such facts he has been able to find into account, it is not hard for him to believe that the deficit in births in the Soviet Union in the four years 1942 to 1945 may have exceeded 10 million.

As regards the excess of civilian deaths, which Timasheff estimates as 18.3 million, the author is more skeptical in spite of the extermination policy of the Germans. There is no doubt that vast numbers of Russians were killed to make room for the settlement of German farmers, nor is there any doubt that the hardships of occupation were deliberately increased in order to produce the same effect where actual murder was not resorted to. Again the hardships involved in the evacuation of vast numbers of people as well as the shortages of goods and shelter must have claimed great numbers of victims. But the author is inclined to remain skeptical of such tremendous losses until and unless an actual count of the Soviet population shows that it did take place. The chief reason for his doubt is the fact that as far as is now known there was no widespread epidemic in the Soviet Union during the war nor any such acute famine as prevailed following World War I and the Revolution. Lorimer estimates excess deaths during World War I and in the following three or four years at more than 16 million. It is altogether possible that the German scourge was more deadly than the scourges in the previous period, but the author feels that we need more evidence than Timasheff presents if we are to accept with reasonable confidence his figure for the excess of civilian deaths during the war.

A French writer [25] says that a Soviet authority gives 10 million as excess civilian deaths. Timasheff cites an officer of the propaganda office of the Central Committee of the Communist Party as saying on Jan. 22, 1946, that the population of the Soviet Union was 193 million [26] (12 million more than his own estimate), and a figure of 190 to 192 million seems to be in quite common use in the Soviet Union for the postwar population. Such state-

[25] Pierre George, "Esquisse d'une étude démographique de l'Union Soviétique," *Population*, Vol. 1, No. 3, p. 406, 1946.
[26] Timasheff, *op. cit.*, p. 148.

ments, of course, only serve to show the divergencies of opinion referred to above.

But, whether the war losses of the Soviet Union were as low as 25 million or as high as 37.5 million, it will be of interest to note how such losses would probably affect the population during the next 20 years. Assuming no war losses and including only the territory of the Soviet Union as of Jan. 1, 1939 (before any annexations), a reasonable expectation of the growth of population would have been from 174 million at the beginning of 1940 to 251 million at the beginning of 1970.[27] If adjustment is made for hypothetical losses in this same territory of a little over 20 million between 1940 and 1945, Lorimer calculates the 1970 population at 222 million, or at approximately 29 million less in 1970 than if there had been no war.[28] This is to be regarded merely as an illustration of how such war losses would affect the growth of a population, other factors in growth remaining unchanged. Larger war losses would, of course, increase the difference between the calculated growth (1970) and the actual growth.

The Birth Rate in World War II. This discussion of the losses of population caused by World Wars I and II cannot be closed without making a few comments on the fact that the birth rate, in Western Europe and in most of the nations chiefly settled from that area, did not decline during World War II as might have been expected from the experience in World War I.

There is no completely satisfactory explanation for this difference in demographic behavior in the two war periods, although the maintenance of a higher marriage rate during World War II was a factor of considerable importance. It may be suggested that this difference arose at least in part from the fact that World War I had been preceded by a period of some years during which economic conditions had been fairly good and there was no large deficit of marriages and births at the time of its outbreak in 1914; whereas in 1939 to 1940, because of the depression beginning about 10 years earlier, there was a large deficit of marriages and of births postponed from the depression years which had to be made up shortly if they were to be made up at all. Moreover, the early years of World War II also brought improved economic conditions to great numbers of people in many countries, and this also encouraged the consummation of postponed marriages and births as well as encouraging earlier marriages among the young people of 1939 to 1943.

While the author thinks that this difference between the prewar economic conditions of the two world wars is a factor of considerable importance, he is by no means satisfied that it is an adequate explanation. He is disposed to believe that the social atmosphere affecting the readiness of young people to establish a family and to raise children under the uncer-

[27] Notestein *et al., op. cit.,* p. 56.
[28] Lorimer, *op. cit.,* p. 183.

tainties of war had changed—that the marriageable generation of 1939 to 1943 was more willing to give hostages to the future than was the marriageable generation of 1914 to 1918. Of course, such a change in attitudes cannot be proved, unless one considers the marriage rates and birth rates themselves as proof of it. In any event there is no doubt that World War II did not have as depressing an effect on the birth rate among the nations of Western civilization as World War I.

Another reason for the smaller losses to the Western peoples in World War II than in World War I is found in the great advances in sanitation and medicine. These affected not only the actual military losses through the reduction of deaths among the wounded and from the intestinal diseases, which had always heretofore taken a heavy toll in all armies, but also the losses among the civilian population.

In the author's opinion there is no reasonable doubt that temporarily war and the hunger and disease which have generally accompanied it have had a large influence in slowing the growth of population and in many cases in actually reducing its size for many years. In the days before the voluntary control of births became widespread in the West and before the economy of most countries became dynamic through the development of new techniques, it is doubtful whether war did more than delay for a few years or a few decades the attainment of as large a population as could be supported considering the resources and the techniques available at that time. Today the situation may be different, although there is no positive proof that it is. Today, among those peoples where the voluntary control of births is widespread and levels of living are fairly good and are rising, the losses of population through war may never be made up in the sense that population will grow to the size where the pressure on subsistence will be as great as it was before the war. There is no proof that this is happening, but it is a possibility. The loss of population through war might become the occasion for the development of a new ratio between resources and the techniques to make use of them, on the one hand, and the size of the population, on the other, which would make possible a higher level of living for the entire population.

When we reflect upon the facts presented in this chapter showing the effects of famine, disease, and war upon the growth of population, we have no trouble in understanding why man's numbers have increased slowly, if at all, throughout the greater part of his existence. What Malthus called the *positive checks* have been quite sufficient to prevent any regular and rapid growth in his numbers throughout the ages. As we shall see later, the gradual elimination of the positive checks to population growth which is now taking place in the unindustrialized areas of the world is creating new pressures of population with which we must deal effectively if we are to prevent international conflict aimed at securing larger resources by the peoples who have only recently begun to grow at a fairly rapid rate and whose industrial potential is also beginning to grow.

Suggestions for Supplementary Reading

BUCK, PEARL S.: *The Good Earth*, 375 pp., The John Day Company, New York, 1931.

BUER, M. C.: *Health, Wealth, and Population in the Early Days of the Industrial Revolution (1760–1815)*, 290 pp., G. Routledge & Sons., Ltd., London, 1926.

CHEYNEY, EDWARD P.: *An Introduction to the Industrial and Social History of England*, rev. ed., 396 pp., The Macmillan Company, New York, 1925.

DEFOE, DANIEL: *History of the Plague in London, 1665* . . . , pp. 1–205, George Bell & Sons, Ltd., London, 1905.

GOLDER, FRANK ALFRED, and LINCOLN HUTCHINSON: *On the Trail of the Russian Famine*, 319 pp., Stanford University Press, Stanford, Calif., 1927.

HECKER, JUSTUS FRIEDRICH KARL: *The Epidemics of the Middle Ages*, 418 pp., translated by B. G. Babington, George Woodfall (The Sydenham Society), London, 1844.

MALLORY, WALTER H.: *China: Land of Famine*, 199 pp., American Geographical Society, New York, 1926.

MORISON, THEODORE: *The Industrial Organization of an Indian Province*, 347 pp., John Murray, London, 1918.

THOMPSON, WARREN S., and C. M. CHIAO: *An Experiment in the Registration of Vital Statistics in China*, Scripps Foundation for Research in Population Problems, Oxford, Ohio, 1938.

WALFORD, CORNELIUS: "The Famines of the World: Past and Present," *Royal Statis. Soc. J.*, Vol. 41, pp., 433–526, 1878.

ZINSSER, HANS: *Rats, Lice and History,* 301 pp., Little, Brown & Company, Boston, 1935.

CHAPTER V

POPULATION GROWTH AND THE INDUSTRIAL REVOLUTION

It is probable that population has grown faster for a relatively long period of time in Western Europe and its colonies since about the beginning of the nineteenth century than had ever happened in the previous history of the world to any population already numbering many millions (perhaps 175 million). Furthermore, this rapid growth of population was accompanied by a very great improvement in the standard of living of the people in these areas. Consequently, it is little wonder that many people, realizing these facts, assume that Malthus was entirely wrong in his views on population and that they are of no interest to us today.

It is true that Malthus never fully realized the significance of the economic changes which were going on about him from the standpoint of their contribution to man's productive capacity and hence of how they might affect the general welfare of great populations. But it is also true that he did realize, as many of his contemporaries did not and as many later students of the relation of population growth to welfare did not, that throughout most of his history man has had a tendency because of his high birth rates to add to his numbers faster than he could find the means to support them.

The reasons why the anomalous growth of Western European populations, which was getting under way in the eighteenth century and which continued until early in the twentieth century, has not led to the dire consequences Malthus predicted are not far to seek. They are to be found in the first instance in the economic changes arising out of that new organization of society which was in process of development in Malthus' day and which is generally referred to as *the industrial revolution*.[1] The second factor of importance, but not of much importance in most countries until the second half of the nineteenth century, was the voluntary control of conception. This will be discussed in later chapters.

At this point attention should be called to the fact that although the great economic revolution of Malthus' day is generally thought of as an industrial

---

[1] Paul Mantoux, *The Industrial Revolution in the Eighteenth Century: An Outline of the Beginnings of the Modern Factory System in England*, rev. ed., Pt. 1, Chap. 3; Pt. 3, Chap. 1, translated by Marjorie Vernon, Harcourt, Brace and Company, Inc., New York, 1928.

revolution it had been preceded by and was also accompanied by what can just as reasonably be called an *agricultural revolution*, and both revolutions arose as a consequence of applying science to the problems of production and transportation.

It was but natural that Malthus should be limited in his outlook by the conditions with which he was familiar. There was much in his surroundings which made it seem probable that the actual size of the population of any given country or area would continue to be limited chiefly by the means of subsistence it could produce and that these would not increase fast enough to permit all persons born to live out the natural "span of life." This being the case, high death rates due to hardship were likely to continue to limit man's numbers. Malthus recognized the fact that a new era in production had arrived, but he did not fully realize how greatly these fundamental economic changes, made possible by the advances in science and technology, would continue to increase the efficiency of productive processes and there is no evidence that he realized how rapidly and how long the opening up of new lands would add to the food and raw materials available to Europeans. Moreover, he either ignored the possibility of the control of population growth inherent in the voluntary control of conception or did not believe it could become of much importance, more likely the latter. It is little wonder, therefore, that he failed to foresee how his doctrines would need modification in the succeeding century in those areas where the agricultural and industrial revolutions were developing and where peoples had access to vast new lands. But the fact that Malthus was unable to foresee clearly what would happen in the dynamics of population growth during the century following his death should not lead us to ignore the important truths in his discussion of population.

1. BIRTH AND DEATH RATES
IN EUROPE PRIOR TO THE INDUSTRIAL REVOLUTION

Malthus was aware, as was shown in Chap. II, that changes were taking place in his day which promised an increase in the welfare of mankind; but he certainly did not foresee the extent to which these changes would, for a time, eliminate the positive checks to population growth in the more favored areas of the Western world, or that they were to issue in the widespread use of a preventive check that would make it comparatively easy for man to keep his numbers within such limits as he might desire.

In order to understand the way in which the industrial revolution acted upon population growth, it will be well to turn attention very briefly to some vital statistics of the eighteenth century and earlier and to compare them with those of our own day. In the decade in which Malthus published his first Essay there were in Sweden, which probably had the most reliable vital statistics in Europe at that time, 33.3 births and 25.4 deaths per 1,000 of the population. Forty years earlier both birth and death rates were about two points higher; hence, the rate of increase was about the same in 1751 to 1760 as in 1791 to 1800.[2] Since there is good reason to believe that the conditions of life in Sweden in the latter part of the eighteenth century were more favorable to the increase of population than in most of the other countries of Europe, we can judge somewhat of the death rates that prevailed generally at the time. In Finland both birth rates and death rates were substantially higher in those periods, but the rate of increase was also greater. Death rates were probably higher in most European countries during a large part of the eighteenth century than in Finland.

In the larger cities, in particular, the growth of population prior to the industrial revolution was probably due solely to migration into them. Thus a record of baptisms, marriages, and deaths in Paris covering a period of twelve years and seven months—1670 to 1675 and 1678 to 1684—showed an excess of 22,790 deaths over births. For an 81-year period, 1707 to 1789, Landry states there were 5,078 more deaths than births.[3] There is also evidence which cannot be ignored that in London the death rate was as high as 50 per 1,000 in 1750 and that it was still over 30 in 1800.[4] It is estimated that in the period from 1700 to 1750 there were 500,000 more deaths than births in London—an excess of deaths over births of about 10,000 per year, which was equivalent to about 20 per 1,000 of the total population.

The decline in death rates in the different parts of Western Europe from a rate of 25 to 50 in 1750 to one of 10 to 12 today is to be attributed largely to the changes in manner of life made possible by the economic revolutions. For the first time in history, man's control over nature gradually became more and more secure so that it was possible for him to live in fairly healthful conditions and thus to avoid the high death rates which had been his usual lot.

Until about the middle of the eighteenth century it was practically impossible to supply any city, even a small one, with wholesome food, good water, a small measure of sanitary sewage disposal, moderately decent housing, and even a minimum of such medical service as then existed. Buer's description of sanitary conditions in the English towns of the medieval period makes this abundantly clear.

The streets of medieval towns were generally little more than narrow alleys, the overhanging upper stories of the houses nearly meeting, and

[2] Sweden, Statistiska Centralbyrån, *Statistisk Årsbok för Sverige, 1950*, p. 52, P. A. Norstedt & Söner, Stockholm, 1950.

[3] Adolphe Landry, "La Démographie de l'ancien Paris," *J. de la société de statistique de Paris*, Vol. 76, No. 2, p. 37, 1935.

[4] M. C. Buer, *Health, Wealth, and Population in the Early Days of the Industrial Revolution (1760–1815)*, Chap. 3, G. Routledge & Sons, Ltd., London, 1926.

thus effectually excluding all but a minimum of light and air. In the seventeenth century Bristol, which still remained typically medieval, the average breadth of the streets was under 20 feet and only trucks and sledges were allowed for transport in the center of the town. In most Continental towns and some English ones, a high city wall further impeded the free circulation of the air. The main streets might be roughly and ineffectually paved with cobbles, the rest of the streets, or rather alleys, would be totally unpaved. Rich citizens might possess a courtyard in which garbage was collected and occasionally removed to the suburbs, but the usual practice was to throw everything into the streets including the garbage of slaughter houses and other offensive trades. By-laws against this practice were quite ineffective, as were the regulations ordering citizens to scavenge the street in front of their houses. Filth of every imaginable description accumulated indefinitely in the unpaved streets and in all available space and was trodden into the ground. The water supply would be obtained either from wells or springs, polluted by the gradual percolation through the soil of the accumulated filth, or else from an equally polluted river. In some towns, notably London, small streams running down a central gutter served at once as sewers and as water supply. The dwelling houses of the well-to-do would be of timber, or timber-framed upon a foundation of brick or stone. Even these, picturesque as they appear to a modern eye, seem to have been designed to admit a minimum of light and air. The dwellings of the poor were mere hovels, built of unseasoned wood and with tiny windows. In the seventeenth century London, which before the Fire largely remained a medieval city, the poorer class house had only a covering of weatherboards, a little black pitch forming the only waterproofing, and these houses were generally built back to back. Thousands of Londoners dwelt in cellars or horribly overcrowded tenements. A small house in Dowgate accommodated 11 married couples and 15 single persons. Old mansions had been converted into 20 or even 30 tenements. It is possible that the overcrowding was worse at this period than during the Middle Ages but there is no proof of this. Another source of unhealthiness were the church vaults and graveyards, so filled with corpses that the level of the latter was generally raised above that of the surrounding ground. In years of pestilence, recourse had to be made to plague pits in order to dispose of the harvest of death. It is not surprising that the deaths in all medieval towns largely exceeded the births, so that the towns only survived by constant recruitment from the country; this drain on the country was supportable, since the town population was relatively very small. But the towns also indirectly decreased the population by acting as forcing grounds for pestilence which spread over the country side.[5]

Anyone who has wandered about Chinese cities at any time during the past three or four decades will be forcefully struck by the fact that he is seeing conditions of living which are almost the exact duplicate of those described above by Buer as existing in England as late as 1700 or 1750.

[5] *Ibid.*, pp. 77–78.

2. CHANGES IN PRODUCTIVITY AND THE DEATH RATE

It is no disparagement of medical science and practice to recognize that the great decline in the death rate that has taken place during the last two centuries in the West is due, basically, to the improvement in production and economic conditions. This economic development made better sanitary practices possible and provided the means for research in medicine and for the establishment of good medical education. These improvements in health depended fundamentally on the development of an economic system which was sufficiently productive to allow of a diversion of considerable quantities of its output to the many aspects of health work. Because of the sanitary improvements thus made possible and because of the improving economic status of an increasing part of the population, it appears probable that for the first time in history it became possible for a few decades for the large towns and cities to have more births than deaths. On the other hand an excess of births was not uncommon in agricultural communities although, as has already been noted, it was not regular and was seldom high. In the United States, after the first settlements were well established, living conditions had been unusually favorable and there was generally a large excess of births over deaths. But even in our cities in the days before 1860 (Civil War) very high death rates prevailed.

The importance of the improvement of sanitation in cities can scarcely be overestimated, since the industrial revolution made more and larger cities necessary and led to a great and steady increase in the proportion of the population living in them (Chap. XIX). If they had continued to kill off each year 2 per cent of their total number in addition to the number born in them, as London probably did between 1700 and 1750, the populations of all Western lands would soon have become stationary; for the rural population which was declining proportionally could not have continued to supply the cities with the surplus that they would have needed to maintain their numbers. Bearing in mind this change in the death rate, which paved the way for a large natural increase of population, let us turn to the consideration of the more basic changes in our social and economic organization which underlay these changes in the death rates.

3. CHANGES WROUGHT BY THE INDUSTRIAL REVOLUTION IN THE SOCIAL STRUCTURE

Changes in Importance of Agriculture. Before describing in more detail the features of the industrial revolution which exerted the most influence on population growth, it will be well to call attention to the fact that throughout man's life on the earth prior to the industrial revolution it had been necessary for almost the entire population to devote its efforts to the production of the agricultural necessities of life. There had never been a time when agricultural work was sufficiently productive to support any very considerable proportion of the population which did not work directly in gathering or producing the products of the soil. The existence of Babylon and Carthage and Rome and Peiping does not disprove this statement. It only proves that, when unusual political organizing ability found opportunity to display itself, food and a few other necessities could be collected from a relatively large area and could be concentrated in one or a few places, and an occasional rather large population could therefore be supported at a particular point. But it is very doubtful whether any of these empires of the past had more than 15 to 20 per cent of their people engaged in nonagricultural tasks. The fact is that until quite recently there was only a small labor supply, except in the off season for agriculture, which could be used to produce nonagricultural goods.

In the century preceding 1750, in Western Europe at least, there had been a very considerable increase in the efficiency of agriculture. It consisted chiefly of the breeding of better livestock, the development and adaptation of better-yielding crops and their transplantation to new areas, and the development of better farm practices. This agricultural revolution had been going on for some time in Great Britain before the real industrial revolution began. This meant that a considerable increase in nonagricultural labor was possible if and when it was needed. Indeed, when more nonagricultural labor was not needed as agriculture became more efficient, there was often great distress among the displaced farm workers. By the time the industrial revolution began to need more nonagricultural workers, agriculture, at least in Great Britain, was in a position to provide food for a larger proportion of such workers. This is a very important point to remember, for it was not until the industrial revolution was well on its way that it contributed directly to the further improvement and extension of agriculture.

Demographic Effects of Changes in Methods of Production and Transportation. Let us now consider the two aspects of the industrial revolution which, in the opinion of the author, contributed most to the growth of the population of Europe and its colonies after about 1750. These are (1) the development of power machines for the manufacture of goods and the more efficient extraction of nature's wealth from the soil, and (2) the application of power to transportation and communication. The second aspect is, of course, only an extension of the first, but it came somewhat later and in many respects gave a second great impulse to population growth.

The improvements in production and transport following upon the application of steam power to machines made it possible for the Western European to free himself to a considerable degree from the action of the positive checks to population growth for more than a century. They enabled him to tap new resources both at home and abroad and to gather a bounty from nature which had heretofore been inaccessible to man. It requires no argument to convince anyone today that this is so and that power-driven machinery has enabled us to produce many times the amount of goods that we could have produced by hand power alone. But probably just as important as the increase in man's power to produce goods was the increase in his power to transport them from place to place. It is extremely difficult for us to realize nowadays how onerous and slow land transportation was a century and a half or two centuries ago. There were very few roads in any country on which a wheeled vehicle could move at all times of the year. The pack horse was perhaps the chief means of moving merchandise over any considerable distance in Europe, while in many parts of the world man was his own beast of burden, either carrying loads on his shoulders or pushing them on a wheelbarrow. Of course, only relatively expensive goods of light weight which could bear a high cost of transportation could be moved any distance in this manner. Under these conditions almost all communities were necessarily self-sufficing, and a very small proportion of all goods produced moved any distance from the point of production. Furthermore, as has already been noted, this inability to transport heavy goods any considerable distance on land was a chief cause of many of the local famines mentioned in Chaps. IV and XV.

When there were no roads and almost no means of transport and communication between localities, even when they were only a few miles apart, any local crop failure was almost certain to result in a higher death rate in the stricken area. Thus in Sweden the death rate increased from 24.8 in 1760 to 32.9 in 1763, which was a year of poor harvests, while in 1773 it rose to 52.4 after two or three years of poor harvests. In 1809 it was again far above the level of preceding years.[6] Since the improvement of transportation there has been no such marked increase in death rates following poor local harvests in Sweden.

Water-borne commerce was in a much better situation than land commerce before the middle of the nineteenth century. The science of navigation was well developed before 1700, and shipbuilders had attained a high degree of seaworthiness in their products. Those countries which had ready access to the sea and had navigable rivers had an advantage over countries which had to depend largely on land transport. This is no doubt one of the reasons for the early and rapid development of modern industrialism and foreign commerce in the United Kingdom.

But the transport of goods is probably of less importance in many respects than the transport of persons and ideas, although the two always go hand in hand. With the rapid extension of commerce during the eighteenth century went an almost equally rapid spread of ideas, which resulted in a quickening of the whole mental life of Western Europe and thus helped to prepare

[6] Sweden, Statistiska Centralbryån, *op. cit.*, pp. 53–54.

the way for the growth of the present social order. With the building of canals and roads, which accompanied or even, in some cases, preceded the actual adoption of the new methods of production, markets became larger and more stable, transport became quicker and cheaper, and a new stimulus was given to human enterprise, particularly in the economic field. Better and cheaper transportation made it possible for new industries to develop in naturally favored localities where costs of production were low, since the product could be shipped where it was needed at a relatively small cost. Cheap transportation also made it possible to import food and other agricultural products from distant lands in the ships which carried out manufactured goods.

The methods and the organization of agriculture were also gradually revolutionized by better transportation; it was no longer necessary for each locality to be wholly self-sufficing in food and fiber production. European agriculturists began to produce staples for markets some distance away, generally cities, as well as for the local community; and this encouraged further revolution in agricultural methods which greatly increased the efficiency of labor on the land.

The improvement of transport and production gradually made it possible not only for a locality to trade with its neighbors but for one country to trade with others at an increasing distance and to trade goods of greater bulk and weight. The new agricultural area in America and elsewhere, the products of which were thus made available to Europe, was enormous. Much of this area was also extremely fertile and easily tilled by the new agricultural machines which began to appear after 1800. Foreign trade in foodstuffs gradually became a regular feature of the commerce of the world during the nineteenth century. By the middle of this century England had definitely become a food-importing country, and in addition food was available in these newly opened lands for such other countries as needed it and had manufactured goods to trade for it. For most practical purposes, the improvement of transport had, by the middle of the nineteenth century, more than doubled the area and resources of Europe.

This vast expansion of Europe's resources, which resulted in the great diminution of the effects of hunger and famine as positive checks to the growth of population for about a century, was not the only important effect of the industrial revolution on the death rate. The industrial revolution also provided the economic means for the study of the causes of those diseases which year after year kept the death rates about twice as high in 1800 as they were in 1900. In the first place, the industrial revolution made possible a better level of living for a more considerable part of the population than in the past. It made possible better housing, fresher and purer food, and more adequate clothing. The improvement in these respects was not large at first, but there was improvement, and in those countries for which good data are available the death rate fell decade by decade throughout much of the nineteenth century with only an occasional relapse. In the second place, in addition to raising the level of living the industrial revolution by increasing the productivity of labor contributed greatly to the surplus (above mere necessities) which could be devoted to the development of science and the application of science to the improvement of health, particularly to the providing of purer water supplies and the installation of more sanitary sewage disposal. In the course of time the greater productivity of labor which made modern science possible and which provided the surplus necessary to apply our knowledge in practical ways also led to the development of modern medicine. But it should be noted that the death rate in Sweden, which in 1801 to 1810 was 28.2 per 1,000, fell to 18.3 in the decade 1871 to 1880, the decade at the end of which Pasteur's great discoveries regarding the nature of disease became known. Prior to 1880 most of the very great decline in the death rate which took place in the Western world must be attributed to the general improvement in the manner of life of the peoples affected by the increased productivity of industry and agriculture which had been taking place during the preceding century. Lack of sanitation and hardship of living always bear heavily on babies during the first year of life; hence any general improvement in living conditions is quickly reflected in the decline in infant mortality. (Infant mortality is generally measured by the number of babies who die under one year of age per 1,000 babies born alive during that year.) In Sweden in the decade 1801 to 1810 the number of babies per 1,000 born who died before they reached one year of age was 198.7. By the decade 1871 to 1880, the last decade without benefit of Pasteur's discoveries, the rate had fallen to 129.9, or by more than one-third. In the next few decades the rate of decline was even more rapid.

The significance of this decline in the death rate, which can be attributed fundamentally to the greater productivity of labor which resulted from more and more use of power machinery, is sometimes overlooked. But it requires only a moment's thought to see that if the death rate declines year after year while the birth rate remains at about the same level the rate of increase of population rises. This is essentially what happened in the Western world during the century after the industrial revolution really became effective, although in some countries the birth rate also began to decline within this period. However, in most of these countries the death rate declined faster than the birth rate for several decades.

In view of this long and rapid increase of population in the West with a rather steady and at times rapid rise in the level of living, many people were bound to ask, was Malthus essentially wrong in maintaining that man *always* tended to reproduce at a rate which would lead to hardship and the operation of the positive checks? I have emphasized the word "always" because I believe this needs qualification. In Malthus' day and earlier, which for him was "always," I believe his description of the factors affecting population growth was essentially accurate just as it still describes what is happening among the greater part of mankind. But Malthus did not foresee how the control of conception might affect his view that man's welfare was always endangered by his tendency to reproduce at a relatively rapid rate, or that production might be increased more rapidly than seemed reasonable in his day.

4. INDUSTRIALISM AND THE BIRTH RATE

There is another aspect of the effect of the industrial revolution upon population growth which we are only now beginning to appreciate but which seems likely in the not-distant future to render Malthus' views on the growth of population as affected by the unchangeability of sex passion of historical interest only. It is that for several decades, at least, the more highly industrialized nations have shown a fairly rapid and steady decline in the birth rate. The reasons for this will not be discussed at this point, but it may not be amiss to say that the very agglomeration of people which was made possible by the application of steam to manufacturing and transport seems to have been instrumental in the development of modes of living which provide very powerful motives for the control of the size of the family. Moreover, it has become quite obvious to everyone who thinks about it at all that when children no longer die like flies and when epidemics are largely under control, survival no longer depends on an unrestricted birth rate. Consequently, the voluntary control of births, chiefly through contraception, has spread rapidly in the West, first in the upper economic groups of the more highly urbanized areas and then slowly, but apparently none the less certainly, to the less favored economic groups of cities and finally to the rural areas. Industrialism, which for almost a century bade fair to flood the world with people, so that not even its continued advance in efficiency could ensure them a good living, has also made it possible to apply effectively a preventive check if people desire to do so. If Malthus had analyzed the tendencies of the new system growing up about him, he might have seen more clearly some of the characteristics which it now exhibits, but it is hard to see how he could have foreseen the rapid spread of the voluntary control of births which has taken place of late years among almost all Western peoples.

The industrial revolution has wrought a revolution in our mental as well as in our economic life. In the past man's mental attitudes were based largely upon the unquestioning acceptance of tradition and custom. In other words, he inherited his social attitudes through the more or less passive acceptance of custom and tradition and institutional organization, just as truly as he inherited his biological traits from his parents. In this new era one of the distinguishing characteristics of our mental life is the readiness to question these traditional beliefs and attitudes and to try to develop more rational modes of conduct. It is not surprising, however, that a large degree of disorganization in conduct accompanies such a great revolution in social organization as we have been and still are passing through; nor could it be expected that man's conduct as regards reproduction would remain unchanged. We are now in the midst of this revolution in reproductive habits, as will be made clear in later chapters. What the end will be no one can tell, but we should not forget that it is the manner of life brought about by the industrial revolution which lies at the root of the changes in population growth which have taken place in the West during the last century and a half and of those upon which other parts of the world are now entering. The techniques of contraception as well as the motives leading to their use must also be regarded as consequences flowing from the industrial revolution.

In looking into the future and attempting to foresee the probable trends of population growth we must, if this analysis of the effect of modern industry on population growth is correct, take account of the probable extension of such industry into new areas and its intensification in areas where already lodged. Only by so doing can we hope to arrive at a reasonable conclusion regarding the growth of any people in the next few decades and foresee the problems which this growth is likely to present. Since no one will deny that our welfare in the near future depends in many ways upon the nature and extent of our population growth, it behooves us to give careful consideration to the effects of modern industrial development upon man's increase and to consider how the most desirable growth in population can be achieved. These matters will be discussed in more detail below (Chaps. XV and XVI).

5. SUMMARY

In concluding this brief discussion of the industrial revolution and population growth it should be pointed out again that the first demographic effect of the increase in man's productive power was to encourage an extremely rapid increase in the population of European origin. The industrial revolution largely removed, for the time being at least, the two great positive checks to population growth which had generally been strongly operative until that time, namely, the lack of the necessities of life and the heavy incidence of disease due to the utter lack of sanitation. The result was just that rapid increase in population which Malthus said would follow the removal of these checks. For more than a century this growth was almost uninterrupted, and it is only recently slowing up because of the application of a type of preventive check which did not enter into Malthus' calculations.

This new preventive check, also an effect of the industrial revolution, is being used in consequence of the new manner of life made possible and necessary by the industrial revolution. It is just as natural and inevitable as the revolution itself, and it bids fair to upset Malthus' predictions of future hardship for those peoples among whom its practice becomes general simply because it is a preventive check, one that reduces the birth rate. Thus, we can look to the future, so far as the increase of numbers among industrialized peoples is concerned, with little misgiving as regards man's ability to control population growth. There is almost no likelihood that the peoples having knowledge of contraception will fail to use it to prevent the decline in their level of living which would very quickly lead to a higher death rate because of the hardships which would soon follow if there were no control over the birth rate. Industrialized man is rapidly learning that a high birth rate and a low death rate cannot long endure together.

This does not mean, however, that the danger of overpopulation is past for all peoples or even for any people at all times. As will be indicated elsewhere, it appears probable to the writer that the United Kingdom is overpopulated today because of changes in world economy which are largely beyond her control. Consequently, she will experience some of the evils of overpopulation until economic conditions change for the better, either through the expansion of her trade and the more efficient use of natural resources or through the decline of population to the point where there will be a better balance between population and natural resources. Thus, even highly—perhaps too highly—industrialized lands may experience overpopulation, but it need not be for more than a few decades, and with more careful appraisal of the situation in advance even such maladjustments of population to economic opportunity should become less frequent and should also entail less hardship. In addition to the temporary maladjustments due to changing conditions which cannot be clearly foreseen or adjustment to which is made too slowly (cultural lag) there will, of course, continue to be the pressures of population on resources which have generally, if not always, characterized preindustrial civilizations. It is to such peoples that Malthus' doctrines apply today and will continue to apply, as long as their conditions of life remain as they are.

In the light of our broader experience today we have far less reason to make the same cardinal mistakes that Malthus did. He assumed that the social and the economic conditions of his time were the normal and usual conditions for all mankind and that they would continue much as they were for an indefinite period. We are accustomed to change, and we should also have learned that no particular social order is more normal, or more usual, or more natural than another. Every social order is natural under the conditions which produce it and which make its continuance possible, but under other conditions other orders are just as natural; and under these different social conditions man is certain to be confronted with new problems which will certainly be somewhat different but may not be less difficult for him to solve.

When in the course of time our present industrialism changes its form or issues in a new type of social organization, then we may confidently expect new factors to enter into the determination of population growth and new problems of adjustment of numbers to resources to arise. With the outlook that we now have, perhaps we may more accurately anticipate some future trends than Malthus and his contemporaries could. But it is not at all unlikely that in many respects we shall fall far short of appreciating fully the influence of the tendencies of our day just as Malthus did in his, even though our greater knowledge gives us less excuse for doing so. For example, there is a strong tendency today to assume that the rapid growth of population which we have witnessed in the West during the last century and a half is the normal or usual condition, with the result that many people are much disturbed now that the birth rate has fallen to a relatively low level and there is prospect of a slowly growing or stationary population in the peoples of Western European descent.

This brief discussion of ways in which the industrial revolution affected population growth in the West during the last century and a half or two centuries was necessary if we would understand what has happened to our population and what is likely to happen in other areas as they industrialize. The significance of the industrial revolution will appear even more clearly as the discussion of the changes in the growth of population and in its composition proceeds.

Suggestions for Supplementary Reading

BUER, M. C.: *Health, Wealth, and Population in the Early Days of the Industrial Revolution (1760–1815)*, 290 pp., G. Routledge & Sons, Ltd., London, 1926.

GEORGE, M. DOROTHY: "Some Causes of the Increase of Population in the Eighteenth Century as Illustrated by London," *Econ. J.,* Vol. 32, pp. 325–352, 1922.

GONNER, EDWARD C. K.: "The Population of England in the Eighteenth Century," *Royal Statis. Soc. J.,* Vol. 76, pp. 261–296, 1913.

LANDRY, ADOLPHE: "La Démographie de l'ancien Paris," *J. de la société de statistique de Paris,* No. 2, p. 37, 1935.

MANTOUX, PAUL: *The Industrial Revolution in the Eighteenth Century: An Outline of the Beginnings of the Modern Factory System in England*, rev. ed., 539 pp., translated by Marjorie Vernon, Harcourt, Brace and Company, New York, 1928.

MOFFIT, LOUIS W.: *England on the Eve of the Industrial Revolution: A Study on Economic and Social Conditions from 1740–1760, with Special Reference to Lancashire*, 312 pp., P. S. King & Son, Ltd., London, 1925.

REINHARD, MARCEL R.: *Histoire de la population mondiale de 1700 à 1948*, 794 pp., Domat-Montchrestien, Paris, 1949. A compendium of information on this subject.

Part II: Population Composition.

THE COMPOSITION OF POPULATION

We are all familiar with the ideas discussed in this chapter, but unless we have had our attention especially called to the significance of the demographic differences between the peoples living in different communities we probably will not attach much importance to them just because of their familiarity.

All of us are sufficiently acquainted with the history of settlement in the United States to know that in the early years of settlement in every part of the country there was a large preponderance of males. Only gradually as the dangers from Indian attack diminished, or the "gold rush" subsided, or the land passed from the hands of speculators into those of cultivators, did the proportion of females increase until there was a near equality of numbers between the sexes. It is also generally known that certain types of communities continue to attract a large proportion of males long after other types cease to do so. Thus communities in which mining is predominant, especially the mining of precious and semiprecious metals, and communities in which cattle ranching on a large scale is well developed, have a high proportion of males long after farming areas come to have only a small preponderance of males and after cities come to have a preponderance of females.

A moment's thought will also lead to the further realization that these predominantly male communities generally are also peculiar in that the people living in them are heavily concentrated in certain age groups. Migrants to predominantly male areas are, as a rule, young adults ranging in age from the late teens to thirty-five or forty years of age. Since there are relatively few women in these communities, there are also comparatively few children, and there are relatively few people over forty-five years of age until settlement has been established for some years. It is also obvious that in the early days of settlement the people who migrated to any community were likely to be engaged in similar occupations. In the Mississippi Valley most settlers were farmers; in northern Michigan most of the men may have been loggers, and in the western mountains most of them were miners or prospectors; on the "high plains" most men were cowboys; etc.

As time passed, many of the early differences in the make-up of the population in different communities became less marked or even disappeared, but functional differences developed which were of a relatively

86

permanent character. In most cities today there is a considerable preponderance of young women, but in a "steel city" there will probably be a preponderance of men, especially at ages twenty to forty. Such a city is also likely to have a larger proportion of children of school age than one in which trade and insurance and light manufacturing predominate. As a consequence, the latter type of city has less need per 1,000 of its population for primary and secondary schools than the former.

Another demographic difference between communities which is of much importance in the United States, although of relatively little importance in many countries, is that in the proportions of the population belonging to different races. Such differences are so important in the United States that the following chapter will be devoted to the discussion of the demographic characteristics of the Negro.

The three traits or characteristics of individuals noted above—sex, age, and race—are hereditary and unchangeable, *i.e.*, neither the individual nor society can alter these qualities of the individual. However, most of the traits or characteristics of individuals which are of social significance can be altered by the will and effort of the individual and the community in which he lives. If a significant change in these physical characteristics of any population as a whole is desired, *e.g.*, a higher proportion of males or more young people, as far as we now know this can only be accomplished by changing the death rates of males relative to those of females, or those of young people as compared with those of older people, or by forbidding or encouraging certain types of persons to migrate. On the other hand, changes in the proportion of the population having given social characteristics, *e.g.,* a college education, can be effected by changing the strength of the inducements and the opportunities to secure such an education.

Some of the differences between communities in the composition of their populations mentioned above may seem so abnormal and temporary as to be of little concern in a general study of population. This is sometimes the case, but many significant demographic differences between the populations of different communities and even between groups within the same community are to be found everywhere and at all times. There are many significant sex, age, and racial differences to be found in different communities in the United States even today, while differences in the social characteristics of their populations are even more numerous and certainly of equal significance. Some of these differences of both types arise out of the earlier conditions of settlement noted above, but most of them arise out of the differences in the economic and social functions served by different communities and groups. Moreover, these differences in composition are still brought about to a considerable extent by the migration into or out of the different communities as was the case in earlier days. This migration is now less obvious than formerly, because it has lost much of its spectacular character and appears more and more a matter of course. It is no less important, however, to know that one community has fewer men than women, or vice versa, than another, that one has more old people or more children than another, or that one has more machinists, or more factory workers, or more people with a good education, or a larger proportion of married persons, and so forth, than another, as will be shown presently.

There are also other characteristics of people living in different communities which are of significance in enabling us to understand the distinctive traits exhibited by different communities. Thus the fact that different parts of the United States were originally settled predominantly by people coming from different European countries or from different regions in those countries, or by those having in common certain beliefs and accepting a certain manner of life, is still manifest in these areas. The fact that New England was settled preponderantly by people of the Puritan religious faith while Virginia was settled chiefly by people belonging to the established Church of England helped to give a different character to the social and economic development of these areas. Later changes in types of migrants have, in turn, effected other changes in social development. Of course, the origin of the migrants was by no means the only factor differentiating life in New England from life in Virginia. Climate, soil, natural resources, and so forth all played their parts, but the fact that one area drew many people having one type of background and social values while another drew more people with a different outlook on life also had its influence in differentiating these areas from one another.

As has already been noted, there were also communities which were settled by people coming from different countries—England, Scotland, Germany, Sweden, and so forth. In some such communities the language of the country of origin is still spoken, although this is no longer common. But many of these communities settled by people from given countries and from particular regions in these countries still retain certain customs and manners which more or less distinguish them from one another.

With the growth in the complexity of social organization connected with the development of modern industry and commerce, we find many other differences arising between people living in different communities and gaining their livelihood by different types of work. When these differences become measurable the student of population is disposed to try to take account of them, to class them as demographic differences, and to regard them as a proper area of study.

Thus the study of the composition of the population tends to expand as we learn more about the social and economic characteristics of people. This expansion of the study of population may not be strictly demographic in the older sense of that term, but the fact that the physical (age, sex, and race), the social (education, religion, and so forth), and the economic (income, rental value of home, occupation and so forth) traits of people are important in understanding many aspects of the organization of community life justifies the student of population in adding the study of social and economic differences to that of the physical differences between people in different communities when he studies the composition of the population.

It will be obvious from what has been said that the composition of the population of a community or an area is not fixed but may change quite rapidly under unusual circumstances, *e.g.*, the location of a military camp or a naval training station. In Europe during and following World War II, the forced mass migration of certain populations changed the character of many communities very greatly. Over a somewhat longer time, but still within a few years, a mining or oil-producing community may spring up rapidly when ores, or coal, or oil is found and may dwindle slowly or even vanish almost overnight when the supplies give out or it becomes uneconomic to recover them. Lumbering is much like many mining enterprises in the instability of the support it provides for a settled population. But even in agricultural and industrial communities, rather rapid changes in the composition of the population may take place under crisis conditions. One of the best examples of change in population in an agricultural community is to be found in the "dust bowl" of the wheat belt in western Kansas and Oklahoma and in northern Texas, where drought coincided with the depression and the shift from horse power to tractor power in wheat farming. Not only was there actual loss in population but there was a considerable change in the composition of the population left behind. In the aggregate, 31 counties in the heart of the dust-bowl area lost almost one-fourth of their population (24.4 per cent) between 1930 and 1940. This was due chiefly to the out-migration of a relatively large number of young adults with their children. Thus persons fifteen to nineteen years of age constituted 11.5 per cent of the total population in 1930, but this same group, aged twenty-five to twenty-nine in 1940, constituted only 8.0 per cent. The actual number aged twenty-five to twenty-nine in 1940 was 19,741, whereas if there had been no migration, death alone reducing their numbers, there should have been approximately 36,101. There is much the same rate of decline in the group aged twenty to twenty-four, from 31,510 in 1930 to 18,025 in 1940, whereas death should only have reduced the number to 30,051. The decline in the proportion of children under ten from 24.0 per cent in 1930 to 19.0 per cent in 1940 is due in part to the decline in the birth rate as well as to the out-migration of young adults with their young children. At the other extreme of life the proportion of persons fifty-five and over rose from 8.8 per cent in 1930 to 13.8 per cent in 1940. Such rapid changes are certain to have considerable effects on life in an agricultural community.

Occasionally changes in industry also effect large and rather sudden changes in the composition of the population in cities. Generally, the sudden changes occur in rather small cities and semirural communities with a rather highly specialized industry or agriculture. This may happen when a factory closes down or moves away because of the consolidation of the industry into larger and fewer producing units, *e.g.*, the abandonment of many small plants by the steel industry, or because the obsolescence of the factories and mills in one area makes it difficult for them to compete with better-equipped plants in some newer area. Likewise changes in labor supply and transportation costs and/or the exhaustion or discovery of raw materials may effect large changes not only in the numbers but in the composition of the population in particular communities. In such cases it is usually the young male adults who move first. Thus the age and sex composition may be quickly altered. Such selective migration, in turn, has an effect on the birth and the death rates. In the Scranton–Wilkes Barre industrial and mining (anthracite) area in Pennsylvania, the fifteen to twenty-four age group constituted 19.8 per cent of the population in 1930, while the twenty-five to thirty-four group in 1940 constituted only 16.5 per cent of the total and the thirty-five to forty-four group constituted only 15.1 per cent in 1950. These declines are all larger than can be accounted for by death alone; hence it is reasonably certain that there was considerable net out-migration of young adults.

But in spite of these rather rapid and significant changes in the composition of the population of some communities, in most communities the changes in composition are not catastrophic but rather slow, so that in comparing demographic conditions in the same community over a decade or two changes in composition may often be so small that they are of little significance. It is never safe, however, to ignore the possibility of significant changes in the composition of population in particular communities when making comparisons of the social and economic aspects of their life.

As will be seen from the above discussion the author is using the phrase *composition of the population* to cover the totality of the measurable qualities of the people that form a given population. The composition of one group or community is said to differ from that of another when one group or community has a larger or smaller proportion of persons with any particular quality than those in another. Generally, however, there are a number of ways in which the composition of one group will differ from that of another as we shall see below. Our discussion here will be concerned chiefly in pointing out differences between communities in the proportions of people having different qualities and in showing why these differences are of more or less importance in understanding many aspects of community life.

Differences between groups and communities in sex and age are universal, but the significance of these differences depends largely upon their size. Where they are large they may be of much importance both as factors determining further demographic changes and also in influencing social and economic development. Other physical qualities which affect the composition of a population are race and what we commonly call today *eugenic quality*, sometimes mistakenly treated as though it were the same as the intelligence quotient.

Because the author considers the question of the quality of population of very great importance, he has not treated quality in this chapter on composition but has given it separate consideration in Chap. XXI.

1. SEX COMPOSITION

It will be well to begin the discussion of the differentials between communities in the composition of their populations with the presentation of the facts showing how they differ in sex make-up.

The sex ratios in the United States, in its different regions, and in several foreign countries for 1880 and for the most recent date available are given in Table 6-1. In 1880 the sex ratio (number of males per 100 females) in the United States was 103.6; by 1950 this had fallen to 98.6. The differences between the regions are much larger. In 1880 the sex ratio in the West was 153.4, while in the Northeast it was only 97.5. By 1950 these ratios were much closer, that in the West having fallen to 102.1, while that in the Northeast had fallen only by about 1.4 point, to 96.1. In most European countries the sex ratios have long been well below that of the United States, and except for Sweden, the European countries shown here still have sex ratios well below that of the United States. India, on the other hand, has had and continues to have a relatively high sex ratio.

The high sex ratio in the United States until quite recently is to be explained primarily by the fact that for a long time we had a large net immigration from abroad in which males predominated. Because of this emigration of males many European countries had relatively low sex ratios. The high sex ratio in India is probably due chiefly to the higher death rates of female infants and young mothers, since there is no generally accepted evidence that the sex ratio at birth (about 105 to 106 males for every 100 females) is different in India from that in European countries. It may also be in part the consequence of an underenumeration of females, although there is no clear evidence on this point.

The ratio of the sexes affects social and economic conditions in a variety of ways. Obviously, if there are more males than females of those ages generally thought of as "marriageable," there will generally be a smaller proportion of married men than in a population where there is an excess of females. As a rule in the United States the proportion of married males under thirty-five is smaller in rural areas than in urban areas, while the opposite holds for females. In many of the European countries, where there has long been a large excess of male emigrants and/or where war has decimated the male population, there will be a relatively large proportion of unmarried women. A high proportion of males also means more workers available for farming and the heavy industries. This is especially true if the sex ratio is high at ages twenty to fifty-five.

The sex ratio is also an important factor in determining the death rate of any population. Women generally have lower death rates than men at most ages in those countries with medium to low death rates; hence, if females constitute more than half of the population, as they do in many communities and in most European countries (England and France, Table 6-1), the total death rate (crude) of the population is appreciably affected by this

Table 6-1. Sex Ratios in the United States and Its Regions and for Selected Foreign Countries, 1950 and 1880

Country[1]	Males per 100 females	
	1950	1880
United States..........................	98.6	103.6
Northeast..........................	96.1	97.5
North Central.....................	99.5	108.0
South............................	98.5	100.3
West.............................	102.1	153.4
England and Wales (1949).............	94.2	94.8
France (1946).......................	90.0	99.5
Germany, Federal Republic (1950)......	88.2	96.3
Indian Union (1951).................	105.8	104.8[2]
Soviet Union (1939).................	92.0	98.7[3]
Sweden (1945).......................	99.0	94.2

[1] Date in parentheses is latest available.
[2] Includes Burma.
[3] Russia, 1897.

fact. Again a scarcity of either men or women at the young adult ages will, by reducing the marriage rate, also affect the crude birth rate. In addition, there is little doubt that school attendance, the extent of the employment of women outside the home, the amount of prostitution, the status of women in the community, and many other social conditions are more or less directly related to the sex ratios of a population, although in particular communities other factors may be more important in explaining such differences between them in social and economic conditions.

Migration and war are probably the two most important factors in producing what may be called "abnormal" differences in sex ratios between particular populations. "Normal" sex ratios arise as a consequence of the effects of death rates, since the sex ratio at birth usually averages about 105 to 106. A "normal" sex ratio by age and for all ages combined can be obtained from any life table (Chap. XI) or from any population where migration is insignificant. At present those countries in which moderate to low death rates have prevailed for some time and migration is small show a declining sex ratio from birth onward because females have lower death rates than males at all ages.

The sex ratios in England and Wales (1911) may be compared with those in the United States white population in 1910 (Fig. 6-1) to indicate the effects

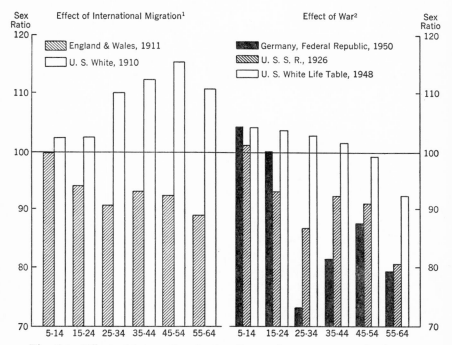

Fig. 6-1. Effect of international migration and war on sex ratios by age.

on sex ratios of rather large-scale immigration and emigration over a considerable period of time. In 1910 the United States had been receiving large numbers of immigrants almost steadily for some decades and the total sex ratio was 106.6; the ratios at ages thirty to fifty-four were from 5 to 10 points higher. England and Wales, on the other hand, had been sending out large numbers of emigrants and had sex ratios below 92.0 at ages twenty to thirty-four and a total sex ratio of only 93.7.

Sex ratios as affected by war are shown by the populations of Germany (1950) and the Soviet Union (1926). Today the differences between communities within a country in sex ratios arise chiefly from the migration of younger people to urban communities, although in the United States the migration of older people to milder climates bids fair to become of importance in the not-distant future in certain states.

2. AGE COMPOSITION

It was impossible to illustrate the differences in sex composition between communities and nations and note the chief reasons for them without also calling attention to differences between different populations in age composition. With only a few exceptions, as noted above, every population has persons of all ages in it, but most communities differ from one another to a greater or lesser extent in their age composition. Where these differences are small, little significance is to be attached to them. In many cases, however, they are large enough to affect the social and economic conditions in a variety of ways, while from the standpoint of understanding the natality and mortality of a community it is of the first importance to know its age composition as well as its sex composition.

Table 6-2 shows some of the age differences in the United States as a whole and in the four large regions, today and in 1880; also for certain foreign countries for about the same dates. It is obvious that when such differences in age composition exist they will help to account for many other differences in social conditions in these areas. For example, the South has long had a considerably younger population than the Northeast. This means it has to provide educational facilities for a larger proportion of its people if they are to be given opportunities equal to those provided in other regions. The South should also have a lower crude death rate than other regions since the rate of mortality mounts rapidly at ages above fifty (Chap. XI). On the other hand, the South has had a somewhat smaller proportion of persons at ages thirty to forty-nine, ages of high productivity. These age differences between the regions would of themselves create social and economic differences if all other factors remained the same, but as a matter of fact they are associated with other differences, *e.g.*, race, which as we shall see are probably even more important (Chap. VII).

The differences in age composition between countries are of the same character as those between regions in the United States. For example, France (1946) has a very small proportion of children under ten (14.1 per cent) and of adults aged twenty to twenty-nine (this group includes the children born during World War I) as compared with most other European countries. In 1950, Germany had a very small proportion aged thirty to thirty-nine. At the older ages—fifty and over—France has had a higher proportion than most other countries for several decades, although some of the other European countries are now approaching its level. In most other Western lands the proportion of older people is now increasing faster than in France. This fact in itself is significant because old people add to the crude death rate, subtract from the crude birth rate, and are less productive economically than younger people, to mention only a few of the more obvious differences. The problem of old age in France has long been of a more pressing character than in most other countries. In this connection one wonders whether the great conservatism of France in business, in family life, in standards of living, and in many other respects is related to the fact that it has long had a large proportion of old people in its population.

Table 6-2.   Percentage Distribution by Age, United States by Regions and Selected Foreign Countries, 1950 and 1880

Country	Year	Under 10	10–19	20–29	30–39	40–49	50–64	Over 65
United States............	1950	19.5	14.4	15.7	15.1	12.8	14.3	8.1
	1880	26.7	21.4	18.3	12.7	9.1	8.4	3.4
Northeast.............	1950	17.3	12.9	15.6	15.7	13.7	16.1	8.7
	1880	22.3	20.0	18.3	13.8	10.5	10.2	4.8
North Central.........	1950	19.0	13.9	15.4	14.8	12.8	15.3	8.9
	1880	26.5	22.2	18.4	12.7	8.9	8.2	3.0
South................	1950	21.7	16.7	16.2	14.6	12.0	11.9	6.9
	1880	31.2	22.0	17.9	11.3	7.7	7.0	2.8
West................	1950	19.6	13.4	15.8	15.8	12.9	14.3	8.2
	1880	22.6	18.2	20.5	16.8	11.7	8.4	1.8
England and Wales........	1949	15.5	12.4	14.8	14.7	15.0	16.8	10.9
	1881	25.7	20.6	16.8	12.7	9.8	9.8	4.6
France..................	1946	14.1	15.7	13.2	14.8	14.9	16.4	11.0
	1881	18.3	17.1	15.8	13.8	12.4	14.5	8.1
Germany, Federal Republic.	1950	14.5	16.3	14.9	12.8	15.8	16.4	9.3
	1880	25.1	19.7	15.9	13.0	10.4	8.0[1]	7.9[2]
India...................	1931	28.4	20.7	18.0	13.9	9.4	7.4	2.2
	1881	27.8	19.1	17.6	14.4	9.7	6.1[1]	5.3[2]
Soviet Union............	1939	23.1	21.9	18.1	14.9	9.0	8.8	4.2
	1897	27.3	21.3	16.0	12.4	9.3	6.7[1]	6.9[2]
Sweden................	1945	15.5	12.8	15.8	16.2	14.1	15.7	10.0
	1880	23.0	19.5	15.7	12.3	10.7	12.9	5.9

[1] Age 50–59.
[2] Age 60 and over.

Conversely, in the United States, are our economic progressiveness and our lack of respect for the customary methods of production and marketing in part a consequence of the high proportion of our population under forty, particularly until about 1930? If so, what will be the effects on our life of an aging population? Will we become more conservative in business, in government, in personal habits, and so forth? Some of these questions cannot be answered with the information now at our disposal; others will be discussed in more appropriate connections, but in passing it may be said there is little doubt that as the average age in the nation mounts we shall find ourselves confronted by many new and puzzling problems. The increase in the proportion of older people has provided much of the drive for the establishment and expansion of the social security program as related to the care of the aged, and the increase in the number and proportion of old people will almost certainly continue during the next six decades. The increase in their numbers can be calculated with considerable exactness, unless some unforeseeable catastrophe intervenes to increase their death rates or unless migration becomes more significant.

Another very serious problem which is now confronting us as a consequence of age changes is that of providing adequate schools for the increase in the number of children now entering primary schools as a result of the rise in the number of births after 1940 and particularly after the close of World War II. In this case the demographer can calculate with reasonable accuracy not only the size of the population coming of school age for six years in advance, but also the total population of school age during this period. He can only guess at future births.

3. RACIAL COMPOSITION

Racial composition will be treated very briefly at this point because it is a matter of but little concern in many, perhaps in most, communities even in the United States. Besides, a separate chapter (Chap. VII) is devoted to the composition of the Negro population in the United States.

In the United States when we speak of race in the composition of the population we nearly always mean the proportions of whites and Negroes in the population under consideration. However, under certain conditions, *e.g.*, during the war with Japan, we are made aware that in certain parts of the country there are significant proportions of other races. Races are quite commonly distinguished from one another by the average person on the basis of skin color and certain differences in facial structure and/or in stature. These rather readily observable differences are quite commonly believed to be very closely associated with certain social, moral, and intellectual differences which are then attributed to the race as a group. As far as the author knows there is no scientific basis for the very widespread belief that the social, moral, and intellectual differences between groups are racial in character. The evidence we have indicates rather that intellectual differences are individual, while social and moral differences arise from differences in customs and institutions. This point will not be labored here but will be treated in Chap. XXI.

Table 6-3.   Racial Composition of the Population of the United States and Its Regions, 1950 and 1880

Region	White			Nonwhite	
	Total	Native	Foreign-born	Negro	Other races
1950					
United States............	89.5	82.8	6.7	10.0	0.5
Northeast...............	94.7	81.6	13.2	5.1	0.2
North Central...........	94.7	88.6	6.1	5.0	0.3
South..................	78.1	76.5	1.6	21.7	0.3
West...................	95.0	87.3	7.7	2.9	2.1
1880					
United States............	86.5	73.5	13.1	13.1	0.3
Northeast...............	98.4	79.0	19.4	1.6	0.0
North Central...........	97.7	80.9	16.8	2.2	0.1
South..................	63.9	61.2	2.7	36.0	0.0
West...................	91.2	68.7	22.5	0.7	8.1

There are many communities in which the proportions of persons belonging to different races vary widely. Since these differences have very important demographic and social consequences, such variations need to be taken into account. Table 6-3 shows that the proportions of whites and Negroes vary greatly in different regions of the United States. The variations between states are even greater. In 1950 Vermont had only about one Negro in each 1,000 of its population while Mississippi had almost 500 in each 1,000. As will be pointed out in the chapter on the Negro such differences have important demographic consequences for both whites and Negroes. But these demographic consequences are of small significance as compared with the social and economic consequences arising from the contact of different races in the same community. This is quite commonly recognized by each of the racial groups involved. This is not the place to discuss such problems, but it may be said in passing that there is probably no community problem that is not made more difficult of solution if the community has a minority racial element amounting to more than a very small percentage of the total. One only need mention the problems connected with schools, housing, travel, employment, income, and so forth, to realize the great influence differences in racial composition exert in the treatment of many social problems.

4. INDUSTRIAL COMPOSITION

The industrial composition of the population of the United States, Iowa, and Connecticut is shown in Table 6-4. These states were chosen because they show wide differences between the proportions of persons employed in different industries and also between the proportions of employed males and females in these industries. It would have been desirable to show the changes in industrial composition during the course of the past several decades because our economy has changed so greatly since about 1900, but a comparable industrial classification does not exist for earlier decades. However, there were substantial changes even between 1940 and 1950. That we have become chiefly an industrial nation with only a minor proportion of our people directly dependent on agriculture is clearly evident from this table, and the end is not yet. The proportion of the persons employed in agriculture has been decreasing for more than a century, while the proportion employed in manufacturing, in transportation, in trade, and in services of all kinds, in the professions, in public work, in construction work, and so forth, has been increasing. Likewise the proportion of women among employed persons has been increasing as more jobs suitable to women have developed in manufacturing, business, and public service.

The proportion of any population engaged in manufacturing, in trade, and in the different services appears to depend upon the function served by the particular area in question. Thus Iowa and Connecticut have quite a different industrial composition. Only a few decades ago all of the United States was much like Iowa, and today even Iowa has about one-half as many persons engaged in manufacturing as in farming while Connecticut has about ten times as many.

Differences in occupational composition naturally follow industrial changes and both affect the life of the community in various ways. The relative decline in agricultural occupations is accompanied many times by an actual decrease in rural population. Thus the rural-urban distribution of population is changed both regionally and nationally (see below). Again, persons in different industries and occupations are subject to different health

Table 6-4. Percentage Distribution of the Employed Population by Sex and Industry Group, United States and Selected States, 1950 and 1940

Area and industry group	Percentage distribution by sex				Percentage distribution by industry			
	1950		1940		1950		1940	
	Male	Female	Male	Female	Male	Female	Male	Female
United States, total	72.0	28.0	75.3	24.7	100.0	100.0	100.0	100.0
Agriculture, forestry, and fisheries	91.5	8.5	94.3	5.7	15.8	3.8	23.5	4.4
Mining	97.5	2.5	98.8	1.2	2.2	0.1	2.7	0.1
Construction	97.1	2.9	98.3	1.7	8.2	0.6	5.9	0.3
Manufacturing	75.0	25.0	78.0	22.0	27.0	23.2	24.2	20.8
Transportation, communication, and other public utilities	84.4	15.6	88.9	11.1	9.1	4.3	8.1	3.1
Wholesale and retail trade	66.4	33.6	73.1	26.9	17.3	22.6	16.2	18.2
Finance, insurance, and real estate	59.3	40.7	69.0	31.0	2.8	5.0	3.0	4.1
Business and repair services	87.0	13.0	91.1	8.9	3.0	1.2	2.3	0.7
Personal services	33.2	66.8	28.3	71.7	2.9	14.8	3.3	25.8
Entertainment and recreation services	74.5	25.5	79.9	20.1	1.0	0.9	0.9	0.7
Professional and related services	41.9	58.1	44.4	55.6	4.8	17.3	4.3	16.6
Public administration	73.8	26.2	80.6	19.4	4.5	4.1	4.2	3.0
Industry not reported	60.6	39.4	65.4	34.6	1.3	2.1	1.3	2.1
Iowa, total	75.6	24.4	80.3	19.7	100.0	100.0	100.0	100.0
Agriculture, forestry, and fisheries	93.2	6.8	98.3	1.7	35.1	8.0	43.8	3.2
Mining	97.5	2.5	99.5	0.5	0.4	0.0	0.9	0.0
Construction	97.1	2.9	98.3	1.7	7.0	0.6	5.1	0.4
Manufacturing	79.7	20.3	83.3	16.7	16.0	12.6	11.9	9.7
Transportation, communication, and other public utilities	84.8	15.2	89.2	10.8	7.8	4.3	7.3	3.6
Wholesale and retail trade	65.7	34.3	73.9	26.1	16.7	27.0	15.5	22.2
Finance, insurance, and real estate	58.2	41.8	67.9	32.1	2.1	4.7	2.1	4.1
Business and repair services	89.5	10.5	92.8	7.2	3.1	1.1	2.4	0.7
Personal services	32.1	67.9	23.8	76.2	1.9	12.3	2.0	25.9
Entertainment and recreation services	71.0	29.0	81.5	18.5	0.8	1.0	0.7	0.7
Professional and related services	39.3	60.7	40.5	59.5	4.5	21.7	4.0	23.9
Public administration	74.7	25.3	79.6	20.4	3.0	3.1	2.7	2.8
Industry not reported	57.1	42.9	69.1	30.9	1.5	3.5	1.5	2.8
Connecticut, total	68.1	31.9	70.2	29.8	100.0	100.0	100.0	100.0
Agriculture, forestry, and fisheries	90.8	9.2	95.7	4.3	4.0	0.9	5.5	0.6
Mining	89.8	10.2	97.8	2.2	0.1	0.0	0.1	0.0
Construction	97.1	2.9	98.1	1.9	8.4	0.5	6.8	0.3
Manufacturing	69.7	30.3	72.3	27.7	43.5	40.6	44.8	40.4
Transportation, communication, and other public utilities	79.7	20.3	85.4	14.6	6.2	3.4	5.9	2.4
Wholesale and retail trade	69.9	30.1	75.5	24.5	17.2	15.9	16.3	12.4
Finance, insurance, and real estate	52.9	47.1	61.7	38.3	3.6	6.9	3.8	5.6
Business and repair services	87.4	12.6	92.2	7.8	3.0	0.9	2.2	0.4
Personal services	39.3	60.7	34.3	65.7	2.9	9.7	3.9	17.8
Entertainment and recreation services	77.0	23.0	82.6	17.4	0.8	0.5	0.7	0.4
Professional and related services	40.8	59.2	42.1	57.9	5.3	16.5	4.8	15.5
Public administration	76.2	23.8	80.1	19.9	3.8	2.5	3.6	2.1
Industry not reported	57.3	42.7	61.8	38.2	1.1	1.7	1.5	2.2

Table 6-5. Percentage Distribution of the Employed Population by Sex and Industry Group, Selected Foreign Countries, Latest Year Available

Industry group	England and Wales, 1931				Sweden, 1945[1]			
	Sex		Industry		Sex		Industry	
	Male	Fe-male	Male	Fe-male	Male	Fe-male	Male	Fe-male
Total...................	70.3	29.7	100.0	100.0	74.9	25.1	100.0	100.0
Agriculture, forestry, fishing...................	94.3	5.7	7.5	1.1	93.7	6.3	30.5	6.1
Mining and quarrying.....	99.4	0.6	8.5	0.1	100.0	....	1.2	
Manufacturing industry....	71.8	28.2	41.1	38.1	82.8	17.2	40.9	25.3
Commerce...............	65.5	34.5	17.7	22.1	54.0	46.0	10.5	26.6
Transportation and communication............	93.6	6.4	10.6	1.7	84.8	15.2	8.5	4.5
Public and professional services...............	68.2	31.8	10.5	11.6	50.5	49.5	6.9	20.2
Domestic service..........	23.3	76.7	3.2	24.7	......	100.0	......	16.4
Not specified............	77.9	22.1	0.9	0.6	82.5	17.5	1.5	9.0

Industry group	France, 1936[2]				Italy, 1936			
	Sex		Industry		Sex		Industry	
	Male	Fe-male	Male	Fe-male	Male	Fe-male	Male	Fe-male
Total...................	63.9	36.1	100.0	100.0	71.3	28.7	100.0	100.0
Agriculture, forestry, fishing...................	59.5	40.5	33.1	39.9	72.5	27.5	48.8	46.1
Mining and quarrying.....	98.2	1.8	2.6	......	98.4	1.6	1.0	
Manufacturing industry....	69.9	30.1	32.0	24.3	73.8	26.2	29.5	26.0
Commerce...............	57.7	42.3	12.0	15.6	72.0	28.0	8.8	8.5
Transportation and communication............	77.6	22.4	7.0	1.8	95.0	5.0	5.1	0.7
Public and professional services...............	69.9	30.1	11.8	9.0	68.2	31.8	6.0	7.0
Domestic service..........	1.3	98.7	0.7	9.1	11.5	88.5	0.6	11.1
Not specified............	84.3	15.7	0.7	0.3	53.6	46.4	0.3	0.6

[1] Sweden, Statistiska Centralbyrån, *Statistisk Årsbok för Sverige, 1950*, pp. 348–349, P. A. Norstedt & Söner, Stockholm, 1950.
[2] Later data for France (1946) are given in United Nations, *Demographic Yearbook, 1949–50*, Table 13, but since similar data are not available for Italy and the comparison of France with Italy is of interest, the 1936 data are used here.

hazards and have different rates of mortality. Miners, blast-furnace workers, tool grinders, brass workers, stevedores, common laborers, and a good many other occupational groups have higher mortality rates than professional workers, clerical workers, managers and officials in business, and those in other more sheltered urban occupations. Since farm people, as a whole, have relatively low mortality rates (Chap. XI), the death rate in a given area will be rather closely related to the relative importance of the different industries and occupations. Occupation also gives some clue to the social and economic status of the worker, although not very precisely.

Occupational differences are often even greater between different industrial communities within a state than between states as different as Iowa and Connecticut. There are many "one-industry" communities such as mining communities, textile cities, steel cities, automobile cities, and so forth. The predominance of a given industry in a community often has distinctive effects. Thus, mining communities differ rather markedly from most other communities. Generally there is little work outside the home for women unless a special effort has been made to bring light industries using female labor into them. When this has happened, as in some of the mining regions of eastern Pennsylvania, there is often rather severe exploitation of female labor under poor working conditions which may depress birth rates and raise death rates. If there is little opportunity for the employment of women outside the home, as in mining communities, in cities where heavy manufacturing predominates, and on the farms, the birth rate is generally higher than in communities where light industry and business employ many women. Thus, in textile cities, a large proportion of women may be employed outside the home, and in many of them a low proportion of women are married; as a consequence the crude birth rate tends to be low and infant mortality tends to be relatively high.

Table 6-5 shows much the same kind of differences in industrial employment between foreign countries as are found in different parts of the United States. The differences between England and Wales on the one hand and Italy on the other are even more marked than those between Connecticut and Iowa. It is very important, then, to know the industrial and occupational make-up of different populations if we would understand not only their demographic data but also many of the differences between them in social and economic conditions. The way in which people make their living influences all aspects of their lives.

5. MARITAL COMPOSITION

Differences between communities in marital composition, like those for the characteristics already examined, are substantial, and like all other characteristics they change from time to time. Table 6-6 shows that there was a marked change in marital condition during the past decade. In the United States as a whole the proportion of single women fourteen years of age and over declined from 27.6 per cent in 1940 to 20.1 per cent in 1950 and the proportion married increased from 59.5 to 65.7 per cent. Likewise the proportion of single males declined to about the same extent, from 34.8 per cent in 1940 to 26.2 per cent in 1950, and the proportion married rose from 59.7 per cent to 67.6 per cent. Much the same change took place in

Table 6-6.   Percentage Distribution of the Population 14 Years Old and Over, by Sex and Marital Status, United States and Selected States, 1950 and 1940

Area	Male			Female		
	Single	Married	Widowed or divorced	Single	Married	Widowed or divorced
1950						
United States............	26.2	67.6	6.1	20.1	65.7	14.2
Vermont................	28.6	64.4	7.0	22.9	62.2	14.9
Connecticut.............	27.3	66.9	5.8	23.3	63.7	13.0
West Virginia...........	27.3	67.1	5.6	21.0	66.6	12.5
Iowa...................	25.5	68.2	6.3	19.5	66.9	13.5
North Carolina (white)....	27.9	68.5	3.6	20.9	67.6	11.5
Oregon.................	22.9	69.6	7.5	15.1	70.8	14.0
1940						
United States............	34.8	59.7	5.5	27.6	59.5	12.9
Vermont................	36.2	57.0	6.8	27.8	58.1	14.1
Connecticut.............	37.6	57.5	4.9	32.8	55.9	11.3
West Virginia...........	35.9	59.6	4.5	28.1	61.5	10.5
Iowa...................	33.7	60.5	5.8	26.8	61.0	12.3
North Carolina (white)....	35.2	61.5	3.4	29.3	60.4	10.3
Oregon.................	32.8	60.1	7.1	22.2	63.8	14.0

all the states listed here. There was some increase in the proportion widowed or divorced for both males and females, but this change was not very large.

Although the increase in the proportion married 1940 to 1950 was large, it may be noted that the proportion of both males and females married has been increasing for some decades, with an almost corresponding decline in the proportion single. In 1890 the proportion of males fifteen and over who were married was 53.9 per cent; by 1940 it had risen to 61.2 per cent. The corresponding figures for females were 56.8 per cent and 61.0 per cent.

There were also large differences between states in 1940 and 1950 in the marital condition of both males and females. In 1940 in Connecticut only 55.9 per cent of the females fourteen years of age and over were married, while 63.8 per cent of this group living in Oregon were married. In 1950 Vermont had a somewhat lower proportion of women of these ages married than Connecticut, but both were well below Oregon. In all the states the rise in proportion married between 1940 and 1950 was large and, as will be noted in Chap. VIII, is an important factor in the rise in the crude birth rate since 1940. There are also substantial differences between states in the proportions of both males and females widowed and divorced.

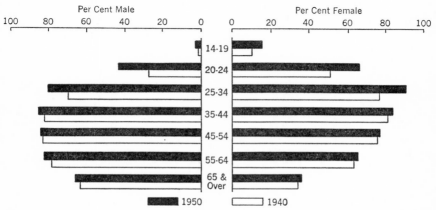

Fig. 6-2. Per cent of population married, by sex and age, United States, 1950 and 1940.

The demographic significance of the differences in marital condition is to be found chiefly in their effects on natality and mortality rates. In general, where a high proportion of females is married the crude birth rate is higher than where a lower proportion of the women is married. Again, both males and females who are married have lower death rates than single, widowed, and divorced persons of the same ages. It follows that knowing the marital composition of a given population will help to understand its vital statistics.

Figure 6-2 shows the changes in the marital state of men and women, by age, in the United States between 1940 and 1950. These changes are very striking and are highly significant in helping us to understand the change in the crude birth rate after 1940. In brief, there was a rather large increase in the proportion of both men and women under thirty-five years of age who were married, the increase being especially large at ages fourteen to nineteen and twenty to twenty-four. In 1940 only 1.4 per cent of the men fourteen to nineteen and 27.4 per cent of those twenty to twenty-four were married, but by 1950 these proportions had risen to 2.5 per cent and 43.6 per cent, respectively.[1] For women fourteen to nineteen the increase was from 9.8 per cent in 1940 to 14.8 per cent in 1950, and for those twenty to twenty-four the increase was from 51.3 per cent to 66.1 per cent. Since such an increase in the proportion of young men and women married cannot long continue, it follows that the effects on the birth rate of this increase in the proportion of young people married is likely to cease in the near future. Hence, until we know how much of the increase in the birth rate is a consequence of the change in the proportion of the young people who are married we must remain skeptical of the view, quite widely held at present, that the increase in the crude birth rate is prima facie evidence of an increase in the size of the average family. This matter will be discussed in some detail in Chap. VIII.

Table 6-7. Percentage Distribution of the Population 15–44 Years of Age, by Sex and Marital Status, Selected Foreign Countries, Latest Year Available

Country	Year	Male			Female		
		Single	Married	Widowed or divorced	Single	Married	Widowed or divorced
England and Wales..	1949	40.8	58.0	1.0	34.5	63.5	2.0
Ireland............	1946	73.0	26.4	0.5	59.4	39.2	1.4
Italy.............	1936	53.8	45.5	0.7	45.5	52.2	2.3
France............	1946	46.1	51.3	2.5[1]	37.3	57.4	5.4[1]
Sweden...........	1945	50.5	47.2	2.3[2]	40.2	56.2	3.6[2]

[1] Includes marital status unknown.
[2] Includes separated.

There are differences between countries in the proportions of married, widowed, and divorced persons which are similar to those between areas and regions within the same nation (Table 6-7). France has long had a higher proportion of married males and females than most other Western European countries, but not as high as in some of the Eastern countries of Europe before World War II, or as high as has been customary in the United States. The recent decline (1946) in France in the proportion of women married is probably due to the war losses, which have substantially reduced the number of marriageable men and kept the proportion of widows higher than that in most other countries.

[1] March, 1950, estimates based on a sample survey, U.S. Bureau of the Census, *Current Population Reports*, Series P-20, No. 33, Feb. 12, 1951.

6. RURAL AND URBAN COMPOSITION

It should be noted at the outset of our discussion of the composition of rural and urban populations that the terms *urban* and *rural* have no precise meaning which is generally accepted. In the United States, before 1950, all people living outside incorporated communities having 2,500 or more inhabitants were classed as rural with the exception that New England "towns" with fairly dense populations, although unincorporated, were classed as urban and a few unincorporated boroughs in other states were also considered urban. A change was made in 1950 to secure "urbanized" areas around cities, although they were not urban under the definition used before 1950. In most other countries the division between urban and rural is made at a different size point, or the terms rural and urban are not used at all and the population is classed merely as living in communities of 1,000 to 1,999, 2,000 to 4,999, etc. In many of these countries the agricultural population lives in villages and not infrequently, *e.g.*, in Japan, villages having well over 2,500 inhabitants are composed largely of people engaged in agriculture. Even in the United States, where in the early days living in places of less than 2,500 and in places above this size distinguished farm from nonfarm population with a useful degree of precision, this method of classification for rural and urban people is rapidly losing its significance because of the spread of people working in cities into surrounding areas having a lower density than the cities but a much higher density than the agricultural population.

It is probable that ever since there were real cities or even moderate-sized villages there have been differences between them and the strictly agricultural areas in the sex and age composition of their populations. In China it is generally believed that the cities, even those of moderate size, have a substantial excess of males due to in-migration and that these males are rather largely concentrated in the fifteen to twenty-four age group. Such little evidence as there is seems to support this view. In India the larger cities all show a great excess of males, some of them having almost twice as many males as females. The urban population as a whole also contains a substantial excess of males. This was probably always the case in all parts of the world until recent times in the more industrialized countries, and there was almost certainly a relatively large proportion of males at ages fifteen to thirty. The rural population, on the other hand, had a higher proportion of females and higher proportions of both males and females in the younger and older age groups.

Although in the modern world areas defined by size and form of political organization (incorporation or some equivalent form) are losing their significance as a basis for determining agricultural and nonagricultural populations, there is as yet no acceptable substitute. The data for the different countries in Fig. 6-3 are not strictly comparable, but they are the best available at present. In the 1950 census of the United States, "urban fringe" populations were counted so that they could be added to the urban populations of the metropolitan areas. This "urban fringe" consists of the urban populations of the Standard Metropolitan Areas, except the central city, plus the more densely settled areas around these cities which are very definitely integrated into the metropolitan area but are not incorporated.[2]

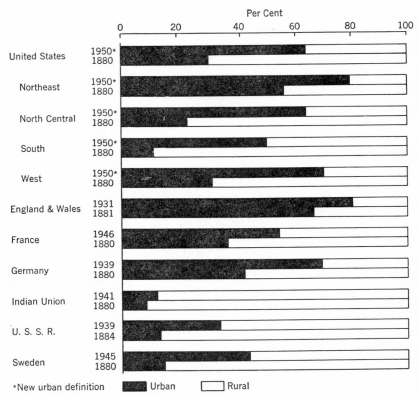

Fig. 6-3. Percentage of the population urban and rural, United States by regions and other selected countries, 1950 and 1880.

Using this new concept of an urban fringe adds about 7.5 million to our urban population as compared with what it would have been if the earlier definition of urban had been used. This number must, of course, be subtracted from the rural population—chiefly from the rural-nonfarm population. Hence, under this new classification the urban population is raised to 64.0 per cent of the total, and rural population is reduced to 36.0 per cent.

[2] There are a few unimportant exceptions.

The urban population is increased by 8.5 per cent, and the rural is reduced by 12.2 per cent. In the author's judgment this is a more realistic classification of people as urban and rural than we had in the past, but it cannot be compared with that of urban and rural populations in other countries with even as high a degree of assurance as the older classification, and, of course, not with our own urban and rural population in 1940 and earlier.

In the 40 years from 1880 to 1920 the proportion of the population of the United States classed as rural (old classification) declined from 70.5 per cent to 48.6 per cent, and it further declined to 41.0 per cent in the ensuing 30 years, to 1950. In 1920 the Bureau of the Census divided the rural population into farm (those people actually living on farms) and nonfarm (the remainder of the rural population), but no separate tabulations of the characteristics of these two groups were made until 1930. Since 1920 there has been a steady and a large decline in the proportion of the total population living on farms—from 29.7 per cent in 1920 to 15.6 per cent in 1950, or by almost one-half. The rural-nonfarm population, on the other hand, has increased slightly in proportion during this period—from 19.0 per cent in 1920 to 20.5 per cent in 1940 and to 20.6 per cent in 1950.[3] Because of the changes in classification, the 1950 urban and rural populations in the United States cannot be compared with earlier urban and rural population with any precision. There can be no doubt, however, that much of what we have heretofore called rural population is now in process of becoming urbanized and will hereafter be enumerated as urban. This is the more realistic procedure.

Even as early as 1880 in the United States there were wide differences in the proportions of rural and urban population in different regions (Fig. 6-3). The South then had the highest proportion of rural population (87.7 per cent), and it still has more than one-half (52.2 per cent) of its people living in rural communities; while the Northeast was predominantly urban (55.1 per cent) even in 1880, and today almost four-fifths of all the people in this region live in urban communities. The West even in 1880 had a substantially larger proportion of urban population than any region except the Northeast.

Table 6-8 shows the age composition (male and female combined) of the population in different sizes of cities and in rural communities in the United States in 1940. It is of interest that the proportion of children under five years old in a community declines as its size increases. In the larger cities with populations in excess of 500,000 only 6.1 per cent of the population was

[3] The 1950 percentages of farm and nonfarm populations are rather seriously affected by the change in classification in 1950. Some persons who were classified as farm population in 1940 became nonfarm in 1950 by reason of paying cash rent for their homes which were otherwise farm homes; some farm people (1940 base) were also transferred to the urban fringe. But the transfers from the farm population were not serious as compared with those transferred from nonfarm to urban fringe, perhaps numbering about 7.5 million.

of this age in 1940, while in the farm population 10.0 per cent of the population was in this age class. There were also differences of the same character for the age group from five to nineteen. At ages twenty to sixty-four, on the other hand, the larger communities had higher proportions than the smaller communities. Migration from smaller to larger communities is the principal cause of the differences in age composition between urban and rural communities at ages of fifteen and over, while at younger ages the differences are due chiefly to differences in birth rates.

Table 6-8.   Percentage Distribution by Age for Population-size Groups, United States, 1940

Area	0–4	5–19	20–29	30–44	45–64	65 and over
Urban....................	6.7	23.4	18.1	23.8	21.2	6.8
Places of:						
500,000 and over.......	6.1	21.9	18.2	25.4	22.2	6.2
100,000–500,000........	6.5	22.8	18.4	24.0	21.4	6.9
10,000–100,000........	7.0	24.2	18.1	23.0	20.7	7.0
2,500–10,000..........	7.7	25.5	17.7	21.8	19.7	7.6
Rural....................	9.7	30.3	16.1	19.0	18.0	6.9
Farm...................	10.0	32.7	15.2	17.3	18.3	6.5
Nonfarm...............	9.3	27.5	17.1	21.0	17.8	7.3

It is also of interest (Table 6-9) that cities of all sizes have substantially lower sex ratios at all ages of five and over than farm communities. These differences are large enough to affect the proportions of both men and women who are married and as a consequence probably have some influence on the crude birth rates, although other factors are probably of more

Table 6-9.   Males per 100 Females by Age for Population-size Groups, United States, 1940

Area	Total	0–4	5–19	20–29	30–44	45–64	65 and over
Urban.................	95.5	103.4	98.8	89.6	95.3	99.9	82.1
Places of:							
500,000 and over.....	97.3	103.6	100.1	90.0	97.4	104.2	80.8
100,000–500,000......	94.4	103.3	98.0	88.3	93.4	98.9	81.7
10,000–100,000.......	94.6	103.5	98.4	89.6	94.0	97.5	81.2
2,500–10,000........	95.8	103.1	98.4	90.9	96.3	97.6	86.5
Rural.................	107.8	103.1	105.3	107.6	106.1	113.8	115.9
Farm.................	111.7	102.9	107.9	117.7	105.4	117.6	134.2
Nonfarm.............	103.7	103.3	101.9	98.5	106.7	109.7	100.2

importance in this respect. The nature of agricultural work is probably the chief reason for the high proportion of males aged twenty to sixty-four in the farm population, just as the job opportunities for women in the cities will account for the high proportion of women twenty to forty-four found there. It is also of interest that at age sixty-five and over the cities have a very high proportion of women (sex ratio about 82) while the farm population contains a very high proportion of males (sex ratio 134).

By definition the farm population shows almost no diversity of occupation no matter where it is found, while the city population shows very great diversity not only within every city but also as between different urban communities. It is probable, however, that the different types of agriculture practiced in different regions induce almost as large social and economic differences between farmers in different areas as do occupational and income differences among city people.

Another respect in which there is a significant difference between urban and rural people is in the amount of education. The farm population contains relatively few persons having more than a high-school education and very few persons with a high degree of technical and professional training.

7. NATIONALITY AND LANGUAGE COMPOSITION

Although racial composition is not of importance in most of Europe—the Nazis, the Fascists, and other followers of the racial doctrines of Houston Stewart Chamberlain to the contrary notwithstanding—it is of great importance for many European countries to know the nationality and/or the language composition of their people. Different language groups within most Central European nations are not as numerous or as large now as they were before Hitler's day, and since the close of World War II there have been further forced migration movements which have had the effect of reducing language and nationality differences within certain territories. In spite of these movements there are still some countries that contain considerable numbers of people who speak languages different from that of the politically dominant group. Not infrequently each of these minority language groups has come to feel more loyalty to the nation whose dominant language it speaks than to the nation in whose territory it resides. It then becomes a matter of pride, as well as of custom, for these minority groups to maintain their language and their distinctive social differences. Under these circumstances the nationality and the language affiliations of the peoples living within the different nations become matters of prime importance. Table 6-10 shows the proportions of the populations in several of the Central European countries that reported their mother tongue as different from that of the dominant group. These data are all for the interwar years, except for Romania in 1948, and will hardly apply to these countries today. The change in Romania between 1930 and 1948 is probably characteristic of those in most of the other Balkan states. Most of the Byelorussians and Ukrainians in prewar Poland have been annexed to the Soviet Union, and most of the Germans in Poland were driven westward into Germany during the last days of the war. The Sudeten Germans in Czechoslovakia were also driven into Germany shortly after the war, and the Germans in East Prussia and east of the Oder and the Neisse rivers have also been driven out.

Table 6-10.   Percentage Distribution of the Population by Language, Selected Countries, Latest Year Available

Country and Language	Percentage	Country and Language	Percentage
Bulgaria (1934)	100.0	Austria (1934)	100.0
Bulgarian	86.8	German	97.5
Turkish	10.2	Slavic	1.9
Hungarian	1.3	Magyar	0.3
German Jewish	0.4	Gypsy	0.1
Armenian	0.4	Other	0.2
Romanian	0.3		
Other	0.6	Poland (1931)	100.0
		Polish	68.9
Czechoslovakia (1930)	100.0	Ukrainian	10.1
Czechoslovak	66.2	German Jewish	7.8
German	22.5	Slavic (Little Russia)	3.8
Magyar	4.9	Byelorussian	3.1
Russian	3.9	German	2.3
Other	2.5	Other	4.0
Hungary (1930)	100.0	Romania (1948)	100.0
Hungarian	92.1	Romanian	85.7
German	5.5	Hungarian	9.4
Slovak	1.2	German	2.2
Croatian	0.3	Yiddish	0.9
Other	0.9	Other	1.8

In addition, the Soviet Union has annexed Lithuania, Latvia, and Estonia, and parts of Poland and Romania. At present it is quite probable that the Soviet Union has a larger number of minority groups than before the war and a larger proportion of its population belonging to these minority groups. These minority peoples may comprise as much as twenty to twenty-five per cent of the entire population. The general status of minority groups in the Soviet Union is described by Lorimer as follows:

> The diversity in ethnic and cultural background is recognized in the political structure of the U.S.S.R. In order to secure the cooperation of ethnic minorities, obviate traditional conflicts, and contribute to the cultural advance of the population, regions containing distinct ethnic groups are organized as "autonomous" republics or districts, with special preroga-

tives, including representation in the All-Union Soviet of Nationalities, and special administrative responsibilities, particularly with respect to cultural affairs. Along with this constitutional recognition there has been a definite policy of encouraging or "sublimating" traditional cultural interests. Measures implementing this policy have included the use of traditional languages in schools, with Russian as a secondary language in non-Russian communities; the encouragement of traditional language publications, which in some cases has necessitated the codification of previously unwritten languages; theatrical performances, festivals, and so forth. Great effort has also been directed toward increasing economic efficiency and improving health and literacy in backward areas, and toward a closer economic and cultural integration of various regions. At the same time, the development of new industrial centers in some of the backward areas and the extensive movements of people across the Soviet Union have tended to break down the distinctive character of various regions. The policy of establishing nomadic groups in fixed residence and the revolutionary character of Soviet economy have also operated to create greater cultural uniformity. In some cases, as among the Kazakhs in the Asiatic steppes, these policies have involved sharp resistances. In general, however, the nationality policy of the Soviet Union has been acclaimed as promoting respect for cultural diversity and a high level of harmonious cooperation.[4]

Not only does the presence of different language groups create many political problems but it also creates social and economic problems many of which have a strongly divisive influence in the national life. Besides, the mere inability of different groups to communicate readily with one another makes for suspicion and reluctance to cooperate fully in matters of national interest. Thus the presence of different language groups may make it more difficult to develop national policies in health matters, in the organization of education, in the use of natural resources, in the organization of the national economy, and in many other respects. Moreover, where there are language groups they are almost certain to be distinguished from one another by certain other cultural characteristics, such as religious beliefs, marriage customs, agricultural practices, dietary habits, and so forth, which make it difficult to weld together all the groups living within a given national territory into a unified nation.

Although language and nationality are not so important in this country as in certain other countries, we have long had a larger and more diverse foreign-born element in our population than any other country.[5] For more

---

[4] Frank Lorimer, *The Population of the Soviet Union: History and Prospects*, p. 54, League of Nations, Geneva, 1946.

[5] Niles Carpenter, *Immigrants and Their Children, 1920: A Study Based on Census Statistics Relative to the Foreign Born and the Native White of Foreign or Mixed Parentage*, 431 pp., G.P.O., Washington, D.C., 1927. (U.S. Bur. Census, *Census Mon. 7.*)

than a century this immigrant group and their children have constituted a substantial proportion of our total population. Since 1900, however, each passing year has witnessed a decline in the proportion of foreign born. If immigration does not rise above the level of recent years, we shall have no considerable foreign-born population within three or four decades. Already it is but little more than half what it was in 1900.

Table 6-11.   Percentage Distribution of the Foreign-born White Population by Country of Birth, United States, 1950

Country of Birth	Percentage	Country of Birth	Percentage
Total	100.0	Eastern Europe	12.0
		U.S.S.R.	8.8
Northwestern Europe	22.8	All other	3.2
England and Wales	5.8		
Ireland[1]	5.1	Southern Europe	16.7
Scotland	2.4	Italy	14.0
Norway	2.0	All other	2.7
Sweden	3.2		
All other	4.3	Canada	9.8
Central Europe	29.0		
Germany	9.7	Mexico	4.4
Poland	8.5		
Czechoslovakia	2.8	Asia	1.8
Austria	4.0		
Hungary	2.6		
Yugoslavia	1.4	All other and not reported	3.5

[1] Includes those from both Eire and Northern Ireland.

Each foreign-born group brought with it certain customs and traditions which tended to create at least a temporary barrier between it and the people already here. Furthermore, every group of any size, except those from the British Isles and the British part of Canada, spoke a language other than English. Hence, there was inevitably a certain amount of cleavage between the natives and most immigrants. This is not infrequently extended to the children of immigrants and prevented these groups from working together harmoniously in communities where there were any considerable numbers of immigrants. Table 6-11 shows something on the heterogeneity of our foreign-born population in 1950. The data in this table should be sufficient to convince anyone that such a diversity of origin in one-eighth to one-tenth of our population as was the case at times in the past was bound to create diversity of outlook on many political and social questions.

But while there is no doubt that the presence of large numbers of foreign-born persons has created problems different in many respects from those which would arise in a more homogeneous native population or even where there were long-established minority language and nationality groups, it should not be concluded from such facts that our country would have been better off without immigration, especially the immigration of the last sixty to seventy years, which included so many people from Southern and Central Europe. This is quite a different matter. This larger question of the effect of immigration upon our social and economic life will not be discussed in this book, but the author wishes to say that he sees no justification for the view that the immigrants are responsible for a large part of the social and economic problems with which we are continuously confronted. In the main, our immigrants have wanted to become Americans, and their children were generally extremely eager to eradicate any marks that smacked of the Old World. This has not been true of the minorities in many European countries. Often they ardently desired to remain as they were and were encouraged in this attitude by people having the same language living elsewhere.

It may be well to say a word here about language differences in certain localities where the spirit of nationality was slower of development than in Europe. China and India have many different language groups, but language does not seem to be as decisive a factor in determining the feeling of belonging or not belonging to a national group as in Europe. In China it would appear that the wide acceptance of the Confucian ethic and the great respect for ancestors it inculcated, the education of the upper classes after a common classical pattern, the similarity of agriculture over a wide area, and the general belief in a common origin, as well as other customs and beliefs which had become almost universal, constitute the basis of the feeling of belonging to the Chinese people. Only rather recently has this feeling of belonging to a people been widely identified with nationality as it is known in the West, and even yet it is doubtful if any large portion of the agricultural classes have a strong feeling of national loyalty. It may be developing more rapidly under the prod of Communist propaganda. The point I would make is that language differences may not have the same divisive effects as regards national unity in China as in Europe. Other cultural factors than language also appear to be more important in India in determining nationality.

8. RELIGIOUS COMPOSITION

The few facts given here relate only to the diversity between countries in the proportions of their populations declaring adherence to recognized religious bodies or faiths. Such differences may be of considerable importance, for they may in part determine the national loyalty of certain groups as well as significant aspects of personal conduct from day to day. Religious influences become inextricably interwoven with the other cultural patterns and thus may exert great influence over behavior even though there may be little awareness on the part of individuals of the operation of religious motives as such.

The direct influence of adherence to definite religious bodies is well illustrated today in India, where the political division of the country into the Indian Union and Pakistan—the feeling of belonging to one nationality rather than to the other—has taken place along the lines of adherence to

Table 6-12. Church Affiliation by Principal Religious Bodies, United States, 1936 [1]

Denomination	Number	Per cent of total population
All denominations.	55,807,366	43.3
Baptist bodies (principal):		
Northern and Southern Baptist Convention.	4,029,199	3.1
Colored Baptists.	3,782,464	2.9
Church of Christ, Scientist.	268,915	0.2
Churches of Christ.	309,551	0.2
Congregational and Christian Churches.	976,388	0.8
Disciples of Christ.	1,196,315	0.9
Evangelical and Reformed Church.	723,877	0.6
Jewish Congregations.	4,641,184	3.6
Latter-day Saints.	774,169	0.6
Lutheran bodies.	4,244,890	3.3
Methodist bodies (principal):		
Methodist Episcopal Church, North and South.	5,571,446	4.3
Methodist Episcopal Church, Colored.	1,177,516	0.9
Presbyterian bodies.	2,513,653	2.0
Protestant Episcopal Church.	1,735,335	1.4
Reformed bodies (principal).	299,694	0.2
Roman Catholic Church.	19,914,937	15.5
United Brethren bodies (principal).	392,897	0.3
Other smaller bodies.	3,254,936	2.5

[1] U.S. Bureau of the Census, *Census of Religious Bodies, 1936*, pp. 10–20, G.P.O., Washington, D.C., 1941.

different religious doctrines and bodies. Adherence to Hinduism, to Mohammedanism, to the Sikh religion, or to some other, apparently takes precedence over adherence to any political body or to the feeling of belonging in a given area. In the effort to give a practical territorial base to these newly established national groups, the Hindu-Moslem migrations of 1947 and 1948 took place, which were probably among the greatest in history. In these countries religious adherence is a strongly determining factor in political life and organization.

In most Western countries adherence to a particular religious body has become less directly determinative of most political behavior than in India. But in spite of this lessening of the area of behavior within which adherence to a religious body determines conduct, religious adherence remains a significant factor, and it is important for every country to know the religious adherence of its people.

Table 6-13. Percentage Distribution of Population by Broad Religious Groups, Selected Countries [1]

Country	Roman Catholic	Greek Catholic	Protestant	Jewish	Mohammedan	Other
Bulgaria (1934).	0.8	84.4	0.1	0.8	13.5	0.4
Czechoslovakia (1930).	73.5	10.4	7.7	2.4	. . . .	6.0
Germany, Federal Republic (1950).	45.4	. . . .	51.4	. . . .	. . . .	3.2
Hungary (1930).	64.9	2.8	27.2	5.1		
Yugoslavia (1931).	37.4	48.7	1.7	0.5	11.2	0.5
Poland (1931).	64.8	22.2	2.6	9.8	. . . .	0.6

[1] Institut International de Statistique, *Aperçu de la démographie des divers pays du monde, 1929–1936*, pp. 136–137; Institut International de Statistique, The Hague, 1939; and *Statistisches Jahrbuch für die Bundesrepublik Deutschland, 1952*, p. 28, Statistisches Bundesamt, Wiesbaden, 1952.

Unlike those of most European countries and of India, the census of the United States does not ask our citizens to state whether they adhere to any religious body and, if they do, the name of that body. Our knowledge of membership in religious bodies is therefore derived from the reports (voluntary) made to the Bureau of the Census by the different religious bodies themselves. Since the rolls of most religious bodies in this country contain many names of people who are no longer adherents, it is probable that such a "census" overstates the number of active adherents of most religious groups. Table 6-12 gives the results of the last such "census" in the United States. Most of these religious bodies now claim considerably larger numbers than those shown here, and because our population has grown by over 25 million since 1936 it seems reasonable to assume that most of these religious groups have also grown since that time. (A new "census" is to be taken soon.)

It appears from these data that a very large proportion of the population of the United States does not hold membership in any definite religious organization. On the other hand, in most European countries a large majority of the people report adherence to some religious body (Table 6-13). There is no means of knowing whether this justifies the belief that adherence to a religious body plays a more important role in the lives of Europeans than in the lives of United States citizens. It may be noted, however, if people in the United States were classified merely as Protestants, Roman Catholics, Jews, Greek Catholics, Mohammedans, and so forth, a large part of the nearly 57 per cent not belonging to any of the groups listed here would be classified as Protestant since their ancestors only a generation or two back were Protestants. This overwhelming Protestantism is reflected in our social, economic, and political life from very early colonial days and is probably more significant than we think.

One of the best proofs of the great significance of adherence to a religious body is found in the efforts of the Communist leaders everywhere to destroy all such organizations and to substitute for adherence to religious beliefs adherence to the doctrines of communism à la Lenin and Stalin.

9. EDUCATIONAL COMPOSITION

Until quite recently little has been known by any nation regarding the extent of the education of its people. Most countries taking censuses know how many of their people are illiterate, that is, how many above a given age cannot read and write. They also know how many are enrolled in schools, but they do not know the amount of schooling that each person has had, that is, what proportions of their people have spent different lengths of time in school and what types of schools they have attended. In our 1940 and 1950 censuses a question was carried regarding the grade of school completed, replacing that regarding literacy. The grade completed for the population aged twenty-five and over, by color and by urban and rural-farm residence for Mississippi and Iowa in 1940 and 1950 is shown in Table 6-14. The chief points of interest are: (1) Urban populations are better educated than rural-farm populations. This holds for both Iowa and Mississippi and for both whites and nonwhites. (2) The whites, especially in Mississippi, are much better educated than the nonwhites, and the urban whites in Mississippi are better educated than the urban whites in Iowa, while the opposite is the case for rural whites. (3) The urban nonwhites in Iowa are much better educated than those in Mississippi. (There are not enough rural-farm nonwhites in Iowa to justify calculating a proportion on the basis of the sample used in 1950.) (4) Between 1940 and 1950 the proportion of high-school graduates increased substantially in both Mississippi and Iowa. There was less increase in the proportion going to or completing college, but the increase was significant except in the urban white population of Mississippi.

One would naturally expect that, with the differences in the amount of schooling shown here, many of the social problems of different communities would take on different forms. Iowa and Mississippi do, as a matter of fact, manifest large differences in their social and economic problems, and some of these differences no doubt arise from the fact that the proportions of the

Table 6-14. Percentage of Persons 25 Years Old and Over Who Have
Completed a Given Grade of School, Urban and Rural-farm, by Race,
Selected States, 1950 and 1940

| State and grade of school completed | White | | | | Nonwhite | | | |
| | Urban | | Rural-farm | | Urban | | Rural-farm | |
	1950	1940	1950	1940	1950	1940	1950	1940
Mississippi, total..........	100.0	100.0	100.0	100.0	100.0	100.0	100.0	100.0
No school years completed	1.0	1.4	2.0	2.5	6.7	8.4	9.2	12.7
Grade school:								
1–4 years............	4.0	4.2	11.3	11.1	31.0	31.3	44.0	44.6
5–6 years............	5.9	7.0	13.6	15.3	21.5	25.3	22.3	23.9
7–8 years............	14.8	18.3	31.1	35.4	20.4	19.7	16.7	12.9
High school:								
1–3 years............	20.6	20.9	22.2	19.4	10.4	8.4	4.5	3.0
4 years..............	27.1	23.5	12.9	9.1	4.6	3.6	1.2	0.9
College:								
1–3 years............	13.2	13.1	3.9	3.7	2.2	1.4	0.6	0.3
4 years or more.......	10.6	10.4	1.9	1.7	1.3	0.9	0.2	0.1
Not reported..........	2.8	1.1	1.1	1.9	1.9	0.9	1.3	1.7
Iowa, total..............	100.0	100.0	100.0	100.0	100.0	100.0	....	100.0
No school years completed	0.6	0.6	0.4	0.4	2.6	4.4	....	6.8
Grade school:								
1–4 years............	3.1	3.3	2.8	3.4	13.3	13.2	....	11.7
5–6 years............	5.2	6.6	5.4	7.8	11.5	13.9	....	13.6
7–8 years............	28.2	35.4	45.0	55.2	25.6	32.2	....	37.2
High school:								
1–3 years............	17.2	17.0	13.4	12.6	21.5	17.2	....	8.9
4 years..............	26.0	20.8	23.8	13.9	14.4	10.5	....	6.1
College:								
1–3 years............	9.9	8.6	5.9	4.5	4.6	3.4	....	3.5
4 years or more.......	7.3	6.3	1.6	1.1	2.8	1.8	....	0.5
Not reported..........	2.5	1.5	1.7	1.0	3.7	3.4	....	11.7

people having different amounts of schooling in the two states are different.
It is probable, however, that other differences—for example, in racial composition, in degree of industrial development, in quality of soil, and in
climate—are of much greater importance. It requires no argument to convince most of us that people who, like the nonwhites in Mississippi, have had
little schooling and few of whom have had any special training for technical
work, will have many mental attitudes different from those of people who
have had better training and have fitted themselves for better and often for
highly specialized jobs. There would be difficulties in working out a health

program, or an economic program, or an educational program among the former which would not arise among the latter. The mere existence of large groups in the population having widely different educational attainments cannot fail to complicate many of the social problems every community must deal with.

In the United States and doubtless in most other Western countries the proportion of persons with only an elementary education or less is declining, while the proportion with secondary education and particularly with some more advanced and specialized education has been increasing rather rapidly. This change no doubt reflects both the improvement in economic conditions making it possible for more persons to stay in school longer and also the need of more and better-trained personnel in industry, commerce, the services, and the professional occupations in these countries.

Table 6-15.   Percentage of Illiteracy (10 Years of Age and Over), by Sex, Selected Countries, Latest Year Available [1]

Country	Male	Female	Country	Male	Female
United States (1947)...	3.0	2.3	France (1936)........	3.4	4.2
Egypt (1937)[2]........	76.6	93.9	Hungary (1941)[4].....	4.9	7.1
Mexico (1940)........	47.6	55.4	Italy (1931).........	17.8	25.2
Cuba (1943).........	23.2	20.8	Poland (1931)........	17.8	27.9
Chile (1940).........	26.5	29.9	Romania (1948)[3].....	14.5	30.9
Belgium (1930)[3]......	5.2	6.0	Yugoslavia (1931)....	32.7	57.1
Bulgaria (1934).......	19.5	43.3	Sweden (1930).......	0.1	0.1
Czechoslovakia (1930).	3.3	4.8	Spain (1940)........	17.3	28.5

[1] *Demographic Yearbook, 1948*, Table 7, United Nations, New York, 1949; U.S. Bureau of the Census, *Current Population Reports*, Series P-20, No. 20, Sept. 22, 1948.
[2] Excludes nomadic population.   [3] Seven years of age and over.
[4] Present territory.

As Table 6-15 shows there are still a number of countries in which censuses are taken where considerable proportions of the people recently were or still are illiterate. However, in most of these countries a rather rapid change is taking place in this respect. This is shown clearly by the large differences in literacy as between the older and younger age groups, *e.g.*, in Poland (1931) 23.1 per cent of all persons ten and over were illiterate, but of those ten to fourteen years of age only 6.6 per cent were illiterate, while 49.8 per cent of those sixty years of age and over belonged in this class. All over the world there is a growing realization that better education is essential to the efficient functioning of a modernized society; hence it seems reasonable to expect that there will be a fairly rapid decline in illiteracy in those countries where there are still large numbers of illiterates and an increase almost everywhere in the proportions of the population with some secondary and higher education. The many ways in which this increase in education will affect social and economic conditions cannot be foreseen with any certainty. But there would seem to be little doubt that economic improvement depends to a considerable degree on the extension of education, particularly in the fields of science, engineering, and economics. The extension of education in any field will almost certainly contribute to the more rapid breaking up of traditional social patterns and thus create an increasing need for new and basic adjustments in social institutions. The effects of increasing education cannot fail to be of great significance in the different groups in our population. We should know what educational changes are occurring if we would understand the broader social and economic changes now taking place.

10. ECONOMIC COMPOSITION

That there are large differences in individual incomes in every community is too well known to need proof. It is not as well known, however, that there are very substantial differences in per capita income payments between different regions within a nation such as are shown in Table 6-16 for the different regions of the United States. The differences in the median incomes of all families and of nonwhite families are even greater than the regional differences and certainly emphasize the fact that the nonwhites of the United States are a badly underprivileged class. There are also significant differences between urban and rural families. The broad social and economic problems associated with these differences in individual and regional incomes do not fall within the province of our discussion.

Table 6-16.   Changes in Per Capita Income Payments to Individuals, United States by Regions, 1929 to 1951 [1]

Region	Per capita income payments, 1951		Per capita income payments, 1929		Per capita income increase, 1929–1951		
	Amount	Per cent of U. S. average	Amount	Per cent of U. S. average	Amount of increase	Rate of increase, per cent	Per cent of U. S. average
United States.....	$1,584	100	$680	100	$904	133	100
New England.....	1,715	108	838	123	877	105	97
Middle East......	1,822	115	926	136	896	97	99
Southeast.........	1,075	68	344	51	731	213	81
Southwest........	1,363	86	464	68	899	194	99
Central..........	1,717	108	720	106	997	138	110
Northwest........	1,507	95	534	78	973	182	108
Far West.........	1,877	118	865	127	1,012	117	112

[1] Robert E. Graham, Jr., "State Income Payments in 1951," *Survey of Current Business*, Vol. 32, No. 8, p. 17, 1952.

It requires no argument to convince anyone that such economic differences between regions and racial groups as are shown in this table tend to differentiate the ways in which people live and to determine to a significant degree the expenditures on most community functions, such as schools, highways, parks, health, etc.

Table 6-17 shows that there are almost unbelievable differences in per capita incomes in different countries. No one will find it difficult to believe that when per capita incomes fall below $300 to $400 per year many public services must be curtailed and many of the amenities of life are no longer possible. Later it will be shown that there is a fairly close inverse relation between per capita income and the death rate—the higher the income, the lower the death rate.

Although most of the data presented here relate to the United States, similar differences in income as between individuals, communities, and regions exist in most other countries. However, owing to differences in

Table 6-17. Per Capita Income, Selected Countries, 1949 [1]

Country	Income, United States dollars
United Kingdom	$773
France	482
U.S.S.R.	308
Italy	235
Greece	128
Japan	100
Iran	85
Union of India	57
South Korea	35

[1] "National and Per Capita Incomes of Seventy Countries," *United Nations Bull.*, Vol. 9, No. 12, p. 720, Dec. 15, 1950.

political organization, in taxation, and in the allocation of taxes collected, the differences between communities in ability to support public services may not be as great as in this country. Thus in many countries taxes collected by the central government are so allocated that they support better public schools in many communities than a region or a local community could support by its own means. This may be likened to the funds for the equalization of educational opportunity found in many of our states. Certain other services which are considered desirable are often supported by the nation at large to a greater extent in other countries than in the United States. It follows, then, that differences in the level of community incomes do not always lead to such differences in community services as they usually do in this country. But as a rule differences between communities in economic status do have much influence on the public services prevailing in them; hence it may be desirable to note some of the community differences in income found in several other countries.

In Denmark [6] the average (mean) income reported for taxation by heads of families in 1949–1950 varied considerably by type of community from 7,834 crowns in the capital, Copenhagen, to 6,167 crowns in the provincial cities and to 5,241 in rural communities. Thus incomes averaged about one-half larger in Copenhagen and over one-sixth larger in the other cities than in the rural communities. There were, of course, rather large differences between individuals in each of these types of communities; but these differences appear to be decidedly smaller than in this country, smaller proportions being found at both extremes of income than here, while larger proportions are found in the middle income groups. I say "appear to be decidedly smaller" because it is impossible to make exact comparisons of income in Denmark and the United States. The figures are not gathered on the same basis. In a small country like Denmark with a homogeneous population one would not expect to find such regional or racial differences as exist in the United States.

In Sweden [7] in 1948 the average (mean) income for employed (active) persons was 4,252 crowns when they lived in rural communities, and 6,495 when they lived in cities, or over one-half larger in the cities. The distribution of these incomes by size is similar to that in Denmark but not identical with it. Sweden appears to have a somewhat larger proportion of city people with incomes of 5,000 crowns and over.

There is no reason to suppose that the differences in economic status by type of community are not basically the same in other countries as in the United States and the Scandinavian countries. But almost certainly regional differences within a country will increase as the size of the country increases. The point of chief interest to us here is that communities everywhere find their public services greatly affected by their economic status, nor can these differences ever be wholly eliminated in spite of many efforts to equalize conditions through the national support of services which the poorer communities cannot provide for themselves. This is the basic reason it is so important to know the economic status of a community when studying its social and demographic development.

11. MISCELLANEOUS ELEMENTS IN THE COMPOSITION OF A POPULATION

The differences between the characteristics of the people in different communities to which attention has been directed above by no means exhaust the list. Practically every community having more than a few thousand people has a prison population, and most communities, even those

[6] Denmark, Det Statistiske Departement, *Statistisk Årbog.*, 1950, p. 267, Bianco Lunos Bogtrykkeri, Copenhagen, 1950.

[7] Sweden, Statistiska Centralbyrån, *Statistisk Årsbok för Sverige, 1950*, pp. 317–318, P. A. Norstedt & Söner, Stockholm, 1950.

which are quite small, have some people who cannot fit into the normal life of the home and the community—the mentally ill, the feeble-minded, the paupers, the deaf, the blind, and so forth. Many of these people do not remain in the local community, but some do. Altogether these people who cannot live a normal life, and as a consequence cannot be allowed the same freedom as normal persons, constitute a significant proportion of the population. In most modern communities the effort consumed in the care of such "abnormal" people takes the form of taxes paid to support the services needed to care for them. The community needs to know how many of its people require special care and the type of care which will be best for them and for the community. People requiring custodial care not only cost the community a great deal economically but interfere seriously with the efficient operation of many community activities and institutions.

12. CONCLUSION

People can be separated into many groups on the basis of their demographic and social characteristics. For many purposes it is not only convenient but essential to do this. However, great care should be taken not to overemphasize any particular trait or characteristic when classifying the people in a community for purposes of studying its structure and its community operations. Any social situation in a community which we wish to understand is almost certain to be easier of comprehension if we know the composition of its people. But this is only one element in a complex social situation, so that even in the effort to understand the differences in the death rates of two communities it is quite possible that after the sex and age differences between them are taken into account and after differences in occupational make-up and in economic status are allowed for we will find a residue of differences which seem to have no relation to the composition of the people. We may have to conclude in the end that some of the difference in death rates is due to differences in social attitudes toward sanitation and hygienic practices which cannot now be measured and which do not seem to have any relation to the measurable differences between groups.

It is the same with many other aspects of group differences. Criminality is connected to some extent with the age and sex composition of a population, but in this case perhaps only a minor part of the differences between two communities in the amount of criminal activity found can be accounted for on the basis of differences in composition. There are subtle differences between the social attitudes prevailing in different communities which may be responsible to a significant degree for differences in criminality and which we cannot yet connect with measurable differences in composition.

We cannot hope to understand many aspects of the life in any community if we do not know the characteristics of the people who live in it, *i.e.*, if we do not know its demographic and social composition; on the other hand, we must be very careful not to try to explain social conditions in a community or differences between conditions in different communities solely by differences in composition. In most cases the explanation of behavior in a community based only on a knowledge of its composition would be misleading, because it would be far too simple and would tend to hinder the search for causal factors the knowledge of which is essential to the intelligent control of social change.

Suggestions for Supplementary Reading

CARPENTER, NILES: *Immigrants and Their Children, 1920: A Study Based on Census Statistics Relative to the Foreign Born and the Native White of Foreign or Mixed Parentage*, 431 pp., G.P.O., Washington, D.C., 1927. (U.S. Bur. Census, *Census Mon.* 7.)

CHEN, TA: *Population in Modern China*, 126 pp., University of Chicago Press, Chicago, 1946.

COLLINS, SELWYN D.: *Economic Status and Health: A Review and Study of the Relevant Morbidity and Mortality*, 74 pp., G.P.O., Washington, D.C., 1927. (U.S. Pub. Health Service, *Pub. Health Bull.* 165.)

COX, PETER R.: *Demography*, 326 pp., Cambridge University Press, Cambridge, 1950. A general discussion of demographic materials and methods.

DUBLIN, LOUIS I.: *Causes of Death by Occupation: Occupational Mortality Experiences of the Metropolitan Life Insurance Company, Industrial Department, 1911–1913*, 88 pp., G.P.O., Washington, D.C., 1917. (U.S. Bur. Labor Statistics, *Bull.* 207, Industrial Accidents and Hygiene Ser., No. 11.)

FRUMKIN, GRZEGORZ: "Pre-war and Post-war Trends in Manpower of European Countries," *Population Studies*, Vol. 4, No. 2, pp. 209–240, 1950.

KIRK, DUDLEY: *Europe's Population in the Interwar Years*, 303 pp., League of Nations, Geneva, 1946. Helpful in many connections.

LANDIS, PAUL H.: *Population Problems*, Pt. 3, American Book Company, New York, 1943.

OGBURN, WILLIAM FIELDING: "The Relationship of Marital Condition to Death, Crime, Insanity, and Pauperism," *Bull. de l'institut international de statistique*, Vol. 22, pp. 441–454, 1926.

THOMAS, DOROTHY SWAINE: *Social and Economic Aspects of Swedish Population Movements, 1750–1933*, 487 pp., The Macmillan Company, New York, 1941.

THOMPSON, WARREN S., and P. K. WHELPTON: *Population Trends in the United States*, 415 pp., McGraw-Hill Book Company, Inc., New York, 1933.

U.S. National Resources Committee: *The Problems of a Changing Population*, 306 pp., G.P.O., Washington, D.C., 1938.

WARDWELL, CHARLES S. R.: *Regional Trends in the United States Economy*, 121 pp., G.P.O., Washington, D.C., 1951.

WHELPTON, P. K.: "Occupational Groups in the United States, 1820–1920," *Am. Statis. Assn. J.*, Vol. 21, pp. 335–343, 1926.

Chapter VII

THE COMPOSITION OF THE NEGRO POPULATION IN THE UNITED STATES

The discussion of the Negro in the United States will be confined to a very brief presentation of the chief demographic and social facts showing differences between whites and nonwhites.[1] It might well be considered merely a more extended treatment of one important element in the composition of our population.

1. GROWTH IN NUMBERS

The Negro was first brought to this country about the time that the Pilgrims were settling at Plymouth. It appears, however, that it was not until about 1700 that the value of the Negro as a laborer in the tobacco fields was fully realized and the importation of slaves on the grand scale began. By 1790 there were over 757,000 Negroes in the United States, and they constituted 19.3 per cent of our total population. The very rapid increase in Negroes during the eighteenth century must be attributed not only to the direct importation of slaves to work in the tobacco fields and for domestic service but also to their rapid rate of natural increase. It is probable that by 1790 about three-fourths of the Negroes in the United States were native born.[2]

[1] In recent censuses many details of composition are given for the nonwhite population rather than for Negroes. In this discussion these two terms will be used interchangeably except where otherwise specified.

[2] This "guess" is arrived at as follows: The census in *A Century of Population Growth*, p. 36, G.P.O., Washington, D.C., 1909, gives estimates of Carey to the effect that about 333,000 Negroes were imported between 1715 and 1808, of whom 70,000 were imported between 1790 (the first census) and 1808 (the date of the prohibition of the importation of slaves). The census indicates, however, that Carey's estimates were probably too low and that the total may have been as high as 400,000. If the Carey estimates were too low by about one-fifth, then the number of Negroes imported before 1790 may have been in the neighborhood of 325,000 to 330,000. Of these probably 140,000 to 150,000 were brought in before 1751 and a large part of them would have been dead by 1790. If it is assumed that about one-third (40,000) of the 130,000 Negroes who were imported between 1751 and 1770 had died by 1790 and that the number of deaths among those brought in between 1770 and 1790 (approximately 50,000) equaled the number of survivors among those imported before 1751, then the total number of Negroes living in 1790 who were born abroad would be in the neighborhood of 170,000 to 180,000, or about one-fourth of the total number enumerated in 1790.

Table 7-1. Negro Population of the United States, 1790 to 1950

Year	Number	Per cent of total population Negro	Percentage increase Negro
1950	15,042,286	10.0	16.9
1940	12,865,518	9.8	8.2
1930	11,891,143	9.7	13.6
1920	10,463,131	9.9	6.5
1910	9,827,763	10.7	11.2
1900	8,833,994	11.6	18.0
1890	7,488,676	11.9	13.8
1880	6,580,793	13.1	22.0
1870	5,392,172	13.5	21.4
1860	4,441,830	14.1	22.1
1850	3,638,808	15.7	26.6
1840	2,873,648	16.8	23.4
1830	2,328,642	18.1	31.4
1820	1,771,656	18.4	28.6
1810	1,377,808	19.0	37.5
1800	1,002,037	18.9	32.3
1790	757,208	19.3	

After 1808 the importation of slaves was illegal, but this did not prevent a large number being smuggled in. Indeed, after the invention of the cotton gin in 1793 the cultivation of cotton became increasingly profitable, and up to the time of the Civil War there was a very brisk demand for slaves on the Southern cotton plantations. After studying the available evidence Dublin [3] concludes, however, that the unlawful trade in slaves could at most have contributed an increase to the Negro population of less than one-half of 1 per cent a year from 1808 to 1860. Hence, the remaining 2 per cent per annum came from the excess of births over deaths (natural increase). But in spite of the fact that a natural increase of 20 per 1,000 per year is a relatively high rate, it was not as high as among the whites at that time. In addition, the rate of growth among the whites was reinforced by immigration to an even greater extent than was that of the Negroes up to the time of the Civil War. There is little doubt, however, that in pre–Civil War days the rate of natural increase among the whites was significantly higher than that among Negroes. This conclusion seems reasonable because the birth rate of the whites is known to have been very high in the first half of the nineteenth century [4] and may very well have equaled or even surpassed that of the Negroes up to the time of the Civil War, while from the time we have any evidence at all

[3] Louis I. Dublin, *Health and Wealth*, p. 256, Harper & Brothers, New York, 1928.
[4] Warren S. Thompson and P. K. Whelpton, *Population Trends in the United States*, p. 263, McGraw-Hill Book Company, Inc., New York, 1933.

regarding death rates those of the whites have always been substantially lower than those of Negroes.

But whatever the cause, the fact is that except for the decade 1800 to 1810 the proportion of Negroes in our population declined steadily from 1790 to 1930. Since 1930, when they constituted 9.7 per cent of our total population, the proportion has increased to 9.8 per cent in 1940 and to 10.0 per cent in 1950. Undoubtedly the almost complete stoppage of Negro immigration after 1860, while white immigration continued until World War I, often at a very high level, contributed materially to the decline in the proportion of Negroes in our population. But the author is disposed to think that their high death rates were also an important factor in keeping their natural increase below that of the whites during most of this time.

Table 7-2.   Urban and Rural Net Reproduction Rates by Race, United States, 1930 to 1947 [1]

Area and race	Total			Urban		Rural-nonfarm		Rural-farm	
	1942–1947	1935–1940	1930–1935	1935–1940	1930–1935	1935–1940	1930–1935	1935–1940	1930–1935
White, United States.........	127	96	97	73	76	115	115	157	157
Northeast................	...	80	84	72	76	104	105	141	135
North Central.............	...	95	95	75	77	114	111	145	142
South....................	...	115	120	73	77	122	127	170	174
West.....................	...	93	88	73	69	117	111	152	143
Nonwhite, United States.....	146	114	107	70	68	121	119	206	192
Northeast................	...	75	70	72	68				
North Central.............	...	83	75	76	69				
South....................	...	125	120	68	68	119	119	208	193
West.....................	...	117	117	72	...	...	...	200	202

[1] U.S. Bureau of the Census, *Population, Differential Fertility, 1940 and 1910, Standardized Fertility Rates and Reproduction Rates*, pp. 20–21, G.P.O., Washington, D.C., 1944; also *Current Population Reports*, Series P-20, No. 18, p. 5, June 30, 1948.

Since about 1924 white immigration has been at a relatively low level and the white rate of increase has no longer received as strong a boost from a large number of immigrants with their relatively high birth rates. Moreover, the birth rates of Negroes have long been considerably higher than those of most whites (quite possibly ever since the Civil War) and the death rates of Negroes have been falling quite rapidly in the past 20 or 30 years. Hence, it is not surprising that the natural increase of the Negroes has been greater than the total increase of whites since the 1920's. The turning point cannot be specified exactly, but it was probably in the later 1920's or early 1930's. The net reproduction rates of whites and nonwhites since the period 1930 to 1935 are given in Table 7-2. The nonwhites have had higher rates than the whites, at least since that time.

As a consequence of their differential rates of growth from 1790 to 1930, the Negro population increased about 16-fold during this 140 years, while the white population increased nearly 35-fold. By 1950 (160 years) the Negro population had increased about 20-fold and the white population nearly 43-fold. The vital statistics of the Negroes will be discussed in later sections of this chapter, but first it will be well to note their geographic distribution and their rural-urban distribution, since their birth rates and death rates have been and still are materially affected by their distribution.

2. DISTRIBUTION

Geographic Distribution. Until recently the Negroes were very heavily concentrated in the South. As late as 1900 almost nine-tenths (89.7 per

Table 7-3.   Number and Percentage Distribution of the Negro Population, United States by Regions, 1860 to 1950

Region	1950		1940		1900		1860	
	Number	Per cent	Number	Per cent	Number	Per cent	Number	Per cent
United States...	15,042,286	100.0	12,865,518	100.0	8,833,994	100.0	4,441,830	100.0
Northeast......	2,018,182	13.4	1,369,875	10.6	385,020	4.4	156,001	3.5
North Central..	2,227,876	14.8	1,420,318	11.0	495,751	5.6	184,239	4.1
South..........	10,225,407	68.0	9,904,619	77.0	7,922,969	89.7	4,097,111	92.2
West..........	570,821	3.8	170,706	1.3	30,254	0.3	4,479	0.1

cent) of the Negroes lived in the South, but by 1950 this had fallen to 68.0 per cent. The increase in the North during the same period was from 10.0 to 28.2 per cent, and in the West from 0.3 to 3.8 per cent. The rather rapid movement of Negroes out of the South began with the need for labor in the North during World War I, but the proportion living in the South was still 85.2 per cent in 1920. During the next decade it declined rapidly to 78.7 per cent in 1930. The movement of Negroes out of the South slackened during the depression of the 1930's and 77.0 per cent were still there in 1940, but the proportion again fell rapidly during the 1940's, to 68.0 per cent in 1950.

Even these data do not give an adequate picture of the high concentration of Negroes in the relatively small area known as the "black belt," before

1910. This region was so named originally from the color of the soil rather than because of the concentration of Negroes in it. In 1890 there were 529 counties, located largely in the black-earth region of the Southern states, which had more than 30 per cent of Negroes in their populations. These counties contained 81.3 per cent of the total Negro population of the United States. By 1950 the number of counties with 30 per cent or more Negroes in their population had declined to 436 and the proportion of all Negroes found in them had declined to 41.7 per cent.

Table 7-4. Urban and Rural Negro Population, United States by Regions, 1950

Region	Number			Percentage distribution		
	Urban	Rural-nonfarm	Rural-farm	Urban	Rural-nonfarm	Rural-farm
United States.....	9,392,608	2,491,377	3,158,301	62.4	16.6	21.0
Northeast........	1,897,799	107,364	13,019	94.0	5.3	0.6
North Central....	2,089,288	100,043	38,545	93.8	4.5	1.7
South...........	4,890,863	2,238,153	3,096,391	47.8	21.9	30.3
West...........	514,658	45,817	10,346	90.2	8.0	1.8

Table 7-5. Percentage Distribution of Negroes, Urban and Rural, United States and the South, 1890 to 1950

Year	United States		United States excluding South		South	
	Urban	Rural	Urban	Rural	Urban	Rural
1950	62.4	37.6	93.5	6.5	47.8	52.2
1940	48.6	51.4	89.1	10.9	36.5	63.5
1930	43.7	56.3	88.1	11.9	31.7	68.3
1920	34.0	66.0	84.4	15.6	35.3	74.7
1910	27.4	72.6	77.4	22.6	21.2	78.8
1900	22.7	77.3	69.9	30.1	17.2	82.8
1890	19.4	80.6	61.5	38.5	15.3	84.7

Rural-Urban Distribution. Before the Civil War the Negroes were overwhelmingly rural, probably 90 per cent or more. After 1860 the urbanization of Negroes went ahead rapidly; by 1930 the urban proportion had grown to 43.7 per cent, by 1940 it had become 48.6 per cent, and by 1950 it was 62.4 per cent. This very rapid urbanization of the Negroes is due primarily to the fact that those who migrate northward and westward go almost exclusively to the cities. In the South, on the other hand, the urbanization of the Negroes has proceeded at a slower pace. In 1950 only 47.8 per cent of the Negroes in the South lived in urban communities. In the other three regions of the United States over 90 per cent of the Negroes now live in urban communities. Thus the Negroes in the United States have quite a different distribution from the whites both regionally and as between rural and urban communities within the several regions (see preceding chapter). Such community and regional differences in racial composition will account in part, at least, for certain other differences in the composition of their populations which will be noted below.

3. SEX AND AGE COMPOSITION

It has been pointed out above how important it is to know the sex and age composition of a population. This is particularly true of the Negroes, who have been migrating in large numbers and whose age and sex composition in many communities has as a consequence changed very rapidly since about 1920. The comparison of the sex and age groups of Negroes in different communities with one another and with those of the whites shows marked differences between them. Knowing these differences is essential to a better understanding of many community problems.

The differences between the age groups of nonwhites in the large Northern cities and in North Carolina are very large, as might be expected in areas affected by large net in- and out-migration. In the Northern cities the highest proportion of nonwhite males is found in the age groups twenty-five to forty-four and the highest proportion of females in the groups about five years younger. In North Carolina, on the other hand, the largest proportions for both sexes are found at ages under twenty, while there are small proportions at ages thirty to forty-four. Among males in North Carolina the fifteen to nineteen group is half again as large proportionally as the group aged thirty-five to thirty-nine; among females, on the other hand, it is only about one-fourth greater than the twenty-five to twenty-nine group.

In the Northern cities over one-half of the entire nonwhite population is between twenty and forty-nine years of age, while in North Carolina only about two-fifths is found in these same age groups. In the Northern cities only about one-fourth of the nonwhite population is under fifteen years of age, but in North Carolina almost two-fifths belongs in this group. In all the population groups shown in Table 7-6 the nonwhites have small proportions of persons over sixty-five as compared with the whites.

It is not surprising, in view of the unusual age composition of the nonwhites in the Northern cities, that these cities have many social and economic problems arising from their peculiar age and sex structure. In the

South, as has already been noted, the nonwhites still live to a considerable extent in rural communities and they constitute a high proportion of the total population in many of these states. The differences in the proportions of children just noted would affect the problem of providing adequate schools in the South even if there were no racial discrimination. The differences in age would also affect family incomes and the proportions married and would likewise determine to some extent the amount and kind of delinquency likely to be found in these different populations. Many other differences between communities are also to be attributed in part to the differences between them in age and sex composition.

Table 7-6.   Percentage Distribution by Age of Nonwhite Population, United States and Selected States and Cities, 1950

Age	United States				New York City, nonwhite		Chicago, nonwhite		North Carolina, nonwhite		Louisiana, nonwhite	
	White		Nonwhite									
	Male	Fe-male	Male	Fe-male	Male	Fe-male	Male	Fe-male	Male	Fe-male	Male	Fe-male
Total......	100.0	100.0	100.0	100.0	100.0	100.0	100.0	100.0	100.0	100.0	100.0	100.0
Under 5....	10.8	10.2	12.9	12.3	11.0	9.3	11.0	10.3	14.7	14.0	14.6	13.5
5–9........	8.8	8.4	10.4	10.0	7.6	6.7	7.9	7.4	12.5	12.0	11.9	11.1
10–14......	7.4	7.0	9.3	8.8	6.7	5.9	6.6	6.4	11.2	10.6	10.4	9.7
15–19......	7.0	6.8	8.1	8.2	6.0	6.2	5.8	6.2	9.8	9.7	8.6	8.5
20–24......	7.4	7.6	7.8	8.7	7.9	10.0	8.2	9.7	8.4	9.0	7.1	8.1
25–29......	8.0	8.2	8.1	8.6	10.7	12.0	10.4	11.3	7.6	7.8	6.6	7.3
30–34......	7.6	7.8	7.1	7.7	9.6	10.7	9.1	9.7	6.5	6.8	5.8	6.5
35–39......	7.4	7.5	7.3	7.8	9.6	10.3	8.9	9.2	6.5	6.8	6.2	6.9
40–44......	6.8	6.8	6.4	6.4	8.5	8.1	7.8	7.6	5.3	5.4	5.7	6.0
45–49......	6.1	6.0	5.8	5.6	7.2	6.5	7.3	6.6	4.4	4.6	5.4	5.4
50–54......	5.6	5.6	4.8	4.5	5.8	4.9	5.9	5.0	3.8	3.8	4.3	4.2
55–59......	5.0	4.9	3.6	3.2	3.6	3.1	4.1	3.5	2.8	2.6	3.6	3.3
60–64......	4.2	4.2	2.7	2.5	2.5	2.4	2.9	2.5	2.1	2.1	2.7	2.5
65 and over.	8.0	8.9	5.7	5.7	3.3	3.9	4.2	4.7	4.4	4.7	6.9	6.9

The large sex differences by age among the nonwhites in different types of communities also create many distinctive problems for them. In New York City females predominate heavily, the sex ratio being 85.9 for the entire nonwhite population (85.9 males per 100 females). But at ages twenty to twenty-nine (sex ratio, 72.9) and thirty to thirty-nine (sex ratio, 78.5) females are even more predominant. Such sex ratios at the ages when people are normally raising families are almost certain to have very disturbing effects on family life and to reduce the birth rate. The sex ratio in Chicago is not as abnormal as in New York City, but at ages twenty to twenty-nine (sex ratio, 81.4) and thirty to thirty-nine (sex ratio, 88.2) there is a very large excess of females. In the United States as a whole the sex ratio for nonwhites is now 95.7. It has been decreasing in late years in much the same degree as that of the whites, so that there is much the same difference between them in 1950 (whites 99.0, nonwhites 95.7) as there was in 1920 (whites 104.4, nonwhites 100.9), although there was somewhat more difference in 1940 (whites 101.2, nonwhites 96.7).

Table 7-7.   Males per 100 Females in the Nonwhite Population by Age, United States and Selected States and Cities, 1950

Age	United States		New York City, nonwhite	Chicago, nonwhite	North Carolina, nonwhite	Louisiana, nonwhite
	White	Nonwhite				
Total..........	99.0	95.7	85.9	92.4	95.6	93.0
0–9..........	104.3	100.0	99.6	98.7	100.2	100.4
10–19........	102.5	98.0	90.6	91.1	98.7	97.3
20–29........	96.3	87.9	72.9	81.4	90.7	83.1
30–39........	96.7	89.0	78.5	88.2	91.5	83.3
40–49........	99.4	97.0	92.4	98.5	92.0	90.4
50–59........	99.8	104.4	100.2	108.8	97.7	98.6
60 and over...	92.7	98.1	79.5	91.0	92.8	93.6

In any population where in-migrants constitute a significant proportion of the total group there are likely to be distinctive age and sex groups. This also holds for areas of out-migration if the number leaving is large. This results from the fact that migrants are generally young people and when the movement is to the cities females usually predominate and they begin to migrate somewhat younger than males. However, one is forced to conclude from the age and sex data for New York City that in all probability the non-white males began to migrate at an earlier date than the females, since the sex ratios are much higher at forty years of age and over than at ages twenty to thirty-nine. It is obvious that age and sex differences of the nature just described would have a marked effect on the proportions of males and females married in the different age groups and hence would almost certainly affect birth rates and possibly death rates also. The predominance of females of younger adult ages would also tend to increase the proportion of women employed outside the home.

4. RACE AMALGAMATION (MISCEGENATION)

Another aspect of the composition of the nonwhite population in this country to which attention should be called is the racial mixture of the whites and nonwhites. This has gone on from the earliest times, but we have no means of measuring it. The census information available on this point is wholly unreliable, and, as Reuter well says,[5] even if the data were accurate they would not tell us the extent to which white ancestry is present among nonwhites. Nor is there any means of knowing whether any change in the proportion of white ancestry is now taking place. Estimates as to the proportion of nonwhites having a white ancestor (or ancestors) at some point in their lineage vary greatly. According to Reuter, some persons believe that three-fourths of the Negroes at some time or another have had a white ancestor and that this proportion is on the increase.

On the other hand, some maintain that the proportion of nonwhites with white ancestry is far less and that there is less race mixture now than formerly. In support of this contention it is asserted that those people with only a trace of nonwhite ancestry are constantly passing into the white population, thus decreasing the proportion of nonwhites with white ancestry. It is also claimed that the fertility of the nonwhites is adversely affected by the mixture of whites and nonwhites—witness the lower birth rates in the North, where the proportion of mulattoes and quadroons is higher. If this latter contention is true, the recognized nonwhite population will tend to become racially purer. Thus the likelihood of racial amalgamation through the increase of white ancestry in the nonwhite population will become less.

Until there is more evidence than we now have it is fruitless to speculate on whether the whites and nonwhites are likely to fuse into a single biological group. It may be pointed out, however, that there is some reason to believe that mulattoes, quadroons, and so forth, are more migratory than nonwhites with more predominant nonwhite ancestry and that, since nonwhite migrants move chiefly to the cities where birth rates are low because of voluntary control, the low birth rates of these groups do not prove their low fecundity but might contribute to a relative increase of the nonwhites of darker color.

5. HEALTH

It has long been known that nonwhites had higher death rates than the whites among whom they lived, although only since about 1930 have the data on nonwhite mortality become sufficiently accurate and comprehensive to permit of reasonably satisfactory comparisons of the rates of whites and nonwhites. Before that time the nonwhites living in the South were not adequately represented in the registration data, since several Southern states

[5] Edward Byron Reuter, "The American Mulatto," *Ann. Am. Acad. Pol. Soc. Sci., Pub.* 2174, 8 pp., November, 1928.

with large nonwhite populations did not come into the registration area until 1925 or later. In addition, the living conditions of the nonwhites in Northern cities with any significant number of such persons were so ab-- normal that their vital rates were of little value. Even today there is little doubt that the registration of deaths in many areas is less complete for non- whites than for whites and that causes of death are also much less carefully reported for them than for the whites. A release by the National Office of Vital Statistics [6] estimating completeness of birth registration in the United States in 1950 gives white registration as 98.5 per cent complete and non- white as 93.4 per cent. There can be no reasonable doubt that there is also some difference in the completeness of death registration as between whites and nonwhites, although no doubt it is less than for births. Because of the greater inadequacy of the death rate for nonwhites in the past any differences in death rates between whites and nonwhites shown by data relating to the period before about 1940 probably seriously understate the real differences. The data bearing on the relative death rates of whites and nonwhites will be reviewed briefly.

In the registration states of 1900 (chiefly the northeastern states, which had comparatively small nonwhite populations which were largely urban) the crude death rate of white males was 17.7 and that of nonwhite males was 25.7; for females the rates were 16.3 and 24.4, respectively. By 1910, the rates were as follows: males, white 15.4, nonwhite 22.3; females, white 13.6, nonwhite 21.0. By 1930 several southern states were included in the regis- tration area and the rates were as follows: males, white 11.7, nonwhite 17.4; females, white 9.8, nonwhite 15.3. In 1940, with all states in the regis- tration area and a very considerable improvement in the registration of non- white deaths, the rates were as follows: males, white 11.6, nonwhite 15.1; females, white 9.2, nonwhite 12.5. In 1949 the rates were as follows: males, white 11.0, nonwhite 12.4; females, white 8.1, nonwhite 9.9. Clearly the crude death rates of nonwhites have been falling very rapidly in recent years —more rapidly than those of the whites. Whereas as late as 1930 the crude rate for all nonwhites was approximately one-half more than that for all whites, it was only one-third higher in 1940 and only one-sixth higher in 1949. However, when the rates are adjusted for age differences the showing is not so favorable (Table 7-8). In 1900 the age-adjusted death rate for Negroes was about 60 per cent higher than that of the whites, and in 1949 it remained about 50 per cent higher.[7] However, the difference is not uniform at all ages or for both sexes.

[6] U.S. Federal Security Agency, National Office of Vital Statistics, *Preliminary Re- sults of the 1950 Birth Registration Test*, mimeographed release dated Jan. 15, 1952.
[7] Although our birth rates and death rates are now generally recorded only for whites and nonwhites, the Negroes constitute such a large proportion of all nonwhites that the nonwhite rate is essentially a Negro rate.

Table 7-8.   Crude and Age-adjusted Death Rates by Race and Sex,
Death Registration States, 1900 to 1949 [1]

Year	Total			White			Nonwhite		
	Both sexes	Male	Female	Both sexes	Male	Female	Both sexes	Male	Female
Crude death rates									
1949	9.7	11.1	8.3	9.5	11.0	8.1	11.1	12.4	9.9
1948	9.9	11.3	8.5	9.7	11.2	8.3	11.3	12.6	10.0
1945	10.6	12.7	8.8	10.4	12.5	8.6	12.0	13.9	10.4
1940	10.7	12.0	9.5	10.4	11.6	9.2	13.8	15.1	12.5
1930	11.3	12.3	10.4	10.8	11.7	9.8	16.3	17.4	15.3
1920	13.0	13.4	12.6	12.6	13.0	12.1	17.7	17.8	17.5
1910	14.7	15.6	13.7	14.5	15.4	13.6	21.7	22.3	21.0
1900	17.2	17.9	16.5	17.0	17.7	16.3	25.0	25.7	24.4
Age-adjusted death rates[2]									
1949	8.8	10.4	7.2	8.4	10.0	6.8	12.6	14.0	11.3
1948	9.0	10.6	7.5	8.6	10.2	7.1	12.8	14.3	11.4
1945	9.6	11.2	8.1	9.2	10.8	7.7	13.5	15.0	12.2
1940	10.7	12.1	9.4	10.2	11.6	8.8	16.2	17.5	14.9
1930	12.5	13.5	11.3	11.7	12.8	10.6	20.1	21.0	19.2
1920	14.2	14.7	13.8	13.7	14.2	13.1	20.6	20.4	21.0
1910	15.8	16.9	14.6	15.6	16.7	14.4	24.1	24.8	23.2
1900	17.8	18.6	17.0	17.6	18.4	16.8	27.8	28.7	27.1

[1] U.S. Federal Security Agency, National Office of Vital Statistics, *Vital Statistics of the United States, 1949*, Pt. 1, p. xliii, G.P.O., Washington, D.C., 1951.

[2] Computed by the direct method using as the standard population the age distribution of the population of the United States as enumerated in 1940.

Age-specific Death Rates. In 1949 the death rate for nonwhite males from birth to one year was 96 per cent higher than for white males of the same age, and for females 102 per cent higher. At ages one to four the proportional differences were not quite as large, and at ages five to fourteen the rate was only two-fifths higher than for whites for both males and females. At all ages fifteen to fifty-four the rates for nonwhites were from two to three times as high as for whites, there being especially large differences in the rates for females aged twenty-five to forty-four. The differences diminished rapidly after sixty-five years of age and after seventy-five years of age the rates for nonwhites were lower than for whites. These facts make it abundantly clear that the death rates of nonwhites are still far higher than those of whites, although in recent years the actual rates for nonwhites have been declining faster than those of whites.

Expectation of Life. In 1929 to 1931 the expectation of life at birth for white males was 59.1 years, and by 1949 this had increased to 65.9 years, or by 6.8 years. For nonwhite males the corresponding figures are 47.6 years and 58.6 years, an increase of 11.0 years. For white females the figure for 1929 to 1931 was 62.7 years and the 1949 figure was 71.5 years, an increase of 8.8 years, but for nonwhite females the figures were 49.5 years and 62.9 years, an increase of 13.4 years. The improvement in the health of nonwhites is going forward rapidly, but it should be noted that the expectation of life of nonwhites is now about where that of whites was 20 to 25 years ago.

Table 7-9.   Death Rates by Age, Race, and Sex, United States, 1949 [1]

Age	White		Nonwhite	
	Male	Female	Male	Female
Total.........................	11.0	8.1	12.4	9.9
Under 1.......................	34.7	26.5	67.9	53.5
1–4...........................	1.5	1.2	2.6	2.2
5–14..........................	0.7	0.5	1.0	0.7
15–24.........................	1.5	0.8	2.9	2.4
25–34.........................	1.9	1.2	5.0	4.0
35–44.........................	4.0	2.5	9.7	8.1
45–54.........................	10.0	5.6	20.1	15.5
55–64.........................	23.0	12.9	35.0	28.1
65–74.........................	51.0	34.7	60.7	52.7
75–84.........................	107.9	86.0	84.6	65.1
85 and over...................	264.4	262.6	116.8	88.2

[1] U.S. Federal Security Agency, National Office of Vital Statistics, *Vital Statistics of the United States, 1949*, Pt. 1, p. xlii, G.P.O., Washington, D.C., 1951.

Since there is no evidence of biological differences between whites and nonwhites which will account for such differences between them in death rates, it must be assumed that these mortality differences arise from differences in living conditions, housing, nutrition, medical service, and so forth. They provide abundant proof of the disadvantages under which nonwhites have always lived in this country.

Causes of Death. The few data already given would lead anyone familiar with mortality data to expect wide differences between whites and nonwhites in their death rates from different causes. The death rate of nonwhites from tuberculosis has always been relatively high and still is. But it should be noted that whereas the nonwhite death rate (per 100,000) from tuberculosis was 262.4 in 1920 it was only 128.0 in 1940 and had fallen to 78.4

Table 7-10.   Expectation of Life by Age, Race, and Sex,
United States, 1929 to 1949 [1]

Age	1949		1939–1941		1929–1931	
	Male	Female	Male	Female	Male	Female
White						
0	65.9	71.5	62.8	67.3	59.1	62.7
10	58.7	63.9	57.0	60.8	55.0	57.6
20	49.3	54.2	47.8	51.4	46.0	48.5
40	30.9	35.3	30.0	33.2	29.3	31.5
60	15.5	18.3	15.0	17.0	14.7	16.0
70	9.8	11.3	9.4	10.5	9.2	10.0
Nonwhite						
0	58.6	62.9	52.3	55.5	47.6	49.5
10	52.8	56.5	48.5	50.8	44.3	45.3
20	43.5	47.1	39.7	42.1	36.0	37.2
40	27.2	30.4	25.2	27.3	23.4	24.3
60	15.3	17.7	14.4	16.1	13.2	14.2
70	11.8	14.4	10.0	11.8	8.8	10.4

[1] U.S. Federal Security Agency, National Office of Vital Statistics, *Vital Statistics of the United States, 1949*, Pt. 1, p. lvi, G.P.O., Washington, D.C., 1951.

by 1948. In the same period the tuberculosis rate for whites fell from 99.5 in 1920 to 36.6 in 1940 and to 24.3 by 1948. Thus the tuberculosis rate for nonwhites is now well below that of whites thirty years ago and is approaching the white rate for 1930. However, the difference between whites and nonwhites is larger when adjusted for age. The same general situation prevails as regards pneumonia and influenza. Since 1940 the death rates from these diseases have fallen rapidly as a result of the use of the sulfa drugs and antibiotics. The fact that there is still a rather large difference between whites and nonwhites in the death rates from them almost certainly reflects the differences in living conditions and in ability to command medical care. On the other hand, nonwhite males now have slightly lower death rates from heart disease than the whites, although for nonwhite females the rate is substantially higher than for white females. These same differences prevail for deaths from cancer and diabetes.

Are those differences due to the fact that nonwhites are peculiarly susceptible to certain diseases while whites are more susceptible to certain other diseases? The most reasonable assumption regarding racial susceptibility to disease, in the light of our present knowledge, is that there is little or no difference between whites and nonwhites in this respect, and hence that the actual differences found arise almost entirely from differences in living conditions (environment) and will disappear when these conditions become practically the same for both races. All over the world death rates are closely

Table 7-11.   White and Nonwhite Deaths per 100,000 Persons by Cause, United States, 1920 to 1948

Cause	Year	Total	White	Nonwhite
All causes (exclusive of stillbirths)...........	1948	988.5	972.1	1,127.5
	1940	1,076.4	1,041.5	1,382.8
	1930	1,132.1	1,076.8	1,633.0
	1920	1,298.9	1,256.1	1,767.5
Typhoid and paratyphoid fever..............	1948	0.2	0.1	0.5
	1940	1.1	0.9	3.2
	1930	4.8	3.7	14.8
	1920	7.6	6.6	19.6
Scarlet fever.............................	1948	.0	.0	.0
	1940	0.5	0.5	0.3
	1930	1.9	2.1	0.6
	1920	4.6	5.0	0.8
Whooping cough..........................	1948	0.8	0.6	2.6
	1940	2.2	1.8	5.9
	1930	4.8	4.1	11.1
	1920	12.5	11.7	20.6
Diphtheria..............................	1948	0.4	0.4	0.8
	1940	1.1	1.0	1.8
	1930	4.9	4.9	4.9
	1920	15.3	16.0	8.6
Tuberculosis (all forms)....................	1948	30.0	24.3	78.4
	1940	45.9	36.6	128.0
	1930	71.1	57.7	192.0
	1920	113.1	99.5	262.4
Cancer and other malignant tumors..........	1948	134.9	139.1	98.5
	1940	120.3	125.0	78.4
	1930	97.4	101.9	56.6
	1920	83.4	86.5	48.5
Diabetes mellitus.........................	1948	26.4	27.4	18.4
	1940	26.6	27.6	17.9
	1930	19.1	19.8	12.8
	1920	16.1	16.9	8.0
Intracranial lesions of vascular origin.........	1948	89.7	87.4	109.1
	1940	90.9	88.6	111.7
	1930	89.0	86.9	108.2
	1920	93.0	93.4	87.7
Diseases of the heart......................	1948	322.7	329.7	262.7
	1940	292.5	297.6	248.5
	1930	214.2	213.1	224.7
	1920	159.6	159.5	160.7
Pneumonia (all forms) and influenza.........	1948	38.7	35.4	66.3
	1940	70.3	64.0	125.4
	1930	102.5	94.4	175.9
	1920	207.3	198.4	304.4
Nephritis (all forms)......................	1948	53.0	49.3	84.3
	1940	81.5	76.6	124.7
	1930	91.0	85.7	138.7
	1920	88.8	86.7	111.1
Puerperal septicemia......................	1948	0.8	0.6	2.4
	1940	2.8	2.4	6.3
	1930	4.6	4.2	8.8
	1920	6.5	6.1	11.3
Violent deaths (suicide excepted)............	1948	72.9	69.6	100.8
	1940	79.8	76.3	110.5
	1930	89.3	85.4	123.9
	1920	77.8	75.2	106.7

associated with the level of living (Chap. IV). Poverty and all its attendant hardships always result in high death rates, and the height of the death rate generally increases as the degree of poverty increases.

Although there is much room for further reduction in the death rates of nonwhites in the United States, these rates cannot be expected to continue to improve at the rapid rate of the recent past. The death rates due to those diseases which are more easily and cheaply controlled are already so low that in many cases their complete elimination would have only a slight effect in reducing the general death rate of nonwhites. This has already happened among the whites for some diseases. Thus, in 1921 when the tuberculosis death rate (deaths per 100,000) for whites was 84.7 there was still opportunity for considerable saving of life, and since the nonwhite rate at that time was 239.3 there was much opportunity to save life by reducing nonwhite deaths from tuberculosis. In 1948, as shown, the rates for tuberculosis were 24.3 and 78.4, respectively. The reduction in this 27-year period was 60.4 for whites and 160.9 for nonwhites. Translated into terms of the crude death rate the white death rate declined during this period by 0.604 per 1,000 and the nonwhite death rate by 1.609 per 1,000 as a result of the reduction in the tuberculosis death rate alone. Obviously the complete disappearance of tuberculosis as a cause of death would have almost no effect on the total death rate for whites (0.243 per 1,000) and only a small effect (0.784) on that of nonwhites. The same is true of all the other infectious and parasitic diseases. However, since the death rate of nonwhites from these other infectious and parasitic diseases is still about three times that of the whites, there is much more room for improvement from this source among nonwhites than among whites. Furthermore, the present relatively low death rates of nonwhites from certain organic diseases seem likely to disappear as those from contagious and infectious diseases are reduced. The pattern of deaths among nonwhites from particular causes seems to be following that of whites with a time lag of 20 to 30 years.

Infant Mortality. Until the last few decades infant mortality has always been high. Even now it has fallen to low levels only in the more industrialized countries of the Western world. This high infant mortality in the past has been one of the chief factors in keeping population increase at a low rate and even in decimating many populations. In the Western countries, however, the level of infant mortality has been declining very rapidly during the past few decades. Today the level of living in a country may be measured fairly accurately by its infant mortality rate—the higher the level of living, the lower the infant mortality. In the United States' registration states in 1916 the total infant mortality rate was 101.0, *i.e.*, there were 101 deaths of children under one year of age to each 1,000 live births in that year. The rate for whites at that time was 99.0 and for nonwhites 184.9, which appears to have been unusually high. The normal rate for nonwhite races was probably 20 to 30 points lower. By 1940 the nonwhite rate had fallen to 73.8 and the white rate to

43.2. Both were substantially less than half as high as in 1916. By 1949 the nonwhite rate had fallen to 47.3—about what the white rate was in 1938—and the white rate had fallen to 28.9. The white and nonwhite rates have been approaching and seem likely to continue to converge, since the further reduction of the white rate by more than 5 to 7 points does not seem probable in the near future. Among nonwhites (1949) infant mortality was about one-fourth higher for boys than for girls, among whites about one-third higher. In 1948 congenital malformations, premature births, and injury at birth accounted for 45.3 per cent of all infant deaths among nonwhites and for 62.4 per cent of those among whites. No doubt deaths from these causes can be reduced somewhat, but they are less amenable to control by presently known practices than are the infectious diseases, particularly the intestinal diseases, which formerly caused such a high proportion of infant deaths.

Table 7-12. Infant Mortality Rates by Race and Place of Residence, United States, 1949 [1]

Area	All races	White	Nonwhite
United States......................	31.3	28.9	47.3
Urban............................	30.1	27.8	46.0
Places of:			
100,000 or more...............	28.2	25.7	40.7
25,000–100,000................	29.6	27.3	48.9
10,000–25,000.................	31.1	28.7	53.7
2,500–10,000.................	34.8	32.4	61.7
Rural............................	33.1	30.4	49.0

[1] U.S. Federal Security Agency, National Office of Vital Statistics, *Vital Statistics of the United States, 1949*, Pt. 1, p. xlix, G.P.O., Washington, D.C., 1950.

Consequently, while the reduction of the infant death rate for nonwhites should be substantial, proportionally, perhaps by 30 to 40 per cent of their present rate, such a reduction will have comparatively little effect on the crude death rate for all nonwhites. It would only amount to a reduction from about 11.2 to 10.9 per 1,000. I do not imply that this is not worth doing; I am only trying to make it clear that the present infant death rates among nonwhites are so low that future reductions will have comparatively little effect on their total death rates.

The infant mortality rates for whites and nonwhites by size of community are shown in Table 7-12. The general pattern is the same for both races—the lowest rates being found in the largest cities and the highest in the smallest cities. The rates for the whites in the medium-sized cities and rural areas are much the same, but for nonwhites they are a little higher in the smaller cities.

The infant mortality rates of nonwhite and white infants from particular causes are shown in Fig. 7-1. The contagious and infectious diseases are still much more deadly for nonwhite babies, while injury at birth is little different for the two races and congenital malformations are much less important among nonwhites.

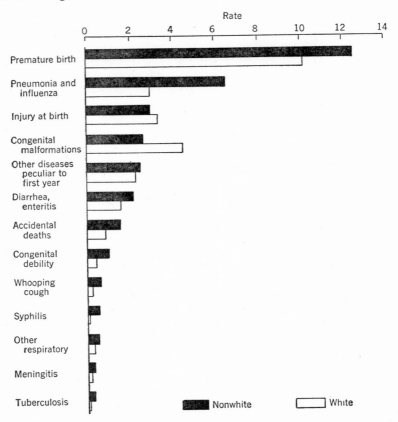

Fig. 7-1. Infant mortality rates, by color and cause, United States, 1948.

6. INDUSTRIAL STATUS

All but a small proportion, 11.0 per cent, of the Negroes in the United States were slaves before the Civil War (1860). Most of the freedmen probably were engaged in nonagricultural industries, and some of the slaves were also household servants and artisans, but the overwhelming majority were employed directly on the land. It is not unlikely that from three-fourths to four-fifths of the employed slaves were engaged in agriculture. In the United States in 1890, the first year for which data are available, 56.1 per cent of the employed colored persons were engaged in agriculture, fisheries, and mining; 32.1 per cent in domestic and personal service; and only 5.8 per cent in manufacturing and mechanical industries. In 1950 the preliminary percentages, for categories as nearly similar to these as it is possible to obtain, were as follows: agriculture and mining, 20.8 per cent; service industries, 32.4 per cent; and manufacturing, 17.9 per cent. In the Southern states the predominance of agriculture was still large. In 1890 in North Carolina agriculture claimed 64.8 per cent of the colored workers who were gainfully employed; domestic and personal service, 24.0 per cent; and manu-

Table 7-13. Proportion of Whites and Nonwhites in the Major Industry Groups, North Carolina and Kentucky, 1950

Industry group	North Carolina		Kentucky	
	White	Nonwhite	White	Nonwhite
Total employed....................	100.0	100.0	100.0	100.0
Agriculture, forestry, and fisheries.....	21.1	36.2	26.8	14.6
Mining..........................	0.2	0.2	7.6	4.2
Construction......................	6.2	5.0	5.7	5.4
Manufacturing....................	31.9	16.2	16.3	9.9
Transportation, communication, and other public utilities...............	4.8	3.5	7.8	6.6
Wholesale and retail trade...........	16.5	7.7	15.7	12.7
Finance, insurance, and real estate....	2.0	0.7	2.2	1.7
Business and repair services..........	2.1	0.9	2.3	1.8
Personal services..................	3.1	19.9	3.5	29.1
Entertainment and recreation service..	0.7	0.6	0.8	1.3
Professional and related services......	6.7	6.5	6.6	8.0
Public administration...............	3.2	1.0	3.1	2.3
Industry not reported...............	1.5	1.7	1.7	2.5

facturing, 6.7 per cent. The analogous categories for 1950 were as follows: agriculture, 36.2 per cent; domestic and personal service, 19.9 per cent; and manufacturing, 16.2 per cent.

These changes in the industrial status of the Negroes were foreshadowed to some extent in the changes in the proportions living in rural and urban communities given above. However, only in one or two of the Southern states are a majority of the employed nonwhites still engaged in agriculture. In Mississippi 56.1 per cent are still employed in agriculture, forestry, fisheries, and mining. The nonwhites like the whites are rapidly becoming urbanized workers, but they must still accept a lower status than white workers, as the following data indicate.

7. ECONOMIC STATUS

It follows naturally from the inferior industrial and occupational status of the nonwhites that they also constitute a relatively poor economic group. Table 7-14 shows that in North Carolina 28.5 per cent of the urban and rural-nonfarm white families reporting incomes received less than $1,500, while 60.3 per cent of the nonwhite persons reported incomes of this size.

Table 7-14.   Proportion of White and Nonwhite Families Reporting Incomes of Different Sizes, North Carolina, 1950

Income	White		Nonwhite	
	Urban and rural-nonfarm	Rural-farm	Urban and rural-nonfarm	Rural-farm
Total..........	100.0	100.0	100.0	100.0
Under $1,000...	19.6	36.8	42.8	60.0
$1,000–$1,499..	8.9	14.7	17.5	16.5
1,500– 1,999..	10.0	12.0	16.0	9.9
2,000– 2,499..	12.0	11.1	10.5	6.1
2,500– 3,499..	18.8	12.7	8.0	4.7
3,500– 4,999..	16.7	7.7	3.4	1.8
$5,000 and over.	13.9	5.1	1.6	0.9

Incomes of $1,500 to $2,499 were reported by 22 per cent of the whites, while 26.5 per cent of the nonwhites reported such incomes. Of the whites 35.5 per cent reported family incomes of $2,500 to $4,999, while only 11.4 per cent of the nonwhites belonged in this class. Of the whites 13.9 per cent reported incomes of $5,000 and over, while only 1.6 per cent of the nonwhites had such incomes. The situation in Kentucky was substantially the same. In the North the relative differences in the incomes of whites and nonwhites would be much the same although the incomes of both would be higher.

8. SUMMARY AND CONCLUSIONS

As was said above, the more fundamental controversial questions relating to the Negro in the United States will not be discussed here. It may not be out of place, however, to point out that the statistical data given here seem to the author to show only that the Negro occupies an inferior social and economic position in American society and not that there is any basic biological difference in the capacity or ability of whites and nonwhites. In matters of health the Negro is clearly in the position of almost all poor people. He lives under relatively harsh environmental conditions. The very natural consequence of this is that he has a high death rate and suffers greatly from debilitating illnesses such as hookworm and malaria, which greatly reduce his economic and social efficiency. It is quite possible that the Negro is more subject to certain diseases than the white man—for example, diseases of the respiratory tract—but we cannot say that this is a fact until the housing conditions of the two races approximate one another far more closely than they now do and until the Negro also has access to equally good medical and hospital care. On the other hand, the Negro apparently is rather immune to scarlet fever and perhaps to diabetes. Under present conditions the only reasonable assumption is that differences in death rates between whites and Negroes are due to differences in the environmental conditions under which they live. But even if the Negro should be more susceptible to certain diseases than the white man, this proves nothing regarding his ability or capacity to share equally in our civilization.

In the matter of natural increase the Negro seems to show the same general tendencies as the whites. He does not breed well in the captivity of urban life, but neither does the white man. In the country the Negro until quite recently had a somewhat slower rate of increase than the whites in the same area, probably because of his higher death rate. But on the whole he seems to feel the pressure of the same conditions which lead the white man to restrict the size of his family, although there is a lag in the control of the size of the family similar to that found among the whites of the southern Appalachians. There is absolutely nothing in any way peculiar about the reproductive life of the Negro which sets him apart from the white man.

As regards his economic status it is increasingly apparent that where opportunity is present the Negro is not content to remain a mere hewer of wood and drawer of water. In all cities with any considerable Negro population there are numerous individuals who show marked business ability and ability to get ahead in the professions. We must not forget that it is only recently that occupations involving more than the use of the hoe, the pick, and the shovel, or the performance of household tasks under close supervision were opened to the Negro; and even yet only a comparatively few are able to afford the long and expensive training essential to entering the better-paid occupations. Surely the progress that the Negroes have made in this respect in the last three or four decades does not indicate that their ability to adjust themselves to the complex industrial order we are developing today is fundamentally less than that of the whites.

In many other lines of activity also it appears that Negroes are beginning to achieve positions which we have been accustomed to deny them in the past. A good education is only very slowly being extended to them, but in spite of this fact they are making fairly rapid progress in many lines. It seems only reasonable to assume that it is the lack of educational, social, and economic opportunities rather than the lack of ability that keeps the Negroes from going ahead both economically and socially much more rapidly than is actually happening.

In art and literature the Negro has done better than in education, business, and industry. Reuter's explanation of this difference, which is to the effect that opportunity in these fields is more open to the Negro than in fields where careful scientific and business training are needed, is convincing. The Negro musician or poet receives far more encouragement than the Negro doctor, scientist, or businessman. Artistic achievement encounters less racial discrimination than educational or economic achievement; hence a larger proportion of such ability among Negroes is developed than of the ability they may possess to compete with the whites in other lines.

In conclusion we may say that the time has come when we should cast aside the multitude of prejudices and prepossessions regarding the Negro which we have absorbed from our past and begin to study him simply as another human being. We are steadily accumulating a body of knowledge regarding Negroes and their modes of life which, if we will make use of it, should very materially assist us in making a truer evaluation of the Negro than we have been able to make in the past. It was inevitable that slavery and its associations should leave us with many beliefs regarding the Negro which rest on no solid foundation. We have just recently witnessed the tendency in the case of our newer immigrants to hold that the actual position people occupy in the community is the measure of their ability. This is exactly the position that we have been accustomed to assume with regard to the Negroes, and it is no more justified in the one case than in the other. Today we must open our minds to the facts regarding the Negro which are becoming available and must accept them for what they are. If we do this, it is difficult to see how we can fail to accept the general position taken by Reuter in his *American Race Problem: A Study of the Negro,*[8] and regard the Negroes as a disadvantaged group whose adjustments to American life have been greatly retarded by social and economic handicaps. When once we become scientific-minded regarding the Negro we shall probably have made the most important step that has ever been made toward a solution of many of the vexed questions of race relations. This does not mean that, once we adopt a scientific attitude in studying the Negro, we shall immediately lose race prejudice and be ready to act justly and rationally toward him, but we shall have taken a long first step in this direction. A generation which has been brought up in this scientific attitude of mind should be in a position to make progress in the solution of our race problems which cannot

[8] The Thomas Y. Crowell Company, New York, 1927. (Crowell's Social Science Series.)

be reasonably expected from a generation brought up with the manifold prejudices that surround us. The accumulation of knowledge of the Negro by the scientific-minded must certainly precede the application of wisdom to the solution of race problems in this country.

Suggestions for Supplementary Reading

DONALD, HENDERSON H.: *The Negro Migration of 1916–1918*, 116 pp., Association for the Study of Negro Life and History, Washington, D.C., 1921. (Reprinted from *J. Negro History*, Vol. 6, 1921.)

DOYLE, BERTRAM WILBUR: *The Etiquette of Race Relations in the South*, 249 pp., University of Chicago Press, Chicago, 1937.

FRAZIER, E. FRANKLIN: *The Negro Family in Chicago*, 294 pp., University of Chicago Press, Chicago, 1932.

GOVER, MARY, and EDGAR SYDENSTRICKER: *Mortality among Negroes in the United States*, 63 pp., G.P.O., Washington, D.C., 1928. (U.S. Treas. Dept., Pub. Health Service, *Pub. Health Bull.* 174, June, 1927.)

HERSKOVITS, MELVILLE J.: *The American Negro: A Study in Racial Crossing*, 92 pp., Alfred A. Knopf, Inc., New York, 1928.

JOHNSON, CHARLES S.: *Shadow of the Plantation*, 215 pp., University of Chicago Press, Chicago, 1934.

KLINEBERG, OTTO: *Negro Intelligence and Selective Migration*, 66 pp., Columbia University Press, New York, 1935.

MYRDAL, GUNNAR: *An American Dilemma*, 2 vols., Harper & Brothers, New York, 1944.

REUTER, EDWARD BYRON: "The American Mulatto," *Ann. Am. Acad. Pol. Soc. Sci.*, *Pub.* 2174, 8 pp., November, 1928.

————: *The American Race Problem: A Study of the Negro*, 448 pp., The Thomas Y. Crowell Company, New York, 1927. (Crowell's Social Science Series.)

SYDENSTRICKER, EDGAR: *Health and Environment*, 217 pp., McGraw-Hill Book Company, Inc., New York, 1933.

THOMPSON, EDGAR T., ed.: *Race Relations and the Race Problem*, 338 pp., Duke University Press, Durham, N.C., 1939.

VANCE, RUPERT B.: *All These People: The Nation's Human Resources in the South*, 503 pp., The University of North Carolina Press, Chapel Hill, 1945.

WOOFTER, T. J.: *Negro Problems in Cities*, 284 pp., Doubleday, Doran & Company, Inc., New York, 1928.

————: *Races and Ethnic Groups in American Life*, 247 pp., McGraw-Hill Book Company, Inc., New York, 1933.

CHAPTER VIII

NATALITY [1]

The fertility of women has always been a matter of vital concern not only to women themselves but also to the communities to which they belonged. Overt expression of this interest is found in the customs and institutions of many peoples that have no written records, while within historical times the literature of most peoples contains numerous references to the unfortunate social status of the barren woman as compared with her fertile sister. But in spite of the abundant evidence of interest in the fertility of the individual woman, the effort to measure the level of natality in a group appears to be of comparatively recent origin. This lack of interest in the fertility of the group as a whole was certainly not due to any lack of interest in group survival, but since the idea of individual fertility was much easier to grasp than that of group fertility, the measurement of the latter received comparatively little attention until modern times.

During the last two to three centuries, however, there has been more and more interest in measuring *vital* phenomena (births and deaths) and the differences between them and in comparing the vital conditions of one community with those of another. Obviously, if valid comparisons of vital phenomena were to be made there must be some standard measure. Some of the more fruitful efforts made to formulate a standard measure of natality will be discussed under the general heading of Natality Rates.

Before discussing natality rates, however, it will be well to notice briefly the content of the words *fertility* and *fecundity*. Among students of population the term fertility is generally used to indicate the actual reproductive performance of a woman or group of women. Thus if, in any specified group of women who had completed the reproductive period, 1,000 of them had borne 2,900 living children, this figure would measure their completed

---

[1] In the chapters on natality and mortality the description of statistical methods will be very brief and elementary. The reason for this rather cavalier treatment of methods is not that they are of little importance but rather that they are too important to be treated adequately in a book of this general character. The reader who is interested in methods will want a great deal more than can be undertaken here, and the reader not interested in methods will need only the brief explanation of a few of the technical terms used in demography. The latter will be supplied here, but the student is referred to Margaret Jarman Hagood *et al.*, *Demographic Methods*, John Wiley & Sons, Inc., New York, 1953, for the former.

fertility. It might equally well be expressed as an average of 2.9 children per woman. But a woman would be considered *fertile* if she had ever borne a child. Fecundity, on the other hand, denotes the ability to bear a child and has no reference to whether or not a woman actually has borne a child. The proportion of all women who are fecund is not known with any precision. In some societies where practically all women marry and where there is strong social pressure to bear children it has been found that as few as 1 or 2 per cent of those married are childless; in most groups the proportion is somewhat higher. Under the conditions just mentioned there is a strong presumption that most of the infertile women are also infecund, but even in such a society infertility is not clear proof of infecundity. There is some reason to believe the proportion of infecund married women is somewhat larger in the United States today than it was in the past and may amount to between 4 and 6 per cent of all married women, but this cannot be stated positively.

We know now that the infecundity of a particular marriage is not proof of the infecundity of the wife, as was quite commonly assumed in the past, but may be due to the sterility of either the wife or the husband, or may arise from the fact that the spermatozoa of a particular male cannot fertilize the ova of a particular female, *i.e.*, to the mutual incompatibility of the individuals' germ cells. In our discussion here we are interested primarily in fertility and will refer only occasionally to fecundity. But it should be remembered that if we measure fertility by the average number of children borne by each woman in a specified group this average will be affected by the proportion of infecund couples and by the proportion of couples that are fecund but childless, as well as by the average number of children borne by the fertile couples. In our study of natality we will use averages because we are more interested in the fertility of the group than in individual fertility.

1. NATALITY RATES

Definitions and Methods of Calculating Natality Rates. The *crude birth rate* of the population in any specified area is obtained by dividing the number of births recorded in that area during a year by its total population, preferably the midyear population, and multiplying by 1,000, thus obtaining the number of births per 1,000 of the population. A *corrected birth rate* is one which is increased to allow for the fact that not all births are recorded. This applies particularly to the United States, for in a good many countries practically all births are recorded. It is obtained in the same manner as the crude birth rate and is subject to the same limitations as the crude birth rate as a measure of fertility. An example is shown in Table 8-1.

The *age-specific birth rates* of an area are obtained by dividing the number of births to mothers of each age by the number of women of this age and

Table 8-1.   Calculation of Corrected Birth Rate, 1940

Area	Recorded births[1]	Popu-lation	Crude birth rate	Per cent of births registered[2]	Corrected birth rate
California, cities of 100,000 or more................	43,204	2,914,546	14.8	98.0	15.1
Kansas, rural............	15,529	1,047,087	14.8	95.5	15.5

[1] U.S. Bureau of the Census, *Vital Statistics of the United States, 1940*, Pt. II, Table 2, G.P.O., Washington, D.C., 1943.

[2] U.S. Federal Security Agency, National Office of Vital Statistics, *Vital Statistics of the United States, 1948*, Pt. I, Table D, G.P.O., Washington, D.C., 1950.

multiplying by 1,000. To calculate this rate the births must be recorded and tabulated by the age of the mother and the age of all the women of child-bearing ages must be known. Births to mothers of unstated age should be distributed proportionally, and allowance should be made for unrecorded births, especially in the United States. In census years there is no necessity of estimating the number of women by age. The figure for *total fertility* is

Table 8-2.   Age-specific Birth Rates, Total Fertility, and Gross Reproduction Rate, 1940

Age of mother	California, cities of 100,000 or more				Kansas, rural			
	Births to women of specified ages		Female popu-lation 4-1-40[3]	Age-specific birth rates	Births to women of specified ages		Female popu-lation 4-1-40[3]	Age-specific birth rates
	Recorded[1]	Corrected[2]			Recorded[1]	Corrected[2]		
15–19[4].........	4,285	4,373	102,624	42.6	1,504	1,578	47,901	32.9
20–24..........	14,467	14,767	122,901	120.2	4,544	4,769	37,525	127.1
25–29..........	13,349	13,626	136,468	99.8	4,313	4,526	35,912	126.0
30–34..........	7,442	7,596	129,634	58.6	2,808	2,947	34,763	84.8
35–39..........	2,949	3,010	124,389	24.2	1,659	1,741	33,303	52.3
40–44..........	643	656	116,031	5.7	608	638	31,689	20.1
45–49[5].........	56	57	108,294	0.5	58	61	30,996	2.0
Not stated......	13	......	....	.....	35			
Total.........	43,204	44,085	....	351.6	15,529	16,260	......	445.2
Total fertility..................	351.6 × 5 = 1,758.0				445.2 × 5 = 2,226.0			
Gross reproduction rate[6]........	1,758 × 48.5% = 852.6				2,226 × 48.5% = 1,079.6			

[1] U.S. Bureau of the Census, *Vital Statistics of the United States, Supplement, 1939–40*, Pt. III, Table V, G.P.O., Washington, D.C., 1943.

[2] Age of mother not stated distributed proportionally and births increased to allow for those not registered.

[3] U.S. Bureau of the Census, *Vital Statistics Rates in the United States, 1900–1940*, Table VII, G.P.O., Washington, D.C., 1943.

[4] Births to mothers aged 15 to 19 include those to mothers aged 10 to 14.

[5] Births to mothers aged 45 to 49 include those to mothers aged 50 to 54.

[6] The decimal of the gross reproduction rate as given here is for 1,000 women. It may be moved one place to the left for 100 and three places for "the average woman."

obtained by adding together the age-specific birth rates for the several age classes and multiplying the sum by five if the rates are calculated for five-year age groups, as is usually the case. This figure shows how many children would be born on an average to 1,000 women passing through the child-bearing age, assuming that the age-specific birth rates of these women remain constant as of the year of calculation and that none of the women die during that period. The *gross reproduction rate* shows how many girls—future mothers—would be borne on an average by 1,000 women passing through the childbearing age, assuming that no woman dies before she is past this age. This rate may be calculated by reducing the figure for total fertility in the same proportion as the ratio between females born and total births. This ratio usually hovers around 48.5 per 100 births. These rates are illustrated in Table 8-2.

The *net reproduction rate*, unlike the gross reproduction rate, makes allowance for deaths occurring among females at successive ages between birth and age fifty. The net reproduction rate shows the ratio between births in two successive generations or the increase or decrease ultimately experienced within a generation by a population whose age-specific birth rates and death rates are assumed to remain constant. The net reproduction rate is computed by applying the age-specific birth rates to the number of years lived in each age group by the survivors of the original cohort after mortality has operated, summing the products, and then applying the ratio between

Table 8-3. Net Reproduction Rate, 1940

Age of mother	Number of years lived in age interval by a birth cohort of 100,000 females[1]	California, cities of 100,000 or more		Kansas, rural	
		Age-specific birth rates	Calculated number of births	Age-specific birth rates	Calculated number of births
15–19	468,365	42.6	19,952	32.9	15,409
20–24	464,119	120.2	55,787	127.1	58,990
25–29	458,832	99.8	45,791	126.0	57,813
30–34	452,593	58.6	26,522	84.8	38,380
35–39	444,922	24.2	10,767	52.3	23,269
40–44	435,129	5.7	2,480	20.1	8,746
45–49	422,084	0.5	211	2.0	844
Total....	....	....	161,510	....	203,451

Net reproduction rate (average per woman).... $\dfrac{161,510 \times 48.5\%}{100,000} = 0.783$ $\dfrac{203,451 \times 48.5\%}{100,000} = 0.987$

[1] 1939 to 1941 United States life-table cohort.

females born and total births (48.5 per cent) and dividing the result by 100,000.

A *standardized birth rate* shows, as a rule, what the birth rate for a group of women would be if these women had the same age distribution as those in some *standard* population. It is computed by taking the age-specific birth rates for women (in a particular population) and multiplying each of these rates by the number of women (in a standard population) in the corresponding age category of each 1 million persons in this standard population. The sum of these products divided by 1 million and multiplied by 1,000—or, more simply, merely divided by 1,000—is the standardized rate.

Table 8-4. Standardized Birth Rate, 1940

Age of mother	Number of females in standard million[1]	California, cities of 100,000 or more		Kansas, rural	
		Age-specific birth rates	Calculated number of births	Age-specific birth rates	Calculated number of births
15–19	35,795	42.6	1,525	32.9	1,178
20–24	35,472	120.2	4,264	127.1	4,508
25–29	35,070	99.8	3,500	126.0	4,419
30–34	34,592	58.6	2,027	84.8	2,933
35–39	34,007	24.2	823	52.3	1,779
40–44	33,257	5.7	190	20.1	668
45–49	32,260	0.5	16	2.0	65
Total...	......	....	12,345	....	15,550

Standardized birth rate per 1,000 population........ $\dfrac{12,345}{1,000,000} \times 1,000 = 12.3$ $\dfrac{15,550}{1,000,000} \times 1,000 = 15.6$

[1] Calculated from the 1939 to 1941 United States life-table population, assuming 105 male births to 100 female births.

Crude Birth Rates. The measure of natality which was in most general use among those interested in such matters until a century or century and a half ago was the ratio of population to births. The equation was population/births = natality and it was expressed as the number of persons in the population at the time under consideration to each birth, *e.g.*, 20 persons to each birth. Thus a population of 500,000 with 25,000 births would have 20 persons to one birth. Until such a measure or rate was devised it was impossible to compare one population with another. The essentials for the calculation of this ratio were knowledge (1) of the size of the population, and (2) of the annual number of births. In time it became customary to invert the above equation, multiply by 1,000, and call the result the *birth rate* (see Table 8-1). The ratio of 20 persons to one birth became a rate of 50 births to each 1,000 of the population. This form of rate came to be preferred to the earlier form, and today it is known as the *crude birth rate* because it does not take into account the fact that different populations vary in age, sex, marital condition, and other characteristics which affect their birth rates.

This crude birth rate is still widely used and is the rate with which the public is most familiar. We have come to realize, however, that because it does not take account of the differences in the composition of different populations it has limited value in comparing the level of natality in different groups. We should be careful not to assume that the crude birth rate tells us

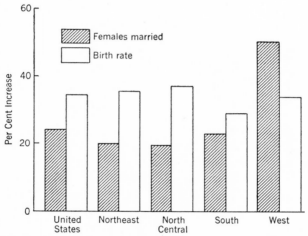

Fig. 8-1. Per cent increase in married females, and per cent increase in crude birth rates, United States by regions, 1940 to 1950.

more than it actually does. *All* it tells us is the number of babies born per 1,000 of the total population in the period under consideration.

Where rather large and sudden changes in the composition of the population have occurred, the crude birth rate can also change rather suddenly, although no change may have taken place in the average number of children born per woman. Such a sudden change in the crude rate is more likely to happen in relatively small populations than in larger national groups. However, rather sudden changes can occur in large groups, and at all times comparisons of the crude birth rates of different groups and in the same group at different dates must be made with caution.

As an illustration of the way in which the composition of a given population may change rather suddenly because of emigration we may refer to the changes in age and sex in the population of a group of counties in the "dust bowl" between 1930 and 1940 shown in Chap. VI, p. 89. These changes in the proportion of women at different ages were so great that a comparison of the crude birth rates for 1930 and 1940 cannot be expected to give more than the merest hint of the trend in the fertility of the women in this population during the interval. Any trend they may indicate may be further distorted by other changes in composition which may have taken place, especially by changes in marital composition due to the postponement of marriage during the depression. Figure 8-1 shows how the proportion of married women in the different regions of the United States changed during the decade 1940 to 1950 and also the change in the crude birth rate. Clearly this increase in the proportion of women married was associated with a large increase in the crude birth rate, although it is not proof that the increase in married women was the only or even the chief cause; but neither can it be treated as proof of a change in the average number of children born per married woman during her reproductive life.

Age-specific Birth Rates. Once the students of vital statistics clearly realized that the age, sex, and marital differences between populations rendered the crude birth rate of doubtful value as a measure of the comparative fertility of different groups, it became reasonably certain that other more useful measures would be devised. One of these is known as the age-specific birth rate (see Table 8-2). This rate can be calculated for single-year age classes or for five-year age classes. There is little practical advantage in calculating it for single-year age classes, since the gain in accuracy is generally slight and the work is about five times as great as for five-year groups (Table 8-5).

It is clear that such a rate eliminates the danger that age and sex differences between groups will affect their birth rates. But the age-specific rate does not eliminate differences in the marital status of the women in different groups, which, as has just been indicated, may exert a large influence on age-specific birth rates. Age-specific birth rates have the disadvantage of showing a different rate for each age class (five-year or one-year as the case may be) thus making difficult a comparison of the fertility of groups as wholes. This multiplicity of rates can be avoided if the age-specific rates for five-year age classes are summed and multiplied by five because each woman spends five years in each such age class. This gives a "total fertility" per 1,000 women based on the assumption that the fertility of each woman at each age is the same as that of the corresponding age group in the particular year to which the data relate. The assumption is also made that none of the 1,000 women entering the childbearing period (age fifteen) die during that period.[3] This rate tells us more about the reproductive performance of the average woman than either the crude or age-specific birth rates, but the assumptions underlying it should not be forgotten.

[3] *Statistical Year-book, 1942–44*, p. 50, League of Nations, Geneva, 1945.

Table 8-5. Age-specific Birth Rates and Total Fertility,
Selected Countries, 1940 to 1949

Country	Year	15–19	20–24	25–29	30–34	35–39	40–44	45–49	Total fertility
United States[1].	1949	81.5	194.6	162.9	99.5	52.6	14.8	1.1	3,035
	1945	48.8	130.1	128.4	94.7	54.6	15.5	1.3	2,367
	1940	48.9	125.0	114.1	77.1	41.8	13.9	1.3	2,110
Netherlands[2]..	1949	12.7	97.0	187.8	172.0	120.2	49.5	4.4	3,218
	1945	9.9	83.7	170.5	162.3	117.5	46.0	3.4	2,966
	1940	10.7	87.7	156.5	141.0	95.1	39.8	3.6	2,672
Japan[2][3]......	1948	17.3	180.4	256.3	211.4	147.9	58.3	4.5	4,380
	1937	19.0	172.0	253.0	201.0	157.0	68.0	9.0	4,396
	1930	31.5	200.2	248.6	217.0	163.1	71.6	10.3	4,712
Sweden[2]......	1947	35.3	128.7	141.3	106.4	65.1	23.4	2.0	2,511
	1945	32.6	127.0	149.4	117.5	72.2	25.4	1.8	2,630
	1940	22.0	88.4	104.2	82.6	52.4	20.6	2.1	1,862
France[2].......	1948	23.3	161.0	183.6	126.1	75.4	26.0	2.3	2,988
	1945	18.6	114.7	138.5	100.0	63.2	23.3	2.0	2,302
	1939	26.2	137.9	129.8	83.0	44.5	14.3	1.3	2,185
New Zealand[2].	1948	25.3	175.9	210.1	148.6	83.1	25.8	1.9	3,354
	1945	18.2	125.3	180.4	143.6	85.5	26.6	2.1	2,908
	1940	21.7	131.2	169.1	121.7	63.4	20.5	1.6	2,646

[1] U.S. Federal Security Agency, National Office of Vital Statistics, "Births by Age of Mother, Race, and Birth Order, United States, 1949," *Vital Statistics—Special Reports* . . ., Vol. 36, No. 9, p. 137, 1951.

[2] *Demographic Yearbook, 1949–50*, Table 18, United Nations, New York, 1950.

[3] *Statistical Yearbook, 1942–44*, Table 11, League of Nations, Geneva, 1945.

Standardized Birth Rates. Another of the early refinements on the crude birth rate used to secure a better measure for the comparison of natality between groups is the standardized birth rate. The earliest form of this was a simple adjustment made to take account of the fact that populations differed in age composition. Such a standardized rate is now generally referred to as an age-adjusted rate. It could not be calculated until age-specific birth rates became available. The rates for different groups calculated on the standard population can be compared directly, with the assurance that the variability in the crude birth rate arising from differences in the proportions at different ages have been eliminated.

In the illustration given in Table 8-4 age-standardized rates are calculated for the large cities of California and the rural areas of Kansas. These populations had the same crude birth rates in 1940 (14.8). However, their age-adjusted rates, standardized on the age structure of the female population of the 1939 to 1941 life table for the United States, were as follows: California cities, 12.3; rural Kansas, 15.6. These rates are much more comparable as measures of the level of natality in these two population groups than are their crude rates. This simple type of age-adjusted rate will be higher than the crude rate in any population where the proportion of young women, let us say women under thirty, is significantly lower than in the standard population, and it will be lower than the crude rate where the proportion of women of these ages is significantly higher. Consequently the age-adjusted rates for cities are generally lower than their crude rates because they contain large proportions of young women, while the age-adjusted rates for rural communities are generally higher than their crude rates because they contain smaller proportions of young women. Other types of adjusted rates may also be calculated when the data measuring different characteristics (marital condition, education, and so forth) are available.

Marital Birth Rates. These rates are usually calculated by dividing the number of legitimate births by the number of married women of the child-bearing ages and multiplying the result by 1,000. The equation is legitimate births/married women 15–44 $\times$ 1,000 = legitimate birth rate. If legitimate births are recorded by age of mother one can also calculate age-specific marital birth rates. This rate can also be standardized or adjusted for age differences between the married women of different populations, thus making the rates still more comparable.

Reproduction Rates. Since none of the rates described above measures the fertility of the average woman in terms of the number of children born in relation to the number needed to maintain a given population, a further refinement of the age-specific birth rates was developed which gave a single figure called the *reproduction rate*.[4] The reproduction rate is usually calculated in two forms: the *gross* reproduction rate, and the *net* reproduction rate.

The Gross Reproduction Rate. The gross reproduction rate is based on the following assumptions: (1) that out of 1,000 female children born at a given time all will live through the childbearing period, *i.e.*, to forty-five or fifty years of age; and (2) that the age-specific birth rates prevailing at the date for which the calculation is made will continue throughout the childbearing life of the group of women under consideration. If the number of girl babies born per 1,000 women is found to be 1,500, then the gross reproduction rate is written 1,500, 150, or 1.50 depending on whether one prefers to think of the number per 1,000, per 100, or per woman. What such a rate tells us is that if 1,000 girls born at a given time all live through the childbearing period and if at each age interval they bear children at the age-

[4] Robert R. Kuczynski, *The Balance of Births and Deaths*, Vol. 1, Chap. 3, The Macmillan Company, New York, 1928; also *The Measurement of Population Growth, Methods and Results*, Chaps. 4, 6, Oxford University Press, New York, 1936.

specific rates prevailing in a given year or period, *e.g.*, in 1950, they would have borne one-half (50 per cent) more daughters than were needed to replace themselves. If, on the other hand, the rate turned out to be less than 1,000, *e.g.*, 950, they would have borne only 95 per cent of the number of daughters needed to replace themselves. This is simply expressing total fertility in terms of daughters. The rate then shows the rate of increase or decrease—above or below 1,000— in a generation, *under the assumptions made*.

The Net Reproduction Rate. The net reproduction rate, unlike the gross, makes allowance for the fact that there will be deaths in any group of females between the time they are born and the time at which they complete their reproductive life. The extent to which taking account of deaths reduces the net reproduction rate below the gross reproduction rate depends on the proportion of women dying between birth and menopause and on the distribution of the deaths by age. If infant and child mortalities are very high, comparatively few of the girls born reach the reproductive age, perhaps only 60 per cent, and another 20 to 25 per cent may die during the age period fifteen to forty-nine. In the United States and a number of other Western countries where mortality is low, about 95.0 per cent of the girls born live to fifteen years of age and about 90.0 per cent live through the childbearing period. The *Demographic Yearbook of the United Nations, 1949–50*, gives the gross reproduction rate of the United States in 1948 as 1.542 and the net as 1.462, while among the Moslems in Palestine (1940) the rates were 3.81 and 2.17, respectively. In the United States the net reproduction rate was only about 5 per cent below the gross, while among the Moslems in Palestine the net was over 43 per cent lower than the gross. Obviously the net reproduction rate is more realistic than the gross if we would measure the probable increase of population in a generation under the assumed conditions, but the gross is the better measure of fertility since it tells us that among the Arabs in Palestine the number of girls born per woman averaged 3.81 and the number of boys born averaged 4.02 (3.81 × 1.055), or a total of 7.83 children per woman.

It is very important to remember the conditions assumed in the calculation of these reproduction rates, namely, that the age-specific birth rates prevailing at a given time apply to the entire reproductive life of the women being studied and, for the net reproduction rate, that the age-specific death rates of this same period also remain constant throughout life. No fault can be found with the statement that in 1948, *on these assumptions*, the women of the United States would increase by 46.2 per cent in a generation (net reproduction rate, 1.462). But since age-specific birth rates may fluctuate rather widely from year to year for a variety of reasons, such as a change in the age at marriage and a change in the spacing of births as well as a change in the average number of births per woman, these reproduction rates may fluctuate in much the same way as crude birth rates. Hence, they do not give an accurate measure of changes in the size of the average completed family or of changes in trends of growth. In the long run, the factors that determine whether a population will increase or decrease, and the rate at which such increase or decrease will occur, are (1) the changes in the proportion of the women in a population having children, and (2) the changes in the average number of their children. Thus all the above measures of current natality are more or less defective as measures of change either in trend of growth or in size of the completed family, chiefly because they either fail to take account of changes in the composition of the population and/or because they assume that current age-specific birth rates apply to the entire reproductive life of that group of women whose natality is being measured. As a consequence, the changes in natality rates and in average number of children shown by these rates must not be accepted as measures of change in the average size of the completed family. This point will be discussed in more detail in Secs. 3 to 5 below.

Intrinsic Birth Rate. This is a rate based upon a *stable* population,[5] *i.e.,* a population having an age-sex composition such as would ultimately result from the indefinite continuance of the age-specific natality and mortality rates prevailing at a given date. The intrinsic death rate is likewise derived by applying a given set of age-specific death rates to the stable population, and the difference between these two is the intrinsic rate of natural increase. Thus the intrinsic birth rate is based on a hypothetical set of conditions which no actual population is likely to attain. Since none of these measures of natality is wholly satisfactory for the purpose of making comparisons between populations, it will be well to go into somewhat more detail regarding the demographic conditions which render them unsatisfactory.

Factors Affecting Measures of Natality. Recent experience has shown very clearly that the age-specific birth rates which constitute basic data for most of the more refined measures of natality are much affected by changes in age at marriage, in the proportions of women married at a given time, and in the spacing of births, *i.e.,* by changes in the length of the intervals between márriage and a first birth, between first and second births, between second and third births, etc.[6] These changes in marital condition and in the spacing of births in early married life appear to be rather closely related to changes

---

[5] For an explanation of the uses of intrinsic rates and the method of calculating them, see Margaret Jarman Hagood, *Statistics for Sociologists,* p. 894, Reynal & Hitchcock, Inc., New York, 1941; U.S. Bureau of the Census, *Population, Differential Fertility, 1940 and 1910, Standardized Fertility Rates and Reproduction Rates,* p. 5, G.P.O., Washington, D.C., 1944.

[6] J. Hajnal, "Aspects of Recent Trend in Marriage in England and Wales," *Population Studies,* Vol. 1, No. 1, pp. 72–86, 1947; P. K. Whelpton, "Reproduction Rates Adjusted for Age, Parity, Fecundity, and Marriage," *Am. Statis. Assn. J.,* Vol. 41, No. 236, p. 506, 1946.

in social and economic conditions; hence, they tend to fluctuate as these conditions change. Thus, in the United States, the marriage rate declined rapidly in the early 1930's as the depression became more severe. In due course this affected the birth rate. In addition, the depression caused a postponement of many births among married couples, thus lengthening the intervals between births and still further reducing both the crude birth rate and certain age-specific birth rates. Later, as recovery ensued the marriage rate rose and many, perhaps most, postponed births were made up. These changes contributed to a substantial increase in natality rates of all kinds. These rates were further raised by an extraordinary number of marriages of men called into military service after 1939. This high marriage rate among men in the armed forces was in sharp contrast to what happened in 1917 to 1918 during World War I, and it came as a surprise to many of us who had long been interested in population changes.

One consequence of these changes in the marital composition of the population and in the age composition of the married population was that the age-specific birth rates for first births in 1942 were so high that if they prevailed regularly there would be 1,084 first births per 1,000 women passing through the childbearing period. This, of course, would be impossible. The remarkable character of such a rate will be even clearer if it is realized that normally only about 800 women out of each 1,000 passing through the childbearing period will have had a first birth, since 8 to 10 per cent do not marry and about another 10 per cent or more are childless.[7] The rather rapid lowering of the age at marriage, the increase in the proportion of the women marrying, and the lessening of the interval between marriage and the first birth, coupled with the first births to older women because of the postponement of such births from earlier years to 1942, led to a very unusual situation in that year. In any given year the unusual distribution of all births by age of mother arising from such changes may give a total fertility and a reproduction rate which is quite unusual and therefore is misleading either as a measure of average size of family or as a measure of the trend in fertility.

Currently there is no fully satisfactory method of telling what portion of the change in natality rates, *e.g.*, in total fertility, in age-specific birth rates, and in reproduction rates, is due to changes in the composition of the population and to changes in the spacing of births within marriage, and what part may be due to a change in the trend of the average number of children born per woman, *i.e.*, in realized fertility. There may be rather large changes in age-specific birth rates and in gross and net reproduction rates with little or no change in the average number of children born per woman. It is important to remember this fact in assessing the significance of changes in the rates described above.

[7] Whelpton, *op. cit.*, p. 503.

Natality Rates and Future Growth of Population. Because the net re-production rate measured the percentage change in the size of a population which would take place in a generation with the continuance of a given set of age-specific birth rates and death rates, it came to be regarded by many persons not only as a measure of fertility under the conditions assumed but also as indicative of probable future growth. This was unfortunate, for the rate certainly was not developed for this purpose. It was intended only to measure the reproductive behavior of different populations more precisely than the other measures in use. Moreover, although there was no basis for assuming that a rise in the reproduction rates was proof of a rise in the average number of children born per woman, and hence of a rise in actual completed fertility, this assumption was often made. As a consequence it was rather widely believed that the "baby boom" after 1940 represented a reversal of the trend in fertility which had prevailed for some time prior to that date. The data available now do not permit of a valid conclusion on this point, although the continuance of a crude rate of 24 to 25 up to the time of going to press makes such a reversal appear increasingly probable. It is important to realize that in a population where control of the size of the family has become largely voluntary, early marriage, the early filling of the family to the desired size, and an increase in the proportion of the popu-lation marrying may change age-specific birth rates and reproduction rates as quickly and to almost as great a degree as they would change the crude birth rate. If follows, therefore, that we cannot be certain of changes in actual completed fertility just because there are changes in the more com-monly used natality rates.

2. ADEQUACY OF THE WORLD'S VITAL STATISTICS

At present it is impossible to calculate natality rates of any kind for a very considerable part of the people in the world because they have never had a census from which a base population could be obtained, or because births are not registered at all, or because registration is so incomplete that the rates calculated are of little value. Generally the first two of these condi-tions are found together.[8]

On the other hand, it should be said that in some countries where the natality rates are known to be quite inaccurate they may have much the same degree of error year after year. Under these circumstances the changes in rates may tell us something about what is happening to the birth rate within a group, although the rates themselves should not be used directly for comparison with other areas or countries. A person who is experienced in the study of vital statistics and who knows the vital rates likely to prevail

[8] A good discussion of the quality of vital statistics in the world will be found in *Demographic Yearbook, 1949–50,* Chaps. 1 and 2, United Nations, New York, 1950.

among peoples living at different levels of comfort can often judge fairly well of the degree of credence to be accorded official data. Thus in a population living in agricultural villages where practically every female marries at an early age, where there is comparatively little interference with the regular processes of conception and gestation, and where the level of living is very low, one immediately becomes highly suspicious of the reliability of data which show a crude birth rate of less than 35 or 40. The same can be said of a death rate in such a population which is below 25 or 30. Such a population is practically certain to have extremely poor sanitation, and modern medical care will be practically nonexistent. Again, a birth rate of less than 25 or 30 is open to suspicion unless the population in question is well started on the road to industrialization and a considerable portion of it lives in cities, while national birth rates of less than 20 are seldom found except in highly industrialized and urbanized lands and death rates of less than 14 or 15 are seldom found except in conjunction with low birth rates.

Actually, therefore, we are not quite as helpless in judging of the level of natality rates in the countries for which the data are lacking, or greatly deficient, as parts of the first statement above might seem to imply. Sometimes there are data for country A, let us say, which are indicative of the level of its natality and mortality rates although precise rates cannot be calculated. In the case of B it may be reasonable to assume, because of similarities in modes of living to those in A, that B's natality rate is much the same as A's. This may or may not be true of their mortality rates. Naturally, as long as we must reason from inadequate data and from general likenesses and differences, we must recognize the uncertainties in our results, but I would argue that we are not quite as helpless in arriving at useful conclusions regarding the natality and mortality among many peoples for whom there are no, or inadequate, vital statistics as would appear at first sight.

An illustration may be given of the way in which the inadequate *vital* data provided by a country may help us to understand its vital phenomena, although they should not be considered precise. The recorded decline in the crude birth rate of India from 33.7 in the period 1935 to 1939, when the registration was probably not more than 75 or 80 per cent complete according to well-informed Indian and foreign scholars,[9] to 27.2 in the period from 1945 to 1948 appears so unusual that the student of population is at once alerted to seek some explanation other than a decline in fertility. To the author the most reasonable explanation is that this decline in recorded rate reflects the deterioration of registration in the postwar years during which there has been much civil disturbance. There are several reasons for doubt-

[9] Gyan Chand, *The Problem of Population,* Oxford Pamphlets on Indian Affairs No. 19, p. 29, Oxford University Press, London, 1945; *India's Teeming Millions,* p. 98, George Allen & Unwin, Ltd., London, 1939; and S. Chandrasekhar, *India's Population: Fact and Policy,* p. 59, The John Day Co., New York, 1946.

ing that the crude birth rate actually declined by 6.5 points, or by almost one-fifth, during this period: (1) there is no suggestion anywhere that the voluntary control of the size of the family is making such rapid headway in India as these figures would imply; and (2) the recent census of India (excluding Pakistan) showed a decennial increase of about 13.5 per cent, or of about 1.3 per cent per year. But if the Indian Union had had a birth rate of only 27.8 for the decade 1941 to 1950, which is the average of the recorded rate for the eight years 1941 to 1948, then it could have had a crude death rate of only about 14.3 during this decade. The average of the recorded death rate was 21.2 for the period 1941 to 1948. This is a death rate almost one-half higher than would have been possible with a birth rate of 27.8 and a decennial increase of 13.5 per cent. (The census count in India is generally believed to be fairly accurate.) But if the recorded birth rate of 33.7 in 1935 to 1939 was only 75 to 80 per cent of the actual, as seems highly probable, and if the recorded decline from 33.7 to 27.2 was due to the increasing inaccuracies of registration, it is probable that the real crude birth rate is in the neighborhood of 40 to 45 and the crude death rate is about 13 points lower, say 27 to 32. The rates arrived at by this line of reasoning seem much more reasonable to most students of demography than the recorded rates. It may be further pointed out that in much of South and East Asia the crude death rate is probably much like that of India, but since in some of these countries the conditions affecting the death rate are even less favorable than in India, it is probable that they have higher death rates and consequently lower rates of increase.

3. THE TREND IN NATALITY

Rather large fluctuations in the birth rate occur many times when there is a great catastrophe. Care should be taken not to confuse these temporary fluctuations with a long-time trend. In addition, what may at first glance appear to be a trend may represent only an improvement or a deterioration in the registration of vital phenomena. Hence, it is often difficult to be certain whether changes in the birth rate indicate a trend or a mere fluctuation which has little significance in the long-time growth of population. At the present moment we may very well be in a period when it is unusually difficult to tell the difference between a mere fluctuation and a longer-time trend even in countries with reliable vital statistics.

As has been noted at several points and as will be elaborated in Chap. XI, the birth rates among peoples with low levels of living are relatively stable when compared with their death rates. It seems to the author quite probable, however, that the amplitude of the fluctuations in the birth rate will increase as the birth rate more and more comes under voluntary control in populations with improving levels of living, because of the increasing possibility of shifting the number of births desired from one date to another when the number does not exceed three or four. If this is the case, then considerable changes in the birth rates now in most general use as well as the continuation of these rates for several years may not indicate a trend in fertility as has been quite commonly assumed. This point will be explained more fully below.

Looking back over the past century, we find that all the measures of natality used agree in one thing, namely, that there has been a rather steady decline in fertility in most European nations lying west of a line drawn from Trieste to Danzig and in those lands peopled chiefly by the descendants of the people living in this portion of Europe. The crude birth rates in Table 8-6 show this, and such a long-continued decline even in these crude rates as is shown in most of these countries could hardly take place without an accompanying decline in the average size of the completed family. This decline in the birth rate is clearly marked in countries as different in many other respects as Sweden and Spain, Great Britain and Hungary, France and Australia. Japan also had a declining birth rate after 1920.[10] The decline of the birth rate in Europe is especially marked since about 1880, and everywhere it seems to have been hastened by World War I.

Although there was a more rapid decline in the crude birth rate in Western Europe since about 1875 to 1880, it should not be assumed as is frequently done that this period represented the end of an era of increasing birth rates in this part of the world and the inauguration of the modern decline in natality.[11] There is no question regarding the relatively rapid decline in the crude birth rate from about 1875 or 1880 to the late 1930's in most Western countries, but I am unable to accept the view that there had been any significant rise in the decades preceding 1880.

There are several reasons for my doubt. For one thing the vital records for Sweden, which has had a good and continuous record since 1749, do not seem to justify the belief that 1875 or thereabouts marks the end of one period and the beginning of another. There have been significant fluctuations in Sweden's birth rate ever since births were first recorded. Between the years 1749 and 1875 (126 years) there were 30 years that had a lower birth rate than 1875.[12] If we use five-year averages, there were three such periods having a lower birth rate than 1871 to 1875. However, there was no 10-year period in which this was the case. The periods of low birth rates generally followed rather prolonged crop failures, and during most of this time the

[10] Elizabeth Boody Schumpeter *et al.*, *The Industrialization of Japan and Manchukuo, 1930–1940*, pp. 92–104, The Macmillan Company, New York, 1940.

[11] G. Udny Yule, "On the Changes in the Marriage- and Birth-rates in England and Wales during the Past Half Century; with an Inquiry as to Their Probable Causes," *Royal Statis. Soc. J.*, Vol. 69, p. 127, 1906.

[12] Sweden, Statistiska Centralbyrån, *Statistisk Årsbok för Sverige, 1950*, pp. 53–56, P. A. Norstedt & Söner, Stockholm, 1950.

Table 8-6. Average Crude Birth Rates, 1808 to 1950 [1]

Year	Austria	Belgium	Bulgaria	Denmark	England and Wales	Finland	France	Germany	Hungary	Ireland
1946–1950	16.6	17.5	24.6[2]	20.6	18.0	26.5	20.9	16.6[3]	18.4[2]	22.1
1938–1942	18.7	14.1	22.2	18.6	14.7	20.2	14.4	18.7	19.6	19.8
1928–1932	16.4	18.2	30.6	18.6	16.1	20.2	17.7	17.0	24.8	19.6[4]
1918–1922	21.9[2]	18.4	34.9	23.7	20.9	23.2	17.3	21.7	27.6	20.6
1908–1912	26.5	23.6	40.9	27.5	25.2	30.0	19.4	30.0	....	23.3
1898–1902	31.4	28.8	39.6	29.7	28.8	32.6	21.7	35.7	....	23.0
1888–1892	31.7	29.1	36.7	30.8	30.9	33.4	22.6	36.3	....	22.7
1878–1882	33.2	31.4	....	31.9	34.4	36.2	24.9	38.0	....	24.8
1868–1872	....	32.1	....	30.2	35.3	33.7	25.3	37.4	....	27.4
1858–1862	....	31.3	....	32.4	34.5	36.8	26.8	36.3		
1848–1852	....	29.8	....	31.3	33.4	36.6	27.0	36.1		
1838–1842	....	33.9	....	29.8	31.6	34.3	28.3			
1828–1832	....	....	....	29.1	....	36.9	29.9			
1818–1822	....	....	....	32.4	....	37.6	31.7			
1808–1812	....	....	....	30.1	....	35.0	31.4			

Year	Italy	Netherlands	Norway	Poland	Romania	Russia	Scotland	Yugoslavia	Spain	Sweden
1946–1950	21.1	25.9	20.7	....	21.9[2]	....	19.0	29.5[2]	21.4	18.2
1938–1942	22.5[5]	20.6	16.1	24.3[2]	25.7	44.2[2]	17.4	26.3[2]	20.2	15.7
1928–1932	25.5	22.7	17.0	31.3	34.8	43.8[2]	19.1	....	28.2	15.2
1918–1922	26.4	26.1	24.2	32.7[2]	36.4[2]	40.9[2]	23.9	....	29.7	21.0
1908–1912	32.7	28.7	26.0	38.2	41.5	45.6[2]	26.6	38.2[2]	32.7	24.7
1898–1902	33.3	31.9	29.8	43.7	39.2	48.8	29.7	38.5	34.3	26.8
1888–1892	37.0	33.1	30.2	....	40.6	48.6	30.9	43.5	35.7	27.9
1878–1882	36.7	35.7	31.0	....	37.6	48.4	34.0	41.7	36.7	29.6
1868–1872	36.9	35.3	29.4	....	33.5	48.9[2]	34.7	43.6	....	29.0
1858–1862	....	33.6	32.9	....	....	....	34.9	....	....	34.1
1848–1852	....	....	31.1	....	....	....	....	....	....	31.5
1838–1842	....	....	28.5	....	....	....	....	....	....	30.5
1828–1832	....	....	31.7	....	....	....	....	....	....	32.5
1818–1822	....	....	32.7	....	....	....	....	....	....	34.2
1808–1812	....	....	....	....	....	....	....	....	....	31.8

Year	Switzerland	Argentina	Canada	Chile	Guatemala	Honduras (British)	Jamaica	Puerto Rico	United States	Ceylon
1946–1950	19.0	24.8[2]	27.2	33.1	50.5	38.8	31.9	40.5	24.1	39.7
1938–1942	16.2	22.7	21.6	32.9	46.8	34.9	32.1	39.2	18.5	36.2
1928–1932	17.0	29.4	23.4	38.8	45.0	37.4	34.8	38.3	18.6	38.7
1918–1922	19.7	33.9[2]	25.0[2]	39.5	41.0	38.5[2]	....	38.3[2]	23.4	38.4
1908–1912	25.1	37.3[2]	26.1[2]	39.5	38.7	41.4[2]	37.4[2]	....	....	37.8
1898–1902	28.7	36.3[2]	20.2	38.4	42.8	....	39.2	26.4[2]	....	38.4
1888–1892	27.6	....	21.6	35.5	44.3	....	37.7	30.0	....	30.7
1878–1882	30.1	....	....	40.0	....	....	....	....	....	25.6
1868–1872	....	....	....	42.3	....	....	....	....	....	25.2
1858–1862	....	....	....	42.2						

Year	India[6]	Japan	Philippine Islands	Algeria[7]	Egypt[8]	Union of South Africa[9]	Australia	New Zealand
1946–1950	26.7	30.9	....	21.9[2]	43.2[2]	26.4	23.4	25.3
1938–1942	31.9	28.9	32.4[2]	22.8[2]	40.9	25.1	18.2	20.5
1928–1932	33.6	33.0	35.4	23.7	44.3	25.6	19.3	18.6
1918–1922	32.5	33.9	33.6	22.9	41.1	28.1	24.7	23.3
1908–1912	38.3	33.8	32.4	29.7	45.0	31.8[2]	27.2	26.7
1898–1902	37.4	32.1	30.8[2]	30.0[2]	45.2[2]	....	27.1	25.7
1888–1892	34.8	28.8	46.6	30.9[2]	43.4[2]	....	34.7	29.5
1878–1882	....	24.7	....	33.9[2]	....	....	35.2	39.7
1868–1872	....	....	....	32.1[2]	....	....	38.6	41.4
1858–1862	....	....	....	38.7[2]				
1848–1852	....	....	....	39.0[2]				
1838–1842	....	....	....	29.9[2]				
1828–1832	....	....	....	19.8[2]				

[1] For the current data on birth rates the reader is referred to *Population Index*.
[2] Austria, 1919 to 1922; Bulgaria, 1945 to 1947; Hungary, 1945 to 1948; Poland, 1938, 1919 to 1922; Romania, 1945 to 1947, 1920 to 1922; U.S.S.R., 1933 to 1935, 1928, 1920 to 1924; Russia, 1906 to 1909, 1876 to 1880, 1866 to 1870; Yugoslavia, 1948 to 1950, 1938 to 1939, 1909 to 1912; Argentina, 1946 to 1949, 1915 to 1919, 1909 to 1913, 1899 to 1902; Canada, 1920 to 1924, 1911 to 1913; Honduras (British), 1922 to 1924, 1909 to 1911; Jamaica, 1906 to 1910; Puerto Rico, 1921 to 1925, 1894 to 1898; Philippines, 1938, 1903 to 1907; Algeria, 1946 to 1949, 1931 and 1933 to 1935, 1901 to 1905, 1891 to 1895, 1881 to 1885, 1872 to 1876, 1861 to 1865, 1851 to 1855, 1841 to 1845, 1831 to 1835; Egypt, 1946 to 1948, 1905 to 1909, 1901 to 1904; Union of South Africa, 1910 to 1914.   [3] Federal Republic.   [4] Irish Free State.
[5] Prewar territory.   [6] 1947 to 1949, Republic of India only.   [7] Europeans only.
[8] Before 1917, Bedouins were not included in population estimates.   [9] Europeans only.

162

fluctuations in the birth rate were due to prior fluctuations in marriage rate rather than to a secular trend. During the period 1800 to 1875 the fluctuations in Sweden's birth rates are such that the author believes it would be stretching the facts to speak of any trend at all, and most certainly no upward trend is discernible. The birth rate in Sweden was considerably higher during the 1850's than during the 1870's, but it was also higher in the former period than at any other time since Sweden's data have been gathered, except during the 1750's. If we assume that Sweden's data have become somewhat more accurate with the passage of time, it is likely that some of the irregularities shown in Fig. 8-2 would disappear, but the data would still contain irregularities which make it appear extremely doubtful whether there was any definite trend in Sweden's birth rate until about 1860, since which time there was a rather steady decline until the later 1930's.

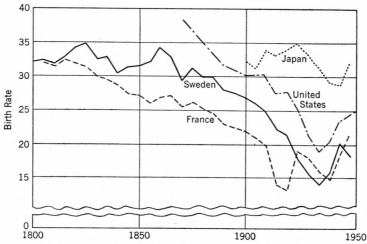

Fig. 8-2. Crude birth rates (five-year averages), France, Sweden, United States, and Japan, 1800 to 1950.

In France and in several other countries for which we have fairly reliable data for most of the nineteenth century (Belgium, the Netherlands, and Scotland) the decline in the crude birth rate was so nearly continuous during most of that century that there is no question of a rise, and where there has been only a small rise the improving completeness of registration may very well explain it (Table 8-6). The rise in the crude birth rates of Denmark, Finland, Germany, and Norway in the period 1878 to 1882 over the preceding decade may very well represent primarily the recovery from the depression of the early 1870's and some improvement in the completeness of registration. Moreover, it seems questionable to the author to regard the rather small rise in the rate for 1878 to 1882 as compared with that for 1868 to

1872 as proof of a rise in the birth rate, for in three of these four countries the recorded birth rate 1858 to 1862 was above that for 1878 to 1882, while in Germany the rising birth rate from the period 1848 to 1852 to the period 1878 to 1882 may very well be due in considerable measure to the improvement in registration.

We have no birth statistics for the United States as a whole until after 1933, but we have had age data given in the censuses in some detail since 1800, and we find that the ratio of children under five to women sixteen to forty-four (Fig. 9–1, page 175), who were likely to be their mothers, had fallen steadily from 1810 to 1940, with the exception of 1850 to 1860, when there was a slight rise, probably due to the great influx of young immigrants during the preceding decade.[13]

Finally, Farr (often called the father of modern vital statistics) did not think that there had been any significant change in the birth rate in England and Wales from the beginning of compulsory registration (1838) through 1876.

> There were in the first year [1838] 30.3 births registered to every 1,000 inhabitants, in the last year [1876] 36.6; and after allowing for any natural increase of the rate in the interval [i.e., for improvement in registration], or any deficiency of registration in the last year of all, I am inclined to think the actual birth rate of living children was 36 per 1,000 during the 39½ years of civil registration.[14]

These facts lead the author to believe that it is impossible to fix any definite time for the onset of the modern decline in the birth rate in Western countries as a group. The evidence seems to him to indicate that it did not occur at the same date in all of them. This is as would be expected if this decline is rather closely related to the passing from an economy in which agriculture was greatly predominant and in which most people lived fairly close to the subsistence level to an economy in which agriculture occupied a decreasing proportion of the population, while nonagricultural work in cities drew an increasing proportion and the level of living was rising. This change in the level of living which seems to have been associated most closely with the decline in the birth rate took place at different times and at different rates in different countries and even in different regions of the same country. Thus in the United States there is no doubt whatever that fertility began to decline in New England some decades before it did in the Middle West and in the latter region earlier than it did in the southern Appalachian region.

[13] Walter F. Willcox, "The Change in the Proportion of Children in the United States and in the Birth Rate in France during the Nineteenth Century," Am. Statis. Assn. Pub., Vol. 12 n.s., pp. 490–499, 1911.

[14] William Farr, Vital Statistics, p. 89, Offices of the Sanitary Institute, London, 1885.

As was indicated above, age-specific birth rates, adjusted birth rates, and reproduction rates where available show the same general trend as the crude birth rate among the Western peoples, and as will be shown below, there is little doubt that the decline in all these rates of natality has been accompanied by a decline in the average size of the family, *i.e.*, by a decline in fertility, although the decline in rates does not measure this decline in fertility with exactness.

4. THE TREND IN FAMILY SIZE

The following data show the change (decline) in the number of children ever born to women at ages forty-five and over in the United States as reported in the censuses of 1910 and 1940. They measure the decline in completed fertility in the 30 years preceding 1940 and 1910, respectively (Table 8-7). The important point to note here is that without exception there is a decline in the number of children born in completed families from the earliest group of women from whom data were secured, namely, those who were aged sixty-five to seventy-four in 1910 and who had completed their families between 1880 and 1889, to the most recent group, namely, those who had completed their families in the five years preceding 1940 (1935 to 1939). The change in the average number of children born to women who completed their families 1880 to 1889 (4.786) and 1890 to 1899 (4.712) was rather small but it is a decline. When these data are considered in conjunction with the ratios of children under five years old to women sixteen to forty-four shown on Fig. 9-1, there is no reason to doubt that the decline in the size of the family in the United States dates from early in the nineteenth century, especially in the less agricultural regions of the country. It may now be in process of stabilization, although the data available up to the time of writing are not conclusive as to trend.

Table 8-7. Number of Children Ever Born per 1,000 Women Aged 45–74, United States, 1940 and 1910 [1]
(Standardized for marital status)

Age of woman	Number of children ever born per 1,000 women	
	1940	1910
45–49	2,758	4,288
50–54	2,891	4,484
55–64	3,066	4,712
65–74	3,364	4,786

[1] U.S. Bureau of the Census, *Population, Differential Fertility 1940 and 1910, Standardized Fertility Rates and Reproduction Rates*, p. 8, G.P.O., Washington, D.C., 1944.

Somewhat similar data in other countries tell the same story. A special study of fertility in England and Wales carried out in connection with the 1911 census showed the number of children ever born to wives with completed families (age over forty-five at census) who were married at different dates. Although the data in Table 8-8 are not directly comparable with those for the United States, there can be no reasonable doubt that the trend in the size of the completed family in England and Wales was downward from the decade preceding 1880 (women married in 1851 or earlier) up to 1946. Although there is some evidence that the change in family size in recent years has been negligible, it is too soon to assert positively that the downward trend has come to an end.[15] It is significant, however, that the rise in

Table 8-8. Average Size of Completed Family, Great Britain, 1946 and 1911

Married women, Great Britain, 1946[1]			Wives over 45, England and Wales, 1911[2]		
Date of marriage	Duration of marriage, years	Average number of children born	Date of marriage	Duration of marriage, years	Average number of children born
1925–1929	17–21	2.19[3]	1881–1886	25–30	5.25
1920–1924	22–26	2.38[3]	1871–1881	30–40	6.05
1915–1919	27–31	2.53	1861–1871	40–50	6.79
1910–1914	32–36	2.90	1851–1861	50–60	7.28
1900–1909	37–46	3.37	Before 1851	60 and over	7.61

[1] United Kingdom, Royal Commission on Population, *Report*, p. 25, H.M.S.O., London, 1949.

[2] Great Britain, Census Office, *Fertility of Marriage*, Pt. 2, p. xcvii, H.M.S.O., London, 1923. (Census of England and Wales, 1911, Vol. 13.) Standardized on all families in England and Wales at each duration of marriage.

[3] Families not quite complete by 1946.

the crude birth rate in Great Britain in recent years is thought by the Commission to be due primarily to the changes in the proportion of persons marrying and the age at which they married rather than to any increase in the average size of the completed family. The Commission does not commit itself regarding probable future changes in family size.

In connection with the censuses of France a study is generally made showing the "productivity of marriages." The fertility of completed families cannot be shown with as much precesion over a period of years as in the above studies because the age of the head of the family rather than that of the wife was used in the 1906 tabulations. The results of the tabulations made

[15] United Kingdom, Royal Commission on Population, *Report*, p. 25, H.M.S.O., London, 1949.

of 1906 and 1931 data are shown in Table 8-9. The average number of children born has almost certainly been declining since about 1890 (head of family born in 1851 or earlier) and the decline was still continuing for women who had recently passed forty-five years of age in 1931. The 1936 census showed an average of 213 children surviving to married heads of families fifty-five years of age and over.[16] In 1946 the number of children surviving per 100 married men aged forty-five to fifty-four was 201.[17] Because of this change in base one cannot be certain about the decline in the size of the average family between 1936 and 1946, but it seems probable that the decline was still continuing at the later date.

Table 8-9. Average Size of Completed Family, France, 1931 and 1906

Women: married, widowed, or divorced, 1931[1]			Head of family: married, 1906[2]		
Date of birth	Age	Average number of children born	Date of birth	Age	Average number of children born
1881–1885	45–49	2.33	1852–1856	50–54	3.43
1876–1880	50–54	2.47	1847–1851	55–59	3.53
1871–1875	55–59	2.64	1842–1846	60–64	3.60
1866–1870	60–64	2.75	1837–1841	65–69	3.58
1861–1865	65–69	2.85	Before 1836	70 and over	3.56
1851–1860	70–79	2.94			
Before 1850	80 and over	3.03			

[1] Statistique Générale de la France, *Études démographiques, No. 1, Reproduction nette en Europe*, p. 35, Imprimerie Nationale, Paris, 1941.
[2] Statistique Générale de la France, *Statistique des familles en 1906*, p. 13, Imprimerie Nationale, Paris, 1912.

It will not be possible to present comparable data for other countries, but there is little doubt that a similar decline in the average number of children born per family has been taking place in practically all countries of European culture, although the time when the decline started and its extent and rapidity have varied considerably from country to country. Thus the level of fertility came to vary considerably at any given time between different peoples and groups even where the general pattern of the culture was much the same.

In what preceded, nations and peoples have been treated as wholes or units. From the standpoint of fertility, however, this is not sufficient if we

[16] Paul Gasc, "Chronique de démographie," *J. de la société de statistique de Paris*, Vol. 86, p. 224, 1945.
[17] Preliminary data sent to the writer through the kindness of A. Sauvy.

would understand the trend in fertility among most Western peoples during the past century. The more detailed trends will be discussed in Chap. IX while the differentials in fertility developing between peoples having different cultural backgrounds will be described in Chap. XII.

5. REPLACEMENT

There has been much interest in recent years in the fertility of a population which would be adequate to replace it or to add to it at a given rate. A short discussion bearing on this point will be inserted here. In the United States in 1949 about 96.5 per cent of the white females born could expect to live to fifteen years of age and 92.4 per cent would live to forty-five years of age. Thus the loss during the childbearing ages was only about 4.1 per cent, and from birth to menopause was only about 8.0 per cent. Another 8 to 9 per cent of those who enter the childbearing period do not marry, according to the 1950 census data, and since the illegitimate birth rate is almost negligible they contribute very little to the total birth rate. (Most women who bear illegitimate children later marry and their children are reported as legitimate.) When allowance is made for women (fifteen and over) who die before they bear a child and for those who do not marry, it is probable that between 10 and 12 per cent of the women who enter the childbearing period do not bear children for these reasons. For purposes of illustration it will be assumed that 11 per cent of the 96,540 females, out of each 100,000 born, who reach fifteen years of age (1949) do not have children either because they do not marry or because they die before they have borne children. Thus about 10,600 must be deducted from the number who enter the childbearing age because they are very unlikely to become mothers. Hence, there are about 85,900 out of each 100,000 females born who marry and who live long enough to have families of average size. This calculation is, of course, only approximate.

Although we do not know what proportion of the married women are not fecund (cannot have children), it probably is not under 4 per cent and may very well be 2 or 3 per cent higher. If 5 per cent of them are assumed to be infecund—in the author's opinion, this is very conservative—then of the original 100,000 girl babies only 81,600 married women remain to provide for the replacement of their generation, *i.e.*, as mothers of the 100,000 daughters needed to replace the original cohort of 100,000 girl babies. To do this each *fecund* married woman must, therefore, have 1.23 daughters. Since, as a rule, 105 to 106 boys are born to each 100 girls, the total number of children each *fecund* married woman would need to bear to maintain the population under the conditions defined above would be about 2.52. If 10 per cent of the fecund married women included in the 81,600 given above remains infertile by choice, then the number of children that would be needed by the average *fertile* woman to replace the original cohort (100,000) would increase to about 2.80. Such calculations cannot be exact. Moreover, for any future period death rates and marital condition and the proportion of infertile marriages may change. However, 2.8 does indicate the approximate average size of the family needed by each *fertile* couple to maintain a population of a given size under conditions similar to those which prevail today. At present the most highly variable element in such a calculation is probably the proportion of fecund couples that remain infertile.

It should be noted that the women of the United States, England, and France for whom completed family size has been given above had higher death rates than those now prevailing. In addition, the age at marriage has been somewhat higher and the proportion married has been somewhat lower in the past than recently. These differences would tend to increase the average size of the family needed by each fertile couple to maintain a given population in the past as compared with the present. On the other hand, it is probable that illegitimate births have been somewhat higher in the past than at present and that fecund but infertile couples have been proportionally fewer. These differences would tend to reduce the average size of the family needed by a fertile married couple to maintain a given population in the past. On the whole the average size of the family needed by a fertile married couple to maintain a given population has probably been declining rather steadily but slowly for some decades, the rate of decline being determined chiefly by the change in the proportion of females dying before they have had time to bear an average size of family, although changes in marital condition are significant.

Obviously the size of the completed family cannot be told until it is completed, but the new techniques of analysis of reproduction by cohorts (women born in a given year), by parity, and by order of birth which are now being developed are much superior to those based on mere age-specific birth rates, such as the reproduction rates described above. In the course of time it seems likely that the use of these techniques will throw new light on the probable reproduction of a given cohort of women some years before they have actually reached menopause. This seems likely because in taking account of the order of birth (first, second, third, and so forth) by age of mother, patterns of reproduction can be established which when related to the social and economic changes likely to effect demographic changes such as age at marriage and the spacing of births, will enable more adequate allowance to be made for temporary changes in age-specific birth rates which may have little or no effect on total fertility.[18] It also seems not

[18] For a complete explanation of the cohort method of studying fertility see P. K. Whelpton, *Cohort Fertility: Native White Women in the United States,* Princeton University Press, Princeton, N.J., 1953.

improbable that the total size of the family desired may prove to be more stable than the distribution of births by age of mother, *i.e.*, the size of the completed family may be less changeable than age-specific birth rates.

Suggestions for Supplementary Reading

CHAND, GYAN: *The Problem of Population*, Oxford Pamphlets on Indian Affairs, No. 19, 31 pp., Oxford University Press, London, 1945.

COOK, ROBERT C.: *Human Fertility: The Modern Dilemma*, 380 pp., William Sloane Associates, New York, 1951.

GREAT BRITAIN, CENSUS OFFICE: *Fertility of Marriage*, 2 vols., H.M.S.O., London, 1917. (Census of England and Wales, 1911, Vol. 13.)

KUCZYNSKI, RORERT R.: *The Balance of Births and Deaths*, 2 vols., The Macmillan Company, New York, 1928–1931. (Brookings Institution, Institute of Economics.)

PEARL, RAYMOND: *The Biology of Population Growth*, 260 pp., Alfred A. Knopf, Inc., New York, 1925.

SPENGLER, JOSEPH J.: *France Faces Depopulation*, 313 pp., Duke University Press, Durham, N.C., 1938.

United Kingdom, Royal Commission on Population: *Report*, 259 pp., H.M.S.O., London, 1949.

U.S. Bureau of the Census: *Vital Statistics Rates in the United States, 1900–1940*, 1051 pp., G.P.O., Washington, D.C., 1943. A similar volume will be published about 1954 adding up-to-date material.

WILLCOX, WALTER F.: *Studies in American Demography*, 556 pp., Cornell University Press, Ithaca, N.Y., 1940.

CHAPTER IX

THE DIFFERENTIAL BIRTH RATE

In the preceding chapter the fact was mentioned that there are considerable differentials in the fertility of different groups. Such differentials are found both between groups and communities within a nation and between different nations or peoples. It is reasonably certain that they are not of recent origin as regards differences between peoples, although they may be greater now than in the past. However, they probably are of more recent origin as between groups within a nation, although we cannot be certain of this.

The extent of the practice of abortion, the rigor with which the segregation of the sexes was enforced at certain periods of life, the practice of allocating young women to the older men as wives, as well as many other practices which might affect fertility, were almost certain to have varying effects on fertility in different clans and tribes and nations. It is also possible that there were certain differentials in fertility as between groups and classes within the same society, although positive evidence of this is lacking. The upper classes of Augustan Rome are generally supposed to have had low fertility. This may always have been true of upper classes because of their strong tendency to succumb to debauchery. We do not know what actually happened. Moreover, we should not conclude that such differentials in fertility, if they did exist, led to differences in rate of growth. If the poorer classes had higher fertility they may have had sufficiently higher death rates to counterbalance their fertility, leaving the rates of increase about equal.

Presumably there would be relatively small differentials in fertility as between groups within a given society or between different societies if it were not for differences in the customs and habits of groups and societies as regards sexual and marital practices and as regards the extent of abortion. Without such limiting factors practically all women would tend to bear children to the maximum of their physiological capacity. As a matter of fact, however, social attitudes which effect a reduction in births below the physiological maximum are so universal that it is almost meaningless to speak of the maximum physiological capacity to reproduce. The significance of this phrase is further impaired because of the very great differences in ability to reproduce between couples as measured by their reproductive performance in the days before there was much voluntary control of conception. There have always been couples where a birth occurs every one and one-half to two years throughout the childbearing years of the woman. For such couples the physiological maximum of reproduction would be very high—possibly 20 to 22 children. However, the author is not aware of any reliable data which indicate an average number of births for any large population exceeding eight or nine. Even such an average would result in a far more rapid increase than any known if as few as one-third of the children born died before they reached the end of the reproduction period. Although it is well known that the fertility of different couples varies greatly,[1] the author has never found any evidence to show that the fecundity, *i.e.*, the physiological capacity to reproduce, was any different in one group or society than in another, and until such evidence is available it must be assumed that differentials in fertility between groups arise as the result of differences in customs, attitudes, and practices which are of social origin rather than as a result of biological differences.[2] In the discussion of differential fertility, therefore, our concern will be with the social factors, using *social* in a very broad sense, which lead different groups to reproduce at different rates. Differentials between nations and peoples in fertility will be discussed in Chap. XII.

1. DIFFERENTIAL FERTILITY IN THE UNITED STATES

In recent years the facts showing differences in the fertility of different social classes have received increasing notice in the popular press. As a consequence it can be taken for granted that many people are now aware

[1] The data on fertility in England and Wales in 1911 which have been referred to in the preceding chapter show that of 30,451 women who were married at 20 to 24 years of age and who had been married 50 years or more in 1911, *i.e.*, who were married in 1861 or earlier, 5.9 per cent had never had a child while 6.4 per cent had had 13 or more children and that over twice as many (24.4 per cent) had borne 10, 11, or 12 children as had borne one, two, or three children (11.9 per cent). All these women were bearing their children at a time when contraception was very little practiced in England and Wales. Great Britain, Census Office, *Fertility of Marriage,* Pt. 2, p. 5, H.M.S.O., London, 1923. (Census of England and Wales, 1911, Vol. 13.)

[2] "Although it is theoretically possible that there has been some decline in the reproductive capacity of the population of Great Britain since the mid-19th century, there is no positive evidence to this effect; indeed, so far as we know, there may well have been an increase. If there has been any decline, it is extremely unlikely that it has been sufficient to account for more than a small part of the fall in family size. Certainly the main cause, and very probably the only cause, of this fall was the spread of deliberate family limitation." United Kingdom Royal Commission on Population, *Report,* p. 219, H.M.S.O., London, 1949.

that in the United States the fertility of rural people is, as a rule, higher than that of city people; also that within city populations there are rather large differences in fertility as between people with large incomes and those with small incomes, between people with a high-school education or better and those with only a grade-school training, and between people engaged in white-collar jobs and those who work with their hands. Increasingly it is realized that the better the economic and social status of a group, the lower is its fertility. This realization has raised many questions in the minds of thoughtful people.

Table 9-1. Average Number of Children per Wife among Pioneer Families Who Originally Settled in New England, by Marriage Periods, 1700 to 1879 [1]

Marriage periods	Average number of children per wife
Total	4.80
Previous to 1700	7.37
1700–1749	6.83
1750–1799	6.43
1800–1849	4.94
1850–1869	3.47
1870–1879	2.77

[1] Frederick C. Crum, "The Decadence of the Native American Stock," *Am. Statis. Assn. J.*, Vol. 14 n.s., No. 107, p. 216, 1914.

Some of the earliest studies known to the author showing clearly that differential fertility existed in the United States were studies whose chief purpose was to show the decline in the fertility of old native stock in New England as compared with that of the immigrants. The differential fertility shown in these studies related primarily to differences between the native-born whites and the foreign-born whites. Hoffman states that in Rhode Island (1885) "the average number of children to a native-born married woman was 3.49 . . . [while] among the foreign-born women, the average number of children . . . [was] 5.38." Crum (1915) states, "Other careful investigators on the subject . . . all interpret the best available data in the same way [as himself] and all arrive at the same general conclusion, namely, that the native element is failing to contribute anything like its proper quota to the new population of this country." Table 9-1 (Crum) shows the average number of children per wife for certain marriage periods. Kuczynski showed that whereas 16.9 per cent of the native Massachusetts women married and aged forty to forty-four at the time of the state census of 1885 were childless, the proportion of the women born in Ireland of the same age and marital condition who were childless was only 10.1 per cent. He also showed that the average number of children born to a native woman aged forty to forty-four was 2.42 while the average number of children per foreign-born woman was 4.94, or more than twice as high.[3]

In 1905 Professor Willcox,[4] using the number of children under five years old per 1,000 women aged fifteen to forty-nine as a measure of fertility, showed that there had long been rather large regional differences. As early as 1850 the northern and western parts of the United States had only 582 children per 1,000 women as compared with 699 in the southern part of the country. Moreover, except in the North and West in 1860, there had been a steady decrease in the number of children per 1,000 women for some decades, and the decrease had been greatest in those states and regions where the development of industry and urban living had been most marked.

When data from the 1910 census became available, the author was enabled not only to carry forward many of the comparisons of the number of children to women made by Professor Willcox but to add to them, and the 1920 census provided still more material on fertility differentials.[5] Suffice it to say that these studies confirmed the results of the earlier studies and also found certain new differentials because of the more detailed nature of the data then available. The chief addition to our knowledge in these later ratio studies was that the ratio of children under five years of age to women twenty to forty-four decreased as the size of the city increased and that there were very considerable differences in the ratios of children to women in different cities although the cities were of much the same size. These differences between cities appeared to be related both to the proportion of "new" immigrants found in the different cities—the larger the proportion of "new" migrants, the higher the ratio of children to women—and also to the types of occupation predominating in a city, steel cities and other heavy-industry cities having higher ratios of children to women than commercial cities. Thus it became clear that there were occupational differentials in fertility, but the data did not yet enable one to study differentials in the detail that soon became possible.

[3] F. L. Hoffman, "The Decline in the Birth Rate," *North American Rev.,* Vol. 189, p. 677, 1909; Frederick C. Crum, "The Decadence of the Native American Stock," *Am. Statis. Assn. J.,* Vol. 14 n.s., No. 107, p. 216, 1914; Robert R. Kuczynski, "The Decrease in Fertility," *Economica,* Vol. 6 n.s., pp. 128–141, 1935.

[4] Walter F. Willcox, *Proportion of Children in the United States,* p. 13, G.P.O., Washington, D.C., 1905. (U.S. Bureau of the Census.)

[5] Warren S. Thompson, *Average Number of Children per Woman in Butler County, Ohio, 1930; A Study in Differential Fertility,* 81 pp., U.S. Department of Commerce, Washington, D.C., 1941; "Race Suicide in the United States," Parts I, II, III, *Sci. Monthly,* Vol. 5, pp. 22–35, 154–165, 258–269, 1917; *Ratio of Children to Women in the United States, 1920,* 242 pp., G.P.O., Washington, D.C., 1931 (U.S. Bur. Census, *Census Mon.* 11); "Some Factors Influencing the Ratios of Children to Women in American Cities, 1930," *Am. J. Soc.,* Vol. 45, pp. 183–199, 1939.

The Bureau of the Census for several years (1923 to 1929) published birth data by age of mother and occupation of the father. These data showed that fertility varied greatly from one occupational group to another, *e.g.*, of the women aged thirty-five to forty-four who became mothers during 1929, coal miners' wives had borne the largest number of children (8.0); close after them came farmers' wives (7.1). At the other extreme we find that the wives of bankers, brokers, lawyers, judges, physicians, and bookkeepers had borne the fewest children (3.4 to 3.7). On the whole, manual laborers' wives had more children than the wives of men in the white-collar jobs. Among white-collar workers the wives of men in the professions had fewer children than wives in other groups, although the difference between them and the wives of clerical workers was very small. A part of the difference

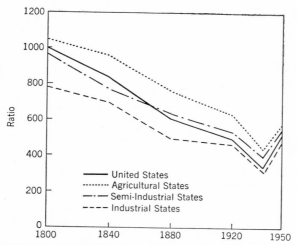

Fig. 9-1. Children under five per 1,000 women sixteen to forty-four, United States and selected states, 1800 to 1950. (Preliminary data for 1950.)

between these groups may have been due to differences in the age composition of the women, in spite of the fact that the differences in age composition have been largely eliminated by using only those women aged thirty-five to forty-four who became mothers during this year. There can be no doubt that these differences in the fertility of different economic and occupational groups as well as between different residence groups were real differences in size of family rather than differences arising solely from demographic differences, particularly differences in age.

That some of these differentials in fertility had existed for decades is shown clearly in the study summarized in Fig. 9-1. When states were classed as agricultural and industrial large differences between them in the ratios of children to women were shown to have existed ever since 1800, and since the semi-industrial states stood in an intermediate position it seemed safe to conclude that fertility had long varied inversely with the degree of industrialization and urbanization.[6]

More recently the Bureau of the Census made a study on differential fertility in 1910 and 1940, some of the data from which have already been used to show the long-continued decline in the size of completed families.[7] This study showed differences in the number of children ever born to women fifty to seventy-four years of age in the different regions of the United States, to whites and nonwhites, and to urban and rural dwellers. In 1910 in the northeastern states 1,000 women aged fifty to seventy-four, when adjusted for age, color, and urban-rural residence, had borne 3,916 children, while an equal number in the South had borne 5,020. In 1910 in the South the white women, adjusted for age and urban-rural residence, had borne 4,934 children per 1,000, while the nonwhite women had borne 6,162 children. By 1940 both the regional differentials and the white-nonwhite differentials had become smaller, although they were still large enough to be highly significant. Urban-rural differentials in fertility were found in all regions in 1910 and 1940 except in the northeastern states in 1910, no doubt because of the great number of foreign-born women having high birth rates found in the northeastern cities at that time (Table 9-2). The same type of differentials in number of children born per 1,000 women were found between many of the states. In general, the more rural a state was, the larger was the number of children per 1,000 women. Always farm women had more children than rural-nonfarm women, and these in turn had larger families than urban women. As between large cities, however, neither the region nor the state in which a city was located seemed to be closely related to the number of children ever born by the older women or to the current reproduction rate. However, on the west coast the families in the large cities were somewhat smaller than in other parts of the country. In the United States there has also been a rather large differential for some decades between the different sizes of urban communities—the larger the city, the smaller the family as a rule—but this differential largely disappeared between cities of 250,000 or more.

In addition to the regional, urban-rural, occupational, and racial differentials noted above there are other differences in fertility between social classes and groups. In broad terms it can be said that for several decades people in better economic circumstances have had smaller families than those in poorer circumstances, that people with good education have had

[6] P. K. Whelpton, "Industrial Development and Population Growth," *Soc. Forces*, Vol. 6, pp. 458–467, 629–638, 1928.

[7] U.S. Bureau of the Census, *Population, Differential Fertility, 1940 and 1910, Standardized Fertility Rates and Reproduction Rates*, p. 7, G.P.O., Washington, D.C., 1944.

smaller families than those with little education, that women who work outside the home have had fewer children than those who did not. The data showing these differentials have become abundant during the past twenty years. Only a few samples can be cited here.

Table 9-2. Number of Children Ever Born per 1,000 Women 50–74 Years Old, Urban and Rural, United States by Regions, 1940 and 1910 [1]
(Standardized for age and color of women)

Area	1940	1910
United States, total	3,094	4,768
Urban	2,666	4,297
Rural-nonfarm	3,318	4,637
Rural-farm	4,211	5,617
Northeast, total	2,681	3,940
Urban	2,607	4,022
Rural-nonfarm	2,810	3,748
Rural-farm	3,380	3,791
North Central, total	2,993	4,916
Urban	2,654	4,527
Rural-nonfarm	3,178	4,766
Rural-farm	3,878	5,652
South, total	3,799	5,526
Urban	2,946	4,581
Rural-nonfarm	3,927	5,238
Rural-farm	4,785	6,179
West, total	2,776	4,631
Urban	2,382	4,057
Rural-nonfarm	3,347	4,941
Rural-farm	3,870	5,851

[1] U.S. Bureau of the Census, *Population, Differential Fertility 1940 and 1910, Standardized Fertility Rates and Reproduction Rates*, p. 8, G.P.O., Washington, D.C., 1944.

In 1930 and 1931 Notestein and Sydenstricker showed that there were large differences in size of family as between certain social and economic classes.[8] The proportion of women who had one or two children or none

[8] Frank W. Notestein, "The Decrease in Size of Families from 1890 to 1910," *Milbank Memorial Fund Q.,* Vol. 9, pp. 181–188, 1931; Frank W. Notestein and Edgar Sydenstricker, "Differential Fertility According to Social Class: A Study of 69,620 Native White Married Women under 45 Years of Age Based upon United States Census Returns of 1910," *Am. Statis. Assn. Pub.,* Vol. 25 n.s., pp. 9–32, 1930; see also Clyde V. Kiser, "Fertility Trends and Differentials in the United States," *Am. Statis. Assn. J.,* Vol. 47, pp. 25–48, 1952.

was significantly higher in the business and professional classes than in the farmer, unskilled-laborer, and skilled-laborer classes, while the proportion of women in these latter classes who had three or more children was correspondingly higher. It is of special interest that these differences were greater for women forty to forty-four at the time of the 1910 census than for women sixty to sixty-four. But even among the women sixty to sixty-four in 1910 whose families were complete about 1890, a significantly larger proportion of the wives of business and professional men than of hand workers were

Table 9-3.   Percentage of Wives Aged 40–44 and 60–64 in Selected Social Classes Who Had Borne Specific Numbers of Children, United States, 1910 [1]

Total children born	Professional		Business		Skilled		Unskilled		Farm owner	
	60–64	40–44	60–64	40–44	60–64	40–44	60–64	40–44	60–64	40–44
Total.......	100.0	100.1	99.9	100.0	100.1	100.1	99.9	100.0	100.3	100.0
0	14.7	19.8	9.6	17.9	8.8	17.4	4.4	16.3	9.0	10.6
1	13.3	19.6	14.0	21.5	13.3	17.0	12.4	14.9	8.8	10.1
2	19.8	24.5	21.1	22.9	16.7	18.0	12.4	16.1	11.8	16.6
3	15.5	18.4	16.7	17.1	15.5	16.2	16.8	14.4	14.8	16.4
4	14.1	9.6	13.0	9.7	12.2	11.0	13.1	9.9	12.7	13.2
5	8.8	4.0	9.8	5.0	9.9	7.2	9.5	6.9	12.5	9.6
6	6.5	2.5	6.8	3.0	7.9	5.2	10.2	5.9	7.9	7.8
7	4.2	0.5	4.2	1.4	5.2	3.0	5.8	4.7	6.3	5.0
8	2.0	0.8	1.8	0.8	4.3	2.3	4.4	4.0	4.9	3.7
9	0.6	0.2	1.7	0.3	2.7	1.9	4.4	2.6	3.9	3.0
10	0.6	0.2	0.8	0.3	1.8	0.5	3.6	2.4	3.9	1.9
11	....	....	....	0.1	1.4	0.2	....	1.2	1.8	1.2
12	....	....	0.4	....	0.2	0.1	1.5	0.5	1.1	0.5
13	....	....	....	....	0.2	....	0.7	0.2	0.4	0.2
14	....	....	....	....	....	0.1	0.7	....	0.3	0.1
15	....	....	....	....	....	....	....	....	0.1	0.1
16	....	....	....	....	....	....	....	....	0.1	

[1] Frank W. Notestein, "The Decrease in Size of Families from 1890 to 1910," *Milbank Memorial Fund Q.*, Vol. 9, p. 184, 1931.

having small families. These data leave no doubt that in the United States such differentials in the fertility of social classes have existed for some decades and that during the decades 1890 to 1900 and 1900 to 1910 these differentials were increasing.

Using 1930 census data for the East North Central states, Notestein has also shown that there was an inverse relationship between the value of the home and the number of children.[9] When the value of the home was less

[9] Frank W. Notestein, "Differential Fertility in the East North Central States," *Milbank Memorial Fund Q.*, Vol. 16, pp. 173–191, 1938.

than $10,000, the lower the value of the home the larger the number of children. When the home was valued at over $10,000, the number of children was slightly higher than in homes valued at $5,000 to $9,999 but smaller than in homes valued at under $5,000. Notestein suggested that the slightly larger number of children in the more expensive homes might represent a reversal of the inverse relation between economic status and size of family which had prevailed in the past. This point will be discussed in some detail later (see page 192).

Kiser [10] using data collected in urban communities in the National Health Survey (1935) found substantial fertility differentials (standardized birth rates) as between occupational groups, educational groups, and groups having different incomes; also for native whites, foreign-born whites, and non-whites separately. However, the differentials by social and economic status were generally less for the nonwhites than for the whites (Table 9-4). Without making any attempt at evaluation of the relative importance of these factors in producing the differentials in the birth rates shown here, one can say there is no reasonable doubt that occupation, income, and education have had a very great influence on fertility whether as direct causes or as causes of conditions which lead to the control of the size of the family.

The second article, reporting results from the Indianapolis Study—a study directed to ascertaining the social and psychological factors affecting fertility—is entitled "Variations in the Size of Completed Families of 6,551 Native White Couples in Indianapolis." [11] These data were gathered in 1941 and show a number of differentials in fertility which can only be summarized here:

1. Significant differences in size of completed family were found as between Protestant and Catholic couples in respect of all the social and economic factors considered. Of the Protestant couples 67.0 per cent had had two or fewer children while of the Catholic couples only 52.0 per cent were in this group. The average number of children to Protestant couples was 2.19 and to Catholic couples 2.74. These differences carry through practically all economic groups, measured by rental value of dwelling unit, except at the very low rentals—below $15 per month.

2. For both Protestant and Catholic couples the number of children declined steadily as rent rose from $15 toward $50 to $59, the smallest number of children being found in families paying rents of $50 to $59 and $60 to $79. It rises somewhat in both groups at rents of $80 and over. The

[10] Clyde V. Kiser, *Group Differences in Urban Fertility,* The Williams & Wilkins Company, Baltimore, 1942.

[11] Clyde V. Kiser and P. K. Whelpton, "Social and Psychological Factors Affecting Fertility: II. Variations in the Size of Completed Families of 6,551 Native White Couples in Indianapolis," *Milbank Memorial Fund Q.,* Vol. 22, No. 1, pp. 72–105, 1944.

Table 9-4. Fertility Rates among White and Colored Wives of Childbearing Age, by Occupation, Education, and Income, 1935 [1]
(Standardized for age)

Occupation, education, and income	Live births per 1,000 wives		
	White		Colored
	Native	Foreign-born	
Occupational class of head: total	96	111	86
Professional	94	86	79
Business	86	109	81
Skilled and semiskilled	100	111	85
Unskilled	115	122	86
Educational attainment of the wife: total	96	111	86
College	87	82	64
High school	91	108	85
Seventh and eighth grade	105	109	85
Under seventh grade	118	125	87
Family income: total	96	111	86
$5,000 and over	78 ⎫	83 ⎫	45
$3,000–$4,999	77 ⎭		
2,000– 2,999	76	90 ⎭	
1,500– 1,999	81	102	60
1,000– 1,499	90	104	73
Under $1,000 and total relief	117	128	90
Under $1,000 and nonrelief	96	108	69
Total relief	147	155	126

[1] Clyde V. Kiser, *Group Differences in Urban Fertility*, pp. 56, 91, and 124, The Williams & Wilkins Company, Baltimore, 1942.

increase in the proportion of families having five or more children with decrease in rents is striking for both Protestants and Catholics but the differences are more pronounced for Protestants.

3. The proportion of couples with five children or more also decreases as the amount of education increases for both Protestants and Catholics but as in the case of increasing rentals the decrease is more pronounced for Protestants than for Catholics. In other words, for Catholics, religion tends to modify somewhat the effects of educational differences in determining the size of the family.

4. The region of birth of the couples also had an effect on the size of the family. In general, fewer couples born in the South were childless and

more had five or more children than among those born in the North. Protestant couples born in the South had substantially larger families than the Catholic couples, practically all of which were born in the North.

Certain other aspects of this Indianapolis Study will be discussed in more detail in the following chapter, since the chief purpose of the study was to investigate the conditions which actually led people to raise families of a given size.

In a study of fertility in the different census tracts [12] of eight large cities, the writer found the following relations: (1) the lower the average rental in the tract, the higher the ratio of children under five years old to women aged fifteen to forty-four; (2) the lower the proportion of employed women, the higher the ratio of children to women; (3) the larger the proportion of the employed population that was engaged in manufacturing, the higher the ratio of children to women; and (4) the higher the proportion of married women, the higher the ratio of children to women. The proportion of married women was no doubt closely related (inversely) to the proportion of women employed.

This study also showed that in only one of these cities (Pittsburgh) did over 41.0 per cent of the white women live in tracts where the ratio of children was high enough to replace the existing population, while in Chicago only 10.9 per cent of the white women lived in such tracts.[13] Thus it appears that there are large differences in fertility within cities. These differences unquestionably reflect the differences in fertility associated with differences in social and economic status which have already been noted.

The significance of the fact that the differentials noted above appear to be diminishing will be discussed on page 195.

[12] Thompson, "Some Factors Influencing the Ratios of Children to Women in American Cities, 1930," pp. 193–194.

[13] *Ibid.,* p. 197. The measure of replacement used here is the *replacement index.* It is merely the actual ratio of children under five years of age per 1,000 women aged fifteen to forty-four (or twenty to forty-four) in a group, divided by the ratio of such children per 1,000 women in the same age group found in a life-table population having approximately the age-specific death rates of the group under consideration. In a life-table population the ratio of children to women shows the number of children per 1,000 women which would maintain that population constant because the number of births is constant and the number of deaths equals the number of births and the distribution of deaths by age is constant. When the index obtained by this division (actual ratio of children to women over life-table ratio of children to women) is over 1.00, the population will increase, when less than 1.00 it will decrease, in a generation by the percentage represented by the variation of the index from 1.00. As an indicator of probable future growth it has the same serious defects as the net reproduction rate, for it assumes a continuation of certain age-specific death rates but a continuation of a given number of births in place of age-specific birth rates.

2. DIFFERENTIAL FERTILITY IN ENGLAND AND WALES

The study of fertility in England and Wales made in connection with the 1911 census also dealt with differential fertility and until recently provided most of the data available on this subject in England and Wales. In this study the age of women at marriage as well as the number of children they had borne and the number surviving was obtained for every woman in the country. This information, when used in conjunction with the other information on the census schedule, made possible an exhaustive study on the fertility of women of England and Wales as it was forty years ago. The findings of this study were not startling, but they gave a more exact picture of differential fertility in a larger population than had previously been investigated in detail. Some of the more significant facts are given in Tables 9-5 and 9-6.

These tables show the number of children born to each 100 couples of completed fertility classified by social status, by duration of marriage, and by age at marriage. There were very large differences in number of children born to women in the different classes when they had completed their families shortly before 1911. But the differentials diminished as the duration of marriage increased, *i.e.*, as their families were completed at earlier dates. One hundred women married in 1881 to 1886 and past forty-five years of age in 1911 had borne only 422 children if they belonged to the upper and middle classes, while 100 women of the unskilled-laborer class had borne

Table 9-5.   Number of Children Born per 100 Couples Where the Wife Was 45 or Over at Time of Census, by Date of Marriage and Social Class, England and Wales, 1911 [1]

Date of marriage	Duration of marriage, years	Total population	Occupied only	Social class[2]							
				I	II	III	IV	V	VI	VII	VIII
1881–1886...	25–30	551	554	422	493	556	562	609	513	684	632
1871–1881...	30–40	605	611	497	567	615	616	652	567	717	667
1861–1871...	40–50	662	673	593	650	679	673	698	633	760	702
1851–1861...	50–60	690	701	625	700	707	700	718	654	759	738
1851 or earlier	Over 60	697	700	605	728	681	740[3]	698[3]	[4]	[4]	746

[1] Great Britain, Census Office, *Fertility of Marriage*, Pt. 2, p. xcviii, Table 44, H.M.S.O., London, 1923. (Census of England and Wales, 1911, Vol. 13.)

[2] Class I, upper and middle classes; Class II, retired and unoccupied, living on private means; Class III, skilled artisans; Class IV, intermediate between Classes III and V; Class V, unskilled workers; Class VI, textile workers; Class VII, miners; Class VIII, agricultural laborers.

[3] Rates based on less than 100 couples.

[4] Less than 10 couples.

Table 9-6.   Number of Children Born per 100 Couples Where the Wife Was 45
or Over at Time of Census, by Age at Marriage and Social Class,
England and Wales, 1911 [1]

Age of wife at marriage	Total popu-lation	Occu-pied only	Social class[2]							
			I	II	III	IV	V	VI	VII	VIII
15–19...............	799	801	637	734	801	804	834	757	904	845
20–24...............	620	619	488	567	622	628	676	566	747	704
25–29...............	428	426	351	404	432	431	470	380	527	510
30–34...............	281	281	230	270	280	283	307	244	349	344
35–44...............	106	107	83	99	106	108	120	97	134	135
45 and over..........	3	3	2	3	3	3	4	4	5	3
All ages (crude)........	487	489	365	435	504	498	533	457	626	572
All ages (standardized)[3]	487	487	389	451	489	492	528	444	585	556

[1] Great Britain, Census Office, *Fertility of Marriage*, Pt. 2, p. xcviii, Table 44, H.M.S.O., London, 1923. (Census of England and Wales, 1911, Vol. 13.)

[2] See footnote 2 of Table 9-5.

[3] Standardized on all families in England and Wales (wives over 45 at census) at each marriage age of wife.

609 children, 100 miners' wives had borne 684 children, and 100 farmers' wives had borne 632 children. At this time, then, the average number of children born to women in these three working-class groups was over one-half higher than the number born to women in the upper and middle classes. For the women marrying 1851 to 1861, the working-class women averaged only about one-sixth more children than the upper- and middle-class women. The data in Table 9-7 leave no reasonable doubt that the differentials in completed fertility between the lower and the upper classes increased rapidly from about 1880 to 1910. The voluntary control of the size of the family had begun in the upper and middle classes and among textile workers in England and Wales some time before 1861 and the differential birth rate between classes kept increasing at least up to 1911. There are no strictly comparable data for the period since 1911, but the recent (1949) *Report* of the Royal Commission on Population [14] gives the estimated size of the average completed family for persons marrying from 1900 to 1929, classified as manual and nonmanual workers. This shows a continuous decline in both groups, but the differential in favor of the manual workers remained practically constant at 41 to 44 per cent during this period, ending in 1946.

Figure 9-2 from the 1911 study of fertility just referred to shows the proportion of all the children produced by different proportions of marriages

[14] *Op. cit.*, p. 29.

when they were arrayed by degree of fertility; unfortunately for our purposes, it does not cross-classify these data by social class. It is of much interest, however, that at the time of the 1911 census the least fertile 25

Table 9-7.   Average Family Size in Each Class as a Proportion of the Average for All Classes Together, England and Wales [1]

Social class	Women marrying	
	1851–1861	1881–1886
I	86	72
II	98	86
III	101	102
IV	100	102
V	105	112
VI	99	93
VII	110	132
VIII	106	113

[1] United Kingdom, Royal Commission on Population, *Report*, p. 28, H.M.S.O., London, 1949.

per cent of marriages of completed fertility had produced only 2.1 per cent of all births, while the most fertile 25 per cent produced 52 per cent of all births. Since there is little doubt that an increasing proportion of the women in the upper and middle classes belonged to the least fertile 25 per cent as

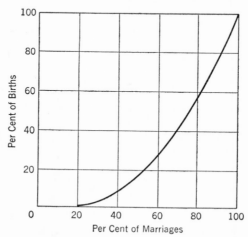

Fig. 9-2. Percentage distribution of births to marriages of completed fertility, England and Wales, 1911.

the date of the completion of the family approached 1911, we can be reasonably certain that the upper and middle classes were contributing relatively less to the next generation than the working classes for several decades prior to that date. The data on manual and nonmanual workers (1946) show that this situation still prevailed in England and Wales. The situation as regards differential fertility in England and Wales appears, therefore, to be substantially the same as in the United States.

3. DIFFERENTIAL FERTILITY IN FRANCE

At the beginning of this century differential fertility appears to have been even more marked in France than in the United States and England and Wales (Table 9-8). It should be noted, however, that the families of

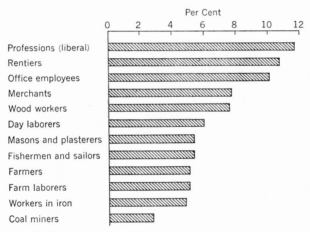

Fig. 9-3. Per cent of couples married over 25 years with no children, France, 1906.

farmers and farm laborers were relatively small (marriages of 25 or more years' duration) in France as compared with such families in the United States and England and Wales and also as compared with a number of other hand-working groups in France. In addition, the proportion of marriages in which no child was born increased as the socioeconomic status of the family improved (Fig. 9-3).

Data for France strictly comparable with those in Table 9-8 have not been tabulated for late years. In 1936 the number of children per 100 families for certain occupational groups where the heads had not yet passed fifty-five years of age (average thirty-eight to thirty-nine years) was as follows:

Extractive industries	211	Public service	152
Agriculture and forestry	203	Manufacturing	151
Fishing	194	Commerce	130
Transportation	165	Liberal professions	129

These data do not relate to completed families as do those in Table 9-8, but they do permit of two conclusions which appear firm enough to be significant: (1) there were still substantial differentials in fertility between

Table 9-8.   Average Number of Children Born per
100 Families Where the Marriage Had Endured
25 Years or More, France, 1906 [1]

Occupation	Children per 100 families
Coal miners	579
Spinners	540
Fishermen and sailors	510
Day laborers	464
Workers in iron	431
Masons, plasterers	427
Farm laborers	426
Woodworkers (own account)	378
Farmers	371
Merchants	342
Army and navy men	325
Rentiers (unoccupied)	321
Professions	312
Office employees	294

[1] France, Bureau de la Statistique Générale, *Statistique des familles en 1906*, p. 115, Imprimerie Nationale, Paris, 1912.

white-collar workers and hand workers, although these differences seem to have been declining proportionally, and (2) the decline in the size of the family among the workers engaged in agriculture and forestry appeared to be less than in most other occupations.

As the result of his exhaustive review of the evidence relating to differential fertility in France, Spengler (1938) concludes, "Although natality was inversely related to wealth in the nineteenth century, data on regional variations and trends suggest that the relationship may be positive today." [15] This result, if established (the author still regards it as questionable in the light of the data cited immediately below), would have come about not

[15] Joseph J. Spengler, *France Faces Depopulation,* p. 102, Duke University Press, Durham, N.C., 1938.

because of an increase in the size of the families of the people with more wealth but because of the relatively greater reduction in the size of the families of people in less favorable economic circumstances. In this connection it may also be noted that, although the size of the family is sometimes larger in the group with fairly large incomes, or of very good economic status, than in the group or groups immediately lower in the economic scale, the author knows of no case, except in the Stockholm study for the period around 1920 to 1930 (see below), where the size of the family in this upper economic group was larger than in the low economic groups.

Some preliminary data from the 1946 census of France indicate that there are still substantial differences in the average number of children per family in the different social and economic classes.

Table 9-9. Average Number of Living Children per
Married Man Aged 45–54, France, 1946 [1]

Occupation	Average number of living children
Total	2.01
Agriculture, total	2.51
Farm operators	2.53
Nonagricultural, total	1.84
Miners and quarrymen	2.72
Employees in trade	1.39
Office employees	1.62
Police, etc	1.94
Employers in trade	1.65
Manual workers in industry and transport	1.89
Professions and employers with more than five employees	1.70

[1] These data were kindly supplied to the writer by Dr. Alfred Sauvy, Director, Institut National d'Études Démographiques, Paris, France. They are preliminary data from tabulations not yet completed and may be changed somewhat in the published report.

4. DIFFERENTIAL FERTILITY IN GERMANY

In Germany, as in these other countries, the birth rate varies greatly from class to class and from one part of the country to another. Bertillon's data (Table 9-10) show how different quarters of Berlin differed from one another over 50 years ago. But these data are now of historical interest only. In connection with the 1933 census the German Statistical Office made a very comprehensive study of fertility, the results of which are of much interest.[16] In the first place it showed that the differential fertility between cities and small communities was still large. Thus women who lived in communities of less than 2,000 and who had been married 21 to 25 years at the time of the 1933 census had borne an average of 3.95 children, while the women of the same duration of marriage who lived in cities of over 100,000 had borne an average of only 2.41 children. In this same duration-of-marriage group of women, 34.7 per cent had families of five or more children when they lived in communities of less than 2,000, but only 12.1 per cent of them had families of this size when they lived in the larger cities. In Berlin only 5.1 per cent of this group married 21 to 25 years had borne five or more children.

Table 9-10.   Births per 1,000 Women 15–50 Years of Age in Sections of Cities Rated According to Economic Circumstances [1]

Economic circumstances	All women				Married women	
	Paris, 1889– 1893	Berlin, 1886– 1894	Vienna, 1890– 1894	London, 1881– 1890	Paris, 1889– 1893	Berlin, 1886– 1894
Very rich........................	34	47	71	63	65	121
Rich.............................	53	63	107	87	94	145
Very comfortable.................	65	96	153	107	96	172
Comfortable.....................	72	114	155	107	109	192
Poor............................	95	129	164	140	128	198
Very poor.......................	108	157	200	147	143	214

[1] Data furnished by Bertillon to Sir Arthur Newsholme and T. H. C. Stevenson for an article on "The Decline in Human Fertility as Shown by Corrected Birth Rates," *Royal Statis. Soc. J.*, Vol. 69, pp. 34–38, 1906.

When Protestant and Catholic groups in communities of the same size were compared, it was found that a larger proportion of the women in the latter group had families of five or more than in the former. There were also fewer childless marriages among the Catholics. Unfortunately the average number of children born to women of different religious faiths, married a given length of time, is not given.

Table 9-11 shows that there was a large difference between occupational classes in the proportion of women, married 20 years or more in 1933, who had borne different numbers of children. The wives of white-collar workers had large proportions who had borne one or two children or none and small proportions with five children or more, while the hand workers (including

[16] Germany, Statistisches Reichsamt, *Volkszahlung vom 16 Juni 1933,* Vol. 452, No. 1, pp. 14–41, Paul Schmidt, Berlin, 1937.

farmers) had smaller proportions with one or two children or none and much larger proportions with five or more.

There was also a close association between the ownership of land and the size of the family, even in the nonagricultural occupations, where the duration of the marriage was 20 years or more. Thus even in the professions only 9.7 per cent of the women were childless if the couple owned land, while 15.2 per cent were childless if the couple did not own land. Moreover, 53.5 per cent of the owning couples had three or more children, while only 39.7 per cent of the nonowning couples had three or more children. The differences were proportionally much the same for other occupa-

Table 9-11. Per Cent of Married Couples Living Together and Married in 1913 and Earlier That Had a Given Number of Children, by Occupational Class, Germany, 1933 [1]

Occupational class	Number of children					
	0	1	2	3	4	5 or more
Independent peasants.......	5.3	7.7	13.1	14.3	13.1	46.5
Agricultural workers........	5.5	6.7	10.0	11.6	12.0	54.2
Agricultural officials........	7.8	15.0	24.8	19.6	12.6	20.2
Independent workers.......	8.6	12.8	19.6	17.4	13.0	28.6
Independent workers in trade and commerce..........	12.4	16.6	22.1	17.3	11.2	20.4
Professions...............	13.5	17.9	24.6	18.5	10.8	14.7
Administrative officials......	10.3	20.0	26.3	18.5	10.9	14.0
Laborers.................	7.9	11.6	16.8	15.9	12.9	34.9

[1] Germany, Statistisches Reichsamt, *Volkszahlung vom 16 Juni 1933*, Vol. 452, No. 1, p. 33, Paul Schmidt, Berlin, 1937.

tional groups; even the laborers in agriculture had larger families when they owned land than when they did not.

This study of fertility leaves no doubt that there were still large differentials between social classes and area groups in Germany as late as 1933 and that in general the lower the economic and social status, the greater the fertility. Some income data given by Burgdörfer, however, led him to believe that in the cities this pattern might be undergoing a change, *e.g.*, the number of children per 100 families having taxable incomes decreased as the size of the community increased.[17] However, the number of children also usually increased as the size of the taxable income increased if the community had 10,000 or more inhabitants. This increase was sufficiently consistent to warrant the statement that the number of children for whom tax

[17] Friedrich Burgdörfer, *Volk ohne Jugend*, 3d ed., p. 59, Vowinckel, Berlin, 1935.

exemption could be claimed increased as income increased. But this does not prove that the size of the family increased as income increased. Until the age of the people in the different income classes and the length of time they have been married are known, we cannot be certain that the relation between size of family and income was positive rather than negative. Older people whose families are completed, or nearly so, are likely to have larger incomes than younger people who belong to the same social class. Although this is the case, the author is inclined to believe with Burgdörfer that the differentials in fertility between poor and well-to-do families have probably become narrower and that they may disappear as the voluntary control of births becomes more general in the poorer classes. Certainly the poor have more economic reason to restrict their families to one or two children than the comfortable and well-to-do, but until more conclusive evidence is available it cannot be said positively that the well-established inverse relation— the lower the economic status the larger the family—has been reversed in Germany.

Table 9-12. Number of Children to Each 100 Persons Entitled to Deductions from Income Tax for Urban Groups and Rural Areas, Germany, 1928 [1]

Income group	Average for all	Under 2,000	2,000–5,000	5,000–10,000	10,000–25,000	25,000–50,000	50,000–100,000	100,000 and over	Berlin
Among those subject to the wage tax									
Under $375......	106	122	111	105	101	98	98	89	77
$375–$ 750...	115	142	132	125	120	115	117	98	75
750– 1,250...	124	158	153	146	138	132	131	104	80
$1,250 and over..	123	173	151	144	138	130	130	103	83
Total, 1928......	114	135	128	123	119	115	116	98	78
Among those subject to income tax									
Under $375......	133	157	138	122	108	103	102	78	56
$375–$ 750...	157	204	166	147	130	122	123	93	69
750– 1,250 ..	153	221	172	151	134	127	128	99	73
1,250– 2,000...	141	211	165	151	136	127	130	103	77
2,000– 3,000...	130	184	158	154	143	136	132	110	90
3,000– 4,000...	127	169	158	146	138	137	134	113	94
4,000– 6,250...	128	163	154	146	139	139	135	115	99
6,250–12,500...	131	157	158	148	144	139	140	121	106
12,500–25,000...	134	170	153	146	144	145	148	125	110
$25,000 and over.	139	174	157	147	162	143	136	132	128
Total, 1928......	144	182	157	141	128	122	122	96	75
Total, 1927......	148	183	163	147	133	126	128	100	78

[1] Friedrich Burgdörfer, *Volk ohne Jugend*, 3d ed., p. 59, Vowinckel, Berlin, 1935.

5. DIFFERENTIAL FERTILITY IN SWEDEN

In connection with the development of a national population policy a special study of fertility was made in Sweden in 1936, the results of which are summarized in Table 9-13.[18] This table shows some variations from

Table 9-13. Average Number of Children Born Alive in Marriages Having a Duration of 20 to 35 Years, by Occupation, Residence, and Income of Husband, Sweden, 1936 [1]

Occupation	Residence	Income							
		Under $150	$150–$250	$250–$375	$375–$500	$500–$750	$750–$1,250	$1,250–$2,500	$2,500 and over
All classes........	Country	4.12	3.85	4.33	4.31	4.01	3.60	3.12	3.32
	City	3.12	3.01	3.38	3.31	3.28	2.92	2.53	2.68
Farmers, agricultural patrons.....	Country	4.30	3.98	4.35	4.69	4.72	4.38	3.97	4.35
	City	4.30	3.17	3.39	3.85	3.78	3.79		
Farm laborers.....	Country	4.92	3.83	5.04	5.39	5.08			
	City	....	....	5.09	4.40				
Other independent patrons.........	Country	3.73	3.62	3.86	3.76	3.55	3.33	3.16	3.14
	City	3.18	3.07	3.34	3.29	3.06	2.88	2.72	2.76
Officials and salaried employees..	Country	3.63	2.86	4.07	3.38	3.21	3.27	2.75	3.04
	City	2.70	2.77	2.62	3.09	2.85	2.84	2.55	2.64
Laborers in industry.	Country	4.16	3.93	4.25	3.96	3.95	3.62	3.37	
	City	3.61	3.49	3.82	3.51	3.44	3.04	2.33	
Other laborers.....	Country	4.55	4.00	4.48	4.37	3.75	3.33	2.67	
	City	3.33	3.29	3.40	3.43	3.36	2.90	2.26	

[1] Sweden, Statistiska Centralbyrån, Statistisk Årsbok för Sverige, 1941, pp. 32–34, P. A. Norstedt & Söner, Stockholm, 1941. The Swedish crown has been converted into dollars at the ratio of four to one. It should not be inferred, however, that the level of living at a given income in Sweden is the same as at this given income in the United States. Four crowns would undoubtedly buy considerably more of certain kinds of goods in Sweden in 1936 than one dollar would buy in the United States.

the usual inverse relation between income and size of family and thus indicates that there may be a trend in the direction of a direct relationship. The largest number of children born alive was found as a rule in the income

[18] Sweden, Statistiska Centralbyrån, Statistisk Årsbok för Sverige, 1941, pp. 32–34, P. A. Norstedt & Söner, Stockholm, 1941.

class $250 to $375 (1,000 to 1,500 crowns); in several social classes the maximum was reached at the next higher income level but in no case at an income level in excess of $500 (2,000 crowns), except among farmers where the maximum occurred at $500 to $750. From the maximum at these relatively modest incomes the number of children generally declined in the income classes $750 to $1,250 and $1,250 to $2,500 and was lowest of all in the latter class. In several groups, however, when the income was in excess of $2,500—the well-to-do group—the number of children rose slightly above the low, but in no case did it rise as high as in the $750-to-$1,250 income group. Thus while the inverse relation between income and size of family in Sweden was more common in 1936 than the direct relation, it can be said that there are enough exceptions as between the group with an income in excess of $2,500 and the next lower ($1,250 to $2,500) income group to suggest that differentials in fertility may be changing to a direct relation between economic status and size of family.

Edin and Hutchinson in their studies of fertility in Stockholm, 1919 to 1922, have, in my opinion, provided the only conclusive evidence of a *direct* rather than an *inverse* relation between socioeconomic status and fertility—the better the socioeconomic status, the larger the family. But it should be noted that these data refer only to women in Stockholm. The data in Sec. I of Table 9-14 refer to all women in the census of Greater Stockholm in 1920 who were living with their husbands at that time, who were under forty years of age, and who had births during the four years 1919 to 1922. Only Group A, the industrial group of lowest social status, showed an inverse relation between birth rate and economic status (income). It also had lower fertility rates at the higher incomes than industrial Groups B, C, and D that were of higher social status. Section II of the same table shows that within specified educational groups the number of children born within the first 10 years of married life was highest for those women whose husbands' incomes were highest. Moreover, as between these educational groups those women whose husbands were best educated had the larger number of children. But since these data relate to the first 10 years of married life only, we cannot be positive that the same relationship would be found between completed families of the different educational classes.

As regards variables which might have affected these results, I cannot do better than quote from Edin and Hutchinson's own summary of that phase of the study from which Sec. II of Table 9-14 was derived.

> The observed fertility rates increased without exception from the lowest to the highest education groups. The validity of this observation was confirmed by demonstrating:
> 1. that the fertility differentials were not produced by a more favorable age distribution or a less frequent employment of wives in the more educated groups;

Table 9-14.   Standardized Fertility Rates for Families by Occupation and
Income and Average Number of Live Births per Family, by
Education and Income of Husband, Stockholm, 1920 [1]

I.   Standardized fertility rates for families in which the wife reported less than 300
kroner earned income in 1920, standardized for age of wife and marriage period

Income of husband, kroner	Occupation group [2]			
	A	B	C	D
Under 4,000	126	110	118	117
4,000–6,000	120	125	123	120
6,000 and over	111	140	147	144
Total	122	129	131	130
Total (unstandardized)	117	125	133	129

II.   Average number of live births per family in the first ten years of marriage

Income of husband, kroner	Education group [3]			
	Total	A	B	C and D
Under 4,000	1.16	1.15	1.18	1.46
4,000–6,000	1.21	1.18	1.34	1.45
6,000–10,000	1.31	1.18	1.35	1.46
10,000 and over	1.74	1.56	1.62	1.85
Under 6,000	1.19	1.17	1.28	1.45
6,000 and over	1.47	1.23	1.45	1.70
Total	1.26	1.17	1.36	1.66

[1] Karl A. Edin and Edward P. Hutchinson, *Studies of Differential Fertility in Sweden*,
pp. 61, 78, P. S. King & Son, Ltd., London, 1935.
[2] A.   Industry, workers: including workers in the printing, textile, chemical, food
products, and building industries, as well as unskilled day labor.
    B.   Industry, others: including technicians, overseers, office staff.
    C.   Trade and commerce: including employees of wholesale and retail stores, banks,
hotels, restaurants, telephone and telegraph service, transportation.
    D.   Arts and professions: including also state and municipal employees, army and
naval officers, hospital staff.
[3] A.   *Folkskolan* or less, the *folkskolan* including the first eight years of education,
from about the seventh to the fifteenth year of age.
    B.   Further education than *folkskolan* but without the matriculation examination.
    C.   With matriculation examination, usually taken at about age 18 or 19 and required
for admission to universities and to the higher civil-service positions.
    D.   Degree from university or higher technical school.

2. that they were not merely a result of the better economic position of the more educated;

3. that they were not a product of temporary changes in fertility during the post-war years [World War I];

4. that in all probability they were not a result of social class differences in the number of children born to the wives before the observed marriages (illegitimate children plus children of former marriages).[19]

These findings are very significant, for they strongly reinforce other findings indicating that a change from an inverse to a direct relation between social status and income, on the one hand, and fertility, on the other, may be taking place. But we shall probably have to wait some years to be certain how rapidly this movement will spread even in a country like Sweden, and whether or not other Western countries will follow the same general pattern, and if they do, under what conditions these new differentials will arise.

6. SUMMARY

There is no need to add further facts regarding the differential birth rate. Everywhere in Europe and in the countries settled by Europeans there are still marked differentials in fertility between the different economic and social classes of the population. The latest data available indicate that these differentials are still preponderantly inverse, namely, that the lower the socio-economic status, the larger is the family. It is reasonably certain, however, that these differentials are decreasing, and in a few communities and under certain conditions, *e.g.*, living in Stockholm, they now appear to be direct—the higher the socioeconomic status, the larger the family. But a higher birth rate at a particular period of time and for certain durations of marriage is not entirely satisfactory proof that the size of the completed families of the different classes will show this same direct relationship.

At present the chief differentials in most countries appear to be as follows: (1) if the population is divided into hand workers and white-collar workers, the former have higher fertility; (2) if hand workers are divided into farmers and others, the farmers have the higher fertility, although this may not hold for some particular groups of nonagricultural hand workers, *e.g.*, miners; (3) within the group of nonagricultural hand workers it would appear that the less skilled and those whose work is harder and dirtier—who, in general, have the lower level of living—have larger families than those whose work is more skilled, less onerous, and cleaner; (4) within the white-collar class it appears that some of the lower-paid groups may have smaller families than the better-paid groups; this appears to me to be a partial explanation of the lower average size of family at some of the middle-

[19] Karl Arvid Edin and Edward P. Hutchinson, *Studies of Differential Fertility in Sweden,* p. 86, P. S. King & Son, Ltd., London, 1935.

income intervals than at the higher-income intervals such as was found in the German, Swedish, and Indianapolis data; (5) when amount of education is taken as a criterion for classifying people, those with smaller amounts of schooling have larger families than those with larger amounts.

It is the author's personal opinion that the differentials in fertility discussed here—those which have apparently prevailed for two or three generations in most Western countries and which still predominate—are largely the consequence of the fact that certain classes in the community learned how to control conception before other classes. The classes that first gained control over fertility lived predominately in the cities and were of better than average socioeconomic status. However, the knowledge of conception control spread gradually—first, to other urban groups of lower socioeconomic status, and later, to rural groups. As this took place fertility declined in all classes, but for some time it continued to decline more rapidly in the upper socioeconomic classes. There is some evidence that more recently the decline in fertility has become more rapid in the less favored socioeconomic classes and that as a consequence the differentials in fertility have become smaller. Since it seems likely to the author that economic considerations are going to play a more and more important role in determining the size of the family as voluntary control increases, it seems not improbable that the less favored economic groups will soon have as small families as the more favored groups, or, perhaps, even smaller. The author is therefore disposed to believe that when a community or nation has evolved demographically to the point prevailing in Western Europe and in the peoples descended from them, the class differentials in fertility with which we are now familiar will tend to disappear. When this happens we shall cease to be as much interested in fertility differentials as we have been heretofore because they will no longer raise such urgent problems.

Before leaving this matter of the differential birth rate it will be well to call attention again to the fact that differential fertility is developing as between nations and that it has already created and will almost certainly continue to create some difficult problems in international politics (Chap. XVII). Many Western nations which were increasing in numbers very rapidly during the last century now have such a low fertility that they will grow but slowly, if at all, during the next few decades.

On the other hand, certain other peoples that have been almost stationary, or have grown only slowly until recently, are beginning to expand at a more rapid rate not because of increased fertility but because of the maintenance of the high fertility which has long prevailed among them while their death rates have begun to decline and will almost certainly decline much more in the near future, if sustenance can be provided, before there is any perceptible change in their fertility (Chap. XV). Since these latter peoples often lack adequate resources to care for their growing numbers for any great length of time at prevent levels of living, to say nothing of improving these levels, we may anticipate that they will make determined efforts to secure the larger resources that they need before the voluntary control of the size of the family becomes widespread among them.

Suggestions for Supplementary Reading

BERENT, JERZY: "Fertility and Social Mobility," *Population Studies*, Vol. 5, No. 3, pp. 244–260, 1950.

BURGDÖRFER, FRIEDRICH: *Volk ohne Jugend*, 3d ed., 536 pp., Vowinckel, Berlin, 1935.

DINKEL, ROBERT M.: "Occupation and Fertility in the United States," *Am. Soc. Rev.*, Vol. 17, No. 2, pp. 178–183, 1952.

EDIN, KARL ARVID, and EDWARD P. HUTCHINSON: *Studies of Differential Fertility in Sweden*, 116 pp., P. S. King & Son, Ltd., London, 1935.

France, Bureau de la Statistique Générale: *Statistique des familles en 1906*, 205 pp., Imprimerie Nationale, Paris, 1912.

HATT, PAUL K.: *Backgrounds of Human Fertility in Puerto Rico*, 512 pp., Princeton University Press, Princeton, N.J., 1952.

INNES, JOHN WARWICK: *Class Fertility Trends in England and Wales*, 152 pp., Princeton University Press, Princeton, N.J., 1938.

KISER, CLYDE V.: *Group Differences in Urban Fertility*, 284 pp., The Williams & Wilkins Company, Baltimore, 1942.

LANDRY, ADOLPHE: *Traité de démographie*, Chap. V, Payot, Paris, 1945. This book contains much information on many aspects of population growth and change and could be used to advantage in connection with most other chapters also.

NEWSHOLME, ARTHUR, and T. H. C. STEVENSON: "The Decline of Human Fertility in the United Kingdom and Other Countries as Shown by Corrected Birth Rates," *Royal Statis. Soc. J.*, Vol. 69, pp. 34–38, 1906.

NOTESTEIN, FRANK W.: "The Decrease in Size of Families from 1890 to 1910," *Milbank Memorial Fund Q.*, Vol. 9, pp. 181–188, 1931.

SPENGLER, JOSEPH J.: *France Faces Depopulation*, 313 pp., Duke University Press, Durham, N.C., 1938.

SYDENSTRICKER, EDGAR, and FRANK W. NOTESTEIN: "Differential Fertility According to Social Class: A Study of 69,620 Native White Married Women under 45 Years of Age Based upon United States Census Returns of 1910," *Am. Statis. Assn. Pub.*, Vol. 25, n.s., pp. 9–32, 1930.

THOMPSON, WARREN S.: *Average Number of Children per Woman in Butler County, Ohio, 1930: A Study in Differential Fertility*, 81 pp., U.S. Department of Commerce, Washington, D.C., 1941.

———: "Race Suicide in the United States," Parts I, II, III, *Sci. Monthly*, Vol. 5, pp. 22–35, 154–165, 258–269, 1917. (See also *Am. J. Phys. Anthrop.*, Vol. 3, pp. 98–146, 1920.)

———: *Ratio of Children to Women in the United States, 1920*, 242 pp., G.P.O., Washington, D.C., 1931. (U.S. Bur. Census, *Census Mon.* 11.)

WHELPTON, P. K.: "Industrial Development and Population Growth," *Soc. Forces*, Vol. 6, pp. 458–467, 629–638, 1928.

CHAPTER X

FACTORS IN THE DECLINE
OF THE BIRTH RATE

What social and economic changes have brought about the large decline in fertility among the Western peoples which has been described above? This question can be put in this form because, as has already been noted, to the best of our knowledge, no fundamental biological change in the capacity of married couples to conceive and bear live children has taken place within the two to four generations during which the decline in fertility has been most pronounced. Our inquiry will, therefore, be confined to a discussion of the changes in social conditions (including economic) which may have had a depressing influence on fertility.

Since there is good reason to believe that this widespread decline in fertility is to a major extent the result of the deliberate control of conception, it may be well to introduce this discussion by presenting the evidence to show that contraception is widely practiced in the West and, as practiced by the majority of the people, is highly effective in reducing the size of their families. However, it should be pointed out that contraception is not the *cause* of the decline in fertility; it is merely the chief *means* used to control the size of the family. The causes of this decline are those conditions of life which lead people to employ contraception as a means of keeping their families within the limits they consider desirable.

1. CONTRACEPTION

Until rather recently there was no very satisfactory evidence regarding the extent of contraceptive practices in any considerable group of people, or regarding the effectiveness of these practices in reducing the birth rate. As long as this was the case it was to be expected that many people would look for biological causes of this decline rather than for the social and economic causes leading to the voluntary control of conception.

In the opinion of the author, the evidence that the practice of contraception is very widespread in the United States, at least, and that it is possible to exercise relatively effective control over the birth rate by this means is now conclusive. In the future the development of safe and effective means for the voluntary control of conception is certain to be regarded as one of the major events in human history. For the first time it has become possible for man to achieve a relatively easy and painless adjustment of numbers to the social and economic conditions prevailing at any given time. In the past, even when a fairly satisfactory adjustment of numbers to the means of sub- sistence was achieved, it was done by methods which entailed far more suffering and hardship than does the voluntary control of conception. Think of the suffering and hardship involved in abortion and infanticide and, when "nature" was allowed to take its course, the terrible toll of infant mortality and hunger and epidemics.

The Extent of Contraception. Pearl[1] found that about 45 per cent of the white women and about 17 per cent of the Negro women included in his study had practiced contraception in some form prior to the conception which resulted in the confinement during which his data were gathered. Pearl believes that the women (about 30,000) who are reported on in this study probably were a representative sample of the general population, as the following quotation indicates:

> In general it may be reasonably concluded that the present material appears to be a fair and representative sample of the general population from which it was drawn in respect of a variety of important variables. The result that it reveals may therefore be accepted with a considerable degree of confidence, as indicative of conditions in the general population, and particularly the urban population, of the United States.[2]

The author is inclined to believe that Pearl was a little overconfident in the typicality of his sample. Nevertheless, there is little doubt that these women were sufficiently like the general population to give his results wide validity. The practice of contraception was certainly widespread in 1931 and 1932 when Pearl's data were gathered, and there is no doubt whatever that this practice has been spreading steadily since that time, not only within the urban communities from which most of these women came but also in those more rural regions where the birth rate had previously been quite high. Pearl's data alone would justify the belief that a large part of the couples in the urban population of the United States are practicing contraception with considerable effectiveness.

More recently the Indianapolis investigation, already referred to in sev- eral places, has shown that among the couples studied intensively, 91.5 per cent practiced contraception in one form or another.[3] Of the couples classed

[1] Raymond Pearl, *The Natural History of Population,* p. 193, Oxford University Press, London, 1939.

[2] *Ibid.,* p. 191.

[3] These were white Protestant couples married in 1927, 1928, and 1929 and inter- viewed in 1941; both husband and wife had completed eight grades of school or more and had lived in a large city most of the time since marriage; the wife was under

as "relatively fecund," over 99 per cent had practiced contraception at one time or another. This group, it will be noted, was not selected as a representative sample of the entire population but rather as a group in which the deliberate control of the size of the family would be about as extensive as it could be expected to become in the entire urban population in the not-distant future. In the population studied, those couples which were relatively

Table 10-1.   Percentage of Contraceptive Effectiveness by Economic Groups, Color, and Age, United States, 1931–1932 [1]

Age	White				Negro		
	Very poor	Poor	Moderate circumstances	Well-to-do and rich	Very poor	Poor	Moderate circumstances
Women reporting at time of first birth							
15–19	43.9	54.8	54.6	84.0	9.2	24.0	
20–24	50.8	53.7	56.8	58.0	10.4	42.0	
25–29	28.6	48.1	43.0	69.3	67.2	51.1	85.0
30–34	79.4	43.7	37.8	42.0			
35–39	....	42.6	−7.3	67.6			
Women reporting at time of second or later birth							
15–19	3.6	22.5	20.3	63.7	3.8	23.1	30.5
20–24	18.7	26.4	31.6	48.7	5.4	8.2	−4.5
25–29	12.5	18.2	23.1	42.1	−22.0	−19.6	67.5
30–34	5.5	9.6	7.3	36.1	10.4	−33.6	66.4
35–39	15.5	· 17.0	20.2	−5.7	−7.8	−38.5	

[1] Raymond Pearl, *The Natural History of Population*, p. 215, Oxford University Press, London, 1939. The percentages given are derived as follows: the mean pregnancy rate per 100 computed ovulations exhibited by each contraceptor subgroup is subtracted from the rate exhibited by the corresponding noncontraceptor subgroup; the difference, with due regard to sign, is then expressed as a percentage of the noncontraceptor mean.

fecund were almost universally trying to exercise voluntary control over the size of their families. Even about 70 per cent of those couples that were "relatively sterile" practiced some form of contraception at some time.

But even granting that the practice of contraception is very widespread and will soon be quite general, it is well known that it has been of highly varying efficacy from family to family and there has been doubt in the minds of many people whether this widespread effort to control conception was

thirty and the husband under forty at the time of marriage. P. K. Whelpton and Clyde V. Kiser, "Social and Psychological Factors Affecting Fertility: VI. The Planning of Fertility," *Milbank Memorial Fund Q.*, Vol. 25, No. 1, pp. 66–67, 1947.

sufficiently effective to account for the large decline in the birth rate during the past several decades.

The Effectiveness of Contraception. It may now be stated categorically that contraception in the manner actually practiced by large sections of the population in the United States is highly effective in reducing the size of the family, and there is no reason to doubt that it is equally effective in most other Western countries. Table 10-1, adapted from Pearl, shows the percentage by which the rate of conception of the women in his sample practicing contraception is lower than that of the women not practicing contraception.

These figures leave little room for doubt that at nearly all ages contraception as actually practiced was highly effective in reducing the rate of conception among the white women in Pearl's sample. It is also of interest that, in general, the effectiveness of contraception increased with the rise in economic status of both white and colored women.

The effectiveness of contraception is also shown in the proportion of married life spent in pregnancy by the women practicing and not practicing contraception (Table 10-2). Among the white women, those practicing contraception spent a significantly smaller proportion of their married lives in pregnancy. This held for all economic classes. Among colored women, how-

Table 10-2. Average Percentage of Married Life Spent in Pregnant (and Puerperal) State, by Color and Economic Groups, 1931–1932 [1]

Items	White					Negro			
	Total	Very poor	Poor	Moderate circumstances	Well-to-do and rich	Total	Very poor	Poor	Moderate circumstances
Women reporting at time of first birth									
Practicing contraception.	26.2	30.9	29.3	25.2	22.0	34.6	36.0	37.6	18.3
Not practicing contraception.	42.3	45.0	45.6	36.3	39.7	37.7	37.7	37.0	54.2
Women reporting at time of second or later birth									
Practicing contraception.	30.4	34.5	31.8	28.1	24.2	38.8	39.8	38.3	32.3
Not practicing contraception.	36.8	37.6	37.4	33.7	36.1	38.9	39.2	38.4	41.4

[1] Raymond Pearl, *The Natural History of Population*, p. 217, Oxford University Press, London, 1939.

ever, there was comparatively little difference between contraceptors and noncontraceptors in the proportion of married life spent in pregnancy in the "very poor" and "poor" classes, but a substantial difference when they were in "moderate" circumstances. Moreover, colored women in moderate circumstances were much like white women both in the proportion practicing contraception and in the proportion doing so effectively.

Pearl found the usual differences in the proportions of the women in the several economic classes who had had four or more live births (Table 10-3). Over two-fifths of all the white women in the very poor class had already borne four or more children, whereas only about one-tenth of the well-to-do and rich had borne four or more children. For completed families the difference would probably be even greater, because it is practically certain that the very poor women would continue to bear children longer as well as more frequently than the well-to-do and the rich.

Table 10-3. Percentage of Women Who Had Produced Their Fourth or Higher-order Live Birth at Time of Record, by Color and Economic Groups, 1931–1932 [1]

Items	White					Negro			
	Total	Very poor	Poor	Moderate circumstances	Well-to-do and rich	Total	Very poor	Poor	Moderate circumstances
Practicing contraception.	24.2	41.3	28.3	15.4	8.6	43.7	48.0	41.6	23.8
Not practicing contraception.	32.9	43.8	32.3	19.5	20.6	40.0	44.8	33.9	29.2
Total.	28.5	42.9	30.3	17.0	10.7	40.8	45.4	35.9	26.7

[1] Raymond Pearl, *The Natural History of Population*, p. 218, Oxford University Press, London, 1939.

Stix and Notestein,[4] using data secured from women who had visited a birth-control clinic in New York City, have shown that contraception as practiced by these women even before visiting the clinic is more effective than among the women in Pearl's sample. This is probably due to the fact that these women were more interested in contraception than those in Pearl's sample, as witnessed by their visits to the birth-control clinic and their payment for its service and for the supplies used for contraceptive pur-

[4] Regine K. Stix and Frank W. Notestein, *Controlled Fertility*, p. 61, The Williams & Wilkins Company, Baltimore, 1940; also "Effectiveness of Birth Control: A Study of Contraceptive Practice in a Selected Group of New York Women," *Milbank Memorial Fund Q.*, Vol. 12, pp. 57–58, 1934.

poses. Table 10-4 shows beyond question that untutored contraceptive practice reduced the rate of conception of these women by over one-half. Furthermore, the degree of effectiveness increased as the duration of the marriage increased. This would appear to be a natural consequence of increased
desire to prevent the birth of additional children after the couple already had
all the children it wanted and also because of the decreasing fecundity of
the women as age advances.

Although the preclinic experience of these women with contraception
shows that it was quite effective in reducing the birth rate, yet they were not
satisfied or they would not have visited the clinic. Did the visit to the clinic
help these women to increase the effectiveness of their contraceptive efforts?
The answer is an unqualified "Yes." Whereas the preclinic rate of conception
for first pregnancies was 41, the postclinic rate was only 7; for second and

Table 10-4.   Pregnancies per Year of Married Life with and without
Contraception, before Clinic Attendance, 1931–1932 [1]

Period of married life	Pregnancy rates	
	No contraceptive used	Contraceptive used
Total rate standardized.......	0.70	0.32
First pregnancy.............	0.91	0.50
All later pregnancies: total....	0.64	0.28
0–4 years since marriage....	0.63	0.32
5–9 years since marriage....	0.66	0.28
10–14 years since marriage..	0.70	0.23
15–29 years since marriage..	0.67	0.14

[1] Regine K. Stix and Frank W. Notestein, *Controlled Fertility*, p. 61, The Williams &
Wilkins Company, Baltimore, 1940.

later pregnancies the rates were 27 and 10, respectively.[5] These differences
are too large to be merely accidental. But it should be remembered that a
considerable proportion of these women came to the clinic because they
already had all the children they felt they could care for or because they
wanted a longer interval between births. Hence, they were ready to practice
contraception more diligently than in the past, and this factor, together with
the knowledge gained at the clinic, accounts for the greater effectiveness of
contraception in postclinic experience.

[5] The pregnancy rate is the number of pregnancies per 100 years of exposure to
conception.

The data collected by Stix and Notestein also throw light on a number of other important aspects of contraception. They show, for example, that a large part of these women plan their families from the beginning of their married life. About 34 per cent planned their families before they had ever had a pregnancy, while about 44 per cent did so before they had a living child. Only 19 per cent planned a pregnancy after they had had two pregnancies and only 10 per cent after they had two living children.

This study also shows that, contrary to a very common belief, the practice of contraception does not render a woman less likely to conceive when a child is desired. "Fifty-four per cent of the 'planned pregnancies' were conceived within a month after contraceptive practice was stopped, and nearly 80 per cent within three months. The 'planned pregnancy' type of non-contraceptive exposure was peculiarly favorable for conception." [6] This is shown by the fact that where contraception was the usual practice but was omitted in order to have a child, the average period before conception took place in the case of first births was 2.6 months, whereas when there was no contraception at all it was 4.0 months. For second and later conceptions the differences were much greater—2.8 months and 9.6 months, respectively. This difference is not surprising, since the natural contraceptive effects of puerperium and of nursing a child have a chance to display their efficacy for those not practicing contraception in the interval between one birth and the next conception, while for those practicing contraception during the early part of this interval this would not be the case.

Another fact of interest in this study is that the Catholic women visiting the clinic were much less given to the practice of contraception prior to their visit than the Jewish women. Whereas the former had practiced contraception for only about six years for one year in which they had not practiced it, the latter had practiced contraception for about 25 years for one year in which they had not practiced it. It also appears that both before and after clinic experience Catholic women practiced contraception less effectively than Jewish women. Likewise the wives of manual workers practiced contraception less effectively than those of white-collar workers, and poor and uneducated women succeeded less often in preventing conception than women in better economic conditions and with more schooling. But the significant point to remember here is that even where contraception had the least effect it still was instrumental in preventing a considerable proportion of the conceptions which would have occurred had it not been practiced.

The Indianapolis Study [7] shows that the effectiveness of contraceptive practices was about 70 per cent; *i.e.*, about 70 per cent of the births to be expected in the absence of contraception were prevented by it. This percentage varied from a high of 85 among 403 couples by whom both the

[6] Stix and Notestein, *Controlled Fertility*, pp. 67–68.
[7] Whelpton and Kiser, *op. cit.*, p. 104.

number and the spacing of children were planned to a low of 38 among 102 couples that had at least two more children than were desired. Clearly contraception as practiced in this Indianapolis group was highly effective even among those couples who were least efficient in controlling the size of their families.

The Royal Commission on Population concludes as follows regarding the effect of the voluntary control of conception on fertility:

> There is thus an overwhelming volume of evidence in this and other countries that the rates of childbearing are at present being greatly restricted by the practice of birth control and other methods of deliberate family limitation below the level at which they would stand if no such methods were practised. That this level is itself as high as it was before 1880 cannot be stated dogmatically. It is just possible that there has been some decline in reproductive capacity, though there is no positive evidence to this effect; indeed, so far as we know, reproductive capacity may well have risen. If there has been any decline, it is extremely unlikely that it has been sufficient to account for more than a small part of the fall in average family size. Of this fall, the spread of deliberate family limitation has certainly been the main cause, and very probably the only cause. Finally, there can be no doubt that if the married couples of today wished to have much larger families than they now have, they would be able to do so; no biological or physiological factor would prevent them.[8]

That the situation as regards the extent and effectiveness of contraceptive practices in other Western countries in which fertility has fallen in recent decades is much the same as in the United States and the United Kingdom admits of little doubt. The voluntary control of conception is the chief *means* by which fertility has been and is being reduced in this part of the world.

2. ABORTION

Abortion has always been and still is an important factor in reducing the birth rate.[9] Dr. Wiehl, who reviewed the evidence on abortion in the United States in 1938, concluded that:

> Total abortion rates for urban samples studied varied from 12.1 per cent to 16.8 per cent; and the weight of evidence favors a rate of approximately 15 per cent of total pregnancies, or 18 abortions per 100 live and still-births.

[8] United Kingdom, Royal Commission on Population, *Report,* p. 34, H.M.S.O., London, 1949.

[9] In medical parlance *abortion* includes spontaneous *miscarriage* as well as induced abortion.

Spontaneous abortions were found to occur in 9 to 10 per cent of pregnancies.

Illegal abortions reported varied from slightly less than 3 per cent to 8 per cent, 4 or 5 per cent of total pregnancies being the most probable rate for married white women in the general population.

Limited data for rural communities suggest that abortions may be somewhat less frequent in the rural areas.[10]

As Taussig shows, there are wide variations in the estimates of the amount of abortion in different countries and areas.[11] It must suffice to say here that the number of illegal abortions, as compared with that of abortions which are spontaneous, is probably quite small, although they are generally believed to outnumber therapeutic abortions by a rather large margin. Since therapeutic abortions are generally performed where the life or health of the expectant mother is at stake, they may be assumed to have comparatively little effect on the size of the population. Often one life is saved while the other is lost and there is no net change. Illegal abortions and many spontaneous abortions, on the other hand, not only result in direct pregnancy wastage but in many cases affect the health of the woman adversely and often result in permanent sterility. Taussig's opinion regarding the effects of abortion is summed up in the following quotation:

When pregnancy is prematurely interrupted by what we term abortion, the human race suffers loss and damage in 3 ways:

First, an infinite number of potential human beings are destroyed before their birth.

Secondly, abortion carries with it a considerable death rate among expectant mothers.

And finally, abortion leaves in its wake a high incidence of pathologic conditions, some of which interfere with the further possibility of reproduction.

It is not possible to estimate the total number of abortions in any population with accuracy. But it is obvious that, if there are a total of 18 abortions per 100 live and stillbirths, then with about 4 million live births and 120,000 stillbirths in 1950 there would have been over 740,000 abortions. It is not known how many of the spontaneous abortions, which constitute much the largest class, are preventable or how many of the illegal and therapeutic abortions prevented a normal live birth. But there can be no reasonable doubt that the number of live births would be significantly larger if all pre-

[10] Dorothy G. Wiehl, "A Summary of Data on Reported Incidence of Abortion," *Milbank Memorial Fund Q.*, Vol. 16, p. 88, 1938.

[11] Frederick J. Taussig in *The Abortion Problem,* proceedings of the conference held under the auspices of the National Committee on Maternal Health, Inc., p. 39, The Williams & Wilkins Company, Baltimore, 1944.

ventable spontaneous abortions were eliminated and if there were no illegal abortions—at a guess, there might be an increase of between 5 and 10 per cent. I would not minimize the importance of abortion in reducing the birth rate or the injurious effects of abortion on the health of women, but it seems reasonably certain that abortion has only a small effect in reducing the birth rate as compared with the practice of contraception. Moreover, it is probably becoming less important as the effective use of contraception increases. Illegal and therapeutic abortions are largely the last expedients resorted to when conception control has failed or has not been practiced. While the effect of abortion in reducing the birth rate should not be minimized, we should not forget that there has always been a considerable amount of abortion. It may well be that we are merely becoming more aware of the amount of illegal abortion and that therapeutic abortion is increasing as a means of saving the expectant mother's life because we know so much more about the need for it. Therapeutic abortion may actually save many more lives than are lost through the removal of fetuses. In any event there is no convincing evidence that any considerable portion of the modern decline in the birth rate is the result of an increase in illegal and therapeutic abortion, or even of an increase in spontaneous abortion.

3. CHANGES IN MARITAL STATUS

It is often claimed that the decline in the proportion of women married has been an important cause of the decline in the birth rate in recent decades. The data do not bear out this contention. There was, as a matter of fact, a rather steady but slow increase between 1890 and 1940 in the proportion of women fifteen to forty-four who were married, but the crude birth rate in the United States declined greatly during this half century, from 31.5 (or more) in 1890 to 20.1 in 1930 and to 17.9 in 1940, with still lower rates in 1931 to 1933. On the other hand, the very large increase in the proportion of married women fifteen to forty-four between 1940 and 1950 was accompanied by a large increase in the crude birth rate (Fig. 8-1). Thus during 50 of the 60 years in which the marital composition of our population was becoming more favorable from the standpoint of fertility its decline was rapid and almost steady, while only in the decade 1940 to 1950 did this favorable change actually go along with a higher birth rate.

At the same time that the proportion of married women fifteen to forty-four was increasing, the proportion married at ages under twenty-five was increasing at an even faster rate than that for all women. This should have increased the birth rate still more from a purely demographic point of view, i.e., from the standpoint of the age changes of married women. It did not do so until the decade 1940 to 1950. Clearly a more favorable marital composition among the women of the United States was not a factor in the decline of the birth rate from 1890 to 1940. The most that can be said is that the birth rate might have fallen even faster if the marital composition had not become more favorable. Since 1940 this situation has changed and a rapid increase in the proportion of young married women, *i.e.*, a more favorable marital composition, has been accompanied by a large increase in the crude birth rate which appears to be in considerable measure due to this change. However, there must also have been some reason for earlier marriage, and a substantial change in attitudes regarding the desirable spacing of children within marriage, to effect such an increase in the crude and age-specific birth rates as has occurred since 1940. This point will be discussed more fully in Chap. XII.

Table 10-5. Number of Single Women Marrying per 1,000 Women Marrying under 45, by Age; and Number of Children 1,000 Women Married at Ages Given Would Have at the Fertility Rates by Age at Marriage in England and Wales, 1911

Age	England and Wales			Sweden			Germany		
	1949	1935	1910	1947	1935	1911–1915	1939	1935	1910
A. Number of single women marrying at given age per 1,000 women marrying under 45									
Under 20	169	88	72	119	66	76	134	57	93
20–24	529	484	490	463	399	419	368	464	531
25–29	199	299	298	254	334	313	322	330	271
30–34	55	87	94	93	134	124	111	103	73
35–39	31	29	33	47	48	48	45	33	23
40–44	17	13	13	24	19	20	20	13	9
B. Number of children 1,000 women married at ages given above would have at the fertility rates by age at marriage in England and Wales in 1911									
Under 20	1,252	652	533	882	489	563	993	422	689
20–24	2,894	2,647	2,680	2,533	2,183	2,292	2,013	2,538	2,905
25–29	708	1,064	1,061	904	1,189	1,114	1,146	1,175	965
30–34	128	203	219	217	312	289	259	240	170
35–39	38	36	41	58	60	60	56	41	28
40–44	5	4	4	7	5	6	6	4	3
Total	5,025	4,606	4,538	4,601	4,238	4,323	4,473	4,420	4,760
C. Proportion of women 15–44 who were married									
	1949	1931	1911	1945	1935	1910	1939	1935	1910
15–44	63.5	50.1	47.7	56.2	44.7	40.6	56.6	52.0	51.4

In England and Wales, in Sweden, and in Germany (Table 10-5) the proportion of women fifteen to forty-four who were married increased between 1910 and 1935, although the increase was comparatively small in Germany. In these countries, then, as in the United States, the change in the proportion of women of childbearing age who were married was favorable to an increase in the birth rate, but the birth rate continued to decline. Hence, the change in the proportion of married women cannot be invoked as a cause of the decline in the birth rate in these countries any more than in the United States. Since 1940, however, in England and Wales and in Sweden it undoubtedly did contribute to the increase in the birth rate and probably in most other Western countries.

In England and Wales the change in age at marriage between 1911 and 1935 was slightly favorable to an increase in the average number of children born per 1,000 married women if the age-specific birth rates for England and Wales at the earlier date are applied to the different age groups of married women of 1935. This increase would have amounted to 10.7 per cent by 1949 if change in marital composition alone had been involved.

The statistics show that in Sweden age at marriage became less favorable between the period 1911 to 1915 and the year 1935 by an amount which would have reduced births by 2.0 per cent on the basis of the age-specific birth rates of England and Wales in 1911, but the crude birth rate actually fell from 23.99 in 1911 to 13.76 in 1935. However, the marital composition among Swedish women became more favorable after 1940, and by 1947 this factor alone would have increased the number of births per 1,000 married women by about 8.5 per cent. In Germany the marital composition changed but little between 1910 and 1935 when measured on the basis of the age-specific birth rates of England and Wales in 1911, but it had begun to be more favorable by 1939. There are no postwar data for Germany comparable to those for Sweden. The point to remember is that although the changes in marital condition taking place for several decades before 1940 were, on the whole, favorable to higher birth rates or at least not unfavorable to the maintenance of the birth rates prevailing in the latter part of the nineteenth century and the first decade of this century, the birth rates were declining rapidly in nearly all Western lands. After 1940 there was an increase in crude birth rates and in age-specific birth rates accompanying changes in marital condition also more favorable to higher birth rates than those which occurred in the half century before 1940. Clearly the changes in marital condition will not satisfactorily explain the different behavior of birth rates at these two periods. However, the marital change since 1940, assuming no change in age-specific birth rates, would explain a part, perhaps a substantial part, of the increase in the crude birth rate since then.

It will help us to appreciate the significance of the different factors which might have affected the birth rate since 1940 if we realize that when the effective control of the size of the family has become quite general and when families of more than three children constitute a rather rapidly decreasing proportion of all families, those couples who do control the size of their families and the spacing of their children have an increasing range of choice as to the age at which they will marry and as to the spacing of their children within marriage. Under conditions of controlled fertility early marriage need not result in an increase in the size of the completed family above that desired, and the birth of the children may be timed to coincide with what the couple believes will be the most favorable conditions. This situation would lead one to expect that while demographic changes, such as an increase in the proportion of women married and in the proportion marrying at an earlier age, might be accompanied by changes in *total* fertility, they may also be accompanied by changes in age of mother at the birth of her children which will affect natality rates at certain ages and in certain periods of time but may have little or no effect on total fertility. The size of the family desired may very well remain fairly stable, while the annual natality rates by which we usually measure fertility may vary considerably over rather short time intervals.

4. CHILDLESSNESS

There can be no reasonable doubt that in most Western countries the proportion of all married couples who are childless had been increasing for some decades preceding the recent rise in the birth rate. As far as the author knows, no thorough investigation has ever been made which shows "normal" childlessness among couples where there was no voluntary control of conception. There are some data, however, showing childlessness under conditions more or less closely approximating uncontrolled conception. These seem to indicate that the "normal" proportion of childless couples may be as low as 2 or 3 per cent, although most figures are considerably higher. Only a few samples of such studies can be given here, and their results do not enable us to say positively what proportion of married couples are fecund.

Crum in examining genealogical records of New England families found: "In the 17th and 18th centuries less than 2 per cent of the wives were childless; in the first half of the 19th century the proportion jumped to over 4 per cent, and this latter figure had doubled by 1870 to 1879." [12] Certainly by 1870 to 1879 voluntary childlessness must have become a factor of some importance in New England and it may well have entered the picture at an earlier date in the group Crum was studying.

[12] Frederick C. Crum, "The Decadence of the Native American Stock," *Am. Statis. Assn. J.,* Vol. 14 n.s., No. 107, p. 218, 1914.

In the report of the Immigration Commission,[13] Hill found that 7.4 per cent of all women included in his sample, married 10 to 19 years and under forty-five at the time of the 1900 census, were childless (had never borne a child). But he also found great differences in the proportions in rural and urban areas and between native and foreign-born women. In Cleveland 8.1 per cent of all the women in the tabulations who were under forty-five years of age at the time of the 1900 census, and who had been married 10 to 19 years, reported that they had never borne a child. In the rural areas of Ohio the percentage for the group with the same characteristics was 5.2. In Minneapolis the proportion of all such women who were childless was slightly higher than in Cleveland, 8.5 per cent, but in rural Minnesota it was only 3.0.

In their study of fertility of native white women Sydenstricker and Notestein, using 1910 census data,[14] found that the percentages of women having no children also varied considerably according to occupational status of the family and the age of the women. Thus, in the professional class 14.7 per cent of the women sixty to sixty-four had had no children; this dropped to 9.6 per cent in the business class, to 9.0 per cent among farmers, to 8.8 per cent among the skilled workers, and to 4.4 per cent among unskilled workers. Where the women were only forty to forty-four, *i.e.*, were 20 years younger, there was a marked increase in childlessness in all classes except farmers, and even there the increase was significant (Table 9-3).

In their study of prolificacy in the United States Whelpton and Jackson [15] found that, in 1919 to 1921, 12 per cent of all married women were childless and that by 1929 to 1931 this proportion would have increased to 23.1 per cent, assuming that the death rates, marriage rates, and age-specific birth rates of 1929 to 1931 prevailed throughout the childbearing period. Under these conditions the proportion for native white married women living to age fifty who were childless would have varied greatly in different regions, from 10.6 per cent in the Mountain states to 23.0 per cent in the Middle Atlantic states, and 26.4 per cent in the Pacific states. The extreme low was found in Arizona (2.7 per cent) and the high in Washington (27.0 per cent) was just ten times as high.

In a study of fertility in a section of Brooklyn (Bushwick) in 1933

[13] U.S. Immigration Commission 1907–1910, *Occupations of the First and Second Generations of Immigrants in the United States, Fecundity of Immigrant Women,* p. 803, G.P.O., Washington, D.C., 1911. (61st Congr., 2d Sess. S. Doc. 282.)

[14] Edgar Sydenstricker and Frank W. Notestein, "Differential Fertility According to Social Class: A Study of 69,620 Native White Married Women under 45 Years of Age Based upon United States Census Returns of 1910," *Am. Statis. Assn. Pub.,* Vol. 25 n.s., pp. 9–32, 1930.

[15] P. K. Whelpton and Nelle E. Jackson, "Prolificacy Distribution of White Wives According to Fertility Tables for the Registration Area," *Human Biology,* Vol. 12, No. 1, p. 42, 1940.

Kiser [16] found that 12 per cent of the native white wives and 8 per cent of the foreign-born wives under fifty years of age and married 10 years or more had had no children. In a more representative study of New York City he found that 11 per cent of the native wives and 7 per cent of the foreign-born wives (9 per cent of all wives) of this age and marital group were childless.

In general, European studies on childlessness, where comparable with the American studies cited above, show somewhat higher proportions childless. In 1910 Körösy [17] found that in Budapest 22.3 per cent of the marriages broken by death (1879 to 1900) where the women had been married 10 years or more were childless. Even where the marriage had endured 30 years or more, 16.6 per cent were childless. In Copenhagen in 1900, where the average duration of marriage was 13½ to 15½ years, the proportion of childless wives varied from 9 per cent among workers to 11 per cent among government employees and professional families.[18] In three sections of Paris, when the women were married at twenty to twenty-five years of age and had been married at least 15 years, the proportions of families without living children varied from 14 per cent in a workers' section to 21 per cent in a section classed as comfortable and to 23 per cent in a rich quarter. In 1901 the proportion of couples in France married more than 15 years having no living child rose steadily as the size of the community increased, from 9.6 per cent of those living in communities having under 2,000 inhabitants to 17.4 per cent in Paris. It should be noted that "having no living child" is not the same as "childlessness."

Data on number of children borne by each woman were collected in the 1912 census of Romania.[19] Of the rural women in Romania who were married, widowed, or divorced and aged thirty-five to thirty-nine at the census only 5.4 per cent were childless, while in urban communities the proportion was 18.2 per cent.

A study showing childlessness among married women in Italy was made in connection with the 1931 census.[20] The following data refer to women married under twenty-five years of age who had lived with their husbands until the time of the census (1931) and were forty-five or over at that time. In the whole of Italy 5.2 per cent of such women were childless, but

[16] Clyde V. Kiser, "Voluntary and Involuntary Aspects of Childlessness," *Milbank Memorial Fund Q.,* Vol. 17, pp. 59–60, 1939.

[17] Josef Körösy, "Weitere Beiträge zur Statistik der ehelichen Fruchtbarkeit," *Bull. de l'institut international de statistique,* Vol. 13, pp. 1–20, 1901.

[18] Lucien March, "Les Statistiques de familles," *Bull. de l'institut international de statisque,* Vol. 17, p 218*, 1907.

[19] Romania, Direction Générale de la Statistique, *Bull. statistique de la Romaine,* Ser. 4, Vol. 16, No. 6–7, p. 102, 1921.

[20] Italy, Istituto Central de Statistica, *Notiziario demografico. Rassegna mensile di dati e notizie sulle populazioni dell' Italia e degli altri paesi,* Vol. 8, No. 8, p. 221, Rome, 1935.

the proportion childless varied from 4.0 per cent among people attached to agriculture to 9.2 per cent among professional people.

The study of fertility carried out in connection with the 1911 census in England and Wales showed that 16.2 per cent of the married women over forty-five had never had a child.[21] This is one of the highest proportions known to the author for an entire country, but it is not surprising if we will remember that England and Wales were more urbanized than any other large country and that the proportion of childlessness among urban women is generally much higher than among rural women.

The 1933 German data throw more light on childlessness in that country than do the data for most other countries, since both the age at marriage and the duration of the marriage are known.[22] In brief summary these data show that (1) the proportion of childless wives had been increasing since early in this century and that the increase was far more rapid in large cities than in rural areas; (2) the proportion of childless wives mounted very rapidly as age at marriage increased, especially above twenty-five; (3) in the same areas there was little difference in the proportions of childlessness among Evangelical and Catholic populations; (4) the proportion of childless women increased steadily and rapidly as social status improved, social status being measured here by type of occupation, beginning with the peasantry and agricultural labor as the lowest and proceeding to the professions and those of independent means; (5) landowners' wives, regardless of social status, had a lower proportion of childlessness than wives of nonlandowners; and finally (6) the proportion of childless wives apparently had been mounting rapidly in the 10 to 15 years prior to 1933, if it is assumed that women married 10 to 15 years and still childless at that time would never have a child. The proportion of wives married in 1918 and childless in 1933 was 17.4 per cent and of those married in 1923 the percentage was 21.8. Clearly childlessness was becoming an increasingly important factor in the growth of the population in Germany.

The data given above furnish slight basis for estimating infecundity.

Voluntary and Involuntary Childlessness. The statement just made will also hold for the few studies of voluntary and involuntary childlessness which are available. However, it will be well to summarize their findings. Lorimer and Osborn [23] analyzed 60 cases of childless women of completed fertility and concluded that from two-thirds to three-fourths of them were involuntarily childless. These were women who had married around 1900

[21] Great Britain, Census Office, *Fertility of Marriage*, Pt. 2, p. xliii, H.M.S.O., London, 1923. (Census of England and Wales, 1911, Vol. 13.)

[22] Germany, Statistisches Reichsamt, *Volkszahlung vom 16 Juni 1933,* Vol. 452, No. 1, pp. 9–48, Paul Schmidt, Berlin, 1937.

[23] Frank Lorimer and Frederick Osborn, *Dynamics of Population: Social and Biological Significance of Changing Birth Rates in the United States,* pp. 257–258, The Macmillan Company, New York, 1934.

and had had much more education than the average woman; as a consequence, they were probably several years older at time of marriage than the average woman. Although no information bearing on age at marriage was available, this may have affected the proportion of involuntarily childless women. On the other hand, Popenoe concluded [24] from his investigations of childless women that about two-thirds of them were voluntarily so. This study was made a little later than that just referred to and related primarily to women in California, where other evidence indicates that the voluntary control of family size is more widespread than in most of the country. In both these cases the authors of the studies are very careful not to draw any definite conclusions and strongly emphasize the need for more study along this line.

Kiser [25] studied a group of childless women in New York City consisting of white wives under fifty years of age and married 10 years or more. It will be impossible to describe this study in detail here, but his results are of unusual interest because the investigation was set up especially to determine the proportions of voluntary and involuntary childlessness and was controlled much more carefully than was possible in the two studies just noted. Kiser found that, of 291 women who had never been pregnant, 217, or 77.8 per cent, had never practiced contraception and that 187 of them, or 66.8 per cent, expressed themselves as disappointed in not having children. Furthermore 157 of them, or 57.3 per cent, had sought medical advice to overcome their childlessness. In addition, there were 90 women who had been pregnant but who had never borne a child; thus of 381 childless women whose pregnancy history was known 291 or 76.4 per cent had never been pregnant and 57 per cent had never practiced contraception as far as is certainly known, since the 90 who had been pregnant but had not borne a child did not report on the practice of contraception.

As Kiser points out, there is some evidence that these women married somewhat later in life than the average woman in the same communities and this may have had some influence in raising the proportion of involuntary childlessness among them, but he thinks this influence could not have been very great, since really late marriages (women over forty) were excluded by the method of selection employed. However, the study of childlessness in Italy referred to above showed that the proportion of *all* married women who were childless was almost twice as high as the proportion of those who were married under 25, and Kiser's data also show that childlessness mounts very rapidly when the marriage age is 25 or over. Kiser is also careful to call attention to the fact that these women were married between 1905 and 1927 and that the importance of contraception in producing child-

[24] Paul Popenoe, "Motivation of Childless Marriages," *J. Heredity,* Vol. 17, No. 12, pp. 469–472, 1936.
[25] Kiser, *op. cit.,* pp. 50–68.

lessness may have changed in recent years. His "tentative conclusion is that, however prevalent may be the practice of contraception for purposes of postponing and spacing pregnancies, such practices cannot be held responsible for any major share of existing permanent childlessness." This conclusion seems to the author to go a little beyond his data.

Pearl's findings regarding the effectiveness of contraception seem to indicate that where contraception is never practiced there is no difference in the fertility of different economic groups except such as can be accounted for by differences in age at marriage.[26] Furthermore, the English data given above show no significant change during almost half a century in the proportion of childless women when they were married under twenty-five.

The results of the Indianapolis Study bearing on the proportion of voluntary and involuntary childlessness are contained in the following quotation:

> The 322 couples who did not conceive may be considered in three groups: (a) The ninety couples that made no attempt to prevent the first pregnancy during the twelve to fifteen years from marriage to interview (only couples married twelve to fifteen years were included in the study), and twelve couples who used contraceptives for a time but later were told by a doctor that they never could have had a child. These 102 couples are classified as unable to have conceived unless treated successfully for sterility. (b) The ninety-three couples that tried to avoid pregnancy during certain periods of their married life but during other long periods discontinued contraception or practiced it only "sometimes." It is assumed that seventy-nine of these couples could not have conceived, and that fourteen would have conceived in from five to eight years if contraception had not been practiced for so long a time. (c) The 119 couples that practiced contraception regularly and successfully all of the time from marriage to interview and the eight that did so for several years after marriage and until an operation was performed which made pregnancy impossible. It is assumed that if these 127 couples had never tried to prevent pregnancy their experience would have been like that of the 513 couples who practiced contraception successfully for a shorter period and stopped to have a child. On this basis 114 would have succeeded, and thirteen would have found themselves unable to do so. Altogether, therefore, 194 of the 322 never pregnant couples are classified as unable to have conceived and 128 as able to have done so.[27]

These results seem to the author to contradict those of Kiser, since almost 40 per cent of the childless couples in the Indianapolis investigation were voluntarily so.

[26] Pearl, *op. cit.,* pp. 218–219.

[27] P. K. Whelpton and Clyde V. Kiser, "Social and Psychological Factors Affecting Fertility: VIII. The Comparative Influence on Fertility of Contraception and Impairments of Fecundity," *Milbank Memorial Fund Q.,* Vol. 26, No. 2, pp. 224–225, 1948.

The Royal Commission on Population doubts that there has been any change in the reproduction capacity of the British people in the last six or seven decades, as the following quotation shows, and also seems to doubt that childlessness is increasing as much as many people suppose.

We have very little direct evidence about reproductive capacity at present, and still less about its past history. Doctors have noticed the increase in recent years in the demand for treatment of involuntary childlessness. But this increased demand may well be due entirely to the spreading recognition, by doctors and the public generally, that treatment can sometimes be efficacious. In former times, only a tiny proportion of the people concerned sought medical help; and an increased demand for treatment cannot, therefore, be regarded as evidence that reproductive capacity has diminished.[28]

In view of the conflicting evidence it is not possible to do more than guess at the proportion of childless marriages which result from infecundity, nor are we in position to say whether infecundity is on the increase. But if most sterile marriages are involuntarily so, as some physicians seem to think and as Kiser's data indicate, then they must be due to biological changes in the race and/or to physiological changes in individuals rendering them infecund, and infecundity must be increasing rapidly. If this is the case it would seem reasonable to assume that these same biological or physiological changes would also reduce the general level of fertility. Such a situation would support Spencer's theory, namely, that as civilization evolves and life becomes more complex man's reproductive power decreases.

On the other hand, the investigators for the Royal Commission were not ready to accept the view that there has been any significant decrease in fecundity. The author is personally disposed toward the Royal Commission's view at the present time, because he does not think that the evidence available justifies belief in any fundamental biological change in man's reproductive capacity in the three or four generations during which fertility has been declining. He is disposed to believe that the increase in childlessness is due primarily to changes in social and economic conditions which issue in a rather large increase in voluntary childlessness, although some of these changes may be of a physiological character which affect the ability of particular couples to have children.

5. GENERAL CONDITIONS FAVORING VOLUNTARY CONTROL OF SIZE OF FAMILY

The Growth of Intellectual Freedom. Many very significant changes in the social and intellectual atmosphere of Western Europe which had been taking place for several centuries came to fruition in the eighteenth century. A

[28] United Kingdom, Royal Commission on Population, *Report*, p. 31.

growing body of people was coming to realize that man could exercise control over many events of the utmost importance to his welfare. Heretofore, man had regarded a large part of what happened to him as outside his province of concern. Intellectually there was little interest in the causal relation of events, and morally the man of the Middle Ages was taught to accept dogma unquestioningly. The development of an atmosphere favorable to freedom of the mind to consider all problems had slowly taken place and may be thought of as the basis of the modern era of human achievement. Such an atmosphere was leading to the development of science and its application to those activities which contributed directly to the improvement of the living conditions of the people. Certain aspects of the practical application of science are known today as the agricultural and industrial revolutions.

The mention of the growth of a new intellectual atmosphere may seem irrelevant to an explanation of how a large part of the people in the Western world have come to look favorably upon the voluntary control of the size of the family. I believe, however, that it is extremely important to realize that the general intellectual atmosphere from the eighteenth century onward favored an open-minded consideration of the problems of human welfare to a degree seldom or never found previously in human history. To ignore this change in attitude is to fail to understand one very important underlying factor making possible a fairly rapid decline in fertility among Western peoples during the past century or more.

The Growth in Productivity. When science was applied to the problems of production great progress was made in reducing the amount of human labor needed to yield a given amount of goods both in agriculture and in industry and also in the effort required to move these goods from place to place. These revolutions soon made possible a large reduction in the death rate through the improvement in living conditions. But before long the application of science to the fields of sanitation and medicine also contributed to still further reductions in the death rate and continues to do so. Malthus was one of the first to gain wide attention for the fact that a high rate of population growth was the natural consequence of a reduction in the death rate if there were no corresponding reduction of the birth rate, and Malthus believed that any considerable reduction of the birth rate was unlikely. In an atmosphere in which people were relatively free to consider the consequences to themselves of a high birth rate accompanied by a declining death rate, it is not in the least surprising that fertility began to decline as soon as means were found to reduce the rate of conception which did not too much offend against the established moral values, which were themselves undergoing rapid change as man came to realize that a lower birth rate coupled with an increase in productivity showed the way to a life relatively free from the positive checks to population growth. I believe that this atmosphere favorable to freedom of thought and experimentation and the increase in level of living accompanying it were very important factors in the rapid and widespread adoption of family limitation.

6. AMBITION

It is quite generally recognized that most people who have a good social status are very desirous of maintaining it and that many of those who have a less desirable status will strive hard to improve it. If we call this urge to maintain or to secure a good social status *ambition*, then it may be said that ambition is one of the most important of all the factors leading to the voluntary control of fertility. It is also probable that the differences in the degree of ambition found in different groups will help to explain the differentials in fertility described in the preceding chapter. It requires no argument to convince anyone that for the great majority of couples, with good social status, it is much easier to maintain that status and to ensure somewhat the same status to their children if families are relatively small. This is even more true of those couples that are striving to rise in status and to improve the status of their children. Therefore, in a society where there is strong competition to maintain and/or to improve social status and where safe and simple means for preventing conception are widely known the restriction of the size of the family is likely to spread rapidly.

Rural-Urban Differentials. One of the most important differentials in the birth rate, as has been noted, is that between country people and city people. A large proportion of city dwellers are migrants or the children of migrants from smaller rural or semirural communities. In the new situation in which these migrants and their children find themselves, their traditional beliefs and modes of conduct avail them little in making the adjustments necessary to establish themselves in their new abode. Under such conditions they are open to a vast number of new suggestions which will be presented to their rural cousins who remain on the land at a later time, if at all. They see differences in modes of living, in incomes, in types of work, in position, in power wielded, in leisure, and in opportunity of which the rural dweller becomes conscious more slowly. These differentiations in city life are so numerous and so striking as compared with those in the country that they excite desires to do, to achieve, and to possess which certainly are not as intense in rural areas. On the farm especially, the traditional modes of conduct are less of a handicap both economically and socially than in the city.

The farmer who carries on in about the same way as his father, does a good job of looking after his land and stock, and provides for his family in reasonable fashion will be approved of by his community even though he may be regarded as rather "old-fashioned" and is not much of an economic success. He is certainly not regarded as a failure if he does not double or quadruple his father's acres and does not otherwise display a strong ambition "to get ahead."

It is much the same with the country woman. She will meet with the approval of her family and her community if she is a good mother and homemaker. She will not be judged to anything like the same extent as the city woman by the way her house is furnished, the clothes she wears, the social items about her in the newspaper, and many other external signs of success. She can still devote her entire energy to her home and her family and feel that she is achieving her full measure of personal development. On the other hand, the city woman has more numerous and distracting contacts —contacts which make her less sure of traditional values and less willing to devote her entire energies to the traditional values centering around home and children.

It is not surprising, therefore, that as between country people and city dwellers there are a great many more of the latter who find that rearing a fair-sized family interferes seriously with the attainment of their ambitions.

Then, too, the higher grades of white-collar work require a long period of rather intensive training and the incomes of workers in such jobs are small until they become well established. Since most young people are eager to live as do other members of their class, and since in a great many cases they cannot possibly do so if they have children, many of them find it decidedly advantageous to postpone children until they are well started on their careers or to limit their families to one or two children if they are started early.

In the country the young man is likely to be quite as able to start his family in his early twenties as he will ever be. His physical vigor is near the maximum, and he has acquired sufficient training to enable him to handle his job satisfactorily. Furthermore, not only are a wife and children not a handicap to his success, as often is the case in the city, but his wife is the economic equivalent of the working wife in the city. In addition, the farm woman's children do not constitute a serious handicap to her in making a substantial contribution to the economic well-being of her family. The handicap of children from the standpoint of the attainment of ambition is therefore a less compelling reason for family limitation among country people than among many classes of city people.

The farm family also remains a more closely knit economic and social unit than the city family. All members of the farm family work at a common task, and each can readily see that his particular work contributes to the welfare of all and that in return he receives from the others many services. This contributes substantially to family unity. Besides, the social life of country communities is still organized around the family unit to a greater extent than in the city.

Another point to be considered is that general farming, which occupies the great majority of our farmers, is a 365-day job and that eight-hour days are unknown during the greater part of the year. Farming requires that the farmer and his wife be at home most of the day and almost every day. Since they must be at home nearly all the time in any event to look after crops and stock, they do not find that children add materially to their immobility. In the case of city people, however, children do add considerably to the immobility imposed by the nature of their jobs and the hours of work. If it chances that travel is one of the things strongly desired by a city family it certainly constitutes a strong motive for family limitation which has been largely absent among farmers in the past.

Other differences between urban and farm living which seem to the author likely to be of some importance in deciding upon the size of the family are the facts that (1) congenial occupations for women, aside from homemaking, are found largely in the city; and (2) work for the children which will be good for them both physically and morally can be provided much more readily in the country. If city children do any regular work they must generally do it away from home where they cannot be supervised by the parents and where the parents have little or no control over the conditions of work or their companions while at work. The scarcity of useful tasks for children not only increases the economic cost of children in the city but also adds to the moral responsibility of the parents without providing them with means of discharging it satisfactorily.

Finally, in pointing out the differences between the country and the city which make for smaller families in the city, we should not forget that information regarding contraceptives has been more widely disseminated in the cities than in the country. No doubt many of the country people who do not yet restrict the size of their families will do so as soon as they learn how. There can be little doubt that, before long, contraception will become as general in the country as in the city. But even so, the author believes it is not likely that the restriction in the size of the family will become as drastic in the country as in many sections of our city population. Children will always interfere less with country people's living as they desire than with city people's living as they desire. It should be noted, however, that with the increased use of the automobile by city workers and with the spread of utilities into rural areas a larger and larger proportion of the nonagricultural workers are moving into suburban areas where they can live a semirural life, so that the differences in living conditions between farmers and village residents on the one hand and city workers on the other are probably becoming less important than they have been during the past four or five decades.

7. REASONS FOR THE DIFFERENTIAL BIRTH RATE IN CITIES

When we turn to the consideration of the differences in birth rates between groups or classes within the city, it appears probable that these differences, too, are to be explained to a significant degree by the way in which children affect the attainment of ambitions by the members of the different groups. It will be recalled that, in general, unskilled laborers have the largest families and that families decline in size as we pass from this group to the semiskilled, skilled, and white-collar occupations; the clerical workers apparently have the smallest families of all. It should not be forgotten, however, that these differences are decreasing and that people in more comfortable circumstances not infrequently have somewhat larger families than those somewhat below them on the social and economic scale.

It will scarcely be questioned that there is far more ambition in the white-collar group than in the hand-working group. In the former there is unquestionably a larger proportion who wish to change and to improve their economic and social position than among the hand workers. Besides, a great many white-collar workers probably have more difficulty in maintaining their present status than do many hand workers. Hence, the additional expense involved in rearing more than one or two children is likely to prove a very heavy handicap to the lower-income segment of the white-collar class. For most of these people it is far easier to keep the family small and thus have more to spend per capita than to increase their income sufficiently to care for a larger family at the desired level of living. In the past this has also been the more certain way to assure oneself of the savings which would guarantee reasonably good living conditions in old age. With the development of social security, however, this may no longer be such an important factor. But it is a fact that for most urban dwellers mere existence depends upon such a variety of factors—employment, prices, ability to continue at work, employer-employee relations, and so forth—over which the individual has little control, that each additional child adds considerably to the uncertainties of life.

The extent to which life is complicated by children and particularly by more than one or two would seem to vary more or less directly with the difference between the way one wants to live and the kind of start he wants to give his children on the one hand, and the means at his disposal on the other. It is obvious that the hand laborer, who has a very modest manner of life to maintain and whose children are generally expected to follow the same pattern of living, has less incentive to keep his family small than the clerical worker who often has even less income but has to dress better, is expected to live in a higher-rent area, and in other ways must at least appear to live at a higher level. If, in addition, the clerical worker, feeling the general insignificance of his position more than the laborer because of his closer contact with the better-paid managerial and supervisory groups, decides that his children must have a rather long and expensive training for a better job than he himself holds, he has a further strong incentive to keep the family small. This situation prevails very widely among the more poorly paid groups in the white-collar class but, of course, is by no means absent among the more ambitious laborers. It is probably an even more important factor in the middle-income groups somewhat above the clerical level that have not yet attained a "well-to-do" status.

The plight of the white-collar workers who are not very well paid is no doubt reflected in the data showing the size of families at different income levels (Chap IX). It will be recalled that in several instances the people having the *higher* incomes had larger families than those with *medium* incomes, although only in Stockholm did we find that the people with the higher incomes also had more children than those in the *lower* income classes.

How differences in ambition operate can readily be seen if we examine the situation in the professions as regards the effect of children upon the advancement of the parents and on the prospects of the children themselves. In the first place, marriage has usually been relatively late in this class because of the long period of preparation involved. In many types of work the period of preparation has been increasing almost steadily during the past two generations until the man who has a sufficient income to live as he is expected to live and to support a wife and one or two children by the time he is thirty is the exception rather than the rule. Even after schooling is over, the the time spent as a "cub" understudy to someone who has already "arrived" or, if an independent practitioner, the period during which a paying clientele is being built up, is relatively long and the income is low. In the meantime the desire to live well, to travel, to be free to go and come as seems best for one's advancement, and a hundred other concrete desires, make it necessary to choose between children and those other activities which contribute directly to "getting ahead." That the decision is often against the baby goes without saying.

The same general type of situation, but with circumstances somewhat altered, is presented to most young couples where the husband is entering business. Children early in life are a considerable handicap, and three or four of them quite generally make it necessary to live so modestly that the neighbors may think one is a failure. Here, as in the professions, the young man generally has a relatively small income during the years when the couple should (biologically) be having its children. Comfort and security are generally attained (if at all) only when it is too late to add to the family.

In the hand-working groups, on the other hand, maximum earning power is generally attained at a relatively early age, perhaps in the age period twenty to twenty-five. This means that the most desirable periods, both biologically and economically, for having children coincide to a larger extent in this group than in the professional and business groups. It is not surprising, therefore, that up to the present the smaller families are found in the better-paid and more ambitious groups. This may not remain so indefinitely, as has been pointed out above, for certainly there are many other motives than ambition, even when defined as broadly as above, leading people to desire small families.

The relatively large number of social and psychological factors which it was believed might affect fertility is shown in the list of hypotheses investigated in the Indianapolis Study.[29]

1. The greater the difference between the actual level of living and the standard of living desired, the higher the proportion of couples practicing contraception effectively and the smaller the planned families. Nineteen questions.

2. The greater the feeling of economic insecurity, the higher the proportion of couples practicing contraception effectively and the smaller the planned families. Twelve questions.

3. The higher the socio-economic status, the higher the proportion of couples practicing contraception effectively and the smaller the planned families. Fifty-five questions.

4. The greater the extent of doubling-up within families, the higher the proportion of couples practicing contraception effectively and the smaller the planned families. Ten questions.

5. The stronger the interest in, and liking for, children, the lower the proportion of couples practicing contraception effectively and the larger the planned families. Twenty-four questions.

6. The interest of children in, and their desire for, brothers and sisters affects the size of the family. Four questions.

7. The stronger the feeling that children interfere with personal freedom, the higher the proportion of couples practicing contraception effectively and the smaller the planned families. Twenty-three questions.

8. The belief that an only child is handicapped is an important reason for having a second child. Four questions.

9. The desire to insure against childlessness is an important reason for having a second child. Four questions.

10. Preferences regarding the sex of children affect the size of the family. Eleven questions.

11. The number, size, and location of communities in which couples have lived affects the proportion practicing contraception effectively and the size of planned families. Twenty questions.

12. Family and childhood situations and attitudes affect the proportion

[29] P. K. Whelpton and Clyde V. Kiser, "Social and Psychological Factors Affecting Fertility: IV. Developing the Schedules, and Choosing the Type of Couples and the Area to Be Studied," *Milbank Memorial Fund Q.,* Vol. 23, No. 4, pp. 394–396, 1945.

of couples practicing contraception effectively and the size of the planned families. Sixty-six questions.

13. Conformity to group patterns affects the proportion of couples practicing contraception effectively and the size of the planned families. Sixteen questions.

14. The greater the adherence to traditions, the lower the proportion of families practicing contraception effectively and the larger the planned families. Twenty-eight questions.

15. The greater the interest in religion, the lower the proportion of couples practicing contraception effectively and the larger the planned families. Twenty-eight questions.

16. The stronger the feeling of personal inadequacy, the higher the proportion of couples practicing contraception effectively and the smaller the planned families. Thirty-five questions.

17. The greater the tendency to plan in general, the higher the proportion of couples practicing contraception effectively and the smaller the planned families. Eighteen questions.

18. The greater the extent to which interest in children is a matter of personal satisfaction, the higher the proportion of couples practicing contraception effectively and the smaller the planned families. Sixteen questions.

19. That member of the couple who is dominant in general family matters tends also to be dominant in determining whether conception shall be controlled and the size of the planned family. Twenty-six questions.

20. The more satisfactory the marital adjustment, the higher the proportion of couples practicing contraception effectively and the larger the planned families. Thirty-two questions.

21. The poorer the health of husband and/or wife, the higher the proportion of couples practicing contraception effectively and the smaller the planned families. Sixteen questions.

22. The poorer the health of the children, the higher the proportion of couples practicing contraception effectively and the smaller the planned families. Six questions.

23. The greater the fear of pregnancy, the higher the proportion of couples practicing contraception effectively and the smaller the planned families. Ten questions.

In addition to the questions assigned to a hypothesis there were others relating to the following topics:

1. Attitudes toward hypothetical inducements to have more children. Sixteen questions.

2. Demographic information about the couple and each child. Twenty-seven questions.

3. Contraceptive practices, menstruation, and lactation. Twenty-three questions (many of them repeated for each practice and for each inter-pregnancy interval).

To supplement the information obtained by questioning the wife and husband, the interviewer herself recorded certain facts and opinions. While the wife and husband were checking categories on the questionnaires the interviewer checked the items on Chapin's Social Status Scale. Soon after the last schedule (Form E) was completed for each couple, she rated the husband and wife with respect to ten of the hypotheses and three other items. Finally she wrote a short analytical summary of the case.

As yet not all of these hypotheses have been reported upon, and the results, while less conclusive than could be desired, are perhaps not much less so than was reasonable to expect in view of the pioneering character of this investigation. The results of several are noted below.

Hypothesis 3 has been reported upon by Whelpton and Kiser. The following quotations summarize their findings in very brief form:

> Despite the relatively low fertility of the "number and spacing planned" group, the fertility rates within this group tend to increase rather than to decrease with rising socio-economic status. Descending the scale by planning status, one finds from these data a rather systematic transition from a direct association of fertility to socio-economic status in the "number and spacing planned" group, to an inverse relation of these variables within the "excess fertility" group. . . .
>
> Finally, with reference to the hypothesis considered in this article, "The higher the socio-economic status, the higher the proportion of couples practicing contraception effectively, and the smaller the planned family," the first part is definitely confirmed by the Indianapolis data but the second part is not. The hypothesis has reference to the "number and spacing planned" and "number planned" groups combined. However, these two groups exhibit marked contrasts in class differences in fertility, and therefore a combination of the two tends to conceal the actual relationships. The second part of the hypothesis is partially confirmed by the experience of the "number planned" but not by the "number and spacing planned" group.[30]

It should be noted, however, that although the highest fertility in the "number and spacing planned" group was found in the group having the highest social status, in the "number planned" group the relation was only partially inverse, while in the "quasi-planned" and "excess fertility" groups the inverse relation was clearly marked. This constitutes further evidence that a change from an inverse relation of socioeconomic status and fertility to a direct relation may be taking place, but only in the upper part of the total group investigated. If and/or when the planning of families becomes practically universal, it seems not unlikely that the direct relation will become more general.

[30] Clyde V. Kiser and P. K. Whelpton, "Social and Psychological Factors Affecting Fertility: IX. Fertility Planning and Fertility Rates by Socio-economic Status," *Milbank Memorial Fund Q.,* Vol. 27, No. 2, pp. 242–243, 1949.

Hypothesis 20 was reported on by Dr. Reed, who summed his findings as follows:

1. A decline in marital adjustment with increasing family size.
2. An increase in marital adjustment with increasing success in controlling fertility according to the desires of the couple.
3. An increase in success in controlling fertility with increasing willingness of both wife and husband to take responsibility for fertility control.[31]

He concludes that the relation of marital adjustment and fertility found here may be affected by other variables:

Although this discussion has been in terms of marital adjustment and fertility without reference to other variables, it is obvious that additional factors are present in the problem. High economic status, for example, has been shown in the past to be associated with low fertility. It is also associated to some extent with good marital adjustment and probably with success in controlling fertility. Thus, differences in economic status or some similar variable may account, in part, for the relationships found between marital adjustment, size of family, and fertility control. It is hoped that further analysis of the couples will throw some light on the influence of the economic and other factors.[32]

Freedman in his analysis of hypothesis 15 says:

A slight negative relationship exists between the effective practice of contraception and degree of religious interest as determined in this study. However, this relationship is mainly a function of socio-economic status. It is not maintained with any consistency within categories based on an Index of Socio-Economic Status. Religious denomination is more closely related to effective planning than is any of the other indices of religious interest or activity which were utilized. . . .

Four denominations have a sufficiently large number of couples to make it worth while to compute fertility rates separately for each fertility planning status. The most significant finding here is that the Presbyterian group, which has the lowest total fertility rate among the four denominations compared, has the highest fertility rate in the two effective-planning categories. This is consistent with a Kiser-Whelpton finding that the negative relationship between socio-economic status and fertility is reversed for effective planners. The Presbyterian group has a much higher socio-economic status than any of the three other groups.

[31] Robert B. Reed, "Social and Psychological Factors Affecting Fertility: VII. The Interrelationship of Marital Adjustment, Fertility Control, and Size of Family," *Milbank Memorial Fund Q.*, Vol. 25, No. 4, p. 423, 1947.
[32] *Ibid.*, p. 425.

On the whole, the findings do not indicate that religious interest is of great importance in explaining variations in reproductive behavior. Neither planning status nor fertility vary in regular gradation with religious interest or participation. It is only when comparisons of extreme religious interest groups are made that the findings indicate a small relationship consistent with the hypothesis. Even the small inverse relationship between fertility planning and religious interest has been shown to be mainly a function of socio-economic status.

It is important to emphasize that the generality of the findings is limited by the nature of the sample—a group of urban native-white Protestants with at least a complete grammar school education.[33]

Whelpton and Kiser in their analysis of hypothesis 2 say:

> The first part of the hypothesis is not borne out by the data. Among the couples studied, success in fertility planning is directly associated with economic security but this relation virtually disappears when socio-economic status is held constant. The second part of the hypothesis is supported by the data. The size of "planned families" and particularly the size of "number and spacing planned" families is directly associated with economic security regardless of differences in socio-economic status. There is a particularly strong tendency for childlessness to be associated with economic insecurity among "number and spacing planned" families. This accounts for much of the direct relation of fertility to economic security among these families. It accounts for virtually all of this type of relation among the total group of "planned families" in the Indianapolis Study.[34]

Little can be said about the relative importance of the different factors investigated in the Indianapolis Study as regards their effects on fertility, but it can be said that the control of fertility shown by the group studied arises from a very complex set of circumstances and motives about which we know altogether too little up to the present. No doubt the analysis of the data bearing on the other hypotheses set up in this study will add to our knowledge, but it must be recognized that this particular study raises as many questions as it answers, if not more. Once the control of the size of the family becomes voluntary, a multiplicity of social, economic, and personal factors come into play, and we cannot hope to understand the *factors in the decline of the birth rate* without careful investigation of all the major forces which operate on individuals to influence their reproductive behavior.

[33] Ronald Freedman and P. K. Whelpton, "Social and Psychological Factors Affecting Fertility: X. Fertility Planning and Fertility Rates by Religious Interest and Denomination," *Milbank Memorial Fund Q.*, Vol. 28, No. 3, pp. 333–334, 1950.

[34] Clyde V. Kiser and P. K. Whelpton, "Social and Psychological Factors Affecting Fertility: XI. The Interrelation of Fertility, Fertility Planning, and Feeling of Economic Security," *Milbank Memorial Fund Q.*, Vol. 29, No. 1, p. 112, 1951.

Suggestions for Supplementary Reading

COOPER, JOHN M.: *Birth Control*, 96 pp., National Catholic Welfare Council, Washington, D.C., 1923.

Great Britain, National Birth-rate Commission: *The Declining Birth Rate, Its Causes and Effects. Being the Report of and the Chief Evidence Taken by the Commission*, 450 pp., Chapman & Hall, Ltd., London, 1917.

KISER, CLYDE V.: "Voluntary and Involuntary Aspects of Childlessness," *Milbank Memorial Fund Q.*, Vol. 17, pp. 50–68, 1939.

LORIMER, FRANK, and FREDERICK OSBORN: *Dynamics of Population: Social and Biological Significance of Changing Birth Rates in the United States*, 461 pp., The Macmillan Company, New York, 1934. Contains much material of general interest.

LOTKA, ALFRED J.: "Sterility in American Marriages," *Proc. Nat. Acad. Sci.*, Vol. 14, pp. 99–109, 1928.

MARCH, LUCIEN: "Les Statistiques de familles," *Bull. de l'institut international de statistique*, Vol. 17, pp. 209–222, 1907.

PEARL, RAYMOND: *The Natural History of Population*, 416 pp., Oxford University Press, London, 1939.

POPENOE, PAUL: "Motivation of Childless Marriages," *J. Heredity*, Vol. 17, No. 12, pp. 469–472, 1936.

RYAN, JOHN A.: *Family Limitation and the Church and Birth Control*, 23 pp., Paulist Press, New York, n.d.

STIX, REGINE K., and FRANK W. NOTESTEIN: *Controlled Fertility*, 201 pp., The Williams & Wilkins Company, Baltimore, 1940.

———: "Effectiveness of Birth Control: A Study of Contraceptive Practice in a Selected Group of New York Women," *Milbank Memorial Fund Q.*, Vol. 12, pp. 57–68, 1934.

TAUSSIG, FREDERICK J., in *The Abortion Problem*, proceedings of the conference held under the auspices of the National Committee on Maternal Health, Inc., 182 pp., The Williams & Wilkins Company, Baltimore, 1944.

U.S. Immigration Commission, 1907–1910: *Occupations of the First and Second Generations of Immigrants in the United States. Fecundity of Immigrant Women*, 826 pp., G.P.O., Washington, D.C., 1911. (61st Cong., 2d sess., S. Doc. 282. On cover: Senate Documents, Vol. 65.)

WHELPTON, P. K., and NELLE E. JACKSON: "Prolificacy Distribution of White Wives According to Fertility Tables for the Registration Area," *Human Biology*, Vol. 12, pp. 35–58, 1940.

——— and CLYDE V. KISER: "Social and Psychological Factors Affecting Fertility," *Milbank Memorial Fund Q.* Seventeen articles in this series have already been published, all of which bear upon various aspects of the subject of this chapter, although only a few of them have been referred to here.

WIEHL, DOROTHY G.: "A Summary of Data on Reported Incidence of Abortion," *Milbank Memorial Fund Q.*, Vol. 16, pp. 80–88, 1938.

WINCH, ROBERT F.: *The Modern Family*, 522 pp., Henry Holt and Company, Inc., New York, 1952. Chap. 5, "The Reproductive Function," utilizes United States materials for consideration of reproduction, childlessness, number of children, and fertility differentials.

CHAPTER XI

MORTALITY

When modern man began to believe that he could exercise some measure of control over his own welfare it was inevitable that he would be interested in reducing mortality, for it was obvious that many of his hardships arose from disease which issued in illness and early death. However, until there was some fairly reliable measure of mortality the deaths of one year could not be compared with those of another, nor could the mortality of one community, or area, be compared with that of others. One of the first measures used was of the same nature as that of births, namely, the ratio of deaths to population, generally expressed as one death for each 20, or 30, or 40 persons in the population. To secure this ratio it was, of course, necessary to know the size of the population and the number of deaths that occurred during the year, just as in the case of births. In time, this was converted into what we now call the crude death rate. This was stated in terms of the number of deaths per 1,000 of the population.

1. MORTALITY RATES

Crude Death Rate. It was soon found that the crude death rate was inadequate for many purposes, especially as a measure of mortality differences between groups in different areas. One of the chief reasons for differences between groups was that they varied from one another in age and also in sex composition, although usually to a lesser extent in sex than in age. Thus what appeared on the surface to be the same rate of mortality was often quite different in fact, while different rates often turned out to be about the same when measured by more refined methods. Moreover, the same population often changed appreciably in age and/or sex make-up from time to time, so that a change in its crude death rate was of little value as an index of basic changes in mortality. This situation could only be corrected by the development of refinements on crude death rates which made more accurate comparisons possible both between different populations and between different time periods for the same population.

The two chief demographic factors to be taken into account in refining or adjusting death rates are therefore the same as for birth rates—age and sex.

Until these differences between groups are allowed for, it is quite impossible to say whether changes in and differences between death rates are merely the effects of age and sex differences and changes or whether they are caused by other differences, chiefly differences in living conditions. It is generally the effects of living conditions on the death rate that we need to know before we can control them and thus change mortality rates for the better. The more customary refinements in mortality rates will only be discussed briefly here because much that was said about the refinement of natality rates also applies to mortality rates and the general references given there also contain a full description of methods for calculating different types of mortality rates.

Age-specific Death Rate. An age-specific death rate (number of deaths of persons of a given age per 1,000 population of that age), generally by sex, can only be calculated with precision if we know the size of the different age groups by sex and if deaths for the same groups are adequately registered. Such rates are the basis for practically all the refinements in mortality rates which are used today. They give an accurate picture of mortality for both males and females at each age. The population base is usually the population in the middle of the period under consideration. If five-year age groups are used there are about 20 age-specific death rates for each sex, and if single-year age groups are used there are about 100. With such a multiplicity of rates only the expert can tell at a glance, and then only approximately, how the mortality conditions of two groups compare. Most of us need a single figure which takes into account age and sex differences if we are to get more than a very hazy idea of how the mortality rates of two populations compare, or how the rates of a particular population have changed over time. Such a rate is commonly called a *standardized* or *adjusted* rate.

Standardized Death Rate. The standardized death rate, based on age-specific death rates, is intended to supply a simple but accurate basis for comparing the death rates of different populations. Assuming that the death rate is standardized for age and sex only, it tells us what the rate would be if the population being studied had the same age and sex composition as some other population which is used as the *standard*. When the death rates of two or more populations are standardized (age and sex) on the same population base (a standard population) their rates can be compared with assurance that any differences found are not due merely to their age and sex differences. Death rates can also be standardized for other known differences in composition, *e.g.*, education, marital composition, and so forth, but such rates are less common.[1]

Death Rate by Cause of Death. The death rate from a given disease is another measure of mortality which is very helpful both in evaluating the

---

[1] Margaret Jarman Hagood *et al., Demographic Methods,* Chap. 14, "Mortality," John Wiley & Sons, Inc., New York, 1953.

effectiveness of present health work in different communities and also in indicating the direction in which the extension of health work is most needed. In the United States this rate is commonly expressed in terms of deaths from a given disease (cause of death) per 100,000 persons in the total population. In this unrefined form it is subject to the criticism that it does not take account of differences in the age and sex composition of different populations. Thus some diseases attack only infants, or at least are not nearly as common among persons above one or two years of age, e.g., enteritis. This disease also seems to be more deadly to boy babies than to girl babies. Since some populations have a larger proportion of children than other populations and since a larger proportion of boys survive the first few days after birth in some populations than in other populations, e.g., in China, such differences need to be taken into account. On the other hand, cancer is seldom a cause of death among children and young adults but rapidly increases in deadliness among people after fifty years of age, as do a number of the organic diseases, e.g., those affecting the circulatory system and other vital organs. The age incidence of certain diseases is made clear by the data in organic diseases, e.g., those affecting the circulatory system and other vital by cause of death in two populations may be quite misleading if one happens to contain proportionally more children or more old people than the other, or if the sex ratio of one population is abnormal.

Table 11-1. Percentage Distribution of Deaths from Certain Diseases by Age, United States, 1948 and 1933

Disease	Year	Under 5	5–19	20–39	40–49	50–64	65 and over
Whooping cough..............	1948	97.0	2.5	0.2	....	....	0.3
	1933	95.5	4.0	0.2	0.1	....	0.1
Diarrhea and enteritis...........	1948	81.2	1.7	3.6	2.1	3.9	7.6
	1933	80.6	2.6	2.8	1.7	3.8	8.5
Cancer and other malignant tumors.	1948	0.4	0.6	4.7	9.8	34.0	50.4
	1933	0.3	0.8	5.9	12.3	34.9	45.8
Diabetes mellitus...............	1948	0.2	0.8	3.1	4.8	31.6	59.6
	1933	0.4	2.6	5.0	7.4	34.8	49.9
Nephritis.....................	1948	0.5	1.1	5.0	6.9	22.3	64.2
	1933	0.6	1.4	5.9	8.6	25.7	57.8
Diseases of the circulatory system.	1948	0.1	0.3	2.4	6.2	25.6	65.3
	1933	0.3	1.4	5.0	7.9	25.7	59.8

Infant-mortality Rate. The infant-mortality rate shows the number of deaths of children under one year of age per 1,000 live births occurring in the same year. Of course, not all the children under one who die in a given year were born in the same year, but usually the changes in the number of births and deaths of children under one year of age are not so great or so rapid over a short period of time that the infant-mortality rate is much different from the death rate of children under one based on the midyear population of children under one. It would generally differ from the latter, however, by a small amount; nor is it identical with the probability of dying as shown in a life table, although as a rule there is little difference among all these rates measuring infant deaths. The age-specific rate from birth to one year of age is calculated on the base of an average or midyear population under one, just as all other age-specific rates generally use a midyear population of the same age. The life-table rate is explained below. The simple infant-mortality rate is generally considered a very good index of the level of living in any population or group—the lower the infant-mortality rate, the better the level of living.

2. LIFE TABLES

The rates of mortality (q_x) which form the basis of the life table differ from the age-specific death rates as usually calculated in that the former show the probability of dying within the specified age interval (*e.g.,* birth to one year) for persons of the exact age specified at the beginning of the period. The age-specific death rate is the rate for persons of a given age dying during the specified interval measured by the number of persons of this age living at the midpoint of the interval. For example, q_{45} shows the probability of dying within one year after the forty-fifth birthday among 1,000 persons alive on that birthday, while the age-specific death rate of persons forty-five is based on the number of persons forty-five years of age dying in a given year per 1,000 persons aged forty-five in the middle of the given interval, *e.g.,* July 1, 1950. Most life tables relate either to males or females, although sex-combined life tables are sometimes calculated. In the United States most life tables assume the birth at a given moment of 100,000 babies, either boys or girls, and by applying the appropriate life-table mortality rates to each age class, *e.g.,* birth to one year of age, one to two, etc. (or, in abridged form, five-year age classes), the number of deaths is obtained. The number of survivors (l_x) at each age from this original cohort is arrived at by subtracting these deaths successively from 100,000. The basic assumption is that q_x rates (probability of dying during a certain period) of the given date (one or more years) continue to prevail throughout the life span of these 100,000 babies. (In Europe it is quite common to use a base number of 10,000.)

Table 11-2. Abridged Life Tables for White Males and Females
in the United States, 1949 [1]

Age interval (period of life between two exact ages stated in years)	Proportion Of persons alive at beginning of age interval dying during interval	Of 100,000 born alive		Stationary population		Average number of years of life remaining at beginning of age interval
		Number living at beginning of age interval	Number dying during age interval	In age interval	In this and all subsequent age intervals	
(1) x to $x+n$	(2) nq_x	(3) l_x	(4) nd_x	(5) nL_x	(6) T_x	(7) $\overset{\circ}{e}_x$
White males						
0–1.........	0.0325	100,000	3,250	97,162	6,587,888	65.9
1–5.........	0.0060	96,750	581	385,259	6,490,726	67.1
5–10........	0.0037	96,169	356	479,859	6,105,467	63.5
10–15.......	0.0037	95,813	355	478,235	5,625,608	58.7
15–20.......	0.0066	95,458	630	475,848	5,147,373	53.9
20–25.......	0.0085	94,828	806	472,182	4,671,525	49.3
25–30.......	0.0086	94,022	809	468,144	4,199,343	44.7
30–35.......	0.0104	93,213	969	463,772	3,731,199	40.0
35–40.......	0.0157	92,244	1,448	457,838	3,267,427	35.4
40–45.......	0.0244	90,796	2,215	448,837	2,809,589	30.9
45–50.......	0.0384	88,581	3,402	434,973	2,360,752	26.7
50–55.......	0.0605	85,179	5,153	413,789	1,925,779	22.6
55–60.......	0.0893	80,026	7,146	383,167	1,511,990	18.9
60–65.......	0.1318	72,880	9,606	341,297	1,128,823	15.5
65–70.......	0.1949	63,274	12,332	286,431	787,526	12.4
70–75.......	0.2708	50,942	13,795	220,813	501,095	9.8
75–80.......	0.3701	37,147	13,748	150,832	280,282	7.5
80–85.......	0.4948	23,399	11,578	86,067	129,450	5.5
85 and over...	1.0000	11,821	11,821	43,383	43,383	3.7
White females						
0–1.........	0.0250	100,000	2,500	97,860	7,150,516	71.5
1–5.........	0.0050	97,500	488	388,499	7,052,656	72.3
5–10........	0.0025	97,012	243	484,356	6,664,157	68.7
10–15.......	0.0023	96,769	223	483,326	6,179,801	63.9
15–20.......	0.0033	96,546	319	482,029	5,696,475	59.0
20–25.......	0.0041	96,227	395	480,224	5,214,446	54.2
25–30.......	0.0051	95,832	489	478,014	4,734,222	49.4
30–35.......	0.0069	95,343	658	475,165	4,256,208	44.6
35–40.......	0.0100	94,685	947	471,208	3,781,043	39.9
40–45.......	0.0147	93,738	1,378	465,506	3,309,835	35.3
45–50.......	0.0221	92,360	2,041	457,081	2,844,329	30.8
50–55.......	0.0334	90,319	3,017	444,603	2,387,248	26.4
55–60.......	0.0496	87,302	4,330	426,485	1,942,645	22.3
60–65.......	0.0769	82,972	6,381	399,993	1,516,160	18.3
65–70.......	0.1287	76,591	9,857	359,774	1,116,167	14.6
70–75.......	0.1988	66,734	13,267	302,005	756,393	11.3
75–80.......	0.2902	53,467	15,516	228,865	454,388	8.5
80–85.......	0.4385	37,951	16,642	146,254	225,523	5.9
85 and over...	1.0000	21,309	21,309	79,269	79,269	3.7

[1] U.S. Federal Security Agency, National Office of Vital Statistics, *Vital Statistics of the United States, 1949*, Pt. 1, p. liv, G.P.O., Washington, D.C., 1951.

A life table or stationary population (L_x) shows the number of persons alive in the specified age interval, assuming a new cohort of 100,000 babies each year. On the assumptions of (1) an unchanging probability of death (q_x) at each age and (2) a new cohort of babies (100,000) each year, there would be no change in number of survivors or in their age distribution after the last baby in the original cohort had died; hence the term *stationary population*. T_x shows the total number of persons in the stationary population in the indicated age interval and all subsequent age intervals.

Another figure of interest derived from a life table is that showing how long, on the average, a person of any given age may expect to live, *e.g.*,

Table 11-3.   Expectation of Life by Age and Sex, United States, Sweden, Canada, and France, Latest Year Available

Exact age	United States, white, 1949		Sweden, 1941–1945		Canada, 1947		France, 1946–1948	
	Male	Female	Male	Female	Male	Female	Male	Female
0	65.9	71.5	67.1	69.7	65.2	69.0	62.5	68.0
10	58.7	63.9	60.4	62.4	59.8	62.8	58.0	62.0
20	49.3	54.2	51.2	53.0	50.5	53.3	48.0	53.0
30	40.0	44.6	42.6	44.0	41.4	44.1	39.0	44.0
40	30.9	35.3	33.6	35.0	32.4	35.0	31.0	35.0
50	22.6	26.4	25.0	26.2	23.9	26.3	23.0	26.0
60	15.5	18.3	17.2	18.0	16.5	18.2	16.0	18.0
70	9.8	11.3	10.5	11.0	10.4	11.4	10.0	11.0

at age forty-five the average white male in the United States (1949) could expect to live 26.7 years. This figure is a simple division of the total number of years remaining to be lived by all members of a given cohort (T_x) by the number of members of the cohort alive at the beginning of the period (l_x).

It can readily be seen that the several types of information contained in a life table are useful in many ways. Thus the q_x rates, probability of dying, for different populations can be compared directly (male and female separately) with the assurance that one is measuring differences in death rates unaffected by age and sex differences and hence that they are a good measure of differences in the health conditions of different populations. The number of survivors at any age (l_x) from the original cohort is also a good indicator of differences in the health conditions that have prevailed up to the age specified, *e.g.*, 100,000 less all deaths to age ten. The total stationary population (T_{0-1}) shows how large a population 100,000 births annually will support at the given q_x rates. Likewise the future expectation of life

($\overset{\circ}{e}_x$) helps to fill out this picture of health conditions. The life-table data also have certain more purely demographic uses such as showing how different q_x rates (in different populations) affect the age and sex composition of the population.

In the United States the differences in expectation of life between whites and nonwhites (chiefly Negroes) are very striking, and in the absence of any evidence showing that these differences have a racial base we must conclude that the health conditions in which the nonwhites live are much less favorable to survival than those in which whites live. (For more details, see Chap. VII.)

In addition, it will be noted that the differences between the sexes in expectation of life are substantial in all the countries for which data are given here. The higher expectation of life for females certainly suggests the possibility that the female organism is biologically tougher than the male organism, but it may be that differences in environment, perhaps chiefly differences in working conditions, will account for the greater average length of life of females. As a consequence of the fact that more women than men survive to old age, the problems of old-age dependency are different from what they would be if the sexes were more nearly equal in numbers at the older ages.

At the death rates of 1949, out of 100,000 white girls born 76,591 would survive to age sixty-five, but out of 100,000 white boys only 63,274 would reach that age. In a population not affected by migration this latter number should be increased to about 66,754, to allow for the fact that as a rule about 5.5 per cent more boy babies than girl babies are born. This difference in survival rates by sex will go far to explain the large excess of older widows in the population. The other factor of most importance here is that wives are generally somewhat younger than their husbands.

Some of the other uses of life-table data are also of interest to the student of population. Thus if 100,000 births of white males annually will support a total population of 6,587,888 at the 1949 death rates, 105,500 male births (the number normally to be expected to each 100,000 female births) will support a male population of about 6,950,200. Since 100,000 white female births annually will support a population of 7,150,516 at the death rates of 1949, each unit of 205,500 births in 1949 will support a total population of 14,100,700. Since the total number of white births in 1949 was 3,171,- 000, or approximately 15.4 times 205,500, the total white population the white births of 1949 would support if this number were to continue indefinitely and if 1949 death rates prevailed, would be approximately 217,150,- 800. Future improvements in health could reasonably be expected to increase this number somewhat.

The nonwhite births of 1949 would support a population of somewhat more than 33 million at the 1949 death rates for nonwhites, and the total population which the 3,722,000 births of 1949 would support, if occurring each year, at the life-table death rates of 1949 would be about 250 million. Since nonwhite death rates will undoubtedly fall considerably more than white death rates during the next few decades, the births of 1949 would support a somewhat larger proportional increase in nonwhites than in whites. If the number of births remained fixed as is assumed in these calculations the crude birth rate would, of course, decline as the population grew. The author cautions against considering the above figures as a projection of future population. They are merely a calculation showing how 1949 death rates and the number of births in that year, if continued, would affect the size of our population by the time all the children born in 1949 had died. Thereafter a continuance of the same conditions would keep the total population at this figure and the age and sex composition would remain constant.

Still another use of the life table is to enable us to calculate the equivalent of a crude death rate when a population has the age distribution of a stationary population with the q_x rates of a given year or period. Thus the life table for white males in 1949 shows that their over-all death rate would be 15.2, and that for white females shows that theirs would be 14.0—a combined death rate for a white stationary population of about 14.6, as compared with a combined crude white death rate of 9.5 in the actual 1949 population. This difference between the general life-table death rate and the actual crude death rate is due to the favorable age composition of the 1949 population as compared with that of a stationary population based on the q_x rates of 1949. This shows us that as we move toward the age composition of a stationary population we must expect that crude death rates will rise, although there will almost certainly be further declines in many, perhaps all, of the age-specific death rates.

A general life-table death rate of 9 would mean that only 9 persons per 1,000 in a stationary population died each year. This could only happen if the q_x rates declined to such an extent that the total life-table population (stationary) rose to approximately 11,100,000, which is also the total number of years lived by each cohort of 100,000 babies in this population; hence, each person in such a hypothetical population would live 111 years, on the average. There is certainly no evidence in the data we possess today that we are likely to approach such an expectation of life in the foreseeable future. Even a general life-table death rate of 12 would mean an expectation of life at birth of 83.3 years, which is about one-fifth higher than that of today.

3. MORTALITY TRENDS

The data on crude death rates in Table 11-4 show that, with only a few exceptions, death rates have long been declining in most Western

Table 11-4. Average Crude Death Rates, 1808 to 1950 [1]

Year	Austria	Belgium	Bulgaria	Denmark	England and Wales	Finland	France	Germany	Hungary	Ireland
1946–1950	12.6	13.0	13.6[2]	9.3	11.7	11.2	13.1	11.0[2]	13.0[2]	13.2
1938–1942	14.3[3]	14.6	13.2	10.1	12.8	16.2	17.0	12.2[3]	14.0[3]	14.1
1928–1932	14.1	13.6	16.7	11.1	12.2	13.5	16.4	11.5	17.0	14.4[4]
1918–1922	18.4[2]	15.5	23.3	12.4	13.7	18.3	20.0	16.7	22.1	15.9
1908–1912	19.8	15.8	23.2	13.4	14.2	16.9	18.5	16.9	....	17.0
1898–1902	22.7	18.0	23.4	16.0	17.4	19.6	20.7	20.8	....	18.2
1888–1892	26.5	20.6	23.1	19.3	19.0	20.8	22.2	23.9	....	18.3
1878–1882	28.7	21.4	....	19.2	20.3	23.0	22.4	25.8	....	18.6
1868–1872	....	23.9	....	19.0	22.2	31.7	26.6	28.0	....	16.7
1858–1862	....	22.2	....	20.1	21.9	26.3	23.4	25.1		
1848–1852	....	23.2	....	20.1	22.6	25.7	23.5	27.0		
1838–1842	....	25.1	....	20.3	22.1	21.9	23.6			
1828–1832	....	....	....	26.8	....	27.3	25.9			
1818–1822	....	....	....	20.7	....	25.6	25.3			
1808–1812	....	....	....	24.9	....	39.8	25.7			

Year	Italy	Netherlands	Norway	Poland	Romania	Russia	Scotland	Yugoslavia	Spain	Sweden
1946–1950	10.8	7.9	9.1	....	20.0[2]	....	12.5	13.4[2]	11.6	10.2
1938–1942	13.9	9.3	10.5	13.7[2]	19.1	20.8[2]	13.7	15.3[2]	17.6	11.1
1928–1932	15.2	9.6	10.9	16.0	20.7	18.9[2]	13.6	....	17.2	12.0
1918–1922	21.1	13.0	13.5	23.6[2]	23.9[2]	21.7[2]	14.8	....	24.4	14.2
1908–1912	20.8	13.8	13.6	21.2	25.6	28.9[2]	15.6	23.7[2]	23.1	14.1
1898–1902	22.6	17.1	15.4	25.0	26.4	31.8	18.0	22.8	27.9	16.2
1888–1892	26.3	20.5	17.7	....	30.2	35.8	19.1	27.0	30.9	16.8
1878–1882	29.0	22.2	16.6	....	30.6	34.9[2]	20.1	28.8	30.6	17.6
1868–1872	29.8	25.8	17.0	....	26.5	36.9[2]	22.2	32.0	....	19.3
1858–1862	....	26.6	18.0	....	....	....	21.1	....	....	19.9
1848–1852	....	....	18.2	....						20.6
1838–1842	....	....	19.3							21.7
1828–1832	....	....	19.4							25.8
1818–1822	....	....	19.5							24.9
1808–1812	....	....	....							33.1

Year	Switzerland	Argentina	Canada	Chile	Guatemala	Honduras (British)	Jamaica	Puerto Rico	United States	Ceylon
1946–1950	10.8	9.5[2]	9.3	17.0	23.2	14.8	12.9	11.5	9.9	14.6
1938–1942	11.5	10.5	9.8	21.7	27.4	19.9	15.2	17.9	10.6	20.1
1928–1932	12.1	12.8	10.6	24.1	21.1	23.0	18.1	21.6	11.5	24.0
1918–1922	14.7	17.1[2]	10.8[2]	31.9	23.1	25.6[2]	....	21.0[2]	13.5	31.6
1908–1912	15.4	17.2[2]	12.5[2]	31.7	21.4	25.2[2]	24.3[2]	....	....	31.1
1898–1902	18.1	18.4[2]	12.1	32.2	20.7	....	21.4	31.0[2]	....	28.2
1888–1892	20.1	....	11.0	35.0	28.2	....	22.6	30.4	....	26.8
1878–1882	22.4	....	....	28.5	....	....	....	....	....	22.7
1868–1872	....	....	....	25.8	....	....	....	....	....	20.9
1858–1862	....	....	....	25.5						

Year	India	Japan	Philippine Islands	Algeria[5]	Egypt[6]	Union of South Africa[5]	Australia	New Zealand[5]
1946–1950	17.6	13.4	....	12.0[2]	22.2[2]	8.9	9.8	9.3
1938–1942	21.9	16.7	16.6[2]	14.3[2]	26.3	9.4	10.4	9.7
1928–1932	24.6	18.8	19.1	15.1	26.9	9.7	9.0	8.4
1918–1922	36.8	24.0	24.9	17.6	29.7	12.0	10.5	10.4
1908–1912	32.8	20.8	21.6	17.9	27.1	10.3[2]	10.7	9.4
1898–1902	31.3	20.6	23.5[2]	21.6[2]	26.5[2]	....	12.7	10.0
1888–1892	29.1	20.4	42.7	25.8[2]	25.1[2]	....	14.4	9.8
1878–1882	....	18.1	....	28.3[2]	....	....	15.2	11.5
1868–1872	....	....	....	26.9[2]	....	....	14.4	11.3
1858–1862	....	....	....	27.5[2]				
1848–1852	....	....	....	43.7[2]				
1838–1842	....	....	....	39.1[2]				
1828–1832	....	....	....	39.8[2]				

[1] For the current data on death rates the reader is referred to *Population Index*.
[2] Austria, 1919 to 1922; Bulgaria, 1946 to 1947; Germany, Federal Republic, 1946 to 1950; Hungary 1946 to 1948; Poland, 1938, 1919 to 1922; Romania, 1945, 1920 to 1922; U.S.S.R., 1933 to 1935, 1928, 1909 to 1924; Russia, 1906 to 1909, 1876 to 1880, 1866 to 1870; Yugoslavia, 1948 to 1950, 1938 to 1939, 1909 to 1912; Argentina, 1946 to 1949, 1915 to 1919, 1909 to 1913, 1899 to 1902; Canada, 1920 to 1924, 1911 to 1913; Honduras (British), 1922 to 1924, 1909 to 1911; Jamaica, 1906 to 1910; Puerto Rico, 1921 to 1925, 1894 to 1898; Philippines, 1938 and 1940, 1903 to 1907; Algeria, 1946 to 1949, 1931 and 1933 to 1935, 1901, to 1905, 1891 to 1895, 1881 to 1885, 1872 to 1876, 1861 to 1865, 1851 to 1855, 1841 to 1845, 1831 to 1835; Egypt, 1946 to 1948, 1905 to 1909, 1901 to 1904; Union of South Africa, 1910 to 1914.
[3] 1938 to 1942 excludes military deaths.
[4] Irish Free State.   [5] Europeans only.
[6] Before 1917, Bedouins were not included in population estimates.

countries and that they have also declined in some of the countries for which data have become available more recently. There are still large portions of the world, however, for which there are no reliable data even on crude death rates. China, the Indochinese peninsula, most of Africa, large areas in the Near East, and some countries in Central and South America either have no demographic data whatever or little reliance is to be placed on those collected. Consequently, such a table is somewhat misleading in that it leaves the reader with the impression that the data are equally good for all countries included in it, which is far from being the case. The *Demographic Yearbook, 1951,* of the United Nations rates the quality of the vital statistics in most of those countries for which such data are available.

However, in spite of the entire lack of data for many countries and in spite of the inaccuracies in the death rates for some of the others, there can be no doubt that in most of the countries for which there are even moderately reliable data the death rate has been declining in recent decades. Even when allowance is made for rather large errors in the recording of deaths in countries like India, or the Philippines, or Chile, it seems reasonably certain that their crude death rates have been declining. The growth of population as shown by successive censuses in India and the Philippines would alone be sufficient to prove a decline in the death rate in those countries unless it could be shown that the birth rate had been rising rather rapidly. There is no evidence of this rapid rise. Moreover, since their birth rates are already very high, the likelihood of any considerable increase is small. It is as certain as $2 + 2 = 4$ that the rates of increase in these countries during the past few decades have not prevailed for any great length of time. In most of those countries where there are no census data and no data on deaths we are forced to fall back on the probability that death rates in them are similar to those in other countries where the conditions determining the death rate are somewhat similar and for which we may have sufficiently reliable data to justify making an estimate.

As we have seen, crude death rates are quite inadequate to give a clear picture of the trend of mortality even in the same population over any considerable period of time, principally because of changes in age composition. For this reason the age-specific death rates for Sweden are given in Table 11-5. Sweden is chosen because, as far as the author knows, it has one of the longest series of reliable age-specific death rates in existence and also because there is no reason to think that the general pattern of change in such rates in Sweden has been fundamentally different from that in other Western countries. The age-specific death rates in Sweden show much the same steady decline from the latter part of the eighteenth century to the present time that her crude rates do when averages for decades are used. When the rates for shorter periods are considered the case is somewhat different, as will be noted in a moment.

Infant Mortality. One of the most important trends in mortality in modern times is the decline in infant mortality. Hence, a few figures showing probable changes over a period of two to three centuries will be of interest.[2] John Graunt, working with parish registers in London, estimated that around 1662 only 640 children survived to age six out of each 1,000 born and only 250 survived to age twenty-six. Dupré de St. Maur calculated that in France prior to 1750 only 540 children out of 1,000 born alive survived to the fifth year, and only 484 to the tenth year. Halley, working on data for Breslau, 1687 to 1691, found 661 surviving to the tenth year, and Süssmilch, basing his calculations on German data prior to 1775, found only 532 surviving to the tenth year. Wargentin, working on Swedish data, 1757 to

Table 11-5. Average Death Rates by Age for Sweden, 1751 to 1948

Age	1945–1948	1881–1910	1811–1840	1751–1780
Total	10.50	16.06	24.08	28.01
0–5	6.98	36.29	63.16	86.61
5–9	.80	5.92	8.25	13.82
10–14	.65	3.60	4.92	7.23
15–19	1.34	4.62	5.40	6.99
20–24	1.95	6.05	7.58	8.53
25–29	1.93	6.29	8.49	10.11
30–34	2.07	6.47	10.67	12.17
35–39	2.45	7.22	12.81	12.21
40–44	3.22	8.25	15.48	16.57
45–49	4.74	9.62	17.75	17.87
50–54	7.28	12.15	23.58	22.97
55–59	11.08	16.31	30.26	27.61
60–64	17.47	23.49	43.29	40.58
65–69	28.95	35.90	61.77	56.94
70–74	47.71	57.22	94.07	89.17
75–79	82.23	93.65	138.90	123.18
80 and over	174.39	184.22	243.25	220.68

1763, found 611 surviving to age ten. At the end of the eighteenth century in Sweden about 200 babies under one year of age were dying per 1,000 live births during the year. Such calculations, except those for Sweden, although based on data which were far less accurate than those to which we are accustomed today, prove beyond reasonable doubt that the mortality of children during the first few years of life was very great in Europe before the agricultural and industrial revolutions had begun to exercise much influ-

[2] Emile Levasseur, "The Tables of Mortality and Survivorship," *Royal Statis. Soc. J.,* Vol. 50, No. 3, pp. 549–554, 1887. (Translated from *J. de la société de statistique de Paris,* March, 1887.)

Table 11-6. Average Infant Mortality Rates in Selected Countries, 1898 to 1950 [1]
(Deaths under one year per 1,000 live births)

Country	1946–1950	1938–1942	1918–1922	1908–1912	1898–1902
Sweden	24	38	65	75	98
New Zealand[2]	24	31	47	61	82
Australia	27	39	63	73	111
Netherlands	31	38	81	111	148
Norway	32[3]	38	58	69	91
United States[4]	32	46	85		
England and Wales	36	54	85	112	152
Switzerland	36	42	80	109	142
Denmark	37	54	84	104	131
Finland	52	70	108	115	138
France	58	73	112	123	154
Belgium	64	86	115	141	157
Japan	65[3]	96	172	159[3]	155
Germany	71[5]	65	140	170	199[3]
Austria	75	74	155	198[3]	220
Spain	76	127	158	152	190[3]
Italy	77	107	141	147	167
Hungary	106[3]	126	193	200	214
India	134[3]	159	212	206[3]	
Chile	161	214	258[3]	314	349
Romania	181	178	209[3]	192[3]	207

[1] For the current data on infant mortality rates the reader is referred to *Population Index*.

[2] Europeans only.

[3] Norway, 1946 to 1949; Japan, 1947 to 1950, 1908 to 1910; Germany, 1901 to 1905; Austria, 1909 and 1910 not included; Spain, 1900 to 1902; Hungary, 1946 to 1948; India, 1946 to 1949, 1911 and 1912; Chile, 1919 and 1920 not included; Romania, 1919 to 1920, 1911 to 1912.

[4] Birth registration area.

[5] Federal Republic.

ence on the economy of this region. However, by the end of the eighteenth century such rates had begun to decline in some countries.

In Sweden after about 1820 infant mortality declined in every decade up to the present time. This was not true for children over one year of age, but in only two or three decades were their mortality rates in a later decade— chiefly in the decades 1851 to 1870—higher than in the decade 1841 to 1850. The net effect of this trend on mortality rates was that, whereas at the death rates of 1757 to 1763 only 611 children out of 1,000 born would have survived to age ten, the 1941 to 1945 life table for Sweden shows that 951 males and 962 females would have lived to age ten. There is no reason to doubt that much the same change in infant and child mortality took place in most other Western countries, although there is some reason to believe that the rates for Sweden were somewhat below those of most other Western countries in these earlier periods just as they still are. For changes in infant mortality since 1900 in much of the West, see Table 11-6.

The Role of Mortality in Determining Population Growth. It has been known from time immemorial that there were frequent and violent fluctuations in the number of deaths in a given population and that they rose to incredible heights at times of famine and when great scourges like the Black Death and the Thirty Years' War devastated whole countries and even whole continents. In these cases the cause (causes) of the excessive number of deaths was generally recognized. It was far less commonly recognized, however, that certain causes of death operated quite regularly to maintain a high death rate.

But even though individuals and communities have always resorted to whatever means were believed to be effective in warding off disease from themselves or in postponing death, it was not until about the end of the eighteenth century that man was in position to begin to control his death rate. Before that, a high and widely fluctuating number of deaths was accepted as a normal condition of existence. This will perhaps explain the seeming lack of interest in the variations in the death rate from year to year among most peoples in the past.

After 1750 we are fortunate in having good statistical data on the death rates in Sweden and Finland, and through them we can secure a fairly adequate picture of the fluctuations during the past two centuries. It is highly probable that in these two countries the fluctuations were smaller during the latter half of the eighteenth century and the first half of the nineteenth than in preceding centuries and also of smaller amplitude than in most other European countries; but they were still large until quite recently. The following data illustrate clearly how variations in the death rate affected population growth until near the end of the nineteenth century.

The death rate in Sweden rose from 27.7 in 1756 to 29.9 in 1757 and 32.4 in 1758 and then fell to 24.8, or by almost one-fourth, in 1760. In 1762 and 1763 it again rose and was above 32.0 in the latter year but fell to 25.1 in 1766. In 1772 it rose to 37.4 and then jumped to 52.4 in 1773, only to fall to 22.4 in the following year (1774). In the war years 1808 to 1810 it averaged 35.5 but fell to an average of 27.0 in the ensuing five years. Variations of 3 to 4 points from year to year were by no means uncommon until the latter third of the nineteenth century. There were even larger variations lasting further into the nineteenth century in Finland than in Sweden. In 1868 (a war year) Finland had a death rate of 77.6 and its population declined by 96,660, or by 53.0 per 1,000.

In France and England there were also rather wide fluctuations in the death rate up to the last quarter of the nineteenth century. In most cases these wide fluctuations can be connected rather closely with food shortages, epidemics, and war. Such data leave no doubt that within the past 200 years there have been wide fluctuations in the death rates even in those countries sufficiently well organized politically and economically to make the recording of the relevant facts possible.

The probable pattern of fluctuations in the death rate before about 1750 among all peoples in the aggregate is illustrated in Sec. B of Fig. 11-1 and may be compared with the fluctuations in the birth rate shown in Sec. A. The solid line (*B*) represents the 10-year moving average of the crude death rate in Finland centering on the date given. The broken line shows the percentage variation of the two-year average death rate, ending in the year

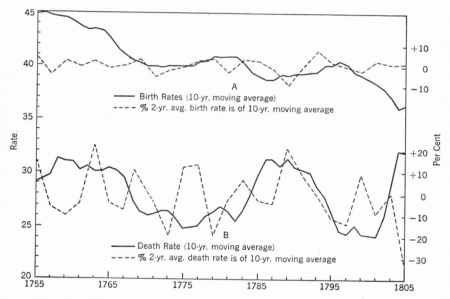

Fig. 11-1. Fluctuations in Finland's birth and death rates, 1755 to 1805.

given, from the 10-year moving average. Section A similarly shows the percentage fluctuations of the two-year average birth rates from the 10-year moving average of the crude birth rates. The point to notice is that, whereas the two-year average birth rate seldom varied from the 10-year moving average more than 3.0 per cent, the two-year average death rate seldom varied from the 10-year moving average as little as 5.0 per cent; in 12 of the two-year periods the variation was above 10 per cent, and in six it was above 15 per cent. The fluctuations of single-year death rates and birth rates around their 10-year averages had an even wider relative variation. It is also of interest that Finland's 10-year average death rates show no clear trend during this period from 1755 to 1805, a condition which probably prevailed throughout man's history until about two centuries ago, with only occasional exceptions.

The preceding discussion on the fluctuations in crude death rates was designed to illustrate the probable roles played by deaths and births in determining population growth throughout most of man's life on earth. There is little doubt that until quite recently the fluctuations in the death rate have been largely decisive in determining changes in the rate of population growth from year to year, while the fact that the birth rate and the death rate averaged about the same over long periods of time will account for the slow change in man's numbers over the centuries. The fact that Finland's death rate was generally well below its birth rate during the period for which there are records merely shows that it had entered upon a period of substantial growth as early as 1750.

I have dwelt upon the point that the variability of the death rate rather than of the birth rate has been the chief factor in determining population growth from year to year throughout most of human history, because it is not generally realized that this has been the case. We have become so accustomed to a death rate showing but small fluctuations from year to year, as well as to a relatively low death rate, that we are inclined to look upon changes in the birth rate as the chief determinant of population growth at any given time. In only a few countries and in recent decades has the death rate come under such secure control that changes in the rate of population growth at any given time are more largely determined by fluctuations in the birth rate than by those in the death rate.

4. SOCIAL AND ECONOMIC FACTORS INFLUENCING THE DEATH RATE

This section will deal chiefly with the influence of social and economic factors other than famines, epidemics, and war in determining the death rate.

Urban and Rural Living. From the time modern vital statistics made it possible to distinguish between deaths in rural and urban communities until quite recently, rural communities have generally had lower death rates than urban communities, although this fact was at times obscured by the failure to adjust death rates for differences in the age and sex composition of such communities. During the last 10 or 20 years, however, there are an increasing number of urban communities that have lower death rates than rural communities, particularly at certain ages.

Dorn's study of urban-rural mortality in Ohio in 1930 is summed up in Table 11-7.[3] This study showed that the lowest crude death rate for native

[3] Similar data are not available for the United States. Harold F. Dorn, *Differential Rural-Urban Mortality in Ohio, 1930,* pp. 90–115, University of Wisconsin Press, Madison, 1933.

white males was found in the largest cities (100,000 and over) and the highest in rural-farm communities and small cities (2,500 to 10,000). Rural-nonfarm communities and cities of 10,000 to 100,000 had rates about midway between these other two groups. The crude rates for females were also highest in the farm population and the smallest cities and lowest in the larger cities. When the rates were standardized for age the above ranking was, in general, reversed. The rate for males showed a consistent decline from the

Table 11-7.   Deaths per 1,000 Native White Population by Age and Sex in Urban Groups and Rural Areas, Ohio, 1930 [1]

Age	100,000 and over		10,000– 100,000		2,500– 10,000		Rural- nonfarm		Rural- farm	
	Male	Female	Male	Female	Male	Female	Male	Female	Male	Female
Total (crude).	9.3	8.1	10.3	9.2	11.7	10.7	10.4	9.9	11.7	11.1
0–4.........	17.2	13.6	17.1	15.0	17.2	13.2	17.3	13.7	16.8	14.0
5–9........	2.4	1.7	1.9	1.0	1.9	1.2	1.9	1.4	1.8	1.7
10–14......	1.5	1.2	1.7	0.9	1.5	1.0	1.4	1.4	1.5	1.3
15–19......	2.4	1.9	2.6	1.7	2.5	2.3	2.7	2.2	1.6	1.8
20–24......	2.7	2.7	2.7	2.5	3.8	3.4	3.6	3.5	3.6	3.1
25–29......	3.1	3.3	3.3	3.1	3.9	3.9	3.4	3.5	4.0	3.7
30–34......	4.4	3.8	3.7	3.3	3.9	3.4	3.5	3.4	3.3	4.3
35–44......	6.4	5.0	5.4	4.5	4.6	4.9	5.2	4.8	4.5	4.5
45–54......	12.3	10.0	10.6	9.0	9.6	9.6	7.8	8.6	7.2	7.5
55–64......	25.8	19.9	24.0	19.1	23.2	17.7	17.0	17.0	16.6	16.2
65–74......	59.1	45.9	58.8	45.1	51.2	41.4	43.9	41.2	43.8	39.5
75 and over..	135.6	114.5	140.9	122.2	140.8	122.2	117.6	123.5	118.0	110.1
Adjusted rate[2]......	10.7	8.7	10.3	8.5	10.0	8.4	9.0	8.4	8.6	8.0

[1] Harold F. Dorn, *Differential Rural-Urban Mortality in Ohio, 1930*, pp. 90, 114–115, University of Wisconsin Press, Madison, 1933. Exclusive of institutional deaths.
[2] Based on the standard million population of England and Wales, 1901.

largest cities to rural-farm communities. The rates for females also declined as the size of the community declined except for the rural-nonfarm communities, where the rate was the same as in the smallest cities.

   In 1940 the crude death rate of Ohio's white population was lowest (10.5) in cities of 10,000 to 100,000, next lowest in cities of 100,000 and over (11.2), followed by rural communities (11.5 in all places under 2,500), and highest in the smallest cities (11.8). When these rates were standardized the different sizes of places ranked as follows in descending order of rate: 100,000 and over, 11.0; 2,500 to 10,000, 9.9; 10,000 to 100,000, 9.7; rural, 9.6 (Table 11-8).

In the United States in 1940, both sexes combined, the crude and standardized rates for the white population in different sizes of communities are also shown in Table 11-8. The crude rates for rural communities were the lowest, followed by the largest cities, the medium-sized cities, and the smallest urban communities in ascending order of their rates. When standardized, the only change in order was between cities of 100,000 and over and those of 10,000 to 100,000. It should be noted, however, that by 1940, in the white population, most of the age-specific death rates at ages under thirty-five were lower in the large cities than in either the rural population or the smaller cities. On the other hand, at ages above thirty-five the larger cities generally had higher death rates than the smaller cities and the rural communities.

More and more frequently since 1920, infant-mortality rates—the number of children under one year of age dying in a given year per 1,000 live births in that year—in the larger cities of the United States have fallen below those in the rural areas. Thus, in 1930 infant mortality in the cities of 100,000 and over (all races) was 61.1 while it was 66.1 in rural com-

Table 11-8.   Deaths per 1,000 White Population by Age and Population-size Groups, United States and Ohio, 1940 [1]

Age	United States				Ohio			
	100,000 and over	10,000–100,000	2,500–10,000	Rural	100,000 and over	10,000–100,000	2,500–10,000	Rural
Total (crude)........	10.9	11.0	12.0	9.5	11.2	10.5	11.8	11.5
Under 1.............	45.7	55.0	66.6	47.8	44.3	46.1	50.4	48.9
1–4................	2.1	2.6	3.3	2.7	2.0	2.1	2.8	2.5
5–14...............	0.9	1.0	1.3	0.9	0.9	0.9	1.0	1.0
15–24..............	1.4	1.7	2.1	1.8	1.5	1.4	1.7	1.7
25–34..............	2.3	2.5	2.9	2.5	2.5	2.2	2.6	2.5
35–44..............	4.7	4.4	4.9	3.9	4.9	3.9	4.1	4.1
45–54..............	10.9	10.0	10.2	7.8	10.8	8.8	8.6	8.1
55–64..............	24.7	22.5	22.4	17.4	24.3	19.9	19.7	18.3
65–74..............	53.3	50.1	49.9	42.4	54.6	47.4	44.7	42.9
75–84..............	118.0	115.8	117.4	108.9	123.0	112.3	113.9	118.0
85 and over.........	210.8	238.2	259.8	241.7	231.1	251.5	264.3	254.3
Adjusted rate[2]........	10.8	10.6	11.2	9.3	11.0	9.7	9.9	9.6

[1] U.S. Bureau of the Census, *Vital Statistics Rates in the United States, 1900–1940*, pp. 198, 205, G.P.O., Washington, D.C., 1943.
[2] Based on the total population of the United States, 1940.

munities. The rates in the cities of 10,000 to 100,000 were about the same as in the rural communities. By 1940 the infant-mortality rate in the large cities had fallen to 39.3 (all races); it rose as the size of the city decreased to 53.4 in cities of 2,500 to 10,000 and then fell to 50.1 in rural communities. Clearly the infant-death rate in the largest cities was falling faster than that in the rural communities, and the highest rates were still to be found in the smallest cities. This was true for the rates of both whites and

Table 11-9.   Ratio of Actual to Expected Deaths as Computed by English Life Tables, England and Wales, 1930 to 1932 [1]

Age	Male			Female		
	County[2] boroughs	Urban districts	Rural districts	County[2] boroughs	Urban districts	Rural districts
5 and over	1.106	0.971	0.858	1.054	0.978	0.934
5–9...............	1.088	0.971	0.847	1.066	1.011	0.840
10–14..............	1.096	0.949	0.929	1.064	0.966	0.906
15–19..............	1.050	1.002	0.921	1.063	0.962	0.937
20–24..............	1.043	0.957	0.971	1.038	0.957	0.975
25–29..............	1.060	0.954	0.932	1.024	0.984	0.978
30–34..............	1.092	0.939	0.902	1.031	0.972	0.983
35–39..............	1.120	0.940	0.850	1.029	0.972	1.002
40–44..............	1.145	0.929	0.800	1.073	0.951	0.921
45–49..............	1.169	0.929	0.763	1.064	0.962	0.916
50–54..............	1.164	0.935	0.756	1.074	0.955	0.911
55–59..............	1.140	0.947	0.796	1.068	0.967	0.909
60–64..............	1.114	0.971	0.815	1.059	0.983	0.907
65–69..............	1.109	0.983	0.835	1.064	0.978	0.913
70–74..............	1.099	1.000	0.841	1.054	0.986	0.908
75–79..............	1.075	1.001	0.905	1.051	0.988	0.945
80–84..............	1.060	1.003	0.932	1.044	0.984	0.963
85 and over.........	1.029	0.963	1.000	1.035	0.988	0.985

[1] Great Britain, Registrar-General, *The Registrar-General's Decennial Supplement; England and Wales, 1931*, Pt. 1, pp. 45–47, H.M.S.O., London, 1936.
[2] Includes London Administrative County.

nonwhites, judging from the partial data which are available for the latter group. Since 1940 there has been a very large further decline in infant mortality in all types of communities, but it was larger in rural communities (34 per cent in the years 1940 to 1949) and in cities of 2,500 to 100,000 (35 per cent) than in the cities of 100,000 and over (27 per cent).[4]

[4] U.S. Bureau of the Census, *Vital Statistics Rates in the United States, 1900–1940*, p. 578, G.P.O., Washington, D.C., 1943; and U.S. Federal Security Agency, National Office of Vital Statistics, *Vital Statistics of the United States, 1949*, Pt. 1, p. xlix, G.P.O., Washington, D.C., 1950.

That differences in death rates between rural and urban communities are not confined to the United States is shown by the data for England and Wales given in Table 11-9. At no period of life except at ages twenty to twenty-four and at eighty-five and over did males in the rural districts of England and Wales have as high a ratio of actual to expected deaths as males in both county boroughs and other urban districts. On the other hand, this ratio among females was higher in the rural districts than in the smaller urban districts at ages twenty to twenty-four and thirty to thirty-nine, but at no age was it as high in the rural districts as in the county boroughs.

In Sweden before 1910 the crude death rates in the rural areas were lower than in the cities but after that date were usually lower in the cities. However, in 1945 to 1946 when the crude death rate for males in rural communities was 11.1 and that for males in urban communities was 10.1, standardizing these rates reduced the rural rate to 10.32 and raised the urban to 11.25. For females in the same year the crude rates were as follows: rural, 11.5; urban, 9.6. Standardizing changed them to 10.87 and 10.37, respectively. The pattern of age-specific death rates was much the same in Sweden as in the United States; urban rates were generally lower at ages under thirty-five than rural rates but higher at older ages.

Since a large part of the deaths at younger ages are due to acute infectious and contagious diseases, it would appear that the cities now possess certain advantages in controlling death from these causes. On the other hand, the fact that the death rates in the larger cities are higher than those of the rural areas at older ages, in spite of the superior health services of the former, must mean that there are some natural advantages in rural communities from the standpoint of retarding the onset of the chronic and organic diseases which develop later in life. More space, fresh air, a slower tempo of life, and possibly a better source of fresh foods may be of significance in this connection.

The most convincing evidence regarding the over-all effects of rural and urban living conditions on the death rate seems to the author to be found in the comparison of the death rates of the rural populations in the more advanced agricultural states in the United States with those in the larger cities which, as a rule, have the best health services. Thus Iowa (1940) had a crude death rate of 8.8 in its rural white population. In Kansas the rural death rate was 9.0; in Minnesota, 8.6; and in Nebraska, 8.6. These rural rates may be compared with the rates in their cities of 100,000 and over: Iowa, 10.2; Kansas, 10.0; Minnesota, 9.8; and Nebraska, 10.7. Moreover, in all these states the age-specific rural death rates, with only an occasional exception, were substantially below those of their own large cities (100,000 and over). With only an occasional exception the age-specific death rates of the rural white population in these four advanced agricultural states were also below those of the large cities in New York, Pennsylvania, and Ohio even at ages under thirty-five. Thus it would appear that the better health services of the larger cities have not yet succeeded in reducing their death rates to the level of those in the better agricultural states, although they are approaching that level, especially at the younger ages.

Marital Status and the Death Rate. Marital status is rather closely associated with differences in death rates in the three countries for which data are shown in Table 11-10. Married persons generally have lower death rates than single persons of the same ages, and single persons generally have lower rates than widowed and divorced persons. This did not hold for the twenty to twenty-four age group in Germany in 1939.

The explanation of these differences in death rates by marital condition shown in Table 11-10 appears to be somewhat as follows:

In the first place marriage is selective, as regards both physical vigor and social adaptability. Men who are in ill-health are likely to avoid marriage

Table 11-10. Death Rates by Age, Sex, and Marital Condition, France, 1933 to 1938; Germany, 1939; and Sweden, 1945

Age	France, 1933–1938			Germany, 1939			Sweden, 1945		
	Single	Married	Widowed and divorced	Single	Married	Widowed and divorced	Single	Married	Widowed and divorced
Males									
20–24	4.50	2.57	.....	3.10	3.52	10.01	3.21	1.43	
25–29	6.41	2.91	7.82	3.78	2.46	7.78	3.48	1.65	4.74
30–34	9.48	4.18	10.61	5.54	2.77	7.39	4.46	1.85	2.25
35–39	12.71	5.75	13.42	8.03	3.81	9.23	5.42	2.25	6.49
40–44	16.44	7.71	17.60	11.19	5.16	12.92	7.00	3.00	6.09
45–49	20.62	10.03	21.21	15.18	7.70	16.02	8.02	4.72	7.45
50–54	25.61	13.69	26.50	20.66	11.34	23.19	11.89	7.51	10.63
55–59	31.92	18.63	31.93	28.56	17.36	30.38	15.46	11.77	15.46
60–64	41.60	26.43	40.07	40.20	26.02	39.67	22.69	17.13	22.99
65–69	56.04	38.00	52.37	58.41	39.50	56.37	37.27	28.29	31.93
Females									
20–24	4.03	3.43	13.67	2.27	2.45	6.49	2.62	1.59	5.71
25–29	5.50	3.47	7.04	3.17	2.34	5.22	3.49	1.62	6.20
30–34	6.13	3.57	6.34	4.01	2.59	5.28	3.61	1.69	5.06
35–39	6.20	4.03	6.83	5.05	3.20	5.99	3.86	2.09	4.41
40–44	7.27	4.88	7.75	6.35	4.02	6.41	4.98	2.80	3.87
45–49	8.98	6.23	8.92	8.34	5.63	7.99	6.67	4.08	5.81
50–54	11.57	8.45	11.26	11.14	8.36	11.02	8.80	6.04	8.05
55–59	14.94	11.47	14.21	15.79	12.91	15.23	10.49	9.78	10.75
60–64	20.98	17.04	19.70	23.69	20.45	23.83	17.57	15.20	16.42
65–69	30.97	25.56	29.19	36.92	33.20	38.74	27.11	25.87	29.81

because of the difficulty of providing for a family. Also, those who for various reasons have little adaptability and do not get on well with other people are likely to avoid family ties. The selective factors among women may be somewhat different from those among men, but reasonably good health would seem to be of equal importance. It may very well be, therefore, that a significant proportion of the 9 to 11 per cent of men and women who do not marry are relatively poor health risks and hence have higher death rates on the average than those who do. However, the selective process involved in marriage no doubt varies considerably from one population to another. In countries like the United States, New Zealand, and Australia where there has been a scarcity of women during much of their history, women are likely to have been more careful in selecting mates than women in countries like England and Wales where there has been a rather large surplus of women.

Another factor which may be of some importance in keeping the death rates of married persons low is the greater regularity of living among the married, particularly among the men. In this connection Newsholme [5] thinks that the "comparative freedom in marital life from the terrible risks of syphilis must be given weight." This factor is probably of less importance now than it was before the development of the antibiotics. Finally, it seems rather probable that marriage represents a better adaptation to life, physically and mentally, than does celibacy.

As regards the relatively high death rates of widowed and divorced persons, it may well be that these groups contain rather an undue proportion of persons who made initial mistakes in the selection of mates from the standpoint of health. In addition, the health of the widowed may have been affected by the conditions arising from having mates whose health was not quite up to normal as well as by the hardships entailed by widowhood. The divorced very obviously have been unable to make a reasonably satisfactory adjustment in marriage, and the instability thus indicated may very well be associated, both as cause and as effect, with constitutional weaknesses. Differences in death rates according to marital status are found in both the urban and rural populations of the United States (Fig. 11-2).

Occupation and the Death Rate. Occupation is an important factor in determining the death rate not only because of the type of work done which may, by its very nature, be detrimental to health, *e.g.*, underground mine work, certain tasks in steel mills involving sudden and large changes in temperature of place of work, occupations in which one breathes much dust, and so forth, but also because occupation largely determines the family income and the physical surroundings of the worker and of his family at home.

[5] Arthur Newsholme, *The Elements of Vital Statistics in Their Bearing on Social and Public Health Problems,* rev. ed., p. 214, George Allen & Unwin, Ltd., London, 1923.

This being the case it is quite surprising there is so little material relating to the death rate by occupation. Most of that now available is quite old; hence it may not reflect accurately the occupational differences which exist today. The author's judgment is that the data given here probably exaggerate the differences in death rates between occupational groups today, both because of the general improvement in living conditions and also because the working conditions of the groups where the death rates were high some years

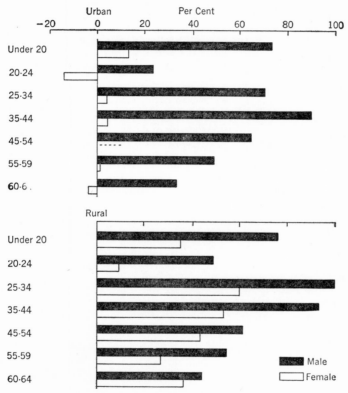

Fig. 11-2. Per cent by which death rates of single persons exceed those of married persons, urban and rural, by age and sex, United States, 1940.

ago are likely to have improved relatively more than for those groups in which the death rates were already relatively low.

Table 11-11 shows the differences in death rates between males of given ages engaged in certain selected occupations in 10 states in 1930. This table speaks for itself, but it may be noted in general that the lower death rates at ages of twenty-five and over are found in those occupations which are better paid and in which the work is lighter. There are some notable exceptions, however. Thus physicians and surgeons forty-five and over have a death rate well above the average, as do restaurant keepers, tailors, guards, watchmen, and so forth, none of which would be thought of as doing heavy or especially unhealthful work. Since physicians could be presumed to have better incomes than those other occupational groups, it would seem quite reasonable to conclude that they encounter rather severe occupational hazards which begin to take a fairly heavy toll in middle life. Some of the other occupational groups having high death rates in spite of being engaged in light work must also encounter heavy occupational hazards, but most of

Table 11-11. Deaths per 100,000 Gainfully Occupied Males 15–64 Years of Age in Selected Occupations, Selected States, 1930 [1]

(Alabama, Connecticut, Illinois, Kansas, Massachusetts, Minnesota, New Jersey, New York, Ohio, and Wisconsin)

Occupation	15–64	15–24	25–44	45–64
All gainfully occupied males in selected occupations...................	906.5	327.2	579.8	1,866.8
Professional men......................	727.2	142.3	316.4	1,633.3
Lawyers, judges, and justices..........	789.1	122.2	292.5	1,778.7
Physicians and surgeons..............	1,068.5	105.3	394.3	1,916.6
Proprietors, managers, and officials.......	927.0	307.6	449.5	1,707.7
Managers and officials (manufacturing)..	723.9	164.3	347.8	1,373.0
Retail dealers........................	981.3	324.9	478.5	1,806.0
Restaurant, café, and lunchroom keepers.	1,171.8	661.6	672.0	2,066.3
Clerks and kindred workers..............	645.4	238.5	430.4	1,727.5
Clerks in stores.....................	511.0	287.1	380.2	1,770.5
Bookkeepers, cashiers, and accountants..	534.7	174.9	348.8	1,631.9
Real estate agents...................	1,008.6	250.0	372.3	1,698.6
Agricultural workers....................	673.9	275.2	384.1	1,267.8
Skilled workers and foremen.............	866.5	302.5	499.9	1,747.0
Mechanics.........................	566.8	307.9	469.2	1,370.4
Machinists.........................	749.0	286.0	424.7	1,674.1
Blacksmiths........................	1,318.4	258.4	669.2	1,915.1
Tailors............................	1,374.1	428.8	637.3	2,283.8
Semiskilled workers....................	900.6	339.7	619.4	2,127.7
Chauffeurs, truck and tractor drivers....	618.7	420.6	549.3	1,454.7
Bakers............................	954.9	303.2	552.9	2,241.6
Guards, watchmen, and doorkeepers.....	2,024.7	229.9	865.6	2,590.5
Unskilled workers......................	1,441.6	502.4	1,059.3	2,746.3
Laborers (manufacturing).............	477.8	186.6	373.5	960.8
Laborers (steam railroad).............	701.3	221.4	509.4	1,303.6
Janitors and sextons..................	1,311.1	274.3	715.6	1,843.8
Factory and building construction laborers	1,696.5	569.0	1,278.6	3,316.2
Draymen, teamsters, and carriage drivers.	1,759.4	470.3	1,117.9	2,991.3

[1] Jessamine Whitney, *Death Rates by Occupation, Based on Data of the U.S. Bureau of the Census, 1930*, p. 30, National Tuberculosis Association, New York, 1934.

them are at the same time in the lower income groups. In addition, it seems reasonable to assume that some of the high-death-rate occupations are rather selective of workers who are already in poor health or are in an age class which would normally have higher rates, *e.g.*, tailors, guards, and watchmen. This may also be true to some extent of the various categories of laborers. Many of them not only are poorly paid but are irregularly employed at heavy work, and this fact would affect not only their living conditions but their general physical condition. Agricultural workers have relatively low death rates at all ages.

As far as one can judge from the scanty data available, the situation was essentially the same in France and England, as long as 60 years ago. In France (Table 11-13) there were rather large differences in the death rates of employers and workers in the same industries in 1907 to 1908 as well as between persons engaged in different industries.

Table 11-12. Deaths per 1,000 Males 35–44 Years of Age Engaged in Selected Occupations, France and England, 1886 to 1891 [1]

Occupation	France	England
All males................................	11	11
Teaching profession....................	6	6
Clergy..................................	7	4
Agricultural laborers..................	8	6
Clerks, etc............................	13	10
Bakers.................................	13	9
Publicans..............................	14	22
Carters................................	17	13
Laborers...............................	20	28
Waiters, etc...........................	22	28
Printers...............................	18	11

[1] Lucien March, "Some Researches Concerning the Factors of Mortality," *Royal Statis. Soc. J.*, Vol. 75, p. 524, 1912.

The best studies of occupational mortality known to the author are those in the decennial supplements to *The Registrar-General's Statistical Review of England and Wales*. Table 11-14 is taken from the latest supplement (1931).[6] The death rates of the different social classes are given here as percentages of the death rate of all occupied and retired civilian males. The differences were large but were decreasing, and they show clearly the effects of different economic and social status on the death rate. The death rate of

[6] The 1941 census for England and Wales was never completed; hence no comparable supplement could be prepared. The 1951 data will not be available for several years.

Table 11-13. Death Rates of Employers and Workers Compared for Selected Occupations, at Specified Ages, France, 1907 to 1908 [1]

Occupation	35–45		55–65	
	Employer	Worker	Employer	Worker
Farming class..................	7	8	21	30
Carpenters and joiners.............	7	10	30	43
Bakers.........................	11	18	37	58
Printers........................	8	22	26	56
Textile industries..................	4	11	13	41
Butchers.......................	17	29	41	86
Builders........................	8	16	28	49

[1] Lucien March, "Some Researches Concerning the Factors of Mortality," *Royal Statis. Soc. J.*, Vol. 75, p. 525, 1912.

the most favored class is but 90.0 per cent of the average, while that of unskilled workers is 112.0 per cent of the average. Expressed in another way, the death rate of unskilled workers is about one-fourth greater than that of the upper class—and this, be it noted, is a standardized figure which makes due allowance for age differences.

Table 11-14. Registered Deaths per 100 Standard Deaths by Social Status of Occupied and Retired Males, England and Wales, 1930 to 1932 [1]

Social class	Age	
	20–65	35–65
All males.........................	101	100
All occupied and retired males..........	100	100
Social class I.........................	90	90
Social class II........................	94	95
Social class III.......................	97	97
Social class IV.......................	103	102
Social class V.......................	112	112
Unoccupied.........................	136	104

[1] Great Britain, Registrar-General, *The Registrar-General's Decennial Supplement; England and Wales, 1931*, Pt. 2a, p. 211, H.M.S.O., London, 1936.

Table 11-15 shows the ratio of expected deaths to actual deaths in certain specified occupations (not for social classes as in Table 11-14), the expected deaths in each case being the number that would have occurred in each occupational group if its death rate had been the same at each age as that for all males of that age in England and Wales.

Table 11-15.   Standardized Mortality of Males 20–65 Years of Age Engaged in Certain Occupations, England and Wales, 1930 to 1932 [1]

Occupation	Registered deaths per 100 standard deaths
All occupied and retired males............................	100
General and undefined laborers............................	119
Building trade laborers......................................	112
Dock laborers..	137
Agriculture:	
Farmers and their relatives...............................	73
Agricultural laborers (including shepherds).................	77
Mining:	
Coal—underground workers, not hewers or getters............	94
Iron ore—underground workers, not hewers or getters..........	116
Makers of bricks, pottery, and glass:	
Potters' millworkers, slip makers, and arkmen................	120
Earthenware, china, etc., kilnmen and ovenmen...............	157
Brick, tile, and pottery, kilnmen and ovenmen...............	119
Glass blowers and finishers, not machine hands..............	160
Metalworkers:	
Puddlers...	166
Iron- or steel-foundry furnacemen and laborers................	132
Metal machinists..	97
Grinders in cutlery trade..................................	240
Textile workers:	
Wool sorters...	118
Cotton blow-room operatives...............................	233
Cotton spinners and piecers................................	105
Dyers..	123
Cutters (not hats, gloves, or boots)........................	91
Makers of foods, drinks, and tobacco:	
Bakers and pastry cooks...................................	77
Skilled workers in ale, etc., brewing........................	112
Tobacco, cigars, cigarettes, snuff..........................	109

[1] Great Britain, Registrar General, *The Registrar-General's Decennial Supplement; England and Wales, 1931*, Pt. 2a, pp. 191–210, H.M.S.O., London, 1936.

These data show startling differences in the age-standardized death rates of males in different occupations. They leave no room for doubt as to what the situation was in England and Wales in 1930 to 1932. All kinds of agricultural work were among the healthful occupations, while most types of factory work were comparatively unhealthful. The professions were healthful as a whole, although barristers and physicians fell well behind the other groups. On the other hand, grinders in cutlery, cotton blow-room operatives, and stevedores had a rate more than twice as high as the average, while nine other groups had rates over 25 per cent in excess of the average. Of course, not the entire amount of the differences in death rates shown here is due to differences in occupational hazards alone. Selection unquestionably plays an important role. Common unskilled laborers, dockers, and stevedores are frequently men who cannot hold regular jobs and in the course of time drift into the poorly paid classes, where work is intermittent and where living conditions are very unhealthful. So it happens that selection picks many of the poorer physical specimens of manhood for the worst-paid jobs, and then poor pay makes decent living impossible. The inevitable result of this combination of circumstances is an extremely high death rate in certain occupational groups. It is, perhaps, the living conditions enforced by poorly paid work, even more than the nature of the work itself, that cause the high death rates in many occupations.

If we bear in mind the differences in the death rates of different occupational groups, we shall have little difficulty in understanding the differences in death rates between certain types of communities. Clearly, a section of a city, or an entire city, in which the textile industry is an important one would be likely to have a higher death rate than a section of a city, or a city, where professional men live, or a residence suburb where only the well-to-do live. As between a rural area in which miners predominate and one in which only farmers live, e.g., some areas in western Pennsylvania and West Virginia on the one hand and the central part of Kansas on the other, there will also be large differences. One may say then that occupation (1) determines the special hazards encountered in one's work, such as those peculiar to mining, metal grinding, working with poisonous materials, whether there are periods of violent exercise alternating with idleness (stevedoring), whether there is exposure to unusual changes in temperature and so forth; and (2) largely determines the income, which in turn determines kind of housing, quality and quantity of food, clothing, medical and dental care, and all the other items which go to make up the level of living. In view of these facts it is surely of the utmost importance to secure more information regarding the death rates of occupational groups. Fortunately, the gap between the death rates of those in the more hazardous and poorly paid jobs and those in the more sheltered occupations yielding larger incomes is being lessened as public health services become more widespread and more efficient and as more effective safety measures are applied in the more hazardous occupations. However, there are still large differences in the hazards encountered in different occupations and in the levels of living resulting from income differentials, and where there are such differences death rates are invariably higher among the disadvantaged than among those whose working and living conditions are reasonably good. In the Scandinavian countries such differentials appear to have been reduced below those existing in most other Western countries.

The Race Factor in the Death Rate. The racial element in the population is so closely associated with differences in death rates that, where there are appreciable elements of different races in a given population, separate rates should be given if the relative health conditions of the races are to be measured. Our own mortality figures generally do this where nonwhites constitute over 5 per cent of the population in any community. (For differences between whites and nonwhites, see Chap. VII.)

The high death rates in countries like India and the Philippines where the white population is of negligible size are undoubtedly due largely, probably entirely, to the unhealthful living conditions of the people rather than to racial differences between them and Europeans. It is possible, of course, that climate, about which comparatively little can be done, is a factor in the relatively high death rates of people living in tropical countries. However, no such assumption should be made until some tropical people has had the opportunity to control disease to the same degree as have the more advanced industrialized countries in the temperate zones. At present the most reasonable view regarding the effect of racial differences on the death rate is that such differences, whether within a country as in the United States, or between different races in different countries, are due to differences in living conditions and not to climatic and/or biological differences. The experience of Japan in very rapidly reducing its death rate since 1945 provides additional support for this view.

5. CAUSES OF DEATH

In the most general terms the causes for the enormous decline in mortality during the past two centuries may be summed up by saying that we have a higher level of living than our ancestors and that, chiefly as a consequence of better economic conditions, making research in sanitation and medicine possible, we have gained an increasing measure of control over the infectious and contagious diseases which have until quite recently been the greatest regular killers of mankind.[7] These diseases have always been especially deadly to babies and young children, and the chief of these regular killers has probably been that group of diseases quite commonly called diseases of the digestive tract (among babies, diarrhea and enteritis).

The control over most of these diseases did not become possible until better means of production were developed which made a surplus of goods above absolute necessity available for better living, for research in medicine and sanitation, and for applying the results of this research to the maintenance of health. Today from the medical and sanitary standpoints there is

---

[7] I express it this way because where famine, undernourishment, and war are present and may be the underlying causes of death, the infectious and contagious diseases very frequently spring up in epidemic proportions.

no reason why there should be any significant number of deaths from those contagious and infectious diseases which have in the past claimed such a large proportion of all human lives. (There are, of course, some infectious diseases which we do not yet know how to control.) The chief benefit from this control over the infectious and contagious diseases has accrued to children, although, as we shall see in a moment, older people have also received large benefits from such control.

In the very nature of the case as people grow older there is more likelihood that they will suffer from the malfunctioning of some of the different organs of the body and from malignant growths (cancer) which very frequently grow slowly and unobtrusively over a period of years. Adults never have suffered from many of the contagious and infectious diseases to the same extent as children, especially children under ten, partly because the children surviving from such diseases as smallpox, measles, whooping cough, scarlet fever, and diphtheria generally have immunity to further attacks and partly because during the later years of youth and the most vigorous years of adult life man is better able to resist the attacks of diseases of the digestive tract. As a consequence, persons from the seven-to-ten age group to the twenty-five-to-thirty group have always had death rates which were low in comparison with those of younger children, who were especially susceptible to infectious and contagious diseases, and also in comparison with those of older people, who suffered more from chronic ailments.

The Swedish data show that in that country persons aged ten to twenty-five have had much lower death rates than children under five ever since 1751. But these data also show that the death rate of children under five in 1941 to 1945 had fallen to about one-ninth of what it was in 1751 to 1760, while the death rate of persons ten to fifteen fell to about one-seventh, that of persons fifteen to twenty to a little over one-fourth, and that of persons twenty to twenty-five to a little over one-third what it was at the earlier date. This difference is due primarily to the fact that the control over infectious and contagious diseases has proceeded at a much faster rate than that over other diseases. But the full effects of this difference in the control of different types of disease are seen only at ages above sixty, where the death rates today are generally at least one-half as high as they were two centuries ago.

Today almost everyone knows that the chronic and organic diseases are old people's diseases—that heart disease and other diseases of the circulatory system, cancer, nephritis (liver), and diabetes (pancreas) are diseases which take a heavy toll of life among older people.

Table 11-16 shows the ten leading causes of death in the United States in 1900 and 1948. In 1900, pneumonia and influenza, tuberculosis, and diarrhea and enteritis ranked first, second, and third, respectively, as causes of death, and combined they accounted for 31.4 per cent of all deaths. In addition, diphtheria and meningitis, also contagious and infectious diseases, ranked ninth and tenth. These five infectious and contagious diseases accounted for 43.7 per cent of all deaths. By 1948 only pneumonia and influenza (sixth) and tuberculosis (seventh), of the infectious and contagious diseases, were still among the ten leading causes of death, and they accounted for only 6.9 per cent of all deaths. On the other hand, in 1948, diseases of the heart, cancer, and cerebral hemorrhage, all diseases of advanced adult life, had become the three leading causes of death, and they accounted for 55.3 per cent of all deaths as compared with 17.9 per cent in 1900. Since the control of the infectious and contagious diseases has, for the most part, saved the lives of children, the inevitable consequence has been a large proportional increase of older people. Among these the chronic and organic ailments are more important causes of death. Thus there would be

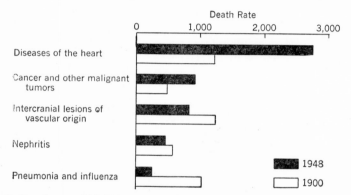

Fig. 11-3. Deaths per 100,000 persons sixty-five years of age and over, by cause, registration states, 1948 and 1900.

an increasing proportion of all deaths from these diseases of later life even if the rates per 100,000 old persons were not increasing. But the fact is that the rates for certain of these chronic and organic diseases have been increasing quite rapidly for the population sixty-five years of age and over (Fig. 11-3). The rate for heart disease in the population sixty-five and over more than doubled between 1900 and 1948 and that for cancer has almost doubled. On the other hand, intracranial lesions of vascular origin as a cause of death declined by about one-third, and nephritis after rising rapidly for two decades declined to somewhat below the 1900 rate in 1948. The greatest decline in rate among the causes of death for older persons was for the one contagious and infectious disease among the five leading causes of death, namely, pneumonia and influenza, which fell in 1948 to about one-fifth of what it was in 1900. In recent years this decline was no doubt due to the development of the sulfa drugs and the antibiotics, but the rate has been going down for the past 50 years and before 1940 this must have been due

Table 11-16.   The Ten Leading Causes of Death in the United States, 1948 and 1900 [1]

Cause	Rank	Death rate per 100,000 population	Per cent of deaths from all causes
1948			
Diseases of the heart................	1	323	32.6
Cancer............................	2	135	13.6
Cerebral hemorrhage................	3	90	9.1
Accidents..........................	4	67	6.8
Nephritis..........................	5	53	5.4
Pneumonia and influenza............	6	39	3.9
Tuberculosis.......................	7	30	3.0
Premature birth....................	8	27	2.7
Diabetes mellitus...................	9	26	2.7
Arteriosclerosis....................	10	19	1.9
1900			
Pneumonia and influenza............	1	202	11.8
Tuberculosis.......................	2	194	11.3
Diarrhea and enteritis..............	3	143	8.3
Diseases of the heart................	4	137	8.0
Cerebral hemorrhage................	5	107	6.2
Nephritis..........................	6	89	5.2
Accidents..........................	7	72	4.2
Cancer............................	8	64	3.7
Diphtheria.........................	9	40	2.3
Meningitis.........................	10	34	2.0

[1] Mortimer Spiegelman, *Health Progress in the United States*, p. 26, American Enterprise Association, Inc., New York, 1950.

chiefly to better medical and hospital care. The five leading causes of death among people sixty-five and over in 1900 had a combined rate of 4,454.9 per 100,000 persons of these ages. By 1948 this rate had risen to 5,166.6, or by one-seventh; the increases in the rates for heart disease and cancer more than made up for the decreases, especially for those in intracranial lesions and pneumonia. But this rise is no doubt due in some measure to the fact that the proportion of persons seventy-five and over among those who are sixty-five and over has increased from 29.0 per cent in 1900 to 31.4 per cent in 1950.

Everyone knows that we cannot yet cure diseases of the circulatory system and cancer and nephritis, as we can pneumonia, by the rather direct and simple medical treatment with the sulfa drugs and antibiotics. It would appear that we shall have to learn how to live so that organic diseases do not develop until the span of life is more nearly complete if we are to reduce the rates from these causes among persons aged sixty-five to seventy-five, but as this improvement takes place it is probable that the rates for these diseases at ages seventy-five and over will increase rapidly. As we learn to reduce the death rates for these diseases at ages sixty-five to seventy-five, *i.e.*, as we learn how to control the social and economic conditions which bring on these ailments in the earlier years of old age and as people adopt the personal habits which will reduce the wearing out of the bodily organs with unnecessary rapidity after forty-five or fifty years of age, it is almost certain that they will wear out more rapidly after seventy or seventy-five years of age. Furthermore, the conquest of cancer would almost certainly lead to a large increase in the death rate from diseases of the circulatory system within a few years. The limits within which we can ward off or postpone the wearing out of the organs of the body are rather narrow, and anything we can do will only postpone the failure of these organs for a few years.

6. FURTHER DECLINE OF THE DEATH RATE

In the future the decline of the death rate in any particular country or area will depend upon the decline already achieved in that area and upon the manner in which those conditions known to be favorable to its further decline can be developed. In general, it may be said that where death rates are already low because of the existence of relatively good living conditions and good health services, the future decline will be rather small and slow, since in these areas the infectious and contagious diseases are already largely eliminated. When 75 to 80 per cent of all children born are still living at sixty years of age, there is little chance for an absolute reduction in number of deaths at any younger age. Since only slow progress is being made at present in reducing death rates at ages over sixty-five, future reductions of the total death rate in such populations will be slow and the future increase in population due to decline in their death rates will also be small. Moreover, in such populations the death rate is not likely to fluctuate much from year to year, except in the event of great catastrophes.

On the other hand, where death rates are now high there may be not only large but spectacular declines in the death rates due to the control of infectious and contagious diseases, since we now know how to control these diseases better than ever before. Such declines would certainly lead to a very rapid growth of population in these areas, even more rapid than that which took place in Europe in the nineteenth century—provided, of course, that the economic basis for the support of such an increase can be found.

Suggestions for Supplementary Reading

Demographic Yearbook, 1951, pp. 9–26, United Nations, New York, 1951.

DICKINSON, FRANK G., and EVERETT L. WELKER: *Mortality Trends in the United States, 1900–1949*, 32 pp., American Medical Association, Chicago, 1952.

DUBLIN, LOUIS I., *et al.: Length of Life*, rev. ed., 379 pp., The Ronald Press Company, New York, 1949.

GHOSH, D.: *Pressure of Population and Economic Efficiency in India*, 109 pp., Oxford University Press, London, 1946.

Great Britain, Registrar General: *The Registrar-General's Decennial Supplement; England and Wales,* 2 vols., H.M.S.O., London, 1936.

MARCH, LUCIEN: "Some Researches Concerning the Factors of Mortality," *Royal Statis. Soc. J.*, Vol. 75, pp. 505–538, 1912.

PELLER, SIGISMUND: "Mortality Past and Future," *Population Studies*, Vol. 1, No. 4, pp. 405–456, 1948.

TITMUSS, RICHARD M.: *Birth, Poverty and Wealth: A Study of Infant Mortality*, 118 pp., Hamish Hamilton Medical Books, London, 1943.

WHITNEY, JESSAMINE: *Death Rates by Occupation, Based on Data of the U.S. Bureau of the Census, 1930*, 32 pp., National Tuberculosis Association, New York, 1934.

WIGGLESWORTH, EDWARD: "A Table Showing the Probability of the Duration, the Decrement, and the Expectation of Life in the States of Massachusetts and New Hampshire, Formed from Sixty-two Bills of Mortality on the Files of the American Academy of Arts and Sciences for the Year 1789," *Am. Acad. Arts Sci., Mem.*, Vol. 2, o.s., pp. 131–135, 1793.

WOODBURY, ROBERT MORSE: *Causal Factors in Infant Mortality: A Statistical Study Based on Investigations in Eight Cities*, 245 pp., G.P.O., Washington, D.C., 1925. (U.S. Children's Bur., *Pub.* 142.)

CHAPTER XII

NATURAL INCREASE AND ITS PROBABLE FUTURE TREND

The crude natural increase of a population is obtained by subtracting its crude death rate from its crude birth rate. After what has been said regarding the various ways of correcting, standardizing, refining or adjusting birth rates and death rates, this may not seem a very meaningful measure of increase. All the crude rate of natural increase tells is the rate of the excess (or deficit) per 1,000 of the total population at a specified time. For many purposes such a rate is quite satisfactory, but we must be careful not to take the crude rate at face value as a measure of anything but current increase. It does not measure trends accurately.

1. PAST TRENDS OF NATURAL INCREASE

Before 1939. The crude rates of natural increase for the leading countries of the world for which such data are available are given in Table 12-1.

In the West the rate of natural increase in most countries appears to have gone through a cycle somewhat as follows: There was a period during the earlier part of the nineteenth century when the death rate fell while there was little change in the birth rate, with the result that there was a rise in the rate of natural increase. In a number of European countries this rate mounted as high as 12 to 15 per 1,000 and remained at about this level for several decades.

The date at which the maximum rate was reached varied considerably from one country to another, but it remained fairly high in most Western European lands until World War I, because although, as noted in Chap. VIII, the birth rate may have begun to decline several decades earlier, the death rate continued to decline, leaving the rate of natural increase about stationary. Since World War I the rate of natural increase has fallen in most Western countries except in parts of Central and South America. It reached a relatively low level in the decade prior to World War II, a level in some countries below that of the period before better living conditions and modern sanitation and medicine became highly effective in reducing the death rate.

At the time vital statistics were first gathered on a country-wide scale in England and Wales the rate of increase was 9.5 per 1,000. It is probable

Table 12-1. Average Rates of Natural Increase, 1808 to 1950 [1]

Year	Austria	Belgium	Bulgaria	Denmark	England and Wales	Finland	France	Germany	Hungary	Ireland
1946–1950	4.0	4.5	11.0[2]	11.3	6.3	15.3	7.8	5.6[3]	5.4[2]	8.9
1938–1942	4.4[2]	-0.5	9.0	8.5	1.9	4.0	-2.6	6.5[2]	5.6[2]	5.7
1928–1932	2.3	4.6	13.9	7.5	3.9	6.7	1.3	5.5	7.8	5.2[4]
1918–1922	3.5[2]	2.9	11.6	11.3	7.2	4.9	-2.7	5.0	5.5	4.7
1908–1912	6.7	7.8	17.7	14.1	11.0	13.1	0.9	13.1	....	6.3
1898–1902	8.7	10.8	16.2	13.7	11.4	13.0	1.0	14.9	....	4.8
1888–1892	5.2	8.5	13.6	11.5	11.9	12.6	0.4	12.4	....	4.4
1878–1882	4.5	10.0	....	12.7	14.1	13.2	2.5	12.2	....	6.2
1868–1872	....	8.2	....	11.2	13.1	2.0	-1.3	9.4	....	10.7
1858–1862	....	9.1	....	12.3	12.6	10.5	3.4	11.2		
1848–1852	....	6.6	....	11.2	10.8	10.9	3.5	9.1		
1838–1842	....	8.8	....	9.5	9.5	12.4	4.7			
1828–1832	....	....	....	2.3	....	9.6	4.0			
1818–1822	....	....	....	11.7	....	12.0	6.4			
1808–1812	....	....	....	5.2	....	-4.8	5.7			

Year	Italy	Netherlands	Norway	Poland	Romania	Russia	Scotland	Yugoslavia	Spain	Sweden
1946–1950	10.3	18.0	11.6	....	1.9[2]	....	6.5	16.1[2]	9.8	8.0
1938–1942	8.6	11.3	5.6	10.6[2]	6.6	23.4[2]	3.7	11.0[2]	2.6	4.6
1928–1932	10.3	13.1	6.1	15.3	14.1	24.9[2]	5.5	....	11.0	3.2
1918–1922	5.3	13.1	10.7	9.1[2]	12.5[2]	19.2[2]	9.1	....	5.3	6.8
1908–1912	11.9	14.9	12.4	17.0	15.9	16.7[2]	11.0	14.5[2]	9.6	10.6
1898–1902	10.7	14.8	14.4	18.7	12.8	17.0	11.7	15.7	6.4	10.6
1888–1892	10.7	12.6	12.5	....	10.4	12.8	11.8	16.5	4.8	11.1
1878–1882	7.7	13.5	14.4	....	7.0	13.5[2]	13.9	12.9	6.1	12.0
1868–1872	7.1	9.5	12.4	....	7.0	12.0[2]	12.5	11.6	....	9.7
1858–1862	....	7.0	14.9	....	....	....	13.8	....	....	14.2
1848–1852	....	....	12.9	....	....	....	....	....	....	10.9
1838–1842	....	....	9.2	....	....	....	....	....	....	8.8
1828–1832	....	....	12.3	....	....	....	....	....	....	6.7
1818–1822	....	....	13.2	....	....	....	....	....	....	9.3
1808–1812	....	....	....	....	....	....	....	....	....	-1.3

Year	Switzerland	Argentina	Canada	Chile	Guatemala	Honduras (British)	Jamaica	Puerto Rico	United States	Ceylon
1946–1950	8.2	15.3[2]	17.9	16.1	27.3	24.0	19.0	29.0	14.2	25.1
1938–1942	4.7	12.2	11.8	11.2	19.4	15.0	16.9	21.3	7.9	16.1
1928–1932	4.9	16.6	12.8	14.7	23.9	14.4	16.7	16.7	7.1	14.7
1918–1922	5.0	16.8[2]	14.2[2]	7.6	17.9	12.9[2]	....	17.3[2]	9.9	6.8
1908–1912	9.7	20.1[2]	13.6[2]	7.8	17.3	16.2[2]	13.1[2]	....	....	6.7
1898–1902	10.6	17.9[2]	....	6.2	22.1	....	7.8	-4.6	....	10.2
1888–1892	7.5	....	10.6	0.5	16.1	....	15.1	-0.4	....	3.9
1878–1882	7.7	....	....	11.5	....	....	....	....	....	2.9
1868–1872	....	....	....	16.5	....	....	....	....	....	4.3
1858–1862	....	....	....	16.7	....	....	....	....	....	

Year	India	Japan	Philippine Islands	Algeria	Egypt	Union of South Africa	Australia	New Zealand
1946–1950	9.1	17.5	....	9.9[2]	21.0[2]	17.5	13.6	16.0
1938–1942	10.0	12.2	15.8[2]	8.5[2]	14.6	15.7	7.8	10.8
1928–1932	9.0	14.2	16.3	8.6	17.4	15.9	10.3	10.2
1918–1922	-4.3	9.9	8.7	5.3	11.4	16.1	14.2	12.9
1908–1912	5.5	13.0	10.8	11.8	17.9	21.5[2]	16.5	17.3
1898–1902	6.1	11.5	7.3[2]	8.4[2]	18.7[2]	....	14.4	15.7
1888–1892	5.7	8.4	3.9	5.1[2]	18.3[2]	....	20.3	19.7
1878–1882	....	6.6	....	5.6[2]	....	....	20.0	28.2
1868–1872	....	....	....	5.2[2]	....	....	24.2	30.1
1858–1862	....	....	....	11.2[2]	....			
1848–1852	....	....	....	-4.7[2]	....			
1838–1842	....	....	....	-9.2[2]	....			
1828–1832	....	....	....	-20.0[2]	....			

[1] For the current data the reader is referred to *Population Index.*
[2] See footnote [2] of Tables 8-2 and 11-4.
[3] Federal Republic.
[4] Irish Free State.

that it was actually somewhat higher than this because of the greater omission of births than of deaths from the records. The rate rose rather steadily from the period of 1838 to 1842 to that of 1878 to 1882, when it reached 14.1 per 1,000, a rate at which the population would have doubled in about 50 years. After 1878 to 1882 it declined slowly until it stood at 11.0 just before World War I. After that it declined rapidly, the rate for 1938 to 1942 being 1.9.

German data are not available until 1848 to 1852, at which time the rate of increase was 9.1, just about the same as in England and Wales a decade earlier. With one setback, 1868 to 1872, this rate rose steadily until about 1900 (14.9) and then began to decline. In the period 1908 to 1912, just before World War I, it was 13.1. As in England the rate fell rapidly after World War I, being 5.5 in 1928 to 1932. It rose, however, to 6.5 in the period 1938 to 1942 under the stimulus of the economic recovery that came with rearmament, of Hitlerian prodding, and of the patriotic urge to military expansion.

It is important also to note that during all this period emigration from a number of the countries of Europe was of such a nature that if it had any appreciable effect on natural increase it tended to reduce the rate, since it resulted in an excess of young unmarried women in countries of emigration. Besides, most of the women who do emigrate are young married women whose births are lost to the homeland. The crude death rate also tends to rise as a consequence of the larger proportion of older people in a population sending out large numbers of migrants, unless the death rate is already very high because of severe population pressure. In this case the death rate may be reduced by emigration and natural increase may rise.

The situation as regards natural increase during the latter half of the nineteenth century was much the same in most of the countries in Western Europe as in England and Wales and Germany, France alone being an outstanding exception. There the highest rate attained since registration was undertaken, until after World War II, was 6.4 per 1,000 in 1818 to 1822. Even at that date contraception was rather widely practiced in France. The rate of natural increase declined steadily in France until about 1880 (allowing for the Franco-Prussian War) at which time it was only about 1.0, and for the ensuing 50 years most people thought of France as having no significant excess of births over deaths. For the period from about 1934 to the end of World War II, France had more deaths than births.

The movement of the rate of natural increase in countries outside Europe settled by Europeans had been of much the same general character as that in Western Europe up to 1939, although there were considerable individual differences.

In the United States the rate of natural increase before 1930 must be estimated from the increase of population, the number of immigrants, and the ratio of children to women (Fig. 9-1) shown in the censuses.[1] It has been estimated that from 1790 to 1830 the natural increase was about 30 per 1,000 per annum; from 1830 to 1860 it was about 25 per 1,000; by 1890 it had fallen to about 15 per 1,000; and in the period 1910 to 1930 it was about 12 per 1,000. These are all crude rates and are only approximations, although the author believes they are substantially accurate. After 1910 there was an increasing registration area to aid in making the estimates. Thus, although the past rate of natural increase in the United States must be calculated in this indirect manner, there is no reasonable doubt that it had been falling for more than a century prior to World War II. The same general downward movement of natural increase was also taking place in Australasia, Canada, and several of the countries in Central Europe.

The rates of natural increase for the other countries of Europe and for the parts of Asia, Africa, and South America for which data are available show indications of following this same general pattern of decline as in the countries surveyed above. We cannot be certain, however, that the time intervals will be the same. Several of them already show a decline in the death rate, and some of these are showing a decline in the birth rate, but as yet in most of these countries the death rate is declining while there is no decline in the birth rate or it is declining more slowly than the death rate so that the rate of natural increase is rising. The result is that in most of the countries, aside from those discussed above, for which we have any data indicating trends in natural increase the rate appears to be rising much as it did in the West a century or more ago.

In that large part of the world for which no data on births and deaths are available or the data are so inadequate that little reliance can be placed on them, there seems no doubt that birth rates are very high—perhaps in the neighborhood of 40 or above—and death rates are also high. In most of these countries the rate of natural increase varies greatly from year to year depending primarily on changes in the death rate. In some of them, however, the censuses clearly prove that the death rates must have declined to some extent in recent years, because their populations are now growing at a rate which could not have endured long or they would have much larger populations than they now do.

After 1939. Since 1939 there has been a considerable change in crude rates of natural increase in a number of Western countries (Chap. VIII and Table 12-1). In most of the Western European countries the crude rate of natural increase reached a low point in the early or middle 1930's during the depression, then rose somewhat in the later 1930's and early 1940's, and rose still more during the later years of World War II and following it. However, the pattern was not identical in all of them. In England and Wales

[1] Warren S. Thompson and P. K. Whelpton, *Population Trends in the United States,* pp. 299–304, McGraw-Hill Book Company, Inc., New York, 1933.

the lowest point in natural increase was reached in 1941, after which it rose slowly but fell off again in 1945, only to rise well above what it had been for some years, in 1946 to 1950. With rather minor variations this pattern was quite common in the West, with the result that population grew faster in most of these countries during the war and following it than appeared at all likely at the beginning of the war, to judge from the demographic experience of this area during and following World War I.

Very little information is available, except for Western countries, for the war and postwar years. The rise in their birth rates and the accompanying rise in natural increase (death rates have continued to decline slowly) is the most important demographic change in recent years (Table 12-2). At the moment, however, we cannot be certain that this increase in the crude rate of natural increase means that families are becoming larger. It may merely

Table 12-2. Crude Birth Rates, Death Rates, and Natural Increase for Selected Countries by Single Years, 1945 to 1950

Country	1950[1]	1949	1948	1947	1946	1945
United States:						
Birth rate.............	23.4	23.9	24.1	25.7	23.3	19.5
Death rate.............	9.6	9.7	9.9	10.1	10.0	10.6
Natural increase........	13.8	14.2	14.2	15.6	13.3	8.9
Belgium:						
Birth rate.............	16.5	17.2	17.6	17.8	18.3	15.7
Death rate.............	12.4	12.9	12.6	13.3	13.6	14.9
Natural increase........	4.1	4.3	5.0	4.5	4.7	0.8
Canada:						
Birth rate.............	26.6	26.9	27.0	28.6	26.9	23.9
Death rate.............	9.0	9.2	9.3	9.4	9.4	9.4
Natural increase........	17.6	17.7	17.7	19.2	17.5	14.5
England and Wales:						
Birth rate.............	15.7	16.7	17.8	20.5	19.2	15.9
Death rate.............	11.6	11.7	10.8	12.3	12.0	12.7
Natural increase........	4.1	5.0	7.0	8.2	7.2	3.2
France:						
Birth rate.............	20.4	20.9	21.0	21.3	20.8	16.5
Death rate.............	12.6	13.8	12.4	13.2	13.4	16.4
Natural increase........	7.8	7.1	8.6	8.1	7.4	0.1
Japan:						
Birth rate.............	28.4	32.8	33.7	34.3	25.3	23.2
Death rate.............	11.0	11.6	12.0	14.6	17.6	29.2
Natural increase........	17.4	21.2	21.7	19.7	7.7	−6.0
Sweden:						
Birth rate.............	16.4	17.4	18.4	18.9	19.7	20.4
Death rate.............	10.0	10.0	9.8	10.8	10.5	10.8
Natural increase........	6.4	7.4	8.6	8.1	9.2	9.6

[1] Preliminary figures.

mean that couples are marrying somewhat younger and that they are having the same number of children as the couples of 10 or 20 years ago but are spacing their children differently now from the way in which their parents spaced theirs. In any event the crude natural increase in many Western countries is higher now than it was most of the time from about 1925 to 1945.

As was just said, in other parts of the world there are only a few areas having reliable demographic data, and the "iron curtain" area is closed to demographic inquiry as well as to other types of free inquiry. In Japan, however, it appears that the rate of natural increase fell for two or three years after 1937 (attack on China), then rose to about prewar level and remained there until 1945, when it became a natural decrease. It rose rapidly after 1946 and in the years 1947 to 1949 attained the highest rate in Japan's history. It now appears to be declining. This postwar rise in Japan is due primarily to the unexpectedly large decline in the postwar death rate, although the postwar birth rate was also quite high.

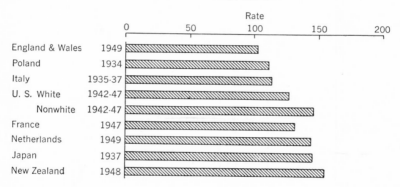

Fig. 12-1. Net reproduction rates for selected countries in recent years.

Net reproduction rates (Chap. VIII) for several countries are given in Fig. 12-1.[2] These net reproduction rates show the same general pattern of growth as between the several countries as do the crude rates of natural increase, although they are more refined and over time take account of changes in age-specific birth rates and death rates as the crude rates do not.

At the moment the rates of increase in the Western world which, on the whole, rose some during the war and considerably more immediately after it show signs of declining, but it is impossible to say with any assurance how

[2] The net reproduction rate as given here shows the number of daughters 100 women would bear if the age-specific birth rates and death rates of the year specified were to prevail throughout their lives to age forty-five or fifty, i.e., until they had completed childbearing (Chap. VIII). With less than 100 daughters born, they would not replace themselves.

rapid this decline will be or how far it will go. But temporarily, at least, the rates of increase in the Western countries are with only a few exceptions about as high as in the period following World War I, but in only one or two countries have the rates risen to the level of the years preceding World War I, France being the most notable instance. In the United States also the crude birth rate since World War II has remained at about the level it maintained for several years following World War I.

2. PROBABLE TRENDS IN DIFFERENT PARTS OF THE WORLD

This substantial rise in the crude rates of natural increase and also in reproduction rates in Western countries has complicated the task of the demographer in trying to describe the outlook for population growth in different parts of the world. Although it is by no means certain that this rise in the rate of natural increase is a permanent feature in the reproductive life of these peoples, it does indicate that changes in the economic and political conditions of life can induce rather rapid changes in social attitudes as regards reproductive practices and thus render the projection of current trends in reproduction even more hazardous than was commonly believed to be the case before World War II.

However, in spite of much uncertainty in the projection of population growth for any given country or area, the author believes that our studies of population have proceeded far enough to permit of some reasonably valid conclusions regarding the probable future trend in natural increase. For some years he has believed that on the basis of probable future natural increase the peoples of the world could be divided into three broad groups.

Group I. The Western peoples who have long been exercising a large measure of control over their death rates through the improvement in the level of living of the masses of the people and the application of science to health problems belong in this group. During the past several decades most of these Western peoples have also come to exercise an increasing measure of control over their birth rates. At present these peoples all have relatively low death rates and birth rates even in spite of the postwar rise in the latter. The dominant factor affecting their rates of increase from year to year is no longer the death rate, assuming no great and uncontrollable catastrophes. It is the birth rate, which as we have seen can and does vary considerably over a relatively short period of time.

On the whole it appears to the author probable that these Group I peoples will have relatively low rates of natural increase in the future. Their death rates are now so low that any further improvement in health will have only a small effect on their rates of growth. In fact, in many of them the crude death rates are likely to rise slowly because of the increasing proportion of old people, whose death rates are the most difficult to reduce (Chap. XI). If for any reason these peoples were to decide to raise larger families, they could do so very quickly, because there is no evidence yet of any significant change in their physiological capacity to reproduce. But it does not seem probable to the author that they will jeopardize their good level of living and their low death rates by any large increase in the average size of their families. To summarize, the Group I peoples have low birth rates and low death rates, both under a large measure of voluntary control, and they seem likely to have relatively small rates of increase or no increase at all as it becomes more difficult to acquire and maintain a good level of living with the resources available to them. In the author's opinion the countries belonging to Group I are the United States, United Kingdom, France, Denmark, Norway, Sweden, the Netherlands, Germany, Austria, Czechoslovakia, Hungary, the Baltic countries (Estonia, Latvia, and Lithuania—now part of the Soviet Union), Belgium, Finland, Switzerland, Italy, Canada (although French-Canadian Quebec still has a large increase), Australia, and New Zealand. They contain approximately one-fifth of the world's population.

Group II. Most of the countries in this group are characterized by a death rate which is coming under control to some extent but which, for most of them, is still at the level which prevailed in Group I countries 50 to 75 years ago. The birth rates of Group II countries are under less control than their death rates, although in some of them there can be no reasonable doubt that the birth rate has begun to decline. As a consequence of these changes in death rates and birth rates their rates of increase are of much the same order as those of the Group I countries around the latter part of the nineteenth century or the beginning of this century—10 to 15 per 1,000. In some cases the rates are even higher. There is, of course, no sharp line of demarcation between Group I and II countries. A country now in Group II may pass into Group I at any time that control over death rates and birth rates becomes more assured. Furthermore, there would be no general agreement among students of population on a list of the countries to be included in each of these groups at any given moment. The decision on this point would rest in part upon one's judgment as to the security of control over the death rate and the extent of the control over the birth rate in the particular country. These Group II countries, sometimes called *areas of demographic transition,* are likely to have relatively high rates of natural increase for several decades to come. As a group, therefore, they will probably grow at a considerably faster rate than the Group I peoples and will contain an increasing proportion of the world's population for several decades to come. The author would place the following countries in this group: Spain, Portugal, Greece, Yugoslavia, Bulgaria, Romania, Poland, South Africa (white), Japan, and the Soviet Union; possibly also Egypt, French North Africa (Algeria, Tunis, and Morocco), Brazil, Argentina, and Uruguay. With all these countries included, the population of this group would amount to a little over one-fifth of the world's total, perhaps 21 to 22 per cent.

Group III. This group would consist of the remaining peoples of the world and would contain perhaps 58 to 59 per cent of its total population. These peoples are characterized by high death rates which are under only a small measure of control as compared with that of Group I and are also substantially higher than those of the Group II countries. In addition, such control as is now exercised over death rates is highly precarious. In these countries the death rate is still the decisive factor in determining the rate of increase at any given moment because the birth rates of all of them are high (probably between 40 and 50 per 1,000) and vary much less from year to year than their death rates (see Chaps. VIII and XI). Among them there is as yet no evidence of any appreciable voluntary control over the birth rate. India is perhaps the best example of such a country for which we can get a fairly reliable picture of what is happening as regards natural increase, although the registration of births and deaths is woefully inadequate. Since India began taking censuses (1872) there were two decades out of the five before 1921 when the decennial increase was less than 1 per cent, *i.e.,* less than one per 1,000 per year. There was also one in which the 10-year increase was only 1.4 per cent. In the three decades since 1921 the rate of increase has varied between 10 and 15 per 1,000, judging from the actual increase in numbers. This is convincing evidence that the death rate is coming under control to some extent. But there is no evidence of any change in the birth rate. This evidence of a decline in the death rate might seem to justify placing India in Group II, but the author is not inclined to do so because the relatively small measure of control over the death rate manifested to date is still so precarious that there is no assurance it can be maintained, especially in view of the fact that the rate of increase in the Indian Union, 14.2 per cent in 1931 to 1941 and 13.3 per cent in 1941 to 1951, is fairly high and in the author's opinion cannot be maintained long without increasing pressure of population on the food supply which is likely to issue in higher death rates.

The important point to notice is that these Group III countries vary in rate of growth from year to year to the extent that the death rate falls, since the birth rate is less variable. Moreover, under prevailing conditions we cannot be at all certain that their death rates can be kept from rising. These countries may be said to have great growth possibilities because of their high birth rates, but they are likely to have highly variable rates of growth because of the great variability in their death rates. Some of the countries or areas in Group III probably are not growing at all because their high birth rates are matched by their high death rates, and others may at times even decline because of famine or disease which raises the death rate above the birth rate. The level of the death rate will determine the growth of the

Group III countries during the next few decades just as it has throughout human history.

Future Population Growth. That the probabilities of growth in these different groups indicated above do not seem to be consistent with the actual growth shown in Table 12-3 is due to the fact that the actual growth during the past decade has been greatly affected by war losses in many areas, while the probabilities indicated arise from an evaluation of the demographic development to be expected during the next few decades. Thus North-West-Central Europe showed an increase in numbers of 8.6 per cent between 1939 and 1949 while Eastern Europe showed a decrease, although the countries in the former area belong in Group I and those in the latter belong in Group II. This shows how a great catastrophe may affect population growth temporarily (Chap. IV). But for World War II, Eastern Europe would have had an increase of perhaps 25 to 30 million and its rate of growth 1920 to 1949 would have exceeded that of Western Europe by a large margin—about 19.5 per cent for the latter as compared with about

Table 12-3.　Population Estimates for Regions of the World, 1920 to 1949 [1]

Region	Reliability of estimates	Midyear estimates, millions			
		1949	1939	1930	1920
World..................	....	2,378	2,195	2,008	1,834
Africa.................	Poor	198	175	155	136
America	....	321	274	244	207
United States and Canada.	Good	163	143	134	115
Latin America..........	Fair	158	131	110	92
Asia[2]	....	1,254	1,162	1,069	997
Near East..............	Poor	74	66	59	55
South-Central Asia.......	Fair	436	394	348	314
Japan.................	Good	83	72	64	56
Remaining Far East......	Poor	661	630	598	572
Europe[3]	....	593	573	530	485
North-West-Central Europe.	Good	214	197	189	179
Southern Europe........	Good	91	84	77	70
Eastern Europe[3].........	Fair	288	292	264	236
Oceania.................	Good	12	11	10	9

[1] *Demographic Yearbook, 1949–50,* p. 10, United Nations, New York, 1951.
[2] Excluding the Asiatic part of the U.S.S.R.
[3] Including the Asiatic part of the U.S.S.R.

35 per cent for the former. This situation emphasizes the need to remember the assumptions on which all population projections are made. Whether it be war, as in the case just mentioned, or war and a change in the pattern of reproduction as in the West, changes in both death rates and birth rates can take place rather rapidly and as the result of conditions which cannot be foreseen. These facts must be remembered when studying projections of probable population growth. The people who make calculations of future growth are generally careful to make their assumptions clear, but the people who use them at times seem to forget what the assumptions were.

We are not so much concerned here with trying to foresee what may happen to the size of the population in any specific country or area as with trying to visualize the probable relative growth of the three groups described above. Consequently little need be added to what has already been said. The great majority of the people in Group I countries not only are definitely aiming to keep their families small enough to prevent any deterioration in their present levels of living but also cherish the hope that they can improve their way of living. The author believes, therefore, that the future rate of increase in the countries in this group will be relatively small and will be more and more controlled to adjust numbers to the resources available for their support.

The peoples in Group II are moving toward membership in Group I but have not yet attained as secure a control over deaths as have the Group I peoples, and they have substantially less control over births. Apart from great unforeseen catastrophes, they should continue to have a fairly rapid rate of natural increase for some time yet—a rate considerably above that of most of the Group I peoples—so that they should become an increasing proportion of the world's population. The growth of population in the Group III countries is highly unpredictable. The information making possible a very rapid extension of control over the death rate is available, but the speed with which such control can be made effective among them depends to a large degree upon the improvement of economic conditions, and there is no way now of answering the question, how rapidly can the economic conditions of the people of India, China, Iran, and so forth, be improved? The improvement of economic conditions depends primarily upon increased per capita production, and this is a difficult and slow process among illiterate and poverty-stricken populations. Furthermore, when the birth rate is very high each addition to the total production of a nation tends to reduce the death rate and thus to keep alive more of the children; hence it tends to prevent any significant increase in per capita production, which is essential to a rise in the level of living. The Western peoples passed through this critical period of a rapidly increasing population at a time when vast new areas, fertile and mineral-rich, were opened to them. The present Group III peoples have no such easy opportunities to open up new lands.

In the author's opinion, as a group they are likely to grow less rapidly for some time than the Group II peoples. But some of them, *e.g.*, the Indonesians, may grow more rapidly than either Group I or Group II peoples, although it is highly uncertain how fast they can colonize the unoccupied areas within their political boundaries. Since the Group III peoples are about three times as numerous as the Group I peoples, the author is inclined to believe that in *rate* of probable increase during the next three or four decades the groups should be ranked, in descending order, as follows: Group II, Group III, Group I. In growth in *absolute numbers* the ranking would be as follows: Group III, Group II, Group I.

Although, as was stated above, our concern here with future population growth is of a general nature, the reader is referred to the calculations of the probable future growth in certain Group I countries and in the Soviet Union by Notestein *et al.*[3] as showing the relative growth of different populations on the basis of the most reasonable assumptions that could be made at that time. The war, of course, is responsible for cutting down the actual population of the Soviet Union by many millions. But this could not be foreseen and allowed for in any such calculations. The future growth of population in the United States will be discussed in Chap. XVIII.

Suggestions for Supplementary Reading

Approaches to Problems of High Fertility in Agrarian Societies, 171 pp., Milbank Memorial Fund, New York, 1952. Eleven papers presented at the 1951 Annual Conference of the Milbank Memorial Fund.

NOTESTEIN, FRANK W., *et al.: The Future Population of Europe and the Soviet Union,* 315 pp., League of Nations, Geneva, 1944.

THOMPSON, WARREN S.: "Recent Trends in World Population," *Am. J. Soc.,* Vol. 34, No. 6, pp. 959–975, 1929.

WHELPTON, P. K.: *Cohort Fertility: Native White Women in the United States,* Princeton University Press, Princeton, N.J., 1953 (in press).

[3] *The Future Population of Europe and the Soviet Union,* pp. 237–315, League of Nations, Geneva, 1944.

CHAPTER XIII

INTERNATIONAL MIGRATION

The movement of men from place to place has taken on many and diverse aspects at different periods in human history. Early in man's history, when society was organized on a kinship basis, most migration was by clans or other small bodies held together by kinship ties. There was little or no independent movement of individuals or families from place to place or from group to group, except where exogamy prevailed. In these early days it would seldom have occurred to an individual that he could act on his own initiative to seek new companions or a new place in which to make a living. If the group moved to the seashore at the time the fish were running in certain waters, he went with it; if it moved to another area when fruit and nuts were ripening, he went there; but it seldom happened that an individual left his group and struck out on his own. No doubt there was always an occasional individual who rebelled against this close confinement within the kinship group and tried to live alone or with a few companions as "outlaws," but such individuals probably soon perished, both because they were regarded as enemies of the organized group and because without the communal organization of the group to support them they found making a living extremely difficult and dangerous.

This type of group migration must have constituted practically all migration until a people settled in a definite area and made their living by agriculture. Only when man began to depend upon what he could grow from the soil for his living and when numbers increased to the extent that the occupied lands became too small to provide for the entire family was there much inducement for individuals and families to strike out for themselves in search of new land, thus severing their relations with the established community. With fixed settlement, trade also expanded and this demanded migratory movement among the merchants. Moreover, even most of the great migratory movements of man, as contrasted with small clan and tribal migrations, have, until quite recently, been group movements rather than individual and family movements such as those to which we are now accustomed. As evidence of this one may cite the great migrations of peoples associated with the names of Attila and Genghis Khan, the Tartar movement into European Russia, that of the Lombards into northern Italy, and that of the Norsemen into France and then to England.

Only gradually as a greater degree of uniformity of civilization (social organization) developed over relatively large areas was it possible for any considerable amount of individual and family migration to take place. Not until the community recognized that the "foreign" individual (or family) could perform some useful service, even though he did not "belong," was it safe for individuals and families to sever themselves from the protection of the community or clan to which they belonged and to risk becoming a member of a different group.

It is this newer type of individual and family migration with which we are concerned here because it has played such an important role in the growth and distribution of population in the modern world, both within and between countries. But we should not assume that because this type of relatively free migration of individuals and families has been a very important factor in population changes in certain parts of the world for several centuries it will continue to be as important in the future. There is evidence accumulating that such migration may be giving way to state-controlled migration, as will be noted below. At this point I will only mention the "forced" migrations of the totalitarian states and in areas where new national groupings are being established (India and Pakistan) and the growing restrictions all over the world on the free movement of individuals across national boundaries.

1. MOTIVES FOR MIGRATION

The motives leading to migration have probably varied but little from age to age, the economic motive being dominant at all times, although not of equal importance in all movements. Clans, tribes, nomadic shepherds, and other regularly migratory groups have always moved as seemed best to them from the standpoint of making a living, although the force exerted on weaker groups by more powerful groups in search of a better living has very frequently made necessary the migration of the weaker group. In the period of European expansion during the past few centuries the motives for migration have, no doubt, been somewhat more varied, since individual circumstances entered more and more into consideration; but, even so, the desire to better one's position economically—the search for better opportunities—has been the dominant motive among both international migrants and internal migrants. Comparatively few peoples or individuals who are reasonably well satisfied with their economic position move to new homes. The more recent "forced" types of migration find their motives in desires and ambitions of political leaders (individuals and/or groups) who show no concern but for their own power in the state. In authoritarian states people are forced to move to preserve life or are shuffled about to serve the purposes of the leaders.

But to say that until these modern forced migrations came into the picture the dominant motive of individual and family migration was economic is not to deny that a good many individuals migrated for noneconomic causes. It is merely a recognition of the fact that far and away the most important cause of migration was the desire to improve economic status. Other causes of significance have been (1) the desire to secure freedom from political oppression, oppression which quite frequently shows itself in the economic disabilities imposed on minority groups; (2) the desire for religious freedom, to find a place where one could believe and worship as he saw fit; (3) personal maladjustments to family and community life; and (4) military and national considerations, which at certain times and in certain places have played an important part in the movement of large bodies of people from place to place.

2. CHARACTERISTICS OF MODERN MIGRATION

The migration of great bodies of people as organized groups and in the direct interest of the migrating group, or of the receiving group, did not play an important part in the modern expansion of Europe or in the internal development of Europe until the rise of totalitarian governments. Prior to World War I we had become accustomed to think of migrants as individuals or families moving rather freely from country to country and from place to place within a country in search of more satisfactory living conditions. As was said above, the motivation was largely economic and individual. The migrant was not often aided in his decision by any public authority, nor was he, as a rule, assisted financially by them in making the move, although at times this was done. By and large it was as often the attraction of the new country as the expulsive force of the homeland which exerted the decisive influence. The knowledge of the attractive features of the new land was conveyed chiefly from relative to relative or from friend to friend by word of mouth and by letter, although not infrequently both private organizations and public agencies in the receiving country made definite efforts to acquaint prospective migrants with the advantages open to them.

The natural result of this relatively free play of forces on the individual was that there was a large movement of people from areas of relatively dense population and low economic opportunity to areas of less density and greater opportunity, provided both areas possessed the same general pattern of culture and climatic conditions were also rather similar. In much of the modern international migration, poor peasants and farm workers with little or no land tended to predominate, both because they predominated in the European populations of their day and because, although poor, they had the qualities which enabled them to become pioneers on undeveloped land. Since the attractions of the new home were made known chiefly by the letters and personal visits of those who had already ventured forth, international migrants were frequently massed in the new home by place of residence in the old home.

But though there were many concentrations of migrants coming from different localities and of different nationalities in various areas of the receiving countries, there was comparatively little advantage to these modern migrants in maintaining the cultural patterns of their home areas unchanged, and there was comparatively little effort on the part of the areas of origin to encourage loyalty to the homeland. On the other hand, since the migrants came as individuals and families and from relatively harsh living conditions, they felt no special obligation to the country of their origin. Furthermore, to remain isolated from the larger community in which they settled generally entailed definite economic and social disadvantages. These were strongly felt by their children, while the lack of pressure, or at most the rather light and intermittent pressure, of the native group did not drive the newcomers to seek safety and refuge in their own community to the same extent as often happened in Europe when two or more nationality groups came into contact. Thus the very nature of modern migration tended to encourage the migrant to adapt himself to the new community, and if the migrants themselves failed to do this because of preference for old and accustomed ways of living and because of difficulties in acquiring a new language, their children tried all the harder. If they failed to achieve full integration in their new homes they failed not primarily because they wanted to remain Poles, or Germans, or Swedes, or Englishmen, and so forth, but because they did not know how to make the transition from foreign to native habits. This was almost as true for those who settled in farming communities as for those who settled in cities, although the former had fewer contacts with outside groups and were necessarily somewhat slower in making the transition.

Thus a large part of the international migration of the last two or three centuries, particularly that of Europeans to countries outside Europe, tended to sever the individual from Old World ties, and to a certain extent from all community ties, and to emphasize the individual aspects of life. Even the increasing ease of transportation did little to maintain the bonds between the migrant and the homeland, except for those who intended to return at some future time. Although there were many who so intended, they were generally a rather small minority. It is not misrepresenting the situation, then, to say that never in the history of the world had a great migratory movement carried with it so little of adherence to traditions and customs; never had the individual found so easy a way to break the bonds binding him to family and community by moving to a new land, leaving behind his past and embarking on a new career. The individual and family character of modern migration is its most distinguishing feature, as it is also the feature most determinative of the migrant's development and of the character of the culture developed in lands where immigrants were many and of varied cultural backgrounds.

3. THE EXTENT OF MODERN MIGRATORY MOVEMENTS

Modern migratory movements of the character just described have far surpassed all known movements, even remotely like them, in past ages. The numbers involved are almost incredibly large. Between 1820, when the United States first began to keep accurate records of immigrants, and 1950 about 39,325,000 immigrants entered the country.[1] Of course, not all of these remained permanently, but probably not far from 32 million remained here and were incorporated into our national life. This is the largest movement of immigrants into any country known to history, and considering the conditions now prevailing in the world, it appears not likely to be surpassed in the near future.

If we add to the immigrants into the United States the immigrants into the other parts of America, there has been a total immigration of approximately 60 million people into the Western Hemisphere since the beginning of the nineteenth century. The proportion of immigrants into South America returning to Europe was probably considerably larger than among the immigrants to North America. The total emigration from Europe since early in the nineteenth century must have been about 5 million larger, because of the movement to Australia and South Africa as well as to other parts of the world where European hegemony had been established. But these movements into other parts of the world were small as compared with that into America and have furnished but a small outlet to Europeans seeking larger opportunities. It would not be far from the truth, probably, to say that 65 million people have gone out from Europe since the beginning of the nineteenth century and that perhaps two-thirds to three-fourths of these remained abroad. There are now probably about one-half as many people of European origin living outside Europe as within it, west of the Soviet Union.

During the last three centuries, while Europe was expanding, there have been other migrations also, but they are of lesser importance. There have been movements from China to the Philippines, the Dutch East Indies, the Malay Peninsula, French Indochina, and Thailand, as well as smaller movements into other areas; for example, into the United States, Peru, and Formosa. The total of these movements from China proper will never be known with any degree of accuracy. In 1922 Ta Chen[2] estimated that there

[1] *Annual Report of the Immigration and Naturalization Service, 1950,* Appendix II, Table 1, U.S. Department of Justice, Washington, D.C., 1950.

[2] Persia Crawford Campbell, *Chinese Coolie Emigration in the Countries within the British Empire,* 240 pp., P. S. King & Son, Ltd., London, 1923; Ta Chen, *Chinese Migrations, with Special Reference to Labor Conditions,* p. 161, G.P.O., Washington, D.C., 1923. (U.S. Bur. Labor Statistics, *Bull.* 340, Miscellaneous Ser.)

were about 8,179,000 Chinese living abroad. The large movement into Manchuria after about 1900 was really an internal movement similar to westward migration in the United States and was probably much larger than all the other movements out of China proper. Although the above figures give no very accurate indication of the total migratory movement of Chinese during recent decades, to say nothing of what has gone on during the last century, they do indicate that there has been a considerable movement out of China over a long period of time. It appears that in recent decades about four-fifths of those who went abroad later returned. Since about 1930 it appears that there has been a considerably smaller movement of Chinese to foreign lands. In fact with the coming of the depression many more than usual returned home, and as the depression lessened the pickup did not bring the movement back to normal.[3] During and following the war the net outward movement became still smaller.

The migration from India has also been fairly large. About 2,130,000 Indians lived abroad in 1924.[4] All but about 100,000 of these lived in other parts of the British Empire—chiefly in Ceylon, Malaya, Straits Settlements, South Africa, Fiji, and Mauritius. With the coming of the depression in 1930 there was an even stronger return movement among the Indians than among the Chinese. Since the outbreak of World War II there has been but a negligible outward movement. The actual number of Indian emigrants now living abroad must be considerably smaller than the estimate given above.

The movement of emigrants from Japan is of quite recent date. Until about the last third of the nineteenth century it was a capital offense to leave the country. Once the restrictions were relaxed and the Japanese began to learn of economic opportunities elsewhere, they started to emigrate. The largest streams to foreign lands went to Hawaii and the United States, until they were excluded, then to Brazil and China. As late as 1909 there were nearly twice as many Japanese in this country as in all Asia outside Japan. By 1920, however, there were several times as many in China, including Manchuria, as among us. After 1931 the number in these areas increased rapidly, and after the attack on China (1937) and with the expansion of the Japanese-held territory in that country, a considerable movement of Japanese civilians took place in order to exploit the conquered area.

For several decades after Formosa (1895) came into Japanese possession and later Korea (1905) there had also been considerable migration from Japan into these areas to further the exploitation of these colonies. Altogether 3 million or more nonmilitary Japanese were repatriated at the close

---

[3] T. E. Smith, *Population Growth in Malaya*, p. 63, Royal Institute of International Affairs, London, 1952.

[4] *International Migrations*, ed. by Walter F. Willcox, Vol. 1, p. 148, Publications of the National Bureau of Economic Research, No. 14, New York, 1929.

of World War II, and practically all of these came from East and South Asia and the adjacent islands. This number includes those from the former Japanese colonies of Formosa and Korea, those settled in Manchuria, and the civilians following the army after 1937. At present most of the Japanese living abroad are found in Hawaii, on the mainland of the United States, and in Brazil and probably number between 600,000 and 700,000.

Korea had also sent considerable numbers of migrants to Manchuria, Russia, and Japan before World War II. Possibly 2.5 million Koreans lived abroad in 1940. When we consider the fact that China, India, Japan, and other parts of Asia and Malaysia probably have five or six times the population that Europe had in 1800, and that the potential rate of increase of these peoples (see preceding chapter) is very high, it is easy to understand that here is a vast reservoir of possible migrants. These Asiatic peoples now have birth rates as high as those of European countries two or more centuries ago, or higher. If any areas of new land were now available to them in proportion to their numbers such as were available to Europeans in 1800, it is probable that they would send out emigrants in the next century which would make the numbers Europe sent out from 1800 to World War I look small. The great movements of Chinese into Manchuria and Malaya and of the Indians into Malaya and to the new irrigation areas developed in India show clearly that these peoples will migrate in much the same way as Europeans when conditions appear equally favorable to them. The fact that no good agricultural areas comparable in extent to those opened to Europeans in America, Australia, and South Africa remain available to Asiatics for settlement undoubtedly accounts, in part, for the relatively small amount of migration to foreign countries from southern and eastern Asia. It should also be remembered, however, that these peoples have not long been allowed to move about as freely as were the Europeans of the nineteenth century.

4. COUNTRY-TO-CITY MIGRATION

Although an increasing proportion of the international migrants of the century preceding World War I who came from rural communities settled in urban communities, the movement from country to city was not primarily an international movement, except to some of the larger American cities. For this reason and also because in most of the countries of Europe there were comparatively few immigrants from abroad, the movement from country to city will be treated below as a phase of internal migration. However, it may be said in passing that when a European peasant went directly to an American city the problems of social adjustment were considerably more complicated than when he went to a farming community which in many cases was composed largely of his fellow countrymen.

5. SOCIAL AND PSYCHOLOGICAL EFFECTS OF MIGRATION

In its simplest terms the migration of a person places him in a situation involving social adjustments greater in degree than he is accustomed to making, and often they are new in kind. If the environment he has left is quite similar to that which he enters, his adjustments are few and relatively easy; hence he is not likely to suffer any very serious disintegration of character, nor is he likely to cause much disturbance in the life of the group and the community into which he enters. If, on the other hand, the adjustments are many and difficult, because of wide differences in cultural patterns between migrant and native, it is practically certain that the migrants and their families will show a large measure of instability in conduct, often resulting in considerable lawlessness and crime. The social controls which the native population finds fairly adequate to direct conduct are not effective for migrants accustomed to quite different controls. Furthermore, where the migrant finds adjustment difficult the receiving community finds the assimilation of the migrant just as difficult, and much mutual antagonism arises. It is this conflict of cultural patterns that is of most importance from the social standpoint in considering the consequences of migration, although the economic conflict of migrant and native is also of great importance and will be considered briefly in the following section. The hereditary differences between migrant and native are of minor significance unless the migrants are of a distinctly different race which is easily distinguishable by its physical characteristics.

The nature of the personal and community problems of adjustment faced by migrants can be illustrated by the brief analysis of a hypothetical case. The Polish peasant coming to the Gary steel mills can have no well-established standards to guide him in his conduct toward his fellow workers, his family, the government, and the bosses. He cannot use his leisure as he did in the old country. Besides, his customary standards give him little assistance in making many other decisions which must be made from day to day. Obviously the traditions of his homeland do not provide him with criteria of conduct for any large portion of his life in Gary. Likewise his experience of personal relations in a rural Polish village gives him no clue to the probable conduct of his fellows toward himself in Gary, nor do they show him how he should conduct himself in his vastly more complex relations with them. In addition, if he has his family with him, he finds that he can no longer have any part in the training of his children for their work in life as he did in the Polish village, where they spent a good part of their time in the fields with him. As a consequence the children rapidly lose interest in their home and parents and he cannot do much to guide them because he does not know what is going on in their minds. The school, which claims them for a good part of their waking time, tends to create a barrier between parents and children that cannot be ignored. Such a man is in a pitiable position, and there is little he can do to help himself in his family and community relations. His relations with his wife also are greatly disturbed by the new kind of life. They can no longer work together in the field; hence, they no longer have a common economic interest. The man's friends may be his fellow workers, while his wife's may be her immediate neighbors. In a hundred ways the traditional family relations are altered, with disturbing and sometimes with disastrous effects.

But sad as is the position of the immigrant and his wife, his children are often worse off. They lack the discipline of a traditional upbringing, and they have no one personally interested in them capable of acting as guide in introducing them to the complexities of a world where status has given place to change—where all is in a state of rapid flux and transition. This is the soil out of which anarchy grows, and it is only surprising that among the children of immigrant parentage so few go completely astray. Their home retains many of the features of a peasant home in Central or Eastern Europe, since the mother knows nothing but Old World traditions and habits, which the children soon come to despise. The mother becomes completely bewildered. She can find no sanctions which the children respect, and the father, being away most of the daytime, finds that he cannot exercise much influence. Physical punishment only makes matters worse. Indeed, physical punishment is quite likely to drive the children away from home altogether at an early age, thus breaking their last ties with the family. Then, too, the children are generally urged to go to work as soon as possible. But as soon as they have jobs they become independent economically, and this adds to their mental chaos. The difficulties experienced in finding a place in community life by both migrants and their children are equally great. The inevitable consequences of such violent uprooting by migration is a high degree of undisciplined individualism. Unfortunately the rather gloomy picture drawn here is only too often reproduced in actual life.

The undisciplined individualism so frequently produced by the conflict of cultures resulting from migration has had a profound effect upon our country as a whole. Not only has it been settled by immigrants from abroad within a comparatively short period, but its internal development has been accompanied by a vast and rapid movement of natives from East to West, from farm to city, and recently from South to North. The consequence is that a large proportion of all our people have experienced a sufficient amount of change in their modes of living at one time or another for it to have an unsettling effect upon their habits of life, issuing in conduct which is likewise uncertain and unstable. In order to have one's conduct orderly and integrated it must be based on a mental development which is orderly and forms a coherent and consistent whole. Migration, particularly where the changes in conditions of life are great, makes such an orderly mental development very difficult and at times renders it wholly impossible. Hence we have a very great number of people whose conduct is a series of actions expressing momentary or short-lived attitudes rather than a well-ordered and integrated mental development. Their lives are very truly lived without law, that is, without the guidance of settled habits and attitudes of mind. Their personalities are disorganized because they lack the unifying beliefs which very naturally grow up in men when they live under more settled conditions and tradition has a chance to do its work.

6. MIGRATION AND THE GROWTH OF POPULATION

In Recent Decades. About 60 years ago General Walker championed the theory that immigration into a country did not constitute a net addition to its population but rather was a substitution of the immigrant and his children for the children of people already there.[5] He pointed out that the birth rate was apparently declining most rapidly in those parts of our country where immigrants were most numerous, and he held that there was a causal connection between these two conditions. He believed that the unwillingness of the natives to have their children compete economically with foreigners was the reason for this decline. If this was the case, then allowing immigrants to enter at will merely meant that we were condemning a like number of children of native parents to remain unborn. Since there is always more or less antagonism between natives and newcomers (immigrants), especially where there are rather large differences in cultural backgrounds, this view was very naturally seized upon by those natives opposed to immigration, as a very effective weapon in their campaign to reduce immigration. We are concerned here only with the truth involved in General Walker's position.

It is quite impossible, of course, to prove conclusively the truth of such a proposition. It is true that native birth rates, if we use ratios of children to women as indicative of these rates in the days before birth registration became adequate, have long been lower in the northeastern states, where immigrants were most numerous, than in most other parts of the country. It is also true that when the rough heavy labor in construction work and factories passed into the hands of the immigrants, many natives did not want their children to enter these tasks. But it does not follow that immigration is the sole factor, or even the chief one, in producing a lower birth rate among the natives who were moving upward in the social scale.

In the discussion of the decline of the birth rate it has been maintained that urbanization and industrialization were the factors most closely associated in Western countries with the decline in the birth rate and in the rate

[5] Francis A. Walker, "Immigration and Degradation," *Forum,* Vol. 11, pp. 638, 642, 1891.

of natural increase in the earlier days of this decline. If this position is correct, then the question to which we are really interested in finding an answer is whether immigration had any effect upon the rate of our industrialization and urbanization. But it must not be forgotten that this is quite a different question from the one as to whether the direct economic competition of immigrants and natives causes the latter to reduce their birth rates.

Even the question of the effect of immigrants upon industrialization and urbanization cannot be answered definitely, but it seems not unlikely that the presence of large numbers of poorly paid immigrants did somewhat hasten this movement. Even while there was still a frontier and while many immigrants were still going directly to the land, our eastern cities were retaining large numbers and employing them in construction work and in factories. The fact that the cities had this abundant supply of cheap labor quite probably did hasten our industrial development by making investment in industry and trade more profitable than it would have been if only higher-priced native labor had been available. But it should be remembered that the immigrants would not have come if they had not been reasonably sure they could find jobs. At the same time that the presence of the immigrants was favorable to a rapid expansion of industry this expansion was probably pushed more vigorously because there was little doubt that an abundance of cheap labor could be drawn from the reservoirs of Europe. Hence, although the causal relation of industrialization and immigration cannot be stated with any great degree of accuracy, it seems to the author quite probable that in an indirect way the coming of our immigrants had some influence in hastening the decline of our native birth rate because it increased the urge of the natives to get into better paid urban jobs and because the people in such jobs were the first to adopt the voluntary limitation of the family.

Thus it is quite possible that immigrants and their children did not constitute a net gain in numbers over what we would have had if the process of industrialization had been slower. But it cannot be proved that we should have had just as many people in this country today as we now have if there had been no immigration since the adoption of the Constitution.[6] We were certain to develop cities and the industry of cities, and the birth rate would have fallen as it did in European cities, but the rate of decline in the native population might very well have been slower.

The effects of emigration upon population growth in the homeland have also attracted much attention and have formed the basis for much heated discussion as to whether the country of emigration gained any relief from population pressure by sending out emigrants. The argument of those who hold that emigration does not really relieve population pressure is based on

---

[6] Warren S. Thompson and P. K. Whelpton, *Population Trends in the United States,* pp. 304–311, McGraw-Hill Book Company, Inc., New York, 1933.

the undoubted fact that, in the past, certain countries have had a rate of increase which does not seem to have been much affected by the variations in the outflow of emigrants. The situation in Italy has frequently been cited in this connection. In Table 13-1 the average annual rate of population increase in Italy since 1862 and the average annual number of permanent emigrants from Italy are given, so far as these data are available.

These data, though not showing the number of permanent emigrants as accurately as could be desired for later years, do show that emigration had no very marked effect on the rate of population increase in Italy until the decade of World War I. Thus the highest annual rate of increase recorded before 1921 is for the period 1882 to 1900, and this was also a period when permanent emigration was increasing very rapidly. It averaged at least three times as much during this period as in the preceding decade, and at the same time the rate of increase was approximately 20 per cent greater. On the other hand, there was an appreciable decline in rate of increase in the

Table 13-1.   Average Annual Number of Permanent Emigrants from Italy and Average Annual Rate of Population Increase, 1862 to 1947

Year	Average annual number of permanent emigrants[1]	Average annual rate of population increase per 1,000 inhabitants
1946–1947	86,072	8.4
1941–1942	−24,772	6.0
1936–1940	20,996	8.6
1931–1935	24,420	8.6
1926–1930	78,886	8.6
1921–1925	159,983	8.6
1911–1920	210,000–220,000	4.6
1901–1910	270,000–280,000	6.5
1882–1900	123,000–125,000	7.4
1872–1881	33,000– 35,000	6.2
1862–1871	15,000– 20,000	7.1

[1] The data for 1921 to 1947 are not strictly comparable with those for the preceding years because they are for net emigration only. The data for the years prior to 1920 are partly estimated.

following decade when the amount of emigration more than doubled. This suggests that a large emigration, as in the first decade of this century, may have had some influence in slowing up the rate of population increase, although the decline in the birth rate may have been the more important factor (Table 8-2). The decade 1910 to 1920 cannot be considered in this connection because there were many other disturbing factors present during World War I. Since 1920, however, and particularly since 1924, the number of emigrants leaving Italy has fallen rapidly and the increase of population has become greater. Thus the slackening of the flow of emigrants has been accompanied, temporarily at least, by an increase in population growth. However, the birth rate declined from 29.2 in 1921 to 23.8 in 1932, fell about a point (1.0) during the middle 1930's but rose to about the 1932 level in 1939 (23.6) and then declined during World War II and did not rise as much after it (1946, 22.7) as in Western Europe and by 1950 had fallen to 19.2. These data permit of no conclusive interpretation regarding the relation of emigration to population growth in the country of origin. The data for Germany (Table 13-2) show even more than those for Italy that in periods of large emigration—1861 to 1871 and 1880 to 1885—the rate of population increase was lower than in periods of smaller emigration or of net immigration—1871 to 1880 and 1895 to 1905.

However, one cannot be certain that the number of emigrants was the only, or even the most important, factor affecting population growth in a given period in either Italy or Germany. The effects of emigration are so

Table 13-2. Average Annual Net Immigration and Average Annual Rate of Population Increase, Germany, 1861 to 1933

Year	Average annual net immigration	Average annual rate of population increase per 1,000 inhabitants
1933[1]	−29,300	5.6
1925[1]	22,800	5.5
1910	−32,000	14.0
1905	10,500	15.2
1900	18,800	15.6
1895	−89,800	11.6
1890	−65,800	11.0
1885	−196,000	7.2
1880	−76,200	11.8
1875	−79,900	10.2
1871	−103,700	7.7

[1] Without Saar Territory.

closely bound up with other social and economic conditions affecting population growth that they probably can never be isolated with any assurance. Thus we should need to know whether increasing industrialization and trade were making it possible for a nation to support a larger population at a higher level of living; whether the efficiency of agriculture was increasing and how fast; what progress the public health movement was making at the several periods; whether the natural resources and capital formation were such as to ensure a long and steady industrial development; whether the agricultural area was being extended, and how much and how easily; whether technical skill and managerial ability were available in such quantities that resources could be more efficiently used; whether the knowledge of conception control was available to the people generally, and how rapidly it was spreading; and a number of additional facts indicating the probable effects of the social and economic conditions which may be assumed to affect birth and death rates and hence to determine the rate of increase.

Some General Conclusions Regarding Sending Countries. It will be impossible to pursue further this matter of determining the effects of migration on population growth in any detail. However, although the author believes that it is not possible to state any generally acceptable conclusions, he will state briefly his own views in general terms. These are based on consideration of far more data than are given here, as well as on much personal observation. If there is a high birth rate and a high death rate in a country, with little or no increase in numbers, this is generally indicative of a considerable pressure of population upon the means of livelihood. Under such conditions emigration probably will not appreciably change the rate of population increase in the sending country. It may, however, raise the rate of natural increase if emigration is at a *high* rate because it will make possible a somewhat lower death rate. The birth rate is unlikely to be much affected, although if a large number of young women emigrate the birth rate may decline a little. In any event it is doubtful whether when these conditions prevail the area of emigration benefits from emigration abroad.

Since there are vast populations in the world today which have high birth rates and death rates and which feel the need of finding relief from the hardships of life through emigration, a word should be said on this point. In the first place, the lands still available to emigrants are small as compared with those available in 1800. There simply is no opportunity for the peoples of China and India and other crowded areas in Asia to find new homes abroad as did the Western Europeans during the nineteenth century. Migration on any scale that is at all practicable would do almost nothing to relieve population pressure at home. As was said above, peoples having the demographic characteristics of the Indians and Chinese—very high birth rates and high to very high death rates—will almost immediately fill any gap left by emigration because of a slight reduction in the death rate. Among the 1,000 million people of South and East Asia who probably have a birth rate in excess of 40 and a death rate of 30 or more, the death rate would need to fall by only 1 point to fill the gap left by the emigration of 1 million people annually. Almost certainly this would happen. How are 1 million of these peope to be moved abroad each year, to say nothing of the 8 million or so who would have to be moved to care for their present natural increase? Even if this could be done in a single year it would have to be repeated year after year for two or three decades merely to give these peoples a chance to raise the level of living in their present (size) populations. One has to assume that every emigrant means one less person in the home population than there would otherwise be in order to believe that emigration from these crowded lands would be of any real benefit to them. All that we know about emigration from lands of high birth rates and death rates seems to me to make this assumption untenable. (For some additional discussion of related points, see Chap. XVII.) Furthermore, these conditions do prevail in most of the countries which most feel the need of emigration for their people.

If, on the other hand, an area has a relatively low birth rate and death rate, emigration is not likely to have much effect on either unless the proportion of emigrants to nonmigrants is appreciable, *e.g.*, 1 to 2 per cent per year. In such a case the effect would probably be in the direction of lowering the birth rate a little and raising the death rate a little and thus reducing natural increase a little. The birth rate would be reduced both because of the emigration of young women and because the marriage rate among those remaining at home would be reduced by the excess emigration of young men. The death rate would be raised because of the proportional increase of older people in the population. Some European countries, or perhaps one should say some sections of these countries, may have benefited in this way through emigration to the United States during the middle and latter part of the nineteenth century, but of course this cannot be proved. It should be noted, however, that countries with low birth rates and death rates seldom send out many emigrants. In such countries conception control is so commonly known and practiced that their growth of population may be rather nicely adjusted to the economic conditions by controlled variations in the birth rate with little or no assistance from emigration. Where conception control is widely practiced, emigration might hasten the adjustment of numbers to the changing economic conditions due to the vagaries of international trade. Thus in the United Kingdom, where the nation's economy is very highly dependent on changes in her relation to the world's economy and where the birth rate is now quite largely under voluntary control, a rather large emigration might very well assist in the solution of her economic difficulties, since it is the babies born 18 to 20 years ago who are now entering marriageable age and are also entering the labor market. Even an actual decline of population might be brought about in part through emigration in such a country. But it is by no means certain that we yet possess the knowledge or the will seriously to undertake the management of migration for such purposes even in the United Kingdom or in other lands where a somewhat similar need exists.

Immigration to Unsettled Lands. As regards the effects on population growth of immigration to new lands by peoples of more advanced culture, there can surely be no doubt in anyone's mind that the population of these new lands is often increased greatly by such emigration. By very definition a more advanced culture (as compared with a more primitive one) means, for one thing, a culture in which the productiveness of human labor is greater. No one denies, for example, that the population of the United States, Canada, Australia, and most of the countries of South America is much greater now than it would have been had the European never entered these lands. So that whatever may be the effect of immigration on population growth after a country is fairly well settled by people of the same general cultural level as the more recently arriving immigrants, the net effect of European colonization has certainly been to increase very greatly the number of Europeans in the world and almost certainly also the total number of people in the world. There can be little doubt that most immigrants in the last 200 or 300 years who have settled in new lands have left more descendants than they would have left if they had remained at home. On the whole, the surroundings of these immigrants have been favorable to a high birth rate and a moderately low death rate, resulting naturally in a very rapid rate of growth, so that we find periods in the life of these European settlements when they have more than doubled their numbers in a generation.

7. SOME OTHER SOCIAL AND ECONOMIC ASPECTS OF MIGRATION

In addition to the aspects of international migration already noted, there are some other points of interest worth mentioning.

Effects on Individuals. From the standpoint of the economic status of the individual there can be little doubt that, in the long run, the migrant is better off as an immigrant than as a native in the homeland. As was said, he ordinarily starts out to improve his economic condition, and he succeeds in doing so in the great majority of cases even though he may remain poor according to the standards of his adopted land. From the standpoint of personality development the balance in favor of the immigrant is less certain. There are no doubt a great many immigrants who feel that they have cast off the shackles of tradition and that they have been released into a larger and more benign world. These people experience an enlargement of spirit which they could never have had at home, and this growth of the spirit can be considered among the finest fruits of the emancipation arising from migration. They are entries on the credit side. The debit side is represented by the broken-spirited and those whose lives have become anarchical. It is quite impossible to strike any general balance in this account. The elements in the case are too imponderable. But the fact is that the consequences of migration on the personality development of the immigrant are so frequently obscured by the economic advantages which are direct and obvious that the immigrant's own judgment is of little value in deciding whether he is spiritually richer for migration. Even his conduct in the matter of inducing his friends to come is conclusive only on the economic side, for the dollars-and-cents argument is no doubt the most generally plausible one and the one which is most frequently decisive. The author thinks there can be little doubt that from the economic standpoint the individual usually benefits from migration; that this is, and will remain, the overwhelmingly predominant motive inducing men to leave their homes and search out new habitations; and that economic improvement will remain the chief criterion by which the immigrant will judge of the benefits of emigration.

Ability of Immigrants. As regards ability, immigrants are probably a little above the average of the groups from which they come, in energy, in knowledge of conditions abroad, and in adaptability. Their going might be a drain on the home community, which would weaken it in the course of time. Too much emphasis should not be placed on this point, however, since economic motives are generally predominant and the selective effects both of economic factors and of personal factors are by no means clear, for comparatively few people who have attained more than average economic success at home are among those who emigrate. Economic success, of course, is not the only criterion of ability, but we have no basis for directly judging the personal characteristics of immigrants which make for good citizenship. In the author's opinion, however, there is no reason to be worried about the hereditary quality of immigrants.

Assimilation of Immigrants. A country of immigration has a problem that is very difficult and perplexing in creating an organic unity of the numerous elements which compose it. Whether or not in the long run it profits from these diverse elements is a matter of much dispute. There are vigorous advocates of the view that diversity of cultural elements is essential to the development of a rich and diversified civilization; but there are also just as vigorous advocates of the view that only a highly homogeneous group can be expected to produce a civilization of a high order. There does not appear to be any very satisfactory evidence for either view; but one is probably safe in saying that the highest achievements in decent and humane living cannot be expected until a high degree of national unity of purpose has been achieved. A fine type of human development necessarily presupposes an integration of personality and an assurance regarding human and aesthetic values which cannot be developed by a people that has not attained a considerable unity of purpose. In so far as immigration retards the integration of the life of all classes and groups into a national whole, it undoubtedly makes the achievement of many of the higher human values more difficult.

Race and Migration. Thus far no mention has been made of the effects of international migration on race contacts. International migration inevitably brings together people having more or less different cultural backgrounds. When these cultural differences are accompanied by visible racial differences the cultural traits of the immigrant group are usually thought of by the native group as in large measure due to racial differences. Thus it has come about that race problems have been multiplied and intensified by migration during the past century or two. This is so obvious that he who runs may see. There is much reason to suppose that these race conflicts will become even more bitter in the future. It is folly to ignore the fact that the expansion of Europe and the importation of Negro slaves into the United States have created many and difficult race conflicts and that the economic exploitation which has accompanied this migration has embittered and is embittering contacts between different races. No attempt will be made here to discuss race contacts, not because they are not worthy of much attention but rather because of the incompetence of the author in that field and because of the limitations of space.

8. THE WAR AND INTERNATIONAL MIGRATION

As has been intimated at several points in the preceding discussion, the relatively free movement of individuals from country to country appears to have come to an end. Ever since the end of World War I there has been a growing tendency to control international migration. This was manifested first in restrictions placed on numbers, and sometimes on sources, by receiving nations and also by the new limitations on the right to migrate from the home country. Our own quota laws, which first came into effect in 1922, both limited numbers and allocated quotas to different countries in accordance with the proportion of our population already composed of the different national stocks. In most European countries restrictions of the rights of immigrants were also increased, or existing restrictions, such as limitation of sojourn without naturalization, were enforced more rigidly, while even in South America more control over immigration, both as to numbers and as to country of origin, gradually came into effect.

Even before the receiving countries became more strict in the regulation of immigration, the Soviet Union had practically forbidden emigration. Totalitarian Italy also soon decided that it was harmful to have a large outflow of young adults and had practically stopped emigration several years before the onset of the depression in 1929.

What international migration had not been stopped before the depression of the 1930's was soon stopped after unemployment began to pile up in the receiving countries. With the access to power of the Nazis in Germany in 1933 emigration was permitted only to those small groups which the Nazis were anxious to get rid of, chiefly the Jews, but owing to the restrictions on the liquidation of their property holdings not many of them were able to leave.

At the same time there developed a strong propaganda in the totalitarian states to the effect that the peoples of similar culture living outside their political boundaries, *e.g.,* Germans in the Baltic States, Poland, Romania, and Italy and Ukrainians in Poland and Romania, should be incorporated into one state. There is little doubt that one of the important causes of World War II can be traced to the desire of these states to "bring home" these migrants either by conquering territory into which they could be moved after driving out the resident population (Germans in western Poland) or by conquering the territory where they then lived and incorporating it into the dominant country (the Soviet Union in eastern Poland with its Byelorussian and Ukrainian populations).

The types of migration resulting from these efforts to unite nationality groups had little resemblance to the relatively free migration of individuals and families which had prevailed before 1914. The totalitarian state did not recognize the right of the individual to move out of the state.

It would be too long a story to follow even the main events of the German migrations undertaken after the fall of Poland in the furtherance of building Hitler's empire. The mere mention of the chief streams will have to suffice. The Balts, the people of German ancestry living in the Baltic states, and the Germans living in northern Italy, in Romania, and in other Balkan states were moved into western Poland as fast as the Poles could be cleared out, and parts of this movement were begun even before the German attack on the Soviet Union. As the German armies advanced into the Soviet Union some of these peoples and also some Germans from Germany proper were moved into the Ukraine. The purpose of all this was to build an empire which would "endure 1,000 years" by creating a solid block of German-speaking people from the Rhine to the Volga, probably reaching as far north as Moscow and south to the Balkans and the Black Sea.

People were moved in mass without regard to personal considerations, and though the exact number moved in this fashion between the fall of Poland and the German reverses in the Caucasus and at Stalingrad is not known, it has been estimated at around three-quarters of a million. It was planned to move several million more as fast as it was possible to do so. Thus several millions of German people who before the war were "minorities" would be added to the solid German bloc by the driving out (forced migration) of perhaps twice as many other people. The successful accomplishment of these grandiose schemes of displacement of Poles and Ukrainians and the resettlement of those areas by Germans were expected to result in an empire of about 80 million Germans containing comparatively small minorities of other peoples.

The understanding arrived at between Germany and the Soviet Union in 1939 gave a large slice of eastern Poland as well as the Baltic states to the latter. Pursuing the policy of eliminating minorities, the Soviet Union allowed Germany to move the Balts, as has been already noted, into what had been western Poland; she herself drove out the Poles in eastern Poland, thus leaving this territory rather completely to the Byelorussians and the Ukrainians. The eastern portion of Romania was also cleared, as far as was possible under the circumstances, of all minorities, leaving it to the Ukrainians to be united with the Soviet Ukraine.

Toward the close of the war, as the German armies retreated, all the German migrants moved into Poland by Hitler and the smaller groups settled in the Ukraine became refugees, and in addition the Germans from East Prussia and the prewar Germans in western Poland joined them in fleeing west of the Elbe and Neisse. Possibly as many as 8 to 10 million persons were involved.

After the war there were still other forced migrations on a large scale. The Sudeten Germans in Czechoslovakia alone numbered 2.5 to 3 million. There was also much migration between the Balkan states, some of it forced and some of it based on the desire of minority groups to join the larger dominant groups speaking the same language but living in other states. There were other movements of vast numbers of people both during the war and following it. The great movement of slave labor into Germany, the crowding of the surviving Poles into a relatively small area in central Poland, the settlement of Germans from the Reich in conquered areas all over Europe from the Atlantic to the eastern Black Sea, the withdrawal of many millions of Russians from German-occupied territory and the similar withdrawal of Balkan peoples from occupied territory, to mention only a few of the major movements, affected at least 30 million people.[7]

9. MIGRATION IN THE FUTURE

At present it seems unlikely that there will again be anything even remotely resembling the relatively free migration between different countries which prevailed before World War I. It seems more likely that the development of exclusion policies in the countries which formerly admitted large numbers of immigrants will keep migration to them at a relatively low level. It also seems likely that the growth of nationalism in Asia (Thailand, Burma, and others) and in the neighboring islands (Indonesia, the Philippines, and elsewhere) will result in the repatriation of the "foreigners" already there rather than lead to further immigration. The forced migration of perhaps 10 to 12 million people between the Indian Union and Pakistan following their establishment as independent nations is a case in point.

Finally, I would mention the possibility that the increase in military power, and as a consequence the increase in political influence, which will ensue upon industrial development in great countries like China and India, and perhaps also in Japan within a decade or so, may lead them to seek outlets for migrants in areas in Africa and in the islands off the coast of

[7] For a good discussion of the entire problem of displacement of peoples as a consequence of World War II, see Eugene M. Kulischer, *Europe on the Move,* 277 pp., Columbia University Press, New York, 1948.

Asia. If this happens and they are successful in achieving their aims, relatively large colonies might be established in certain parts of Africa and in large islands like Borneo, New Guinea, Madagascar, and Celebes within a relatively short period. In the opinion of the author such colonies would do little or nothing to relieve the pressure of population in the countries of emigration, with the possible exception of Japan, but it might effect a great change in the character of the population in the receiving areas and in the type of society that would develop there. Certain other aspects of such a movement of Asiatic peoples into the territories but little developed at the present time will be discussed more fully in Chap. XVII.

Suggestions for Supplementary Reading

CAMPBELL, PERSIA CRAWFORD: *Chinese Coolie Emigration to the Countries within the British Empire*, 240 pp., P. S. King & Son, Ltd., London, 1923.

CHEN, TA: *Chinese Migrations, with Special Reference to Labor Conditions*, 237 pp., G.P.O., Washington, D.C., 1923. (U.S. Bur. Labor Statistics, *Bull.* 340, Miscellaneous Ser.)

International Migrations, ed. by Walter F. Willcox, 2 vols., Publications of the National Bureau of Economic Research, No. 14, New York, 1929–1931.

International Union for the Scientific Study of Population: *Cultural Assimilation of Immigrants*, 118 pp., Cambridge University Press, London, 1950. (Supplement to *Population Studies*, March, 1950.)

ISSAC, JULIUS: *Economics of Migration*, 285 pp., Kegan Paul, Trench, Trubner & Co., London, 1947.

KULISCHER, EUGENE M.: *The Displacement of Population in Europe*, 171 pp., International Labour Office, Montreal, 1943.

————: *Europe on the Move*, 377 pp., Columbia University Press, New York, 1948.

PLANT, G. F.: *Overseas Settlement, Migration from the United Kingdom to the Dominions*, 186 pp., Oxford University Press, London, 1951.

Postwar Problems of Migration, Conference of the Milbank Memorial Fund, Oct. 29–30, 1946, 173 pp., Milbank Memorial Fund, New York, 1947.

"Reappraising Our Immigration Policy," *Ann. Am. Acad. Pol. Soc. Sci.*, Vol. 262, 259 pp., March, 1949.

SCHECHTMAN, JOSEPH B.: *European Population Transfers, 1939–1945*, 532 pp., Oxford University Press, New York, 1946.

TAFT, DONALD R.: *Human Migration*, 590 pp., The Ronald Press Company, New York, 1936.

WALKER, FRANCIS A.: "Immigration and Degradation," *Forum*, Vol. 11, pp. 634–644, 1891.

Chapter XIV

INTERNAL MIGRATION

The causes of internal migration—moving within national boundaries—are not essentially different from those of international migration, but it is probable that personal motives of a noneconomic character play a somewhat more significant role in internal movements. It is also likely that differences in political and social conditions furnish a less important motive for migration between the several regions within a nation than between nations. Finally, although differences in economic status and opportunity within a nation may be large and are better known than those between nations, they probably are smaller relatively than those between nations which send out and receive migrants. Thus in spite of the fact that during the productive years of life most people who migrate any considerable distance within a country probably do so in order to secure a better living, there are certainly considerable numbers who migrate because of personal and family reasons. These differences render internal migration far less a one-way stream than international migration, except for the seasonal movements of laborers between a few countries, and consequently the net gain to most communities through internal migration is generally a relatively small part of the whole.

The volume of internal migration has never been recorded with any degree of accuracy in most countries. However, a few European countries have kept account of the movement of people from community to community during recent decades. The Swedish data, which are certainly among the best, will be noted in Sec. 4 below. However, as interest in migration has grown, an increasing number of studies dealing with migration within different countries have been made. The amount, the direction, and the personal characteristics of the migrants are steadily becoming better known.

1. THE SOURCE OF INTERNAL MIGRANTS

It has long been known that during the period of modern industrial development the prevailing net movement has been from agriculture to the nonagricultural industries—from the farm and agricultural village to industrial village or town and city. This was the natural result of a continuing agricultural revolution closely associated with, and no less fundamental than, the industrial revolution of the last two centuries.

294

In addition to the general change in the economy of the West making relatively fewer agricultural workers necessary and providing jobs for more non-agricultural workers, the agricultural population has for some decades had a higher birth rate than the urban population (Chap. IX), and since it has also had a lower death rate, with only minor exceptions, it is the usual thing for it to have a higher rate of increase. Thus the agricultural population of the Western lands, within the period with which we are concerned here, has generally had a surplus population that could not be employed to advantage in agriculture except at times when new lands were being settled rapidly or in areas where agriculture was being greatly intensified. A considerable proportion of this surplus population has been going to the cities, and this has been the chief source of internal migrants in modern times. Before the industrial revolution cities had never been able to keep alive enough of their children to maintain their own numbers, to say nothing of providing for growth; hence it is highly probable that the rural areas have always been the chief source of internal migrants. This may be in process of change at present because of the increasing number of migrants between urban communities and the decreasing proportion of the farm population.

In older countries where most of the good cropland has been occupied for centuries, internal migration has long been primarily a country-to-city movement, but until the industrial revolution had gained some momentum this movement must have been relatively small. This would certainly have been the case in countries like China and India where there was no fundamental change in the economy for centuries. The situation was much the same in Europe until about two centuries ago. Moreover, as long as the productivity of agriculture was so low that it took the labor of four agricultural families to supply the essential needs of themselves and one urban family, it is obvious that the movement of people from country to city could not have been large. In new lands, on the other hand, internal migration supplied not only a considerable part of the population of the cities but also a large part of the people settling on the new lands.

2. MIGRATION WITHIN THE UNITED STATES

In the United States the westward movement of young people leaving the East to take possession of new lands in the West was long the dominant movement. Such vast internal movements of people, chiefly between rural areas, in search of new homes were, of course, peculiar to those countries which had great unsettled agricultural areas which were attractive to immigrants. However, even in the United States during the period of rapid land settlement there was a much larger proportional increase in the urban population, small though it was in absolute numbers, than in the rural population as a whole. There were, however, many rural areas in the western part of the

United States which grew even more rapidly than most cities until about 1880 to 1890, by which time the better agricultural lands had been occupied.

Redistribution of Population during the Nineteenth Century. The tremendous effect which internal migration in the United States had upon the growth of population in the newer regions of the country is well illustrated by what happened in the East North Central states during the nineteenth century (Table 14-1). In 1790 there was no enumeration of population in the territory now comprising these states. In 1800 there were only 51,000 people enumerated in this entire area. The column headed "estimated population" shows approximately what the growth would have been if the rate of natural increase for the actual population enumerated in 1800 had been 100

Table 14-1.   Estimated and Enumerated Total Population and Enumerated Foreign-born Population, East North Central States, 1800 to 1950

Year	Estimated population[1]	Enumerated population	Foreign-born population	Per cent of U.S. population in E.N.C. states
1950	4,500,000	30,399,000	. . . .	20.2
1940	3,600,000	26,626,000	2,579,000[2]	20.2
1920	2,400,000	21,476,000	3,232,000	20.3
1900	1,600,000	15,986,000	2,625,000	21.0
1880	800,000	11,207,000	1,917,000	22.3
1860	400,000	6,927,000	1,197,000	22.0
1840	200,000	2,925,000	. . . .	17.1
1820	100,000	793,000	. . . .	8.2
1800	51,000	51,000	. . . .	0.1

[1] Assuming a natural increase of 100 per cent each 20 years and no migration, 1800 to 1900; 50 per cent each 20 years, 1900 to 1940; 25 per cent, 1940 to 1950.
[2] Includes foreign-born Negroes, Chinese, and Japanese but not other foreign-born nonwhites.

per cent in each 20 years up to the end of the century, 50 per cent from 1900 to 1940, and 25 per cent during the last decade—very high rates of natural increase as compared with the actual rates in the United States in these different periods. The next column shows what the population actually was at 20-year intervals. The following column (foreign-born) shows the number of persons living in the area who had come from abroad (not available before 1850), and the last column shows the change in the proportion of the population (United States) living in this region. Not until after 1860 did the population fail to double in 20 years. Clearly a large part of the increase until the beginning of this century must have come from internal migration, since it cannot be accounted for either by natural increase or by the influx of immigrants from abroad.

The growth of any other group of states west of the Appalachians during the period of their rapid settlement would illustrate this point just as well. Moreover, this east-to-west movement still continues, for during the decade 1940 to 1950, 80 to 85 per cent of the increase of population in the Pacific Coast states came from migration, and nearly all of this was internal. For the past two centuries, but especially since 1800, this east-to-west movement of population will go far to explain the growth of population in the different regions of the United States.

But this east-to-west migration was by no means the only internal movement of importance during the nineteenth century, although it must have been much the largest in numbers until the last quarter of the century. Table 14-2 shows that with the single exception of the decade 1810 to 1820 the urban population of the country has grown much faster than the rural population, generally several times as fast. Even during the period 1790 to 1830, when there was comparatively little immigration from abroad, the rate of growth of the urban population averaged about twice that of the rural. If there had been no migration to the cities from the country the rural population would have grown faster than the urban, for even before 1830 the rural population had a higher birth rate and a higher rate of natural increase than the urban population. However, not until after 1880 did the urban population grow more in absolute numbers than the rural.

Redistribution of Population since 1900. The two movements just noted, *i.e.*, the east-to-west and country-to-city, probably account for a large part of the internal migration in the United States before about 1900. Since about 1900 other streams of migration have become of increasing importance. The industrial cities of the North have drawn more and more workers from the South, both white and Negro. For the past few decades the South not only has had a higher birth rate than the North but also, being more rural, it has offered fewer opportunities in its cities to the surplus population from the farms, which surplus has been increasing rapidly as a result of mechanization. This movement northward increased rapidly after World War I shut off immigration from Europe, and with the restriction of immigration during the 1920's it was maintained at a high level until 1930. During the depression it practically disappeared as a net movement, and the proportion of the people born in the South and living in the North declined slightly between 1930 and 1940. This movement northward again became of considerable importance when rearmament began in 1940 and has remained so since that time, in spite of the fact that now the South is becoming more industrialized and offers more opportunities for nonagricultural workers. The 1950 data on migration between the states will not be available for some months (see Tables 7-3 and 14-3).

In recent decades although the westward movement of population has continued on a large scale, as indicated above its character has changed

Table 14-2.   Urban and Rural Population of the United States, 1790 to 1950

Year	Number			Percentage of increase		
	Total	Urban	Rural	Total	Urban	Rural
1950[1]	150,697,361	96,467,686	54,229,675			
1950[2]	150,697,361	88,927,464	61,769,897	14.5	19.5	7.9
1940	131,669,275	74,423,702	57,245,573	7.2	7.9	6.4
1930	122,775,046	68,954,823	53,820,223	16.1	27.3	4.4
1920	105,710,620	54,157,973	51,552,647	14.9	29.0	3.2
1910	91,972,266	41,998,932	49,973,334	21.0	39.3	9.0
1900	75,994,575	30,159,921	45,834,654	20.7	36.4	12.2
1890	62,947,714	22,106,265	40,841,449	25.5	56.5	13.4
1880	50,155,783	14,129,735	36,026,048	30.1	42.7	25.7
1870	38,558,371	9,902,361	28,656,010	22.6	59.3	13.6
1860	31,443,321	6,216,518	25,226,803	35.6	75.4	28.4
1850	23,191,876	3,543,716	19,648,160	35.9	92.1	29.1
1840	17,069,453	1,845,055	15,224,398	32.7	63.7	29.7
1830	12,866,020	1,127,247	11,738,773	33.5	62.6	31.2
1820	9,638,453	693,255	8,945,198	33.1	31.9	33.2
1810	7,239,881	525,459	6,714,422	36.4	63.0	34.7
1800	5,308,483	322,371	4,986,112	35.1	59.9	33.8
1790	3,929,214	201,655	3,727,559			

[1] New urban definition.
[2] Old urban definition.

greatly. There are comparatively few migrants now going into agriculture in our West. In the decade 1940 to 1950 when the Pacific Coast states had almost a 50 per cent increase in numbers there was almost no change in the number of persons working on farms in this area. These far western states are now among the highly urbanized areas of the country. California, in particular, now ranks with Pennsylvania and New Jersey in the proportion of its population living in urban communities. Clearly internal migration is of great importance not only in effecting a regional redistribution of population in the country but also in effecting a rural-urban redistribution. However, this regional redistribution of population through internal migration is no longer as closely associated with the movement from rural communities as in the past, although the movement from east to west and from south to north is still in part a movement from country to city.

Regional shifts in population in the United States are more and more supported by the movement of people between communities of the same general character, *e.g.*, between large cities and between metropolitan

Table 14-3.   Native Population Born in the North and Living in the South, or Vice Versa, 1900 to 1940 [1]

Region	1940	1930	1920	1910	1900
Population born and living in the North[2] or in the South[3] and with state of birth reported.........	106,812,818	97,746,825	83,852,590	72,581,780	62,098,675
Born in the North..............	64,637,806	59,468,321	51,341,156	43,975,391	37,941,559
Living in the North...........	62,562,327	57,590,129	49,619,807	42,526,162	36,920,109
Living in the South...........	2,075,479	1,878,192	1,721,349	1,449,229	1,021,450
Per cent of total born in the North...................	3.2	3.2	3.4	3.3	2.7
Born in the South..............	42,175,012	38,278,504	32,511,434	28,606,389	24,157,116
Living in the South...........	38,718,033	34,981,175	30,359,885	27,079,282	22,861,263
Living in the North...........	3,456,979	3,297,329	2,151,549	1,527,107	1,295,853
Per cent of total born in the South...................	8.2	8.6	6.6	5.3	5.4
Net gain of the North (excess of persons born in the South and living in the North over persons born in the North and living in the South)...................	1,381,500	1,419,137	430,200	77,878	274,403

[1] U.S. Bureau of the Census, *Sixteenth Census of the United States, 1940, Population, State of Birth of the Native Population*, PSR 11, p. 4, G.P.O., Washington, D.C., 1944. Persons born or living in the West and the small number of native persons born outside continental United States and persons for whom state of birth was not reported are omitted from this table.
[2] The North here includes New England, Middle Atlantic, East North Central, and West North Central divisions.
[3] The South here includes South Atlantic, East South Central, and West South Central divisions.

communities. On the other hand, the larger proportional increase of population in metropolitan communities than in the nation as a whole can only come from the migration of people out of rural communities and small cities to these metropolitan communities since there is no longer a large immigration from abroad. The farm population of the United States which now constitutes less than one-sixth of the total can no longer furnish enough migrants to provide for large regional shifts in population, although it can still furnish not only its total natural increase but some of its present numbers to increase the proportion of our people living in cities, particularly in metropolitan communities.

Migration in Metropolitan Areas. Finally, since about 1920 a new movement within metropolitan areas has developed which is a very significant factor in changing the structure of these areas, namely, the centrifugal movement from the central city to the area surrounding it. This is by no means the only factor in the very rapid growth of satellite areas, but it is an extremely important one. The significance of this growth of satellite areas will be discussed in the chapters on the city, but a few of the facts showing this growth may be given here. In 1900 the central cities of the 44 Metropolitan Districts of that time contained 77.3 per cent of the metropolitan population, but in 1940 they contained only 67.1 per cent of the population in those same districts. The number of Metropolitan Districts increased from 44 in 1900 to 140 in 1940, but the story is the same. The proportion of the metropolitan population living in the more densely settled central cities has been decreasing, and that living in the satellite areas has been increasing. Moreover, between 1900 and 1910 the central cities (44) absorbed 74.9 per cent of the total metropolitan increase, while between 1930 and 1940 the central cities (140) absorbed only 43.9 per cent.

The census no longer recognizes Metropolitan Districts but now uses Standard Metropolitan Areas defined by county lines. These Standard Metropolitan Areas contained 52.6 per cent of the nation's population in 1940 and 56.0 per cent in 1950, a larger increase in proportion than in the Metropolitan Districts of any preceding decade. In 1940 the proportion of the population of the Standard Metropolitan Areas living in the central cities was 61.7 per cent, but during the decade it declined to 57.6 per cent. Thus, though the Metropolitan Districts and Standard Metropolitan Areas are not strictly comparable, there cannot be the least doubt that the central cities are attracting a smaller and smaller proportion of the metropolitan increase.[1]

There are no summary data for the United States showing the size of the centrifugal movement out of central cities to the satellite areas around them, but a study of the data for migration within Ohio, 1935 to 1940, will throw some light on this point.[2]

The data on migration within Ohio between 1935 and 1940 show beyond doubt that much of the increase between 1930 and 1940 in the satellite areas surrounding the eight cities of 100,000 and over was due to the movement from central cities to their own satellite areas. Almost 124,000 migrants living in satellite areas in 1940 reported that they lived in the central city of the same metropolitan area in 1935, while only 23,000 reported that they moved from a satellite area to its central city during the same period. This left a net outward movement of 101,000 persons. In addition, of the 35,000 migrants from central cities to other metropolitan areas only a little over 21,000, or about 61.0 per cent, went to central cities while about 14,000 went to rings (satellite areas), and out of somewhat over 9,000 migrants from rings to other metropolitan areas only about 4,000 went to central cities; the remainder went to other rings.[3] Thus the satellite areas had a net gain of about 10,000 through intermetropolitan migration. The third source of gain by the rings from intrastate migration consisted of about 31,000 migrants to them from the nonmetropolitan areas of the state which was

[1] Donald J. Bogue, *Population Growth in Standard Metropolitan Areas, 1900–1950, with an Explanatory Analysis of Urbanized Areas,* G.P.O., Washington, D.C., 1953.
[2] Warren S. Thompson, *Migration within Ohio, 1935–40: A Study in the Re-distribution of Population,* p. 16, Scripps Foundation for Research in Population Problems, Oxford, Ohio, 1951. Similar studies can now be made for other states.
[3] *Ibid.,* p. 34.

largely canceled by a loss of 24,000 migrants from rings to nonmetropolitan areas, leaving a net gain of about 7,000 for the rings. Thus of the total net gain of about 118,000 in the rings through intrastate migration about 85 per cent came from their own central cities. Since the total increase of the ring population, 1930 to 1940, was approximately 145,000, about 70 per cent is to be attributed to this centrifugal movement from their own central cities during the last five years of the decade. The proportion of the growth of satellite areas arising from such a movement will almost certainly vary greatly from one metropolitan area to another and from state to state, but there can be no reasonable doubt that it is providing an important part of the entire increase in satellite areas.

Migration from 1935 to 1940. In 1940 for the first time our census collected information regarding the place of residence of persons who had crossed a county or a large city boundary between Apr. 1, 1935, and Apr. 1, 1940, the date of the census. Since all the personal data usually collected in the census were also available, it became possible for the first time to count the people in the different streams of migration and to tell something of their characteristics. Not all the data regarding migrants were tabulated, but enough has been done to increase greatly our knowledge regarding internal migration in the United States. However, in the use of this material one should remember that it relates to the period 1935 to 1940, a time when recovery from the depression was started but by no means completed. Both the number of migrants and their characteristics may have been significantly affected by this fact. Moreover, the definition of migrants used was as follows:

> Migrants are those persons who lived in different counties (or quasi counties) in 1940 and 1935. In this classification, a city of 100,000 inhabitants or more is treated as a quasi county, and the remainder of its county as another. Thus, migrants comprise: (a) Those living in different counties in 1940 and 1935; (b) those living in 1940 in a city of 100,000 or more in 1940 but living elsewhere in the same county in 1935; and (c) those living in a city of 100,000 or more in 1935 but living elsewhere in the same county in 1940.[4]

This definition may also have affected both the number and the characteristics of the migrants between different areas to differing extents.

Here it will only be possible to mention a few of the more important results of this census of migrants. Of the population enumerated in 1940 about 15.7 million, or 12.0 per cent, were migrants; of these, 52.3 per cent were living in urban communities and 47.7 per cent in rural communities in 1940. Of the migrants living in urban communities 51.4 per cent came from

[4] U.S. Bureau of the Census, *Population, Internal Migration 1935 to 1940, Color and Sex of Migrants*, p. 1, G.P.O., Washington, D.C., 1943.

within the state, 21.6 per cent from contiguous states, and 27.1 per cent from noncontiguous states. When the migrants lived in large cities the proportion coming from noncontiguous states rose to 37.4 per cent, while for migrants living in rural farm communities only 11.4 per cent came from noncontiguous states. About two-thirds of all migrants coming from noncontiguous states lived in urban communities, and over one-third (35 per cent) lived in large cities. Bogue and Thompson [5] found that whereas 88.6 per cent of all the migrants to rural-farm communities came from the two nearest zones (from within a state and from contiguous states) only 62.1 per cent of those to large cities came from the same distance zones.

When the urban population (1940) was considered by regions it was found that 21.3 per cent of the urban population of the West consisted of migrants, while only 6.4 per cent of the urban population of the Northeastern states belonged in this category. The West was still drawing large numbers of migrants from the eastern states, but only about one-fourth as many were settling on farms as in urban communities and only about one-half as many on farms as in rural-nonfarm communities, *i.e.*, only about one-seventh of the total migrants living in the West were on farms and only about 38 per cent of them came from noncontiguous states. Westward migration to farms was about over.

The distribution of net gains from migration during the decade shows that most of the states east of the Rocky Mountains lost on the interstate exchange unless like Maryland, Virginia, and Connecticut they were affected by growth in the ring of a large city, or cities. Michigan, which had a fairly large net gain, was probably feeling the effects of the rearmament program more than any other state in 1940. Florida must be added to the states having a large net gain through migration. But it is significant that a large part of the net gain through migration accrued to the western states, most of it to the Pacific Coast states, and it is the *net* gain or loss of population through migration that produces most change both in distribution and in composition.

It is also of much interest that only a very few of the cities of the United States having over 100,000 inhabitants in 1940 showed a net gain through migration between 1935 and 1940. No doubt their losses through migration were somewhat exaggerated by the fact that when migrants reported their place of residence in 1935 they were prone to name the nearest large city which might be known to the census enumerator rather than some satellite or other small city, or the rural area near it, in which they actually lived. This type of error probably increased with distance. But even so there can be little doubt that many of the larger cities actually sent out more migrants (chiefly to their own rings) than they received. Hence very

[5] Donald J. Bogue and Warren S. Thompson, "Migration and Distance," *Am. Soc. Rev.,* Vol. 14, No. 2, p. 241, 1949.

few metropolitan areas lost population through this interchange of migrants.

It has frequently been suggested that the migration from farms to the larger cities took place by stages—farm to small city to large city—rather than directly. The Ohio study dealing with intrastate migration in some detail shows that, whereas the nonmetropolitan urban population constituted only 42.4 per cent of the total nonmetropolitan population, it furnished 50.6 per cent of the migrants to metropolitan communities and 56.3 per cent of those to the central cities, but that the nonmetropolitan rural-farm population which constituted 30.5 per cent of the nonmetropolitan population furnished only 20.1 per cent of the migrants to metropolitan communities and only 16.0 per cent of those to central cities.[6] This certainly does not prove that the movement from farms and rural communities is by stages, but it seems to the author to add a little confirmation to this view.

3. SOME CHARACTERISTICS OF MIGRANTS [7]

Quality of Migrants. There has long been considerable discussion regarding the kind of selection, if any, that takes place when people move from one type of community to another of different type. Students have been especially concerned to find out whether the rural community and the small town lost their best, their poorest, or their average citizens to the city. When rural-urban migration first attracted attention there was a marked tendency to assume as a matter of course that the brighter and more energetic boys and girls were leaving the farms and villages and going to the city. It seemed quite logical to believe that it took more than an average amount of energy and initiative to sever one's home ties and move into unknown conditions.

Later, as the problems arising from foreign immigration to the cities multiplied and became baffling, there was a rather violent reaction from this belief in the all-round superiority of the migrant, and there was much talk that they were the "scum" of the population, the "dregs of humanity," and so forth. This point of view was also adopted as regards internal migrants by some writers, although it was never applied to them in the extreme form in which it was applied to foreign-born immigrants. More recently there is an increasing disposition to believe that internal migrants are a pretty good sample, as far as their hereditary qualities are concerned, of the people in the communities from which they come. The data on

---

[6] Thompson, *op cit.*, Table 49, p. 82.

[7] U.S. Bureau of the Census, *Population, Internal Migration 1935 to 1940, Color and Sex of Migrants,* 490 pp., G.P.O., Washington, D.C., 1943; *Age of Migrants,* 382 pp., 1946; *Social Characteristics of Migrants,* 270 pp., 1946; *Economic Characteristics of Migrants,* 223 pp., 1946.

internal migrants in the United States, 1935 to 1940, do not throw any light on this old controversy, but they do shed some light on the social and economic characteristics of migrants in different streams. Only a very few points can be mentioned here.

Sex Ratios. For white and nonwhite migrants combined there were 101 males for each 100 females (sex ratio 101) when the migration took place within a state. When the migration was between contiguous states the sex ratio was 102.7 and when it was between noncontiguous states, 110.5. Clearly the farther migrants moved the higher was the sex ratio. Whites (100.4) had a substantially lower sex ratio than nonwhites (109.3) when the movement was within a state. Between contiguous states the situation was mildly reversed (whites 103.0 and nonwhites 99.6), while among migrants between noncontiguous states (whites 111.8 and nonwhites 93.3) the excess of white males was very large. In urban communities the sex ratio of migrants (94.8) was quite low, while in rural-farm communities it was quite high (116.7). In urban communities the white migrants had a substantially higher sex ratio (95.3) than the nonwhites (87.8), but in rural-farm communities the sex ratios of whites (116.8) and nonwhites (116.2) were about the same.[8]

Age. That migrants differ substantially from nonmigrants in age has long been known. The former are rather heavily concentrated at ages fifteen to thirty-four with proportionally more females under twenty and more males over thirty-five. Old people show little tendency to migrate, although the mild climates of Florida and California attract considerable numbers. Paradoxically, however, unusually high ratios of old people in a given area in the United States, while due to migration, do not arise from the migration of the old people themselves but rather from the migration of young people, thus leaving behind a large proportion of older people. The highest ratios of old people in the United States are found in some of the New England and Middle West states from which there have been large movements of young people (ages fifteen to thirty-four). Older women are somewhat more likely to migrate than older men. People moving to cities, especially from nonmetropolitan subregions, are younger than those leaving cities. In the movement from central cities to their rings there are relatively large numbers of men at ages thirty to forty-four and of women at ages twenty-five to forty-four.

Education. In general, migrants are better educated than the nonmigrants among whom they settle. The migrants to metropolitan areas contain a low proportion with only a common-school education and a high proportion who have completed high school and college. People with a good education, especially those with a college education or more, have a high rate of

[8] U.S. Bureau of the Census, *Population, Internal Migration 1935 to 1940, Color and Sex of Migrants,* p. 5.

migration, *i.e.*, a high ratio per 1,000 persons of the same educational status in the community in which they settle, as compared with migrants with only a common-school education. The nonmetropolitan areas lost well-educated people to the metropolitan areas. Migrants (aged twenty-five to thirty-four) between noncontiguous states contain a much higher proportion of persons with a college education or better (15.5 per cent) than those between contiguous states (11.4 per cent), and these in turn contain a higher proportion of this educational status than migrants within a state (10.2 per cent). Such educational differences between migrants in different streams and the residents of receiving communities aid materially in the development of significant differences in educational attainment between different types of communities, although they probably are not the major factor.

Occupation. The differences in educational attainment between migrants and residents, just noted, would also lead one to expect certain differences between migrants and residents in occupational status. In general migrants are most numerous relatively in the occupations which require the most training, *i.e.*, have higher proportions than the residents in such occupations. White-collar workers are much more mobile than hand workers, and the higher the social status of the white-collar workers the more mobile they are. This large relative migration of better-trained persons reflects not only their

Table 14-4. Percentage Distribution of the Migrant Population 25–34 Years of Age, by Years of School Completed and Migration Status, United States, 1940 [1]

Years of school completed	Migration status		
	Within a state	Between contiguous states	Between noncontiguous states
Total..........................	100.0	100.0	100.0
Grade school:			
Less than 5.................	6.1	5.3	3.1
5–6.........................	6.1	6.1	4.1
7–8.........................	22.2	21.7	18.8
High school:			
1–3.........................	20.6	19.6	19.0
4............................	24.1	24.7	26.3
College:			
1–3.........................	10.7	11.3	13.3
4 or more..................	10.2	11.4	15.5

[1] U.S. Bureau of the Census, *Population, Internal Migration 1935 to 1940, Social Characteristics of Migrants,* p. 13, G.P.O., Washington, D.C., 1946.

greater knowledge of opportunities elsewhere but also their financial ability and their readiness to take advantage of these opportunities. Migrants to rural-farm communities do not contain high proportions of well-trained persons.

Other Differences between Migrants. There are many other social and economic differences between migrants in different streams which cannot even be mentioned, but a few should be noted. (1) A smaller proportion of migrants to metropolitan areas had low wage and salary incomes (under $1,200) and a higher proportion had incomes over $2,000, than for those to nonmetropolitan areas. Migrants from central cities had the smallest proportion with low incomes and the highest proportion with incomes of over $2,000, while the reverse held for migrants from nonmetropolitan areas. (2) In general, in the population fourteen years of age and over, a larger proportion of migrants than of residents was employed (probably on account of the differences in age composition already noted above). (3) Central cities drew small proportions of married migrants as compared with their rings, especially their other urban and rural-nonfarm communities.

When the data on migration (1935 to 1940) both within states and into particular subregions from other states are analyzed in greater detail, we shall be able to tell much more about the size and the direction of the streams of migration, and we shall also know more about the characteristics of the migrants in the different streams. But until the 1949–1950 migration tabulations are completed we shall not know how far these data for 1935 to 1940 are to be regarded as showing "normal" migratory movements within the United States.

4. GROSS AND NET MIGRATION

It has long been known that the total number of migrants moving into and out of a given area within a country was, as a rule, vastly larger than the net gain or loss in that community from migration. It will be of interest, therefore, to note some of the findings of studies bearing on this point.

Sweden. Thomas [9] has shown that in Sweden net gain or loss through migration is only a small portion of the gross intake or outflow. This holds for all types of communities. Thus in the year 1895 the out-migration from agricultural communities amounted to 56.8 persons per 1,000 of their average population, but their net loss was only 10.3 per 1,000. In 1933 the net outflow (8.0 per 1,000) was a still smaller proportion of the total out-movement (63.7 per 1,000). In rural industrial communities which had a net inflow, an even smaller proportion of the total in-migrants remained—

[9] Dorothy Swaine Thomas, *Social and Economic Aspects of Swedish Population Movements, 1750–1933,* pp. 299–303, The Macmillan Company, New York, 1941.

in 1895 only 6.8 per 1,000 out of an in-migration of 62.4 per 1,000 and in 1933 only 1.1 per 1,000 out of 59.1 per 1,000. In large industrial towns, where there was always a net inflow, this was also a very small proportion of the total in-migration even in periods of rapid growth. Thus in 1895 the net inflow to these communities was 30.8 per 1,000 of their population while the gross inflow was 118.0 per 1,000. Only about one out of four was net gain. By 1933 this had fallen to 9.1 net out of 93.5 gross—one in ten.

Gross internal migration in Sweden is greatest in proportion to net effect on numbers in the smaller industrial or semi-industrial communities. Such places probably draw large numbers of people from surrounding agricultural areas for seasonal work, who return to their home communities when work slackens. In general one gets the impression that in- and out-migration is easier in the small communities than in the larger places. One can but wonder whether these smaller industrial communities are not increasingly becoming the areas where seasonal and unusual manufacturing demands are met simply because they are able to get extra workers quickly and for a short time from surrounding agricultural areas.

In Germany much the same general pattern as regards net migration was found by Dr. Heberle.[10] The net out-migrants from rural areas constituted only a small proportion of all out-migrants from these areas, and the net in-migrants were but a small proportion of all in-migrants in the urban areas gaining from internal migration. Furthermore, as in Sweden, it appears that the *net* out- or in-migration is becoming a smaller part of the *gross* out- and in-movements; in other words, the population appears to be getting more mobile. This would seem to be a natural consequence of the increasing ease of communication and transportation and of the increasing unevenness of industrial operation.

Moore [11] in her study of Swedish migration gives data showing differentials in the movement of people between different types of communities. Some of her findings may be summarized briefly: (1) a smaller proportion of rural-born than of town-born people find their way to Stockholm (4.37 and 5.90 per cent, respectively); (2) a slightly smaller proportion of rural-born people are found in towns (18.19 per cent) than of town-born in rural communities (19.82 per cent); (3) a smaller proportion of rural-born (49.75 per cent) than of town-born (61.5 per cent) are found in the community in which they were born; and hence (4) more rural-born (32.06 per cent) than town-born (18.93 per cent) move to similar types of communities. The two points of special interest are here (2) and (4)—that a

[10] Dorothy Swaine Thomas *et al.*, *Research Memorandum on Migration Differentials*, p. 289, Social Science Research Council, New York, 1938.

[11] Jane Moore, *Cityward Migration*, 140 pp., University of Chicago Press, Chicago, 1938.

larger proportion (not number) of town-born people were living in rural communities than of rural-born who were living in towns, and that a smaller proportion of town-born people moved to other towns than of rural-born people to other rural communities. The explanation of this second point is probably to be found in the fact that when industry and commerce are expanding people born in towns do not need to go elsewhere to find jobs, while when agriculture is expanding the new lands lie outside the existing agricultural communities and hence necessitate moving.

Moore's data also show that a larger proportion of town-born people than of rural-born people who move to Stockholm, 57.91 per cent and 21.84 per cent, respectively, move there directly from community of birth, while conversely a larger proportion of rural-born people than town-born people, 78.16 and 42.09 per cent, respectively, make intermediate moves between community of birth and Stockholm. People born in small industrial and mixed agricultural-industrial communities occupy an intermediate position in these respects.

United States. No exact comparisons on these points can be made between migrants in Sweden and the United States, but as was indicated above, there is some reason to think that rural people in the United States also reach the larger cities by stages rather than in a single move. As regards the small ratio of net migration to gross migration, there can be no doubt that the situation in the United States is much the same as that in Sweden and Germany, although the data are somewhat different in character. The 1935 to 1940 data show the number of migrants to and from each state. In general the gross movement is several times as large as the net gain or loss in numbers, but the ratios of net to gross vary greatly from state to state. Thus there were somewhat over 360,000 in-migrants into New York State and over 417,000 out-migrants to other states, leaving a net loss for the state of 57,000 or a net loss of one person for each 7.3 out-migrants. In Nebraska the loss was 1 to 1.5 out-migrants, while in California the net gain was 1 to 1.3 in-migrants.[12] The extent to which in-migration compensates for out-migration, or vice versa, depends upon the particular conditions prevailing in the area under consideration. But in any event the mere interchange of population is so great that the net change due to migration is rather small except in a few areas. In spite of this fact internal migration is generally, though not always, the chief agency through which the redistribution of population takes place. In a few areas differentials in natural increase may be more important than net migration in accounting for differentials in rate of growth and hence for changes in distribution, but in general migration is of greater importance.

[12] U.S. Bureau of the Census, *Population, Internal Migration 1935 to 1940, Color and Sex of Migrants*, p. 18.

5. FACTORS DETERMINING INTERNAL MIGRATION

If the volume of migration as well as its direction is determined primarily by the economic differences between communities, as has been contended here, and if in consequence people generally move from areas of low earning power to areas of higher earning power, it should be possible to predict with fair accuracy the general direction of net internal migration in the United States, or in any other country, for a few years in advance. This assumes, of course, that unusual conditions like those prevailing during war, or when defense production is urgent, do not dominate the migration picture. Areas of low earning power are such for three chief reasons: (1) they may have a low ratio of natural resources to the population depending on them for their livelihood—poor land, relatively small mineral deposits, an unfavorable climate, and so forth—or may be so isolated that transportation costs are high; (2) the community may lack the technical personnel, the organization, and the capital to make good use of its resources; (3) the changes in economic processes and the shifts in the location of industry may be so rapid that what was only an adequate population under former conditions has become an excessive population under the changed conditions or vice versa. For example, the very rapid mechanization of cotton farming in the Mississippi Delta and westward is having significant effects on the living of the agricultural population in all the cotton states. The Southeast, the old cotton area, has been most affected by these changes.

It should be observed that the conditions making for low earning power are seldom found singly. As a rule, most or all are found in the same locality—each, in fact, being causally related to all the others. When this is the case, such areas are almost certain to be areas of *net* out-migration.

Areas of Out-migration, United States. Bearing in mind the conditions favorable to out-migration, there is little difficulty in picking the chief areas from which a large part of our net out-migrants are likely to come: (1) the hilly and mountainous areas of the southern Appalachians, of central Kentucky and Tennessee, and of the Ozarks, where the birth rate is high, the land poor, and industrial development lacking; (2) the cutover areas of the northern Great Lakes and of the South, where formerly lumbering furnished a livelihood to a considerable population; (3) the cotton South, especially the Old South, which can no longer compete with the Delta and the new cotton country in Texas and California; (4) the western wheat lands (dust bowl), where drought and the mechanization of agriculture have already combined to oust a considerable number of farmers and where mechanization is not yet complete; (5) the corn belt, where mechanization is also proceeding at a rapid pace and seems likely to continue to do so for some time to come; and finally (6) those areas in which there is a more or less sudden change in industrial employment due to the exhaustion of natural resources (coal or copper mines, and so forth) or to the discovery of new resources elsewhere which are cheaper to exploit, or where temporary conditions have made it expedient to assemble a population which cannot be supported there under normal conditions, or where a long-time shift in industry is taking place, e.g., a shift in the textile industry from New England to the Southeast. The conditions likely to attract in-migrants are, of course, just the opposite of the above.

In the future, therefore, we may look for a considerable part of our net internal migration, the part which will exercise an effect on the distribution of population, to come from the areas just described and to go to areas where industrial development is proceeding at a rapid pace. But we should not overlook the fact that a large proportion of all internal migrants will continue to pass from city to city, from farm to farm, and from village to village and between different combinations of these areas. They will leave little net residue in most of them. The net movement out of or into any given area will depend upon the nature and strength of the expulsive and attractive forces prevailing at the time. Farmers left the "dust bowl" in great numbers for two or three years because drought drove them away, but the mechanization of wheat farming, a somewhat less spectacular factor, added its expulsive force to that of drought. The expellees went west partly, no doubt, because of our national tradition that opportunity lies to the west, but also because they were told that jobs could be found there or that farm land was still available in that region. This will account for the fact that in about two years and nine months over 250,000 people who were dependent upon their work for a living went into California by auto.[13]

But though the areas of greatest probable out-migration can be predicted in a general way, it is impossible to foretell the future contributions of a particular area, since this depends upon many factors which are quite beyond our power to foresee. Another drought in the dust bowl might drive out a high proportion of the farmers still living there; the rapid replacement of cotton by synthetic fibers might place special compulsion on the Negro population of the cotton belt; a few prosperous years in the corn belt might enable farmers to purchase even more efficient machinery and thus spare more young people to the city, while military demands for goods might aid in producing this effect. All such contingencies are possible, but who can say which is the most probable?

Areas of In-migration, United States. It is even more impossible to say where migrants are likely to go. Will new industries (for example, plastics) seek new locations? Will new pipe lines carry crude oil to be refined on the

[13] *Migrants: A National Problem—and Its Impact on California,* 51 pp., California State Chamber of Commerce, San Francisco, 1940.

eastern seaboard or gasoline which has been refined in the Southwest? Will the expansion of existing industries take place at present locations or in new locations? Will the increasing use of electric power tend to break large manufacturing plants into smaller units scattered more widely in smaller communities? Will the automobile affect the distribution of industry and commerce in different ways in different parts of the country, *e.g.*, in the South and in the North? Will cheaper and more satisfactory telephonic communication decentralize the great business offices of the Northeast? There is no answer to these and a hundred other questions which should be answered if we are to predict the amount and the destination of migration with even a moderate degree of accuracy. The most probable guess would be that past trends will continue and that any significant variation from the present pattern will proceed slowly. But for any given locality even this is a most hazardous guess. Only national planning on a large scale would supply the answer to where our migrants are likely to go.

6. PROBLEMS OF PERSONAL ADJUSTMENT

The problems of personal adjustment and integration with the life of the community confronting internal migrants are different from those confronting foreign-born immigrants only in degree. They consist essentially in the adjustment of the mental attitudes and habits of living of the migrants to those in the new community to such an extent that the migrants are accepted as members of their community and are allowed to participate fully in community activities. There are, of course, many degrees of difficulty in making these adjustments in a new community. They range all the way from practical negligibility to very basic changes in social attitudes and ways of living. Thus one can be reasonably certain that the open-country youth who stays in the open country, in the same county or one nearby, does not encounter any very difficult problem of adjustment unless his social status (renter, or hired hand, or owner) also changes. If he happens to move into a community where most of the families are related to one another and rather resent outsiders, his problems of adjustment may be more difficult.

On the other hand, a brief statement of some of the new conditions confronting young people from the Kentucky hills when they move to an industrial community in the North may help to show some of the more difficult problems of adjustment encountered by internal migrants. In general, a boy from the Kentucky hills has made his living by a desultory sort of mountain agriculture, supplemented by a certain amount of lumbering, hunting, and fishing. He has always lived at some distance from his neighbors, so that his sanitary habits made little difference to anyone but himself. He will find it difficult to understand the sanitary regulations of the city, and he may make the enforcement of its sanitary code almost impossible, at least in certain parts of the city. Regular hours of work, observance of safety regulations, and the strict discipline essential to working in crews on a common task, all demand the formation of new habits in connection with earning a living. At the same time, living in a relatively densely settled community demands a different conception of personal obligations to neighbors and family. Moreover, a more cooperative attitude toward established authority and also toward employer and fellow workers has to be developed. It is little wonder that such migrants often fail to make quick and satisfactory adjustments to these new conditions. It is almost inevitable that there should be much demoralization among them and that they should present many serious problems to the local authorities in the city, to their bosses in the factories, and to the labor organizations in the industry. The family often fails to exert its customary control over the conduct of husband and wife and of children. Indeed in this case the problems of adjustment are probably almost as perplexing as those of the European peasant moving to an American city. The Kentucky migrant has the advantage of the peasant in speaking English, but he has the disadvantage of less group discipline and of a deep-seated individualistic outlook on life which makes it very hard for him to fit into the highly organized life of the modern urban community.

As I see it, the problems of personal adjustment of the internal migrant to his new home lie all the way between the extremes I have tried to picture —between the problems of the farm boy moving to a farm not far from home, and those of the Kentucky boy leaving the hills to become an industrial laborer. The difficulties of adjustment are to be measured largely by the cultural differences between the migrant and the dominant group into which he moves. On the average these differences are probably substantially less in the case of internal migrants than in the case of foreign-born migrants, but certainly this is not always the case.

I would not maintain, however, that cultural differences are the only factor in the personal adjustments of internal migrants to their new homes. There can be no reasonable doubt that at times these problems of personal adjustment are so intimately bound up with the volume of migration and the economic conditions prevailing that it is impossible to tell which is the more significant. The very rapid building up of some of our defense industries provides striking examples of the effects of a great influx of migrants into a community not equipped to provide for their physical needs and not organized to absorb them into its daily life. But even so, the problems arising from too great a volume of migration are largely problems arising from the clash of cultures in the broader sense. Where migrants fit into the pattern of life of the natives and where they supply services needed and wanted by the community, they are seldom considered outsiders for any great length of time, nor do they long remain hostile to the customary community controls in their new homes.

If the problems of personal adjustment arise primarily from cultural differences, then a considerable proportion of all internal migration can be said to involve so little adjustment that it loses interest except as a matter of increase in numbers and as a change in the composition of the population. The farmer moving from farm to farm within the community or to a nearby community; the family moving from one part of the city to another, or even from city to city, with no appreciable change in economic status; the movement of professional men and executives from place to place commonly associated with advancement in their work—these and many other types of movement involve comparatively easy adjustments for all members of the family. On the part of the migrant there is no violent uprooting of old habits, no period of personal disorganization while groping for new connections in the community; and on the part of the community there is no holding at arm's length of the newcomer, no assumption that the community must use force to impose minimum standards of decency. Such migration, while large in volume, does not require much attention from the community because the migrant is able, without outside aid, to make the few and relatively small adjustments needed, and unless the economic situation should be such as to make all outsiders suspect, his presence will scarcely be noticed. On the other hand, considerable differences in general manner of life will create cleavages between the migrant and the native, between the migrant and the community, which are very difficult to close; and if there is also competition for jobs, with the migrant accepting lower wages, the difficulties are much intensified.

There are many other aspects of internal migration, for example, Negro migration,[14] the Okies, the hobo, and so forth, which cannot be discussed here. These are all of interest, but I believe that they do not present essentially different problems from those outlined above. Since I believe, however, that internal migration, almost to the exclusion of foreign immigration, is going to be the means by which we will effect a redistribution of our population in the future, I think that it will behoove us to direct much more attention to this movement of population within the country than we have in the past.

Suggestions for Supplementary Reading

ANDERSON, NELS: *Men on the Move*, 357 pp., University of Chicago Press, Chicago, 1940.
GALPIN, C. J., and T. B. MANNY: *Interstate Migrations among the Native White as Indicated by Differences between State of Birth and State of Residence*, 105 pp., U.S. Department of Agriculture, Bureau of Agricultural Economics, Washington, D.C., 1934.

[14] Henderson H. Donald, *The Negro Migration of 1916–1918*, 116 pp., Association for the Study of Negro Life and History, Washington, D.C., 1921.

GEE, WILSON, and J. J. CORSON, 3d: *Rural Depopulation in Certain Tidewater and Piedmont Areas of Virginia*, 104 pp., Institute for Research in Social Sciences, *Mon*. 3, University of Virginia, Charlottesville, Va., 1929.

GIST, NOEL P., *et al.:* "Selective Aspects of Rural Migrations," *Rural Soc.*, Vol. 6, pp. 3–15, 1941.

JEROME, HARRY: *Migration and Business Cycles*, 256 pp., National Bureau of Economic Research, New York, 1926.

LORIMER, FRANK, *et al.: Foundations of American Population Policy*, 178 pp., Harper & Brothers, New York, 1940.

MOORE, JANE: *Cityward Migration*, 140 pp., University of Chicago Press, Chicago, 1938.

NELSON, LOWRY: *Rural Sociology*, 567 pp., American Book Company, New York, 1952.

QUINN, JAMES A.: *Human Ecology*, 561 pp., Prentice-Hall, Inc., New York, 1950.

THOMAS, DOROTHY SWAINE: *Research Memorandum on Migration Differentials*, 423 pp., Social Science Research Council, New York, 1938.

VREELAND, FRANCIS M., and EDWARD J. FITZGERALD: *Farm-City Migration and Industry's Labor Reserve*, 67 pp., National Research Project, Work Projects Administration, 1939.

ZIMMERMAN, C. C., and J. J. CORSON, 3d: "The Migrations to Towns and Cities. Number 6," *Soc. Forces*, Vol. 8, pp. 402–408, 1930.

CHAPTER XV

POPULATION GROWTH AND AGRICULTURE

In spite of the fact that man can now make many products essential to the maintenance of a moderately comfortable existence out of products which he has not grown, agricultural production remains the basic source of most of those goods which are essential to life. If other products which grow, namely, those of the forests and in the waters on the earth, are included with agricultural products, it can be said that the limit of population in the world is the limit of man's ability to grow those products essential to his life.

1. SYNTHETIC PRODUCTION OF FOOD AND FIBERS

Some thirty-odd years ago there was considerable optimism over the possibility that the chemist assisted by the engineer would soon be able to produce by synthesis much of the food and fiber essential to human life. If this were done, the relative importance of agriculture would diminish and the limits which agriculture placed upon population growth would be lifted. The tide of thinking along this line was running so strongly in this direction that Alsberg, a leading chemist of that day, considered it desirable to discuss the relation of chemistry and population theory.[1] The following quotation shows how he looked upon the possibility of synthetic food production at that time:

If it is true that agriculture utilizes the solar radiation so inefficiently and that labor in agriculture is so little productive, why has not the synthesis of food elements been attempted? To the physiologist and the chemist the reasons are obvious. How completely the simple food elements that the chemist already knows how to produce can be substituted for natural foods has not yet been determined adequately. It is only a few years since it has been known that amino acids may be substituted at least in great part for proteins. Not all the amino acids have as yet been synthesized. Methods for obtaining large quantities of carbonic acid must be devised. The methods of producing simple sugars and fatty acids are laboratory procedures involving many steps and many difficult operations. Probably

[1] Carl L. Alsberg, "Progress in Chemistry and the Theory of Population," *Ind. Eng. Chem.*, Vol. 16, p. 524, 1924.

few of the methods now in use are suitable for large-scale operations. Even if adequate quantities of cheap power were available, it would still be the work of years to translate laboratory practice into large-scale production. It is, however, very doubtful that energy from our common sources of power—coal, oil, water—is at present cheap enough to permit food synthesis to compete with agriculture. Whether the values of agricultural products and of energy from our present sources of power will ever bear such a ratio to one another as to make competition between agriculture and chemical industry feasible, it is, of course, impossible to say. It is more than probable that such competition will not be possible before the advent of some nonbiological method for the utilization of the solar radiation.

In view of the great progress in photochemical theory in the last decade, the problem is far from hopeless. No one could venture to predict when the theoretical and experimental problems will be solved. The solutions may be nearer than most men think. What is most probable is that the practical application will wait on economic necessity. The work in pure science is likely to be completed before this necessity arises. The chemist's task may be done before the engineer is set to work. If the problem is not solved earlier, it will boldly confront us with the exhaustion of the world's coal and oil reserves. The solution of the world's food and fuel problem will be the same. When it is achieved, a more profound social revolution must follow than followed the invention of the steam engine, for the importance of land and agriculture will diminish; and it will remove to a far more distant horizon the bounds that now tend to limit the growth of population.

Since the above was written much has happened. Synthetic fibers utilizing timber and coal as raw materials have increasingly displaced annual fiber crops for clothing and are steadily finding new industrial uses. In so far as timber is being used in the place of annual crops of fiber plants, it simply means that for a time we can draw on the capital already accumulated on the surface of the earth instead of being dependent on what we produce currently. The same is true of the use of coal and oil and other mineral products as the raw material for fiber, plastics, rubber, and so forth, which may take the place of annual crops. In so far as the capital of the earth, its stored resources, can be used in the place of its annual product, the land no longer needed for these products can be used for food and the size of the population that can be supported at any given level of living can be increased.

Some other ways in which the synthesizing of various products may affect the demand for natural agricultural products may also be noted. Research in vitamins and amino acids has made it possible to synthesize many of them more cheaply and thus put them into manufactured products, so that a complete diet from the standpoint of nutrition can be obtained while the bulk of the energy-producing food comes from products which may be lacking in these vital elements. As yet this increasing knowledge of nutrition has been used largely to supply the deficiencies of a diet from which vitamins have been removed or destroyed by the processes of manufacture and distribution that have come into use in supplying food to vast city populations. This does not mean, of course, that our newer knowledge of nutrition is limited to such uses. It is quite possible that crops like corn and soybeans, which are now used largely for livestock feed and industrial purposes, can be made into palatable and dietetically satisfactory foods at only a fraction of the cost of converting them into food by way of feeding them to cattle and hogs and then eating meat, milk, butter, and cheese.[2] A large part of the earth's population actually consumes directly the crops grown, and it is only because they do so that countries like China, India, Japan, Java, and a number of the other poorer countries of the world are able to support their present populations.

Thus, while it would be folly to assert that the existing agricultural limits to population growth are permanent, it would be equally foolish to assume that they have been abolished or are likely to be abolished in the near future. As yet no progress has been made in converting minerals into organic compounds which can be used for food. One cannot say that this will never be done, but as a practical consideration in trying to assess the limits which agriculture places to population growth in the foreseeable future we must assume that practically all our food will continue to come from current agricultural production. The limits agricultural production places on population are, however, being relaxed in two ways. One of these has already been mentioned, namely, the more direct and efficient use of agricultural products such as the direct consumption of grain, the supplying of the nutritional elements lacking in cheap foods, and possibly the conversion of the indigestible parts of such a crop as soybeans into digestible products. The calories in our corn crop alone are more than sufficient to meet the needs of a population three times as large as we now have.

The second way to push back the limits on population growth imposed by agriculture today is to produce more efficiently. Agricultural advance has been so rapid in recent years that we seem to be entering an era in which the optimistic predictions of increase in agricultural yields remind one of similar predictions regarding the likelihood of the production of synthetic foods 30 years ago. The author would not for a moment underrate the possibilities of securing larger yields of most of our staple crops. Indeed, he believes that because of his long-continued interest in such matters and because his personal hobby is farming he is more fully aware of the possibilities of increased crop and livestock yields than most amateurs. But he

[2] O. E. Baker, "The Population Prospect in Relation to World's Agricultural Resources," *J. Geog.*, Vol. 46, No. 6, p. 213, 1947.

is also more aware of many of the practical difficulties that stand in the way of securing these yields than many persons who have not had the personal opportunity to observe closely the practical application of science to farming, or the opportunity to observe, from a background of interest and experience, agriculture as it is practiced in many of the more backward areas of the earth. It will therefore be worth while to explore these agricultural limits a little, although too briefly.

2. AGRICULTURAL POSSIBILITIES OF THE EARTH

There is little point in trying to calculate the capacity of the earth to yield agricultural products, but it will be worth while to point out that it is not as simple a matter to calculate how many people can be provided with a sufficiency of agricultural products, as many persons seem to think. To point out some of the difficulties involved in expanding agricultural production seems to the author especially needed at this time because there seems to be an upsurge of optimism regarding agricultural possibilities, encouraged chiefly by men who are considered experts. This is not the easy optimism of the people of 30 years ago who thought that because Texas was about as large as France or Germany it could support as many people on its agricultural products. There is today a much wider realization that there are great areas of the earth's surface that are practically useless agriculturally and perhaps still larger areas which will yield but meager returns because of lack of rainfall, or shortness of the growing season, or poor soils, or rough and mountainous terrain—conditions which are modifiable by man to a limited extent only. Practically one-fourth of the earth's surface is desert or semidesert, having a rainfall of less than 10 inches annually, and only a very small fraction of this area can be irrigated. Almost one-third more has a rainfall of 10 to 20 inches. The part of this which has less than 15 inches can only be classed as poor grazing land except in those temperate regions where the rainfall is rather heavily concentrated in the spring and early summer months or where irrigation is possible. In the whole area where the rainfall is 10 to 20 inches the likelihood of crop failures is great because the annual average is made up of years in which the rainfall is too scanty to produce even a moderate yield of grass as well as of years in which it is adequate to produce fairly good yields of grain.

On those areas receiving 20 to 40 inches of rain annually (about one-fifth of the earth's surface) crops are more certain, yields are much higher, and the variety of crops grown is much greater than in the lower rainfall areas, always excepting irrigated areas. But it must not be forgotten that much of this area with more adequate rainfall is rough, mountainous, and unsuited to tillage and yields but scanty returns at best, as in our own Appalachian highlands (150,000 to 200,000 square miles) or in our

Cumberland, Ozark, and western mountain areas. Moreover, in the large portion of this 20- to 40-inch-rainfall area, the part of it having 20 to 25 inches is rather frequently subject to drought or semidrought, as we well know in the United States from our experience in the 1930's.

Much of the tropical land of the earth suffers from too much rain, so that the soil is badly leached of plant food and subject to serious erosion. Clearly it makes little sense to talk of the tremendous productivity of the tropics or even of a particular nation in the tropics unless we specify more definitely just what areas we are talking about. Practically all land in the tropics as elsewhere is a definite type of land, and its productivity is determined to a considerable extent by the quality of the soil. Again the tundras of Asia, North America, and Europe are of very limited value as regards the agricultural products they can furnish man. Land must be classified as to fertility, rainfall, length of growing season, and many other criteria which enter into crop production before we can have any clear picture of the agricultural potentialities of the earth. But even if we could place all the land area of the earth into definite categories on the basis of its potential production we could still tell little about how likely the land in any fairly large area was to yield crops of a given size. We should need to know the agricultural practices of the people using this land, and if, as is generally the case, it is not being used efficiently we should need to know the economic and cultural obstacles to improvement before we could form a reasonable guess as to the length of time that must elapse before agricultural practice could be so improved that actual yields would approximate potential yields under favorable conditions.

But if there is little profit to be gained by talking about the agricultural potentialities of the world, this is not the case to the same extent if we will ask whether a given area or country can support a larger population at the same level of living or the same size of population at a better level of living.

The new wave of optimism regarding agricultural production which was referred to above is largely based on actual achievements in production already made in certain lands or areas. The assumption is then made that similar yields can be obtained from similar lands elsewhere under similar climatic conditions where cultural conditions are also much the same. To illustrate, rice culture in China is quite similar to rice culture in Japan, and climatic conditions and rainfall in Japan are also quite similar to those in some of the best rice areas of China; yet there is no doubt whatever that in Japan the yields of rice per acre are much larger, probably from 50 to 100 per cent larger than in the good areas of China. Obviously, in the light of these facts it would seem reasonable to maintain that China can raise yields to equal those of Japan and hence that she can support from 50 to 100 per cent more people than she now does in these rice areas, as far as food is concerned—assuming, of course, no substantial change in food requirements. The author himself has little doubt that food production can be doubled on a significant proportion of China's tilled land. But assuming this is correct he hastens to add that this does not prove that there is no shortage of food in China or that there is no need to give serious consideration to the pressure of population on food supply until China's population is increased by one-half, or is perhaps doubled, by which time agriculture will again have improved so that another large increase in the food supply will be possible.

The real crux of the problem of population and food supply is not whether China or any other country can support as many people per square mile of tillable land as Japan or Java or some other densely settled area having somewhat similar conditions determining production, but whether there is likely to be much improvement in the manner of life in China even if there is a large increase in agricultural production. Of what advantage is it to China and the Chinese to have twice as many people as now if they live with about the same degree of hardship as at present? What China and all other such countries need is not merely an increase in total production but an increase in per capita production. The real problem is to secure this increase in per capita production as long as the birth rate remains high and the death rate is reduced year by year in almost the same degree that total agricultural production increases. Under these conditions an increase in per capita consumption is very difficult to achieve.

Furthermore, we should be very careful to recognize that the possibility of doubling China's agricultural production is one thing and that the actual attainment of this doubled production is quite another. It is one thing to be *able* to make two blades of grass grow where one grew before and quite another to grow those two blades so quickly that a larger per capita income becomes available to the mass of the people.

The author wants to make it clear, however, that he is personally convinced that the total agricultural product of Chinese agriculture can be increased in a number of ways. In the first place, he is convinced from personal observation as well as study that the tilled area in China can be considerably enlarged. But this enlargement must come chiefly in regions where rainfall is relatively low and where *extensive* agriculture is practical. Such areas are now largely untilled because the primitive methods of cultivation in use do not ensure the tiller a living. But areas which, because of light rainfall, will not yield a living to the farmer, with primitive methods of tillage may do so if farmed on a larger scale with the use of modern machinery as in our own western winter-wheat belt. Such farming, however, requires relatively large farms and the most up-to-date machinery as well as a complete change of attitudes toward farming on the part of the Chinese farmers. I see no reason why the Chinese farmer in northern China should not, in the course of time, use this land. On the other hand, I see many reasons to believe that the development of these areas will be slow, that it will take several decades, and since time is crucial the question again becomes not whether this land of low productivity can be tilled but how long it will take to bring it into use. The reason for this emphasis on the time element will be made clear shortly.

In the second place, in the author's opinion, the plant breeders and the agronomists who maintain that the development of better varieties of the staple Chinese crops and better practices in the care of these crops would yield larger returns per acre are undoubtedly right. The Japanese have greatly increased the yields of rice and wheat and barley as well as those of many other crops in this way. No one who knows even a little about agriculture should hesitate to accept the view of these experts on this matter. But I should like to see a timetable for the accomplishment of these improvements which is based on a thorough knowledge of the mind of the peasant and a full realization of the economic and social problems involved as well as on a knowledge of agricultural possibilities. I believe in the possibility of great improvements, but I do not believe in the *probability* of attaining them in time to ensure much per capita increase in consumption as long as the birth rate remains at its present level.

I have talked in the field with Chinese agricultural workers who might be compared to our own county agricultural agents, and the stories of their difficulties in attempting to spread the knowledge and practice of a better agriculture were heartbreaking. It is not a question of the ability of the Chinese to do what the Japanese have done in the improvement of their crop yields, but it is a question of how long it will take to break through the extremely thick and tough "cake of custom" and secure the adoption of more efficient varieties of crops and methods of tillage. If crop yields can be increased by 2 per cent a year and population grows by 2 per cent, where is the gain to the individual Chinese?

In the third place, the extension of irrigation even in areas of seemingly abundant rainfall to control the use of water when most needed could add considerably to the agricultural production of China, but this generally costs large amounts of money and involves the cooperation of people over large areas, which simply does not exist. How long will it take to develop the essential types of cooperation for the building and maintenance of large public works? I certainly do not know. A government devoted to the public interest might force the pace considerably, but I cannot see a rapid extension of irrigation in China. I believe we must think in terms of decades rather than of years.

In the fourth place, the use of the gentler slopes of hills and mountains for tree crops and for crops not requiring standing water while growing could undoubtedly become the means of adding largely to the variety as well as the bulk of the diet of the people. At present the hills of China—and China is a land of hills and mountains, with relatively small valleys and plains as compared with many parts of the Americas and Central and Eastern Europe—are almost bare of trees. The weeds, shrubs, and grass they produce annually are gathered to provide the pitifully small fuel supply essential to the cooking of the cereals and vegetables which constitute almost the entire diet of the mass of the people. How can these hillsides be put to more profitable use as long as the people are in such urgent need of the scanty fuel they produce? In addition, erosion is rampant in the hills and mountains where they are stripped of their forest and shrub coverage. Hence, not only are the hillsides becoming more sterile but the stones, sand, and clay from them are being washed into the small valleys, where they destroy land already being intensively tilled. Such conditions cannot be changed by fiat. They grow out of the necessity to use today what is now available without regard to greater future advantage. This necessity always arises when there is dire poverty, and it results in practices which are inimical to the improvement of living conditions in the future, even in the future only a year or two away. I very much doubt that these destructive practices in the use of hill lands can be changed in a few years. As in the adoption of the other practices which would really add substantially to the agricultural produce of the country, it is more likely to take several decades than several years to put them into effect.

Let us return now to the basic reason for trying to get a realistic evaluation of the time it will take to secure the larger agricultural product which the author, at least, believes can be secured in China and in other lands where agriculture is much the same as in China. (I use China here merely as illustrative and not because the situation there is fundamentally different from that in most of southern and eastern Asia and in the neighboring islands and in most of the Near East.)

The birth rate in China is not known, but what little is known justifies the guess that it is 40 per 1,000 per year or above. Likewise the death rate is unknown, but all will agree that it is very high. The author, unlike a good many Westerners and Chinese, is very skeptical of any increase in population in China since the beginning of the Taiping Rebellion over a century ago. He is disposed to believe that over this century the death rate has equaled the birth rate, except in Manchuria and parts of the northwest, and that there has been little or no increase in population. During this period and throughout most of man's history the factors determining population growth are what Malthus called the *positive* checks—war, hunger, and disease. When the death rate was high, population did not grow or even declined; when these positive checks were relatively mild, population grew because the death rate fell. What determined the severity or mildness of the positive checks has always been, first and foremost, the agricultural production.

Now to come to the nub of the matter. Suppose that China or any other country similarly situated undertakes the improvement of her agriculture; what will be the probable course of this improvement and what effect will it have on population growth? We must talk in terms of what is reasonable to expect in the light of such knowledge and experience as we possess. I have given my reasons above for believing that agricultural improvement will, at best, be slow. In my judgment, it is much more likely that the increase in total production will be less than 2 per cent per year than it will be above that rate. As far as we can tell from what has happened in the past, the first demographic effect of such an increase will be to reduce the death rate by raising the level of living a little. It will have little or no effect on the birth rate for some time, perhaps for several decades, unless there is a deliberate and successful effort to encourage family limitation. At present this appears highly unlikely for some time. Even a widespread effort to encourage family limitation could not be effective for some years. As long as the death rate only is reduced while the birth rate remains relatively stable, the population will grow about as fast as total agricultural production increases. We are thinking here of those peoples who have high birth rates. Since among the Western peoples today a death rate of 15 to 20 is considered high and since such death rates can be attained although great poverty and hardship are only mildly alleviated, it is clear that a natural increase (birth rate minus death rate) of 15 to 20 per 1,000 can be attained without much difficulty once the level of living begins to rise slowly. India and the Philippines have at times had such rates in the recent past and our own rate has been higher at times (25 to 30). Our own high rates occurred long before modern sanitation and medicine really became effective in reducing the death rate.

The point to be remembered is that unless the rate of increase of agricultural production is higher than the rate of population growth there is no increase in per capita product. Malthus was essentially correct in his belief that the rate of increase in population in his day was determined by the rate of increase of *subsistence* and that the lack of *subsistence* resulted in the operation of the *positive* checks—those conditions which raised the death rate. Hence he was also correct in saying that the only way to mitigate the hardships which resulted in a high death rate was to bring into play the *preventive* checks which would reduce the birth rate. Where he was in error was in his belief that the delay of marriage to a later age was the only feasible method of reducing the birth rate.

It will no doubt be argued that the author's position regarding the effect of an improvement of agriculture on population growth, which is essentially that of Malthus as regards those unindustrialized countries which are very largely dependent on agricultural production for *subsistence*, is unjustified— that they will not in fact increase in numbers nearly as fast as their agricultural production increases. The crucial questions are (1) how fast can agricultural production be increased? and (2) will the growth of population follow closely the growth in agricultural production? I have argued above that agricultural production in the backward areas of the world must necessarily increase slowly. I believe this to be the most reasonable view because of the great practical difficulties which stand in the way of a rapid increase, and I believe that the actual experience in countries like Japan, Java, India, and the Philippines supports the essential soundness of this view.[3] That under the most favorable conditions imaginable agricultural production in the Philippines, for example, could be increased as rapidly as population could possibly grow for a few years I would not deny, but I would hold that the most favorable conditions for agricultural development are so unlikely to be attained in any of the larger backward areas that it is unrealistic to talk of their expansion of agricultural production in terms of the technical possibilities of increase while ignoring the social and economic obstacles which must be overcome to make the technical improvements possible.

It took Japan 50 to 60 years to double, or a little more, her agricultural production and push up her per-acre yields of rice and other staple grains well above those of other peoples living in South and East Asia, and when she had succeeded in doing so she found that she also had about twice as many people. Furthermore, Japan in the meantime had become to a high degree the "workshop" of Asia much as Great Britain had become the "workshop" of the world a century earlier. (The place of industry and commerce in the support of population will be discussed in the following chapter.) Japan had also acquired a colonial empire from which she, like the European colonial powers, could draw food for her people and raw materials for her industry at a relatively low cost in terms of the labor required to produce the goods exchanged for them. (The price was low only directly to the users both of food and industrial raw materials. The indirect or hidden costs of empire made such goods fairly expensive to the nation as a whole, although the possession of empire did assure the possessor, to a certain extent, against an arbitrary control of its markets and sources of supply by other nations through tariffs, trade quotas, etc.)

The fact we are interested in here is that Japan's population did grow almost as fast as her supply of food increased—almost, but not quite; hence, there was a small margin for improvement in the level of living. Moreover, the government-backed industry and commerce grew rapidly as a result of relatively favorable trade conditions, and by 1920 the practice of contraception began to acquire importance in the cities. Since that time and to an increasing degree this *preventive* check has operated to keep Japan's population growth at a more moderate level than would have been the case otherwise and has thus been a factor of importance in raising the per capita con-

[3] Howard R. Tolley, "Farmers in a Hungry World," *Proc. Am. Philosophical Soc.,* Vol. 95, No. 1, pp. 54–61, 1951.

sumption of the country. But, be it noted, the further fall of the death rate as the level of living rose and as public sanitation improved kept the rate of increase from falling faster than the birth rate until Japan became heavily involved in war.

It is the author's belief that the conditions which made it possible for Japan to expand her agricultural production very rapidly and to employ a rapidly increasing proportion of her population in industry and commerce are highly unlikely to be duplicated in most of the countries which already have large and dense populations almost wholly dependent on agriculture. In addition, attention should also be called to the fact that some of the practices which led to the reduction of Japan's rate of population growth in the past among which abortion and infanticide played an important role, probably continued to operate to a certain extent after modern industrial development began and were of some importance in keeping her birth rate below that of most other Asiatic peoples. In modern times it is probable that Japan's birth rate has never been above 35.

The chief reasons the author believes that the conditions which favored a rapid improvement in Japanese agriculture are not likely to be duplicated in most of these other regions can only be mentioned here. They are as follows: (1) Japan had a strong central government at the time her passage from feudalism to a modern economy began and has had such a government ever since; hence, the people were accustomed to much direction from above. (2) This central government saw the need of increased agricultural production, supported a great deal of research, and saw to it that the results of this research were made known to the farmers. (3) The fact that there were a large number of big landlords who had the capital to improve their lands and to undertake the new and more efficient practices undoubtedly made their adoption quicker and easier. (4) The rapid industrialization of the country, in which the government played a large part, resulted in an expansion of the market for agricultural products and prevented the piling up of population on smaller and smaller farms to the degree that would otherwise have happened. (5) The government also assisted in the development of irrigation and flood control and thus made possible better crops on much land. (6) Finally the unity of Japan in culture, in language, in religion, and in many other ways gave her a great advantage in the development of a modern economy, both agricultural and industrial, over large countries like China and India which possess highly diverse populations requiring quite different handling in building a new economic structure. The problems of developing a unity of national action to improve agriculture and industry are far greater in these countries with vast populations unaccustomed to a central authority. I am not saying that it is impossible to unify such countries or that they will not come to act as political units in the development of a more efficient economy, but I do maintain that the difficulties of doing this are far greater than they were in Japan and that in consequence progress in this direction will be slower. I further believe it is only reasonable to hold that, if economic progress is slower, population will continue to press about as heavily as in the past on the subsistence it can produce, so that the mass of the people will only slowly develop the new modes of living which have hitherto been associated with the adoption of contraceptive practices leading to lower birth rates.

It may be thought that the possibility of increasing agricultural production through the development of Point 4 programs in these backward areas has been overlooked. This is not the case. It is rather that I do not believe substantially increased agricultural production can be obtained in a few years in these backward areas under Point 4 programs. Agriculture is a way of life as well as one of the processes of production in an economic system. Improvement in agriculture is dependent not only on providing the proof that it is possible and may be profitable but also in convincing the agriculturist that it is consistent with the manner of life to which he is accustomed and which he wishes to continue. Agricultural improvement cannot be obtained with the sureness and speed of industrial improvement even where there is clear proof that it is possible. Even in our own country, where farmers have become accustomed to taking part in a more or less continuous agricultural revolution, much of our farming remains relatively inefficient. The practical difficulties are not only economic but cultural, and in these backward lands they are very great. It is the firm conviction of the author that they will prevent any agricultural revolution rapid enough to keep production increasing over a period of years at a rate much, if any, above that of the increase of population as long as the birth rate remains at about its present level. I do believe that there will be some improvement in the level of living as time goes on, but it will be slow and it will never be sufficient in any large area to keep the death rate at what we now consider a reasonable level as long as the birth rates of these countries remain high.

One other point regarding the development of agriculture in relation to population growth needs to be made clear. It has become the fashion to speak of a world food problem almost as though world agricultural production and world consumption or need could be balanced against one another. Under this assumption one can argue quite plausibly that the world production of agricultural commodities can be increased by 1 per cent per year, about equal to the present rate of population growth, and hence that there is no need to worry about the world's food problem. It may be true that the world's food supply can be increased as fast as world population is now growing or even a little faster, but this is not the crucial point in trying to assess the probability of agricultural production keeping up with or ahead of population increase. In some countries there is little doubt that if the prices of agricultural products are good their production can be increased by 2 or 3 per cent per year, or even more, for some time to come. But the fact is that the surplus agricultural product of the United States, or Argentina, or Australia, is available to the people of China or Japan or India only if they have something which we want equivalent in value to trade for it. To ignore this simple fact and to speak as though any increase in agricultural production in the United States (or any other country) were available to feed the increase of population in India or some other needy area is wholly unrealistic in the world in which we live. This fact seems so obvious that it should not need mention. But because of it, the only really sensible questions regarding the relation of population increase and increase in subsistence must relate to national or, perhaps, regional entities. The conditions that actually prevail or those which can reasonably be expected to prevail in the near future make this necessary.

It is not, then, a question of whether the world can produce food sufficient to care for an additional 10 million or 20 million each year, but whether India can produce enough food, or can trade for enough, to provide for the 5 million or more persons she is likely to have each year, if subsistence is available, until such time as her birth rate is reduced faster than her death rate.[4]

On this matter I must confess to a considerable degree of pessimism.

Suggestions for Supplementary Reading

ALSBERG, CARL L.: "Progress in Chemistry and the Theory of Population," *Ind. Eng. Chem.*, Vol. 16, pp. 524–531, 1924.

BAKER, O. E.: "The Population Prospect in Relation to World's Agricultural Resources," *J. Geog.*, Vol. 46, No. 6, pp. 203–220, 1947.

BENNETT, MERRILL K.: "Population, Food, and Economic Progress," *Rice Institute Pamphlet*, Vol. 39, No. 2, pp. 1–68, 1952.

BRODY, SAMUEL: "Facts, Fables, and Fallacies on Feeding the World Population," *Federation Proc.*, Vol. 11, No. 3, pp. 681–693, 1952.

FORSYTH, W. D.: *The Myth of Open Spaces: Australian, British and World Trends of Population and Migration*, 226 pp., Melbourne University Press, Melbourne, 1942.

JONES, WELLINGTON D., and DERWENT S. WHITTLESEY: *An Introduction to Economic Geography*, 603 pp., Vol. 1, *Natural Environment as Related to Economic Life*, University of Chicago Press, Chicago, 1925.

KING, F. H.: *Farmers for Forty Centuries*, 379 pp., Jonathan Cape, London, 1927.

SMITH, J. RUSSELL: *The World's Food Resources*, 634 pp., Henry Holt and Company, Inc., New York, 1919.

STAMP, L. DUDLEY: *Land for Tomorrow: The Underdeveloped World*, 230 pp., In-

---

[4] Warren S. Thompson, "Some Reflections on World Population and Food Supply during the Next Few Decades," p. 85, in *Studies in Population* (proceedings of the annual meeting of the Population Association of America), ed. by George F. Mair, Princeton University Press, Princeton, N.J., 1949.

diana University Press, Bloomington, Ind.; American Geographical Society, New York, 1952.

STEFANSSON, VILJALMUR: *The Friendly Arctic*, 812 pp., The Macmillan Company, New York, 1943.

TAWNEY, R. H.: *Land and Labour in China*, 270 pp., Harcourt, Brace and Company, Inc., New York, 1932.

THOMPSON, WARREN S.: "Some Reflections on World Population and Food Supply during the Next Few Decades," in *Studies in Population* (proceedings of the annual meeting of the Population Association of America), ed. by George F. Mair, pp. 80–92, Princeton University Press, Princeton, N.J., 1949.

Chapter XVI

INDUSTRY AND COMMERCE AS BASES FOR THE SUPPORT OF POPULATION

In contrast with agriculture, industry and commerce appear to have been less dependable in their support of population over rather long periods of time. They have occasionally drawn together relatively large populations, but not infrequently they have been unable to maintain these populations for any length of time, and many centers of commerce and industry have disappeared altogether.

1. RISE AND FALL OF TRADE CENTERS

It is a well-known fact that, in general, centers of commerce and industry rise through some definite advantage which stimulates their growth, that they flourish for a time and then decline in power, absolutely and/or relatively. Sometimes they disappear altogether as did Troy, Mycenae, Carthage, and numerous others. Sometimes they become second-rate market towns serving only a restricted area, as did some of the Hanseatic towns. Sometimes they decline only relatively, owing to the more rapid growth of other centers, as in the case of Venice and Nice. If in more recent times they seem steadier and more dependable sources of support to certain cities and countries, it is probably due to the shortening of our historical perspective as regards modern cities. London, Paris, Antwerp, Amsterdam, Canton, Bombay, and a number of other cities have held positions of much economic importance for several centuries. Certain countries have also been dependent on commerce and, more recently, on industry for considerable periods. But even so there have been rather numerous and rapid changes in their relative importance. In the Orient, particular cities have been important centers of industry and commerce for comparatively long periods, but even here the relative importance of different cities changes quite rapidly. Witness the decline of Peiping (Peking), Kyoto, and other older centers of industry and commerce and the rise of Tientsin, Shanghai, Tokyo, Osaka, and other new centers more advantageously located in respect of transport and communication costs.

Since the industrial revolution, we have seen a growing tendency for whole nations to rely upon industry and commerce as bases for the support of their populations. Great Britain was, of course, the leader in modern economic development and for about a century relied more and more on her industry and commerce to furnish the means for the support of a rather rapidly growing population. Her political power, too, was largely the outcome of her preeminence in industry and commerce. Her great and continued success in wielding vast influence in world affairs because of her industrial and commercial strength led her to rely more and more on these pursuits. This is witnessed by the fact that, for some time, agriculture has employed less than one-tenth of her population and furnished the food for only about two-fifths of it; in addition to food, native agriculture furnishes probably about one-half of the wool consumed, while practically all other agricultural products used in industry are procured abroad in steadily increasing amounts. At present a determined effort is being made to expand food production.[1] Great Britain's mineral resources have been utilized more fully than her agricultural resources, because they contributed directly to her industrial and commercial supremacy and because minerals were more expensive to import.

Some years ago I argued that Great Britain was unlikely ever to regain the position of industrial and commercial preeminence she held before World War I.[2] Her position seems decidedly worsened as a result of World War II, and now even her mineral resources are becoming less and less adequate to support her position as a manufacturing and trading nation. Moreover, Great Britain now has more numerous and more efficient competitors than ever before, and Japan is just beginning to bid again for her share of postwar world trade. Finally, all over the world there is a strong movement toward autarchy, and as long as the danger of war persists this movement is likely to remain strong and may even eventuate in a reduction of the volume of international trade. As a result of these world economic trends Great Britain finds herself today in much the same position that a commercial and industrial city of former times found itself when new trade routes were opened up, or when new sources of the products in which it specialized were discovered, or when substitutes for them were developed. There is a very serious question today whether Great Britain can maintain her present population at a level of living commensurate with that of other countries where the dependence on industry and commerce is relatively less.

The conditions which make it possible for any city or country to attain great preeminence in industry and commerce and to support a large part of

---

[1] A. M. Carr-Saunders and D. Caradog Jones, *A Survey of the Social Structure of England and Wales as Illustrated by Statistics,* pp. 39–40, Oxford University Press, London, 1927; United Kingdom, Royal Commission on Population, *Report,* pp. 48–50, H.M.S.O., London, 1949.

[2] Warren S. Thompson, "Britain's Population Problem as Seen by an American," *Econ. J.,* Vol. 36, pp. 177–191, 1926; also *Danger Spots in World Population,* Chap. 12, Alfred A. Knopf, Inc., New York, 1929.

its population by trading with other areas are necessarily uncertain and temporary because, as a rule, they arise out of the exercise of some monopoly of skill in production, or experience in trade, or in the possession of certain natural resources which make for low production costs. These advantages can seldom, if ever, be long maintained in the face of competition from other peoples and other areas.

2. CONDITIONS OF TEMPORARY MONOPOLY, NATURAL

The conditions upon which a temporary monopoly is based are of two kinds: (1) natural, and (2) acquired. If the natural resources of an area in certain materials are practically inexhaustible, are not progressively difficult to exploit, are essential to the welfare of large numbers of people, are the only such resources available, and are ones for which no substitute can be found, then and then only are the industries based on them and the trade growing out of their use likely to be permanent. Very few if any of the resources under the control of any nation meet the conditions just noted. Either they are exhaustible, or they exist elsewhere in as available a form, or there are substitutes for them, or they are not essential to the life and happiness of any great part of the human race. Even the potash of Germany, often spoken of as a natural monopoly, does not meet these conditions. It is certainly not inexhaustible—in fact, there is comparatively little of it—and the most permanent agriculture that we know, the Chinese, manages to get along without commercial fertilizers in which potash is generally an important constituent; finally, other potash deposits have been found from time to time, so that Germany's deposits have steadily become less important to the world. Hence, it was inevitable that they should become less important to Germany as a source of income. The lack of important mineral resources, like the lack of agricultural resources, can become a source of embarrassment and even a national danger in a world in which war is a constant menace. There is probably no instance in which a natural monopoly is of more than passing significance in human history. Although it is always dangerous to prophesy, it seems probable that natural monopolies will play a less significant role in the lives of nations in the future than in the recent past because of the increasing ability of the chemists—and, shall we add, the physicists and the engineers using their discoveries—to substitute synthetic products for the natural products which have heretofore been in use.

In the light of our present knowledge it is clear that there are no natural monopolies on which any people can rely for more than a few years as the basis of support of any considerable number of people. It will be sufficient merely to mention a few of the important minerals to indicate the fact that they are far from being monopolized in any given area or by any particular nation.

Coal and iron are, of course, basic to our present type of industry. Considering all types of coal and iron ore, they exist in relatively large quantities in most parts of the world, although their lack, or perhaps more often the lack of certain qualities of them, can be and is a source of industrial weakness in certain areas and to certain nations. But as our technology improves we are progressively able to use inferior qualities with little or no increase in the human effort required to produce given amounts of the desired goods. In addition, we are also finding it possible to substitute certain other products for iron in some cases. This substitution has not reduced the total need for iron up to the present, but as the cost of producing aluminum, magnesium, and titanium (no doubt other minerals will be added to this list) decreases the relative importance of iron may decline.

It is too soon, of course, to say whether atomic energy will replace coal and oil as a source of power in everyday use. It would be foolish to deny this possibility, but it certainly would not be wise to count on this as the basis for the support of a larger and larger population in the foreseeable future. It is reasonable, however, to expect that we shall continue to make progress in the more efficient use of nature's stored fuels (coal and oil). Obviously, if one pound of coal or oil can be made to do the work of two, a larger population can be supported at any given level of living. But the point we are especially concerned with here is that the developments of our science and engineering tend to lessen the likelihood of monopoly through the possession of particular natural resources redounding to the advantage of any particular nation. This seems to the author to be a fact, and it should be given due consideration when the population policies of different peoples are under consideration.

Other minerals which are of great importance in modern industry and which apparently are more unevenly distributed in nature than iron and fuel are copper, tin, manganese, tungsten, vanadium, chrome, nickel, and a few others. The lack of these can certainly be the cause of acute embarrassment, or even of danger in time of war, but it is not because they are the monopoly of any other power but rather because of the increased difficulty of importing them under the conditions brought about by war and of finding quickly substitutes or new processes dispensing with them at a time when much of the energy of a nation is being devoted to the production of military supplies.

It should be clearly understood that I am not arguing that the possession of large natural resources of a quality such as to make them readily usable with the techniques we now possess is not a great advantage. It is, and there is no doubt that a larger population can be supported at any given level of living than would be possible if these resources were less abundant. But to possess large resources of good quality is far different from possessing a monopoly on which to build an industry and a wide trade through which a large population can be supported indefinitely. It must not be assumed that because an area or a nation possesses large resources it can count on a long-continued and profitable trade with less favored areas, a trade which will make it possible to exchange its manufactured goods for food and raw materials indefinitely and hence to support a large and growing population dependent on manufactures and trade. This support of a large population by industry and foreign trade is apparently merely a stage in the development of our modern economy and not a permanent feature in the life of any given nation. It may appear more or less permanent if there are good natural resources which at the time seem to be inexhaustible or to be natural monopolies. When they later prove to be neither monopolies nor large in amount, a difficult situation as regards the support of population may arise.

Thus there was a time in the development of the economy of Great Britain when it no doubt appeared probable to many of her economic leaders that she could long maintain a preeminent position in industry and commerce because of her possession of large amounts of good coal and iron and considerable amounts of tin. The ease of transportation of both raw materials (including food) and finished products throughout the world, to which should be added the possession of a high degree of skill and "know-how" in her industry, were also valuable assets to Great Britain, but they are no longer able to ensure her people a superior level of living.

Today it is abundantly clear that Great Britain has no basis in her own natural resources for a permanent position of preeminence in manufacturing and commerce. No more have the other countries which have recently been competing with Great Britain and have been slowly displacing her as the economic leader of the modern world. Germany, the United States, and Japan, the most active foreign competitors of Great Britain in recent years, have also been competing actively with one another. Germany and Japan are momentarily greatly handicapped in competing for world trade, but this condition is likely to pass. Each of these competitors probably has certain natural advantages of resources, of climate, or of location, which will enable it to carry on certain industries or to cultivate the trade of certain peoples better than the others. But these advantages are not large in any one of them, and it would be folly to base a hope of economic supremacy in world trade upon them and to assume, therefore, that a relatively large population can be supported indefinitely by any trade monopoly they may now possess or are likely to develop in the foreseeable future. The author, at least, is not surprised that as the difficulties of maintaining a large population dependent on foreign trade become apparent, leaders of the peoples lacking adequate resources are inclined to demand larger resources (Lebensraum, empire) and that they often urge the forcible seizure of these resources.[3]

But if it appears that what are frequently thought of as natural monopolies and large resources are slim reeds on which to rely for the permanent

[3] Thompson, *Danger Spots in World Population,* pp. 10–15.

support of any particular population through manufacturing and commerce, we should not overlook the fact that advantages of location are probably the most permanent of all natural advantages in the struggle for foreign trade, although even these are greatly modified from time to time by the development of new means of transportation and communication and the shifting of trade routes. Venice, as was mentioned before, declined upon the establishment of an all-water route to the East. Great Britain's very favorable location for trade in the North Atlantic is, on the whole, less favorable now that a larger proportion of the world's trade enters the Pacific and Indian Oceans. Japan should always gain some advantage from her location off the east coast of Asia, and the United States should derive some permanent benefits from her ready access to the markets of both the North Atlantic and the North Pacific as well as to certain parts of South America. Anything that cheapens transportation, however, tends to equalize the value of different locations, and it seems probable that differentials in commercial activity due to locational advantages will be less in the future than in the past.

Another advantage which is quite permanent and which will exercise more or less influence upon the commercial prestige of a nation is its climate. Thus, textiles of certain kinds are more easily manufactured in certain climates than in others. However, the artificial creation of favorable manufacturing conditions within factories is rapidly rendering such advantages of little consequence. Possibly some other types of industry may also be better adapted to particular climates, e.g., steelmaking to the temperate latitudes, but it seems likely that climate like location will play a less important part in industrial and commercial success in the future than in the past. It is in agricultural production, of course, that climate appears as the most important determining factor, but even here it does not seem that any country possesses a monopoly of any particular kind of climate adapted to the economical production of some important crop. Consequently, climate can furnish no basis for the enduring preeminence of any people or nation in industry, commerce, or agriculture thus enabling it to continue for long to support a population based on the advantages of climate. In addition, many highly specialized agricultural products are being supplanted by synthetic products. One need only mention rubber (butadiene) and quinine (atabrine and chloroquine) to indicate some of the ways in which monopolistic agricultural production is also being rendered of less advantage in the world of today, and hence of less and less dependability as the basis for the support of population in a particular area.

So far, then, as one can see there is no sound basis for any country to hope for a position of leadership in world industry and commerce lasting any great length of time because of its superior natural advantages in resources, in location, or in climate. This means that the support of a population dependent upon what are commonly thought of as natural monopolies or advantages is more and more precarious because of the changes in modern industry and transportation and also because of the opening up of new agricultural areas suitable for the growth of crops which have heretofore been grown in limited areas which possessed a temporary (advantage) monopoly. If any country is to attain and hold for any length of time a monopolistic position in an industry or in certain lines of trade it must be on some other basis than the endowments that nature has given it. It is, of course, impossible to separate neatly the natural and acquired advantages which may give a temporary monopoly or a partial monopoly to a given area or nation.

3. CONDITIONS OF TEMPORARY MONOPOLY, ACQUIRED

The acquired advantages, aside from the use of force, which give any people a temporary monopoly may be summed up under two heads: (1) advantages of technique, and (2) advantages in the accumulation of capital. The second probably flows largely from the first, although differences in the social organization of two countries may determine the distribution of the goods produced between different groups and thus the rate of capital accumulation. Whether any surplus of goods above *necessary* consumption will take the form of consumption goods and be widely distributed and consumed or will take the form of production goods and fall into the control of a small group accumulating them for further production is probably due chiefly to the social structure of the society under consideration. It was largely to the advantages arising out of the development of superior industrial techniques, including the skills of her industrial workers, that Great Britain owed most of her industrial and commercial preeminence and hence her political leadership during the century preceding World War I. The application of steam power to manufacturing processes and the development of the skills essential to the efficient use of this power at once gave her a long lead over the Continental countries. Her workmen and engineers soon developed technical processes and skills which made her industry far more productive and profitable than the old hand industries. Her economic leadership arose largely out of this monopoly of the technique of machine production which was hers for some decades. But this factor is decidedly one of temporary nature. The proof of this lies in the rapidity with which the productiveness of many British industries has been equaled and surpassed by those of other countries.

It requires no argument to convince anyone that the training and knowledge of the engineers of any country are readily acquired by those of other countries and that the skill and experience of the workers in machine industry are just as rapidly diffused. The types of organization developed both in the productive processes and in the distributive processes of modern nations are also open to the inspection of the world. There is no reason why efficient processes and effective types of organization, with the necessary local adaptations, should not spread over the whole world in a comparatively short time. Japan's success in adopting and adapting the economic processes developed abroad abundantly proves the ease with which these can spread under fairly favorable conditions. The success of the students from the Orient and South America in the technical schools of Europe and North America shows how readily technical knowledge can be diffused, and the rapid industrial development of the Soviet Union also proves that a peasant people can quickly acquire both technical skills and administrative capacities.

One might go on almost indefinitely to point out how the techniques which gave one nation an advantage over others at one stage of industrial development have either been acquired by the others or been rendered obsolete by the development of new processes, new methods, and new machines, not infrequently among the more recently industrialized peoples. In these latter days nations tend very rapidly to approximate each other in the techniques of their industry. Patents and secret processes somewhat retard this movement, but probably the habits of the workers as they affect their use of tools and their adoption of new methods of work and the attitudes of the employers toward the newer methods of industrial and business organization do far more to account for the differential element in the productive capacity of different countries than the actual lack of skill on the part of workmen and engineers. Today, therefore, no country or area dares rely on this acquirement (the possession of unusual skill and technical training) for the permanence of its economic position. Such qualities have too little of the monopoly element in them to give one country any long-continued advantage over another, and the probable duration of such advantages as may be acquired is almost certainly decreasing.

The second advantage mentioned above is the greater ease with which capital is accumulated in one social group than in another. Before there can be any appreciable accumulation of capital there must be a surplus of products above the customary consumption of the population. In Western Europe the institutions of society were well adapted to make it possible for any such surplus to be gathered into the hands of a very small proportion of the population, and nowhere was this easier than in Great Britain. For several centuries prior to the industrial revolution the rights of laborers as against employers had been the subject of restrictive legislation which had quite effectually brought the laborers under the control of the employing class. All that was needed to make possible a rapid accumulation of capital was the presence of a considerable surplus above the customary consumption of the people. This was furnished by the application of water power and steam power (particularly the latter) to the driving of machinery. In a comparatively short time, therefore, the entrepreneur class in Great Britain had accumulated large amounts of capital. It was this new command over capital that gave Great Britain her firm grip on the economic life of the world. Never was the truth of the saying "to him who hath shall be given" better exemplified. There is no doubt that even the recipients of this accumulating surplus were astonished at its size. But shortly they accepted it as their rightful portion, and economists developed the theory which justified it as such. Thus, the large returns of machine industry to capital were fastened upon the new industrial system as a basic charge.

Great Britain had a good head start in the modern race for capital accumulation, and it was necessarily some time before any other country could come within hailing distance of her. It is not surprising, then, that until well on toward the beginning of the twentieth century Great Britain was not even aware of the approach of industrial and commercial competition.

More recently the development of industry in Japan and the Soviet Union shows that there are other systems which may render the accumulation of capital and the acquirement of industrial skills even more rapid than the laissez-faire economy under which the West developed. Under such circumstances the policy of dependence of any given country on production for foreign trade as the means of support of any considerable part of its population becomes steadily more questionable, *i.e.,* the period of time during which dependence on foreign trade can be relied upon as a certain support of population is decreasing and likely to decrease more rapidly in the future. I am not predicting the decline in the total volume of foreign trade or even the decline in the per capita volume, but I am saying that the advantages which a nation like Great Britain possessed because of her earlier development of modern power industry are now largely nullified by like developments elsewhere and that the prospect is for their still further diminution in the future.[4]

4. PRESENT POSITION OF GREAT BRITAIN

It will be interesting and instructive to trace very briefly the process by which, under modern conditions, a nation like Great Britain rises to power and then after several decades loses her position of preeminence.

Great Britain had good natural resources, particularly fuel and iron. She had also a trade of long standing in woolen goods and in some other lines which made her merchants familiar with the ins and outs of foreign commerce. In addition to this the very happy invention of machines to utilize her fuel, machines for working textiles, and new methods of smelting iron gave her a greatly increased productive power and furnished the basis for

[4] United Kingdom, Royal Commission on Population, *Report of the Economics Committee,* Papers of the Royal Commission on Population, Vol. 3, p. 11, H.M.S.O. London, 1950.

the accumulation of capital at an unprecedented rate. It was not long before she had capital and to spare. Her leadership in finance was based upon her ability to make large foreign investments. Thus, Great Britain became the economic dictator of the Western world during a good part of the nineteenth century. Never had any other country enjoyed such economic ascendancy. To many of her leaders her ascendant position seemed impregnable. It looked to them as though she had so far outdistanced other nations that she need not fear their competition, particularly under a capitalist system in which the supplier of capital became the controller of the industry, whether at home or abroad.

In considering the factors at work in the development of the economic life of Great Britain, it seems rather curious (until we look about us today and see much the same lack of vision) that the economic leaders of Victorian Britain did not realize more clearly the certain outcome of a preponderant dependence upon foreign trade and investments. It was inevitable that other countries should profit by Great Britain's experience and financial strength to further their own economic development. They borrowed her capital only to make for themselves the machines and the goods that would in time render them not only economically self-contained but to a high degree competitive with her. They adopted her techniques of production and forms of organization and imported experienced managers and workers. Thus they rapidly caught up with their teacher and banker in the efficiency of their industry.

The self-sufficiency of a newer (industrial) country develops gradually, and it is not apparent at first that the capital that it borrows will ultimately reduce its dependence on the lending country, for foreign loans, whether private or public, are generally devoted to developing, first, transportation and, later, industry. The development of transportation in new countries greatly stimulates trade by extending the area of trade as well as by creating a direct demand for the goods necessary to construct railways, canals, and so forth. However, it is not long before capital is also invested in industrial plants in the new country, which shortly come into competition with those of the investing country. Thus, the greater the success that attends the efforts of a country to accumulate capital and acquire interests abroad, the sooner is it certain to feel the competition of its borrowers, at first in the home markets of the borrowing country and later in the markets of other countries. It is just the competition of the industries of the countries which were but a short time ago Great Britain's borrowers, or are even yet borrowers (the United States, Japan, Germany, Australia, Canada, South Africa, and so forth) that has brought upon Great Britain the crisis she has faced ever since World War I. It is one of the ironies of history that the greater the success of a highly industrialized country in accumulating capital and in making investments abroad, the more quickly comes the time when its home industries will be sick unto death because of the competition encouraged by these investments.

But this is not the only disadvantage of giving hostages (loans and capital investments) abroad. It creates such a deep interest in the affairs of the debtor areas that we find all manner of expedients resorted to in order to ensure the integrity of these investments. Of course, the cost of this insurance (military expeditions, navies, protectorates, and elaborate foreign services of various kinds) is borne by the nation at large, while the benefits accrue to a few investors; naturally, the powerful investors regard it as a matter of *national honor* that these investments be kept sound.

But even in the heyday of the power and wealth of a country like Great Britain, depending on external resources for so much of her raw materials and foods, she was at the mercy of every adverse wind that blew. A civil war in the United States caused untold suffering to her cotton-mill workers because of the inability to get cotton, and as a consequence during that war she pursued a policy toward the North which every self-respecting Britisher blushes to remember. A new tariff act in Australia causes consternation in the woolen industry of Yorkshire. The possibility of preferential tolls to American ships going through the Panama Canal is viewed with alarm as an obstacle in the path of British commerce. A new constitution and its enforcement in Mexico cause the withdrawal of a diplomatic representative as a protest against the diminution in value of certain investments.

Our own conduct of foreign relations in the West Indies and Central America shows numerous incidents of the same nature, due to our efforts to preserve the value of our investments abroad. A country depending largely on industry and commerce for prosperity is at the mercy of economic vicissitudes in all parts of the world. She can know no peace of mind and her policies must be governed by the interests at stake in each particular case. Hard times in India due to the failure of the monsoon with the resulting famine, a boycott in China, an earthquake in Japan, overexpansion of agriculture in Argentina or the United States or Canada, and so forth, are causes of much concern to the nation which has far-flung capital investments and especially to the nation that needs to sell a substantial portion of its annual product abroad. We are becoming more and more aware of the inconveniences and dangers of dependence on foreign trade. The country which is supposedly fortunate in having a highly developed industrial organization based upon the trade of a considerable proportion of its manufactures for goods and raw materials from all over the world is necessarily much affected by the economic vicissitudes of all other countries. It has the least freedom to go its own way, and its people dare not follow their natural impulses of generosity and justice in dealing with the less industrialized peoples of the world. Its economic organization is too delicate to withstand the loss of markets and raw materials, and so it must needs "stand up for the *rights* of its nationals" (property rights in general) and regard any infringement of the customary rights of its nationals by another nation as "an affront to its national honor." The economic effects of changes in the flow of trade are of the utmost importance to all countries depending on the export of manufactured goods for a considerable share of their incomes. The international relations of such countries are largely determined by the effort to ward off economic action by other countries which will adversely affect employment in the manufacturing and trading country. In the world of today it is dangerous from the standpoint of individual and of national welfare for a nation to become highly dependent on manufacturing, a large proportion of the products of which must be traded abroad for the food and raw materials it must have. In a world in which peace was well established and trade was largely unrestrained, the situation might be quite different, but competition for trade would, in general, be even keener, and whether countries with a relatively high level of living could survive such competition is a question that cannot be answered at present. But since the fact is that we do not live in a world of free competition, it behooves every country to be prudent in trying to foresee the means it will have available for the support of its people in the world as it is and is likely to be for some time to come.

Fortunately, the imperialism which prevailed up to World War II is rapidly passing and will no longer supply the motive for the development of a large manufacturing and trading population in the metropolitan center of empire. But before World War II countries like Great Britain, Germany, and Japan had already developed such a dependence upon foreign markets that they were having great difficulty in keeping the markets already established and still more trouble in opening new markets as their industrial capacity expanded. Today their problems are even more complicated. How they will adjust to postwar conditions no one knows, but there is no doubt that the process of adjustment will be prolonged and painful. A country may very well be overpopulated when the conditions determining its national income change as has been the case in those countries which are heavily dependent on the exchange of their industrial products for food and raw materials.

5. DURATION OF PROSPERITY BASED ON INDUSTRY AND COMMERCE

Japan, Germany, the United States, and the leading self-governing dominions of the British Empire should study carefully the problems arising from a high degree of dependence on manufacturing and trade abroad as exemplified in the development of Great Britain before they decide to go farther in this direction in a world as unsettled as that in which we live. Of course, none of these lands can reasonably expect to attain an economic hegemony over the world such as Britain held for some decades even if one of them should chance to attain it for a brief time.

It would certainly seem that the difficulties Great Britain has experienced since the beginning of this century, but especially since World War I, by reason of the dissolution of her empire and in maintaining and expanding her foreign trade should give serious pause to the plans of other nations to follow in her footsteps. The situation in which Great Britain found herself in 1914 made it practically inevitable not only that she would be almost immediately involved in any sizable war which broke out anywhere on the globe, but also that she would lose some of her hold on her foreign markets and some of her claims to imports through the disruption of trade during the war and the liquidation of her foreign holdings. The important point is that when any nation becomes economically dependent on its ability to trade on a large scale with the world at large it becomes highly dependent on the maintenance of the *status quo* for its very existence. This seems likely to be even more true in the decades ahead than it has been during the past century. This is the reason why any nation which is contemplating a large increase in its industry a large proportion of whose products are to be traded abroad should proceed cautiously. Certainly the economic position of Great Britain today is anything but enviable, and its outlook for the future is still more bleak.

In all lands where machine industry is established or is being introduced, people seem to think that there is some magic power in it which will free them indefinitely from the limitations imposed upon the production of wealth by the older agricultural economy. It is true that the term of the increases in man's efficiency in transforming raw materials into consumers' goods is not in sight, and that the amount of goods that can be used to advantage is limited, in the long run, only by the ability to produce them. But the ability of any nation to produce is itself limited at a given time not only by the resources available to it at that time but by a great number of economic and social conditions over which it has little or no direct control. Even when it seems reasonable to believe that a large increase in the production of nonagricultural goods is possible, it does not follow that this increase can be disposed of to advantage either at home or by foreign trade. Only under the semimonopolistic conditions which favored Great Britain for some decades before 1900 is any country again likely to find foreign trade so easy and so advantageous. In the opinion of the author the conditions which made it possible for Great Britain to support a growing population for some decades through the expansion of her foreign trade are not likely to recur in the foreseeable future.

6. THE PRESENT SITUATION IN JAPAN

The need of Japan for industrial expansion and for the sale of much of the increased produce abroad is, perhaps, even greater than that of Great Britain. Without such a development it is hard to see how Japan can support the probable increase of her population during the next two or three decades at the present level of living, to say nothing of raising that level. Consequently, it may be of some interest to note briefly what happened in prewar Japan and to evaluate the postwar outlook for Japan—the probability that she can reasonably expect to increase her industry and trade to the extent necessary to care for her probable growth in population.

For some time before World War II many well-informed Japanese realized that it was going to be very difficult to increase food production to any great extent within the home islands. Since it was also quite clear that Japan could add to her colonial empire only by war, many of the men of good will came to look to industry and commerce to provide for Japan's growing population. They pointed to the huge exports of manufactured goods sent out by Great Britain and the fact that with these exports she bought more than half the food consumed by her people, as well as a large proportion of the raw materials for her factories. They believed that it would be possible for Japan to do likewise. They also pointed with pride, and wholly justifiable pride, to the rapid industrial and commercial development that had already taken place in Japan, and they did not believe it unreasonable to assume that Japan could continue to expand her industry and foreign trade fast enough to keep pace with her growing needs as population increased.

This line of analogical argument was apparently convincing to many people. For my own part, however, I never considered it sound. The comparison between the situation of Great Britain and that of Japan is misleading in a number of respects. In the first place, Japan never had the natural resources of the Great Britain of 100 years ago. She had but very meager supplies of coking coal, iron, copper, and other important minerals. Without doubt the rich mineral deposits of Manchuria constituted one of the chief attractions of this area, although the possibilities of an increase in trade with its 40 million people were not without influence in the decision to take over this region.

In the second place, Great Britain developed her industrial strength in a world that was predominately agricultural. She had but little competition to meet in placing her manufactured products on the world markets. Besides, she had a large and rapidly increasing body of English-speaking people living abroad that looked to her for manufactured products. Japan, on the other hand, had to meet very keen competition from other industrial lands from the very beginning of her industrial and commercial expansion. In addition, she had no large body of Japanese living abroad who preferred to buy Japanese products.

In the third place, both capital and technical knowledge and skill are more mobile and more abundant now than in the days when Great Britain was establishing her industrial supremacy. This fact makes it increasingly difficult for any nation to retain markets, even when they are once gained, to say nothing of establishing a semimonopoly in trade in any line of goods.

In the fourth place, there is a very marked tendency in the world today to foster home industry by raising protective tariffs, by "safeguarding," by trade quotas, by exchange control, and so forth. This not only tends to make the expansion of foreign trade more difficult than it would otherwise be, but it also renders its continuance more uncertain. Japan has had to face, and will continue to have to face, a much more difficult situation in expanding her industry and commerce than Great Britain did a century ago.

In the fifth place, by 1900 Great Britain had accumulated a very large investment abroad, the interest on which was sufficient to pay for vast imports. Moreover, the mere existence of this investment carried with it many advantages in trade which Japan did not have and which it would take some years to acquire even if she were extremely fortunate in the relations her merchants established abroad.

In the author's opinion it was in part, at least, the recognition of the obstacles which lay in the path of a rapid expansion of industry and trade as the basis for the support of a rather rapidly increasing population that had much to do with the decision of Japanese expansionists to take over Manchuria and prepare for further conquests as the solution of their country's economic troubles. Their ventures have ended disastrously, but they were right in believing that increased industrialization and foreign trade would not ensure the permanent support of their growing population in the world as it was organized before World War II.

Since World War II Japan's situation has become even more precarious in that her empire is dissolved and any advantage she enjoyed in trading with her colonies as compared with trading with independent nations has vanished. In addition, temporarily at least, the accumulation of capital for the modernization and expansion of her industry has become more difficult. Her merchant marine was destroyed and must be built up anew. Many of the new industrial processes require better-trained engineers and technicans, and more of them, and her educational facilities are not adequate to the job. She has no consular service and trade organization such as she possessed before 1941. Competition in foreign trade is even keener than in the past, and besides it is not at all certain that even when she is ready to export on a large scale the Chinese and the other Asiatic peoples will allow her to trade freely with them. One does not wish to be a pessimist, but at the same time the facts must be faced, and it seems to the author that the facts point to greater difficulties in the near future than in the past for the country depending heavily on industry and foreign trade for its economic welfare.

Unfortunately there is almost nothing any particular country can do to overcome most of the obstacles to the expansion of its own trade. They arise in large part from world conditions which will require an economic reorganization of the world to ensure the expansion of the economy of all peoples. The first condition is the assurance of peace. A second condition is the progressive removal of the barriers to trade. A third condition—in the author's opinion, the most important—is the control of population growth so that the need of ever larger resources and ever increasing agricultural and industrial production will become less urgent. But even in the case of a country like Great Britain, where population is growing rather slowly and there is a considerable amount of emigration, it is not certain that peace and freer trade will solve her economic problems. She may need to reduce the size of her population as well. In the author's opinion, Japan and Italy are in even greater need of a large increase in foreign trade because their populations are growing more rapidly, but their greatest need is to reduce their rate of population growth. Only in this way can many of the more crowded areas of the world keep from becoming so dependent on foreign imports of raw materials that they can be reasonably certain of maintaining present levels of living, to say nothing of raising them. This is not to say that autarchy is desirable; it is merely to recognize the fact that for the foreseeable future it is dangerous for any nation to rely to any great extent on the exchange of its industrial products for the food and raw material essential to the welfare of its people.

Suggestions for Supplementary Reading

ABRAMS, MARK: *The Population of Great Britain, Current Trends and Future Problems*, 51 pp., The London Press Exchange, London, 1945.

ADLER, JOHN H.: *The Underdeveloped Areas: Their Industrialization*, 30 pp., Yale Institute of International Studies, New Haven, Conn., 1949.

BALLARD, GEORGE A.: *The Influence of the Sea on the Political History of Japan*, 311 pp., E. P. Dutton & Co., Inc., New York, 1921.

CLAPHAM, J. H.: *An Economic History of Modern Britain: The Railway Age, 1820–1850*, 623 pp., Cambridge University Press, London, 1926.

FAIRGRIEVE, JAMES: *Geography and World Power*, 2d ed., 373 pp., University of London Press, Ltd., London, 1921.

MOORE, W. E.: *Industrialization and Labor, Social Aspects of Economic Development*, 410 pp., Cornell University Press, Ithaca, N.Y., 1951.

PENROSE, E. F.: *Food Supply and Raw Material in Japan*, 75 pp., University of Chicago Press, 1929.

SCHUMPETER, ELIZABETH BOODY, *et al.*: *The Industrialization of Japan and Manchukuo, 1930–1940*, 944 pp., The Macmillan Company, New York, 1940.

THOMPSON, WARREN S.: "Britain's Population Problem as Seen by an American," *Econ. J.*, Vol. 36, pp. 177–191, 1926.

———. *Danger Spots in World Population*, 343 pp., Alfred A. Knopf, Inc., New York, 1929.

United Kingdom Royal Commission on Population: *Report of the Economics Committee*, Papers of the Royal Commission on Population, Vol. 3, 64 pp., H.M.S.O., London, 1950.

CHAPTER XVII

POPULATION GROWTH AND
INTERNATIONAL POLITICS

The economic and, as a consequence, also the political problems arising out of the differential rates of increase of nations are among the important problems the world faces today (Chap. XII). The task before us here is to investigate some of the ways in which these differential rates of increase are affecting and, in the future, are likely to affect the relations between nations.

1. HOW POPULATION GROWTH CREATES POLITICAL PROBLEMS

Unfortunately there is a very general impression not only that the tensions arising between nations do not concern the average citizen but that the circumstances giving rise to them are quite beyond his comprehension. World War I did something to shake us in the United States out of our lethargy over international affairs; World War II did still more to awaken us to the need of thinking about the causes of tensions between nations; and the "cold" war of the past few years has further educated us in the need of understanding our relations to other peoples and the factors which determine their actions as well as our own. However, there is still a widespread feeling that the causes of international tensions are so complex and recondite that only the deeply initiated can hope to understand them and that the worry over them should be left to this expert class. This may be true of many of the fine technical or legal aspects of international relations, but it is not true that some of the most basic causes of international tensions cannot be understood by the average man.

We are concerned here with but one of the factors affecting international tensions, namely, how changes in population growth may affect the relations between peoples and may add to the tensions between them. As we have seen above, different nations have different rates of growth largely because they have different birth rates and death rates. Since the natural resources of peoples are also different in amount and in quality, these differentials in rates of growth affect the needs of nations differently. If a people has fairly adequate resources now and if it is growing slowly or not at all, its need for more resources will not be pressing—perhaps for some decades. If, on the other hand, it has quite inadequate resources and is growing rather rapidly it may soon come to feel the need of more land for agriculture, more coal, iron, copper, rubber, sulfur, salt, and so forth, as an urgent matter affecting the welfare of all its people in vital ways.

The author has long believed that the differential growth of the populations of nations was a basic factor in international relations because it was bringing about changing needs for resources of many kinds and at the same time was altering the military status of nations. Differential population growth is not, of course, the only factor at work in effecting changes in relative military and political power. The degree of industrialization is an extremely important factor both in determining the need for resources and in building up the military power of a given country to the point where it may feel strong enough to undertake the conquest of larger resources. However, it seems to the author that the growth of population and especially the differential growth of peoples has been an underlying factor of great importance in bringing about both a change in the need of a people for resources and a change in the military power essential to conquest. Hence, a world in which large differentials in population growth exists is likely to be an unstable world and one in which the acquisition of larger resources by the growing peoples would be governed chiefly by their ability to take them forcibly from weaker peoples. This belief rests, in part, on the further assumption that even if unused resources needed by the more rapidly expanding peoples were available they would not be made accessible to them by the peoples that already hold title to them. It has long appeared to the author, therefore, that the changing needs of peoples for resources, arising, in part, from differential rates of population growth was a very significant factor in creating international tensions which could readily lead to war.[1]

It should be said at the outset of this discussion that the view presented here, namely, that differential changes in the pressure of population on resources due to differential rates of population growth are likely to increase the danger of war, is not *universally, perhaps not generally,* accepted even by those whose knowledge and experience entitle them to opinions on this matter. Many such people hold that Japan, Italy, and above all Germany had no basis in fact for their demands for more ample resources. Many people believe that the outcry against the "dog in the manger" attitude of the great colonial powers was only a "blind" to conceal the real purposes of the cliques controlling these countries, namely, their desire to expand their empires and enhance their own power. In support of this view they cite as one important proof the efforts of the leaders of these "have-not" peoples to induce them to increase their birth rates, or at least to prevent

[1] Warren S. Thompson, *Danger Spots in World Population,* pp. 10–17, Alfred A. Knopf, Inc., New York, 1929.

their further decline, and then to use the increase in numbers as a reason for demanding larger space.[2]

In the past those who did not believe that changing population pressures were of any great significance in determining the efforts at territorial expansion usually also denied that the possession of great colonial areas by the "haves" placed any restriction upon the economic use of these areas by the "have-nots." According to this argument the Japanese or the Germans had just as much opportunity to exploit territory under the control of other European countries as did the nationals of these countries. This question cannot be argued here, but it may be asked why, if this was the case, the great colonial powers were so anxious to retain possession of the areas under their control, many of which they were unable to exploit effectively. Rather strangely, the advocates of this view have been equally certain that, conditions being reversed, they could not thrive in German or Japanese colonies. The great difficulty, of course, was that no nation trusted another to treat it fairly in the use of the natural resources of an area over which another possessed control.

There are numerous ways, most of which never appeared on the statute books or in the executive orders and administrative regulations, of hampering the economic activity of a rival when one also holds political control in a colonial area. But the most convincing proof that political control was generally believed to give an economic advantage to the nationals of the governing country is found in the reluctance to hand over this control to an international authority even when it was clear that the governing country could not exploit the resources of the area advantageously.

At present the argument regarding the advantages of holding colonies and more or less excluding other nations from a share in their exploitation in the prewar manner is in process of becoming academic. The spirit of nationalism abroad in the world has already resulted in the independence of many former colonial areas and will undoubtedly lead to the independence of the remainder in the not-distant future. However, there appears to be developing a new type of colonialism under the Soviet Union. Its form we can only dimly discern at present, but judging from the information seeping through the "iron curtain," it seems likely to be far more exclusive and more ruthlessly exploitative than the colonialism of the past. Certainly there is no evidence that the mere breakup of the prewar type of colonialism will automatically lead to a more just access to the world's resources, nor is there any evidence that Communist colonialism recognizes that differential rates of growth of population call for an effort to reallocate the access to natural resources. Indeed, the classical Marxian view is that there can never be real pressure of population on resources, since poverty in modern indus-

[2] Sir Norman Angell, *Raw Materials, Population Pressure and War,* pp. 41–42, World Peace Foundation, New York, 1936. (World Affairs Books, No. 14.)

trial society is caused by a capitalistic social system which does not give people an opportunity to use the resources they already possess. In any event it does not appear that the change in the form of colonialism and the adoption of a new ideology eliminate the problems raised by the differential rate of growth between nations. These changes alter the form of the problem, but they do not solve it.

The thesis here is, then, that the changing rates of population growth in different nations help to create changes in the pressure of populations on the resources available to them and that as these changing pressures come to be felt more and more they are almost certain to lead to violent attempts to effect new adjustments more favorable to the growing peoples. Moreover, the tensions thus created are likely to become greater as the industrial power of these growing peoples increases and as their political organization enables them to act in a more unified manner to undertake to enforce what they come to feel are just demands for a larger share in the world's resources. It is the author's belief that World War II was in large measure the consequence of past disregard of these changing pressures of population on resources accompanied by changes in military and political power. With this brief introduction we shall proceed to examine some of the facts on which this conclusion is based.

2. LANDS HELD OUT OF USE

The expansion of Europe's population which has taken place since about 1700 was accompanied by a preemption by certain European powers of vast areas of the earth's surface which previously were under the control of tribal peoples or of loosely organized agricultural civilizations. The peoples in possession of these areas at the beginning of this era had comparatively little power to resist European encroachments. In some cases European settlers migrated in rather large numbers and took complete possession of the land, carrying on agriculture, establishing industry, and developing trade with their own labor. The United States, Canada, Australia, certain parts of South America, and to a lesser extent South Africa are examples of the settlement and exploitation of new lands by Europeans with their own labor.

On the other hand, European peoples also occupied by military force great areas which they never made any attempt to settle. In these areas they generally depended on the native labor of the colored races for the exploitation of the natural resources. One need only mention the occupation of India, Burma, and the Malay Peninsula by the British, the parceling out of the important islands of the Western Pacific and Indian Oceans (except the Philippines) between the Dutch and the British, the conquest of Indochina by the French, and finally the dividing of practically the whole of Africa among the interested European powers, to realize the extent to which the control of Western Europe over the resources of the world grew as its population increased and its industry expanded.

In this expansion of European control in Africa, Asia, and the neighboring islands, the British came out a long first, with France and the Netherlands getting huge areas, while Belgium and Portugal received not inconsiderable territories in Africa; Germany and Italy, at that time not great military powers, were later given a few scraps of territory which were of little value economically. Japan also came on the scene too late to secure large colonial areas with as little effort as the European colonial powers.

The Americas were included in this colonial expansion of Western Europe, but with the loss of the thirteen British colonies which became the United States a process of colonial disintegration set in which resulted in the practical elimination of European control over any considerable territory in the Western Hemisphere by the middle of the nineteenth century. Hence, this region has not been much concerned with the politics of European expansion since that time.

Of all the territory in Africa and Asia and in the Western Pacific which came under European control, only Australia and New Zealand have actually been settled and developed by Europeans. Other areas were located largely in the tropics, and as long as they remained colonies the Europeans made no settlement there which could be compared to those they made in the temperate zones. In the tropics the European remained primarily an exploiter; he took what he could and went back home to enjoy his spoils. With only a few exceptions he did not make his home in such colonies and become a true settler interested chiefly in the welfare of his adopted home.[3]

The result of the colonial policies followed by the European powers and the reluctance of Europeans to take up permanent settlement in the tropics was that a large part of these tropical possessions in Africa and in the Pacific islands remained very thinly peopled by the indigenous inhabitants. But the European did not hesitate to bring in other nonwhite laborers, chiefly Chinese and Indians, wherever his exploitation would be made more profitable thereby. He was, however, reluctant to open these areas to people having strong national sentiments which might in time lead them to oppose the existing political control, even though there were large areas whose settlement and use might be hastened by the encouragement of such immigration.

Regardless of the absence of definite prohibitions against the settlement of the Japanese and the Indians and the Chinese in most of these colonies,

[3] Ellsworth Huntington, "Man and Nature in Hot Climates. How a Tropical Setting Affects Racial Culture and Density of Population," *Asia*, Vol. 27, pp. 822–829, 1927.

the practical effect of their control by Europeans was to retard the expansion of these peoples into many areas. Thus the exploitation of the natural resources of these areas by non-Europeans was made relatively difficult, and even Europeans who were not nationals of the governing power found that their participation in the exploitation of these tropical areas was not welcomed. As a result great areas of the world were practically being held out of use by the great European colonial powers which, even while their populations were still increasing rapidly, showed no ability to settle them.

So far as Europe was concerned this situation was further aggravated by the fact that, as was shown above, new differentials in population growth and in the need for natural resources were developing among the peoples of Central and Western Europe. The Germans and Italians, in particular, felt that they were being unfairly handicapped in their efforts to make a better living because they were denied *free* access to the great and largely unused areas held by the more favored peoples.

As was said above, this is too large a subject to discuss adequately here, but it is also too important to ignore in a general survey of population problems. Only a concrete case or two can be given brief consideration here.

3. JAPAN'S PROBLEM

Japan's economic situation had been growing increasingly difficult for some time before 1930. Her population had been growing quite rapidly, and she had but meager natural resources with which to support her increasing numbers. From an estimated population of about 33 million in 1872, Japan had grown to 63,870,000 by 1930 and to 71,540,000 by 1940. Thus in 70 years her population had grown by approximately 115 per cent and there were perhaps 2 to 2.5 million more in her colonies and in Manchuria.[4] For some time the rate of growth had been holding at about 12 to 15 per 1,000 per year. It did not fall below this rate until after the attack on China (1937) when large numbers of soldiers were sent abroad. In 1938 and 1939 the natural increase fell to 9 or 10 per 1,000. However, it should be noted that there was clear evidence as early as 1920 that the birth rate was falling in the cities of Japan and also in certain rural areas, chiefly those surrounding the larger cities. But the death rate generally fell as fast as the birth rate, or faster, until the close of the 1930's. Under the circumstances prevailing in 1940 and even after the attack on Pearl Harbor it seemed reasonable to assume that Japan's population would increase by 10 per cent or a little more during the 1940's unless war losses were extremely heavy and the absence of military personnel overseas had a more depressing effect on the birth rate than then appeared probable. Actually the birth

[4] *A Brief Report on Public Health Administration in Japan*, 27 pp., Ministry of Welfare, Japan, 1951.

rate averaged slightly higher during 1940 to 1943 than in the preceding five years (1935 to 1939), while the death rate averaged somewhat lower, so that the rate of natural increase was a little higher during 1940 to 1943. During the last year of the war (1945) the death rate rose rapidly as hardships increased and the birth rate fell as more men were sent abroad, so that there was an excess of deaths over births amounting to 6 per 1,000. Between Oct. 1, 1945, when the population was estimated at 72,410,000 (about 1.0 million more than in 1940) and Oct. 1, 1950, Japan's population grew by about 11 million, to about 83 million. Of the increase during 1945 to 1950 the major part, over 6 million, came from the excess of births over deaths from Jan. 1, 1946, to Oct. 1, 1950 (the date of the 1950 census). The remainder were repatriates—military personnel plus civilians returned from Manchuria, Korea, Formosa, and other Japanese settlements, as well as civilians who followed the armies to exploit the territories.[5]

The large postwar natural increase began about the middle of 1946 and was due, on the one hand, to the return of military personnel to their families, the addition of the civilian repatriates, and the increase of marriages among the returning soldiers. The second factor aiding increase was the very precipitate decline in the death rate after 1946. By 1948 the death rate had fallen to about 12 per 1,000 from a prewar rate of about 17 and by 1950 had fallen to about 11. The official rates of natural increase for 1948, 1949, and 1950 were 21.8, 21.3, and 17.4, respectively. By 1950 the birth rate (28.3) was substantially below that for prewar years, but even so the rate of natural increase was over 2.0 points above the high rate of the early 1930's.

It is anybody's guess as to what Japan's rate of growth will be during the next decade or two, but it seems reasonable to assume that it will be within the range of 10 to 15 per 1,000 unless the birth rate falls much faster than now seems likely and/or unless the death rate rises because of the economic difficulties of caring for such an increase in numbers. This last statement calls for a very brief survey of Japan's economic development during the past three or four decades.

Prior to 1930, Japan was securing some relatively cheap food and raw materials from her colonies—Korea and Formosa—and also from Manchuria, a part of which was virtually in colonial status. With the coming of the world depression in 1930 and the increasing difficulties of maintaining foreign trade Japan's economic situation became more and more precarious. The political liberals were driven from power by a program of assassination engineered by the military clique. The rise of this clique to power was probably in part the consequence of growing economic pressures. In the fall of 1931 the army felt strong enough politically as well as militarily

---

[5] The net gain through repatriation was reduced by about 1.2 million through the moving out of foreigners settled in Japan, chiefly Koreans and Chinese.

to take over Manchuria. This lauched the new program of expansion into Asia which later (1937) led to a direct attack on China and in 1941 to the attempt to supplant the United States and the Western European powers throughout the whole region of the Western Pacific.

Japan is but a small country and not more than one-fifth of her area can ever be cultivated. Most of this is already being tilled. In consequence Japan is the most densely crowded country in the world, if we measure density by the number of persons per square mile of arable land (Table 17-1). On the average, all her arable land has to carry as dense a population as does the best land in China, India, and Java.

Table 17-1.   Persons per Square Mile of Arable Land, Selected Countries, 1950

Country	Persons per Square Mile	Country	Persons per Square Mile
Canada	98	Union of India	786
Australia	149	Italy	936
United States	293	Belgium	2,155
Spain	459	Switzerland	2,406
Sweden	489	Netherlands	2,395
New Zealand	634	United Kingdom	2,551
France	511	Japan	3,575

Possibilities for Agricultural Expansion in Japan. As has been said, there is little opportunity for the expansion of the agricultural area in Japan proper. Indeed it is highly probable that the use of fairly level land for the expansion of city areas, the establishment of airfields, and the modernizing of main highways will equal or exceed the area that can be added to the tillable land. Moreover, the land yet to be added is of inferior quality. Hence one is justified in saying that Japan has reached the practicable limits of expansion in tillable land. This does not mean that total agricultural yields cannot be somewhat increased as better varieties of rice, fruits, wheat, and so forth, are developed, as more fertilizer is used, and as new crops, or at least crops which are not yet staple, are introduced and accepted as an essential part of the diet of the people. But this addition to the food supply must come quite largely from increased yields per acre in a country where yields are even now far superior to those of other countries in that region. The Japanese are already using excellent varieties of their staple crops. They are familiar with the use of commercial fertilizers; they tend their crops meticulously; they have good agricultural experiment stations and well-organized means for informing the farmers of new and improved crop varieties and better farming practices. Hence the further improvement of yields of the staple crops in Japan will be slow and difficult. To add one-fourth or one-third to the yield of crops which already is high is quite a different matter from adding a similar percentage to the yield of crops which is low or medium as a result of inferior agricultural practices.

The matter of increasing the production per acre of Japanese crops is even more important now than before 1940, since Japan no longer has colonies with which she can trade on highly favorable terms. Moreover, Japanese agriculture has never produced any significant amount of animal food; hence there is no cushion or reserve to be had by substituting a more highly vegetable diet for meat. Actual increase in yields per acre and imports paid for through foreign trade represent the only sources open to Japan at present to add substantially to her food supply. The large postwar increase in Japan's population has been made possible by the heavy food imports provided by the United States outside the regular channels of trade.

It seems to the author that at the present time Japan faces a much more difficult food situation than she did in 1940 both because of her loss of colonies and because of her large growth of population in the home islands. The pressure of population on food in Japan may be expected to mount rapidly in the near future. The Japanese will strive hard to maintain their present low death rate, and even though the birth rate may continue to fall fairly rapidly, they will almost certainly have an 8 to 10 per cent increase per decade for the next two decades *if they can secure a reasonably adequate food supply.*

Trade and Industry in Japan. The importance of trade and industry in Japan has been discussed in Chap. XVI, but it will be in place here to add a little regarding her situation in these respects in the postwar (World War II) period. Japan now finds herself with a rather feeble organization for placing her goods on the world market and up to the fall of 1951 was not allowed to develop any such organization. As of 1952, then, Japan had to start almost from scratch in redeveloping her foreign trade. She is undertaking this task with a factory system badly damaged by the war and handicapped by the lack of the capital necessary to modernize quickly her manufacturing facilities in many lines of industry. She also lacks the credits to purchase the raw materials which must be imported. Nevertheless to feed herself and to secure the raw materials absolutely essential to the revival of her industry she must export large quantities of manufactured goods, and she must give a larger *quid pro quo* than she was accustomed to giving the people in her colonies. In this respect, as already indicated, Japan and the United Kingdom are in much the same situation. They must both have a large foreign trade, and in order to develop and maintain such trade they must meet the most severe competition that has ever existed in this field. The Japanese will find this even more difficult than the British in many respects. On the other hand, they may be able to produce more cheaply than the British because of the lower level of living of their workers. This will in some measure compensate for other disadvantages. But it must be remembered that China and India are also preparing as fast as possible to compete with Japan for Asia's trade.

The situation as regards population growth in postwar Japan and the difficulties she will encounter in reestablishing and expanding her prewar industry and commerce, sketched so briefly above, inevitably raise a question which we must consider with the utmost care. Will the leaders of the Japanese people of 1960, or thereabouts, feel that they must undertake adventures in empire building similar to those undertaken by their predecessors in 1940? It seems not improbable that the hardships of Japanese life will increase during the next decade or two and this condition may exert a powerful pressure on her leaders to provide larger resources. To the author this seems almost certain to happen unless the United Nations makes real progress toward freer access to the world's unused resources than now seems probable, and unless international trade is made much freer than it now is, or unless Japan's population ceases to grow in numbers more rapidly than now appears probable.

It should be obvious to all peoples that modern war does not pay in the sense that they will be better off after the war than before, but it is doubtful whether this fact will deter a nation from going to war in the effort to secure access to larger resources if the people can be led to believe that they are being unjustly deprived of the opportunity to use resources which they might possibly capture by war. In any event we should face squarely the problems encountered by the peoples with meager resources when they are growing in numbers in a world where there are no longer large unclaimed areas but where there are large differentials in rates of growth of population as well as in resources. It is the author's belief that the problems arising out of differential population growth leading to increasingly inadequate resources among certain peoples are going to dominate international relations more and more as time passes and that in no country are they more likely to do so than in Japan.

4. CHINA—POPULATION PRESSURE

The war and the rise to power of the Communists in China have not yet essentially changed the population situation in that country, but the domination of the country by the Communists has made China a far greater immediate threat to peace than it has been in the past.

The population conditions in China can be described but briefly here, and the description must necessarily lack precision. In the first place, we do not know the size of China's population within 50 to 100 million. It may be as small as 350 million, or it may be 450 million or more. The author believes that there is no convincing evidence of any growth in China's population for about a century, except in Manchuria and the neighboring parts of

Inner Mongolia. The reasons for this belief are many and cannot even be enumerated here, let alone discussed convincingly. However, a few of the chief reasons must be mentioned.

The Taiping Rebellion began in South China in 1848 and spread over a vast area, including much of the Yangtze valley. It lasted for about 20 years, and it is often claimed that its direct and indirect effects together caused the death of 50 million people. Its very happening attests the weakness and ineptness of the central government.

All during this past century there have been many severe famines in different parts of China due to drought and flood and political disturbances. The victims of these famines and of the epidemics which always accompanied them must be numbered in the tens of millions. Since the Boxer troubles (around 1900) there has been constant turmoil in much of China, with local "war lords" in control. There has also been a vast amount of intermittent conflict. At times war on a rather large scale took place between the more important war lords. This domestic conflict was somewhat interrupted by the Japanese invasion but, as is well known, was resumed on a grand scale after the Japanese surrender. Now the country appears on the road to unification again by a strong conquering central government.

In addition, during this past century there does not appear to have been any significant improvement in agriculture through the extension of irrigation, the introduction of new and better crop varieties, the reforestation of the hills and mountains, the improvement of farm practices, or any other important development. If anything, within China proper the agricultural area has probably diminished in size because of erosion, rather than grown. Likewise there has been no significant improvement in health conditions except in very small populations in the more favored portions of the Treaty Ports or occasionally in some small rural area.

Under the conditions that have prevailed during the past century it seems more probable to the author that in China the death rate and birth rate have about balanced than that the death rate has fallen substantially below the birth rate as has happened in India in recent decades. It should be emphasized again that we do not know what has happened in China. We can only weigh probabilities and try to arrive at a reasonable conclusion as to changes in population in rather recent times. What has just been said applies only to China proper. In Manchuria there is no doubt about a large increase in population since 1900, perhaps a growth from about 10 million to about 40 million. During much of this time there has been a large emigration from northern China to Manchuria, and because of somewhat better conditions of life on the new lands in Manchuria, the death rate has probably been somewhat lower than in North China while there is no evidence of a decline in the average number of children born per family.

As yet it does not appear that the Communists have done anything to change this situation. In fact it is probable that the postwar years have been more destructive of life than the Japanese invasion. However, from the standpoint of possible population changes in China the potentialities of the Revolution should not be overlooked. For the first time in more than a century it appears that China is on the road to possessing a strong central government. I am not predicting what its actions may be, but with the power it seems to have it can take actions which may have a momentous effect on the growth of population in China. The actions which could be taken quickly would almost certainly reduce the death rate while they would have little or no effect on the birth rate. They would consist of direct health measures and of measures to increase production, both of which would reduce the death rate.

Direct Actions to Reduce the Death Rate. We have now accumulated a great body of knowledge and experience which make possible a reduction of the death rate the like of which has never been known in the past. The experience of the Soviet Union in the reduction of the infant and child death rates even among illiterate peasants through the improvement of sanitation shows that death rates in such groups can be reduced to a relatively low level in a few years. The accomplishment of Ceylon in almost wiping out malaria in two or three years proves what can be done in controlling one of the most destructive diseases in the Far East. The accomplishments of Japan assisted by the Occupation show how a death rate already low for the Orient (about 17 in prewar Japan) can be brought down almost to the level of that in Western countries in three or four years. That the death rate in China, or in any other country in a somewhat similar situation, *can* be thus reduced admits of no question, *if such a reduction is purely a health problem.* Such marvels have been realized and will be realized more frequently in the daily life in different parts of the world. But they must have a sound economic base if they are to be maintained. Will the Chinese Revolution provide this essential economic base?

As the author has indicated in Chap. XV, he is convinced that China can expand her agricultural production very considerably in the next few decades, but the real question to consider is how fast this improvement in agriculture is likely to take place. Will it proceed fast enough not only to provide for the very considerable increase in population which will almost certainly take place when production begins to expand but also to provide for an increase in per capita consumption? No one can answer this question with assurance, but it may be pointed out that there are many well-informed Indians who believe that the considerable agricultural expansion and improvements in India during the past 50 years have brought no increase in per capita consumption but rather a decrease, *i.e.,* that her population has grown faster than her production. But it is a well-established fact that it would not require a very great expenditure of time and money on health to reduce China's death rate so that a natural increase of 20 to 25 per 1,000 per year would ensue if it were merely a problem of controlling the more important causes of death. This would mean, however, that agricultural production would have to increase by 2.0 to 2.5 per cent a year merely to maintain per capita consumption at its present very low level. It is extremely doubtful that such a rate of increase in agricultural production over a period of years can reasonably be hoped for in any country where most of it must come from better yields rather than from the settlement of new and fertile lands. Hence, with no rational expectation of any substantial reduction of China's birth rate during the next two or three decades, it seems highly probable that any increase in agricultural production will be absorbed almost entirely by the increase in population. There may even be a worsening in per capita food consumption if health work is *too successful*, and any worsening of the food situation will almost certainly retard the further decline of the death rate. It might even lead to an increase in it.

Industrial Production. China is probably better supplied with industrial raw materials than Japan. Although according to Western and Soviet standards, China cannot be said to have an abundance of industrial raw materials, except in coal, she has sufficient to permit of a fairly rapid industrial development for some years if other conditions are favorable. However, except for an increasingly strong central government and its great desire to expand industrial production, other conditions are much less favorable to the development of industry in China today than they were in Russia 35 years ago following the 1917 Revolution—capital is scarcer, trained managers and workers are relatively fewer, transportation is far less adequate, and the social organization of China has a far thicker "cake of custom" to be cracked than was the case in Russia in 1917.

Not much more can be said here on this point, but it is worth noting that students of our own economy believe that over the past several decades our average annual rate of increase in *total* production has been about 3 per cent. If this is the best we can do in the United States, one must certainly question seriously whether a country like China can be expected to average half as high a rate for at least two or three decades even under the best conditions imaginable. We do not know what has happened in the Soviet Union, but it does seem reasonably certain that for all its great industrial advances, per capita production is still quite low when compared with that in the more industrialized countries of the West. It does not seem likely that the rate of industrial production in China will add much to the per capita consumption of industrial products during the next two or three decades. As in the Soviet Union a great part of the increase will probably go into capital and armaments for some time to come.

The reader may be wondering what this discussion of China's population and production has to do with the differential increase of nations and its effect on international relations. I will try to be brief. Whatever China's population may be, it is a vast population and because it has a very high birth rate—probably 40 to 45—it will increase rapidly if its death rate can be reduced substantially. A rate of increase of 20 to 25 per 1,000 per year is quite within the bounds of reason, that is, it might easily double within 28 to 35 years. China does not have either the agricultural or industrial resources and organization to support such a rate of increase in numbers in the near future at a rising level of living. Under these conditions, why should we expect that the leaders of China will be more ready to keep their hands off areas that promise to supply new lands and larger resources than were the leaders of Japan after 1905? Furthermore, there is a militancy about communism at present which will almost certainly reinforce the pressure of population as a reason for expanding their territory. We only need to look at the Soviet Union to be convinced of this. But we should not underestimate, as we have in the past, the way in which national leaders can play upon the desire of their peoples to maintain their present level of living and to improve it in order to induce them to support the leaders in the conquest of any seemingly weaker people possessing desirable resources. The pressure of population on resources, when real (and sometimes when not very real), can be rather readily exploited by unscrupulous leaders as we well know. There is no reason to hope that the leaders of the peoples who now have the high potential increases (Group III) will be more scrupulous than Hitler, Mussolini, or Tojo in exploiting population pressure as a reason for the expansion of empire.

5. HOW POPULATION PRESSURE LEADS TO WAR

Population pressure is not an absolute quantity which can be measured by some generally accepted standard such as the number of persons per square mile, or per acre of arable land, or even by some standard measure of poverty. The poorest country is not necessarily the country in which the pressure of population is most likely to lead to efforts at alleviation by the forcible acquisition of new and larger resources. In order for population pressure to become dangerous to peace, the people of a given country must feel this pressure and believe (rightly or wrongly) that something can be done about acquiring larger resources by force. Hence a country may be very densely settled and the people may be desperately poor, but as long as they are not led to believe that there is a possibility of improvement by the conquest of larger resources and as long as they are politically unorganized for aggressive action, they are not likely to disturb the peace of the world. In the author's opinion such a situation prevailed in China until quite recently. When, however, a people comes to feel that it is being kept from lands and resources it really needs by peoples who are not using them or are using them in only a limited way, we have a dangerous situation.

The feeling of population pressure which will lead a people to justify its aggression against another people is no doubt a compound of many attitudes and beliefs which arise from the comparison of its actual economic and political status with that of other peoples. Thus a people may come to feel that it merits a much better economic status than it possesses and may decide to take by force what it feels is its due. All I would urge is that it is the feeling of the pressure of population on resources, however it may have been developed, that leads people to undertake forcible expansion—that poverty by itself is not a sufficient motive for aggression, especially in the modern world where numbers and need count for little against organized military power. The greatest feeling of population pressure probably comes as a consequence of having made some progress in better living and coming to realize that still more progress is possible if only larger resources can be acquired. People who have had a taste of better living are those who will make the greatest—and perhaps one should add, the most unscrupulous—efforts to gain more.

I would not give the impression that I believe the poverty of resources in relation to population is the only cause of war, but I do believe that the economic differences between nations are a source of international friction and that these economic differences in turn often arise out of the changing ratio of population to resources as new differentials in population growth develop.

6. THE WAY OUT

When I first became seriously interested in the changes in population growth as a factor in determining international tensions there were only a little over three-fourths as many people on the earth as there are today. I was convinced then that, if we would honestly face up to the situation that was developing new pressures of population in areas which previously had felt little pressure, we could provide for all peoples an increasing volume of the good things of this world without fighting to determine who should have the lion's share. I was never so unrealistic as to believe we would deliberately undertake to divide the resources of the world more justly, but I hoped that we might make a beginning and that we could thus buy enough time to make it appear worth while to make still greater efforts to render access to the world's resources relatively free to all peoples. I did not expect that we would be able to avoid another war or two brought on by the desire on the part of certain peoples to gain a larger share of the world's resources for themselves. For this I was regarded as a pessimist by many of my friends and especially by those who had had little opportunity to see how the poverty under which the greater part of mankind eked out its existence was resented by the "have-nots" who had begun to enjoy a few of the advantages of better living.

As I look back on my own experience I see that I was too optimistic rather than too pessimistic. I believed two things which led me astray: (1) I believed that men of good will would have more influence in the world than proves to have been the case; and (2) I thought we had more time to work out a solution of the problem of the equitable distribution of the world's resources than has proved to be the case. I did not expect that the population of the world would grow by about one-third in forty years. The two world wars that have taken place during that time and a third which may be in the making have done little or nothing to remove the problem of acquiring adequate resources from the field of military conflict. European imperialism which stood in the way of attempting a humane effort to distribute the world's resources more justly until after World War II is now a dead issue in spite of a few feeble attempts to maintain it. The "white man's burden" is now being replaced by the "Communist's burden," which bids fair to be a much heavier burden on the backs of satellites—but enough of this.

If there is any way in which population pressure can be eliminated as a cause of war, it seems clear now what it must be, namely, the reduction of the rate of population growth through the reduction of the birth rate. There can be no rational hope of providing a world population growing at the rate of about 1 per cent a year with a reasonable abundance of the things needed for a decent life for any considerable period of time. The real question we face today is, will a large part of the world's people continue to breed at a high rate while insisting on reducing their death rates? If so, there can be little doubt that we will continue to fight one another for the necessities and a few of the luxuries of life and thus destroy most of them for everyone. In the long run, as Malthus clearly stated long ago, man must reduce his rate of reproduction if it is not to cause him constant hardship, because his rate of production cannot long proceed apace. Man cannot make use of his knowledge of how to reduce his death rate and fail to reduce his birth rate without suffering the hardships of overpopulation—of pressure of his numbers on the available resources. As long as this is the case he is quite likely to make periodic attempts to secure the larger resources he feels he needs, even though he knows he is taking a long chance. The attempts to improve the ratio of population and resources by acquiring larger resources to match growing populations will quite naturally come from those countries and areas where population is growing fastest in relation to resources, i.e., the ratio of population to resources is probably worsening most rapidly. In general these are the countries which are now coming into a period of relatively rapid population growth.

Suggestions for Supplementary Reading

ANGELL, NORMAN: *The Great Illusion, 1933,* 308 pp., Pt. 3, "The Verdict of the Events," G. P. Putnam's Sons, New York, 1933.

————: *Raw Materials, Population Pressure and War,* 46 pp., World Peace Foundation, New York, 1936. (World Affairs Books, No. 14.)

BAIN, H. FOSTER: *Ores and Industry in the Far East,* 288 pp., Council on Foreign Relations, Inc., New York, 1933.

DAVIS, KINGSLEY: *The Population of India and Pakistan,* 263 pp., Princeton University Press, Princeton, N.J., 1951.

DUTCHER, GEORGE MATTHEW: *The Political Awakening of the East. Studies of Political Progress in Egypt, India, China, Japan, and the Philippines,* 371 pp., Abingdon Press, New York, 1925.

EAST, EDWARD M.: *Mankind at the Crossroads,* 360 pp., Charles Scribner's Sons, New York, 1923.

International Labour Office: *Social Policy in Dependent Territories,* 185 pp., International Labour Office, Montreal, 1944.

MUKERJEE, RADHAKAMAL: *Races, Lands, and Food: A Program for World Subsistence,* 107 pp., The Dryden Press, Inc., New York, 1946.

MYRDAL, ALVA, and PAUL VINCENT: *Are There Too Many People?* 48 pp., Manhattan Publishing Company, New York, 1950. (UNESCO Project—Food and People.)

PENROSE, E. F.: *Population Theories and Their Application with Special Reference to Japan,* 347 pp., Food Research Institute, Stanford University, Stanford, Calif., 1934.

SEMPLE, ELLEN CHURCHILL: "Japanese Colonial Methods," *Bull. Am. Geog. Soc.,* Vol. 45, pp. 255–275, 1913.

THOMPSON, WARREN S.: *Danger Spots in World Population,* 343 pp., Alfred A. Knopf, Inc., New York, 1929.

————: *Population and Peace in the Pacific,* 397 pp., University of Chicago Press, Chicago, 1946.

————: "Population Growth and Control in Relation to World Peace," *Yale Law J.,* Vol. 55, No. 5, pp. 1242–1257, 1946.

Chapter XVIII

THE FUTURE GROWTH OF POPULATION
IN THE UNITED STATES AND SOME
OF ITS CONSEQUENCES

The probable future growth of population in any nation is of interest to its people for many reasons. Obviously any long-time plans for national development will be more realistic if they are based on estimates of future changes in the size of the population made in the light of the best information available rather than being based on mere guesses. This also holds as regards the different communities within the nation which must plan their own public works. If certain characteristics of the population can also be foreseen with reasonable accuracy this is an additional advantage of considerable value.

The need for population projections can be seen most clearly when concrete problems arise for consideration, *e.g.*, in planning to meet our transportation and communication needs in the nation, in the several states, and in local communities, there *must* be some projection of the number of persons in different areas likely to make use of the different means of transportation and communication as well as estimates of the changing per capita needs. I am not saying that accurate projections of population can be made for any or all of these different areas needing them for any considerable future period, but only that projections taking into account the best information available regarding all the aspects of population change which are of importance to the community are more likely to be helpful in planning for future needs than mere guesses or the mere extension of past trends.

One cannot mention any type of planning for the future development of a nation or a community that does not involve, either directly or indirectly, some assumptions regarding the size of the future population similar to those needed in planning transportation and communication, and many plans depend upon estimates of the population having certain characteristics as *e.g.*, age and sex (Chap. VI). Local communities must plan how the services and utilities in daily use can be kept adequate to the needs of the community, how industrial and residential areas are to be developed, and where schools are to be located; in a hundred other ways they must try to foresee the problems which will arise as population grows or declines in number and changes in character if they are to avoid unnecessary waste and confusion. Without the best estimates possible regarding the number and the kind of people who will be affected by these different services some very serious and costly mistakes are sure to be made which might have been avoided by more careful study of population changes in the area concerned. It should be realized, however, that, in general, the errors in projection are likely to increase as the size of the population decreases, as the projections are extended in time, and as they are made more specific as regards the characteristics of the group. Such errors are inherent in the nature of population growth, on the one hand, and in the changes in economic organization and activity, on the other.

Changes in the size of the population in any specified area arise from differences between birth rates and death rates and from variations in the net amounts of in- and out-migration. Birth rates, death rates, and migration are closely related causally to social and economic changes and in turn are the causes of many changes in the characteristics of a population, since the social and economic conditions determining both natural increase and net migration may vary rather considerably between localities and regions within a country. Even when there is but little change in the population of the nation as a whole there may very well be rather wide local fluctuations in population growth and rather rapid changes in the composition of local populations.

The greater variations in the growth of a portion of the United States than in the nation may be illustrated by showing how one region—the Pacific states—has grown in comparison with the United States during the past half century. The examination of the data in Table 18-1 shows that rather powerful local forces must have operated to effect such differences in ratios of regional growth to national growth from decade to decade. The Pacific states have grown much more rapidly than the remainder of the country during their entire period of settlement, but when the nation was still growing fairly rapidly (21.0 per cent) in the first decade of this century, the rate in the Pacific states bore a ratio of 3.5 to the national rate (unity) as it did again in the 1940 to 1950 period when the national growth was 14.5 per cent. However, when the national rate declined during the decade of World War I, at a time when our manufacturing was still highly concentrated in the Northeast and along the Great Lakes, the ratio of growth in the Pacific states to that of the nation was only 2.2. This was also the ratio when the national rate of growth fell rather precipitately during the 1930's. In the last decade when the national rate of growth rose to twice its 1930 to 1940 level the rate of growth in the Pacific states rose to 2.6 times its own 1930 to 1940 rate and as already noted bore a ratio of 3.4 to the national rate. Thus it appears that while the growth of the Pacific states has by no means been independent of the national rate of growth, it seems to have had a somewhat different rhythm from the country as a whole. It appears that the conditions

Table 18-1.   The Rate of Increase of the Population of the United States
Compared with That of the Pacific States, 1900 to 1950

Decade	Rate of increase of population, per cent		Ratio of national rate of increase to rate of Pacific states
	United States	Pacific states	
1940–1950	14.5	48.8	1 :3.37
1930–1940	7.2	18.8	1 :2.22
1920–1930	16.1	47.2	1 :2.93
1910–1920	14.9	32.8	1 :2.20
1900–1910	21.0	73.5	1 :3.50

which led to a rather slow growth of population in the United States (as compared to past decades) led to an even slower relative growth in the Pacific states, while those which led to a relatively rapid growth in the United States were even more stimulating to growth on the Pacific Coast. Such variations are even larger in smaller areas within regions.

1. THE FUTURE POPULATION OF THE UNITED STATES

Estimates of the future population of the United States have taken several forms which may be described roughly as (1) guesses, usually based on a rather simple extrapolation of past percentage trends; (2) mathematical formulas, estimates arrived at after a careful study of trends and the embodiment of these trends in some mathematical formula which was believed to describe a general pattern of population growth, e.g., the logistic curve as used by Pearl and Reed; (3) empirical methods of projection, which sometimes used trends in the components of population change such as birth rates and death rates to calculate probable future changes in the size of given cohorts and modified such changes by those which would occur if the number of immigrants attained a given level. When this method was used it also yielded age and sex projections because it started with actual age and sex cohorts, e.g., the empirical method as used by Whelpton and Thompson. In many local projections a variety of empirical methods have been used. Natural-increase figures are the basis for most of them, but many ingenious ways of estimating migration changes have also been employed—changes in school attendance, changes in number of water, gas and electric users (number of meters), number of building permits issued, number of auto licenses issued, and other changes which are believed to be more or less closely associated with changes in the number or the composition of the people in the area involved. This matter of methods involved in making population projections cannot be pursued here, nor will space permit of any discussion

Table 18-2. Estimates of the Future Population of the United States,
1920 to 1980
(In thousands)

Year	Whelpton estimate of 1928[1]	Thompson & Whelpton		Whelpton estimate of 1947[4]		Pearl & Reed estimate of 1920[5]	Census
		Estimate of 1933[2]	Estimate of 1943[3]	With no immigration	With immigration		
1980	. . . .	155,200	165,358	. . . .	. . . .	174,941	
1970	171,460	153,800	160,494	160,604	163,656	167,945	
1960	162,670	149,800	153,355	154,093	155,801	159,230	
1950	151,620	142,900	144,396	146,259	146,759	148,678	150,697
1940	138,250	133,100	132,532[6]	132,532[6]	132,532[6]	136,318	131,669
1930	123,600	122,800	. . . .	. . . .	. . . .	122,397	122,775
1920	106,290	. . . .	. . . .	. . . .	. . . .	107,394	105,711

[1] P. K. Whelpton, "Population in the United States, 1925–1975," *Am. J. Soc.*, Vol. 34, p. 266, 1928.
[2] Warren S. Thompson and P. K. Whelpton, *Population Trends in the United States*, pp. 316–317, McGraw-Hill Book Company, Inc., New York, 1933. Based on medium birth rates, expectation of life, and immigration. This was the projection preferred by the writer at the time it was made. The fact that there was practically no immigration during the 1930's would have reduced the 1940 population a little.
[3] Warren S. Thompson and P. K. Whelpton, *Estimates of Future Population of the United States, 1940–2000*, p. 74, National Resources Planning Board, 1943.
[4] P. K. Whelpton, *Forecasts of the Population of the United States, 1945–1975*, pp. 76, 80, Bureau of the Census, G.P.O., Washington, D.C., 1947.
[5] Raymond Pearl and Lowell J. Reed, "On the Rate of Growth of the Population of the United States since 1790 and Its Mathematical Representation," *Proc. Nat. Acad. Sci.*, Vol. 6, pp. 275–288, 1920.
[6] Census population plus an allowance for underenumeration.

of local or community projections. Our brief discussion in what follows will therefore relate only to the United States as a whole.[1]

It will be noted at once that all the projections for the United States shown in Table 18-2 are significantly in error at some point when they relate to a time 10 or more years away from the date on which they were made. They agree, however, in showing a decline in rate of growth with a virtual cessa-

[1] Raymond Pearl and Lowell J. Reed, "On the Rate of Growth of the Population of the United States since 1790 and Its Mathematical Representation," *Proc. Nat. Acad. Sci.*, Vol. 6, pp. 275–288, 1920; Warren S. Thompson and P. K. Whelpton, *Population Trends in the United States,* Chap. 10, McGraw-Hill Book Company, Inc., New York, 1933; also *Estimates of Future Population of the United States, 1940–2000,* National Resources Planning Board, G.P.O., Washington, D.C., 1937; P. K. Whelpton, *Forecasts of the Population of the United States, 1945–1975,* G.P.O., Washington, D.C., 1947. (U.S. Bureau of the Census.)

tion at varying times toward the end of this century. The differences between the results of using the logistic curve and the cohort methods tended to increase with the passage of time, the logistic curve giving the larger population except for Whelpton's 1928 projection [2] which he himself ceased to use after later projections were made and to which he did not return even when making his 1947 projections. The fact is that estimating the population of the United States for more than a few years ahead has not been highly successful, but these estimates have served to introduce an element of reasonableness into projection making which was sadly lacking in earlier years.

The chief reason for the rather substantial errors in the projections for particular years based on the empirical cohort method of projecting trends for the components in population growth has proved to be the rapid rate at which the birth rate can change—the very rapid decline for several years preceding 1934, the surprising (to the author) recovery in the 1940's during the war, and the maintenance of the expected postwar recovery for a longer period than that following World War I. Whelpton's 1928 projections were considerably in error in 1940 because the decline of the birth rate during the depression was greater than the trend indicated at the time these projections were made. That they came very close to the actual population in 1950 was due to the fact that the rise in the number of births after 1940 compensated for most of the deficit of 1930 to 1940. In the 1933 projections, in which the author participated, too much weight was given to the short-time change (downward) in birth rates, i.e., the short-time fluctuation was treated as though it were a trend. In the 1943 projections this rapid downward movement in birth rates was still given too much weight as was also the case in Whelpton's 1947 projections. The longer-time projections made before the rather violent fluctuations in the birth rate after 1930 may prove to be more accurate, although it now appears likely that both Whelpton's 1928 and Pearl and Reed's 1920 projections for 1960 and 1970 will be substantially too low. However, it seems to the author that there is now some danger that, in shying away from past projections as being too low, new projections that are too high may again become current as was quite common before 1930. But after all, projecting total population is only one aspect of population projections. Important as it is to secure the best projections possible for the total population of the nation (or of any given area), it is probable that the changes in age are of even more importance from the practical standpoint of planning for the better living of the population. Consequently much of our discussion here will be devoted to future changes in age composition.

[2] P. K. Whelpton, "Population in the United States, 1925–1975," *Am. J. Soc.*, Vol. 34, pp. 253–270, 1928.

2. PROBABLE CHANGES IN AGE STRUCTURE IN OUR FUTURE POPULATION

The discussion of mortality (Chap. XI) made it clear that there could be a considerable measure of certainty in estimating the future size of some age groups because we know the age-specific death rates and we know the limits within which they are likely to move during the next two or three decades. On the other hand, during the period since 1930 we have had a good example of the way in which the birth rate may fluctuate (Chap. VIII) over relatively short periods of time. Consequently we are well aware today of the large element of uncertainty in projecting future births and hence the number of persons not yet born that are likely to be found in the population (at the younger ages) during the next several years.

The Age Group under Twenty. None of the persons of this age at the beginning of 1975 will be born until 1955. Hence, there is necessarily chance for a large margin of error in estimating the size of this group between now and 1975. In the rough calculations the author has made for this chapter (Table 18-3) he has assumed a rather rapid decline in the number of births between 1952 and 1960 to 1964. He has done this for several reasons but

Table 18-3. Future Population of the United States by Age, 1950 to 1975
(In thousands)

Age	1950		1955		1960		1965		1970		1975	
	Number	Per cent	Number	Per cent	Number	Per cent	Number	Per cent	Number	Per cent	Number	Per cent
Births [1]	18,465		16,500		15,300		16,500		17,700			
0–4 [2]....	16,164	10.7	16,715	10.4	15,000	8.6	13,953	7.8	15,077	8.1	16,206	8.3
5–19...	34,935	23.2	42,031	26.0	48,414	27.6	51,086	28.7	48,614	26.0	46,925	24.0
20–44..	56,691	37.6	56,998	35.3	57,554	33.7	59,762	33.5	65,572	35.1	72,362	36.8
45–64..	30,637	20.3	32,638	20.2	35,370	20.7	38,021	21.3	40,778	21.8	42,155	21.5
65 and over..	12,270	8.1	13,079	8.1	14,197	8.3	15,536	8.7	16,932	9.1	18,734	9.5
Total.	150,697	100.0	161,461	100.0	170,535	100.0	178,358	100.0	186,973	100.0	196,382	100.0

[1] Births for the five-year period beginning in the year indicated.
[2] The population in the 0–4 age period is obtained by applying a survival rate to the number of births in the preceding five-year period and then reducing this number by 6.1 per cent to allow for underenumeration in the 0–4 age group by the census.

principally because the small number of children born during the depression are now coming to marriageable age and will be having a large part of their children during the next 12 to 15 years. By the middle 1960's, on the other hand, the increase in number of children born after 1940 to 1941 will raise appreciably the number of marriages and the number of births, and by 1968 to 1970 the very large increase in births since 1946 would normally lead to further large increases in number of marriages and births. This projection of the number of births assumes that there will be no such violent fluctuation in economic conditions as we have had since 1929 but that there will be a substantial decline in age-specific birth rates from those which have prevailed since the war, which were enhanced at the younger ages by many earlier marriages and at ages over twenty-five and thirty were raised by marriages and births which had been postponed during the depression.

The group under twenty years of age constituted 33.9 per cent of the total population in 1950. On the assumptions made here, this will only decline to 32.3 per cent by 1975. (This decline is less than I had previously thought probable.) With the number of births used here the number of persons of these ages will increase from 51.1 million (1950) to about 63 million in 1975, an increase of over one-fifth. Since the sex composition in this group in 1975 is almost entirely determined by death rates and sex ratio at birth, the males will outnumber the females by about 4 per cent. Because of differential errors in reporting age to the census the sex ratio at the census may be somewhat different.

On the basis of the number of births used here, children under five years of age will decline proportionally from 10.7 per cent of the total population in 1950 to about 8.0 or 8.5 per cent in 1975, and those from five to nine will decline from 8.8 per cent to about 8.2 per cent, while those from ten to fourteen will remain at about 7.4 per cent and those from fifteen to nineteen will increase by about one percentage point. Part of the increase in the fifteen to nineteen age class as projected will be due to the fact that it loses none through the misreporting of ages, since it is a calculated group, not a census group.

The two most probable general changes in the age group under twenty are the large increase from about 51.1 million in 1950 to about 63.0 million in 1975, and the decrease of about 2 percentage points in the proportion of the total population found in this age group. If such a change were to take place at a uniform rate throughout the period it would attract little attention and would not create any very serious problems of adjustment beyond those now confronting us in providing schools, playgrounds, and adequate housing for the largely increased number of families and children since 1940. However, for reasons already explained, even assuming no great catastrophe (depression or war) it appears probable that in 1955 there will be about 58.7 million in this group out of a total population of about 161.5 million. Thus they would amount to about 36.4 per cent of the population. After that the number would rise to about 65.0 million in 1965 in a total population of 178.3 million, while the percentage would be practically unchanged (36.5). It would then decline to 63.1 million in 1975, or to 32.3 per cent of the population, which would number approximately 196.0 million. Even if the number of births used here is too high, their distribution over this period is likely to follow the pattern indicated here, with a fairly rapid increase of persons in this age group in the next dozen years and then a decline of around 2 million by 1975.

We are already feeling the effects of the increase in number of children in several ways. The number entering school is increasing, and this increase will continue up to 1958 even if the number of births should fall off more rapidly in the next several years than indicated here. In 1960 there will be about 48 million children aged five to nineteen as compared with 34.9 million in 1950, an increase well over one-third. Most of the children of these ages will be in school.

Such an increase in the number of children will require increasing expenditures for all the goods and services needed by them, in addition to the expanded educational facilities. Moreover, the considerable variation both in proportion and number of persons under twenty years of age will neccessitate rather large adjustments in the industries supplying children's goods, although if times continue prosperous the smaller number of children toward the end of this period might have little effect on the increase in demand for such goods because of the rising level of living. The chief problem the changes in the number and proportion of persons in this age group will impose on us would seem to be those related to furnishing adequate educational and recreational facilities and new housing. The net effect of a relatively large child population on the general economy should be somewhat stabilizing. People are quite likely to cut into savings more quickly where the welfare of their children is at stake than where only the expenditures for themselves are concerned. Moreover, public action to ensure child welfare can also be expected to be less affected by economic changes than action affecting chiefly the welfare of adults. Finally, the consumption expenditures for children fall more largely in the class of necessities than do those of the total population; hence it seems reasonable to assume that an increase in the proportion of children or even a relatively stable proportion of children should work toward stabilizing production. The larger the proportion of our total consumption classed as "necessities" for children, the less variable is the total production likely to be.

The Twenty to Forty-four Age Group. Since the only estimates of births involved in projecting this age group between now and 1975 are for the years 1953 and 1954, there should not be any very considerable error in calculating the number of persons in this group during this period. Even if the number of births in these two years declines somewhat more than estimated, the size of the group as a whole will not be affected greatly. The increase in numbers should be from about 56.7 million (counted) in 1950 to about 72.4 million (calculated) in 1975. This would be a growth of about 28 per cent. Because of the larger number of births since about 1940 there would be only a small decline, if any, in the proportion of the population in this group during the period being considered—from 37.6 per cent in 1950 to 36.8 per cent or a little less in 1975. A depression which would substantially reduce the number of births during the next two years would, of course, reduce in the same degree the size of the age class twenty to forty-four in 1975.

In making comparisons between age groups in 1950 and 1975 it should be remembered that there are always errors in reporting age at any census which are perpetuated in the calculated population starting from that count. Hence, the calculated population aged twenty to forty-four in 1975 contains the errors in the age group under twenty years in the 1950 census plus those in estimating the under five age group in 1955, while the twenty to forty-four group in 1950 contains those errors peculiar to it as a census age class. The errors in these two groups are not the same. For this reason not too much weight should be attached to small differences in the size or the proportion of two groups of the same age at two different dates when one is a census group and the other a calculated group. The decrease in the proportion of the twenty to forty-four age group from 37.6 per cent in 1950 to 36.8 per cent in 1975 may or may not be real, but the increase from about 56 million to about 72 million is fairly firm, assuming no great unforeseen catastrophe. Although it seemed desirable to call attention to the fact that a calculated population of a given age for a later date is not directly comparable with a census group of the same age, it is doubtful whether the differences are large enough to nullify any conclusions we may draw as to probable age and sex changes between 1950 and 1975.

As has just been noted, any change in the proportion of the total population in the twenty to forty-four age group is likely to be small between 1950 and 1975 but may be either upward or downward. Hence there will be little proportional change in the most vigorous portion of our labor force during the next 25 years. However, because of the large number of births since 1940 there will be a large increase in the number of persons and especially in those aged twenty to twenty-nine who were born in 1945 to 1954, from about 23.7 million in 1950 to 35.8 million in 1975. This should lead to a very large increase in number of new families after 1965 as well as to a rapid increase in the labor force, although between now and 1965 the number of persons aged twenty to twenty-nine will grow relatively slowly because of the small number of births during the 1930's.

The Forty-four to Sixty-four Age Group. In 1950 there were approximately 30.6 million people of middle age (forty-five to sixty-four) and they constituted 20.3 per cent of the total population. By 1975 there will be about 42.2 million in this age group and they will comprise 21.5 per cent of the total population if the number of births estimated here is approximately correct. With a smaller number of births the proportion of middle-aged persons will be somewhat larger. The major part of the increase will occur in the fifty-five to sixty-four age class, this group growing by 48.4 per cent as compared with 29.3 per cent for the age group forty-five to fifty-four. The increase in this group as a whole will approximate 38 per cent, while the proportional increase will be only 1.4 percentage points. Here, too, there is some distortion of age for the reasons noted in the preceding section. This renders comparisons between the 1950 census population forty-five to sixty-four and the 1975 calculated population less exact than could be desired. Taking the figures as they are in 1950 and projecting them to 1975, we find that the number of males will increase from 15.3 million in 1950 to 20.5 million in 1975, or by about 34 per cent, while the number of females will increase from 15.3 to 21.7 million, or by about 42 per cent. Whereas females of these ages constituted 20.2 per cent of all females in 1950, they will constitute 22.1 per cent in the projected population of 1975 and males forty-five to sixty-four will rise only from 20.5 per cent of all males in 1950 to 20.8 per cent in 1975. Because of the lower death rates of females, the larger proportional increase as well as the larger absolute increase of females is in the direction to be expected. The increase in proportion in this age group while significant is not large, but the rate of growth is high. The increase in the population aged fifty-five to sixty-four (48.4 per cent) is, perhaps, the most significant change in this group, although the excess of females amounting to almost 6 per cent in 1975 is also of much importance.

There can be no reasonable doubt that the proportion of middle-aged persons as well as their number will increase substantially by 1975. There are, however, certain factors which may have a modifying effect on the proportional increase in this group as regards its productivity. In the first place, the general improvement in health which has taken place in the past 30 years should leave a great many of the members of this middle-aged group in better shape physically than the people now of these ages who did not enjoy such good living conditions in their childhood and youth. Then, too, the continuing mechanization of many of the heavier jobs in industry and farming should materially add to the productivity of these older workers. Finally, it is now realized as never before that there is need for retraining many middle-aged workers in the new processes being constantly developed so that they may retain their productivity to a later age. Because of these conditions it would seem to the author reasonable to expect that, even in spite of the proportional increase in the middle-aged workers and especially in those fifty-five to sixty-four, there not only would be little or no decrease in their per capita productivity but perhaps even an increase. It would also seem reasonable to expect a rather considerable increase in the number of women over forty-five working outside the home if they marry younger, raise relatively small families, and find that they are still vigorous enough to meet the requirements of many kinds of light manufacturing, sales, and office tasks. It may be, however, that the larger increase in women workers outside the home will come in the preceding age group, namely, in their thirties and early forties, after their children are old enough to go to school. But even if this is the case many of these women will continue to work, if jobs are available, until later middle age.

The Sixty-five and Over Age Group. On the assumptions made above regarding births and survival rates, there would be approximately 18.7 million persons aged sixty-five and over in 1975 as compared with 12.3 million enumerated in 1950, and they would constitute 9.5 per cent of the entire population as compared with 8.1 per cent in 1950. The increase will probably be greater than that indicated by these figures, since the 1950 enumeration contains errors of inclusion in this age class through the intentional reporting of an age in excess of one's actual age in 1950, or earlier, in order to gain pension or social security benefits. The 1975 projections, on the other hand, carry forward only the age distortions of the population forty years of age and over in 1950, and comparatively few of the people sixty-five and over in 1950 will be alive in 1975 to perpetuate the errors in their ages. In any event there will be a substantial increase in the proportion of old people in the population, amounting to at least 1.4 percentage points and an increase in numbers of about one-half. It may also be noted that the proportion of elderly females will increase (8.5 per cent in 1950 and 10.5 per cent in 1975) appreciably faster than that of males (7.7 per cent in 1950 and 8.6 per cent in 1975) because, disregarding differences in age errors, females of these ages continue to have lower age-specific death rates than males just as they had at younger ages.

The economic consequences of a large increase in the sixty-five and over age group will certainly be highly important. It is obvious that an average increase of 2.0 per cent a year in the number of old people will require far greater expenditures on pensions, on medical and hospital care, on homes for the aged, and on all other goods and services needed by old people than we have been accustomed to in the past. How this increase in older people will affect national productivity it is very difficult to say. The same health considerations which may help to make better workers out of persons in later middle age (fifty-five to sixty-four) will also extend to old people, so that the amount of assistance required by old people from the community may not increase as fast as their numbers. Moreover, there is a growing feeling on the part of many old people, and many others as well, that retirement should not be dependent on age alone but that ability and desire to do useful work should be taken into account. There is also increasing discussion of part-time work and adjustment of jobs to the capacities of older people which, if put into effect in a large way, might very well enable many of them to remain self-supporting for several years beyond sixty-five. But even when these possible adjustments intended to lengthen working life are taken into account, there is no reasonable doubt that the nation must expect a very substantial increase in expenditure for aid to the aged, and in the opinion of the author this will also figure out at an increase in the proportion of the national income that will be devoted to this use. We are becoming an older people and must face this fact.

Although the author is disposed to believe that the aging of the population will have comparatively little direct depressing effect on the per capita productivity of workers during the next 25 years, he does believe that it may have some indirect effects which may be harmful.

The older established workers will almost certainly try to keep the better jobs for themselves and to monopolize skilled work, if it appears at all likely that there will be a scarcity of such jobs. Already many labor-union rules and regulations are designed to ensure the better jobs to the older men now holding them. These older workers are coming to feel that they have a right to a privileged position. This might become a matter of considerable importance in determining the level of labor productivity, since it might result in increasing opposition by the older workers to the spread of more efficient techniques. It would not be surprising if they were less inclined than the younger men to learn new techniques and to take their chances on getting a fair share of the increased product that better methods will produce.

Again it is quite generally recognized that the control of property rests largely in the hands of people above fifty. The accumulation of property is relatively slow during the early years of adult life, even in those classes which ultimately do accumulate appreciable amounts; hence the rapid increase in the numbers and in the proportion of old people will probably tend to increase the economic power of this age group through this increasing control of property. Moreover, it is probable that a larger proportion of old people now have significant property holdings than when the number of children in the family was larger. Just because of fewer children a larger part of the families with appreciable savings could save more for investment and their estates are less frequently broken up into small parts at death. However, the accumulation of property by those who depend largely on savings is clearly undergoing considerable modification with the recent changes in tax laws. But in spite of this it seems probable that the older people of the upper middle class and the wealthy class are acquiring more and more control over our economic life through their possession of an increasing proportion of our property.

Another significant aspect of this increasing economic control of older people arises from the very common practice among men whose property accumulations are modest (say $100,000 and under) of leaving the entire estate, or a large part of it, to the widow. Since widows are from two to three times as numerous as widowers at all ages over forty-five, there can be no doubt that older women are steadily coming into the possession of an increasing portion of the nation's property.

Under these conditions it would seem only reasonable to expect that investment and the direction of economic enterprise would tend to assume patterns calculated to assure the comfort and stability of life of these older people for the few years remaining to them. Thus investment policies may also strengthen the basically conservative tendencies of private capitalistic economy. On the other hand, the increased urge for security in investment might possibly give our economy a strong push in the direction of state capitalism. This could happen if there were a growing feeling that government bonds offered greater security than the bonds and stocks of private business enterprises, a feeling which grew rapidly during the depression of the 1930's.

3. SOME ECONOMIC PROBLEMS RELATED TO POPULATION GROWTH

Changes in Rate of Population Growth. At any given level of living a slower rate of population growth means a slower increase in the demand for the goods customarily consumed at that level. When population increased at only about 0.70 per cent per year (1930 to 1940) the rate of increase in the amount of goods needed to support the increase at a fixed level of living was obviously only about one-half as much as was needed to support the population growth of 1940 to 1950, about 1.40 per cent per year. Likewise the rate of increase in capital needed to provide for the 1930 to 1940 increase in population would not have been more than one-half that needed in the decade 1940 to 1950. This difference alone would have had an important effect on the general level of economic activity in the two decades, other things being equal. But whether or not the relatively slow growth in numbers between 1930 and 1940, which began in the later 1920's, played a causal role in reducing economic activity during that decade, and if it did, how important a cause it was, the fact is that the slow growth of population was a significant factor in leading to much discussion of a "saturated" economy, of a "lack of economic opportunity," or of a "stagnation of enterprise." The possibility that we no longer needed a rapidly expanding economy because of slow population growth without doubt reacted very strongly on the willingness of businessmen to employ more labor and expand their activities, and this in turn depressed the marriage rate and the birth rate and thus reduced still more the rate of population increase.

I am not suggesting that a relatively slow rate of population growth necessarily leads to economic stagnation, but I am suggesting that it may be an important factor in the minds of businessmen when they see the number of new customers increasing more slowly than has been customary and are powerless, through their individual actions, to improve the purchasing power of their existing customers. This seems a reasonable conclusion, although there is no inevitable causal connection between these two phenomena. My personal belief is that even with a stationary population there can very well be a thriving and expanding economy, but I also believe that as long as we tend to associate a growth in numbers with economic expansion this association is itself an important psychological element in determining the vigor of enterprise. But in addition to the psychological factors involved in adjusting the economy to a more slowly growing population, there are other more tangible difficulties of a very formidable character involved in this adjustment.

Better Customers. The main difficulty in adjusting the economy to a slower growth of population so that it will operate steadily at a high and increasing level of efficiency seems to me to lie in learning how to make better customers out of a population expanding more slowly than it has been in the past. Over a period of time the pattern of distribution of the national product tends to become adjusted to the expansion of the population, to the rise in the level of living, and to the need for capital investment. As a consequence any sudden or rapid change in the need for goods arising from a change in any of these claims on the national product is highly disturbing to the steady operation of the economy and therefore to its efficient operation. It is not an easy matter either to arrange for the rapid absorption of a larger portion of a national product which is increasing at a given rate by a population growing more slowly, *i.e.*, to increase per capita consumption more rapidly than it has been increasing, or to turn more of this national product into capital goods if that is needed. Production tends to become specific— wheat, beef, carpets and rugs, houses, machine tools, etc.—and cannot be shifted from one type of goods to another without considerable friction and delay. It is not easy to make sufficiently better customers out of 130 million people so that they will keep the economic machinery as well employed as 140 million if the change in rate of growth takes place too quickly. It is not that the 130 million could not use as large a total production as 140 million would have used, but that (1) they would not be the same goods, and (2) for them to use the same total would involve a much more rapid change in the incomes of certain groups than in those of others and also a shift in the proportion of all products being used for capital and consumption, and there is no economic machinery to effect such a change without considerable delay and friction.

It should also be noted that when we speak of the increased efficiency of our economy we mean an increase in the productivity of a given unit of labor and capital as well as in our total production. If the increase in total production amounts to an average annual rate of about 3 per cent, as seems to have been the case for the past half century, it means that we have about this much more to distribute, on the average, each year than in the preceding year. If population is also growing at a rate of 3 per cent a year these two will just balance and there probably will be a very slow change, if any, in the general level of living and in the shares being used for capital and for consumption. The situation in this country for the century and one-half preceding 1860 might be considered illustrative of what would happen under these conditions. Total production may have been growing somewhat more rapidly than population, but the difference was not great and there was but a slow improvement in the level of living for the great majority of the people. When population began to grow more slowly than production there was a larger volume of goods per capita available, and this could be used to increase the level of living and/or to add to the capital stock. No doubt some of the additional goods was used in both ways. If the change in the ratio of population to production were quite slow, *i.e.*, if the per capita increase in production were quite slow, the adjustments in the distribution of the national income needed to maintain the customary level of economic activity would be likely to be made almost without awareness that they were being made; but if the change in per capita productivity came more rapidly, both because of increase in efficiency and because of a slower population growth, the problem of the proper distribution of the increased per capita product would be more acute. Up to the present time we have found no way to determine what the proper distribution of the per capita increase would be. By "proper" here is meant that distribution of the goods produced which would maintain a given level of economic activity, the *desirable* given level being full employment as currently defined. But even if we knew what the proper distribution of the increased per capita product was, *e.g.*, if we knew that two-thirds of any per capita increase should be used to increase consumption and one-third for additions to capital, we have no economic machinery to accomplish this redistribution. Furthermore we do not know how the shares going to consumption on the one hand and to industries for capital on the other should be distributed to different industries. A free economy is assumed to accomplish all this automatically, but it obviously does not or we would not have had the two very severe and prolonged depressions, 1892 to 1898 and 1929 to 1938, to say nothing of several of lesser severity and duration in the past 60 years. The fact is that the increase in per capita production which takes place in a progressive and expanding modern economy is distributed in accordance with the power which can be wielded by the different groups taking part in economic activities, and the idea of the "general welfare" plays little part in this scramble to secure the benefits of a more productive economy.

The reader may be asking what all this has to do with a more rapidly or less rapidly increasing population. The point I would make is that a change in the rate of population growth, if it is rather sudden, if it is downward, and if it comes at a time when the per capita productivity of the economy as a whole is increasing, is almost certain to disturb the equilibrium of the system severely and may be a rather significant element in prolonging if not in causing a depression. The more sudden the transition to a slower growth of population the more quickly the readjustment of the shares allotted to consumption and production must be made, and hence the less likely it is that such a shift in shares will be adequate to prevent a decline in economic activity.

A fairly sudden increase in the rate of population growth, on the other hand, is a stimulus to economic activity because it immediately increases the need for customary goods and thus calls forth the latent power to produce such goods already available and also encourages new investment. The point we are concerned with here is that slower population growth tends to aggravate any disturbance to the economy arising from oversaving, *i.e.,* placing too large a proportion of the national income in the hands of the savers, and if it comes rather suddenly at a time when over-all efficiency is increasing, it adds to the difficulty of effecting a satisfactory relation between the shares of the national product allotted to consumption and production.

It follows from the above analysis that wages and salaries and farmers' incomes should not only increase in total amount but should, if efficiency in the use of capital is increasing, also be an increasing proportion of the national income. Moreover, per capita income in these groups should increase even faster at a time when population growth becomes suddenly slower than at times of normal growth. Unfortunately, at times of relatively slow population growth these groups are in the least favorable position to secure per capita increases in income because of growing unemployment and falling prices. Again we do not know how much of the increase in the proportion of the national income should be allotted to consumers, but it should certainly be more when population is increasing slowly than when it is increasing at a normal rate, if the economy as a whole is to be kept at a high level of efficiency.

It may be of some interest to look at the facts of population growth and investment during the 1920's to illustrate how slower population growth may affect economic activity.

In the five years and three months from Jan. 1, 1920, to Apr. 1, 1925, there were 14,966,000 births and 7,179,000 deaths in the United States and net immigration amounted to 2,061,000. Thus the net increase in population in that period was approximately 9,848,000. In the five years from Apr. 1, 1925, to Apr. 1, 1930, the number of births (13,355,000) declined by over 1.5 million and the number of deaths (7,271,000) rose by about 100,000 while the net immigration declined by about 750,000. The net increase in population during this period (1925 to 1929) was, therefore, only 7,385,000, or somewhat less than three-fourths as much as in the slightly longer period from 1920 to 1924. For the entire census period (123 months) the growth was over 17.23 million and equaled the entire population of Belgium and the Netherlands together. This was the largest absolute increase the nation had ever had. About 57 per cent of this increase took place before April, 1925.

In the decade 1930 to 1940 the annual increase was more uniform than in the preceding decade, but the total was only a little over half as great (8,890,000). This means that as compared with the 1920 to 1930 census period the population growth during the 1930 to 1940 period fell short by an amount approximately equal to the entire population of Belgium in 1938. Thus we needed to expand our economy during the decade 1930 to 1940 by an amount only sufficient to build and maintain a complete Netherlands as compared with the need to build and maintain a complete Netherlands plus a complete Belgium during the 1920's. It does not seem unreasonable to assume that such a change in rate of growth would make necessary many significant adjustments in our economy if total production were to be increased at a rate equal to that of the 1920's. I would argue that the chief adjustment needed was a rapid and relatively large increase in the proportion of the national income going into wages and salaries and farmers' incomes (to consumers), a very large part of which is spent currently.

By the later 1920's our economy was prepared not only to care for a population increasing at a rate of about 15 per cent in 10 years but to provide the goods which would enable all of us to live better than in the past, although the rate of population growth was declining rather rapidly after 1925. The rather sudden falling off of employment in 1929 and 1930, and the rapid decline in the birth rate which ensued in due time, even further modified the need for new capital.

During the 1920's the net addition to our capital averaged $7.5 billion annually.[3] This does not include the maintenance of the existing stock of capital. Since our population increase averaged 1.7 million each year, an average of about $4,400 in new capital was added annually for each person added to the population. But as we have seen the average annual population increase before Apr. 1, 1925, was considerably larger (1,875,000) than in the next five years (1,477,000). If we assume that $4,400 in new capital was needed for each person added to the population during the 1920's, the annual need before 1925 was about $1.75 billion greater than after 1925 and the capital need was further greatly reduced as the birth rate began to fall even more rapidly in late 1930 and the three following years. In addition there was very little immigration after 1930. It would seem rather obvious that such a declining need for additional capital to maintain a given

[3] Simon Kuznets, *National Income and Capital Formation, 1919–1935*, 86 pp., National Bureau of Economic Research, Inc., New York, 1937.

level of living could not fail to have rather far-reaching consequences on the whole investment market and in turn upon the level at which the entire economic system would function. I am not arguing that as large an amount of new capital as was used during the 1920's could not have been used during the 1930's, but only that for this amount to be used would have required changes in the allocation of capital to the different industries and in the shares of both capital and consumption goods allotted to different groups engaged in economic activity, changes which our system was not prepared to care for automatically. Hence, when population growth was cut in half as it was after 1930, the need for this alteration in shares became more urgent if the equilibrium of the economy was to be reestablished. Rather drastic redistribution of the national income, as between consumption and production during the latter 1920's and early 1930's would have made it possible for the more slowly increasing population to absorb the goods which could be produced. A rather large per capita income increase in the lower income groups, which contribute very little to savings, would have been especially helpful in this situation.

In the decade just passed our population again attained an absolute growth greater than ever before—about 19 million. These 19 million people (1940 to 1950) plus the 8 to 9 million added since Apr. 1, 1950, needed a vast increase in essential commodities and housing in addition to the goods required for improvement in the level of living attained by the entire 159 million of us, and this in turn required a vast capital investment which stimulated our economy greatly. My argument is that the difference between the spirit manifested by our economic leaders in the 1930's on the one hand and the 1920's and 1940's on the other is in part a difference due to the rate of our population growth in these two periods. However, I believe that if we had known how to adjust the shares of the national income going to the different groups in the population engaged in economic activities and if we had been willing to act on this knowledge during the latter 1920's and early 1930's the decline in the rate of population growth would not have been as large and need not have had any serious effect on the level of economic activity. On the other hand, the greater increase in population since 1940 has lessened the need for a rapid and drastic adjustment in the division of the national income between investment and consumption. But this need for readjustment is continuous in an economy increasing in efficiency and may again become urgent if the birth rate declines rapidly while per capita productivity goes on increasing.

Even though there may be no rapid or sudden decrease in the rate of population growth, it is often argued that a very slow growing or stationary population is likely to lead to an unprogressive or stagnant economy, *i.e.,* one in which there is very little or no increase in per capita product and no substantial change in the level of living. The chief reasons advanced for this belief are: (1) In an area or country where population is growing little, if any, and where death rates are low the average age of the population will be relatively high and will be increasing. Hence it is said the productivity of labor is likely to decrease and the goods available for capital are likely to be insufficient to ensure an increase in per capita productivity. (2) When population is not increasing the stimulus to improve productive processes is lacking, *i.e.*, the psychological atmosphere is unfavorable to the improvement of techniques. (3) The level of living is more likely to become relatively fixed in an older stationary population and thus the desire to raise it is less likely to provide sufficient stimulus to ensure the more efficient use of both labor and capital than where population is growing. This again is a psychological factor.

The author would not deny that these demographic and psychological factors may be and probably are of importance in rendering the economy of a stationary population in an industrialized country less dynamic than that of a growing population if adequate resources are available to both, but he is very much inclined to doubt that the mere lack of growth and the age changes accompanying it, *i.e.*, the demographic aspects of slow or no population growth, are of primary significance. The lack of growth may and probably does have a psychological effect in determining what people will regard as worth-while economic activity, especially if the population has been growing fairly rapidly in the past. I should be disposed to believe, however, that the accepted economic values were the consequence of the whole social situation prevailing in a nation rather than of the lack of growth in the population.

I should also be inclined to believe that the increase in the proportion of old people and in their economic power would be of more importance than the fact that population is growing but slowly or not at all. For some time yet in most countries a slower growth of population will necessarily be accompanied by an increase in average age, especially by a rapid increase in the *number* of old people and also by a growing *proportion* of old people. Hence it is unlikely that for some time yet we shall be able to separate many of the effects of aging from those due to slow growth.

Aside from the general effects of slow population growth, or no growth, on the economy as a whole, it is reasonably certain that different segments of the economy will be affected differently by the changes accompanying a low rate of population growth. It will not be possible to discuss such matters here in any detail, but one or two points may be noted in passing.

Agriculture. Farming even more than industry and commerce is likely to suffer adverse effects if and when the growth of population declines rapidly and becomes practically stationary, while agricultural efficiency is still increasing, since the need for agricultural goods is less elastic than that for most other kinds of goods and services. On the other hand, the improvement in the diet of the people might soften the effects of slower population growth until such time as agriculture may be called upon to furnish more of the raw materials of industry, *e.g.,* cellulose for plastics and alcohol for fuel and rubber, since in most countries the area of good tillable land is not readily extensible. The relatively slow growth of population in the United States, 1930 to 1940, almost certainly aggravated the economic problems of agriculture during that decade, in part, no doubt, because it also coincided with a period of rapidly increasing efficiency in production due to the mechanization of many types of agriculture and the improvement in yield of some of the more important crops. The larger increase in population in 1940 to 1950, together with the improvement in diet, have increased the need for agricultural products, raised agriculture out of its 1930-to-1940 depression, and made much better customers out of farmers as a class although there are now fewer of them than in 1910.

Land Values. In another direction one would expect that real estate values would grow slowly when population grew slowly and would mount rapidly when population grew rapidly. This would apply especially to farm lands. The value of real estate in each city, however, depends largely on local growth; hence changes in the value of real estate in particular localities may have little relation to the national growth of population. Thus when the area of California centering around San Francisco–Oakland grew in numbers by 53.3 per cent (1940 to 1950) while the Scranton, Pa., area decreased by 14.6 per cent there can be little doubt in anyone's mind what the respective changes in real estate values were. Such changes in population in given localities may take place no matter what the rate of growth of the nation's population may be, but large increases will almost certainly be less numerous when the nation's population is growing slowly than when it is growing fairly rapidly. Hence real estate values are likely to become more stable and also to grow more slowly in most areas as population growth declines. But the redistribution of population resulting in the rapid growth of the rings of metropolitan areas has certainly enhanced real estate values in the areas surrounding most large cities more than in the cities themselves.

Optimism and Population Growth. In the United States, even more than in most other Western countries, we have taken it for granted that economic activity would expand steadily and at a fairly rapid rate. This has been an axiom of our economic thinking, not always, perhaps not generally, in the forefront of consciousness of the businessman and the politician, but just for this reason all the more basic to our economic thinking and activity. It is probable that very few people have fully realized how much the belief in a constantly expanding economy rested on the assumption of a rapidly growing population.

Once the belief in a steadily and automatically expanding economy became general a number of corollary beliefs followed inevitably. The one we are most interested in here is the belief that the need for capital would continue to expand indefinitely and at so rapid a rate that savings would generally be inadequate and would therefore be immediately put to use to provide additional productive equipment. The existence of such a belief is abundantly attested by the great virtue attached to thrift and saving not only in copybook maxims but in economic theory as well. Such an emphasis on saving as a primary virtue and as an essential to economic progress could only have developed in a society in which there was large opportunity for the profitable investment of all available capital. The high interest rates which prevailed in the United States until about 1930 also attest to the fact that new capital was greatly needed to expand our industry and commerce. In retrospect this belief in the naturalness, indeed, the inevitability, of a steadily expanding economy and the very general economic optimism it engendered appear to be in large measure the natural consequence of a steady and rapid population growth rather than a quality inherent in the nature of our economic universe, as many people still seem to think.

Will an economic system which has developed in connection with a rapid and continuous growth of population and which has, on the whole, worked well, work as effectively when population growth rather suddenly slows down and population appears likely to become stationary? The author believes that an *automatically* expanding economy is closely related to a growing population and that when population growth ceases or becomes quite slow the economy can be kept efficient and expanding only by conscious community effort; that the success of our laissez-faire economy owes far more than is generally realized to the fact that it operated in a rapidly expanding population; and that many of the qualities manifested in our economic system are not inherent in the nature of economic activity but are to a very significant extent an outgrowth of the great expansion of population which has taken place in the Western world since about 1750. Since this expansion of population is nearing an end in many countries, one can but wonder whether the easy optimism it engendered is not likely to pass away with it. I would argue that in the future we must consciously undertake to expand economic activity if we are to keep our economy functioning effectively in the new stage of human growth upon which we are entering.

Slower Population Growth and the Level of Living. I believe that the slowing up of population growth in the Western world can be made to contribute substantially to a better manner of life. It also seems reasonable to me to hope that the increasing efficiency of our economy will provide us more time to devote to nongainful pursuits than in the past if we do not allow pressure on resources to become unduly great. Whether or not we will actually derive these and other benefits from slower population growth will depend on our willingness to control population growth as well as our ability to reorganize our economic system so that we can steadily make better customers of that large portion of our people who still lack the essentials of decent living. But we should also bear in mind that many of the features of satisfactory living depend fully as much upon what we value in life as upon the economic level at which we are producing, once the essentials of decent living are available to all. Some of the European countries, notably the Scandinavian countries in which the level of economic productivity is well below our own, seem to have been more successful than we have been in assuring all their people reasonably comfortable and satisfactory living conditions. They thus demonstrate that mere efficiency in production alone is not sufficient to produce highly satisfactory living conditions. They have shown that the virtual abolition of *poverty* is essential to the attainment of a high level of personal development and that this can be done even if per capita production is less than our own. These countries, while not yet having stationary populations, have had relatively low rates of increase for some time. Furthermore, as a consequence of having obtained the goal of a fairly adequate economic situation, they seem to have more time than we to devote to the organization of ways to make their freedom from poverty serve better living. A slower growth of population should give us, too, larger opportunities for using our economy for humane ends, but it will not of itself assure such an attainment.

4. OTHER CHANGES IN THE CHARACTER OF THE FUTURE POPULATION

There will be many other changes in the characteristics of our population in the future which will have little or nothing to do with the natural processes of birth, death, and aging. These changes arise from social and economic causes. Many of these cannot be foreseen, but certain of them seem so likely to take place that it may be worth while mentioning them.

A More Urban People. In the future we shall almost certainly be an even more urban people than we now are, if by *urban* we mean that a larger proportion of our people will depend directly on nonagricultural work for their livelihood. This does not necessarily mean that more of us will live in the type of urban community which we now call a city (Chap. XX), but it probably does mean that urban attitudes of mind will become increasingly predominant. Whether this will lead to an intensification of the urban-rural conflict cannot be told. It should be pointed out, however, that we possess the means of developing a better understanding between urban and rural dwellers than any people has possessed heretofore. It remains to be seen whether we use our greater mobility and our excellent means of communication to develop a more sympathetic understanding between urban and rural dwellers or merely to arouse new antagonisms. Certainly the growing preponderance of city people will not of itself allay the urban-rural conflict, which appears to be as old as the establishment of towns.

A More American Background. As a consequence of the smaller number of immigrants being admitted, our population will tend more and more to have a purely native background. Just what the social advantages or disadvantages of this may be no one can tell. But we cannot assume, as many people seem inclined to do, that this increasing homogeneity will be all to the good. The fact that we can take certain attitudes of mind for granted as being widespread, or almost universal, among our people should have some rather obvious advantages. On the other hand, there can be no guarantee that this situation will not raise new problems and difficulties fully as perplexing as those arising from the presence of a large foreign-born population. This increasing homogeneity of background will certainly tend to remove the problem of political blocs due to foreign birth and background and will make it easier for all groups to communicate with one another, but we cannot be assured that it will not result in some cultural loss, nor dare we assume that the area of social and group conflict will be automatically diminished as the proportion of immigrants and their children decreases.

Certain other changes now taking place may be suggested by questions, although their consequences cannot be discussed here. Are we becoming more migratory? Are we going to modify (decentralize) still further our large metropolitan communities? Will we continue to increase the period of school attendance? If so, how will this longer preparatory period react upon our economy and our manner of living? We cannot now answer many of the questions regarding our future population which are of interest, but as we become more convinced of the need for such knowledge it is probable that we shall find answers to those questions which will be most helpful in planning for the future.

Suggestions for Supplementary Reading

BANCROFT, GERTRUDE: "Older Persons in the Labor Force," *Ann. Am. Acad. Pol. Soc. Sci.*, Vol. 279, pp. 52–61, Jan., 1952. Present status and future prospects in the United States.

BORRIE, W. D.: *Population Trends and Policies: A Study in Australian and World Demography*, Chap. 11, Australasian Publishing Company, Sydney, 1948.

BOWLEY, A. L.: *Estimates of the Working Population of Certain Countries in 1931 and 1941*, 19 pp., submitted to the preparatory committee for the International Economic Conference, League of Nations, Geneva, 1926.

Federal Security Agency: *Man and His Years: An Account of the First National Conference on Aging*, 311 pp., Health Publications Institute, Inc., Raleigh, N.C., 1951.

HAGOOD, MARGARET J., and JACOB S. SIEGEL: "Projections of the Regional Distribution of the Population of the United States to 1975," *Agricultural Economics Research*, Vol. 3, No. 2, pp. 41–52, 1951.

HANSEN, A. H.: *Economic Policy and Full Employment*, 340 pp., McGraw-Hill Book Company, Inc., New York, 1947.

———: "Extensive Expansion and Population Growth," *J. Pol. Econ.*, Vol. 48, No. 4, pp. 583–585, 1940.

KUZNETS, SIMON: *National Income and Capital Formation*, 86 pp., National Bureau of Economic Research, Inc., New York, 1937.

MYRDAL, GUNNAR: *Population: A Problem for Democracy*, 237 pp., Harvard University Press, Cambridge, Mass., 1940.

PEARL, RAYMOND, and LOWELL J. REED: "On the Rate of Growth of the Population of the United States since 1790 and Its Mathematical Representation," *Proc. Nat. Acad. Sci.*, Vol. 6, pp. 275–288, 1920.

REDDAWAY, W. B.: *The Economics of a Declining Population*, 270 pp., George Allen & Unwin, Ltd., London, 1939.

REED, LOWELL J.: "Population Growth and Forecasts," *Ann. Am. Acad. Pol. Soc. Sci.*, Vol. 188, pp. 159–166, 1936.

TAEUBER, IRENE B.: "Literature on Future Populations, 1943–1948," *Population Index*, Vol. 15, No. 1, pp. 2–30, 1949.

TERBORGH, GEORGE: *The Bogey of Economic Maturity*, 263 pp., Machinery and Allied Products Institute, Chicago, 1945.

THOMPSON, WARREN S.: "The Economic Consequences of Slow Population Growth in the United States," *Proceedings*, 1939 Ohio Conference of Statisticians on Business Research, Ohio State University, Columbus, Ohio, pp. 3–11, 1940.

———: "Future Population Growth and Real Estate Values," *J. Real Estate Appraisers*, Vol. 3, pp. 34–41, 1934.

———, and P. K. WHELPTON: "Counting Tomorrow's Customers: How Will America's Growth Affect Your Business?" *Nation's Business,* Vol. 17, pp. 41–42, 154–155, February, 1929.

WHELPTON, P. K.: *Forecasts of the Population of the United States, 1945–1975*, 113 pp., U.S. Bureau of the Census, G.P.O., Washington, D.C., 1947.

CHAPTER XIX

FACTORS IN THE GROWTH OF THE
MODERN CITY

The growth of urban population and its concentration in large cities is one of the distinctive characteristics of the present industrial age. Nothing like it has ever been witnessed by man.[1] We can say this with assurance, even though we do not know positively the size of most of the larger cities of the past. We do know, however, that the technological conditions essential to the existence of really large cities—swift and cheap transport and communication, and efficient sanitary engineering—are of recent development. We also know that the productivity of the economic systems of past civilizations was such that no considerable part of the population of any of them could possibly have lived in cities. Only recently (within two centuries) did agriculture become sufficiently productive to spare more than 20 to 25 per cent of the people from agricultural labor.

So far as one can judge, every people has developed cities or towns, or some equivalent form of agglomeration, to the extent that its productive techniques and economic organization have permitted. Even the size of the tribal group and the degree of its stability in a given locality seem to have depended to a large extent upon the amount of the agricultural surplus available for the support of nonagricultural workers. But tribal aggregation, even though at times showing some of the characteristics of the town or city, generally lacked sufficient permanence of location to encourage the complexity of civic organization that towns and cities had. The retinues maintained by the more important tribal chiefs do show us, however, that man forms some kind of nonagricultural agglomeration to avail himself of the benefits of specialization in occupation to the extent that the productivity of the different segments of his economy permits. The city, or perhaps one should say the urban community, appears to be as *natural* as a rural community, a thunderstorm, or sheepherding. Man apparently never loses an opportunity to use any surplus agricultural production (above the mere necessity of the agricultural workers) to establish more or less permanent centers where he can trade and where he can employ his fellows in special-

[1] Adna Ferrin Weber, *The Growth of Cities in the Nineteenth Century: A Study in Statistics,* 495 pp., Columbia University, The Macmillan Company, New York, 1899. (Columbia University Studies in History, Economics, and Law, Vol. 11.)

ized occupations to make things which satisfy his craving for a greater variety of goods. This, I take it, is the *natural* basis of the city.

1. THE GROWTH OF CITIES SINCE THE USE OF STEAM

All civilizations have had their cities. Indeed the only evidence we have today of the existence of many civilizations is the ruins of their cities, so that we have almost come to think of the city and civilization as synonymous terms. It is obvious, of course, when one thinks of it that the city must always subsist on the surplus drawn from the earth by the tillers of the soil, the miners, the fishers, and the foresters—unless, and until, we find cheap methods of synthetically producing these basic resources. The efficiency of these basic extractive industries, therefore, determines the proportion of the people in any civilization which can live in towns and cities. It is because of this necessary connection between the efficiency of the basic extractive industries and the proportion of the people in cities that we can say with absolute assurance that nothing like the growth of modern cities has heretofore been possible. We can also be certain that even the largest of cities in older civilizations could not have approached in size our largest cities of today, because they did not have the mechanical means of supplying the necessities of life to populations such as we find in New York, London, Berlin, Paris, Moscow, and other of the larger cities.

We may perhaps get some notion of the limits to the size of cities imposed by the use of the packsaddle, the cart, and the canalboat from the populations of the larger cities in China and India before the era of steam transportation. A survey of Peiping [2] gives reason to believe that in the heyday of the Manchus this great capital could not have contained many more than 1 million people and probably somewhat fewer. Canton and Hankow may have been somewhat larger, because they had good water communications, but it is extremely doubtful whether any of these cities reached this size before modern steam transport came to their aid.

In India we have more precise information regarding the size of the large cities two or three decades after the time steam transport came into use. At the census of 1881, Calcutta (with suburbs) had 829,000 and Bombay had 773,000 inhabitants. Hence we shall not be far wrong if we asume that the largest cities India supported in presteam days had not much in excess of 500,000 to 600,000 inhabitants. The great cities of antiquity were probably not much larger, although we cannot be sure that Rome under Augustus or Babylon at the height of its power did not approach 1 million. But certainly 1 million must represent about the upper limit in size for cities in the presteam age. The problem of supplying an appreciably larger num-

[2] Sidney D. Gamble, *Peking: A Social Survey,* 538 pp., Doubleday, Doran & Company, Inc., New York, 1921.

ber of people, living in a compact group, with food, fuel, and the materials of manufacture was unsolvable so long as transport depended upon manpower and the use of domestic animals and the boats that could be navigated without steam on both natural and artificial waterways. Thus the conditions of transportation limited the size of the individual city, and the economic system prevailing determined within rather narrow limits the proportion of the nonagricultural population in any society. It is quite safe, therefore, to say that large cities, and particularly the multiplication of large cities, are phenomena unique to our own age.

Table 19-1 shows the growth of several of the world's largest cities since 1800. This table gives us a fairly adequate picture of what has been happening in city growth during the period characterized by the application of steam to transport and to the operation of machinery. This does not mean that the use of steam is the sole factor in this very rapid growth of the cities. But it should be clear from what has already been said that the great

Table 19-1. Population of the World's Largest Cities, 1800 to 1950 [1]

City	1950	1930	1900	1850	1800
New York	7,891,957	6,930,446	3,437,202	696,115	79,216
Tokyo	4,555,565	2,070,000	1,819,000		
Moscow	4,137,018	2,781,000	1,174,673	332,878	188,654
Chicago	3,620,962	3,376,438	1,698,575	29,963	
Shanghai	3,489,998	3,000,000	457,000		
London	3,348,000	4,396,821	4,536,267	2,363,341	959,310
Berlin	3,199,938	4,227,000	2,712,190	429,217	172,846
Leningrad	3,191,304	2,228,000	1,439,613	487,300	220,200
Paris	2,853,000	2,891,000	2,660,559	1,053,262	547,756
Buenos Aires	2,620,827	2,100,000	821,293	76,000	140,000
Calcutta	2,108,891	1,485,582			
Cairo	2,100,506	1,307,422	570,000		
Philadelphia	2,071,605	1,950,961	1,293,697	121,376	41,220
Rio de Janeiro	2,014,185	1,469,000	687,699	166,419	43,376
Los Angeles	1,970,358	1,238,048	102,479	1,610	
Detroit	1,849,568	1,568,662	285,704	21,019	
Vienna	1,798,659	1,836,000	1,727,073	446,415	231,949
São Paulo	1,776,000	962,295	240,000		
Nanking	1,755,300	633,452	270,000		
Osaka	1,690,072	2,453,000	996,000		
Rome	1,653,935	1,008,000	463,000	184,000	153,000
Peiping	1,556,364	1,297,718	1,000,000		
Bombay	1,489,883	1,161,000	776,000		
Sydney	1,484,004	1,254,000	487,932	53,924	2,537
Mexico City	1,448,422	1,007,672	345,000		

[1] These are actual city populations as far as it is possible to judge from the data. A different basis of classification would yield different results.

Table 19-2.   Percentage Distribution of Gainful Workers by Industry Group,
United States, 1820 to 1950

Year	Agriculture	Manufacturing and mechanical pursuits	Trade and transportation	Domestic and personal service	Professional service	Mining
1950	12.5	32.0	32.5	6.2	13.7	1.7
1940[1]	18.8	28.0	28.7	8.9	12.1	2.0
1930	21.4	28.9	28.6	10.1	6.7	2.0
1920[2]	25.6	30.8	25.1	8.1	5.2	2.6
1920	26.1	30.6	24.9	10.1	5.0	2.6
1910	31.2	28.4	21.3	11.3	4.6	2.6
1900	36.8	27.0	18.7	10.6	4.2	2.0
1890	41.9	25.6	15.6	10.3	4.1	1.8
1880	48.9	24.1	12.2	9.3	3.5	1.5
1870	53.4	21.2	10.4	10.2	2.9	1.4
1860	59.7	18.4	7.4	9.5	2.9	1.6
1850	64.5	16.4	5.4	9.6	2.7	1.2
1840	68.6	14.6	3.8	9.6	2.7	0.3
1830	70.4	13.3	3.1	9.8	2.8	0.3
1820	71.9	12.2	2.5	10.0	2.8	0.3

[1] Not exactly comparable to previous figures because of difference in classification.
[2] According to the 1930 census classification.

agglomerations of human beings found in our larger cities today could not possibly come together and survive except for the increased speed and efficiency of transport arising in the first instance from the use of steam and now being assisted by the use of the internal-combustion engine and of electricity. This improvement in transport not only ensured a more certain supply service for large cities by increasing the number, the variety, and the size of the areas from which they could draw food and raw materials, but at the same time made it possible for these cities to sell their goods and services to people scattered throughout the world and for their inhabitants to move quickly from place to place in the cities themselves.

Before proceeding to discuss the role of steam in the building of our modern city, let us notice briefly the shift of population from the country to the city which has been so characteristic of our time. The data in Table 19-2 for the United States are rather typical of the changes which have taken place in most Western lands, but of course this urbanward movement did not begin at the same date in all countries and did not proceed at the same pace. More recently a similar movement has begun in other parts of the world, Japan, India, China, the Soviet Union, and elsewhere. The economic significance of this vast movement to cities is summed up in the changes in the industrial classification of workers. Agriculture, which occupied about 72 per cent of the workers in the United States in 1820, now occupies only about 12.8 per cent, while those engaged in manufacturing are about two and one-third times as numerous now as at the earlier date, those in professional service are relatively over four times as numerous, and those in trade and transportation are relatively over eleven times as numerous. In many other countries the same type of change—the shift from agriculture to manufacturing, to commerce, and to the services—has also taken place (Table 19-3). The Soviet Union, India, and Bulgaria were still predominantly agricultural countries on the basis of the latest data available, but even there the movement to urban communities is well begun and in the Soviet Union there has been a tremendous swing to the cities since the war.

No other data are needed to call attention to the great change in the distribution of population between town and country which takes place as agriculture becomes more efficient and more people are freed from the work of producing agricultural goods. We are all aware of this change because most of us need go back only a generation or two to find forebears who tilled the soil or who lived in rural villages and supplied the farmers with the few and simple things they could not make for themselves. But in spite of this consciousness of having detached ourselves from the soil only a few years or a few decades ago, most of us do not realize the fundamental

Table 19-3.   Percentage Distribution of Gainful Workers by Industry Group, Selected Countries

Country	Year	Agriculture, forestry, and fishing	Manufacturing and mining	Trade and transportation	Army and navy	Public and professional service	Domestic and personal service
England and Wales..	1931	5.7	46.6	27.2	1.3	9.6	9.6
	1871	16.7	51.8	8.2	1.4	5.5	16.5
Germany..........	1939	26.1	42.1	17.6	2.3	8.1	3.9
	1882	44.7	37.4	10.5	5.2	....	2.2
Australia..........	1947	16.8	36.6	27.3	[1]	19.3	[1]
	1891	25.4	37.0	19.4	....	6.3	11.8
France............	1946	37.4	29.9	15.9	[1]	16.8	[1]
	1866	41.2	28.8	8.2	2.5	4.1	15.3
Italy..............	1936	48.2	29.3	12.6	1.1	5.2	3.6
	1881	58.7	28.6	4.1	1.1	3.4	4.1
Bulgaria..........	1934	76.3	10.4	4.9	1.5	6.0	0.9
	1900	83.5	7.6	3.7	1.6	2.3	1.2
India.............	1931	71.5	10.9	7.1	0.6	2.2	7.6
	1901	72.4	17.0	2.8	0.1	3.8	3.9

[1] Included in public service.

changes in our mode of life which have resulted from this detachment from the soil. If we would envisage our social order of only a few decades ago, we must visit India, or China, or Java today where a large majority of all workers are still to be found on the land. The occupational distribution in these countries is not greatly different from that which prevailed among us a century ago.

It is not exaggerating to say that the changes in the social order which have occurred since the beginning of the nineteenth century in the industrialized areas of the world are much greater and more profound than those which occurred in Europe from the time of the Greeks down to 1800. We cannot attempt here even to enumerate these changes, to say nothing of discussing them. It will be necessary, however, to mention briefly the chief factors that underlay these changes and to show how they affected the distribution and growth of population and led to the development of the modern city.

2. THE AGRICULTURAL REVOLUTION

As was noted in Chap. V, an agricultural revolution was in progress before what is commonly called the *industrial revolution* began and has accompanied the latter throughout its development. The two did not always move with equal speed, but the basic effects of both were the same as regards the productivity of labor. Agriculture the world over was extremely inefficient until this modern revolution, and it probably required 75 to 80 per cent of the total population to provide agricultural products at the very low level then prevailing for themselves and for the 20 to 25 per cent of the population that was engaged in nonagricultural occupations. This situation still prevails in much of the world; even in India, which is somewhat ahead of most of South and East Asia in the development of industry, over 70 per cent of the people were engaged in agriculture at the time of the 1931 census, the latest for which such data are available. (The proportion is probably somewhat less today.) Clearly there could be but little nonagricultural industry and very little trade until the efficiency of agriculture improved so that instead of four persons (perhaps one should say families) in agriculture being needed to produce the necessities of life for five it was reduced to three, then two, and then one. The preliminary data from the 1950 census of the United States indicate that just over one-eighth of the employed persons were then engaged in agriculture. The first requisite for the development of the nonagricultural industries and the expansion of trade appears then to have been an increase in the efficiency of agricultural labor. Once this had begun, more labor became available for the expansion of industrial enterprises and for new developments in both domestic and foreign trade as well as in professional services and many other white-collar occupations.

As soon as the modern agricultural revolution made it possible for more and more people to leave the land and engage in nonagricultural tasks, towns and cities began to grow rapidly. In England this change began during the latter half of the eighteenth century, and London had a population of almost 1 million by 1800. A similar development took place elsewhere in the West as the agricultural revolution spread to other areas.

Since the agricultural revolution of the past two and one-half centuries or more has been less publicized than the industrial revolution, it will be well to review its development briefly.

Throughout the Middle Ages and into early modern times the agricultural surplus produced by the Western European peasant was very small indeed. His tillage practices were quite primitive. He knew little or nothing of fertilizing his fields, and he kept a considerable part of them, one-fourth to one-third, fallow. He did not know how to select good seed, and he knew almost nothing about animal breeding. He knew just as little about producing milk and meat efficiently with the crops that he did raise, while he never dreamed of more productive varieties of the crops he was accustomed to raise either for human or for animal food. As for new crops, they were quite beyond his power of imagination. In a word, his ignorance of agriculture was profound; nor were most of the lords of the manors, their bailiffs, or other landed proprietors much better than the peasant in any of these respects. The landlord all too often encouraged thriftlessness by appropriating to himself all the benefits of any improvements in production which were made.

Each country, of course, had its own distinctive agricultural problems. Those of France were different in many respects from those of Germany, and these in turn differed from those of Italy or England. But everywhere in Europe until modern times agriculture was extremely inefficient and therefore could support only a very small nonagricultural (urban) population. No matter if better manufacturing processes were well known or if more people might desire to enter trade, little development along these lines could take place until the agricultural production per worker was increased, thus enabling a smaller proportion of the workers of the nation to produce the agricultural necessities for a given population. Without going into detail, it may be interesting to indicate some of the improvements in English agriculture which made it possible for England, while still self-supporting agriculturally, to employ a larger and larger proportion of its population in nonagricultural pursuits. Lord Ernle says of English agriculture in the eighteenth century:

> The gigantic advance of agriculture in the nineteenth century dwarfs into insignificance any previous rate of progress. Yet the change between 1700 and 1800 was astonishing. England not only produced food for a population that had doubled itself, as well as grain for treble the number

of horses, but during the first part of the period became, as M. de Lavergne has said, the granary of Europe. [The advances in agriculture during this period] may be summed up in the adoption of improved methods of cultivation, the introduction of new crops, the reduction of stock breeding to a science, the provision of increased facilities of communication and of transport, and the enterprise and outlay of capitalist landlords and tenant farmers.[3]

We cannot take time to show how these improvements in agriculture enabled a smaller proportion of the people to produce the food and clothing of the nation. It must suffice to say that improved methods of tillage literally caused two grains of wheat, or two tons of hay, to grow where one had grown before; new crops provided better feed for cattle and, in conjunction with better breeding of cattle, produced two pounds of meat or milk or wool where one pound had formerly been produced. Enclosure of open fields accompanied these changes in agriculture and drove many people from the rural districts to the towns and cities, since they were no longer needed on the land. Thus it came about that an agricultural revolution in England to a certain extent preceded and made possible the industrial revolution. Too often this fact is overlooked, and it is not realized that the improvement in standards of living and comfortableness of life for the masses of the people was inaugurated by this improvement of agriculture some decades before modern industry began to develop.

As Lord Ernle says, the improvements in agriculture accomplished during the eighteenth century, though great, were almost as nothing compared with those of the nineteenth, and this progress still continues. The consequence is that we have had a constantly diminishing proportion of the population in Western lands needed to produce our agricultural necessities and to add many luxuries to them. The data for Australia show that only 15.6 per cent of the employed persons were engaged in agriculture in 1947, and Australia still exports vast amounts of wheat, wool, and meat.[4] The story is the same wherever science is being applied to agriculture and industry.

3. THE NATURE OF URBAN GROWTH

Having noted briefly the changes in agriculture making urban growth possible, let us now turn our attention to the more detailed consideration of the factors giving our urban communities the particular forms they assumed in the course of the evolution of the modern city. Until quite recently the modern city in the West has been essentially a mononucleated

[3] Roland Edmund Prothero, First Baron Ernle, *English Farming, Past and Present,* p. 148, Longmans, Green & Co., New York, 1922.

[4] *Demographic Yearbook, 1949–50,* p. 274, United Nations, New York, 1950.

community. At least most of these cities have had one nucleus which was far more important than any of the others, and indeed as a rule it has had a "downtown" or "central" area in which were congregated most of the important offices, stores, hotels, amusements, and public buildings. This form of structure necessitated the coming together of great numbers of people during the working hours of the day and their dispersal to more or less distant residence areas at night. Why have our modern large cities assumed this mononucleated form, which has only recently begun to undergo substantial modification?

It may be pointed out that the larger cities built in presteam days were not mononucleated to the same extent as our modern cities. One can see this very clearly by studying the organization of economic activity in some of the older European cities. In Paris and Naples, for example, a far larger proportion of the people has no reason to go to the downtown or central section of the city than is the case in our own cities. This is also true of London. The fact is that in these older European cities, which were formed by the amalgamation of rather distinct towns that were themselves old, the separateness of these units has never been entirely effaced, so that they still retain an individuality and an economic and social independence which can scarcely be found in any of the more recent industrial and commercial cities, e.g., Berlin and Milan in Europe and most American cities.

But it is in the Orient that we see the large city of the past best exemplified. Where modern means of transport were lacking, the large city was necessarily organized so that most people could work either at home or in the immediate neighborhood of their homes. Furthermore, before the days of steam power the factories were small, and the amount of office work involved in carrying on the business of any particular firm was very little; hence there was no economic reason for the concentration of any large number of people in a given place for work. So it is that we can see today in the structure of some of the large cities of China the city much as it must have been at all times and in all lands until the development of steam transport and steam-driven machinery. In wandering about these cities one is impressed with the lack of a central business area, with the large amount of home manufacturing, and with the resultant uniformity of most parts of the city. The highly differentiated sections—business, retail and wholesale, factory, railroad, residence, and so forth—to which we are accustomed are largely lacking, and one gets the impression of going through a series of small cities rather than one large city of the modern type. There is, however, even in these Chinese cities a very considerable amount of differentiation of areas for the production and sale of jewelry, furs, textiles, pottery, and other major types of goods. However, it is only where Western influence is decidedly marked, as in the newer port cities, that a more centralized structure prevails, and even in them centralization is much less marked than in the West. The Western influence is more clearly marked in such cities as Tokyo and Osaka, Shanghai and Tientsin, than in Kyoto and Peiping. In the latter the older form of city structure has persisted longer.

It was steam transport and the application of steam to the driving of machinery that led to the greater differentiation in the various quarters of the modern city and concentrated great numbers of people in small areas for their working hours. Thus we came to have the modern city with a structure quite different from anything that had existed in the past. The economic and "social" life of the city came more and more to center in the downtown or central business area—the real nucleus of the modern city—although the heavy manufacturing always tended to locate outside this central business area nearer the marshaling yards of the railroads.

Little space need be devoted to pointing out how the city was affected by steam transportation. The area with which a city could trade was greatly extended, both at home and abroad. In the course of a day's wandering in any large city one can see goods being unloaded from ships or railway cars, or both, which came from every part of the earth. And, of course, goods are being sent out in exchange for them. This fact is too commonplace to attract attention, but we must not forget that better transportation (and communication) made possible a concentration of population working in small areas which is unique in human experience.

Of no less importance, although its effects upon the form of our cities is less generally realized, was the application of steam to the driving of machines. It is in the very nature of steam power when applied directly for manufacturing that it is more economical if it is applied to large units and to machines concentrated within a comparatively small area. When used directly for power—as it was almost exclusively until about thirty years ago, when the individual electric motor began to come into use on an increasing scale—high-pressure steam cannot be carried any considerable distance, and it cannot be applied economically to the operation of individual machines. The large factory, built around a central steam plant, is the natural development of the direct use of steam for power, since the power from the steam engine was transferred to the machinery by the use of shafts, pulleys, and belts, and efficiency diminished rapidly as the distance from engine to machine increased.

When the owner of the small water-power cotton mill supplemented his water power by the use of steam or changed to steam entirely, he frequently found that an increase in the number of units in his mill was accompanied by lower costs. He was thus in a more favorable position to undersell his competitors. Naturally he was encouraged to increase still further the size of his factory. The situation was much the same if he occupied a water-power site capable of furnishing large additional power. Both water power and steam encouraged the development of manufacturing plants in which growth in the number of producing units of machinery was profitable as long as they could be kept within a short distance of the source of power—where the shaft-pulley-belt system of power transmission was fairly efficient. This increase in factory size was, of course, accompanied by an increase in the number of employees.

The more economies the large-scale steam plant made possible, the more successful the business was and the more funds were available for its extension. Nothing was more natural, then, if business expanded, than the building of an addition to the existing plant and the employment of still more workers. The very nature of steam and water power as direct motive power for factories was to encourage the concentration of population in comparatively small areas where the workers could get to the factories by walking. Steam was not well adapted to local urban transportation in small units. Since the business offices were at first located in the plants, where the owner or manager, generally the same person in the early days, could have both the manufacturing and commercial ends of his business under his immediate control, these locations also drew an increasing number of white-collar workers.

Long after it was possible to get cotton from the United States for the Lancashire mills and to sell the product in all parts of the world, it was rather tedious and difficult for the factory owner to look after his affairs very satisfactorily if he lived at any considerable distance from his factory and office. The same held for employees until local transportation was electrified. This will account for the tenement type of building, the lack of open places, the terrible room crowding, and most of the other hideous features of congestion with which we are only too familiar in many of the older parts of modern cities. In its early days the steam-powered factory continued and extended the concentration of population which was characteristic of the small walled city of the Middle Ages. In the days when our modern cities were taking form, there was probably no alternative to this crowding. The growth of industry and trade and the lack of rapid local transportation made it inevitable.

It could never have occurred to most of the men who were the enterprisers in developing the modern factory system that the growth of their businesses could be accomplished in any other way than by an addition to their existing plant and office space. But after a time, when rail transport between cities became more efficient, it did occur to many men that these industrial cities they had created were not very pleasant places in which to live. They began to find it possible to live in some more congenial locality some distance away from the factory and to commute by train daily. They also found that they could turn more and more of the technical work of manufacturing over to some engineer or technician and need not visit the factory every day. But as a rule they still thought of an enlargement in output as necessarily connected with an addition to the existing plant. Furthermore, once the actual owners had left the plant, they forgot how bad were the living conditions that had grown up around it, and they did not realize how the new addition was going to make living conditions still worse for their employees. Consequently they did not stop to consider whether the form in which their enterprises were developing could be changed to make the living conditions of their employees more satisfactory.

When the owner moved his own office away from his factory he took part of his office force with him. At first he frequently visited the factory. If he had moved to Boston or London or Paris or New York he found that he could still get to his factory in a few hours and spend a day there occasionally. This worked reasonably well, because, in any event, it was rapidly becoming impossible for businessmen to keep up with the technical developments in their industries. Production and distribution were becoming more highly specialized, and the businessman found that his visits to the factory were becoming less necessary, while general management required more and more information about all aspects of the business, production, sales, financial control, and so forth. Thus grew up the very common practice of almost complete separation between factory and the general management of an enterprise which is so common in business today and which has led to the development of so many large central offices in downtown business areas.

It also soon became apparent that there were certain advantages to a firm in its owners' and general managers' having their offices in the neighborhood of other owners and managers with whom they did business. It is easy to see how this was the case in the pretelephone days and even in the days when the telephone first came into use. At that time the use of the telegraph also was slow and costly, and most business had to be transacted in person or by letter carried by train. In other words, the use of steam rendered certain forms of business organization more efficient than others, in the same way that it determined the size and concentration of factory production. It requires but little imagination to see how the owner of mills at Lawrence might, in pretelephone days, profit by living in Boston, where he was in close touch with the men who were likely to buy his goods, with specialty suppliers, and with technically trained men whose services he often needed. If he remained in Lawrence, he had to depend largely on letters to keep in touch with these people, and he was then at a distinct disadvantage as compared with his competitors who had moved to Boston and maintained closer personal contact with them.

As business increased in size and the amount of capital needed increased, it also became more important for the industrialist to keep in close touch with his bankers. More and more the expansion of enterprise came to require the concentration of capital in large amounts, and the banker organized the service by which this could be done. In all these financial arrangements personal contacts played a large part, so that it was often of distinct advantage for the enterpriser to live in the financial center.

It is out of this general situation that the habit of concentrating offices in downtown areas under the immediate supervision of the "big boss" became general. As the business of a firm grew, the amount of office work in most cases grew even more rapidly, so that today we have some prodigiously large offices that have apparently grown up just as the factories did, that is to say, without much consideration on the part of the men in charge as to whether it was better to add another floor or another building to their present office space or to attempt a new form of decentralized office organization. The invention and use of the skyscraper in this country apparently has solved the problem of increase in office staffs, so far as our managers are concerned. It seems never to have occurred to them that they were rapidly making the large city of today an almost impossible place for the masses of the people to live in. What the factory did for the hand-working people in the way of crowding people together and making life hideous—so hideous that the enterpriser moved away—the skyscraper is doing for the white-collar workers in our offices, in spite of very much improved transport facilities within the city.

4. THE DISAPPEARING NEED FOR THE PRESENT ORGANIZATION OF THE CITY

Today it is hard to understand the need for such a great number of people working in downtown areas in our large cities. The conditions which originally gave impetus to this crowding together in centralized districts no longer exist, but the inertia of this movement still maintains the dominance of the central area, although there are clear signs that the degree of dominance of this area is beginning to diminish. Recently, many firms have found out that there are advantages in building branch factories instead of adding more to the original plants and in moving their factories out of their earlier locations to the fringes of the enlarged cities of today. In contrast to the outward movement of factories, branch offices as well as the offices of the larger local industries are still being located in the "downtown" or central areas. The men who are responsible for the location of offices do not seem to realize that the conditions of communication which made it advantageous for them to be near buyers and bankers, as well as to have their office staffs close at hand and in a central location, are no longer as compelling as they were. The development of the telephone, the telegraph, and air mail have changed the need for doing as large a part of the office work of a large business in one place as was formerly the case and have also made a downtown office for many local businesses quite unnecessary. These facts are being recognized in the establishment of more branch offices and to some extent in the location of more office work at the plant site, but the decentralization and dispersion of office work is proceeding more slowly than is that of production facilities.

In spite of the changes which are taking place in the structure of the modern city, it still retains most of the form derived from the direct use of steam for power and communication. If electricity and methods for its use had been developed simultaneously with the use of steam, it is quite probable that our whole industrial-urban civilization would have assumed quite a different form; possibly even its basic organization would have been different. Some of the social and economic possibilities inherent in the use of electricity and the gas engine will be discussed later.

There is another factor in the development of the modern city which seems to me to have been of considerable importance in encouraging the concentration of businesses in the downtown areas of large cities, a factor which is of a less tangible character but still of great importance, namely, the association in the minds of many people of the idea of huge size with that of great efficiency. There is little doubt that in the early stages of modern industrial development there was a very close connection between the size of the plant and office and the efficiency of the business as a whole. The really efficient producer was then, as has generally been the case, the one who made the greatest financial success in his business. He was therefore the one who had the most capital to spend upon the expansion of his enterprise and the one who could most easily raise additional capital through the banks. Expanding size, therefore, was a proof of success, and great size in itself came to be regarded as one of the most important factors making for success, if indeed it was not an indispensable factor. In the course of time any business or city that had grown to large proportions came to be regarded as more efficient and more desirable than one that was smaller, and having an office in a large city, perhaps at some distance from the plant, also came to be a visible badge of success. There cannot be the least doubt that the prestige which has come to attach to mere bigness has driven or drawn many men who have developed their enterprises in smaller communities away from their factories into the larger cities. When they make this change they very frequently take with them their offices and office staffs and most of the professional workers needed to carry on all those phases of business not directly concerned with factory management. Table 19-4 shows the occupational trend in some of our larger cities.

These data show that in all these large cities, except Los Angeles, the number of persons employed in transportation, communication, and other public utilities, in business and repair services, and in public administration has increased faster than that in manufacturing. However, in all these cities, except Detroit, the number engaged in manufacturing increased faster than the total number employed so that there was a proportional increase in persons engaged in manufacturing although not as large as the proportional increase in these other industries where the increase in numbers was larger.

Unfortunately such data do not tell us in what kinds of work the persons engaged in these several industries were engaged. The preliminary data for the United States relating to the major occupational groups show, however, that the largest proportional increases were in "clerical and kindred workers" (from 9.8 per cent in 1940 to 12.1 per cent in 1950) and the "craftsmen, foremen, and kindred workers" (from 11.4 per cent in 1940 to 13.7 per cent in 1950). Other substantial proportional increases were found in "pro-

Table 19-4.   Percentage Increase of Employed Workers in the Broad Industrial Groups, Selected Large Cities, 1940 to 1950

Industry group	New York	Chicago	Philadelphia	Los Angeles	Detroit	Cleveland	Saint Louis	Boston
Total....................	15.4	19.4	17.6	36.2	21.3	22.2	13.3	15.2
Agriculture, forestry, and fisheries..............	49.1	52.2	18.8	3.8	43.3	18.9	23.0	12.8
Mining..................	15.1	17.0	−23.0	−46.3	50.0	90.1	−17.8	−7.0
Construction............	9.7	27.0	37.2	52.7	34.2	49.0	10.4	30.4
Manufacturing..........	22.8	28.7	17.3	71.7	18.3	27.8	16.5	24.2
Transportation, communication, and other public utilities..............	23.1	25.1	34.3	31.3	41.0	34.2	26.6	25.4
Wholesale and retail trade.	21.6	10.8	17.0	28.8	23.8	11.8	6.8	10.6
Finance, insurance, and real estate............	8.1	9.0	15.4	24.2	16.8	10.0	2.4	23.9
Business and repair services.	50.6	33.7	34.9	63.8	45.0	36.6	22.5	34.2
Personal services..........	−21.1	−18.5	−11.6	−4.0	−14.1	−12.5	−24.2	−22.0
Entertainment and recreation services...........	16.4	6.5	4.8	8.2	20.1	23.2	11.8	−3.6
Professional and related services.................	17.9	26.2	19.8	51.1	37.3	22.8	21.5	15.8
Public administration.....	24.8	41.5	41.2	47.5	37.7	42.6	75.6	35.0
Industry not reported.....	−22.2	43.0	−7.4	35.6	41.6	22.8	80.2	−19.6

fessional, technical, and kindred workers" (from 7.9 per cent to 8.9 per cent); in "managers, officials, and proprietors" (from 8.3 per cent to 9.0 per cent); and in "operatives and kindred workers" (from 18.2 per cent to 19.8 per cent). Similar data are not available for these large cities, but since for the entire country the four groups which can be identified fairly certainly as white collar increased from 32.5 per cent of all employed persons in 1940 to 36.7 per cent in 1950, while the two groups which furnished most of the wage workers in manufacturing increased slightly less, from 29.6 per cent in 1940 to 33.5 per cent in 1950, it would appear probable that the white-collar group continued to increase somewhat faster than the wage-worker group in the country as a whole, and it is almost certain that this was the case in the larger cities. Today it is reasonably certain that our larger cities owe the major part of their growth not to the increase of wage workers in manufacturing but rather to the continued concentration of professional and clerical workers in large corporation offices and to the increase in service workers of many kinds as more and more mechanical devices come into general use.

It may seem that this discussion of the development of the large modern city is somewhat beside the point. But this is not the case; it is very much to the point if we would understand the population problems which now confront us. As was said above, a larger and larger part of our people are going to work at nonagricultural tasks for some time to come. Are these people going to live in large cities of the present type, or is some new form of urban organization going to emerge? Probably no definitive answer can be given this question at present, but with each passing decade it appears that the rebellion against the modern highly centralized city is growing. More and more people want to live in urban communities, but they are not satisfied to live in the densely settled large city. A change in the distribution of population is taking place, and this will almost certainly have a profound effect on the structure and function of the modern city.

In the not-distant future the distribution of the population over the face of the land will come to be regarded by social scientists as one of the major problems of the age. The horror, the strain, and the inhumanness of living in modern large cities, where 75 to 90 per cent of the people have too little space in their homes and too little room about their homes for play and recreation, where they have the constant irritation of noise and dust and smoke, where going to and from work—instead of providing wholesome exercise and relaxation—is the most wearing part of the day's work, and where the commuter seeking space in which to live has almost no time to become acquainted with his family, are so clearly evident that we cannot much longer ignore their effect upon the quality of our civilization. The time has come when we must begin to ask ourselves whether we cannot reorganize our urban communities so that people will find them better places in which to live and work. Instead of judging a city by the number of its inhabitants, we shall ask what part of its people have a chance to have real homes in which a wholesome family life is possible and in which they will be willing to raise at least enough children to replace themselves. For, of course, a city civilization in which the deaths exceed the births—a condition which has already come to pass in many quarters of our larger cities—cannot long endure and can be regarded only with misgiving by those who look some distance into the future. A civilization whose most perfect fruit is the modern large city is certainly doomed to early decay. Some of the reasons for this judgment will be given in the next chapter.

Suggestions for Supplementary Reading

BURGESS, ERNEST W., ed.: *The Urban Community*, 268 pp., University of Chicago Press, Chicago, 1926. (Selected papers from the proceedings of the American Sociological Society, 1925.) See pp. 122–132, H. B. Woolston, "American City Birth Rates"; pp. 133–138, C. E. Gehlke, "Some Economic Factors in the Determination of the Size of American Cities"; pp. 139–143, Hornell Hart, "The Expectation of Life in 2000 A.D."; pp. 144–150, Ernest P. Goodrich, "Statistical Relationship between Population and the City Plan."

ERNLE, ROLAND EDMUND PROTHERO, FIRST BARON: *English Farming, Past and Present*, 504 pp., Longmans, Green & Co., Inc., New York, 1922. See Chap. 15, pp. 290–315, "The Rural Population, 1780–1813."

GAMBLE, SIDNEY D.: *Peking: A Social Survey*, 538 pp., Doubleday, Doran & Company, Inc., New York, 1921.

HAWLEY, AMOS H.: *Human Ecology*, 456 pp., The Ronald Press Company, New York, 1950. See Chap. 19, "Expansion—The Growth of the City."

MCKENZIE, RODERICK D.: *The Metropolitan Community*, 352 pp., McGraw-Hill Book Company, Inc., New York, 1933.

MUMFORD, LEWIS: *The Culture of Cities*, 586 pp., Harcourt, Brace and Company, Inc., New York, 1938.

PARK, ROBERT E., *et al: The City*, 239 pp., University of Chicago Press, Chicago, 1925. See Chap. 2, pp. 47–62, Ernest W. Burgess, "The Growth of the City: an Introduction to a Research Project."

THOMPSON, WARREN S.: "Urbanization," *Encyclopaedia of the Social Sciences*, Vol. 15, pp. 189–192, 1930.

WEBER, ADNA FERRIN: *The Growth of Cities in the Nineteenth Century: A Study in Statistics*, 495 pp., Columbia University Press, The Macmillan Company, New York, 1899. (Columbia University Studies in History, Economics, and Public Law, Vol. 11.)

CHAPTER XX

THE FUTURE OF THE LARGE CITY

In what kind of cities or communities will our nonagricultural workers live in the future? No doubt all of us have seen sketches of the future city, with hundred-story buildings and two or more levels of streets with moving sidewalks and escalators, and with several levels of tracks for passengers and freight service. If all Manhattan were built up in this fashion, it could no doubt house from one-third to one-half of the present population of the nation, and the engineer would have proved his prowess in construction. It is extremely doubtful, however, whether the human race could survive under such living conditions or would wish to do so. Indeed, to judge from their birth performance before 1940, a rather small minority of the dwellers in large cities manifested an effective desire to survive, that is, had enough children to ensure their own replacement in the next generation. The building of such supercolossal cities would therefore probably prove a major catastrophe to man, just as Frankenstein's monster proved his undoing.

1. THE FUTURE CITY

This whole matter of city living and what it means to man economically, socially, culturally, and morally has attracted more than its usual meed of attention recently. Chase [1] has pointed out that even the engineers are beginning to question their ability to build ever more and larger structures on a limited area and ensure these modern cliff dwellers the goods and services essential to decent living. The problem of servicing the modern great city is becoming so complex that real catastrophe due to a breakdown in these services merely because of increased congestion is by no means improbable. To the danger of a breakdown in the services supplied to cities arising from engineering and human limitations must now be added the danger from aerial bombing, in particular from the atom bomb and possibly, before long, from the hydrogen bomb.[2] This threat of destruction by bombs seems not unlikely to gain more and quicker consideration for the need to decentralize large

[1] Stuart Chase, "The Future of the Great City," *Harper's Mag.,* Vol. 160, pp. 82–90, 1929.

[2] Warren S. Thompson, Chap. 12, in *Cities Are Abnormal,* ed. by Elmer T. Peterson, University of Oklahoma Press, Norman, Okla., 1946.

cities than all the discussion on this point by sociologists, economists, and city planners during the past two or three decades. But even though military considerations may prove to be the decisive factor in hastening decentralization they cannot occupy our attention here, because we do not yet know what kind of a community can best be defended against aerial attack, or whether this threat is to remain a relatively permanent factor in national and city planning. Leaving aside for the present, therefore, the military considerations affecting the organization of the modern city, we shall confine our discussion chiefly to the social and economic factors indicating the need and the possibility of reorganizing the structure of the large city.

Mumford [3] is convinced that the physical difficulties arising with increasing congestion which Chase emphasizes are of little import as compared with the impoverishment and the warping of the human spirit which inevitably accompany congestion. He believes that the large city sets up values and modes of living which are basically opposed to those humane and biological values by which man must guide his conduct if he is to survive—that man must choose between reconstructing the city so that it will provide the essentials of the good life and dying out. The modern city is destroying him both biologically and spiritually.

It was shown in Chap. IX that for some time past city people had not been reproducing themselves. This situation may have changed somewhat since 1940, but we do not yet have any basis for assurance that such a change has occurred or that if it has occurred it is permanent. We still need to ask in all seriousness whether any civilization which so nearly sterilizes a large class of its citizens (dwellers in large cities) can long survive. Mumford says "No," and the author agrees with him. Our discussion here will be confined largely to those factors which may bring about the redistribution of population within the larger urban areas known as metropolitan communities and between urban and rural areas, even though in so doing we ignore many of the most interesting aspects of city life.[4]

2. THE QUALITIES OF STEAM AND ELECTRICITY CONTRASTED

In the preceding chapter the author has argued that the use of steam as the direct motive power in industry, transportation, and communication largely determined the pattern of population distribution in Western cities until within the past two or three decades. The modern mononucleated large city represents this development in its most extreme form. This form of urban organization continues to flourish today in spite of the fact that we

---

[3] Lewis Mumford, *The Culture of Cities,* 586 pp., Harcourt, Brace and Company, Inc., New York, 1938.

[4] Niles Carpenter, *The Sociology of City Life,* 502 pp., Longmans, Green & Co., Inc., New York, 1932.

now substitute electricity or the internal-combustion engine for many operations where steam was used directly in the past. In doing this we have acquired a new basis for the redistribution of population and for the reorganization of our economic activities, but we have made little progress in actual reorganization.

It is not particularly strange that the type of city developed at the time of the direct use of steam should still be with us, for it is only about thirty years since the significance of using electricity for power and communication began to be realized even by the initiated, and it is only now that we are beginning to understand how electricity and the use of the internal-combustion engine may contribute to the enrichment of life for the masses of the people.

Even though it involves some repetition, I wish to contrast very briefly the qualities of steam and electricity before undertaking to point out the possibilities inherent in the wider use of electricity for the improvement of human living by making possible a more rational distribution of population. In the first place, steam, if used *directly* for power, must be used quite close to the place where it is produced. Its power must be transmitted through shafts, pulleys, and belts. High-pressure steam cannot be carried any great distance from the source of generation. Moreover, steam cannot be used efficiently in small and varying amounts in accordance with the requirements of each machine being operated, nor can it be kept in readiness for instantaneous use as desired. On the other hand, electricity need not be used at or near the source of production. It can be distributed at comparatively small cost over considerable distances. Electricity can also be used in almost any amount with almost no price differential, at any point within the range of efficient distribution. This makes it possible to operate every machine in a factory at a relatively high level of efficiency as regards the power it consumes. Electricity can also be used in many types of industrial furnaces to obtain a better and more uniform product than can be obtained by the use of any other form of heat. Because of these differences in the character of steam and electric power, the basic organization of industry may become quite different in the not-distant future. The size and the location of plants, the organization of the factory, and the capital investment might all be quite different when electricity furnishes the power for industry. Today we must also begin to look forward to a new type of productive unit, electronically controlled, which may be far more efficient than even the most completely electrically operated factory of the past. The internal-combustion engine, of course, shares honors with electricity in supplying readily portable power for many types of work, but it is not yet a serious competitor of steam in the production of electricity.

In the second place, as a means of communication the steam engine was, of course, a vast improvement over the stagecoach and the sailing vessel, but as compared with electricity, steam and all other means of actual physical movement of ideas must remain extremely slow and cumbersome. It cannot provide for direct personal communication, as does the telephone, or for the rapid transmission of information as does the telegraph. This point needs no elaboration.

In the third place, in transportation, steam holds its own better than in the application of power to machinery and to communication; but even in this field it is rapidly giving away to electricity produced by the internal-combustion engine (diesel and gas turbine). The children of the coming generation are likely to look upon a steam locomotive as a museum piece.

As was shown above, the very nature of steam power made it inevitable that efficiency should come to be closely associated with large size and compactness of plant in the minds of men in the early days of the industrial revolution. With the increasing use of electricity for power and communication and for the control of operations and with the increasing use of the internal-combustion engine for transportation, it is probable that the concentration of production in big plants will appear less and less efficient. It is becoming increasingly clear that the size of a business and the size of an individual plant need have little relation to one another. The efficiency and speed of communication may become more and more determinative of the size of the business, while the efficiency of actual production at particular points will determine the size of factory.

We now have the basis for a complete reorganization of the physical structure of our economic system, which will in turn result in a redistribution of our nonagricultural population. Economically we no longer need the intense concentration of factories, offices, and people within a small area which the direct use of steam not only made possible but also made almost inevitable. Our new sources of power, new means of communication, and new forms of transport can give us almost a new world in which to live if we will but take advantage of the greater opportunities for better living which they offer.

3. POSSIBILITIES OF DECENTRALIZING INDUSTRY

The use of the electric motor, the electric furnace, the internal-combustion engine, and electric communication opens up possibilities of decentralizing the economic activities of large cities which have only recently become apparent. The new technology of production and of centralized policy control based on these new sources of power and means of communication is also making it possible to disperse many economic activities over a much wider area. Today a single power station, advantageously located, may supply power to industries within a fairly large radius at rates which practically equalize power costs between the small plant using a few thousand units a day and the large plant using many tens of thousands of units daily, or between the plant next door to the power station and that many miles away. The large factory with its own efficient steam plant, whether steam is used directly to drive machinery or whether it is used to produce electricity which is then used for power, as is increasingly the case, is losing much of the advantage of lower power costs which it formerly possessed. Besides, this ability to buy cheap power from a central station saves the man who may want to establish a small factory the capital expense of installing any power plant of his own.

But perhaps of greater significance than the equalizing of power costs between the small and the large producer is the fact that the large producer can now break up his factory into smaller units and place them at strategic points as determined by other considerations than power costs and nearness to his place of residence—for example, by nearness to markets or raw materials; by the relation of size of plant to costs of management and to the ease of securing good managers; by the efficiency of workmen living under varying conditions; by rentals; by wages; by ease of access to satisfactory transport facilities; and by many other factors which may be of importance in the successful operation of particular enterprises. In other words, the use of electricity and of the internal-combustion engine has increased the potential mobility and the flexibility of industry within the last 20 or 30 years as much as the introduction of steam power increased these same qualities in the industry of England in the latter part of the eighteenth century.

The development of flexible transportation units through the use of the gas engine should not be overlooked when we are considering the possibilities of a redistribution of industry in the present age. It is now possible for factories located in small communities having only a single railway line to avail themselves of the railway facilities in neighboring towns and cities at no greater cost than is incurred by factories in large cities for like services. Ten or twenty miles of driving over paved roads in the country may cost little more than driving as many blocks in the large city with its congestion and consequent delays. Already the truck has largely supplanted the railway for certain kinds of traffic—for example, local freights and the hauling of livestock—and has thus robbed the large city of some of the advantages of its superior railway facilities. In the meat-packing industry truck transportation of livestock bids fair to bring about a genuine reorganization, in which smaller centers will take an increasing proportion of the business away from the larger centers. The long-distance moving of household goods is already in the hands of the truckers, and there can scarcely be any doubt that still other kinds of traffic will take to the truck as time goes on. Thus some of the transportation subsidies enjoyed by our larger cities because of our present freight-rate structure are being removed, and the smaller places will be in a position to compete with them more purely on a basis of efficiency than they have been in the past.

In discussing the effects of more flexible transportation upon the redistribution of industry we must also take account of the airplane. On the assumption that both passenger and freight service by air are going to increase rapidly in the future, the nearness of landing fields to the factory may become a matter of great importance in freight traffic by air. In this respect the factory in the small city and even in the village will have obvious advantages over the factory in the city, once plane-load lots become common. Whether these advantages will be sufficient to weigh much in the location of new factories or in the establishment of branches cannot now be told. For many types of airplane service the large city will for some time have advantages over smaller communities, just as it has in its railway service, but with the development of air-taxi service this advantage may become less decisive.

4. DECENTRALIZATION OF OFFICES AND IMPROVED COMMUNICATION

The development of electric communication and air travel also makes it less and less necessary that the men in charge of large enterprises should have any considerable proportion of the office staff of the enterprise in their immediate vicinity. These technological developments in communication are far from being used to the full to decentralize offices within the metropolitan areas, while still less use is being made of them to disperse the office work of large concerns over the country. As a result many millions of people are compelled to live in the congested quarters of our large cities, while the better-paid executives flee to the suburbs. Thus, although we now have the technical base for a vast reorganization and dispersion of all manner of business operations, we are as yet taking little advantage of this ability to disperse population into areas where people can have more space in which to live and at the same time not have to spend an excessive proportion of their incomes as well as a large part of their leisure time in commuting to work.

If, for example, the great life-insurance companies of New York, and other great central offices, were to decide to move three-fourths of their workers out of New York City, as they no doubt could do with profit to all concerned, by reorganizing their operations and by making full use of electric and airplane communications, there is little doubt that the building of more skyscrapers and subways in New York could be postponed for a few years or perhaps forever. Once it was made clear by actual demonstration that the huddling of enormous numbers of workers in huge offices in great cities is neither good economics nor good social policy, thousands of businesses would be encouraged to reorganize their office operations and to search for new locations for at least a part of their white-collar workers. In the long run the efficiency of workers of all types depends in considerable measure upon their having good living conditions. There would seem to be no good economic excuse for maintaining a traditional pattern of operations either in factory or office which requires people to live in congested slums and under conditions in which they are unwilling to reproduce themselves when we possess the means for reorganizing all manner of economic activities in such a way that a large proportion of our people could enjoy the much better living conditions dependent upon having more space for living. After all, conditions of life which yield a high degree of personal satisfaction are also quite likely to be the same as those conducive to a high degree of individual efficiency, *i.e.*, the efficiency of the economic system is closely related to personal efficiency. It is high time that we began to give more weight to human considerations in the reorganization of the structure of industry and business with a view to making better community life possible to the great majority of workers.

Finally, although it is not yet possible to say what effects military considerations will have on the size and the structure of our cities, it is reasonably certain that they will be of great, possibly of prime, importance as long as we fail to work out the means for the peaceful settlement of international disputes. But it cannot be assumed at this time that military considerations will greatly hasten either the decentralization of our large cities into their "rings" or the dispersion of their populations into many smaller communities. Strategic considerations may conceivably work in the opposite direction. They may dictate a very great concentration of industry and of white-collar work in a few great metropolitan areas which can be so fully protected from aerial bombardment that little damage is likely to be done them. It is useless to speculate further on this point at this time.

5. THE NEW CITY

Apart from military considerations and in spite of the reluctance of the men in positions of power to make use of the developments in communication and transportation and in the distribution of electric power to decentralize and to disperse their operations and hence, of course, their personnel, these processes are going on slowly today. Here we are concerned primarily with the decentralization of large cities, *i.e.*, with the relative decline of population and industry in the central city itself and the building up of the suburban area in these respects. The wider dispersion of population and industry over the country at large is a different matter and will be discussed elsewhere.

The most important change in the form of the large city is its rather rapid expansion into a larger metropolitan community. Most large cities are no longer the relatively complete and self-contained communities they were even 20 to 30 years ago. The city as a political unit is more and more becoming merely the center of a metropolitan aggregation which as a whole is assuming many of the economic and social functions performed by the city of the past and occasionally has also taken over some of its political functions. This movement toward the integration of the life of the city and of the surrounding area received great impetus when the automobile began to make personal transportation feasible and the bus made local transportation routes more flexible. At the same time the truck began to provide suburban industry with more adequate freight facilities, and the marshaling yards of the railroads were improved to give suburban manufacturing areas better service. The suburban movement was further encouraged by the extension of the public utilities—water, gas, electricity, telephones, highways, and so forth—into the more thinly settled areas around cities. People were not slow to take advantage of these developments in their search for more comfortable living quarters. Business leaders were slower in realizing that business, too, was being released from the space and distance restrictions to which they had become accustomed.

Clearly it is no longer feasible merely to set up "city plan" commissions; they must be "area plan" commissions. As a matter of fact, the mononucleated city as the important social and economic unit of modern industrial society is being replaced by the polynucleated metropolitan area, and the movement in this direction is probably only well begun—assuming that military considerations do not interfere seriously with this development. The data on the growth of Metropolitan Districts from 1900 to 1940 and of the Standard Metropolitan Areas from 1940 to 1950 show beyond doubt that the central city may be said to be losing its identity or to be in process of absorption by the metropolitan area.

At present, in most cases, this process of transforming the city and its environs into an integrated metropolitan community is greatly retarded by the forms of political organization and by the checks on the change of political boundaries which were established some decades ago. As a result the changes in the structure of the metropolitan area—politically, socially, and economically—which would enable it to make full use of the improvements in transportation and communication to improve community life are slow and are made piecemeal. However, this movement is making headway in spite of great difficulties, and in the future planning commissions will be compelled to work more and more with metropolitan areas of which the city is only a part, albeit an extremely important part.

It is not possible to foresee, except in a very general way, the form and structure of the future metropolitan area, but I shall take the risks of a few general prophecies. The metropolitan area is quite clearly going to have several subnuclei, although the "downtown" area will probably remain the chief nucleus for some time, at least for the performance of certain highly specialized functions. The downtown nucleus is becoming more specialized and in the larger metropolitan communities may even be split into two or more nuclei, which may be some distance apart but which will probably be closely connected by rapid-transit facilities. Already in some metropolitan areas it is possible to find outlying portions which are almost as independent of the downtown center (or centers) as are the smaller communities a hundred miles away.

These subnuclei will strive to make available most of the highly specialized services formerly only provided in the downtown areas, while enabling people to avoid the tedium and the delay of a trip downtown. It is not yet clear just how large a population these subnuclei must serve to accomplish their purposes or just what their relation to the downtown area will be. In retailing and banking it seems probable that the "branch" may be the answer. Policy control will still remain with downtown headquarters. In providing professional service, however, it would seem probable that these subnuclei will differ considerably from one another. They may be expected to develop fairly adequate medical and hospital service. The legal services they provide will probably be adequate to serve most of the needs of individuals, while the more specialized needs of corporations and business generally are likely to remain downtown, except where a particular subnucleus also happens to be the headquarters of numerous business enterprises needing specialized legal services. As for schools, these subnuclei will be self-sufficient until the students are ready for college. It will then be necessary for many of them to "go away" to school or to make rather long daily trips to other parts of the metropolitan area. There should be little difficulty in finding adequate amusement facilities in all the larger subnuclei.

These subnuclei will all provide relatively large parking areas. Indeed, they will be developed largely on the assumption that people will seek most of the services they desire in areas where they can park their cars with comparatively little difficulty, for as long as is necessary to tend to their affairs, and with little or no direct charge.

Many of the highly specialized business services of the metropolitan area will be slower to leave the central area, e.g., wholesaling and jobbing, which are now generally found on the fringes of the downtown area. The central offices of banks, the offices of public bodies dealing with area matters, the general offices of local business enterprises which have been removed from the factory, and the branch offices of concerns doing a national business will probably be among the last to leave downtown, if they ever do. Many other services which draw their business from the entire metropolitan area or serve it as a whole, e.g., advertising agencies, newspapers, and engineering groups, will also remain in the downtown area. The larger transient and convention hotels are also likely to remain there. It seems to the author unlikely that there will be any sudden withdrawal of workers from downtown areas, but there may be a slow decline in actual numbers as business learns how to reorganize its office operations. The readiness of workers to move to the suburbs and even to neighboring smaller cities will also increase as both factories and offices stablize employment so that workers find it less and less advantageous to live in a central location from which they may go to jobs in any one of several directions.

Industry has already begun to move from the increasing congestion of quarters once regarded as peripheral to still more peripheral locations and even into rural areas within metropolitan communities. Judging by the extremely rapid growth of population in these same areas, it seems clear that the workers are also building homes in these new industrial areas. The development of better "crosstown" or around-the-town roads and highways and the increasing use of the automobile by workers are rapidly removing the objections of industrial workers to living away from the center of the city, namely, that living at some distance from the center makes it more difficult for them to move from job to job. Up to the present, however, there are few of the larger metropolitan areas in which decentralization is taking place fast enough to prevent the increase of traffic congestion in central areas and to keep the costs of doing many types of business in these areas from mounting more rapidly than in other parts of the metropolitan area.

6. THE GROWTH OF METROPOLITAN AREAS

It is impossible to foretell with any precision the future growth of metropolitan areas as a whole, and the likelihood of serious error increases rapidly when the growth of particular areas is in question. For at least 50 years the metropolitan areas have been growing faster than the remainder of the country. Two tables will be used here. Table 20-1 shows the growth of Metropolitan Districts from 1900 to 1940, while Table 20-2 shows the Standard Metropolitan Areas as of 1950 for 1900 to 1950. The Metropolitan Districts comprise the central cities and the minor civil divisions surrounding them which had a relatively high density of population at the time of the census. The Standard Metropolitan Areas include the central city or cities and the county, or counties, which are considered to belong to the particular area in question.

In the decade 1900 to 1910 the total population of the nation grew by 21.0 per cent, but the 44 Metropolitan Districts of 1900 grew by 34.6 per cent or about two-thirds faster.[5] Even at that time the central cities (33.6 per cent) did not grow quite as fast as the sattellite areas (38.2 per cent) around them. In the next decade, 1910 to 1920, when the national popula-

---

[5] In these comparisons the same area was used at both the beginning and end of the decade to avoid the inclusion of new territory.

Table 20-1. Per Cent Increase of the Population of Metropolitan Districts and Their Constituent Parts, by Decades, 1900 to 1940 [1]

Area	1930–1940 (140 districts)	1920–1930 (97 districts)	1910–1920 (58 districts)	1900–1910 (44 districts)
Total......................	8.1	28.3	26.9	34.6
Central cities..............	5.1	22.3	25.2	33.6
Satellite areas..............	15.1	44.0	32.0	38.2
Urban..................	7.4	37.7	30.7	35.9
Rural..................	30.0	56.0	35.1	43.2

[1] Warren S. Thompson, *Growth of Metropolitan Districts in the United States, 1900–1940*, p. 45, G.P.O., Washington, D.C., 1947.

tion grew by 14.9 per cent the 58 Metropolitan Districts of 1910 grew by 26.9 per cent, the central cities by 25.2 per cent, and their satellite areas by 32.0 per cent. The movement to the satellite areas was beginning to gain momentum. In the decade 1920 to 1930 the total population of the country grew by 16.1 per cent, the 97 Metropolitan Districts of 1920 by 28.3 per cent, and the central cities by 22.3 per cent, while the satellite areas increased by 44.0 per cent. Thus the satellite areas grew practically twice as fast as the central cities. This was the decade in which it first became practical for any considerable number of people to use the automobile for transportation to and from work. In the decade 1930 to 1940, the 140 Metropolitan Districts of 1930 grew but little faster (8.1 per cent) than the total population (7.2 per cent). But the satellite areas (15.1 per cent) grew almost three times as fast as the central cities (5.1 per cent) and over twice as fast as the total population. In the decade just ended, the Standard Metro-

Table 20-2. Percentage of United States Total Population in Standard Metropolitan Areas and Their Constituent Parts, 1900 to 1950 [1]
(United States total equals 100 per cent)

Area	1950 (148 S.M.A.'s)	1940 (126 S.M.A.'s)	1930 (116 S.M.A.'s)	1920 (95 S.M.A.'s)	1910 (72 S.M.A.'s)	1900 (53 S.M.A.'s)
Total.........	56.0	51.1	49.8	43.7	37.6	31.9
Central cities..	32.3	31.6	31.8	28.9	25.0	21.2
Rings.........	23.8	19.5	18.0	14.8	12.7	10.7
Urban......	12.0	10.5	10.3	8.0	6.5	4.9
Rural.......	11.7	8.9	7.6	6.8	6.2	5.7

[1] Donald J. Bogue, *Population Growth in Standard Metropolitan Areas, 1900–1950, with an Explanatory Analysis of Urbanized Areas*, G.P.O., Washington, D.C., 1953.

politan Areas having over 100,000 in 1950 grew by 21.8 per cent as compared with a national population growth of 14.5 per cent. The central cities (13.7 per cent), for the second time, failed to grow as fast as the total population. However, satellite areas grew by 34.8 per cent and the rural parts of these areas grew by 41.3 per cent as compared with 29.1 per cent for the urban parts. Furthermore, in the larger S.M.A.'s (Standard Metropolitan Areas) the central cities grew more slowly and the rings more rapidly than in the smaller areas. Within the rings the growth was faster in rural areas than in urban areas, and in general this rural-urban difference was greatest in the largest S.M.A.'s. Throughout the last half century except for 1930 to 1940 the S.M.A.'s having over 100,000 population at the end of the decade have grown much faster (about one-half) than the total population. The 53 S.M.A.'s of 1900 having a population of 100,000 or more contained 31.9 per cent of the nation's population while the 148 S.M.A.'s in the same size group in 1950 contained 56.0 per cent of the total. The proportion of our total population living in the central cities grew from 21.2 per cent in these S.M.A.'s in 1900 to 32.3 per cent in 1950. The rings, which contained only 10.7 per cent of the total population in 1900, have grown steadily, and in 1950 they had 23.8 per cent of the total or almost three-fourths as many people as the central cities compared with about one-half as many in 1900. The proportion of our people living in the central cities of the S.M.A.'s is now about stationary, in spite of the large growth in the proportion of the total population living in the S.M.A.'s. Of our entire national increase 1940 to 1950, the S.M.A.'s drew 80.6 per cent, 31 per cent going to the central cities, while their outlying portions drew 49 per cent. The remainder of the country drew only about 19.4 per cent. Obviously the movement of the population toward the metropolitan areas was greatly speeded up during this decade.[6]

The above data on metropolitan growth seem to justify two general conclusions regarding the future distribution of population, assuming no great catastrophe such as atomic bombing: (1) the proportion of our population living in the S.M.A.'s is likely to increase much faster during the next two or three decades than that living in the remainder of the country; (2) within the metropolitan areas the central cities are growing comparatively slowly while the outlying areas are growing rapidly. The number of large metropolitan areas in which the outlying population is greater than that of their central cities will almost certainly increase during the next few decades. These data seem to the author to justify the statement made earlier that the large city is rapidly being transformed into a metropolitan area which will have a political, social, and economic structure quite different from that of such communities today.

[6] Donald J. Bogue, *Population Growth in Standard Metropolitan Areas, 1900–1950, with an Explanatory Analysis of Urbanized Areas,* G.P.O., Washington, D.C., 1953.

Naturally the population changes noted are to be regarded partly as symptoms of the basic changes in social and economic organization which are taking place and partly as causes of further changes in structure which will take place. The desire of people to move away from highly congested areas could be realized much more readily once the automobile came into general use and the utilities were extended to the areas surrounding the cities. This in turn had an effect on the moving of industry to the more open fringes of the city. Both such movements encourage the development of subnuclei within the metropolitan area and tend to reduce the relative importance of the city itself in the life of the people living in the area. Such a movement once under way gains momentum. At present this development of a metropolitan area, not as a city of the conventional pattern but as a large urbanized area with a new and different distribution of population and with a growing decentralization of many of the accepted functions of the city, seems to be in full swing. To the author this presages a new type of urban life, and it is to be hoped it will be a more satisfying life and one into which people will be more willing to bring enough children to replace themselves. When 60 to 70 per cent of our people live in metropolitan areas the remainder (30 to 40 per cent), of whom only one-half to two-thirds will live in rural areas, cannot make up for any large replacement deficit which may occur in these metropolitan areas.

Suggestions for Supplementary Reading

BOGUE, DONALD J.: *Metropolitan Decentralization: A Study of Differential Growth,* 17 pp., Scripps Foundation for Research in Population Problems, Oxford, Ohio, 1950.

————: *The Structure of the Metropolitan Community: A Study of Dominance and Subdominance,* 210 pp., Horace H. Rackham School of Graduate Studies, University of Michigan, Ann Arbor, Mich., 1949.

HILBERSEIMER, L.: *The New City, Principles of Planning,* 192 pp., Paul Theobod, Chicago, 1944.

PETERSON, ELMER T., ed.: *Cities Are Abnormal,* 256 pp., University of Oklahoma Press, Norman, Okla., 1946.

THOMPSON, WARREN S.: *Growth of Metropolitan Districts in the United States, 1900–1940,* 59 pp., G.P.O., Washington, D.C., 1947. (U.S. Bureau of the Census.)

Chapter XXI

THE PROBLEM OF QUALITY

The problem of the quality of the population is not a new problem. It has from time to time occupied the thoughts of statesmen and philosophers who were interested in a better society or an ideal state. We are not concerned at this point to recount the theories which have prevailed regarding the quality of the population or with the practices adopted to maintain quality in the past. It will suffice to recall that the exposure of infants has at times had a eugenic purpose as well as that of restricting population growth. The selection of wives and of concubines has also, at times, been effected with eugenic intent. But by and large man has not been much concerned with the problem of his quality. The economic and social status of the family has been much nearer his heart. Concern over the eugenic quality of the nation's people has developed slowly as our increasing knowledge of heredity and of the processes of population growth have shown the possibilities of the deliberate control of quality.

It will be recalled that knowledge of the nature of heredity and of the processes of evolution grew apace—that as we became familiar with such ideas as "struggle for existence," "survival of the fittest," and "natural selection," we were also made aware of the significance of heredity in human development. In this connection it should be mentioned that Malthus' exposition of the processes of human growth had great influence on the thinking of Darwin and Wallace when they were working to explain the "origin of species" and hence on their formulation of the doctrine of evolution. But it was not until the latter part of the nineteenth century that the knowledge of the processes of human population growth coupled with the growing knowledge of heredity led to much interest in the quality of human stock. By that time the doctrine of heredity which was quite generally accepted was that heredity was not changed by use and experience but that the individual was merely a carrier of traits which he passed on unchanged. Since it was also becoming known that not all people left the same number of offspring, that is, that differentials in birth rates were quite usual (Chap. IX), the stage was set for a rapid increase of interest in the quality of the population. Obviously, if heredity was, for practical purposes, unchangeable and if people were reproducing at different rates, it was important to know what kind of people left the largest number of offspring. On this depended the future character of the race.

Under these circumstances it is not surprising that many people were quick to assume that many of the differences actually found between individuals in mental development, in social position, in economic status, and even in general attitudes toward life and society were due to hereditary differences, that is, to differences in the traits or characteristics carried in the germ plasm and, hence, beyond man's control, except through elimination.

This biological approach to the problems of quality in man led many to believe that the destiny of the individual, whether he would be a rich man or a poor man, a leader or a follower, an aristocrat or a beggar, a banker or a worker, was determined, largely if not entirely, by his heredity. Such an extreme position, of course, aroused the antagonism of those who believed that man's destiny lay in his own hands. These "perfectionists," as they were called in Malthus' day—"environmentalists," we would call them —came forth with equally extreme views to the effect that heredity was of little consequence in individual development, since it supplied only a plastic material which environment could mold in any way that society might desire. The extreme environmentalist at times even went so far as to deny that heredity placed any limits whatever on the development of individuals. Thus the battle was joined, and the problem of quality in the population largely took the form of a discussion of the relative importance of heredity and environment in determining the quality of individuals.

1. HEREDITY AND ENVIRONMENT [1]

We cannot hope to arrive at any satisfactory understanding of the problem of quality in man without a sound view of the relation of heredity and environment in the formation of the individual's personality. Unfortunately discussions on this matter have generally taken the form of an attempt to answer the question, is heredity or environment more important in the development of human character? The very form of this question assumes that, *as a general thing*, one of these factors must exercise a more or less exclusive influence on conduct. It is perfectly clear, however, when we come to examine the matter carefully, that heredity and environment are complementary elements in the life of the individual and that it is only as related to the individual that the discussion of their importance has any significance. Heredity and environment are simply two aspects of the life of every organism. Both are essential in producing life and in its develop-

[1] R. S. Woodworth, *Heredity and Environment: A Critical Survey of Recently Published Material on Twins and Foster Children,* 95 pp., Social Science Research Council, New York, 1941.

ment. It is foolish to try to show that, in general, one is more important, or less essential, than the other.

But we must hasten to say that, though both are always at work in an individual and though they are complementary, yet in particular cases it may very well be that one or the other exercises a decisive influence. Thus no one would deny that heredity very narrowly determines the limits within which environment can exercise its influence in the case of certain types of feeble-mindedness. Environment cannot supply traits which one did not inherit, nor can it change the characteristics represented by the inherited genes. This is commonly recognized in the case of physical traits like skin and eye color and many deformities which are known to descend in family lines, although some hereditary deformities can be rendered harmless to the individual. But this does not affect their hereditary nature. In general it can be said that environment can only encourage or repress the development of those plastic traits which the individual inherits. Thus the vital question becomes, what inherited traits are plastic and susceptible of development, and how far are they (in particular individuals) modifiable by training and experience? There may very well be many people of talent or genius— "mute, inglorious Miltons"—who never develop their superior qualities because environment gives no opportunity for their expression, while many others of only moderate ability attain a considerable degree of eminence because they have had every possible opportunity to develop their capacities. It is a great mistake to suppose that genius "will out" in spite of any and all conditions. Indeed, there are certain types of genius which are probably unusually sensitive to the influence of environment and which without the most favorable surroundings would never be developed.

Some concrete examples may help us to appreciate how heredity and environment cooperate to produce some of the most significant types of personality. Goethe will certainly be recognized as one of the great men of his time, perhaps of all time. In discussing his own achievements he fully recognized his debt to other people and ages, that is, to his environment, and was not in the least loath to acknowledge it. He saw heredity and environment as cooperating forces in his own life, as the following quotation clearly shows:

> I read some pieces of Molière's every year, just as, from time to time, I contemplate the engravings after the great Italian masters. For we little men are not able to retain the greatness of such things within ourselves; we must therefore return to them from time to time, and renew our impressions.
>
> People are always talking about originality; but what do they mean? As soon as we are born, the world begins to work upon us, and this goes on to the end. And, after all, what can we call our own except energy, strength,

and will? If I could give an account of all that I owe to great predecessors and contemporaries, there would be but a small balance in my favor.[2]

In whatever direction one looks, one finds this intimate and intricate relation between the hereditary qualities of the individual and the environment in which they develop. One cannot read the life and letters of Charles Darwin, for example, without being very deeply impressed with the fact that the fine hereditary qualities of the man were so dependent upon a favoring environment for their fruition that it would have taken very little to render him scientifically sterile. It is almost impossible to image Darwin earning a living for himself and his family and yet having the energy to produce scentific work of great significance. Probably the very qualities which made him such a fine observer of nature also rendered him so sensitive to his surroundings, both physical and social, that he could not participate in the affairs of everyday life to any considerable extent and yet have the energy and insight essential to scientific achievement. It not infrequently happened that a trip to London to meet some other scientists, or to read a paper before the Royal Society, left him so wrought up that he could do no work for days or even weeks. One could readily mention a dozen factors in Darwin's environment which, had they been slightly different, might easily have made his scientific work largely impossible.

This delicate and involved interplay of heredity and environment is always present. That it is not always so manifest as in the lives of men of genius does not prove that it does not exist, but only that the lives of most of us are not scrutinized so carefully as those of the men who make unusual contributions to human progress. Besides, it is probably true that most of us are less sensitive to what is going on about us than are men of unusual talent, so that we are not so fully aware of the sources from which we derive our ideas, sentiments, and habits as are the men of genius. There is no doubt a continuous gradation of susceptibility to the influence of environment on mental and personal development, from the idiot, whose susceptibility is too small to measure in most cases, to the genius, who has apparently a vast capacity to receive and make use of certain of his contacts with the life about him out of which he can make creations of great significance. In every case heredity sets the limits within which environment may act, but in no case can the actual realization of hereditary capacity go beyond the opportunity offered it by the surrounding environment. This may seem so obvious that it need not be said, but as a matter of fact there are many people who talk as though either heredity or environment alone were sufficient to account for much or all that has meaning in the conduct of men.

[2] Johann Peter Eckermann, *Conversations of Goethe with Eckermann and Soret,* p. 154, translated from the German by John Oxenford, rev. ed., George Bell & Sons, Ltd., London, 1909.

It cannot be emphasized too strongly that the individual personality as we know it at any moment is the resultant of the hereditary qualities a person possesses as developed by the particular environment in which he has lived.

If we accept this view of the complementary nature of heredity and environment, it is absurd to look upon most, or all, social problems as arising from hereditary deficiencies, as many whose primary interests are biological are prone to do, or as being merely the consequence of the inadequate organization of environment, as many environmentalists do. Little headway can be made in understanding and solving not only the problems of human quality but also most other social problems as long as these particularistic attitudes prevail. Problems of poverty, of crime, and of housing, for example, cannot be understood in their true relations by the person who believes that personal shortcomings are chiefly the result of defective heredity any more than by the person who believes that they are always the result of environmental conditions.

Let us consider for a moment the matter of poverty. Many people are inclined to believe that poverty is largely a matter of defective heredity and that it can be done away with if we can rid society of those who have less than the normal power of adjustment to the economic circumstances of life. No one who is at all familiar with poverty and with people in poverty would for a moment deny that many people have inherited capacities of such a low order that they can be developed very little by training and experience and, hence, that they are more likely to become poverty-stricken than people with normal or superior mental powers who are capable of a wide range of adjustments. The latter are far more likely to make a reasonably good adjustment to the economic and social circumstances in which they find themselves. To be unable to adjust oneself to the exigencies of the existing economic order generally results in a low income and all its attendant evils. On the other hand, to argue that being in poverty proves that an individual has inferior hereditary powers of adjustment which inevitably doom him to poverty is unrealistic.

Quite obviously, many social and economic circumstances contribute to the poverty of many people who are quite "normal" in mental equipment. A prolonged period of depression resulting in unemployment always brings into need many people who are normally self-supporting. Sickness, however caused, is also at the basis of much poverty. Likewise in many industries the wages, which are too low to maintain decent standards of living, lead to much illness, which in turn causes poverty. The intermittent employment so characteristic of certain segments of modern industry is also a frequent source of poverty. There is perhaps less need to call attention to the non-hereditary factors producing poverty today than there has been at any time since the settlement of America began, but unfortunately there are still many who believe that poverty is generally the consequence of hereditary deficiencies and that if we could prevent the propagation of this group among the poverty-stricken we could eliminate a large portion of all poverty.

If we investigate any particular case of poverty with sufficient thoroughness we can probably find out whether it is primarily due to (1) some personal hereditary deficiency, or (2) social circumstances such as accident, sickness, or unemployment. We can deal with the poverty-stricken individual or family intelligently only when we know the causes, both hereditary and environmental, and are willing to undertake the particular adjustments needed in each case.

This may seem a considerable digression from the problem of quality in a population. It is not so, however, for we cannot hope to understand the problem of quality nor can we hope to devise the proper means of maintaining the desired quality until we can evaluate the roles of heredity and environment realistically. Moreover, it should be made clear that we know the manifestations of heredity in a particular individual only as they are developed in a particular environment and that at present we possess no means of telling how far the personal traits of an individual which are most significant in determining his relations to his fellows have their origin in heredity or how far they are due to the development of his hereditary qualities in the environment in which he has been raised. Actually all that any *test* tells us is that the individual responds in a given way at a given time and under certain conditions; except for a few persons in whom hereditary deficiencies are rather clearly marked, we must be extremely careful in interpreting a given type of response as arising chiefly from heredity or environment. We must also know whether the environment encourages or discourages a given type of development, and even then we cannot be certain, in most cases, of the relative importance of these two factors. Consequently we must be extremely careful how we make use of the results of "intelligence" tests, personality tests, and other devices in arriving at judgments regarding the inherited capacities of individuals. It is no doubt true that the more closely similar the environments of individuals have been, the more the differences in their responses in a given situation are dependent upon inherited differences. Nevertheless the idea needs constant reiteration, in view of current practices and doctrines, that no two people, even in what appear to be the same environments, do actually have the same environmental influences exerted upon them; just as, except in the case of identical twins, no two children even of the same parents have the same hereditary character. The actual response of any person at any moment to a given situation is an extremely complex product, and it cannot be analyzed into its hereditary and environmental components with any exactness. Personality, as it manifests itself in daily conduct, is a far more subtle compound than the most complex organic compounds with which the chemist has to deal.

Because of the large hereditary differences between individuals, even children of the same parents, we have almost no basis at present for judging of the hereditary qualities of groups. The fact that some particular group, as a whole, responds somewhat differently to a particular test from another group cannot, except in rare circumstances, be interpreted as proof of a group differential in hereditary qualities. This differential may be due to differences in heredity, but until we know that it could not be due to a difference in experiences of people living in different environments we must not assume that group differences are hereditary. This is a very important matter, since there has been and still is a strong tendency to interpret group differences in the scores attained in certain tests as due to hereditary differences between them. Only in very small groups, generally in groups of blood kinship, is there any basis for assuming that particular hereditary traits of intellect and personality are characteristic of certain groups.

This means that we cannot judge of the inherited intellectual and personality qualities of individuals or of groups from the social status that they occupy at any given time or from their responses to a particular situation with which they are confronted, such as an intelligence test or a personality test.

The frequency with which a personality of high quality does come out of Nazareth should make us very slow to generalize regarding the inherited quality of people who may be found in lowly position. Real ability does appear in the most unpromising places and is often absent from the progeny of men and women of remarkable ability. The fact is that except for bodily traits and extremely marked cases of mental aberration we know very little about the relative importance of heredity and environment in the personal development of any individual and even less regarding their influence in the development of different classes or groups in the community.[3]

Although the author believes that what has just been said is sound doctrine, he would not leave the impression that we can learn nothing definite about the ways in which heredity and environment contribute to the development of the individual. The psychologists are slowly learning how to separate hereditary and environmental factors in personality development and thus to measure the effect of each while the other remains unchanged. But only a beginning has yet been made. It was just because there was almost complete confusion on this matter that the early work in mental testing left many people with such wrong impressions regarding the relation of heredity and environment in determining the development of the individual and his status in society. It was too readily assumed in these early studies that what was being measured was the native, or hereditary, capacity of the individual. It was quite natural, therefore, when rather wide differ-

[3] Julian Blackburn, "Family Size, Intelligence Score and Social Class," *Population Studies,* Vol. 1, No. 2, p. 175, 1947.

ences in intelligence quotient were found as between different economic and social groups, to assume that these also were the result of hereditary differences between these groups; *e.g.,* that a man was a common laborer because he had the intelligence appropriate to that job, and that the banker also had hereditary qualities which made him a banker rather than a laborer. The fundamental error in this type of thinking is the failure to recognize that the individual is always a complex organic product of heredity and environment and that as yet we know far too little of their interaction to make any precise statements of their relative roles in personality development. We are even less justified in attributing differences between groups in test scores to hereditary differences.

The early studies of particular families which had been a heavy social and economic burden to their communities for some time because of their poverty and crime—the Jukes, the Kallikaks, the Nams, and so forth—all suffered from the same defect. The results were frequently used to show how defective heredity produced thieves, drunkards, prostitutes, paupers, and ne'er-do-wells of many kinds. There is little doubt that in many of these families there was defective heredity, but the facts gathered made just as good a case for the influence of environment in producing individuals who were a public menace. The problem of individual adjustment to life is far more complicated than it appeared to these early workers. Fortunately the study of the relation of heredity and environment is being pursued in a more scientific spirit today, and we are beginning to get results which should prove extremely useful in the formulation of future population policy as it affects the quality of the people.

Space will not allow the detailed description of even the more interesting of the recent studies of heredity and environment, but it will be necessary to indicate briefly some of the results. As is generally known today, identical twins arise from the splitting of a single fertilized egg (ovum). Thus they have exactly the same hereditary qualities. Therefore, the differentials between them that develop during life must be attributed to differences in environment. Identical twins reared together should show appreciably more likeness to one another in personal qualities which can be measured than identical twins reared apart, and under all circumstances identical twins might be expected to show less difference from one another than fraternal twins or other children of the same parents whether reared together or apart. The study of Newman, Freeman, and Holzinger [4] shows that identical twins were more alike in height, in weight, and in intelligence quotients than fraternal twins of like sex. There was, however, practically no greater likeness between identical twins than between fraternal twins in personality traits, in school achievement, and in arithmetic. Furthermore, it seems to

[4] Horatio H. Newman, Frank N. Freeman, and Karl J. Holzinger, *Twins: A Study of Heredity and Environment,* 333 pp., University of Chicago Press, Chicago, 1937.

the author important that, while fraternal twins differed more from one another in height, weight, I.Q., and achievement than identical twins, these differences between fraternal and identical twins became less as one proceeded from measurements of physical qualities such as height and weight to that of mental qualities and social adjustments, as the following quotation indicates:

> In certain instances, namely, arithmetic, nature study, history and literature, tapping, will-temperament, and neurotic disposition, the correlations of identical twins are but little higher than those of fraternal twins. This seems to indicate that inheritance is a greater factor relatively in producing likeness or difference in some traits than in others.[5]

When identical twins who had never been separated were compared with identical twins reared apart these relations were confirmed. But environmental differences did seem to make a significant difference between identical twins in certain characteristics:

> In one of the physical traits, weight, and in intelligence and school achievement the differences [that is, the differences between identical twins reared apart as compared with those between identical twins reared together] are significantly greater, demonstrating the effect of environment on these traits. In height, head measures, and the score on the Woodworth-Mathews test, on the other hand, no significantly greater difference is found.
>
> When the amount of difference between the separated twins is compared with the estimated amount of difference between their environments, highly significant correlations are found.[6]

The study of *own* and *foster* children has also provided new information regarding the influence of heredity and environment in individual development. In general it appears that foster children show a somewhat stronger resemblance to their true parents in I.Q.'s than to their foster parents and certainly less resemblance to their foster parents than children in a control group showed to their own parents. But these differences are not large, and in the judgment of the author, the control of environmental factors in these studies is not as satisfactory as in the twin studies, since it consists largely in rating the biological parents of adopted children by their social or economic status, which leaves a far larger unknown element in environmental conditions than where children are brought up in the same family.

In the author's judgment these studies, even where they do show a more significant association between the I.Q.'s of the children and the social status of the biological parents than of the foster parents, do not conclusively prove that this arises from heredity. Furthermore, they cannot be

---

[5] *Ibid.*, pp. 352–353.   [6] *Ibid.*, pp. 356, 357.

expected to do so until means are devised by which the influence of both hereditary and environmental factors can be measured more accurately than has been done thus far. All one can say at this stage of our knowledge of the relative influence of heredity and environment gained from these studies is that, although there is no doubt that the social and economic status of the individual is frequently determined by his heredity, we have no unmistakable evidence that heredity is a significant determinant of differences between social and economic classes as wholes. This is not to say that there is any reasonable doubt that when certain groups of the population can be segregated, *e.g.,* certain classes of the feeble-minded, they will have a high proportion of children manifesting the same hereditary characteristics. But there is no reason to believe that defective or inferior heredity characterizes any racial or national group as such, or any social or economic group of appreciable size found in the normal community. The only hereditary differences about which we can be reasonably sure are those between individuals. A person who consistently falls in the lower 5 or 10 per cent in intelligence tests given to people in his own group is quite probably (assuming no accidental cause) of less hereditary capacity in certain respects than one who is consistently in the upper 5 or 10 per cent. But differences of a few points in I.Q.'s between social and economic classes or groups do not seem to the author to be of decisive significance as regards the hereditary quality of classes and groups as wholes. They *may* be due to differences in heredity, but they seem to him just as likely to be due to differences in opportunity associated with differences in social status, especially if the small percentages of clearly defective individuals, who are no doubt more frequently to be found in the lower social classes, are left out of account.

The upshot of these studies of the influence of heredity and environment on twins and foster children as well as of those of a more general nature carried out through the use of intelligence and personality tests is to show beyond question that heredity does place definite limits to the development of the individual in certain respects. However, in most respects important in determining social adjustments these limits are very broad. Environment can also produce significant differences between individuals even when they have what would generally be recognized as sound heredity. Moreover, the more significant the characteristics are from the standpoint of the adjustment of the individual to the community, the broader seems to be the field within which environment can act on the traits provided by heredity. The author believes that the modifiability of those traits which have to do with the determination of I.Q.'s, of school achievement, and of knowledge of arithmetic, nature, history, and literature and with the development of personality is so great that there would be little need to worry about the hereditary quality of the population if only that small portion of the people having defective and unstable mental traits could be prevented from reproduction. As we shall see, *nature* has already provided for this in a considerable proportion of these cases.

What has been said above about the relation of heredity and environment does not mean that we should not concern ourselves about the improvement of the hereditary quality of the population through the improvement of human heredity; but it does mean, as will be pointed out later, that we shall probably make far greater progress in improving the over-all quality of our population by providing an environment favorable to the development of the hereditary qualities already existing in the population than by concentrating any considerable amount of effort on the elimination from the population of those qualities or characteristics which show little susceptibility to improvement through environmental action. This interpretation of the relations of heredity and environment also means that from the standpoint of changing the hereditary quality of the population it is doubtful whether the differential birth rate is of much significance. In the opinion of the author the differential birth rate is of very great social significance but not primarily because it issues in an increase of the hereditarily inferior or superior. It is of significance chiefly because the social classes having the larger families have the least opportunity to give their children a reasonably good start in life, and this prevents as rapid an improvement in personal development as would otherwise take place.

But even though the author does not believe that the chief improvements in human life during the next few decades will come because of a better quality of heredity, he does believe that it is important to inquire into what can be done to eliminate defective hereditary capacity in our population without overstepping the bounds of reasonableness due to our lack of knowledge of how to select the carriers of defective heredity.

2. FEEBLE-MINDEDNESS

The very term *feeble-minded* implies that the persons in this group are not capable of responding in normal ways to the stimuli of their environment. We now know that many feeble-minded persons have hereditary defects which will prevent them from ever sharing fully in the life of the community. They can neither give to nor receive from the community the benefits which come from normal communication. Unfortunately even now we do not know how many feeble-minded persons there are in the nation, or which of these are carriers of defective heredity. Estimates made by well-informed and unbiased individuals regarding the number of feeble-minded in the population vary by as much as 100 per cent and generally fall between 1 and 2 per cent. A conservative estimate (1 per cent) would place the total number at not less than 1,500,000, of whom only about 120,000 to 130,000 are found in institutions [7] while, of course, an estimate of 2.0 per cent would double this number. What proportion of these feeble-minded are carriers of hereditary defects and what proportion are lacking in ability to make normal adjustments because of accidents, illnesses, and other environmental causes is likewise unknown. But, assuming that one-half, or even a smaller proportion of the feeble-minded are carriers of defective heredity, it is clear that the prevention of their reproduction would be a great gain in society.[8]

In the judgment of the author the community should take measures to prevent the reproduction of the feeble-minded as fast as we can identify them with reasonable certainty and can devise methods of sterilization which will be supported by public opinion. This curb on reproduction should be placed not only on those who carry defective heredity but also on many of those who are accidentally defective. For even though the latter probably will not have defective children, they are generally so handicapped both in personal development and in the matter of the opportunities they can offer children that their offspring will have little chance to develop as normal members of the community.

There are at present several serious obstacles in the way of preventing the propagation of the feeble-minded: (1) it will be a long time before we can provide adequate facilities to segregate those who should not reproduce; (2) there is widespread public opposition to the compulsory sterilization of such people; and (3) we do not yet have fully satisfactory tests enabling us to divide the feeble-minded from the normal. In fact the use of the word *normal* in this connection implies an arbitrary classification which will certainly continue to be challenged until we have more objective measures of normality than we now possess.

It is quite possible that much of the opposition to segregation and to physical sterilization would disappear if we had better methods of separating the feeble-minded from the normal.[9] Progress is being made along this line, but we know now that there are no sharp breaks between different grades of mental capacity. At whatever point in any kind of a scale it was decided to make a break and to say that those having less than a given score were feeble-minded while those having a higher score were normal, there would be a significant proportion of all persons so close to this point that they would have to be considered "borderline" cases and would have

[7] Frederick Osborn, *Preface to Eugenics*, p. 31, Harper & Brothers, New York, 1951.

[8] In this connection it should be noted that the lowest types of the feeble-minded are incapable of reproduction, so that the harm they do the community is confined to their economic cost, to the strain they put on their relatives, and to the generally demoralizing effects of having subnormal people at large in the community.

[9] Ezra S. Gosney and Paul B. Popenoe, *Sterilization for Human Betterment: A Summary of Results of 6,000 Operations in California, 1909–1920*, p. 117, The Macmillan Company, New York, 1929.

to be treated arbitrarily. Human capacity is a continuum. What we can hope to do as time passes is to say that certain individuals are incapable of doing certain tasks and of making certain adjustments and that because of this the community has decided they cannot be allowed to propagate. At present borderline cases are probably far more numerous than those that can be positively classed as feeble-minded. We should go slow in the matter of extending the stigma of segregation and/or sterilization to borderline cases. It is especially important just now that we go slow in extending the right of any man, or body of men, to prescribe sterility for additional groups in the population. This power in the hands of people who believe in the superiority of certain classes and races may easily become the means of eliminating those classes of the population that are considered a threat to the interests of the people who happen to be in power. It has taken some centuries for the mass of mankind to gain a modicum of personal rights and privileges and we should be extremely careful in abrogating these rights. The common good and not the advantage of certain classes and groups should be our sole criterion in denying the right of reproduction to any man.

Furthermore, this matter of preventing the reproduction of the feeble-minded is not so urgent as is often assumed. It has already been noted that the lowest grades are incapable of reproduction. The higher grades have children but do not rear them at a rate which need occasion great alarm. Even though their birth rates may be fairly high, the death rate of their children is high and they themselves are apt to die at a comparatively early age. This is not given as an argument against preventing the reproduction of the feeble-minded far more than is now being done. It is merely presented as a reason for proceeding slowly in broadening the classes of persons who are to be denied the right of reproduction. The community has always protected itself against those among its own members who endangered its welfare. What it considers its welfare constantly changes, and there is not the least doubt that we are now moving to protect ourselves against the burden of the feeble-minded, but we should not allow our enthusiasm for the more exact methods of identifying the feeble-minded which are being developed lead us into a too rapid inclusion of additional classes of people among the feeble-minded.

3. MENTAL DISEASE

The feeble-minded are not the only class of the population which has a harmful effect on its hereditary quality. Many mentally diseased persons are such because of some defect or weakness in heredity. They have less than the normal capacity to adjust themselves satisfactorily to the life of the community, not because of lack of ability but because of mental instability. It is extremely difficult, in fact impossible, at the present time to say what portion of the population is mentally diseased and of the mentally diseased to say what portion inherits and passes on some defect which makes it likely to succumb to mental disorders. We do not know what conditions may so enhance different types of mental instability that their possessors will become a menace to the general welfare. One estimate of the extent of mental disease is to the effect that at any given time 1.5 per cent of the adult population is more or less affected by mental ailments, while 10 per cent is affected at some time during life.[10] Estimates of the part played by heredity in the onset of mental diseases are at present of little value, but there can be little doubt that mental disorders are considerably more common in some families than in others, enough so that even the similarity of environment can be ruled out as the decisive factor within particular families.

It would appear that mental disorder is not usually inherited as a definite trait or group of traits but rather as some general instability of personality which makes one more than ordinarily susceptible to certain types of environmental influence. Whether this susceptibility will actually lead to a definite mental disturbance and breakdown will depend largely on the type of environmental influences that surround one. If this view is correct, then there is nothing hereditarily inevitable in most cases of mental disease. However, there can be little doubt that schizophrenia [11] (dementia praecox), which comes on fairly early in life, and manic-depressive psychosis,[12] which comes on later in life and is recurrent, are both of hereditary origin in many cases, that is, there is an inherited predisposition which is likely to lead to definite mental disturbance in a certain portion of the population.

From the standpoint of the hereditary quality of the population, however, even the most common types of mental disease are of less significance than might at first be assumed. Schizophrenia, as has already been mentioned, comes on early in life (at puberty or soon after), so that its victims have a far lower rate of reproduction than the general population. This is also true of the reproductive rate of manic-depressives, although they probably leave more offspring than schizophrenics. These two types of mental disease account for nearly three-fifths of all hospitalized cases of mental disease in the United States.

No doubt people suffering from the other types of mental disease which come on later in life have higher reproduction rates than the two just dis-

[10] Carney Landis and James D. Page, *Modern Society and Mental Disease,* pp. 19–25, Farrar & Rinehart, Inc., New York, 1938; Carney Landis and M. Marjorie Bollis, *Textbook of Abnormal Psychology,* p. 132, The Macmillan Company, New York, 1947.

[11] Characterized by (1) general apathy and indifference, or (2) paranoia, including delusions of grandeur and persecution, or (3) a general refusal to cooperate and sometimes mutism, or (4) silliness and bizarre ideas.

[12] Characterized by a very unstable emotional life, with violent swings from depression to a high state of excitement and rapid action.

cussed, but even these do not in general have high rates. There is a rather strong current of selection operating to reduce the proportion of the population in which the predisposition to mental disease is hereditary. There is no reason, however, why people suffering from such disease should not be encouraged to be sterilized and in most cases should not be compelled to be sterilized if they are to be turned back into the general population while still of reproductive age. But in view of what has been said it will be clear that we should not expect a great deal of improvement in the hereditary quality of the population from such measures.

4. OTHER TYPES OF DEFECTIVES

There are still other types of individuals who by their propagation contribute dangerous or weakening elements to the population. It is not easy to recognize the part played by heredity in causing many ailments, for example, blindness, deafness, mutism, the susceptibility to diseases such as cancer, tuberculosis, and so forth, but as fast as it is possible to be certain that heredity is a significant factor in any family, it would be well to encourage the afflicted individuals to be sterilized and where the community suffers serious injury through their propagation even to enforce sterilization or segregation. However, until we have clear evidence on the hereditary nature of the defect, no compulsory action should be taken.

Thus far, most that has been said about improving the hereditary quality of the population has been negative, that is, it deals with reducing the amount of hereditary defect in the population. The general conclusion is that in certain respects the community could reasonably expect to benefit by preventing the propagation of those having definite hereditary defects, but the extent of the benefits to be expected is quite limited.

5. CONCERN OVER A DECLINE IN MENTAL ABILITY

In recent years the discussion of the quality of the population seems to the author to be centered less on the elimination of the demonstrable carriers of defective heredity and more and more on the decline in the average mental ability of a population which would be expected to follow from the higher birth rate among people of less than average ability as compared with that among the people having average ability or better. It is perfectly obvious that *if* at any given moment 5 to 10 per cent of the people belong in a group in which the members tend to *inherit low mental capacities*,[13] and *if* these same people have a substantially higher birth rate than the 5 to 10 per cent at the other extreme of inherited ability, and *if* the children of this group of low ability survive in approximately equal proportions with those of the

[13] Osborn, *op. cit.*, p. 36.

group having better inherited ability and again reproduce in larger numbers, the average ability of the population is likely to decline. But it will be noted that there are many if's in the above, none of which can be taken for granted.

In the first place, our data on the differential birth rate (Chap. XI) relate chiefly to social and economic groups, which are far from being homogeneous groups from the standpoint of heredity. Moreover, such data as are available showing that parents of low hereditary ability have relatively high proportions of children with similar ability deal almost entirely with birth rates or number of births and make no allowance for differences in survival rates. Often it seems to be taken for granted that the improvement in health conditions in recent decades has, for practical purposes, eliminated differences in survival rates between social and economic groups and that as a consequence the differentials in their birth rates measure their differentials in increase. The data on infant mortality and on occupational mortality do not bear out this assumption. Unfortunately most such data (Chap. XI) are now rather old, and conditions may have changed quite recently, but I do not believe we can assume that differential birth rates measure differential rates of increase until more data are available. At present our data indicate that the poorer economic classes still have higher death rates than the more comfortable classes. Finally, as we have seen in Chap. IX, the differentials in birth rates between social and economic groups appear to be declining and may disappear altogether in the near future. This does not mean that there may not remain substantial birth differentials between the groups ordinarily spoken of as "inferior" and those of higher mental capacity; but it is between these same groups that we should expect the largest differences in survival rates. I know of no study showing the differences between the survival rates in such groups. The available data relate to birth rates or to number of births per family. Obviously these are not the same as survival rates or number of children per family surviving to reproduce. In view of these conditions it seems to me that there is not infrequently a tendency among those greatly interested in the quality of the population to exaggerate the harmful effects of the differential birth rate and the improvement in the death rate on the quality of the population.

6. A EUGENIC PROGRAM FOR ENCOURAGING THE GROWTH OF THE DESIRABLE

We have still to consider the positive aspects of the problem of hereditary quality, namely, the encouragement of the more rapid growth of those who would generally be judged to have good (sound) heredity. There are three questions to answer if we are to make any headway in understanding this aspect of the problem of quality: (1) Who are the fit, or the people of good stock? (2) How are matings between the fit to be secured? (3) How is the proper number of children to be ensured after the matings of the fit have been consummated? In what follows, considerable space will be devoted to the analysis of the widely accepted views regarding what constitutes superior stock, but no attempt will be made to define it exactly. All the author will attempt to do here is to show some of the practical difficulties in securing a more rapid propagation among people whose hereditary fitness no one would seriously question. Since every well-defined group or class tends to think of "good stock" in terms of the way certain qualities in other groups and classes affect its own welfare, there is no reasonable hope of securing in the near future more than a very modest measure of agreement regarding what constitutes "good" heredity.

But the difficulties of the positive eugenist have only begun when he has defined good stock. Supposing that an agreement is reached as to what constitutes good stock and how to identify it, the next difficulty is to secure matings between people of good stock. There is no sure way of doing this in a democratic country, but there is good reason to hope that a sensible and thorough education for parenthood will render many people less willing than now to mate with those whose heredity is known to be of doubtful quality. To this end there is need to encourage a legitimate pride in family achievement which is not, at the same time, snobbish. People should be encouraged to consider whether the children issuing from a contemplated mating will be able to uphold the family traditions and/or to contribute satisfactorily to community welfare. We have had far too little genuine family sentiment in this country. We have been prone to think that family pride and snobbery were synonymous. Unfortunately this has all too often been the case. But a real pride in the achievement of one's family is altogether consistent with the most humane and democratic sentiments. We may well develop in legitimate family pride a strong eugenic force. This family pride need by no means be confined to the small percentage of people who contribute conspicuously to the life of their time. Many humble workers have a right to feel that they are making a very important and necessary contribution to community welfare and to feel proud of their work. There is not the least reason why all of us should not encourage our children to carry on the family tradition of thorough and honest work. Such family pride should not only contribute materially to an improvement in family life but also lead to more consideration of the quality of offspring. But, of course, we must recognize that education for parenthood and family pride, although capable of becoming eugenic forces of no mean strength, will probably be more important in their social than in their biological consequences. They will accomplish more in the better standards of family life they set for people to aim at than in the actual increase in the proportion of the population having good heredity.

Even supposing that matings between people of good stock are secured in an increasing portion of our population, we still have the problem of whether they will be as fruitful as—or, preferably, even more fruitful than —those less desirable eugenically. There is, of course, no way of telling how fruitful such marriages would be; we may, however, adduce some considerations which have a bearing upon this matter. At present we place heavy personal economic penalties on those people whose preparation for life is long and expensive, if they undertake to rear fair-sized families. Since, in this class as a whole, inherited property is of little consequence and incomes are both small and uncertain until one is, perhaps, thirty-five years of age, the rearing of a fair-sized family is both arduous and precarious. Furthermore, promotions and raises in pay generally come more slowly to those who have fair-sized families early in life than to those who have small families or, indeed, no families. Such preferential treatment of the bachelor, or the near-childless man, may be justified from the standpoint of the value of these men to the employer as compared with the man rearing a fair-sized family, but it certainly puts a penalty on the rearing of children which few will endure when contraception is easy and "success" gauged by economic standards is a strong social ideal. This is one reason, and a very important one, for great numbers of childless marriages and of one- and two-child families in certain groups of white-collar workers. In the laboring classes somewhat different motives may operate, but for many of them the urge to small families is hardly less pressing—the desire to give their children a larger opportunity than they themselves had, the irregular employment, and the uncertainty of being able to rear a fair-sized family and still lay something by for old age.

One way, then, to encourage greater fertility in matings where the stock is good is to remove some of the penalties for rearing children which our present system places upon those who are most likely to give some weight to eugenic considerations in their mating. There are many ways in which this may be done, as will be brought out in the discussion of national population policies (Chap. XXII). But there is one point not brought out in the policies thus far adopted to which the writer would like to call attention here. In modern industrial society, money is the chief measure of the value the community attaches to any and all types of activity. This being the case, the woman who prefers to give the best years of her life to rearing a family finds little or no public reward or recognition of this service in our society because she can earn no money. Society recognizes the economic value of the woman who goes to the factory to knit stockings for children but does not recognize any economic value in her staying at home and darning those stockings or in her doing the much more essential tasks concerned with the care of the physical and mental welfare of children. In fact she is often made to feel that she is a parasite—that in bearing children and taking care of them while they are dependent she is not rendering an essential service but is adding burdens to the family budget. In the opinion of the author an industrial society paying money rewards for useful work should recognize the service of the mother and pay her for it; there should be a mothers' wage. This is not *buying* children; it is merely providing women with the tangible evidence that the community does value mothers' services as well as the services rendered to industry and commerce by women who work outside the home. The question of whether it is better for the community to ease the cost of rearing children by providing services—health, housing, school, and so forth—or in the form of cash will come up for discussion in the chapter on national population policies.

The removal of the economic penalties of rearing a family should also do much to reconcile the desire for individual development, which is characteristic of many of those having a little more than average ability, with the urge to biological survival. These two elements of our nature can never be wholly reconciled, but much can be done to remove the economic handicaps of fair-sized families from those who would like to rear such families.

The author believes that if the economic handicaps of fair-sized families are largely removed many of the social handicaps will automatically disappear. But much might also be done to encourage families of the proper size (every couple that has children must now have approximately three to keep the population at its present size) by an education which would make it clear that biological survival as well as personal success is needed to make a well-rounded life. Our whole scheme of education today, particularly our education of women, is most woefully defective in this regard. There appears to be little chance for fair-sized families from good matings, even when the social and economic handicaps have been removed, until we develop some quite different notions than are now current regarding the relations of the individual and the race. Naturally any considerable change along this line will take time. We should not, therefore, anticipate any very rapid progress in increasing the proportion of the next generation that comes from those groups and classes which would generally be admitted to have good heredity. Whether this is considered a dangerous situation calling for urgent action will, of course, be determined by our judgment as to whether or not the present processes of population growth are dysgenic and, if so, to what extent.

7. NATURAL SELECTION AND SURVIVAL

There is a very widespread belief among those who have interested themselves in the hereditary quality of the population that in the past *natural* selection worked toward the improvement of the quality of the population while the *artificial* processes of selection in operation today are dysgenic, that is, lead to the more rapid increase of those having defective or inferior heredity. This view assumes that natural selection as regards man was a process with which he interfered very little in the past and that its results were always beneficial to the race, while the processes of selection operating in Western society today are *artificial*, that is, are now being interfered with by man's control over social conditions and are more or less detrimental to the quality of the population. We are told that the general improvement in economic conditions, the development of medical science and practice within the last half century, and the organization of charitable relief on a large scale are the nefarious agents which have gradually nullified the action of natural selection until today artificial selection, that is, selection controlled by man's interference with these earlier natural processes, is the chief factor in determining who shall survive.

The questions that arise in connection with selection in the mind of one studying the processes of population growth are (1) whether there is any valid ground for calling the processes of selection *artificial* today as contrasted with *natural* yesterday; (2) whether the processes of selection going on today are any less rigorous and beneficial than they were yesterday.

The answer to the first question, as to whether there is any real difference in the character of the selective processes called natural and artificial, appears to be "No." There has never been a time in the history of man when his habits, his customs, his institutions, and his social attitudes have not been important factors in determining what groups and individuals would survive to reproduce. He has always tampered with his environment to the extent of his ability, in order to survive with as little effort as possible. In this sense there has always been an artificial (social) element in what has been called "natural selection." Man has also always made changes in his social organization, the larger part of which were probably made without his being conscious that he was trying to adapt his modes of life so that he could ensure himself more certain survival. Obviously, whenever these man-made changes in environment, in social institutions, and in customs, proved of advantage they led to greater certainty of survival and thus increased the social (artificial) element in what is customarily called natural selection. The difference between the natural selection of the past and the artificial selection of today is not in kind but merely in degree. Man has always guided the processes of selection to the degree he has been able to do so to ensure group survival.

At any given time the selective processes which were actually operating may or may not have been beneficial from the standpoint of the quality of any particular group. Without doubt many groups have perished. There is not now and there has never been any assurance that the types of men most honored by their fellows would leave the greatest number of survivors. Nature, if one may personalize her, has never been interested in anything but the survival of traits or qualities. She has never encouraged evolution "upward" (whatever that may mean) in direction because man considered it upward but rather has judged the goodness of traits solely by their survival value to the group. To put the matter very bluntly, if imbeciles have traits—for example, a strong sexual urge, with reasonably strong parental inclinations—which make for survival, while on the other hand, geniuses have a strong bent toward self-development and but slight urge to rear children, nature prefers the imbeciles and always has. She has never had any respect for group judgments as to what traits were or were not socially valuable at any given moment of time; she has been interested only in those traits which ensured the survival of the group. Fortunately, however, the same traits have often had both social value and survival value.

Supposing, then, that we drop the distinction often made between natural and artificial selection and regard all the processes affecting survival as natural in the circumstances under which they operate since this is the attitude which science dictates. Is there any reason to suppose that the selective processes are less rigorous today than they were ten centuries ago? In a considerable part of the world they have changed but little in ten centuries or so; hence they are of the same kind and intensity as of yore. Therefore, in attempting to answer this question, we need not consider the regions and peoples where there has been little or no change during the last few centuries. But in most of Europe, North America, Australia, South Africa, Japan, parts of South America, and a few other places, great changes in modes of living have taken place in the last century or two. Have these changes lessened the rigor of the selective processes to which these people are subject?

Before we can say whether the rigor of natural selection is being mitigated today, we must make sure that we understand what is meant by *rigor* in this connection. Many people seem to think that natural selection is not as rigorous today as formerly, merely because our death rate is only one-third or less as high as it was a few decades ago. This one fact seems to them to prove that the rigor of the selective process has been greatly abated of late years. The simple fact is, however, that in the process of evolution it is of little significance whether or not the individual lives and reproduces. The rigor of the selective process is to be judged, not by the height of the death rate which shows only the proportion of the individuals in a population dying in a given period, but by the proportion of the family strains that survive and the relative rates of increase of these different family stocks.

Judged by this standard, it is probable that selection is more rigorous now in industrialized lands than ever before; that more strains of family stock are now dying out in each generation than in most past ages. It is also likely that many of the family strains in certain groups in the population are becoming a smaller and smaller proportion of the population in each succeeding generation. The quarrel, then, is not with the change in the character or in the rigor of natural selection but with the criterion which nature applies, namely, survival value. People who believe in the harmful consequences of "artificial" selection are in effect saying that for untold ages the survival of the fittest was good, *i.e.*, the fittest were not only the best from the standpoint of survival but also the fittest (best) from the standpoint of community welfare. They believe that today the processes of selection for survival and for social fitness no longer coincide; hence, we must try to arrange matters so that once again the fittest to survive will also be the fittest socially.

8. THE EUGENIC CHARACTER OF NATURAL SELECTION

The view that we need to modify or change the processes of selection operating in modern society assumes that formerly the differential death rate removed the ne'er-do-wells, the defectives, the incompetents, the vicious, and the poor at a much more rapid rate than it did the people of more than average ability, the successful, the rich, and the powerful and that, as a result of this process, the race has, in the past, grown more largely from the middle and upper classes, who were of superior stock, than from the lower classes who were inferior in ability.

It is by no means certain, however, that the processes of selection in past ages were so simple and so eugenic as this view implies. In the first place, there is no satisfactory evidence that the classes of superior ability, as measured by success, actually have increased any more rapidly than have the lower classes in past ages. In the second place, it is rather doubtful whether the superior groups, by which is generally meant the upper social and economic classes, did and do contain a higher-than-normal proportion of the all-round superior type of human being upon whom progress in human welfare depends. With regard to the higher survival rate of the rich and powerful in past times, a few considerations may be set forth which will make this appear less axiomatic than is generally assumed.

One of the chief occupations of the upper classes in most communities in past times has been war. And it should be borne in mind that in many groups this occupation was reserved exclusively for the upper classes. The peasants and laborers were only indirectly involved in it. It is exceedingly questionable whether this fact alone is not sufficient to counteract the greater incidence of nonviolent deaths upon the lower classes, if indeed this incidence was significantly greater before the days of the industrial revolution. In addition to the losses from war, upper classes always and everywhere have been inclined toward debauchery and this frequently resulted in the dying out of the family in a few generations. A study of European nobilities shows that in the legitimate line they are not very long-lived. Again, even in China, where family ties are unusually strong, the powerful and exalted appear to have been rather easily corrupted so that they died out within a few generations. From these two considerations alone it would appear doubtful whether in the past the race has actually been bred so much more from the upper classes as is commonly assumed.

We must also recognize that in times past the quick-acting germ diseases —smallpox, typhus, typhoid, cholera, diphtheria, plague, and so forth—were the causes of a very considerable proportion of all deaths and that these diseases were but indifferent respecters of social status. They made little distinction in their attack between the mighty and the lowly in the days when they were regarded as inevitable visitations of the wrath of a supernatural being and when sanitation was equally unknown in the hovel and the castle. Even in the incidence of infant mortality there cannot have been a very great difference between the poorest and the richest, for the first principles of infant feeding and care were utterly unknown. Besides, it is likely that upper-class women have always avoided nursing their own children far more than have poor women. It may be that the avoidance of nursing their own children by upper-class women did not increase infant mortality so greatly as might be supposed because of the ease with which wet nurses could be secured, but even so it is probable that the turning of babies over to wet nurses by well-to-do women has resulted in higher infant-mortality rates than if they had more generally nursed their own children.

Furthermore, it is by no means certain that the improvements in health conditions which are often supposed to have mitigated the force of natural selection on the lower classes have actually been of more benefit to them than to the upper classes. The most recent comprehensive data on occupational mortality known to the writer show that in England and Wales as late as 1931 the death rate of the unskilled workers throughout their working life was often 25 per cent in excess of that of the upper and middle classes but was even greater than that at the ages when reproduction is taking place. As late as 1939 in England and Wales infant mortality was over twice as great (60.1) in the lowest social class as in the upper and middle classes (26.8), and a large part of the difference took place in the period between four weeks and one year of age from causes which were closely connected with environment, the rate in the poorest class from infectious diseases being 22.7 while that in the upper and middle classes was only 3.6.[14]

In 1938 the death rate of white male industrial policyholders in the Metropolitan Life Insurance Company aged twenty and over was 43.6 per cent above that of ordinary policyholders in the same company. A careful inspection of the occupations of these industrial policyholders shows beyond doubt that they were among the better paid of those falling within the industrial classification. Hence, the difference between industrial workers of lower economic status and ordinary policyholders must have been considerably above 43.6 per cent. The fact that the industrial policyholders in the Metro-

[14] United Kingdom, Royal Commission on Population, *Reports of the Biological and Medical Committee,* Vol. 4, pp. 11–26, H.M.S.O., London, 1950.

politan Life Insurance Company had a very much higher death rate than the regular policyholders, although in 1938 they had a death rate only 78 per cent as high as the white male population of the United States of the same ages, is certainly of great significance. Thus, while the data are far from being satisfactory, there can be little doubt even today that there are substantial differences in the death rates of different social and economic classes in the population. There is no clear evidence that the differential in favor of the upper social and economic groups as compared with the lowest social and economic groups is less today than in the past.

If there is any significant change in the relative survival rates of the upper and lower classes in the past century, it probably arises not from the relative easing of "natural" selection on the poor but from the fact that at the moment they are less given to the practice of conception control than the well-to-do. Since practically all students of population growth are disposed to believe that the large differentials in the birth rates which have characterized different economic classes and groups during the last few decades are temporary, it would seem that we need not be concerned much longer over the higher birth rates in the lower social and economic classes.

9. SOCIAL AND ECONOMIC SUCCESS AS RELATED TO SUPERIORITY

There is a widespread disposition to assume that the very fact of having attained a certain measure of success in the community proves the possession of superior hereditary traits which it would be desirable to pass on. The author believes there is little justification for this view. The attainment of success is proof only of satisfactory individual adaptation to the conditions determining success according to the standards of the group at that time. Social and economic success is not proof of an all-round ability in the person who thus succeeds, nor is it proof of the possession of qualities which will contribute largely to the development of a progressively humane social order. As a matter of fact, many people who attain success, particularly along economic and political lines, do so because they are thick-skinned and lack the imagination to see the ways in which their success reacts adversely upon the welfare of others and upon the organization of community life. There is nothing inherent in the nature of contemporary social success to ensure that the person who attains it will also possess those qualities which will add to the fullness and richness of community life.

It would not be at all difficult for anyone who knows a number of successful people to pick out several of them who owe their success largely to the qualities which they share in common with the bully, the prize fighter, the ward heeler, the racketeer, and the fox. Otherwise how can one possibly explain the callous indifference of a not insignificant fraction of successful men to the living and working conditions of their employees, to the effects of their business practices on the national economy, and to those of their political machinations on the welfare of the people? There is not time or space to go into the nature of the social processes selecting people for success, but no one can study the people who attain a little more income and prestige than the average without feeling that an appreciable proportion of them have attained their position by the exercise of highly antisocial qualities, by manipulating common human weaknesses for their own enrichment and aggrandizement, by crawling through legal loopholes ferreted out for them by clever lawyers, or by a lack of insight into how their conduct reacts upon the welfare of other people. In other words, an appreciable proportion of the successful owe their success to their rather dull moral and social sense, which sees nothing out of the way in exploiting their fellow men as long as they can avoid legal penalties, or to the fact that they have not the capacity to see themselves as others see them. In either case can it be seriously contended that such people are the salt of the earth and that their failure to reproduce is a serious loss to the community? Even if, as is probably the case, the antisocial qualities which the successful all too frequently manifest are the product of experience (environment) more than heredity, the chances are that their children will develop many of the same qualities through their family contacts. But no matter whence arise those qualities which are commonly associated with the terms "hard-boiled," "shyster," "slicker," "corner cutter," the people possessing them make life harder and more difficult for great numbers of people, and it is certainly stretching a point to call such qualities "superior" just because they are so frequently associated with economic and political success.

In addition, at present we do not know that the size of the family is the same for all types among the successful. In fact what we do know would lead us to expect rather large differences within this group just as appears to be the case in those groups for whom we do have some information. Indeed, there is some reason to think that those who take their success seriously and who endeavor to give society value received in return for its generous recognition of their ability, rear larger families than those who regard the world as their "oyster" and are concerned chiefly with opening it to secure the meat. It is the latter type that we may well spare; there will always be too many of them.

Finally, it may be suggested that, as the size of the family comes more and more under control, the differential birth rate will come to express real differences in outlook upon life. Those people who see some meaning and purpose in life and who wish to contribute their mite to the development of this meaning and purpose will be ready to make considerable personal sacrifice to have children to carry on. A cherished desire to participate in the future through offspring might then be regarded as far better proof of desirable hereditary qualities than most of the qualities now making for economic success. If at some future time the population should spring more largely from such people, the world would be a better place to live in than at present. Until now, at least in the West, the combative, acquisitive type of individual has played altogether too large a role in the development of our ideals and our forms of social organization.

10. ECONOMIC HANDICAPS AND THEIR CONSEQUENCES

There is not the least doubt that there has been a rather close association between economic status and size of family for several decades—the poorer the group, the larger the family size. A considerable amount of evidence on this point has already been cited in Chap. IX. Data were also presented there showing that this differential natality may now be passing.

This matter of the relation of *success* to *superiority* cannot be left without some additional remarks regarding the handicaps which certain social and economic conditions impose upon the personal development and the social status of certain groups.

It is now generally recognized that for various causes there are rather large areas and regions in the United States in which economic conditions are much harder than in other regions. The economic conditions of people living in mountainous areas, in cutover areas, and in areas where a once rich soil has been so eroded that it will only produce meager crops are usually much below those of people living on better soils and in urban areas. An examination of the fertility of these different groups of people shows that there is a rather close inverse relation between economic condition, measured by level of living, and fertility—the lower the level of living of an area, the larger the number of children under five years of age per 1,000 women aged twenty to forty-four.[15] Going into somewhat more detail, one finds that the rural people in the poorer counties in practically every state have a higher fertility than those in the more prosperous counties. As late as 1940 there were almost no exceptions to this generalization. It is not surprising, therefore, to find that in most states the counties with the highest ratios of children were also those with extremely low expenditures for education per pupil and with low expenditures for health, for roads, and for other public services. This situation is being improved to some extent in a number of states through the development of state activities in different fields, *e.g.,* through the equalization funds for education. But it is still generally true that the areas with the highest fertility have the poorest schools, the least health service, and the poorest roads, as well as the poorest housing and the

[15] Carter Goodrich *et al., Migration and Planes of Living, 1920–34,* 111 pp., University of Pennsylvania Press, Philadelphia, 1935.

lowest level of living. Can anyone doubt that these conditions impose a severe handicap on the children in these poorer areas?

Although the handicaps of poverty in city populations are not the same as those in the rural population as regards schools and certain other public services, they are highly significant as regards quality of housing, opportunities for recreation, adequate nutrition, and so forth. The point is that wherever poverty is found, in spite of the improvements in public services being made, low incomes do impose handicaps on children which make the manifestation of what are commonly thought of as superior qualities a far more difficult matter for such children than for those brought up under more favorable economic and social conditions.

Another type of handicap to children reared in poor families is shown in the division of the family expenditures between different types of goods and services in families of different sizes. In Chicago it was found that the expenditure for food per meal per adult equivalent declined as the size of the family increased, income being held constant. With the proper adjustments for the fact that a child does not need so much food as an adult, the couple with no children paid 22.5 cents per meal per adult equivalent; the couple with the one child, 18.8 cents; the couple with two children, 16.2 cents; the couple with three or four children, 13.8 cents. Thus the couple with three or four children spent only about three-fifths as much per meal as the couple with no children in the same income class. There can be little doubt that the children in these larger families did not get fully adequate nourishment. There simply was not enough money in many families to enable the parents to get what was needed to ensure good health, although these larger families spent a larger proportion of their budgets for food. The families with three or four children spent 38.6 per cent of their budgets for food, while the childless couple at the same income level spent only 31.1 per cent.[16]

This larger expenditure for food in the larger families left less to be spent for other goods and services. The proportion of the budget going for rent in the three- and four-child families was slightly higher than in the two-child families but somewhat lower than in the no-children families. The three- and four-child families spent no larger a proportion of their income for clothes than other families; hence they must have had poorer clothes. They spent no more on medical care; hence it had to be stretched thinner, or they had to depend more largely on the public health services.

Another respect in which low family income imposes a heavy educational handicap on all children in such families, in addition to the inferior quality of the public schools in poor rural areas, is in the years of schooling the children received.

[16] Frank Lorimer and Herbert Roback, "Economics of the Family Relative to Number of Children," *Milbank Memorial Fund Q.,* Vol. 18, No. 2, pp. 119–125, 1940.

Bell found that, out of over 13,000 Maryland youths interviewed who were permanently out of school, 39.1 per cent did not go beyond the eighth grade. But this proportion varied greatly in families of different sizes.[17] Thus if there was only one child in the family only 22.2 per cent did not go beyond the eighth grade, while if there were four the percentage rose to 35.0, if there were seven it was 52.4, and with nine or more it was 66.1. But perhaps it is even more significant that only 7.6 per cent of the children of fathers who were classed as professional-technical men stopped school at the eighth grade or earlier, while 66.1 per cent of the children of unskilled workers stopped at this point and 86.3 per cent of the children of farm laborers. On the other hand, 32.8 per cent of the children of professional men finished high school before stopping, while only 10.7 per cent of the children of unskilled workers did so. The children who attended school four years or more beyond high school came even more largely from the professional-technical group, over 21.1 per cent of them going on four years or more, while less than 0.4 per cent of the children of unskilled laborers had this much schooling.

There is certainly no evidence in the difference between these groups in intelligence-test scores which would lead one to expect such differences between the children of professional men and unskilled workers in their hereditary capacity to do high-school and college work. The only reasonable conclusion is that such differences in proportions going to high school and college are very closely related to the economic opportunity the family is able to provide.

The significance of all this from the standpoint of the quality of our population is that the social and economic status a family occupies in the community is quite largely dependent upon the opportunities a man has in youth, always excepting, of course, that small group of whose inability to profit by opportunity we can be reasonably sure. If this is the case, then it follows that any considerable improvement in the social quality of our population depends very largely on removing the handicaps to good health, to adequate training, and to generally decent living which depress, both economically and socially, such a large proportion of our people. The presence of such economic handicaps means that we can never know what the capacities of people really are until we provide much more ample opportunities to the underprivileged groups than those they now have. It also means that the opportunity for generally decent living must be dissociated from higher socioeconomic status as now reckoned. We can no longer justify the wide differences in opportunity for health, for education, for decent housing, for recreation, and for a steady and adequate income, on the basis of the belief that people are what they are because of basic hered-

[17] Howard M. Bell, *Youth Tell Their Story*, pp. 57–61, American Council on Education, Washington, D.C., 1938.

itary differences about which nothing can be done. The real improvement in the quality of our people which will fit us to develop a more humane and a more democratic civilization must come chiefly by increasing the opportunities of the underprivileged and not by breeding from superior stock, although people of good stock should be encouraged to raise families of at least average size.

Suggestions for Supplementary Reading

ECKERMANN, JOHANN PETER: *Conversations of Goethe with Eckermann and Soret,* 583 pp., translated from the German by John Oxenford, rev. ed., George Bell & Sons, Ltd., London, 1909. (Bohn's Standard Library.)

GOODRICH, CARTER, et al.: *Migration and Planes of Living, 1920–1934,* 111 pp., University of Pennsylvania Press, Philadelphia, 1935.

GOSNEY, EZRA S., and PAUL B. POPENOE: *Sterilization for Human Betterment: A Summary of Results of 6,000 Operations in California, 1909–1929,* 202 pp., The Macmillan Company, New York, 1929. (Human Betterment Foundation Publication.)

HOGBEN, LANCELOT: *Genetic Principles in Medicine and Social Science,* 230 pp., Williams & Norgate, Ltd., London, 1931.

HOLMES, SAMUEL J.: *The Eugenics Predicament,* 232 pp., Harcourt, Brace and Company, Inc., New York, 1933.

LANDIS, CARNEY, and M. MARJORIE BOLLIS: *Textbook of Abnormal Psychology,* 576 pp., The Macmillan Company, New York, 1947.

LANDMAN, J. H.: *Human Sterilization: The History of the Sexual Sterilization Movement,* 341 pp., The Macmillan Company, New York, 1932.

LEVEN, MAURICE, et al: *America's Capacity to Consume,* 272 pp., Brookings Institution, Washington, D.C., 1934.

LORIMER, FRANK, and HERBERT ROBACK: "Economics of the Family Relative to Number of Children," *Milbank Memorial Fund Q.,* Vol. 18, pp. 114–136, 1940.

NEWMAN, HORATIO H., et al.: *Twins: A Study of Heredity and Environment,* 369 pp., University of Chicago Press, Chicago, 1937.

OSBORN, FREDERICK H.: *Preface to Eugenics,* rev. ed., 333 pp., Harper & Brothers, New York, 1951.

———: "Significance of Differential Reproduction for American Educational Policy," *Soc. Forces,* Vol. 14, pp. 23–32, 1935.

PENROSE, L. S.: *The Biology of Mental Defect,* 285 pp., Grune & Stratton, Inc., New York, 1949.

THOMPSON, WARREN S.: "Eugenics as Viewed by a Sociologist," *Monthly Labour Rev.,* Vol. 18, pp., 11–23, 1924.

WOODWORTH, R. S.: *Heredity and Environment: A Critical Survey of Recently Published Material on Twins and Foster Children,* 95 pp., Social Science Research Council, New York, 1941.

Chapter XXII

POPULATION POLICY

At the outset of our study (Chap. I) it was shown that from time immemorial man has been concerned with the control of the size of the group in which he lived, not infrequently with the distribution of the group in space, occasionally with its quality; it was also shown that some of his practices had the effect of changing the composition of the group, *e.g.,* the killing of the aged and the preferential infanticide of girl babies. However, as a rule and at any given time, it is not likely that the individual was fully aware that the customs and institutions through which control was exercised had developed because of the need for population control as an element making for group survival. To him these practices merely represented the customary reactions of the group and as such were generally conformed to without raising a question regarding their survival value.

Carr-Saunders has argued that man's efforts to adjust his numbers to his environment have, on the whole, been highly successful, so that actual population and optimum population have usually been about the same. The author cannot agree with this view if it implies that man has generally been able to keep his numbers at the most desirable level considering the conditions under which he lived. He can agree with it still less if it is implied that the characteristics of the people, demographically and socially, were also those best suited to contribute to his welfare. If by an optimum population nothing more is meant than that the actual population was of the best size merely because it was not generally too large to live on the resources available to it with the existing technology, although it was too large at times of famine, the statement has little meaning since it is an obvious fact. There are never more people alive than can be kept alive on the *necessities* that are available. But to regard a population of 10 to 12 million people in certain provinces of northwest China as an optimum population in July of 1930 and to regard from 3 to 5 million fewer as an optimum population six to nine months later after a severe famine had swept the area seems to the author to rob the term optimum of all meaning. The whole history of mankind shows that man's numbers have varied directly with the volume of the necessities the group could produce from its resources with the technical skills it possessed. Hence, since the natural phenomena of climate—rainfall, length of growing season, mean temperature, and so forth—constitute

446

extremely important but highly variable factors in the production of any group, it would seem to the author that the concept of optimum population to be of value must take into account the *long-run* capacity of the area to support population.

This is not to deny that the form of social organization established by a group is a factor of importance in its population growth, or that it has a direct influence on the number of births and deaths and also determines to a large extent the ability of the group to make quick and useful adaptations to its environment. I would agree that man has made many efforts to adjust his numbers to his environment so that he would be less at its mercy, but I would not agree that he has thus far been very successful in these efforts.

In recent years the discussion of the optimum population as a goal of population policy has been largely confined to the economic optimum. Such an optimum has generally been defined as that population which can produce the *maximum* per capita amount of goods with the resources and means of production available to it. In a dynamic economy in which changes in the means of production are taking place almost constantly, although their effects on efficiency are by no means constant, it would seem to the author that the concept of optimum (economic) population must change so rapidly that it is of no practical value as a goal of policy. The concept of an economic optimum might be practically useful in an economy which is relatively static, *i.e.,* one in which productive techniques do remain relatively fixed over considerable periods of time and in which, therefore, the new natural resources discovered would continue to require a relatively fixed amount of labor for their exploitation. Since we know that such a situation is not likely to develop in the foreseeable future, the author regards the concept of an economic optimum population as of no practical importance today.

However, there is considerable interest in an economic optimum population, and not a few people are ready to argue that particular countries or areas have already exceeded the optimum number, or are well below it; hence, it will be well to devote a few paragraphs to the theory of the optimum population.

1. THE THEORY OF OPTIMUM POPULATION

As a matter of theory it it quite conceivable that there is one certain quantitative relationship between labor, capital, and resources which will yield the highest per capita product under any *assumed set of conditions.* Since the productivity of a particular economy at a given time is the resultant of an extremely complex interplay of the components of these generalized factors, the influence of only a few of which can be measured with any precision, and since even these few can be measured only on the assumption of static conditions, the concept of maximum per capita production seems certain to remain hazy and unrealistic for some time to come.

The theoretical argument underlying a judgment of what constitutes the optimum population in any given area at a given time rests on the assumption that there is a point where the marginal productivity of labor, as an algebraic sum of all economically productive activities, would be at a maximum. An increase or decrease of labor (population) from this point would reduce per capita production. In the opinion of the author, even though it might be possible to arrive at a figure for the optimum population of a given area under the assumption of a static economy, such a figure would have no practical value, for the one thing we can be certain of today is that the marginal productivity of labor as applied to many, perhaps most, economic activities will be different tomorrow. This statement regarding marginal productivity may be challenged; hence, it may be well to examine briefly the basis on which it rests in the simplest case—the use of land for agriculture.

Let us assume that the tillable land of the United States is divided into 20 grades with a decrease of five points in productivity in each lower grade when a similar amount of labor is applied. If the highest grade is given a productivity rating of 95 to 100, then the lowest would be 0 to 5. The land rated 95 to 100 probably would not constitute 5 per cent of the total. Moreover, land of the highest quality would be found widely scattered, and it would be of first quality only when used for the crops to which it is best adapted—corn, cotton, wheat, fruit, and so forth. Marginal productivity would be lower on all other grades of land, other conditions remaining equal. Therefore, from the standpoint of securing maximum per capita agricultural production only a small part of the land could be used. What has actually happened in agriculture during the past century is that much of the labor expended on lower grades of land today has a higher productivity than that expended on first-grade land 50 or 100 years ago. However, differentials in marginal productivity still remain, although they may not be the same as a century ago.

It is inconceivable to the author that the present techniques and improvements in agriculture leading to much higher per capita productivity today on land of lower quality than on land of the highest quality 50 to 100 years ago could ever have been developed if only the land having the highest productivity had ever been tilled. It does not seem reasonable to him to assume that if only the best of our tillable land had been used because of the differential in per capita production, we would have developed the improvements in farm practice and in machines which now make possible per capita production on lands of lesser productivity far above the per capita production on the best lands two or three generations ago. Would we ever have gained the means to apply science to plant breeding on a large scale, or would we ever have studied the control of plant and animal diseases as we actually have, if only the best grade of land had been in use? If we were to return to the use of this smaller area could we even now retain the efficiencies in agricultural production we have already developed, to say nothing of developing still more efficient techniques in the future? Such questions cannot be answered positively, but I would maintain that "No" is a much more probable answer than "Yes." However, no one questions that, other things being equal, productivity of grade 1 land would be greater than that of grade 2 or 3, and so forth, at any given stage of agricultural development. Hence, if agricultural production were the only type of production in any society and if a given level of technical efficiency is assumed, the maximum per capita product could be obtained only if cultivation was confined to grade 1 land.

The same situation would exist as regards the use of other natural resources. More labor would be used in the extraction and preparation of natural resources to a given standard suitable for further use, in the exploitation of all *natural* products as their quality deteriorated, or as difficulty of recovering them increased, *e.g.,* as the depth of the mines increased, or as the distance involved in the delivery of the raw products and of the semi-manufactured products became greater. The labor involved in the mining and smelting of grade 1 iron ore and of making it into iron or steel suitable for further processing is less than that involved in using grade 2 ore, all other conditions remaining the same. This is true of all other *natural* resources. Hence, the maximum per capita productivity in the use of all natural resources can be obtained only when the quality is of the best and when all the conditions of extraction and preparation to a given standard for further use are not less favorable than those involved in the use of grades 2, 3, etc. Labor costs for transportation vary largely according to the weight, distance, and ease of handling the product being shipped. Hence, it may cost less at a given time to use lower-grade raw materials than better grades because of the distribution of people and raw materials. However, by definition of optimum population on a given area, a distribution of people such that it demands the use of lower-quality raw materials by part of them reduces the average per capita product of the entire population. Transportation does not introduce an essentially new element into the situation. Hence, if all production were confined to agriculture and what are called the *extractive industries* (including the preparation of natural resources to a given standard of quality suitable for further manufacturing) only the use of the highest-quality resources would yield the maximum per capita product.

Factory costs, however, belong in a somewhat different category. Once steel of a given quality or other standardized product used in manufacturing has been delivered to a plant, the cost of fabrication depends upon the efficiency of the processes used, the division of labor, the general organization of the factory, and so forth. There is no *natural* difference in marginal productivity of labor applied under such conditions, except the *natural* difference in human ability. This is also true of services of many kinds. These differences in per capita productivity in the nonextractive industries and in services are due to factors under rather complete human control, and costs per unit of product can be reduced in all factories and service organizations as long as human ingenuity can devise better methods of utilizing labor. There is no *natural* differential here.

Per capita production in manufacturing and services may continue to increase long after per capita production in the extractive industries (including the preparation of raw materials to standard quality) has fallen below the maximum because of the use of inferior resources. If the per capita gains in the former economic activities (manufacturing and services) more than offset the per capita reduction due to the use of inferior land and resources, average per capita production of all goods will continue to increase, but a *maximum* per capita return is not assured merely because of an *average* increase in per capita return.

The theoretical optimum population, as already noted, is that yielding the maximum per capita production. It must be calculated as of a given moment with a given set of conditions assumed, for obviously the optimum population in a predominantly agricultural society will be quite different from that in a society in which industry and services are highly developed. Precisely because the optimum population as generally defined can only be conceived as that of a particular society with a particular set of economic conditions as they exist at a particular moment, it seems to the author that it is of no significance as a goal of population policy.

As has already been said, an optimum population can be calculated only in a society in which economic conditions are static. Perhaps no society is ever completely static for any considerable period, but in some of the underdeveloped areas of the world this condition has been approached for rather long periods. Such societies are predominantly agricultural, and their agriculture is of the era preceding the modern agricultural and industrial revolutions, *i.e.,* let us say, before 1700. In a highly dynamic society the author can see no possible way by which the optimum population can be calculated even approximately. But if by some miracle of calculation we could say that with economic relations as existing in June, 1952, per capita product would be increased by a given amount if our population were decreased or increased by a certain number, we could not be certain this would be true in 1953, to say nothing of later years. The one thing we can be reasonably certain about is that economic efficiency will not be the same in 1953 as in 1952.

Furthermore, the basic assumption that the per capita productivity of the nonextractive industries and the services, which are not subject to natural limitations due to differences in the quality of natural resources, will increase sufficiently to raise total per capita product if fewer people are engaged in the use of inferior natural resources is open to question. If several million fewer people in the United States were engaged in agriculture and in the exploitation of other natural resources of less than the highest quality, it is not at all certain that the present efficiency of labor in the nonextractive activities could be retained. The efficiencies attained in all our economic activities depend in large measure on the size of the markets, *i.e.,* on being able to dispose of certain amounts of products. If the amounts of many products that could be disposed of were substantially smaller because of satiation of wants for particular goods in a smaller population, there is no assurance that the present efficiencies of many industries could be retained. Hence, it is quite possible that the gains in per capita productivity that might be expected if only the better lands and the better minerals were used would be offset largely, or entirely, by decreases in the efficiency of other industries if the population were smaller and a smaller product were demanded of them. The reduction in total product of the nonextractive industries which might very well take place under these conditions might make it impossible to maintain many of our present efficiencies. If it is said that the reduction in population needed to reduce it to the optimum would not involve any reduction in total product especially in nonagricultural products, then it seems obvious that the mineral resources now being used would have to continue to be used and there could be no increase in over-all per capita efficiency arising from abandonment of the use of inferior agricultural, mineral, and forest resources.

If the miraculous calculation referred to above showed that per capita production would be increased by a certain amount if population were increased or decreased by a given number, we would still only know that this would hold as of a given moment, *i.e.,* with economic relations remaining fixed in the pattern assumed in the calculation. Because of the unrealistic character of such calculations, even if they were possible, it seems to the author that any statement regarding the size of the optimum population in any given area is quite meaningless as a guide to a practical population policy. The very heart of the theoretical argument supporting the view that a population is larger than the economic optimum is that if this were not the case it would be unnecessary to use land and other resources of inferior quality, the per capita returns from which are less than those from the use of the better resources. But of almost equal importance is the assumption that if the population were reduced by the number of persons dependent upon the use of these inferior resources the people engaged in other types of work would retain their present efficiency and thus the average per capita product would be increased and would more nearly approach a maximum.

In the author's opinion, we shall do much better to forget about the economic *optimum* population and ask merely whether the per capita income is increasing or decreasing and how it is likely to be affected by future changes in population and, in turn, how changes in per capita income are likely to affect population growth. It will be better, from the practical standpoint, to adopt this approach not because these questions can be answered with entire satisfaction but because answers can be arrived at which will be convincing to most reasonable people and which will be of just as much value in determining population policy as though we could say definitely that the optimum population for the United States, or for France, or for any other country is a given number plus or minus some small percentage.[1]

2. A PRACTICAL POLICY AS REGARDS NUMBERS

In those countries where the economy is dynamic, *i.e.,* where the techniques of production and the organization of the economy are changing fairly rapidly, the level of living is generally well above subsistence. In some of these countries, perhaps in most of them, there is no reasonable doubt that per capita production has been and probably still is increasing. The level of living has also been rising in most of them. (A rise in the level of living does not necessarily accompany a rise in per capita production, since the increase in production may be used for some time to increase capital goods, or may even be wasted in war, rather than being used to increase consumption goods.) Whether it is desirable to adopt a population policy encouraging population growth, or one which will discourage further growth, or one intended to reduce numbers does not depend in any way upon knowing what is an optimum (economic) population. It is sufficient to know what is happening to per capita production and what the aim of the community is as regards a desirable level of living. If per capita production is increasing and if the level of living among the less favored classes in the community is rising fairly rapidly, there certainly is no urgent call for a policy which will change the current rate of population growth unless an unfavorable change in per capita production is clearly foreseen, or a more rapid rise in level of living is desired. Indeed, if at present population is growing at a moderate rate a policy calculated to reduce this rate, if successful, *might*—we cannot say "will" or "will not"—interfere with the progressive improvement in per capita production and level of living.

If a population which has a fair to good level of living and in which per capita production has been increasing for some time finds that the rate of increase in per capita production is becoming lower or has ceased altogether,

[1] P. K. Whelpton, "Population Policy for the United States," *J. Heredity,* Vol. 30, No. 9, p. 403, 1939; Alfred Sauvy, *Richesse et Population,* p. 252, Payot, Paris, 1944.

so that there is slower improvement in level of living or none at all, it would seem that this situation at least ought to be regarded as a warning signal. It should be asked whether it means that population is increasing faster than there is any reasonable hope of increasing the goods needed to improve the level of living, or whether the level of living is likely to fall. Such a question probably cannot be answered positively, but in the absence of definite reasons to believe that per capita production will continue to increase, it would seem reasonable to consider means by which the growth of population might be reduced or even turned into a deficit.

Where there is a good level of living, a fairly rapid rise in per capita production and also a fairly rapid increase in population, it would seem to the author that no definite policy as regards numbers is called for unless there is rather clear evidence pointing to the improbability of a continuance of these conditions.

The actual adoption of a policy intended to affect population growth will in most countries not depend entirely, perhaps not primarily, on economic considerations (see Sec. 3 below), but at least the probability that further growth in population at the current rate may curtail improvement in the economic conditions of life deserves more careful attention than it has received in the past. The fact that the improvement in the level of living in most Western countries has been accompanied by a decline in the birth rate and in recent decades by a decline in the rate of growth seems highly significant. It does not seem probable to the author that the connection between slower population growth and an accompanying rise in the level of living is purely fortuitous. This situation should furnish food for thought to those peoples who have not yet attained a level of living much above subsistence and whose economies have not yet become dynamic, or only mildly so.

In countries which have long had a relatively static economy and are only now breaking through the "cake of custom" and tradition which has been a factor in keeping per capita production at a very low level, population policy as regards numbers seems to the author a much more urgent matter than in the countries with a dynamic economy. The reasons for this opinion will involve repeating a few facts already set forth in preceding chapters.

Most countries with a relatively static economy have the very low (subsistence) levels of living and the high birth and death rates which characterized practically all peoples until a century and a half or two centuries ago. Many of them also have large and relatively dense populations almost entirely dependent on agriculture. In addition, we now know how to prevent most deaths due to contagious and infectious diseases, and we are beginning to apply this knowledge in these underdeveloped areas.

On the other hand, most of the countries with dynamic economies have fair to good levels of living and low birth rates and death rates. The death rates are low because hunger and contagious disease no longer take a heavy toll. The birth rates are low because of a complex of reasons, among which the desire to maintain a good level of living is certainly of much importance. These peoples no longer want the large number of births which characterize the unrestricted family and which were regarded as necessary to survival when high death rates prevailed universally. In the countries which are only now breaking away from a relatively static economy, the sudden realization of a rate of population growth which would be high in relation to past growth is therefore more probable than in the countries whose economies began to become more dynamic 150 to 200 years ago and whose birth rates and death rates are now low. Moreover, because it is easier and cheaper to reduce the death rates in those countries now having high death rates than it is to raise their productivity, there is a strong likelihood that their populations will increase about as fast as their total production. This likelihood is further enhanced by the relative lack of emigration opportunities and of unused tillable lands to which they can move, both of which factors have played an important part in raising per capita production in the Western world since 1800.

However, even in these countries with a relatively static economy until now, it is probable that per capita production will increase slowly as their economies become more dynamic even if there is a completely "hands off" policy as regards population growth. But considering the practical difficulties many of them face in increasing total production—lack of skilled workers and technically trained men, lack of capital, lack of men experienced in business organization, lack of new land, and so forth—and the high probability of an increase in numbers whenever per capita production rises even a little above subsistence it seems reasonably certain that improvement in the level of living will be very slow and uncertain. In most of these countries, therefore, if a fairly rapid rise in level of living is desired the most rational population policy as regards numbers is easy to state. The rapid reduction of the birth rate is essential to a moderate and sustained improvement in per capita production. China and India may be able in the course of time to support considerably larger populations at substantially higher levels of living than now prevail, but their progress in this direction will be slow as long as the birth rate remains high enough to produce an annual rate of increase of 2.0 to 3.0 per cent because of increasing control over the death rate whenever production substantially exceeds subsistence.

Enough is already known regarding the relation of population growth to welfare under certain conditions to enable these underdeveloped peoples to decide upon population policies likely to hasten the rise in the level of living they so greatly desire. There is no need for them to concern themselves with the question of the optimum population. All that they can possibly do in the near future is to undertake measures looking to the reduction of the rate of growth, and no measures which are practicable in this present situation are likely to reduce the birth rate fast enough to prevent the continuing hardship arising from hunger and disease for a period of several decades, although it may be hoped that a gradual alleviation of these hardships will take place.

We do not know, of course, how fast the birth rate of any people can be reduced if a vigorous public effort is made to acquaint the people with the advantages of a lower birth rate and with the means by which this can be achieved; nor do we know how fast total production can be increased in these countries under the conditions now existing. We are told, however, by those who have studied our own economy very carefully that for the past 50 years or so the increase in total production has averaged about 3 per cent per year. But ours is a highly dynamic economy, and during this period of rather rapid increase in production our population has never increased at more than about 2 per cent a year and most of the time at about 1.5 per cent or less. Clearly there has been a considerable amount of product available for per capita increase in consumption. This situation is basically the same in a number of other Western lands. Is it reasonable to assume that in those lands where the economy has long been relatively static total production can be increased by more than 1.5 to 2.0 per cent per year in the near future? Just because it is easier to reduce the death rate than to increase the rate of production, and because the birth rate is high and will fall more slowly than the death rate, any rapid rise in the level of living is precluded, but it will certainly rise more rapidly if the birth rate can be reduced, thus reducing the rate of population growth.

3. OTHER CRITERIA FOR DETERMINING OPTIMUM POPULATION

Thus far the discussion of population policy as regards numbers has centered on economic considerations. There are, however, other criteria which some people would prefer to use in determining the satisfactory size of a population. Thus a people intent upon increase in military power will not think of the optimum number primarily on the basis of economic welfare, but will ask what size of population will provide the greatest amount of military power. Clearly Hitler, Mussolini, and the prewar Japanese leaders thought of the best population as a rapidly growing population which would provide not only sufficient manpower for full production in agriculture and industry but also sufficient men for a military establishment great enough to ensure the expansion of their empires. In other words, they wanted a surplus of population above economic needs to use for "cannon fodder."

Other ideals have also determined the desired size of the population in the eyes of different peoples at various epochs. Thus the concept of a God who glories in a large number of worshippers, much as a monarch might preen himself on the adulation of great numbers of people, has at times led to the belief that the increase in the number of worshippers was of more importance than the earthly welfare of these worshippers. Naturally such values would lead to the approval of practices calculated to keep population large at the expense of improving welfare. However, deliberate efforts to put into effect policies leading to the increase of numbers at low levels of living have never been very effective as far as we can judge. By far the most effective stimulant of population growth throughout human history has been the acquirement of larger *usable* resources leading to larger and more stable production. Until quite recently the acquirement of additional tillable land has been the most potent of all stimuli in encouraging population growth. However, for some decades now the acquirement of larger mineral resources has been of increasing importance in this respect.

4. MODERN PRACTICES INTENDED TO MAINTAIN OR TO INCREASE NUMBERS

It will not be possible to give any details of the practices which have been initiated by different governments in recent decades to encourage an increase in the birth rate. They center around a fact that is now quite generally recognized, namely, that the development of the modern industrial state has led to very fundamental changes in the relation of children to the economy of the family as compared with their position in the family in the predominantly agricultural economy of the preceding era. This change has had a strongly depressing effect on the birth rate.

It is the recognition of this change in the economy of the family which lies at the basis of most practices adopted to increase the birth rate, or to prevent it from further decline. In an industrial economy children can do little to contribute to their own support until they have completed the years of schooling required by law. Moreover, an increasing proportion of them must have a rather long period of training beyond the minimum required by law. In an agricultural economy, on the other hand, they begin to help in supporting themselves at a fairly early age by working with the parents on the land and in the home.

The general character of the measures adopted today to encourage larger families or to prevent further decline in the birth rate may be described by the term *family allowances*. These allowances are intended to assist parents in meeting the increasing economic burden in raising enough children to maintain or to increase the population while also enjoying a good level of living. The allowances have taken many forms, only a few of the more important of which can even be mentioned here. Medical care for the pregnant mother, aid in providing the layette for the baby, and payment of the hospital costs of confinement cover entirely or help to reduce the family outlay up to the time of arrival of the baby. Medical advice in the care of the baby, the providing of certain essential foods for it, and often a periodic payment in kind, or in money, as long as the child is in school relieve the parents of a part of the cost of raising the child. Sometimes the housing needs for a family with children are partly provided for. Where the government is making great efforts to induce people to raise families large enough to ensure an increase in population the periodic payments (*e.g.,* monthly payments) on account of children are generally increased for each child beyond one or two up to five or six or more, and in the Soviet Union handsome bonuses are given to mothers of truly large families.

In Sweden, where there is no desire to increase the population, the emphasis is placed on providing allowances in kind which can be used only to ensure better health, better living conditions, and better education to the children. Where mere increase in numbers is the object, as was the case in Hitler's Germany and in Italy under Mussolini and apparently in the Soviet Union today, there is, as a rule, much less emphasis on ensuring better opportunity for the children. The state wants the children to use as its dictators see fit.

The author knows of no country which is now following deliberate policies intended to reduce the size of its population, although the emigration policies of England and the Netherlands and especially the large amount of talk about the need for emigration from these countries suggest the possibility that some of their leaders are coming to believe that it would be better if their populations were actually smaller. But not only is there no official recognition in any country of the need to reduce the *size of the population* there are, as far as the writer knows, only a few tentative official efforts to reduce the *rate of population growth* with the idea of arriving at a relation between numbers and resources which would be likely to lead to increased per capita production.

The organization of the public health centers in Japan with legislation allowing, if not actually encouraging, birth-control clinics is a tentative step in this direction. However, adequate funds to support such clinics are not yet available, and it remains to be seen whether the conception-control movement will be encouraged or discouraged by the Japanese leaders when the shadow of the Occupation is removed.

The leaders of India have also shown some interest in a lower birth rate, but as yet no definite effort has been made to inform the people of the need for conception control or to supply them with the means to exercise this control. It is encouraging, however, to have political leaders manifest an interest in the relation between population growth and economic welfare. This is an essential preliminary step toward a policy of encouraging a lower birth rate, but it is only a feeble first step. Even with the most earnest of intentions the Indian leaders may not be able to proceed rapidly in this matter. In the author's opinion, the control of population growth in India will almost certainly proceed slowly.

The author also sees little hope of substantial improvement in living conditions in most Group III countries (Chap. XII) until their birth rates are so reduced that the natural increase will be at a lower rate than now prevails because of their declining death rates. It is to be hoped that the promising interest in policies intended to lead to a slower population growth in Japan and India may develop into such effective control that an increase in per capita production will be possible in these countries in the not-distant future and that many other countries will follow their lead in this respect. Because of the very urgent need of many peoples to reduce their birth rates if they are to enjoy higher levels of living, it may be of some interest to describe a little more fully the population situation which has developed in Japan since the war and the plans which are being mooted for the control of population growth.

5. POPULATION CONTROL IN JAPAN

After the war the Occupation was confronted with the task of repatriating about 6 million military and civilian Japanese from overseas, while also occupying the country and keeping order in a population of about 73.0 million (1945). The people to be repatriated were scattered all over East and Southeast Asia and the islands of the Western Pacific. Without very careful and efficient health work some very devastating epidemics were to be expected. Suffice it to say that the health work was so efficiently organized that there was no serious outbreak of disease, either among the repatriates themselves or among the people of Japan, as a consequence of this vast movement of people. The few epidemics that did occur were of a minor character and had little influence on the death rate after the first few months of the Occupation.

This health work was extended, chiefly under direct Japanese control but with the advice and the very substantial assistance of the Public Health and Welfare Section of SCAP, to the whole of Japan. The almost immediate effect was that the crude death rate of Japan, which had remained about stationary at 17 to 18 per 1,000 for several years before the war and was about 29 in 1945, fell to the prewar level in 1946 and to 14.6 in 1947. By 1950 it had fallen to 11.0 per 1,000, or to about 60 per cent of the prewar rate. This is the best illustration known to the author showing how the intelligent and vigorous application of modern health knowledge in a large population can further reduce the death rate even when that death rate has already been brought to a moderately low level. The Occupation reduced the death rate in Japan about as much in three or four years as we did in the United States in the 30 years from 1900 to 1930.

In Japan, as elsewhere, the return of the military personnel led to the reunion of families and to a large number of new marriages so that the birth rate rose as precipitately as the death rate fell, and by 1947 the rate of natural increase rose well above that in any previous year. Since Japan no longer had any overseas territory and since both her agricultural and mineral resources are quite limited, such a rate of increase at once raised very serious problems both for the Occupation and for the Japanese.

The postwar health work in Japan was implemented locally through "health centers." The plan was to have one of these for about each 100,000 of the population with subcenters as needed. As a result of the discussion of the problems raised by this great increase in population (1.5 to 1.75 million per year) accompanying the decline in the death rate, certain laws were enacted providing for a eugenic and family consultation office in the health centers. Among other services this office was empowered to give advice on family limitation. Thus it became possible with the sanction of the government to spread the knowledge of how the size of families might be controlled. As a matter of fact this family consultation service has not yet become very active in most of the health centers because of the lack of funds and personnel. However, there may also be some feeling that this plan to spread knowledge of family limitation was an Occupation policy rather than a Japanese policy and that there was no indigenous demand for vigorous efforts in this direction. There can be no doubt, however, that the legal basis has been laid for a public effort to encourage smaller families, or that a larger and larger number of thoughtful Japanese are in favor of such a policy.

The crude birth rate in 1950 fell to 28.4 from 32.8 in 1949. This is a decline of over one-eighth—a very substantial decline, indeed, but even so it only reduced the rate of natural increase to about 17 per 1,000, which was well above the prewar rate. Only time will tell whether the decline in rate of natural increase will continue and how rapid it will be. However, it is *possible* that a population policy aimed at reducing the birth rate may become effective in Japan within a few years. The organization through which a very rapid dissemination of the knowledge of family limitation could take place is now in existence, the need for a slower population growth is more and more widely felt, the public is discussing population problems, and the press is giving wide publicity to this discussion. The author is not predicting the general acceptance of family limitation by the Japanese people within the next few years, but he does believe it is possible that the Japanese birth rate may fall quite rapidly if the government wholeheartedly supports this policy and *if* some very *simple,* very *cheap,* and highly *effective* means of preventing unwanted conceptions is found.

At present no one can say whether the substantial reduction of the birth rate in 1950 and apparently again in 1951 is the result of a definite policy of the Japanese government and people or is merely a temporary fluctuation. Japan has only recently gained complete independence of action, and its people are only beginning to think for themselves. It will be several years before we can know whether what appears to be an established official policy is such in fact. My personal hope is that Japan will lead the way among the peoples of Asia in making an adaptation of numbers to the means of support which will render a continued effort to secure larger and larger resources, by force if this seems to be the only way, an unnecessary element of national policy (Chap. XVII).

6. POLICIES AFFECTING QUALITY

As has already been noted (Chap. I), there have been population policies in the past the purpose of which was to maintain or to improve the quality of the stock. The particular quality aimed at was generally wholeness and soundness of body. Cripples and deformed persons as well as those seeming to be of feeble constitution were frequently exposed as infants (infanticide), and where such persons survived infancy they were often neglected and abused so that their death rates must generally have been high. The chief motive for the neglect and infanticide of children showing some abnormality was probably the economic hardship involved in supporting them, but the fear of the unusual which is so common among "primitive" peoples must also have played its part. Occasionally, however, the desire for stout men as workers and soldiers and for hardy women as workers and mothers seems to have led to the deliberate policy of doing away with children who appeared weak and with those who showed physical abnormalities. Mental abnormalities were, perhaps, less often eliminated by deliberate selection, since "unbalanced" people were often regarded with rather awesome respect and not infrequently were believed to be favorites of the supernatural powers.

In recent times interest in quality arose as knowledge of heredity increased and it became evident that many types of abnormality, both physical and mental, were passed on from parents to children. Once it was proved that certain undesirable qualities, chiefly mental abnormalities, could be transmitted from parents to children, that they could thus be perpetuated, and that possibly the people possessing them would increase in relation to the remainder of the population, it is not surprising that many people began to think of the possibility of improving the quality of the national stock by preventing the people inheriting these undesirable qualities from passing them on to their descendants. The modern movement to prevent the reproduction of persons having undesirable hereditary qualities is only

60 to 70 years old, and its beginning is most frequently associated with the name of Francis Galton, a cousin of Charles Darwin. At first, and before the Mendelian theory of heredity was rediscovered, it was assumed that many mental traits were inherited as wholes and that the prevention of births to people having these undesirable mental traits would improve the average quality of the population. It has turned out to be a much more complicated problem to eliminate undesirable mental traits, even when they are hereditary, than Galton and his early followers suspected. Comparatively little headway has yet been made toward this end.

Two general types of effort to eliminate undesirable heredity have been tried, but neither of them with sufficient consistency to justify referring to them as *population policies*. Elimination of undesirable hereditary traits may be accomplished either by making reproduction physiologically impossible or through the segregation of the afflicted males and females. Sterilization by operation is practiced to a limited extent in several states in the United States and in a few other countries, but it is not yet a widely accepted practice. Segregation in institutions is a more generally used method of rendering certain classes of people infertile, but is so costly that it is only applied to a small proportion of those mentally defective and unstable persons who are most likely to transmit their defects to posterity. It would appear that policies looking to the improvement of the hereditary quality of the population will be adopted slowly until we know a great deal more about the inheritance of mental defects and instability than we now do.

The other type of effort to carry out a policy of eliminating undesirable qualities, genocide, has been tried in modern times, notably by Hitler. In general it assumes that the qualities it is desired to eliminate are racial qualities, *i.e.,* qualities which all the members of some identifiable group (usually called a "racial" group by the people practicing it) possess and that the most effective way to eliminate such qualities is to destroy the race possessing them. In the opinion of most people qualified to have an opinion, there are no racial differences of any significance from the standpoint of hereditary quality. In a word, differences in hereditary quality are individual and family differences, not racial differences. Hence, genocide as a means of eliminating people of undesirable heredity can be advocated only by people with diseased imaginations, those having such violent prejudices that reason has no place in their thinking on problems of quality, or those who are so ignorant of the findings of the students of heredity and anthropology that they mistake their own mental aberrations for knowledge.

It seems to the author likely that most of the improvement in the quality of the population during the next few generations will come from the adoption of policies such as those of Sweden which are intended to improve social quality by improving the living conditions of the disadvantaged classes in the population rather than by eliminating family lines which are the carriers of defective or diseased heredity. In this way the differences in opportunities between classes and individuals will gradually be diminished, and we shall learn to distinguish with greater certainty hereditary from social deficiencies. Only when we have gained the ability to do this can we really hope to make much headway in improving the hereditary quality of the population by the gradual elimination of the hereditarily unfit. The Swedish policies referred to above aim at the equalization of opportunity and are based on the implicit assumption that the social gain achieved by this improvement will more than offset any increase in the number of people who are carriers of defective heredity. In the present state of our knowledge regarding the transmission of hereditary defects, this assumption seems to the author fully justified, and he regards the social policy of Sweden as the population policy best calculated to improve the welfare of a nation's population in the near future. In so far as other peoples follow Sweden's lead, we may reasonably hope for a fairly rapid improvement in the ability of people to adjust themselves to the increasing complexities of modern living, to enjoy better health, and to develop a social organization in which the minimum of welfare is well above that prevailing anywhere today.

7. THE DISTRIBUTION OF POPULATION

A third aspect of population change regarding which formation of policy is of increasing importance is the distribution of population—distribution as between the different nations and regions of the world, between urban and rural communities, between different sizes of urban communities, between the different regions of a nation, and between different occupations and industries. In the modern era most matters affecting population distribution were, until rather recently, left to the supposedly free play of economic forces. Actually there has always been a large element of control, private rather than public, in the distribution of population. The "free play" of economic forces in modern migratory movements, in the location of modern transportation routes, in the location of factories, and occasionally even in the location of cities has been subject to much interference from and direction by individuals and groups that were primarily interested in their own profits or power. This private control of distribution has been exercised in a great variety of ways, most of which cannot even be enumerated here. The point in which we are interested is that the distribution of population never does represent the "free play" of economic forces either as between countries or within a country. It has always been managed, more or less, to serve the advantage of nations, of individuals, and of groups. This is true of broader regional patterns of distribution as well as of the local distribution of population within a given area.

In modern times there are but few examples of public policies intended to determine the distribution of population, except in the authoritarian states. The Soviet Union from the inception of its five-year plans deliberately followed a policy which would spread industry over a vast area and thus render it less vulnerable to destruction in case of war. This policy was openly avowed and, although not carried out with complete consistency, has remained in effect. Where the population was reluctant to move to the new centers of industry, a great variety of means were employed to effect such migration, some of them involving actual compulsion. When it was believed that dissident elements might interfere with state plans if allowed to remain where they were, no means were considered too drastic to force the desired migration. Many workers were *sent* to areas where they were needed without regard to their desires. One need only mention the sending of kulaks to the northern forest areas to get out the needed lumber, and the manning of the Siberian mines with "dangerous" elements, to indicate the nature of these forced migrations which had a marked effect on the distribution of population in the Soviet Union and which are a reversion to feudal serfdom in the name of the welfare of the state.

Hitler's Germany could not locate new industry out of range of aerial attack and could not send dissident elements to far places to carry out public works. Hence, the concentration camp took the place of the Siberian work camp. It was not until after the attack on Poland and the clearing of the Poles out of the Western part of the country that Hitler had opportunity to "bring home" many minority German elements from the Baltic states, from the Balkans, and from northern Italy. Migration of these peoples into the annexed provinces of Poland on a rather large scale was begun as soon as possible. The purpose was to concentrate all the German-speaking people of Europe in a solid bloc in Central Europe.

War always has had its accompanying migratory movements, but this last war and its aftermath produced such movements on a scale undreamed of hitherto. Many of these migratory movements were the result of mere military maneuvers and produced no lasting effect, but some seem to have been the consequence of more enduring policies and may be mentioned. In the closing months of the war practically all German-speaking people were driven out of the territory east of the Elbe and the Neisse; the Poles were cleared out of eastern Poland, and the Ukrainians out of parts of the present Poland. Soon after the war the Sudeten Germans were driven out of Czechoslovakia and many minority groups were shuffled about in the Balkans. With the establishment of the Indian Union and Pakistan, millions of people, perhaps as many as 12 million, were forced to flee from one to the other. One cannot say whether or not the forced migration of minority groups will continue until there are no such groups, but the fact is that it has been going on in a large way for the past decade or two and is causing a considerable change in the composition of the population in certain localities. It has, perhaps, had more effect on nationality composition than on numbers, but the social consequences of such policies are highly significant and need to be borne in mind.

Local Redistribution. Until recently little attention has been given to what might be called public policies which might effect a redistribution of the population within a nation. This is probably due to the fact that there is as yet comparatively little realization that the present distribution of people within the nation may be inimical to the best interests of the community at large, as well as detrimental in many respects to the welfare of the family and its members.

Today one scarcely needs to argue with well-informed people that slums breed many evils which not only destroy individual integrity but are extremely costly to the community, and yet any proposal to replan a city with a view to developing a new pattern of residential and industrial distribution meets with almost insuperable opposition from the interests which profit from the present distribution. The difficulties encountered in trying to change the distribution of people within most of our larger urban communities (metropolitan areas) are too well known to need elaboration. But in the United States the development of private automobile transportation and the spread of utilities in suburban areas are effecting a veritable revolution in the structure and organization of metropolitan communities through the redistribution of population in spite of the efforts of vested interests to maintain the existing structure. Apparently free people will not put up with the inconveniences of living in crowded cities if they can find any relief. As a consequence there is some indication today that public policies looking toward urban redevelopment are forming. It seems reasonably certain that these policies will become of increasing importance in effecting a new pattern of population distribution within enlarging metropolitan areas (Chap. XX).

Regional Redistribution. There is also some evidence that an increasing body of people are thinking of the advantages which might be gained from a different distribution of population between the different regions of the nation. This may presage the formulation of national policies which will have an important effect on the regional distribution of population. At the moment, however, the national policies which will most affect the regional distribution of population are probably not recognized as policies likely to effect a redistribution of population. They are thought of in quite different terms.

Thus the conservation of water resources in the western half of the United States is thought of quite largely in terms of land reclamation through new irrigation projects. However, if the water which might be used to add to the irrigated area were to be used for household and industrial purposes it would support several times as many people. In this region the determination of the use of water may, therefore, turn out to have a very important effect on the distribution of population between the regions of the United States, although there may be little or no thought of changing this distribution when the use of the water is decided upon.

Strategic Considerations. The factor which is most loudly calling for the development of a national policy for the redistribution of population at present is the danger of the destruction of the huge metropolitan concentrations of population and economic activity by atom and/or hydrogen bombs. As far as the author can ascertain, such strategic considerations have not yet had any influence on national policies affecting the distribution of population, except in the Soviet Union, and even there they have only resulted in the wider dispersion of industry and population over a vast territory and not in the development of new forms of urban aggregation which would be less vulnerable to aerial attack. In the United States there has been some official pressure to induce certain industries vital to defense to move inland, but this has not been great and certainly has not been consistent. The changes in the distribution of population within metropolitan areas which are actually taking place in the United States and a few other countries are largely a consequence of technological changes and changes in economic organization. They have been effected by the relatively free play of social and economic forces and do not represent a public policy aimed at the redistribution of population. The changes in the pattern of distribution now in process are slow, perhaps too slow to ensure national survival to most peoples in a world where war is imminent, even if they were in the right direction. Moreover, as was shown in Chaps. XIX and XX, they are concentrating more and more of our total population and industry in a few areas highly vulnerable to attack with atom and hydrogen bombs.

It is altogether probable that to minimize the destruction that may be caused by such attacks we shall have to develop entirely new forms of urban aggregation. If this is the case it seems clear that only governmental authority can undertake such a vast redistribution of population as is implied in the concept of a metropolitan area which will suffer minimum damage from bombs being delivered through the air.

8. MIGRATION POLICIES

Little need be said here of migration policies as an aspect of population policy (Chaps. XIII and XIV). Clearly any such redistribution of population as would be required to minimize the dangers of aerial bombing will demand the public control of the migration of people within the country. This will run contrary to all the notions of free movement which have been developing ever since the feudal system began to break up. Only the policies followed by totalitarian governments in recent years have taken this backward step in the cancellation of human rights, but their efforts to spread totalitarian control may force a reconsideration of the right of free movement by other peoples if they are to survive and retain even a vestige of individual freedom. It appears to the author that we may be entering a period when legal controls over migration, both internal and international, will increase. The basis for this judgment is the fact that at present there is no evidence that the totalitarian powers desire to work out a *modus vivendi* with the relatively free peoples which would make it possible for them to permit the continuance of the relatively free internal migration of the postfeudal era.

As regards international migration, the past 40 years have seen a great change in the degree of freedom to leave one country and to enter another. Only the totalitarian powers have placed a general prohibition on emigration, but many peoples have put more and more restrictions on immigration. About all that can be said at the moment concerning international migration policies is that restrictive immigration policies are developing in many of the free countries and that they seem likely to become more widespread as time passes. As far as the free countries are concerned, these policies are largely determined by what the people themselves consider essential to their economic welfare under the existing conditions. As regards the totalitarian countries, the considerations governing immigration are largely determined by a ruling clique much more afraid of the interchange of ideas accompanying immigration than of the economic consequences. It would appear, therefore, that migration policies, both as regards internal and international migration, are likely to bulk larger in the formation of population policies in the future than they have in the past.

But it should not be supposed that the considerations noted here as likely to have a decisive influence on migration policies will not also have an important influence on over-all population policy—as affecting numbers, quality, and distribution in all their aspects. Population policies, like all public policies in free countries, arise from the public judgment of what will contribute most to the general welfare. In totalitarian countries the ruling clique, not the public, decides what is the general welfare, and this is generally found to coincide with the maintenance of the power of this clique. As long as this clique follows policies calculated to maintain and enhance its own power, it can force many policies upon the free peoples which they would otherwise never consider seriously. This is just as true of population policies as of foreign policies, trade policies, policies affecting domestic welfare, and so forth. The fact is, then, that population policies looking to the increase of the general welfare will almost certainly be greatly modified when they must give first consideration to the maintenance of national independence and the amount of freedom allowed must be subordinated to this.

It is devoutly to be hoped that we and all other peoples will soon be freed from these considerations of survival in the determination of population policies as well as of all other public policies. Until that happens we cannot fully use our knowledge and our understanding of population growth and changes to determine policies which will enhance the general welfare.

Suggestions for Supplementary Reading

GLASS, D. V.: *Population Policies and Movements in Europe*, 490 pp., Clarendon Press, Oxford, 1940.

LORIMER, FRANK: "European Governmental Action Regarding Population," *Ann. Am. Acad. Pol. Soc. Sci.*, Vol. 262, pp. 55–61, March, 1949.

MYRDAL, ALVA: *Nation and Family: The Swedish Experiment in Democratic Family and Population Policy*, 441 pp., Harper & Brothers, New York, 1941.

————: "A Programme for Family Security in Sweden," *Int. Labour Rev.*, Vol. 39, pp. 723–763, 1939.

SAUVY, ALFRED: *Richesse et Population*, 327 pp., Payot, Paris, 1944.

WAGGAMAN, MARY T.: *Family Allowances in Various Countries,* 62 pp., G.P.O., Washington, D.C., 1943. (U.S. Bur. Labor Statistics, *Bull.* 754.)

INDEX

References to tables and figures are indicated by **boldface** numbers